RABBI
NACHMAN'S
STORIES

RABBI NACHMAN'S STORIES

(Sippurey Ma'asioth)

The Stories of Rabbi Nachman of Breslov

Translated

with notes based on Breslover works

by

Rabbi Aryeh Kaplan

PUBLISHED BY THE BRESLOV RESEARCH INSTITUTE

ISBN 0-930213-02-5

Library of Congress Catalog Card Number: 83-70201

Copyright © 1983
Breslov Research Institute

First Edition

For further information:

Rabbi Chaim Kramer
Breslov Research Institute
POB 5370
Jerusalem, Israel   91053

cover design: Ben Gasner

Photo-composition by:
HaNachal Press — דפוס הנחל
of the Breslov Research Institute

PUBLISHER'S PREFACE

"To separate between the light and the darkness" (Gen. 1:4). The Midrash explains: "The light is a reference to the *ma'asim* of the Tzaddikim, the darkness is a reference to those of the wicked" (*Bereshith Rabbah* 20).

In Hebrew, the word *ma'asim* has a double meaning: deeds and stories.

The teaching of the Midrash is that there are differences as great as the difference between day and night, not only between the deeds of the nations but also between their *stories.*

Our sages knew that in the latter generations the Jews would be exiled and would fall into a profound lethargy.

"And it came to pass that, when the sun was going down, a deep sleep fell upon Abram; and lo, a dread, even a great darkness, fell upon him" (Gen. 15:12).

The sleep, the dread, and the darkness, were a vision of the four exiles. The downfall is symbolically represented by the idea of sleep (*Bereshith Rabbah* 44).

There are many who have fallen into this deep sleep. Some people believe they are serving God, but they are really sleeping. The years pass by and what are they left with in the end? There are others who are in such a deep slumber that they do not even know they are asleep (*Likutey Moharan* 60).

The only way to wake people up, Rabbi Nachman tells us, "is through stories."

The Torah is a powerful light which can illumine even the thickest darkness.

Just as a person who has been deprived of light for a long time must not expose himself to glaring sunlight all of a sudden, so too, one who is ignorant of Torah can only be exposed to it in a veiled form at first.

The veil of the Torah is the *ma'asioth*, stories. These stories are a gate which is accessible even to those who are still infinitely far from God. The stories can awaken and revive them.

Our Sages themselves used this method. The Midrash tells us: "When Rabbi Akiva noticed in the course of a lecture that his pupils were getting sleepy, he told them the following story; 'Why did Esther merit to rule over one hundred and twenty-seven provinces?...et.' " (*Esther Rabbah* 1). Similarly we find that when Rabbi Yehuda the Prince noticed that his listeners were beginning to get sleepy, he interrupted his lecture and said: "A woman in Egypt gave birth to 600,000 babies!" When his pupils shook themselves out of their drowsiness and asked him what he was talking about, he answered: "It was Yocheved, who gave birth to Moses, who was equal to the 600,000 Jews in Egypt." (*Shir HaShirim Rabbah* 1).

When Rabbi Nachman first started telling his stories, he declared: "Now I am going to tell you stories." The reason he did so was because in generations so far from God the only remedy was to present the secrets of the Torah — including even the greatest of them — in the form of stories. There was no other way to achieve the necessary impact in order to heal us.

Rabbi Nachman was especially concerned that his teachings should be available to all, and this is why he wanted translations in Yiddish and Hebrew.

The Breslov Research Institute of Yeshivat Chasidei Breslov in Jerusalem, has begun translation of the major works of Rabbi Nachman into different languages, for the benefit of those who are interested in his teachings and stories. The present work is the third in a series of translations of the major works of Rabbi Nachman. It follows *Rabbi Nachman's Wisdom*, and *Advice*.

There have been a number of translations of Rabbi Nachman's stories. The present work, however, includes a running commentary drawn from the traditional commentaries by Rabbi Nachman's students and followers, giving insight and understanding as to what Rabbi Nachman may have been alluding to. This is the first time that this material has been accessible to the English-speaking reader.

We advise the reader to read through the story first before attempting to study the explanations. The commentary on earlier parts of any given story often contains references to later parts, and without a thorough knowledge of the story itself the reader may not enjoy the full benefits of the commentary.

To achieve a perfect translation without veering from the original by one iota is an impossible task. It is equally impossible to express the exact intention of the author without falling into a laborious literalness. Our intention has been to achieve a translation which is both readable and at the same time sufficiently close to the original that the intention of Rabbi Nachman has been fully conveyed.

The Breslov Research Institute wishes to extend its most heartfelt thanks to Rabbi Aryeh Kaplan for this most exacting work. Besides the translation of the stories themselves, collecting and correlating the commentaries from the many different sources was a project of monumental difficulty. This has never been done before, even in the Hebrew editions. This will now pave the way for similar work to be done in the Hebrew, French and other language editions.

Gratitude is due to Rabbi Nachman Burstyn, Rabbi Shmuel Moshe Kramer and Rabbi Moshe Schorr, for their valuable assistance in reviewing and editing the manuscripts for publication. Additional thanks are due to the editors, typists, proofreaders, and staff at our typesetting plant — HaNachal Press — for their dedication in bringing this book to publication.

May the Almighty accord us the merit of hearing the end of the thirteenth story, "The Seven Beggars," with the coming of *Mashiach* and the rebuilding of the Holy Temple, Amen.

Chaim Kramer
Shevat, 5742

TRANSLATOR'S INTRODUCTION

Rabbi Nachman's stories are among the great classics of Jewish literature. They have been recognized by Jews and non-Jews alike for their depth and insight into both the human condition and the realm of the mysterious. As a result, almost a half dozen translations of these stories have already been made.

When the stories were first published, the book contained both a Hebrew and a Yiddish version of the stories. While both versions are essentially the same, minor variations do crop up, and these have generally been noted.

There is also a huge Breslover literature on the stories, that, for the most part, has been ignored by translators as well as commentators on the stories. Here, this literature has been gathered together on page notes to make it readily accessible. Many other allusions to the Bible, Talmud, Midrash and Kabbalah are also included in these notes.

It is hoped that these stories will be an inspiration in translation as they were in the original.

Aryeh Kaplan
21 *Marcheshvan*, 5742

להתודע ולהגלות

אַז אִיטְלִיכְס װָארְט װָאס דָא שְׁטֵייט, אִין דֶעם הֵיילִיגֶען סֵפֶּר, אִיז קוֹדֶשׁ
קָדָשִׁים לוֹיטֶער סוֹדוֹת הַתּוֹרָה. מֶען זָאל נִישְׁט מֵיינֶען אַז דָאס זֶענֶען חַס
וְשָׁלוֹם פְּרָאסְטֶע מַעֲשִׂיוֹת. װָארִין, דִיא מַעֲשִׂיוֹת װָאס אִין דֶעם סֵפֶּר
שְׁטֵייֶען, הָאט דֶער צֵיילְט דֶער גְרוֹיסֶער צַדִיק, דֶער קָדוֹשׁ עֶלְיוֹן, דֶער
הֵיילִיגֶער רֶבִּי, ר' **נחמן זצ"ל**, זַיין זְכוּת זָאל אוּנְז בֵּיא שְׁטֵיין. זַיין
כַּוָּנָה אִיז גֶעװֶען אוּנְז צוּא לֶערְנֶין װִיא אַזוֹי דֶעם אֵייבֶּערְשְׁטִין צוּא
דִינֶען. אוּן הַלְװַאי מִיר זָאלִין פַאר שְׁטֵיין דִיא גְרוֹסֶע סוֹדוֹת אוּן דֶעם
מוּסָר װָאס עֶס שְׁטֶעקְט אִין דִיא מַעֲשִׂיוֹת. װֶעלִין מִיר זַיין פְרוּמֶער
יוּדֶען אַזוֹי װִי מֶען דַארְף צוּא זַיין. אוּן הַשֵׁם יִתְבָּרַךְ װֶעט אוּנז שִׁיקֶען
דֶעם גוֹאֵל צֶדֶק בַּאלְד, אִין אוּנזֶערֶע צַייטִין, בִּמְהֵרָה בְיָמֵינוּ, אָמֵן.

*To make known and to reveal, that every word that is written in this
holy book is Holy of Holies, according to the secrets of the Torah.
One shall not think that these are simple stories. For the stories that
are in this book were told by the great Tzaddik, Rabbi Nachman of
Breslov, may his merit protect us. His intention was to teach us how
to serve God. Would it be, that we should understand the great
secrets and moral guidance that are in these stories. Then we will be
proper Jews, as we should be. May the Almighty send us the
Messiah, quickly, in our time, Amen.*

TABLE OF CONTENTS

INTRODUCTION

"Whatever he was, his name has already been given, and it is known that he is Man" (Ecclesiastes 6:10).

This is the Torah of the holy man[1] — one who was worthy of completing the Form of Man[2] — for this is the entire man.[3]

We are speaking of our glorious master, teacher and rabbi, the crown of our glory,[4] the pride of our strength,[5] the holy, awesome rabbi, the great lamp,[6] the highest lamp, the beautiful, holy lamp — his name is holy — our master and rabbi, the Master, Rabbi Nachman (may the memory of the saint and holy man be a blessing).[7] He was a great-grandson of the holy, awesome, Godly rabbi, the Baal Shem Tov[8] (may the memory of the saint and holy man be a blessing).

The people Israel have already enjoyed his enlightenment in his holy, wondrous works which have already been published.[9]

---

1. Paraphrase of Numbers 19:14.
2. See Genesis 1:26, 27. This indicates that Rabbi Nachman was the paradigm of man, and that he was able to perfect the concept of the supernal Man.
3. Ecclesiastes 12:13.
4. cf. Jeremiah 13:18.
5. Leviticus 26:19.
6. See *Zohar* 1:4a.
7. Proverbs 10:7. This expression is used after mentioning the name of a deceased righteous man.
8. Rabbi Israel ben Eliezer (1698-1760) was the founder of the Chassidic movement.
9. The *Sippurey Maasioth* was first published in Ostrog, 1816. The only Breslov works published prior to this were *Likutey Moharan*, Ostrog, 1808, and a second portion, *Likutey Moharan Tinyana*, Mohalov, 1811.

Many saw [them] and rejoiced, and the upright were ecstatic.[10]
The truth has shown its own way.[11]

Now you can see what else is in our pouch. It is a collection of
wondrous, awesome tales, which we were worthy of hearing
"mouth to mouth"[12] from [the Rebbe's] holy lips. He perceived,
and he pondered and composed many parables.[13]

[The Rebbe] disguised high and mighty concepts, and hid
them in his stories in wondrous, awesome ways.

This was the way things were originally done in Israel,
through redemption and interchanging.[14] When people wanted to
speak of God's hidden mysteries, they would speak in allegory
and parable, hiding in many disguises the concealed secrets of the
Torah, the King's hidden treasury.

Thus, after telling the story of "The Exchanged Children"[15]
the Rebbe said that in ancient times when the Initiates discussed
Kabbalah, they would speak in this manner, [making use of
stories and parables]. Until the time of Rabbi Shimon bar Yochai
(author of the *Zohar*),[16] they would not openly use explicit
Kabbalistic terms.

In most cases, after a number of stories, [the Rebbe] would
reveal [some hints to the mysteries alluded to in the story]. There
would be some allusion as to the significance of the words, but it
was very little, less than a drop in the ocean. We will discuss some
of these allusions given after the stories in their proper place.

Until now, we kept these stories in our private files. But many
people have said to us, "Why don't you show us this good?"[17]

---

10.   From the High Holiday *Amidah*. See Job 22:19.
11.   A folk saying. See Ibn Ezra on Proverbs 9:1.
12.   Numbers 12:8.
13.   Ecclesiastes 12:9.
14.   Paraphrase of Ruth 4:7.
15.   See below, p. 231.
16.   Rabbi Shimon bar Yochai (circa. 150 C.E.) and his disciples were the authors of the
       Zohar, the major classic of Kabbalah.
17.   Psalms 4:7.

Many members of our group have a deep longing and yearning[18] to be able constantly to hear the words of the Living God[19] that were spoken by our holy rabbi, especially in the stories that he told.

Until now, the stories were not available except in the form of handwritten manuscripts, produced by various scribes. These manuscripts contain so many errors that the main point is often lost. Therefore, people came to us with great yearning, and persuaded us with great longing, until we had no other choice but to fulfill their desire and bring [this work] to press.

The Rebbe himself also expressed such a desire. Once he declared that he wanted to print the *Sippurey Maasioth*, saying in the presence of many people, "I would like to print the book of stories. It should have the Hebrew written on top, and the [Yiddish] vernacular on the bottom."

He also once said, "What can people find to complain about this? After all, they are nice stories to tell...." We heard words such as these from his holy lips.

This is what motivated us to bring [this work] to press. Of course, we are not deluding ourselves, since we realize full well that [the Rebbe] has had much opposition. However, truth is its own witness.[20] We have an obligation to do [God's] will, and God will then do as He sees fit.[21] He who wants to listen will listen, and he who wants to refuse will refuse.[22]

Also, thank God, Providence has helped us so that [the Rebbe's] sacred works have become popular among the holy people. In every congregation in the community of Israel, his words provide the people with joy and happiness. They are as

---

18.   Psalms 84:3.
19.   Jeremiah 23:36.
20.   A folk saying. See Rabbi Yosef ibn Caspi, *Adaney Kesef* (London, 1911, Volume 1, p. 66).
21.   2 Samuel, 10:12.
22.   Ezekiel 3:27.

sweet as honey in their mouths.[23] All of them are satiated and
enjoy his good.[24] It is like marrow and fat that satisfies their souls
so that with joyous lips, their mouths sing praise.[25]

More people are on our side than are on the side of those who
dispute the truth, speaking about the Tzaddik with arrogance,
pride and scorn,[26] and making up accusations that are totally
unimaginable. We cannot speak at length about this, since it is
among God's hidden mysteries. How many worlds are turned
upside down because of the disputes that have currently become
more prevalent between scholars and tzaddikim? What can be
done by a person who comes after the King? What has been done
is done.[27]

Nevertheless, we wish to inform everyone that our intent in
printing these stories is solely for the sake of members of our
group, who wish to find shelter in [the Rebbe's] holy shadow,[28]
yearning, seeking and searching to hear these holy words. The
words may be printed in a book, but they are the same as if they
had been proclaimed in a great congregation.

Moreover, we see that these stories have already begun to
spread in writing through many manuscripts. There is no
difference between words in a handwritten manuscript and words
in a printed book. Furthermore, the words were never meant to
be kept secret.

Whoever has eyes will see, and whoever has a heart will
understand. [Regarding these stories, it can be said,] *It is not an
empty thing from you* (Deuteronomy 32:47). [As our sages teach,]

23.   Ezekiel 3:3.
24.   cf. Friday night *Amidah*.
25.   Psalms 63:6.
26.   Psalms 31:19.
27.   Ecclesiastes 2:12.
28.   See Judges 9:15; Isaiah 30:2; Psalms 57:2. Rabbi Nathan includes this disclaimer
      because of the great opposition that he was encountering. A number of Chassidic
      leaders who felt that they understood these stories claimed that they were too holy
      for publication.

"If it is empty, then it is from you"[29] [that is, it is your own fault].

The words [of these stories] stand in the highest places. We heard [the Rebbe] say explicitly that every word of these holy stories has tremendous meaning, and that anyone who changes even a single word of these stories from the way that they were told is taking very much away from the story.

[The Rebbe] also said that these stories are original concepts (*chidushim*) that are very wondrous and awesome. They contain extraordinary, hidden, deep meanings. They are fit to be preached in public and one may stand in the synagogue and tell any one of these stories. They are extremely lofty, awesome, original concepts.

Moreover, if a person's heart has attained perfection, and he is expert in the sacred works, especially in the books of the Zohar and the writings of the Ari,[30] then if he fully concentrates his mind and heart on these stories, he will be able to understand and know a small portion of the allusions found in them.

Also in most places, these stories contain wondrous, highly motivating moral lessons (*mussar*), which an intelligent person can understand by himself. Most of [these stories] will arouse the heart and draw it very close to God. They will cause a person to repent before God with ultimate sincerity, so that he will dedicate himself fully to Torah and serving God at all times, turning away completely from all worldly vanities. If a person looks at these stories sincerely, he will see this with his mind's eyes.

The ultimate meaning of these stories, however, is far above the grasp of normal human intelligence. It is deep, deep, who can discover it?[31]

It does not pay to praise these stories overmuch, since they are far above our understanding. The more one tries to praise their

---

29.   *Yerushalmi, Peah* 1:1; *Zohar* 1:163a.
30.   Rabbi Yitzchak Luria (1534-1572), known as the Ari, was considered one of the greatest Kabbalists of all time. Knowledge of his writings is essential in order to understand much of the Kabbalistic teachings after his time.
31.   Ecclesiastes 7:24.

greatness and depth, the more one takes away from them. The only reason that we have spoken at all was to arouse the hearts of the members of our group, so that they not forget the wonders [the Rebbe] showed them. Through the few allusions that he revealed to us after each story, he showed the implication of the words; but still, it was only like seeing gestures from a great distance.[32]

It is true that we have written down some of the allusions that we heard from his holy lips. However, it is obvious to any intelligent person that seeing something in a book is not the same as actually hearing it from the author. This is all the more true of allusions such as these, which are not comprehensible except through such gestures as the movements of the head, winks of the eye, motions of the hand, and the like. Only by seeing these can one begin to understand, and one is even then astounded by what one's eyes have seen. From the distance he will see the greatness of God and His holy Torah, clothed in many garments, as explained in all the sacred texts.

This is how far we can go with a few words, even though they contain very much. Our hearts are still filled with terror; where is the scribe and where is the one who can weigh [the outcome]?[33] From where will our help come?[34] Who will be moved for us for what has been consumed?[35] Who will stand up for us?

We lift our hearts in our hands to God in heaven.[36] Into His hands we entrust our souls.[37] To You, God, we lift up our souls.[38] Until now, Your mercy has helped us. Help us, for we are

---

32.   See *Berakhoth* 46b; *Chagigah* 5b.
33.   Isaiah 33:18.
34.   Psalms 121:1.
35.   The expression used here, *mi yanud*, is found in Isaiah 51:19, Jeremiah 15:5, Nahum 3:7, etc. However, the reading here may be, *mi yagur lanu esh okhelah* — "Who among us shall dwell with the devouring fire?" (Isaiah 33:14).
36.   Lamentations 3:41.
37.   Psalms 31:6.
38.   Psalms 25:1.

depending on You.[39] May God's pleasantness rest upon us,[40] until the Righteous Teacher comes to our community, and our holy, glorious Temple is rebuilt. May we look upon Zion, the city of our solemn gatherings;[41] may our eyes behold the King in His glory[42] — quickly, in our days, Amen.

These are my words as writer, typesetter and transcriber, to eat to satisfaction and to cover ancient things.[43]

Signed:

The insignificant Nathan,[44] son of my father, our rabbi and master, Naftali Hertz[45] (may God protect him and keep him)[46] of Nemerov, and son-in-law of the great rabbi, the saintly one, renowned all over the world. His holy, honorable name is our master, Rabbi David Tzvi[47] (may the memory of the righteous be a blessing in the World to Come), who was head of the rabbinical court in the holy congregation of Kreminetz and its environs, the holy congregation of Sharograd, and the holy congregation of Mohalov and its environs.

Before [the Rebbe] began telling the first story in this book, he declared, "Many hidden meanings and lofty concepts are contained in the stories that the world tells. These stories,

---

39. Daily liturgy.
40. Psalms 90:17.
41. Isaiah 33:20.
42. Isaiah 33:17.
43. Isaiah 23:18, according to Midrashic interpretation.
44. Rabbi Nathan Sternhartz of Nemerov (1780-1845) was the leading disciple of Rabbi Nachman, and the editor of most of his published works. See above, p. 3.
45. Rabbi Nathan's father, R. Naftali Hertz of Nemerov, was very wealthy, having many stores in Nemerov, Berdichev and Odessa (*Kokhavey Or*, p. 9). Rabbi Nathan's mother was the daughter of Rabbi Yitzchak Danziger (*Avenehah Barzel*, p. 3; *Tovoth Zikhronoth*, p. 13).
46. The abbreviation *NeRU* indicates that Rabbi Nathan's father was alive at this time.
47. Rabbi David Tzvi (ben Aryeh Leib) Ohrbach (died 1808). Rabbi Nathan married his daughter in 1792 (*Yemey Maharnat* 6a. Also see *Avenehah Barzel*, p. 4).

however, are deficient; they contain many omissions. They are also confused, and people do not tell them in the correct order. What begins the story may be told at the end, and the like. Nevertheless, the folk tales that the world tells contain many lofty hidden mysteries.

"The Baal Shem Tov (may the memory of a tzaddik and holy man be a blessing) was able to bring about a Unification (*Yichud*)[48] through telling a story. When he saw that the supernal Channels were defective, and it was not possible to rectify them through prayer, he would rectify and unify them by telling stories."

The Rebbe spoke about this. Then he began to tell the story on the following page.[49] He said, "I told this story while on a journey...."[50]

It is important to realize that the stories here are for the most part (if not all) completely new stories that have never before been told. [The Rebbe] created them with his holy mind, based on the lofty perception that he gained through divine inspiration. He would clothe his perceptions with a particular story, and the story itself would be a demonstration of the awesome, great, lofty perception that he experienced, as well as what he saw in the place that he reached.

[The Rebbe] would sometimes relate ordinary folk tales, but he would embellish them. He would change the order of the story, so that it was very different than the original folk tale. In this book, however, only one or two such modified folk tales are included. All the other stories are totally new and original.

When the Rebbe (of blessed memory) began telling stories, he said, "I am now beginning to tell stories" (*ich vell shoin an-heiben maasios der-tzeilen*). His intent was as if to say, "[I must tell

---

48.   A *Yichud* is the unification of two spiritual forces that have been separated.
49.   In the first edition, there was no second introduction, so the stories began on the page after the introduction.
50.   See below, p. 31.

stories] because my lessons and conversations are not having any effect in bringing you back to God." All his life, he made great effort to bring us close to God, but when all this did not help, he began to engage in telling stories.

It was around this time[51] that [the Rebbe] taught the lesson that begins, "Rabbi Shimon said, 'It is a time to do for God, they have disregarded Your Torah' "(Psalms 119:126)...[52] This is speaking of the Torah of the Ancient One[53]... It is printed in the first book on page 157.[54]

At the end of this lesson, [the Rebbe] speaks a bit about stories. He says that people may be asleep all their lives, but through stories told by a true tzaddik, they can be awakened....See what is written there.[55]

There are some stories that are "in the midst of years."[56] However, there are other stories from ancient times that are included in the concept of the Ancient One.[57] If you study the entire lesson well, you will have some awareness and understanding as to the lofty implications of these stories as well as [the Rebbe's] holy intent [in telling them].

In most cases, even the plain, simple meaning of these stories can strongly motivate a person toward God. All these stories consist of awesome mysteries, but aside from their secret meanings, they have great power to motivate everyone toward God. Be strong.

51.　This lesson was said on Rosh HaShanah, 5567 (1806), about two or three weeks after the first story was told (*Yemey Moharnat* 12a; *Chayay Moharan* 34a #1, 22b #14). See note on p. 31.

52.　*Likutey Moharan* 60. The quotation here, which opens the lesson, is from the *Zohar* 3:128a.

53.　In Aramaic this is Atik (see Daniel 7:9, 13, 22), which is the highest of the supernal *partzufim* or persona.

54.　In the first edition of *Likutey Moharan*, Ostrog, 1808.

55.　*Likutey Moharan* 60:6.

56.　*Ibid.* from Habakkuk 3:2. This is a story that is obviously related to a Torah lesson.

57.　See note 53.

SECOND INTRODUCTION[1]

When we printed these stories the first time, we heard an uproar[2] declaring that it was not proper to publish stories such as these. To repeat their words, however, would merely be superfluous.

In our [first] introduction we have already quoted the words of the Rebbe who said that he wanted to have these stories published. [He said,] "What can people find to complain about this? After all, they are nice stories.[3] Innumerable stories have been published in the world, and no one opens his mouth to complain."

Also, most of the stories that the Rebbe told teach very important lessons. Good examples are such stories as "The Master of Prayer," and "The Seven Beggars." Moreover, when one delves into most of the stories, aside from the hidden meanings, one will find lessons of wisdom and good conduct.

Furthermore, we have published notes after these stories, along with some wondrous, awesome allusions that the Rebbe himself revealed, as discussed earlier.

Nevertheless, we resolved that we would bring up a number of other points, which, according to our humble opinion, cast some

---

1.   This Second Introduction was first printed in the edition of *Sippurey Maasioth* of 1850 (no place given), some five years after Rabbi Nathan's death. From the wording, it appears that Rabbi Nathan of Nemerov wrote it as an introduction to a second edition which he never got a chance to print (see *Nevey Tzaddikim*, pp. 45, 46). However, since portions of *Likutey Halakhoth* are mentioned (see below, pp. 25,26), this introduction was certainly written toward the end of Rabbi Nathan's life, probably around 1845.

2.   Isaiah 66:6.
3.   See above, p. 3.

light on the allusions contained in the stories. Whoever wishes to add to this may do so.

It is known that in all the books of the *Zohar* and *Tikkuney Zohar*,[4] as well as in the writings of the Ari,[5] the "King's Daughter" alludes to the Divine Presence (*Shekhinah*) and the Congregation of Israel, as it were. We have been given authority to use such allegorical language from the earliest masters, whose words are our very life.

Thus, both King David and his son Solomon made considerable use of such expressions. The expression, "King's Daughter," is used in this sense in the verse, "All glorious is the King's Daughter indoors" (Psalms 45:14). There are also many similar expressions. Furthermore, the entire Song of Songs, which is "holy of holies, to the extent that the entire world is not fit for it,"[6] is built on this foundation.

Such usage is also found in many places in the writings of the Ari and the books of the *Zohar*. It is thus taught, "He who kills the Snake is given the King's Daughter — which is prayer."[7] This is even more explicit in the teachings of the Old Man (*Sava*) in the *Zohar*, which speaks of "the Beautiful Girl who has no eyes."[8] There are too many cases such as these to recount.

Similarly, in the *Yehi Ratzon* ("May it be Your Will") prayer recited before saying Psalms, we use the expression, "...to attach the Wife of Youth with her Beloved..." Likewise, in the *LeShem Yichud* ("For the Sake of Unification") prayer found in *Shaarey*

---

4. *Tikkuney Zohar* (*Rectifications of the Zohar*) consists of seventy chapters on the first word of the Torah, by the school of Rabbi Shimon bar Yochai (see p. 2, note 16). It was first printed in Mantua in 1558, and, with a different arrangement of pages, in Ortokoi, near Constantinople (the latter being used in all subsequent editions). The *Tikkuney Zohar* contains some of the most important discussions of Kabbalah, and is essential for understanding the system of the *Zohar*.
5. Regarding the Ari, see above, p. 5, note 30.
6. *Yadayim* 3:5.
7. *Tikkuney Zohar* 13 (29b). Also see *Tikkuney Zohar* 21 (43a).
8. *Zohar* 2:95a. See *Rabbi Nachman's Wisdom*, p. 198.

Tzion[9] to be recited before putting tefillin, we say [that it is being done so that] "the Bridegroom [should embrace the Bride, with his left hand under her head] ..."[10] See the entire prayer in this source.

It is immediately apparent from the writings of the Ari that the entire foundation of Kabbalah involves the unification of the concepts of the Bridegroom and the Bride... These writings explain that all the Divine Names, and Emanations (*Sefiroth*), as well as the entire linkage (*hishtalshaluth*) of the Supernal Universes, depict the form of a human male.... Every part of the body has a precise spiritual counterpart. Also discussed in these writings are the concepts of union, intercourse, pregnancy, birth, nursing, and raising a young boy and girl until they come of age... These are discussed at very great length in the *Etz Chaim*[11] and *Pri Etz Chaim*.[12] There are also allusions to these in the *Idra Rabba*[13] in the portions of *Naso*[14] and *HaAzinu*.[15]

---

9.   *Shaarey Tzion* (*Gates of Zion*) is a collection of Kabbalistic prayers by Rabbi Nathan Nata (ben Moshe) Hanover, first published in Prague, 1662. We have used the Brooklyn, 1974 edition, which is a reprint of the Przemysl, 1917 edition, where this prayer is found on p. 92.

10.   See Song of Songs 8:3. When the supernal Man, wearing tefillin on his left hand, places his left hand under the Woman's head, then the hand tefillin are in the place of her brain. The hand tefillin thus provide the consciousnesses (*mochin*) of the Female.

11.   *Etz Chaim* (*The Tree of Life*) by Rabbi Chaim Vital (1542-1620) is the foremost classic of the Ari's Kabbalah. It was first published in Koretz, 1782. We have used the Ashlag edition, Tel Aviv, 1960.

12.   The *Pri Etz Chaim* (*Fruit of the Tree of Life*) is the Kabbalistic classic that applies the principles of *Etz Chaim* (see previous note) to meditations based on observances. First published in Koretz, 1782.

13.   The *Idra* (*Assembly*) is one of the most mystical parts of the *Zohar*. It consists of the *Idra Rabba* (*Great Assembly*) in the portion of *Naso* and the *Idra Zuta* (*Lesser Assembly*) in the portion of *HaAzinu*.

14.   The portion of *Naso* is Numbers 4:21 - 7:89. The *Zohar* is structured as a running commentary on the Torah, and the *Idra Rabba* occurs in this portion. Here Rabbi Shimon bar Yochai assembles his disciples and reveals to them mysteries which hitherto have been kept concealed. This section contains the basis for much of Kabbalah's dynamics.

15.   The portion of *HaAzinu* is Deuteronomy 32. It contains the *Idra Zuta*, where Rabbi

This is also a major theme in the Song of Songs, which speaks of all the parts of the Bridegroom's body, as praised by the Bride,[16] and all the parts of the Bride's body, as praised by the Bridegroom.[17]

In the Midrash, our sages also liken the giving of the Torah to a wedding. Our sages thus comment on the verse, "On the day of His wedding..." (Song of Songs 3:11), stating that it alludes to the giving of the Torah.[18] Commenting on the verse, "[Moses brought the people out of the camp] to greet God" (Exodus 19:17, our sages state, "Like a bridegroom going out to greet his bride."[19]

The holy Sabbath is likewise referred to as both a bride and a queen. [We thus inaugurate the Sabbath with the song,] "Come my friend to greet the Bride..." [We conclude by saying,] "Come O Bride..."

As mentioned earlier, our sages likened the entire joining of the Supernal Universes to their Root to the joining of the Bridegroom to the Bride. This is "because in the image of God He made man" (Genesis 9:6).

Thus, all the parts of both the male and female body form the "image of God." It is thus written, "God created man in His image, in the image of God He created them, male and female He created them" (Genesis 1:27).

We also say in the Wedding Blessings, "[Blessed are You God...] Who created humanity in His image, in the image of His structure's form, and through him made a structure that will last for all time..."

All this is because man and woman are literally a counterpart of the Divine. Between them man and woman have the letters of the Tetragrammaton (YHVH). If a couple is worthy, the Divine

---

Shimon reveals additional mysteries associated with those in the *Idra Rabba,* and then dies.

16.   Song of Songs 5:10-16.
17.   Song of Songs 4:1-5.
18.   *Taanith* 26b.
19.   *Mekhilta*, Rashi, *ad loc.*

Presence rests between them, since he provides the *yod* (ׁ) of the Divine Name, and she provides the *heh* (ה).[20]

All this is well known and obvious to all. All the Ancients used this type of language, alluding to the closeness between God and Israel as the joining of the Bridegroom and the Bride. In its highest Root, our entire mode of serving God alludes to the joining of the Bridegroom and Bride, that is, the joining of the Blessed Holy One (*Kudsha B'rikh Hu*) and His Divine Presence (*Shekhinah*). This is discussed in all the books of the *Zohar*, and forms the main theme of the writings of the Ari.

Also in the Kinoth for Tisha B'Av, in the elegy beginning, "Then when Jeremiah went...."[21] where we bewail the exile of the Divine Presence and the Congregation of Israel, we say, "[Jeremiah] found a beautiful woman who had become repulsive."[22] Furthermore, the Rectification of the Three Watches,[23] taken from the *Zohar Chadash*,[24] also uses such an expression, "Thus She bewails her husband...." See the exact wording there.

From all this, and from many similar cases, it is obvious that the exile of the Divine Presence and the Congregation of Israel is alluded to as an account of the loss of the King's Daughter and her being far from her Beloved...

---

20.   *Sotah* 17a, Rashi *ad loc.* s.v. *Shekhinah*.
21.   An elegy by Rabbi Eleazar Kalir. In the *Authorized Kinot* (London, 1965), p. 135.
22.   *Ibid.* p. 136. In most editions, this is presented as part of the next elegy. The Woman, who represented the Divine Presence, had become repulsive from mourning for the Temple.
23.   Special prayers said during the three watches of the night; see *Berakhoth* 3a.
24.   The *Zohar Chadash* (*New Zohar*) is part of the Zoharic literature, consisting of sayings and texts found in manuscripts of the Safed Kabbalists after the printing of the *Zohar*. These were assembled by Rabbi Avraham (ben Eliezer HaLevi) Berukhim (1516-1593) and first printed in Salonika, 1597. It was called the *"New Zohar"* simply because it was printed later than the original *Zohar*. In the printed editions of the *Zohar*, many expositions break off in the middle, and these are completed in the *Zohar Chadash*.

In the Bahir,[25] cited in the Additions to the Zohar,[26] the text comments on the verse, "Come My beloved, let us go out to the field..." (Song of Songs 7:12). It speaks of a King who lived in the innermost of chambers.... "The King married off [his Daughter] and also gave her away as a gift. Because of his love for her, he sometimes calls her, 'My Sister,' since they both come from the same place. Sometimes He calls her 'My Daughter,' because she is his daughter; and at other times He calls her, 'My Mother'."

Commenting on the verse, "The crown that his mother gave him" (Song of Songs 3:11), our sages speak about [a king who had a daughter] whom he loved so much that he called her "My Mother."[27]

Throughout the entire Book of Proverbs, faith and the Torah are referred to as the "good wife," "the woman of valor." Conversely, false belief and heresy are referred to as an evil woman and a prostitute.[28] This is explained in Rashi's commentary and in all the words of our sages.

There is also a story told by the Baal Shem Tov at the very end of *Toledoth Yaakov Yosef*[29] which speaks of a merchant and his wife who were at sea... [That work] explains that the "God-fearing woman" is the Congregation of Israel.

Since God has revealed all this to us through His early prophets, saints and sages, one can study these stories with an eye

25. *Bahir* 63 (Margolioth Edition). The *Bahir* is one of the most ancient Kabbalistic texts, attributed to the First Century school of Rabbi Nechunia ben Hakana, and first revealed around 1175. It was first printed in Amsterdam, 1651, and an English translation has been made by Rabbi Aryeh Kaplan.

26. *Zohar* 1:265b.

27. *Shir HaShirim Rabbah ad loc.* This may be related to the Yiddish endearment *mamaleh*, used for a child, which literally means "little mama."

28. See especially Proverbs 6, 7, 31.

29. *Toledoth Yaakov Yosef* (Koretz, 1780), p. 202b. This was the major classic of Chasidism, and the first Chasidic work to be published. It was written by Rabbi Yaakov Yosef (ben Yehudah HaKohen) of Polonoye (died circa 1782), one of the leading disciples of the Baal Shem Tov.

to the truth, trying to understand them and plumb their depths, and one will discover wondrous, awesome concepts. Admittedly, it may be impossible to grasp the true meaning of the stories, or their construction and sequence from the beginning to the end. Nevertheless, even if a person gains only a very small amount of understanding, it will be very sweet to his soul.

The first story is "The Lost Princess." This is speaking of the mystery of the exile of the Divine Presence (*Shekhinah*). This exile of the Divine Presence began even before the creation of the universe, this being the mystery of the Shattering of Vessels.[30] This is the mystery of the verse, "These are the kings who reigned [in Edom before any king reigned in Israel]" (Genesis 36:31).[31]

Immediately after Adam was created, he had the task of rectifying this. He was to bring all the Supernal Universes back to their proper places. Thus, immediately after the world was created, God's Kingdom would have been revealed, just as it will be in the Messianic era. However, [Adam] was not careful to avoid eating from the Tree of Knowledge. In the story, this is alluded to by the King's viceroy not standing up to the test and eating from the apple.[32] Through [eating from the Tree of Knowledge, Adam] brought a great spiritual blemish to the world. This caused the Divine Presence to descend even lower, until it was in the [realm of the] Other Side, as is known.

---

30.   At the very beginning, God created vessels to hold the power (light) of His creation. (These vessels were the Sefiroth). These vessels however, were not strong enough to hold the light, and shattered and fell to a lower level, forming the realm of evil. These vessels were the earliest manifestation of the Female Principle (*Malkhuth*) and the Divine Presence (*Shekhinah*). The shattering and falling of these vessels was thus the first manifestation of the exile of the *Shekhinah*.

31.   The kings mentioned in these verses are seen as manifestations of the vessels that shattered, and hence, the Torah records that each of the kings died. The vessels are referred to as "Kings" because they are an aspect of Kingship or Royalty, *Malkhuth*, in Hebrew, which is the Female Principle. It is called a female principle because it is meant to hold, just like the female womb. It is also referred to as "Kingship," since this is what holds the power of the king. See note 40.

32.   See below, p. 39.

Later, Noah wanted to rectify this. He was unsuccessful because he drank wine and became drunk, this being the mystery of the verse, "He drank the wine and became drunk...." (Genesis 9:21). This is explained in the sacred texts as being the concept of, "What is man that he should become drunk?"[33] Noah failed the test by drinking wine, as the Torah explicitly states.[34]

From that time on, all the saints of each generation were involved in completing this rectification. This will continue until the Messiah comes, when the final rectification will occur.

[But besides speaking of the search for cosmic rectification] this story also alludes to every person in every time. Every individual experiences almost every phase in this story. Every Israelite must constantly engage in this rectification, elevating the Divine Presence from exile, raising up the Divine Presence from the dust, and bringing the Holy Kingdom out from among the idolators and [forces of] the Other Side, into which She has fallen.

This is the mystery of everything that we do to serve God — all the observances, good deeds and Torah study that we engage in throughout our lives. All these revolve around this point, as discussed in the sacred texts.

This is true of even the most simple people among the masses, who do not know right from left. Even they can be worthy of following the straight path according to their level, so as to turn aside from evil and do good.[35] Even the simplest person, if his eye looks straight ahead,[36] knows what the Torah forbids, and can turn away from evil and choose good. If he does that, then all the rectifications in the supernal worlds are automatically made through him, and he is worthy of raising the Divine Presence from where it has fallen. It all depends on how much he can sanctify and purify himself.

Therefore, every Israelite is actively engaged in searching for

---

33. *Zohar* 1:73a; *Bereshith Rabbah* 36:4.
34. In the story, the viceroy also drinks wine. See p.41.
35. Psalms 34:15, 37:27.
36. Proverbs 4:25.

the King's Daughter so as to return her to her Father, just as she was in her girlhood. This is the mystery of the verse, "She shall return to her father's house as in her girlhood, and then she can eat of her father's bread" (Leviticus 22:13).

Israel as a whole is likened to the King's viceroy, since they rule the world. Just as [God] brings the dead to life and heals the sick, so does Israel. [Commenting on the verse, "Say to Zion, 'You are My people' " (Isaiah 51:16), the *Zohar* says,] "do not read *am-i* (עַמִּי) [meaning 'My people'] but *im-i* (עִמִּי) [meaning 'with me,' " making the verse read, "You are with Me"]. [God says,] "Just as I can make heaven and earth with My words, so can you."[37] There are many similar teachings.

Therefore, to the extent that each individual serves God, he is, as it were, searching for the Divine Presence and the Congregation of Israel, to bring it out of exile.

Conversely, as it were, the Divine Presence reveals itself to that person. From the deep exile where she has concealed and hidden herself, she comes to him secretly, and reveals to him where she is dwelling and what he can do to find her.

This is expressed in the story, where the King's Daughter reveals to the viceroy what he must do to free her. The methods provided there are explained in a very simple and transparent manner. (It is the Rebbe's way, in most stories, that in the course of the story he provides words of encouragement according to the simple meaning, as one who reads the stories can see.)

Thus, a person must choose a place for himself, and set himself a routine of repentance and fasting, constantly and steadily yearning for God, so that he will be worthy of having a conception of Him. One must desire that He reveal His Kingdom in the world so that, "Every created thing should know that You have made him, everything formed should know that You have

---

37. *Zohar* 1:5a.

formed him, and all who have breath in their mouths...."[38] and that "His Kingdom rules over all."[39]

The raising of the Divine Presence from exile consists primarily of bringing about the recognition of God's Kingship in full faith and truth.[40] Then, everyone, great and small alike, will be aware of God, and the Kingdom will be God's....

A person begins to do this, and chooses for himself a place for meditation and serving God, longing and yearning for Him. Sometimes, after a while, he can be very close to reaching his goal and having [the Divine Presence] reveal itself to him so that he experiences a revelation of God's Kingdom according to his level. But then, on the very last day, this person is tested according to his level. On that day, when everything depends on the person's actions, the Evil One and all his cohorts overcome him in a very powerful manner.

They speak to him and convince him to take their advice, so that he sees "that it is pleasant to the eyes and desirable...."[41] He takes the fruit and eats a little bit, failing the test that he had to pass in order to be purified.

He then immediately falls asleep. This "sleep" denotes a loss of the correct states of consciousness (*mochin*). One then loses the knowledge and wisdom that enlighten him, this being the mystery of Cain, when "his face fell" (Genesis 4:5). It is written [that God asked Cain,] "Why has your face fallen?" (Genesis 4:6).

In the lesson which begins, "Rabbi Shimon said..." (*Likutey Moharan* 60), it speaks about the spiritual blemish brought about through the lust for food. This causes a person to lose his "face," which denotes the correct states of consciousness, and he then falls into the concept of "sleep."[42] If you look up what is written

---

38.   High Holiday liturgy. The viceroy in the story also had to find a place for himself.
39.   Psalms 103:19.
40.   Thus the Divine Presence (*Shekhinah*) is God's Kingship (*Malkhuth*). See above, p. 16, note 31.
41.   Genesis 3:6.
42.   *Likutey Moharan* 60:6.

there, you will understand, since there is considerable discussion of the concept of stories and how they can awaken one from such "sleep."

During the period that a person is in such a sleeping state, all sorts of bad things can happen to him. In the story, this is alluded to by all the troops that passed by the viceroy when he was sleeping.[43]

When the viceroy woke up, he realized that he had been sleeping and he went back to where the King's Daughter was. She told him how pitiful both he and she were, since because of one day, he lost everything. She was then more lenient in her requirements, telling him that he need not fast completely, but merely that he must abstain from wine, so that he not fall asleep.

Then he strove for a long time, serving God so as to free the King's Daughter, but then on the last day, he failed the test again, even though it was relatively easy. He saw a spring flowing with wine, and fooled himself so that he began being drawn to it. He said to his servant, "Don't you see that this is a spring? How can it possibly contain wine?" With that, he took a small amount of the wine and tasted it, immediately falling asleep. He then slept for a very long time.

But this is the way of the Evil One and his temptors. When they want to trick a virtuous person who wants to avoid temptation, they fool him little by little. They cause him to be curious about the things he desires and wonder about them. Then, when the desire is well entrenched in his mind, the Evil One overcomes him and causes him to sin.

The Torah presents this sequence explicitly regarding the Tree of Knowledge. First the snake engages the woman in conversation and says to her, "Did God then say [that you may not eat from any tree in the garden]" (Genesis 3:1). [The snake wanted to get the woman to think about the tree and wonder about it. It is then written,] "The woman saw that the tree was good to eat and

---

43.   Below, p. 42.

desirable to the eye" (Genesis 3:6). Look carefully and you will understand.

This is the way of all desires and tests. If a man has true intelligence and is truly concerned that his soul escape destruction he will want to stand up to a test. In order to do so, he must direct his mind away from the object of his desire completely. He must not confront the desire at all, nor should he even speak, think, or wonder about it at all. He should totally avoid letting his thoughts confuse him.

It is thus written in the "Alphabet Book,"[44] "Do not engage in arguments with the one who wishes to tempt you." (See what is written there.)

Rather, a person must take his mind off his desire completely. He should open his mind to the Torah, or even discuss business or other affairs until he is saved from this temptation. When similar thoughts or ideas return, he must again overcome them and take his mind off them. This he must do over and over, being very stubborn, until he finally wins the battle.

The viceroy in the story failed the test a second time, and he once again fell asleep for a long time. This time he slept for seventy years.

The concept of sleeping for seventy years is discussed in the lesson which begins, "Rabbi Shimon said..." (*Likutey Moharan* 60). Some people fall asleep [so that they are unconscious of] all "seventy faces of the Torah,"[45] which is the concept of "seventy years." In such a case, it is impossible to arouse them except by telling stories of ancient times[46].... Look carefully at what is written there.

When the King's Daughter, which is the Root of a person's

---

44. This is now usually referred to as *Sefer HaMiddoth* (*Book of Attributes*). It was first published in Mohalov, 1811. The quote here is in *Niuf* 10.

45. *Otioth-DeRabbi Akiva*; cf. *BaMidbar Rabbah* 13:15; *Zohar* 1:47b, 1:54a, 3:216a. This indicates that there are seventy ways to interpret the Torah.

46. *Likutey Moharan* 60:6.

soul, passes by, and sees that the person has fallen asleep for so many years, she weeps very much. Both he and she are very greatly to be pitied. Then she tells him that she is not in the same place where she originally was, but in another place, on a mountain of gold....

The parallel is clear. No matter what he did and regardless of how far he fell during this long period, the Divine Presence nevertheless tries to awaken him over and over again. Each time She gives him new advice how to find Her and find his holy Root, which is the concept of the King's Daughter.

We thus see that this viceroy failed the test twice, and fell asleep for such a long time. He experienced so much travail and suffering in order to find the King's Daughter, and then, because of what happened on the last day, he lost everything. He fell twice in this manner, as we have seen earlier. Nevertheless, he did not give up hope. Rather, he went out to seek and find the Golden Mountain and the Castle.

Then, with tremendous effort and difficult wanderings, he set off to find the mountain and the castle. Finally he found a giant carrying a huge tree.... The giant put him off and told him, "There is positively no such mountain or castle." The giant tried to talk him out of it and dissuade him so that he would return home.

The viceroy, however, refused to be dissuaded or discouraged. He said, "I'm certain that the mountain and castle do exist!" Finally, he got the giant to call together all the animals, but they too insisted that the mountain and castle were nonexistent. The giant told the viceroy, "You can see with your own eyes that it is nonexistent. Why are you striving so much for nothing? Take my advice and go back!"

The viceroy did not pay any attention to this, and replied, "I'm certain that it exists!" The giant then told him that he should go to his brother, who was in command of all the birds. The viceroy went and expended much effort finding the brother, but when he found him, the second giant also discouraged him and tried to talk him into turning back. The giant insisted, "I'm positive that this mountain and castle do not exist!"

The viceroy refused to accept this discouragement. The second giant had to call together all the birds, but they all replied that there is no place in the world where such a mountain or castle exists. The second giant told the viceroy, "You can see with your own eyes that you are striving for nothing. Go back!" The viceroy, however, also refused to pay attention to the second giant, insisting that he has absolute faith that the mountain and castle definitely existed.

The second giant then told the viceroy to go to his brother who oversees all the winds. The third giant also discouraged him very much, and he called together all the winds, who answered that no such thing exists. The third giant then said, "See! You must realize that you have been making all this effort in vain. It is obvious that no such thing exists! Return home!"

The viceroy realized that he had come to the end of the trail, and he did not have anywhere else to turn. But deep inside he was still strong in his faith, and he knew for certain that the mountain and castle existed, and that the King's Daughter was there. Because of the great suffering and bitterness that he felt in his heart, he began to weep very much.

God then had mercy on him, and a wind arrived and informed him that it had been the wind which had carried the King's Daughter to the mountain and castle. [The giant] then gave him a purse from which he could take any money he needed, so that lack of money would not be an obstacle. The viceroy then went there, and worked hard to devise a plan until he found the King's Daughter. Happy is he.

If one looks at this with an honest eye, one will understand well how strong a person must be in serving God. One must realize that in serving God, one's stubbornness must be without measure or limit. This is true of every single person according to his level, no matter how high or low he goes, and no matter what happens to him.

One can then look at this story and understand how much struggle and effort the viceroy underwent, only to twice fail an easy test and fall asleep for as long as seventy years. Nevertheless, he did not give up hope. He continued striving and did not pay attention to any obstacles or discouragement placed in the way of his finding his goal.

He ignored discouragement and strengthened himself until the giants changed their minds and began to help him. Each one gathered the animals, birds or winds under his charge. It is true that they subsequently discouraged him all the more, saying that they could not discover anything like this to exist. But still, he ignored their discouragement, and then each one told him about his brother, until he came to the one who oversaw the winds, and was then able to reach his goal.

Even this last giant discouraged him, but he remained strong in his mind, never giving up, no matter what happened. Then, in one instant, everything was reversed, and all the obstacles and hindrances became means of helping him. All the negative influences became positive influences and means of attaining the goal. In the end a wind came and told him that it was the one that had brought the King's Daughter to the mountain and the castle, and finally this wind carried the viceroy there as well.

Look, understand and see. In each detail of the story, you will find allusions and wondrous encouragement, telling how much a person must strengthen himself to probe, seek and find a way of finding God at all times. This follows from the verse, "Seek His presence at all times...." (Psalms 105:4).

It may be true that the story itself is higher than our understanding. We have no idea at all what is the meaning of the Golden Mountain, the Pearl Castle, or any of the other concepts mentioned in the story. Nevertheless, all these allusions fit into the general framework, and can be understood in the context of the story. One can derive one's own interpretations if one wants, and thus find great encouragement. The wise man will hear and expand the lesson.[47]

---

47.   Proverbs 1:5.

The same is true of all the other stories.

(The concepts of the Golden Mountain and the Pearl Castle allude to the great wealth, obtained in a holy manner, that one needs for true contemplation.... This is discussed in the lesson, "Rabbi Shimon said..." (Chapter 60 in the first part [of *Likutey Moharan*]).[48] Look into this carefully, and you will understand, since this lesson is a commentary on this story, as we understood it from the Rebbe himself.)

One can go from one concept to another, and delve into the story of "The Sophisticate and the Simpleton." To some degree, it is obvious that the lesson of the story is that the main goal is to live with simplicity, without any sophistication. If a person looks at the story carefully, then in every word he can see wondrous allusions which will strengthen him in the ways of simplicity. This is the main goal in life in this world, and certainly in the next.

Moral lessons beyond compare can also be found in the story of "The Exchanged Children," "The Master of Prayer," and all the more so in "The Seven Beggars." In this last story, each beggar teaches wondrous, incomparable moral lessons. Each one boasts of his great separation from the worldly in the ultimate sense.

Thus, one boasts that he has always been blind, never looking at the worldly at all, since the physical world is no more than the blink of an eye. The deaf beggar boasts that he is totally deaf to all the voices in the world, since they are all deficient. He does not consider the world worthwhile, that he should listen to its shortcomings. Another one boasted that he had never spoken any words other than praise of God, and therefore he has a severe speech impediment when it comes to speaking of worldly matters. Still another boasted that he did not want to add to the vanities and "vapors" of this world. The same is true of all of them.

48.   *Likutey Moharan* 60:1.

This must be studied very carefully. If you look with an honest eye, you will stand and tremble in astonishment, and you will become aware of the wonderful moral lesson and encouragement toward God that is found in this story. There is nothing that can be compared to it.

Look at our words in *Likutey Halachoth*.[49] In many places God has enlightened us, and we have been able to interpret the allusions in a number of the stories.

Thus, in the Laws of Tefillin, there is a discussion of the first beggar, the one who was blind.[50] In the Laws of the Morning Blessings, we discuss the story of "The Exchanged Children."[51] In the Laws of Prayer, we discuss the story of the "Master of Prayer."[52]

In *Yoreh Deah*,[53] in the Laws of Worms, we discuss the story of the sixth beggar, the one without hands, who told the story of the King's Daughter who ran to a castle made of water.[54] In *Evven HaEzer*,[55] in the Laws of Women, we discuss this same story further, especially insofar as the remedy for the King's Daughter is ten types of song.[56] If you look in other places, you will also find pleasure, with God's help.

Look in the Laws of Vows regarding the story of the fourth day [in the Seven Beggars], about the two birds.[57] In the Laws of

---

49. *Likutey Halakhoth* (*Anthology of Laws*) is an exposition of Breslover Chasiduth written by Rabbi Nathan of Nemerov in the form of a commentary on *Shulchan Arukh* (the accepted code of Jewish law).

50. *Likutey Halakhoth, Orach Chaim, Hilkhoth Tefillin* 2.

51. *Likutey Halakhoth, Orach Chaim, Birkhoth HaShachar* 3. In the book, the story is referred to as "The Exchanged Children."

52. *Likutey Halakhoth, Orach Chaim, Tefillah* 4.

53. *Yoreh Deah* is the section of *Shulchan Arukh* dealing with the laws of kashruth and other laws requiring rabbinical decision.

54. *Likutey Halakhoth, Yoreh Deah, Tola'oth* 4.

55. *Evven HaEzer* is the third section of *Shulchan Arukh*, dealing with marriage and divorce.

56. *Likutey Halakhoth, Evven HaEzer, Ishuth*, 6:3, 10.

57. *Likutey Halakhoth, Yoreh Deah, Nedarim* 4:24, 36.

Charity, there is a discussion of the story of the third day, regarding the beggar with a speech impediment, the heart of the world, and the spring which was above time.[58]

May God show us the wonders of His Torah, and may we be worthy to add to our understanding of the allusions in the stories and the words that we were worthy of hearing from this great light.

We also found the following among the writings. It is a defense that he offered for writing the stories in such a simple manner:

"We would like to make people who read the Book of Stories aware that they should not denigrate them because of the somewhat coarse language that is sometimes employed. Thus, in the first story, he uses the expression, 'He became angry at her.' Likewise, in the story of the 'Exchanged Children,' he says, 'He took himself to drinking.' In all these cases we must give the story the benefit of the doubt. It was an error uttered by a ruler,[59] for some important reason."

This is what we have found, and we copied it letter for letter.

One can see clearly that he[60] wanted to write a reason for [using such expressions]. However, it appears that something interrupted him in the middle, and God did not allow us to be worthy of having what he himself wrote. But thank God that we were worthy of being able to copy the above words.

Whenever he wished to write a word, so that it be revealed to this world, there were many, many obstacles Because of this, he was very diligent in writing, as you can see with your own eyes.

---

58. *Likutey Halakhoth, Yoreh Deah, Hilkhoth Melamdim U'Tzedakah* 13.
59. Ecclesiastes 10:5.
60. This is apparently referring to Rabbi Nathan of Nemerov; see below, notes 62, 63. Thus, it appears that the above quote is also from Rabbi Nathan. This section was most probably added by Rabbi Nachman of Tulchin, a leading disciple of Rabbi Nathan.

He always told us that he would make himself all the more diligent to overcome the obstacles and write what he wished immediately. He never knew if he would have another opportunity to write it, for many reasons that were known only to him.

Now, because I heard that he stated that he wanted to print [this work] again,[61] and write the reason for what we have discussed earlier, I will not refrain from writing one of the many concealed and hidden reasons that he had. This is what I heard from him (may his memory be blessed).[62]

Our master, Rabbi Nachman (may the memory of a tzaddik and holy man be a blessing) told the stories in the Yiddish spoken in our land. Then Rabbi Nathan (may the memory of the righteous be a blessing),[63] the Rebbe's foremost student, translated them into Hebrew. He was very careful to use simple language so as not to change the meaning for reading them in Hebrew, and so that they should be understood exactly the same as they were when [Rabbi Nachman] told them in the Yiddish that is spoken among us.

This is the reason that such simple Hebrew expressions are found in many places. It was meant to be as simple as possible.

This is besides the hidden reasons that we were not worthy of hearing from him. It is not farfetched to believe that there are other hidden reasons. It is obvious from his other works that he was a great master of language, but here he lowered himself especially to use simple language. It is therefore fitting to believe that he had an important reason for this. A man of faith shall abound with blessings.[64] Amen. May this be His will.

---

61. From here we see that Rabbi Nathan wanted to reprint the *Sippurey Maasioth*; see p. 10, note 1.
62. That is, from Rabbi Nathan of Nemerov.
63. Here we see that this section was written after Rabbi Nathan's death.
64. Proverbs 28:20.

THE
THIRTEEN
TALES

1

THE LOST PRINCESS*

[The Rebbe] spoke up and said,* "While on my journey* I told a story. Whoever heard it had a thought of repentance."* *(and this is the story).*

There was once a king* who had six sons* and one

The Lost Princess. Literally, "Loss of a King's Daughter," *Avedath Bath Melekh* in Hebrew.

This story is one of the most transparent of all the stories here, and the most easily interpreted. There is also a wealth of information in the various commentaries on this story.

[The Rebbe] spoke up and said. This is not in the Yiddish, which merely begins with the quote.

While on my journey. It was Rabbi Nachman's custom to travel from Breslov to Tchehrin, Terkovitz (and Medvedevka) on *Shabbath Nachamu*, the Sabbath after Tisha B'Av (*Chayay Moharan* 30a #24; see *Sippurim Niflaim*, p. 160). On *Shabbath Nachamu* 5566 (11 Av; July 25,1806), while Rabbi Nachman was in Medvedevka, he told this story (*Yemey Moharnat* 12a; *Chayay Moharan* 15b #59; *Parparoth LeChokhmah* 60:1).

A short time before this, after Shavuoth, Rabbi Nachman's son, Shlomo Ephraim, had died. Rabbi Nachman later said that this child could have been the Messiah (*Yemey Moharnat* 11a, *Chayay Moharan* 33b #1).

thought of repentance. Rabbi Nachman later taught that, no matter how deeply one is sleeping (spiritually), one can be awakened by stories from ancient times (*Likutey Moharan* 60; *Biur HaLikutim* 60:6, 62:6). This lesson, *Likutey Moharan* 60, was taught on Rosh HaShanah after the story was told (Shabbath, September 13, 1806), and it is said to contain the key to this story. (See Introduction p. 9. Also see *Chayay Moharan* 22b #14, *Likutey Halakhoth; Yoreh Deah; Yeyn Nesekh* 2:8.)

king. This refers to God (Rabbi Rosenfeld, tape). God is called a King because He plans the direction of the world, and decrees how things should go. This is known as Providence (*hashgachah*).

The first stage of this planning was the creation of the Vacated Space, in which He would create all things. This is described in the Zohar: "In the beginning of the authority of the *King*, the Lamp of Darkness carved out a space in the supernal Light" (*Zohar* 1:15a; *Zohar HaRakia ad loc.; Shefa Tal.* See *Likutey Moharan* 49).

daughter.* This daughter was very precious to him and he loved

Kabbalistically, the term "King" can relate to any of the upper three of the Ten Sefiroth. These upper three sefiroth are Kether (Crown), Chokhmah (Wisdom) and Binah (Understanding). (See *Zohar* 1:229; *Zohar Chadash* 45d; *Or HaGanuz* on *Bahir* 9, 16, 24, 37, 53; *Pardes* 23:13.) These may be represented by the three letters in the Hebrew word *melekh*, meaning king. They represent the intellectual powers that God created, through which He would direct the world. (Also see the beginning of story #2, p. 55.)

six sons. The six sons and the daughter allude to the seven most basic forces of creation, that is, the lower seven of the Ten Sefiroth. Their names are found in the verse, "Yours, God, are the [loving] greatness (1), the strength (2), the beauty (3), the dominance (4) and the empathy (5) for all that is in heaven and earth (6); Yours, God, is the Kingdom (7)" (1 Chronicles, 29:11, interpreted Kabbalistically). (*Biur HaLikutim* 60:20).

These seven forces are reflected in the six days of creation and the Sabbath. These also parallel the six basic directions (north, south, east, west, up, down) and the center point (*Sefer Yetzirah* 4:3; *Maharal, Tifereth Yisroel* 2; see *Rimzey Maasioth*).

The six masculine forces (sons) are basically seen as parts of the power to give and create. Hence, they are also related to the six days of creation. They are the ways in which one reaches out to the six directions of creation.

The seventh force, known as Malkhuth (Kingship), is seen as being feminine. Like the womb of the female, it is seen as the power to receive and hold (and eventually give back something more perfect). It is thus the Sabbath which gives us the power to hold on to the original forces of creation and integrate them into our lives. It is also the center point, where instead of looking outward, we look inward, and integrate holiness into ourselves.

It is noted that there is a significant parallel to this in the Torah. Leah also had six sons and one daughter, Dinah (Genesis 46:8-15; *Zohar* 1:153b). Like the King's Daughter (Malkhuth), Dinah entered Shechem, the place of evil (Genesis 34:2), and could only be taken out with a clever plan (Genesis 34:13; see end of the story; *Biur HaLikutim* 60:62, 69; *Rimzey Maasioth, Hashmatoth*). One reason for this is that Leah is related to Binah, the supernal Mother (*Etz Chaim, Shaar HaKelalim* 12; *Shaar Yaakov VeLeah* 4, p. 199).

daughter. The identity of this daughter is the key to the entire story. As we see from the context, this is the Sefirah of Malkhuth (Kingship, government), the feminine force of creation. When a king is in his chambers, he has no interaction with his subjects. It is only when he sits on his throne, and exercises kingship (Malkhuth) that his subjects can relate to him. Malkhuth also denotes government, the means by which the people receive their direction from the king. (See *Biur HaLikutim* 60:66.)

Thus, Malkhuth is seen as the ability to experience God's presence. In this respect, it is also known as the Shekhinah (Divine Presence), from the root *shakhen*, meaning to dwell (See Introduction, 18). This is related to prophecy, because when a person has a prophetic experience, the Shekhinah is said to rest upon him (See *Sanhedrin* 11a).

It is also known as the Congregation of Israel (*Knesseth Yisroel*) (Introduction, p. 14). This is because Malkhuth is like the collective soul of Israel, allowing Israel to interact with

her* very much. He spent much time with her.*

God (*Shaarey Orah* 1, p. 16a; Introduction, p. 14; *Likutey Etzoth, Ratzon* 3; see *Likutey Halakhoth, Nedarim* 4:25).

As mentioned earlier, the King is God's Intellect, represented by the three highest sefiroth, Kether, Chokhmah, and Binah. The feminine concept, through which we can receive and grasp God's Intellect, is Malkhuth, and hence it is referred to as "The King's Daughter."

The King's Daughter is thus seen as our ability to understand, especially the mysteries of the Torah (*Rimzey Maasioth, Hashmatoth; Biur HaLikutim* 60:86; see *Zohar* 1:114a, 3:248a).

Since our awareness of God's presence is enhanced through prayer, the King's Daughter is also seen as an aspect of prayer. This is also an aspect of Malkhuth. (Introduction, p. 11; from *Tikkuney Zohar* above; see *Zohar* 1:24a, 253a, etc; *Shaarey Orah*, p. 22a).

The main place where God's imminence (as well as prophecy) is enhanced is in the Land of Israel. Therefore, the King's Daughter is also seen as alluding to the Holy Land (*Zimrath HaAretz*). The Holy Land is also an aspect of Malkhuth (see *Shaarey Orah*, p. 16b; see *Zohar* 1:166a, 222b, 3:84a). This also relates to the soul of the Messiah (*Biur HaLikutim*, p. 60).

In one of the earliest interpretations of this story, Rabbi Nathan states that the King's Daughter is faith (*Alim Leterufah* 2, 26 Nissan, 5582 [1822]). [This was written before the second introduction.] However, it is primarily through faith that we are aware of God's imminence. Hence, faith is also an aspect of Malkhuth (*Zohar* 3:16b, 230a, 1:230b; *Tikkuney Zohar* 5a; *Likutey Moharan* 35:7).

On a simpler level, the King's Daughter is the spouse or soulmate that every individual seeks in life (*Biur HaLikutim* 60:14, 87, *Rimzey Maasioth, Hashmatoth*). The Talmud thus teaches that it is the way of a man to seek what he has lost (Niddah 31b). In a sense, a man's search for a wife parallels his search for the spiritual, since an unmarried person cannot be spiritually complete. (See *Zohar* 1:181b, 136a, 3:65a.)

In general, then, the King's Daughter is man's ability to experience the Divine. This is the Shekhinah (Divine Presence), which Kabbalistically is known as the Sefirah of Malkhuth.

loved her. As mentioned earlier, the King denotes God's intellectual plan to create the world. The purpose of creation was so that God would be able to do good for another, and thus reveal His loving-kindness to the world (*Likutey Moharan* 64:1). The means through which this would be attained would be through Malkhuth, the King's Daughter. Since the King's Daughter is the means through which the King's purpose is accomplished, he wishes to be as close as possible to her, and hence, he loves her. (See *Pardes Rimonim* 18:3; *Biur HaLikutim* 60:84.)

spent much time with her. Or "frolicked with her." This is God's playing with the Torah before creation (Proverbs 8:30). According to the Midrash, God spent 2000 years before creation, frolicking and delighting with the Torah (*Bereshith Rabbah*). Kabbalistically, this

One time, he was alone with her on a certain day* and he became angry at her.* He inadvertently said,* "May the Evil One take you away!"*

---

represents the forces of creation going through the sefiroth of Chokhmah and Binah (*Avodath HaKodesh*). In Kabbalistic terms, this represents the light of the King entering the Vessels, which are represented by Malkhuth. As we have seen, Malkhuth, the Daughter, is the ability to grasp and hold.

alone together. At the beginning of the first day of creation, all the six masculine forces were being readied to create the universe. They were all expressed on the first day, since everything was created on that day (Midrash).

became angry at her. This is the concept of *tzimtzum* (constriction), where God withdraws His power (*Biur HaLikutim* 60:17). Kabbalistically, God withdrew some of His power from the vessels (Malkhuth) so that they would not be able to hold His light. The vessels would then shatter when the light of creation entered them. (See *Etz Chaim, Shaar Mati VeLo Mati*, Chapter 2, end.)

The Talmud states that when a person becomes angry, "If he is wise, his wisdom is taken away" (Pesachim 66b). Thus this anger could relate to the removal of the mental power of Chokhmah from the vessels.

The anger might have come about because God foresaw the deeds of the wicked. Therefore, He withheld the light of creation, and created physical light (Rashi, Midrash). Thus, even though God's creative power is called light, the world was originally dark (Genesis 1:2).

inadvertently said. Literally, "A saying was thrown from this mouth" (Heb. ונזרקה מפיו) or, "a word slipped out," Yiddish (*arois-ge-chapt*).

The purpose of the shattering of the vessels was to allow free will to exist (*Etz Chaim, Shaar Derushey Nekudoth* 6, p. 116). Without a realm of evil, it would be impossible to choose between good and evil.

However, if free will is to exist, God must constrict (and restrict) His knowledge of the future. Otherwise, we become involved in the paradox of free will and God's knowledge of the future (*Likutey Moharan* 21:4). Thus, the creation of free will through the shattering of the vessels also involved God's withdrawing His knowledge from creation. Thus, the first word of God created the realm of evil (*Biur HaLikutim* 60:76).

May the Evil One take you away. Literally, "The no good should take you." This is seen as the shattering of vessels (*shevirath ha-kelim*), where the shattered vessels (Malkhuth) fell into the realm of the evil husks (*klipoth*). (Second Introduction, p. 16.) This means that the power to perceive God would not be perfect in the world.

The lack of perception of God is alluded to in the darkness that existed at the beginning of creation (Genesis 1:2). Thus, Rashi points out that God's name is not associated with darkness, and the Torah therefore says, "The darkness *He* (not God) named night." (Genesis 1:5)

It is significant that the expression "the no good" is used here. The ten sayings of

At night* she went to her room. In the morning, no one knew* where she was. Her father was very upset,* and he went here and there looking for her.

---

creation represent the Ten Sefiroth. Then, the 11th saying of creation begins with "no good" — "It is no good for man to be alone." (Genesis 2:18) This represents the realm of the *klipoth*, which is below the Ten Sefiroth. (See *Shiur Komah* 55.)

The original vessels consisted of the lower sefiroth, corresponding to the days of the week (along with Daath). Since the vessel, which is the feminine element (Malkhuth), was shattered, we would expect that the feminine element of each day would be damaged. Indeed, darkness and night are the feminine element of the first day, and God would not associate His name with them (Rashi). On the second day, the lower waters wept. On the third day, the fruit (feminine) did not extend its taste to the entire tree. On the fourth day, God reduced the moon, which also represents Malkhuth (*Chullin* 60b; see *Rimzey Maasioth*). On the fifth day, the female leviathan was killed. Finally, on the sixth day, it was Eve who was first tempted to sin.

The exile of Malkhuth to the realm of evil was later reflected in the exile of the Shekhinah with the destruction of the Temple (Rabbi Rosenfeld). It was also reflected in the fact that the Holy Land was occupied by other nations (*Zimrath HaAretz*).

The fact that the feminine element is trapped in the realm of evil is also represented later by the fact that the wives of the patriarchs were taken by the Philistines. This was true of both Sarah (Genesis 12) and Rebecca (Genesis 26) (*Rimzey Maasioth, Hashmatoth*). It is also reflected by the fact that King David, who represents Malkhuth (royalty) originated from an act of incest, after his ancestor Lot left Sodom. David was a descendant of Moab, who was born from a liaison between Lot and his daughter (Genesis 19). The Midrash thus says, "Where did God find David? In Sodom" (*Bereshith Rabbah* 41:4, 50:10; *Yebamoth* 77a, *Rimzey Maasioth, Hashmatoth*).

That night. Night is seen as the time when the forces of evil have power (*Biur HaLikutim* 60:21). The shattering of vessels took place during the original darkness that existed at the beginning of creation.

no one knew...(See *Rimzey Maasioth*). At the time of creation, Malkhuth left the universe of Atziluth (closeness), which is the universe of the Sefiroth, and entered Beriyah (creation), the universe of the throne (see Ezekiel 1:26). This, however, is also the realm of the *klipoth* (see *Shaar HaKavanoth, Derushey HaLaylah* 4, p. 352; *Pri Etz Chaim, Tikun Chatzoth* 1).

upset. It is thus written, "For a short moment I forsook you, but with infinite kindness I will have compassion on you" (Isaiah 54:7). God also said, "Bring an atonement for Me because I reduced the moon" (*Chullin* 60b; *Rimzey Maasioth*). The Talmud also teaches that God said, "I am with him in trouble" (Psalms 91:15) (Rabbi Rosenfeld, notes) and that God mourns the destruction of the Temple (*Berakhoth* 3a; Rabbi Rosenfeld, tape). Also, God weeps because of the exile (*Berakhoth* 59a; Rabbi Rosenfeld, notes). (See *Shiur Komah* 56).

The concept is that God created the world to do good. However, in order to give free

The viceroy* realized that the king was very upset. He stood up and asked [that the king] give him a servant,* a horse,* and

will, God had to create evil, as discussed earlier. Moreover, in order to maximize man's reward, God made the challenge as great as possible (*Avoth* 5:23, see *The Handbook of Jewish Thought* 3:25). This would mean that those who passed the test would have the maximal reward, but it also meant that many others would fail. Since God's purpose would not be realized through these people, God (the King) is said to grieve. It is thus written, "God regretted that He made man on the earth, and He grieved in His heart" (Genesis 6:6).

viceroy. *Sheni lemalkhuth* in both Hebrew and Yiddish; literally, "second in the government". This is the viceroy, chamberlain, or prime minister. The identification of the viceroy is very important, since he is the second main character in the story.

In general, the viceroy is identified with Israel as a whole (Introduction, p. 17), especially the souls of Israel (*Rimzey Maasioth*). Israel is seen as God's second in command when it comes to directing the world and bringing about the final goal. Thus, the word *sheni* (שני), can be seen as an abbreviation of *shoresh nishmoth yisrael* (שורש נשמת ישראל), "the root of the souls of Israel." The viceroy also represents every Jew, who is seeking out the King's Daughter, and trying to find the Divine (Introduction, p. 17; *Zimrath HaAretz*).

But in particular, the viceroy represents the righteous man or tzaddik in each generation (Introduction, p. 17). Thus, as we shall see historically, he takes the form of both Adam and Noah.

In general, the one time that the Torah speaks of a "second to the king" is in relation to Joseph (Genesis 41:43). Joseph is the concept of tzaddik (*Zohar* 3:26a, 101a, 236a). This is related to the sefirah of Yesod (foundation), as it is written, "The tzaddik is the world's Yesod" (Proverbs 10:25). Yesod usually denotes the concept of penetration; hence the viceroy must penetrate the realm of evil in order to free the princess.

This is very much like Joseph, who penetrated the defilement of Egypt to become a tzaddik (in rejecting Potiphar's wife, Genesis 39:8), and the "second to the king." The chain of events is that after becoming a tzaddik, he became second to the king.

Since Yesod is the sixth sefirah, it represents the 6th day of creation, when man was made. Hence, the viceroy can also represent mankind as a whole, or Israel, who is the heart of mankind.

In Kabbalah, Rachel is very often identified as the Shekhinah (see *Shaar HaKavanoth loc. cit.*). She was also in exile, brought up in the home of the wicked Laban. Jacob, who was the tzaddik of his time, had to free her from this realm of evil (*Biur HaLikutim* 60:26, *Rimzey Maasioth, Hashmatoth*).

servant. This is the soul (*Rimzey Maasioth*). This was left behind before the viceroy went to find the gold mountain. From the context, however, it appears that the servant here represents human logic (see below).

horse. The body (see *Rimzey Maasioth* 6; see *Likutey Moharan* 12:4; *Tikkuney Zohar* 70:134a). The horse was left behind outside the first castle.

some money* for expenses, and he went to search for her. He searched for her* very much, for a very long time, until he found her. (Now he tells how he searched for her until he found her.)

[The viceroy] traveled back and forth for a long time, through deserts, fields and forests. He searched for [the princess] for a very long time. Finally, while traveling through the desert,* he saw a path to the side.* He thought it over.* "Since I have traveled for so long in the desert and cannot find her, let me follow this path. Perhaps it will bring me to an inhabited area."

He continued traveling for a long time until he finally saw a castle.* Many soldiers* stood around it. The castle was beautiful,* and the troops around it were standing in a fine order.

[The viceroy] was afraid that the soldiers would not let him

---

money. This is wordly goods (*Rimzey Maasioth*). Money will be of no avail on the golden mountain. Later, the viceroy receives a purse with which he can have all the money he wants. It seems that money may refer to merit or good deeds.

He searched for her. Going to seek the princess is, in itself, a very great thing. The forces of evil want us to feel that awareness of God is a mere illusion (*Rimzey Maasioth*).

desert. *Midbar.* The world *midbar* comes from the root *davar,* meaning "to speak." This alludes to words of prayer. Also, the desert is a place of isolation, where one is alone. Hence, the desert refers to *hithbodeduth*, individual, isolated prayer and meditation (Rabbi Rosenfeld, tape and notes).

According to Rabbi Nachman, the desert also alludes to faith, since going into the desert with Moses was a supreme act of faith on the part of the Israelites (*Likutey Moharan Tinyana* 5:15).

A desert is also a dry place. It may denote the fact that when one first sets out to serve God, one does not feel any accomplishment; one feels that one's worship is dry and lifeless.

path to the side. This indicates that in order to find the princess, the tzaddik must leave the well-trodden path, and seek the side paths (see *Likutey Moharan* on *hithbodeduth*). There is a Breslover tradition that this side path is *hithbodeduth,* meditation.

thought it over. Meditated on it and thought it over well (Rabbi Rosenfeld).

castle. (*mivtzar* in Hebrew; *schloss* in Yiddish). Later, she would be in a pearl castle. Now, however, she was in the realm of evil. Kabbalistically, *mivtzar* denotes the universe of *Beriyah* (see *Kehillath Yaakov*).

soldiers...These are the troops of evil that guard its realm. They are reflected in the armies of occupation that held the Land of Israel (*Zimrath HaAretz*). These soldiers can also denote a person's fantasies and imaginations (see *Likutey Moharan* 25:1,3).

beautiful. The realm of evil resembles the realm of good, but it is illusory (Rabbi Rosenfeld).

enter. But he thought it over, [and said to himself,] "I will go ahead* and see what happens."

He left behind his horse* and went up to the castle. [The soldiers] let him [come in], doing nothing to stop him.* He went from room to room without being challenged.

Finally he came to the main hall.* He saw the king* sitting there with a crown [on his head].* There were also many soldiers, as well as musicians with their instruments in front of them. It was [all] very pleasant and beautiful.*

Neither the king nor anyone else asked him any questions.* He saw delicacies and fine foods* there, and he ate.* Then he

---

I will go ahead... The tzaddik does not fear the realm of evil (Rabbi Rosenfeld). The Talmud says that a perfect tzaddik cannot be harmed by evil (*Berakhoth* 7a). "Also when I walk in the valley of the death shadow I will fear no evil, because You are with me." (Psalms 23:4)

He left behind his horse. That is, he left behind his body (see *Rimzey Maasioth*). This indicates that this was completely a spiritual experience. Meditation and prayer can bring one to "divestment of the physical" (*hithpashtuth ha-gashmiuth*) (*Orach Chaim* 98:1). Moreover, if this is speaking of Adam, as we shall see, then he was entirely on a spiritual level (Ari, *Likutey Torah*).

doing nothing to stop him. The viceroy can enter unhindered, since Evil has no power on its own.

main hall. *Paltin*, literally palace; *palatz* in Yiddish. *Hekhal* denotes Malkhuth (see *Zohar*). This might indicate Malkhuth of Beriyah (universe of creation).

Actually, the light of Malkhuth is in Chesed of Beriyah (*Etz Chaim, Shaar Shevirath HaKelim* 3, p. 126).

king. This is the king of evil (see *Likutey Moharan* 1).

with a crown...There is Kether on the side of evil, just as there is one on the side of good (see *Likutey Moharan* 242; *Etz Chaim, Shaar Derushey ABYA* 3,4). The *Zohar* also speaks of the "Crowns of Evil" (*Tikkuney Zohar* 69:108b).

pleasant and beautiful. But in the realm of evil, all beauty is an illusion (Rabbi Rosenfeld, tape).

questions. No one questions him. It is easy to enter the realm of evil, and no one questions you. There are no barriers (Rabbi Rosenfeld). "He who comes to defile himself, they open up for him" (*Yoma* 38b). This is in contrast with the giants, who later interrogate him and discourage him.

delicacies and fine foods. In the realm of evil, all worldly enjoyments can be found (cf. *Zimrath HaAretz*).

He ate. It appears that it was permissible for him to eat the food. Possibly, he did not

went to lie down* in a corner to see what would happen.

He saw the king issue a command to bring the queen. [People] went to fetch her. There was a great uproar as they brought forth the queen, and the orchestra played and [the choir] sang.* [People] set up a throne for [the queen], and sat her next to [the king].

She was the [lost] princess!* As soon as the [viceroy] saw her, he recognized her. The queen looked around, and seeing someone lying in the corner, recognized him.* She stood up from her throne, and went over and touched him. "Do you know me?" she asked.

"Yes," he replied. "I know you.* You are the king's daughter who was lost."

He then asked her, "How did you get here?"

She replied, "It happened when my father said [that the Evil One should take me]. This is the place of Evil."*

He told her that her father was very grieved and had tried to find her for many years. "How can I get you out of here?" he asked.

---

realize that he was in the place of evil and could not eat the food. This may have been the reason that he was weakened. It may have also been the reason that he did not have the power later to refrain from eating.

he went to lie down. He was merely an onlooker, not a participant. This may have been the result of his eating there.

orchestra played... This is obvious from the Yiddish. The Hebrew is somewhat ambiguous. It is interesting that music plays an important role here. Rabbi Nachman says that music comes from the birds (*Likutey Moharan* 3). Music from the Other Side comes from the birds of the Other Side (cf. *Zohar* 1:217b). These derive their life energy from the "breasts" of Malkhuth (*Etz Chaim, Shaar HaKlipoth* 2; *Likutey Moharan* 3). Hence the King's Daughter is the one who nourishes the entire realm of the Evil One, basically through this music.

She was the [lost] princess. Not only is the princess a captive there, but she is also a queen. This is because the Other Side gets all its nourishment from Malkhuth. (See previous note.)

recognized him. This is because the tzaddik is always close to the Shekhinah. All his prayers are for her (Rabbi Rosenfeld, tape).

I know you. Thus the tzaddik is able to find the holy sparks, even in the realm of evil. He sees good even in the midst of evil.

of Evil. Literally, "of the no good." This is the physical world (see *Zohar* 2:223b).

She said,* "It is impossible to get me out unless you choose yourself a place* and remain there for an entire year.* All that year you must long* to get me out. Whenever you are unoccupied you must only yearn, seek and look forward to freeing me. You must [also] fast.* Then, on the last day of the year,* you must

---

She said. The Shekhinah itself tells the person how to free her (Introduction, p. 18).

choose yourself a place. In order to free the Shekhinah from the realm of evil, a Jew must choose for himself a place and sit there each day; whenever he has time. He must seek her and look forward to freeing her (*Likutey Etzoth, Ratzon* 3).

remain there for an entire year. Or, "sit there..." This cannot mean an actual year, since the first test is a manifestation of Adam, and Adam ate from the tree of knowledge on the day he was created (*Sanhedrin* 38b). However, as we shall see, a year also denotes the understanding of one of the 70 aspects of the Torah. Thus, he was to remain there until he understood an aspect of the Torah. Adam understood an aspect of the Torah on the day he was created; therefore, he was able to name the animals (Genesis 2:19, 20). He was aware enough of the essence of the Torah to give the animals names that would be appropriate for the Torah.

you must long. The way to free the Shekhinah is to yearn constantly for her (Introduction, p.19). This was King David's task (*Shaar HaKavanoth loc. cit.*). He constantly yearned: "My soul thirsts for God, for the living God (Psalms 42:3), and, "For my soul thirsts for you; my flesh longs for you" (Psalms 63:2) (*Zimrath HaAretz*).

fast. This is to purify the body. The Torah uses anthropomorphisms, wherein all aspects of God's providence are likened allegorically to parts of the body. Therefore, the human body reflects the entire structure of the divine realm. Thus, by fasting, one purifies the body, and at the same time rectifies all spiritual concepts (*Biur HaLikutim* 60:85).

Also, it is taught that the brain is usually nourished by the body. When one is fasting, however, the body is nourished by the brain (*Shaar Ruach HaKodesh*, p. 25). This helps bring a person to a state of expanded consciousness (*mochin de-gadluth*). When seeking to free the Shekhinah, one needs to be in this particular state of consciousness, and hence must be especially careful regarding eating and drinking (*Biur HaLikutim* 60:8).

When a person is not careful regarding eating, it is easy for him to forget his goal. It is thus written, "You should not eat and be satiated... and forget God your Lord" (Deuteronomy 8:12, 14). (*Zimrath HaAretz*; see *Likutey Moharan* 17:3) Fasting thus helps keep a person in the necessary state of longing and desire. Nowadays, since fasting is difficult, the main thing is to maintain desire (*Likutey Etzoth, Ratzon* 3).

It is also possible that he had to fast to rectify his eating in the place of the No Good.

last day... That is, when the new level of understanding is complete. This is Rosh HaShanah, the holiday that comes when the new moon is seen. As mentioned earlier, the moon was reduced in size as a result of the King's statement. When the new moon is seen, the moon begins to increase in size, and this is seen as the beginning of the rectification of

fast and go without sleep for the entire twenty-four hour period."

[The viceroy] went and did [exactly what she told him]. On the last day, at the end of the year, he fasted and did not sleep. Then he stood up, and was headed toward [the castle], when he saw a tree* with very, very beautiful apples. It was very desirable to the eyes,* and he ate an apple.* As soon as he ate the apple, he immediately fell asleep,* and he slept a very long time.

His servant* tried to wake him up, but he could not. When he finally woke up, he asked his servant, "Where in the world am I?"

Malkhuth. It is thus written, "Seek God when He can be found" (Isaiah 55:6), and our sages (cf. *Rosh HaShanah* 18a) say that this refers especially to Rosh HaShanah. This is also the time that the Shekhinah can be found and freed (*Rimzey Maasioth, Hashmatoth*). Rosh HaShanah was also the day Adam was created.

he saw a tree. On the last day, the Evil One makes it particularly difficult (Introduction, p. 19). The princess herself says this to him. It is thus written, "Evil will come to you in the end of days" (Deuteronomy 31:29). At the last minute, the forces of evil marshal all their powers.

It was very desirable to the eyes. This is a paraphrase of Genesis 3:6. There it relates to Eve. This was the test of the first humans, Adam and Eve. The viceroy here represents the first humans. Adam and Eve had the first chance to rescue the King's Daughter. (See *Tikkuney Zohar* 65:98b; *Etz Chaim* 1:111, 113; *Shaar Derushey Nekudoth* 3.)

apple. It is interesting that the story has the fruit as an apple. In the Midrash and Talmud there are various opinions as to what the fruit was. Some say that it was a fig, a grape, an ethrog, and even wheat (*Berakhoth* 40a etc.; see *Zohar* 2:15b).

asleep. This denotes the loss of the higher state of consciousness (Introduction, p. 19; see *Etz Chaim, Shaar HaNesirah* 1). As such it is like a spiritual death, one sixtieth of death. This is reflected in the Torah, where, during the ten generations from Adam to Noah, essentially nothing of significance happened. It is as if the human race was in a state of sleep during this time. But at this time, humanity was still one, and it could have been easily rectified.

This sleep is reflected in the exile that the Israelites underwent in Egypt (*Biur HaLikutim* 60:76, 79; see *Zohar* 2:189a, b). This exile was a result of Adam's sin (see *Shaar HaKavanoth, Pesach*, 1, p. 137). The Egyptian exile also came as a result of a lack of faith on the part of Abraham, as we see from his speech, "How will I know..." (Genesis 15:8; *Biur HaLikutim loc. cit.*). As we have seen, faith is one aspect of the King's Daughter.

servant. The servant is not affected by this. The main effect is in the viceroy, Zer Anpin, the supernal man. Even the souls are not affected by this sleep. The servant represents intellect. The person fell into desire, so his intellect tried to wake him. During the second sleep, the servant did not try to wake him.

[The servant] told him exactly what had happened. "You slept for a very long time — for many years. I survived by eating this fruit."

[The viceroy] was very upset. He went [to the castle] and found [the princess].* She lamented to him, "If you had come [directly] on that day, you would have freed me from here. But because of one day, you lost [everything]. But it is very difficult not to eat, especially on the last day, when the Evil Urge* is very strong."

"Now find yourself a place again, and remain there for another year. This time, you are permitted to eat* on the last day, but you may not sleep. Do not drink any wine [on that day] so that you will not fall asleep. The main thing is [avoiding] sleep."*

[The viceroy] went and did [as she had instructed him]. On the last day, as he was heading toward [the castle],* he saw a flowing spring.* It was red in color and smelled like wine. He asked his

---

and found [the princess]. After the first incident, the princess is still in her original place and it is easy for him to find her (*Rimzey Maasioth*). This is because humanity was still one. Humanity did not have to change its status to rectify the Shekhinah.

Insofar as this sleep represents the Egyptian exile, this means that after the exile, prophecy still existed. One could have the Divine Presence rest on him through prophecy. Indeed, the greatest revelation of all would take place at this time, as well as the prophecy of Moses, the greatest that would ever exist. (See *Biur HaLikutim* 60:79.)

Evil Urge. *Yetzer Hara* in Hebrew.

you are permitted to eat... This time it is easier.

main thing is [avoiding] sleep. In order to free the Shekhinah, one must be in a proper state of consciousness. Moreover, the forces of evil have power over a person when he sleeps (*Biur HaLikutim* 60:24). This is why we must wash our hands when we awaken from sleep (cf. *Shabbath* 108b; *Rimzey Maasioth, Hashmatoth*).

heading toward [the castle]. He was going toward Malkhuth. This is speaking of Noah. The Kabbalists say that the vineyard that he planted (Genesis 9:20) represents Malkhuth (Recanti). Wine can help a person reach the correct state of consciousness to interact with Malkhuth; this is why we make kiddush on wine on the Sabbath. But, misused or forbidden wine has the opposite effect (Recanti).

saw a flowing spring. A spring is seen as a means of purification. Therefore, it should represent something that could be of help to him. But the Evil Urge always tries to disguise evil as good. (Also see *Biur HaLikutim* 60:74).

servant,* "Do you see this? It's a spring and should contain water. But it has a red color and smells like wine."

[The viceroy] went and took a taste* from the spring, and he immediately fell asleep for many years. He remained asleep for seventy years.*

He asked his servant. The first time, he simply ate the fruit because he desired it. This time, he discussed it with his servant. [This would seem to indicate that his servant was his intellect and logic.] As soon as one begins to use formalistic reasoning where something forbidden is concerned, one is on the way to one's downfall (Introduction, p. 20).

In the first case, the viceroy was drawn by simple desire. Here the problem is more one of intellectual curiosity. This is a mental desire rather than a physical desire. He needed an excuse, because he knew that wine would take away his mental capacity.

took a taste. The viceroy is now in the role of Noah. Noah could have freed the Shekhinah and brought about the final rectification, but he lost the opportunity by getting drunk (Genesis 9:21; Introduction, p. 16; see Recanti, *Adir BeMarom* 11b). Wine brings on sleep (*Likutey Halakhoth, Yeyn Nesekh* 2:8).

This is related to the wine of Achashverosh at the end of the seventy year period of exile (*Likutey Halakhoth, Purim* 1:1; *Biur HaLikutim* 60:76).

Mankind thus fell in two ways, once through Adam and once through Noah. The Talmud says that one of the sages used to pray, "Lord of the universe, we wish to do Your will, but we are held back by our subjugation to the nations and by the leaven in the dough" (*Berakhoth* 17). Rashi explains that the leaven is the Evil Urge.

The Evil Urge came about through Adam's sin, because afterward evil became internalized in man. The Midrash speaks of Adam as the dough (*issah*) of the world (see *Shabbath* 33). Thus the "leaven in the dough" is the internalized evil in man.

Subjugation to kingdoms, on the other hand, came about from Noah's sin. Immediately after the account of Noah's drunkenness, the Torah speaks of how the world was split into seventy nations. (There are seventy nations mentioned in Genesis 10; see below.) This is the second element that makes it more difficult to free the Shekhinah.

seventy years. In *Likutey Moharan* 60, which is said to be a key to this story, Rabbi Nachman says explicitly that a seventy year sleep means that one is in such a state of constricted consciousness, that he is blocked from all seventy faces of the Torah (Introduction, p. 19; *Likutey Halakhoth, Yeyn Nesekh* 2:8; see *Zimrath HaAretz*). This indicates that one is in the lowest level of defilement (*Biur HaLikutim* 70:70). It is taught that "there are seventy faces to the Torah" (*Otioth-DeRabbi Akiba*), that is, the Torah can be interpreted in seventy different ways. In Hebrew, the word *shanah* (שָׁנָה) means a year. The same word (שָׁנָה) can also mean "study" as well as "difference."

Thus, Noah's sleep was considered to have been seventy years because it resulted in the world being divided into seventy nations and seventy languages. This also led to the rise of secular wisdom, which draws a person away from the seventy faces of the Torah (*Likutey Halakhoth, Orach Chaim, Kaddish* 7).

Meanwhile, many soldiers* passed by, along with their baggage trains* with their equipment. The servant hid* himself because of the soldiers.

Then a chariot* and carriages* passed by, carrying the

The seventy year sleep also alludes to the seventy years of exile in Babylon after the destruction of the First Temple. Of this exile, the psalmist says, "We were like dreamers" (Psalms 126:1). (*Zohar* 2:189b; *Biur HaLikutim* 70:71; see *Shaar HaKavanoth, Purim*). This is the significance of the story of Choni HaMaagal I (the grandfather of the one who made the circle), who slept during the seventy years of the Babylonion exile (*Taanith* 3:9, 16b; *Likutey Moharan* 60:9; *Biur HaLikutim* 60:80). This was related to Noah's wine; and at the end of the seventy years, Achashverosh made a feast with wine (Esther 7:2; *Likutey Halakhoth, Purim* 1:1).

It is significant that this exile was in Babylon, the place where the world was divided into seventy languages. The exile in Babylon was thus meant to rectify Noah's sin (*Bereshith Rabbah* 36).

The seventy years also allude to a person's life (Psalms 90). The average person can live an entire lifetime and not rise above constricted consciousness. Of course, if he is worthy, during his seventy years, he can rise through each of the seventy faces of the Torah (*Likutey Halakhoth, Sefer Torah* 2:11; *Kibud Rabi VeTalmid Chokham* 2:3).

The two episodes therefore relate to the two main tests that a person has in life. The apple represents simple desire. A person can fall from his level (sleep) because he succumbs to his desires, but he does not sleep "seventy years," and the Divine Presence is still there waiting for him when he wakes up.

But a person can also fall because of intellectual curiosity, and thus become involved in atheism and disbelief. When a person drinks this "wine," he falls away from all seventy faces of the Torah. Moreover, when he wakes up, the Divine Presence is no longer waiting for him. (This is the *Shibud Malkhuth* mentioned earlier which is gentile wisdom.)

It is therefore significant that although the servant tried to wake him the first time after he had eaten the apple, this time the servant made no such attempt. Furthermore, since the servant has been co-opted, when the viceroy continues his quest, the servant will be left behind.

soldiers. Some say that these were the soldiers from the castle bringing the princess (Rabbi Rosenfeld, tape). The soldiers also represent the troubles that a person undergoes (Introduction, p. 19). They also represent fantasies (*Likutey Moharan* 60:9).

baggage trains. *Obazin* in Yiddish (See Story #12, p. 322).

servant hid. Since the servant had been an accomplice this time.

chariot. *Merkavah* in Hebrew. This is the *merkavah* that Ezekiel saw after the first exile. This was the last prophecy that occurred during the exile. The chariot-*merkavah* is what is carrying the princess, as we see later. *Merkava* represents the Shekhinah going into exile.

carriages. *Agaloth tzav* in Hebrew. See Numbers 7:3, where it is usually translated "covered wagons" (see *Living Torah*). These were the wagons that carried the Tabernacle when it was transported.

princess. She stopped there next to [the viceroy] and descended, sitting next to him. She recognized him and tried very hard to wake him up,* but he could not be awakened.

She then began to complain* to him. He had spent so much effort and great toil for many years to free her, but then on the very day that he would have been able to free her, the opportunity was lost. She wept very much. "It is a very great pity, both upon him and upon me. I have been here such a very long time, and I cannot leave."

She then took the kerchief* from her head, and wrote on it· with her tears,* leaving it next to him. She then got up, sat in her chariot, and left.

---

tried... to wake him up. The Shekhinah itself tried to wake mankind (Israel) up but it could not (Rabbi Rosenfeld, notes, tape). When a person loses faith because of intellectual curiosity, then even manifestations of the Divine cannot arouse him.

complain. The Divine Presence complains that we do not free her (see *Zohar* 3:42a, b).

kerchief. *Patsheila* in Yiddish. The kerchief here is worn around the head. It therefore denotes the surrounding forces (*makifin*) around the mentalities of the Shekhinah (*Zimrath HaAretz*).

The concept of *makifin* (surrounding lights) denotes ideas that the intellect cannot grasp (*Likutey Moharan* 21:4; *Likutey Moharan Tinyana* 6:7; also see *Likutey Moharan* 35:9). By giving him her kerchief, she is giving him an idea that his mind cannot grasp. Logically, she cannot be found. In order to find her, the viceroy will have to be able to transcend logic.

This may refer to the prophecies of redemption that were given during the seventy years of Babylonian exile.

This is the first mention of her kerchief. Some say that it denotes the Torah that he lost, and now cannot understand (*Rimzey Maasioth, Hashmatoth*; see below).

wrote... tears. The Talmud speaks about God weeping and shedding tears for sending His children into exile (*Berakhoth* 49). Rabbi Nachman explains that these tears denote God's providence over the Israelites to keep them from harm (*Likutey Moharan* 250). The message is that the Shekhinah is still involved in watching the Israelites. Also, Rabbi Nachman teaches that tears have the power to push out the evil side of Malkhuth (*Likutey Moharan* 36:4). Therefore, her tears will give him the power to push out the power of the evil Malkhuth, and be wholehearted in seeking her.

It is also possible that in doing this, she teaches him the power of tears. Later, we will see that whenever his faith is questioned, he weeps, and thus overcomes all obstacles. This is to be contrasted with the first time, when she gave him specific instructions. This time she writes it in tears, which can barely be seen.

When [the viceroy] woke up, he asked his servant, "Where in the world am I?" [The servant] told him everything that had happened. [He told him] that many troops had passed by, and that a chariot had come. [A woman] had wept over him and had lamented that it is a great pity both on him and on her.

[The viceroy] then noticed the kerchief* lying next to him. "Where did this come from?" he asked.

[The servant] replied that [the woman] had written on it with tears.

[The viceroy] took it and held it up to the sun.* He began to see the letters and could read what was written on it. [It contained] all her lamentations and grief. [He also read] that she was no longer in the castle.* He must now search for a golden

It is significant to note that Moses wrote about his own death with tears (*Bava Bathra* 15a).

noticed the kerchief. When he wakes up, his intellect (the servant), makes him aware of the Torah that he has lost (*Rimzey Maasioth, Hashmatoth*).

the sun. Rabbi Nachman teaches that the sun is the wisdom in each thing (*Likutey Moharan* 1). Thus, we are only aware of the providence of the Shekhinah through Chokhmah, consciousness.

Rabbi Nachman also teaches that the sun is the tzaddik (*Likutey Moharan* 49:7). If one wishes to see the true power of tears and faith, one must hold it up to the light of the tzaddik (Rabbi Rosenfeld, tape).

The kerchief is *makifin*, which cannot be understood. Only when one holds it up to the "sun" can one begin to read its message. Otherwise the writing is invisible.

This may also denote the way to *ruach ha-kodesh*. Until the destruction of the First Temple, it was common (*Megillah* 14a). But after those seventy years, prophecy ceased to exist, and the only way to reach *ruach ha-kodesh* would be through *maaseh merkavah* — the message left by the princess on the *merkavah*. This was not something open and obvious to all; it was written in invisible ink, that could only be understood when held up to the sun. *Merkavah* can only be taught to *"chokham, ha-meven mi-dato."* One must have the light of Chokhmah to learn it (*Chaggiah* 11b).

no longer in the castle. After the first time, she was still in the castle, but now she had moved far away (*Rimzey Maasioth;* see *Biur HaLikutim* 60:79).

After Adam's sin, the Divine Presence was still in a place where she could be freed by any human being. But after Noah's sin, only the descendants of Shem, and then of Abraham and Israel could free her. She is thus in a much more distant place.

This is reflected in the two exiles. After the exile from Egypt the Divine Presence could still be found through prophecy. But after the Babylonian exile, prophecy ceased to exist.

mountain* and a pearl castle,* and there you will find me.

To find the Divine Presence would thus be a much more difficult task.

Also, at first the viceroy was able to choose any place he desired. Now he would have to find the golden mountain before he could free her.

golden mountain. This is the key to the entire second part of the story. From the context, the fact that the mountain is made out of gold alludes to the fact that ordinary wealth and riches are not worth anything there. This is obvious from the last giant's question, "What is valuable there?" Thus, the Shekhinah is hidden in a place of untold wealth. As we shall see from the context of the story, this appears to be the World to Come.

In the lesson which is said to be the key to this story, Rabbi Nachman teaches that for deep understanding of the Torah (finding the Shekhinah) one needs great wealth. Thus, in order to find the King's Daughter, one must first find a golden mountain. (Introduction, p. 24; see *Likutey Moharan* 60:9).

The need for this wealth is alluded to in the ark, which was covered with gold. Paralleling the ark in the Temple on earth, there is one in the Temple on high (see below, p. 53). Thus, the mountain can allude to the Temple on high, which is on the Temple mount. This would be the source of wealth from the side of holiness (see *Rimzey Maasioth, Hashmatoth*).

One reason that it is so difficult to find this, is because the ark does not take up any space (*Bava Bathra* 99a).

Perhaps the mountain represents the ark, since prophecy came from between the two gold cherubs, over the golden ark. This is now hidden on high.

This may allude to the place of souls. Indeed, it is taught that the purification of souls parallels the purification of gold (*Shaar HaKavanoth, Pesach* 1; *Pri Etz Chaim, Shaar HaMatzoth* 1). It is also taught that the Shekhinah walks through paradise, the place of the souls of the righteous, in the universe of Beriyah (*Shaar HaKavanoth, Tikun Laylah* 4; see *Pri Etz Chaim*). This may be related to *Aravoth*, where God keeps His treasures as well as souls (*Chagigah* 12b).

Originally, the Shekhinah could be freed by keeping the seven commandments of Noah. But now it requires keeping all 613 commandments of the Torah. It does not take any money to keep the seven commandments, but keeping all 613 requires money. There are many ritual objects that one must purchase.

From the context of the story, the golden mountain seems to be the World to Come (See end of story #7, p. 152).

Some say that this is alluded to in the verse: "Its stones are the place of sapphires, and it has gold dust. No bird of prey knows that path; neither has the falcon's eye seen it. The proud beasts have not trodden on it; nor has the lion passed it by" (Job 28:6-8). Hence, later in the story neither the birds nor the beasts know it (*Biur HaLikutim* 60:67; *Rimzey Maasioth, Hashmatoth*).

Significantly, according to the Talmud, this is speaking of the wealth of Sodom (*Sanhedrin* 109a; *Zohar* 1:106a). Therefore, this is wealth that has fallen into the domain of evil, and must be lifted up again (see *Sichoth HaRan* 4).

[The viceroy] left his servant behind* and went alone to find her. He traveled for many years. He concluded that he certainly would not find a golden mountain and a pearl castle in any civilized area,* since he was an expert in geography.* Therefore, [he said,] "I will go into the deserts."

He searched for her for many years in the deserts. Finally, he met a huge man.* He was such a huge giant that he could not be

---

However, the verses go on to say, "But where can wisdom be found... it cannot be gotten for gold..." (Job 28:12, 15). It then says "From where does wisdom come... It is hidden from the eyes of all life (beasts; *chai*), and kept shut out from the birds of the air... But God understands its way and knows its place... When He makes a weighing for the wind..." (Job 28:20-26). This can denote the Torah (see *Zohar* 3:256b).

According to the *Zohar*, this is speaking of Yesod of Chokhmah (Rabbi Chaim Vital on *Zohar* 3:193b; also see *Zohar* 1:29b, 2:123a, 3:61b). This is the pleasure (Yesod) that one has from intuitive knowledge (Chokhmah). The pleasure that one can have from a flash of insight can be much greater than that of gold. This insight may be the golden mountain that the viceroy is seeking. People discourage him and say that it does not exist.

pearl castle. Some say that this is the Holy of Holies in the Temple on high (Proverbs 3:15; *Rimzey Maasioth, Hashmatoth*). Furthermore, this may relate to Abraham, who had both a daughter (*Bava Bathra* 16a) and a pearl (*Bava Bathra* 16a). This pearl also denotes wisdom (Rashba on *Eyn Yaakov;* see *Biur HaLikutim* 60:73; *Rimzey Maasioth, Hashmatoth*).

A pearl is said to be related to dreams (*Tikkuney Zohar* 70, 129b). (See *Bahir* 41. This is related to the vowel point *cholem* which denotes Tifereth.)

Earlier she was in an ordinary castle, but now she is in a castle of pearl.

left his servant behind. In the first quest, he left behind his horse. Before the first test, he merely had to overcome bodily pleasures. This time he also leaves behind his servant. He must leave behind his intellect and operate with pure faith (*Rimzey Maasioth*). According to those who maintain that the servant is the soul, this denotes extreme purification, where even the lower portions of the soul are left behind (Rabbi Rosenfeld, tape).

not... in any civilized area. "It is not found in the land of the living" (Job 28:13; *Biur HaLikutim* 60:67).

geography. *Land kart* in Yiddish; literally "the world map."

huge man. In this part of the story, the viceroy encounters three huge giants. The Hebrew is *adam gadol*; Yiddish: *groise mench*, which can also mean a "great man."

This is related to the concept of the four universes, Atziluth (closeness), Beriyah (creation), Yetzirah (formation), and Asiyah (making), alluded to in the verse, "All who are called by My name, for My glory (Atziluth), I have created them (Beriyah), formed them (Yetzirah), and made them (Asiyah)" (Isaiah 43:7). As mentioned earlier, the sefiroth were originally in Atziluth, but Malkhuth (the princess) fell to Beriyah.

The *Zohar* teaches that there are three men "a man of Beriyah, a man of Yetzirah, and

considered human. He was carrying an immense tree.* In
civilized areas such a large tree would never be found.

"Who are you?"* asked the stranger.

"I am a human being," he replied.

"I have been in the desert for many years now," said [the
giant] in amazement. "I never saw a human being here before."

[The viceroy] told him the entire story, and [said] that he was
looking for a golden mountain and a pearl castle.

[The giant] said that he was certain that no such thing
existed.* He discouraged [the viceroy] and told him that he had

---

a man of Asiyah" (*Tikkuney Zohar* 19:42a; *Zohar Chadash* 33c). These are the three great
men whom the viceroy encounters (*Rimzey Maasioth*).

These three men represent the three levels of the soul: *nefesh, ruach* and *neshamah.*

In encountering the three men, the viceroy can be taking on the aspects of the three
patriarchs, Abraham, Isaac and Jacob (see *Zohar Chadash* 33c; also see *Likutey Moharan*
60:4).

The three giants also represent three of the four faces that Ezekiel saw. Thus, the first
giant, who was king of the beasts, is represented by the lion, and the second, the king of the
birds, is represented by the eagle (*Biur HaLikutim* 60:86; but see *Tikkuney Zohar* 70, 122b
top).

The giant can also represent literally "a great man," that is, a tzaddik (Rabbi
Rosenfeld).

tree. In general, the tree is the array of the Ten Sefiroth in each of these lower three worlds
(*Rimzey Maasioth*).

Also, the tree is the root of souls (*Zohar* 2:99a; *Likutey Moharan* 15:4; *Rimzey
Maasioth*).

On a simple level, if the man represents a tzaddik, then the tree may represent the
Torah, which is called "a tree of life" (Proverbs 3:18).

Who are you. Unlike the first quest, where no questions were asked.

no such thing existed. Each giant gives him such discouragement initially. But later, when
the viceroy insists, each giant helps him go further in his quest (see Introduction, pp.
23,24).

On a Kabbalistic level, before entering each of the upper universes, one encounters the
forces of the *klipah*. These are the forces that discourage and confuse a person (*Zohar*
3:123a). The three *klipoth* are represented by the "storm winds, cloud and fire" that
Ezekiel saw, (Ezekiel 1:4), and by the "wind, earthquake and fire" that Elijah saw (1 Kings
19:11, 12). (*Zohar* 2:203a, b; *Biur HaLikutim* 60:86). Since the "viceroy" fell from all
seventy faces of the Torah, the giants holding the Torah tend to discourage him. Also all
the higher powers discourage him (*Rimzey Maasioth; Likutey Moharan* 25:3).

been convinced by foolish tales; certainly, no such place existed.

[The viceroy] began to weep very bitterly.* He was certain that it must exist some place, even though [this giant] was discouraging him and [saying] that [people] had obviously told him foolish tales. [The viceroy] insisted, "It certainly does exist!"*

[The giant] said to him, "In my opinion it is mere foolishness. But since you are so stubborn,* I will do something for you. I am in charge of all the animals.* I will summon them* all together. The animals run all over the world. Perhaps one of them knows something about this mountain and castle."

He summoned all types of animals, large and small, and asked them. They all replied that they had not seen* [anything like that].

He said to [the viceroy], "See! People have told you foolish

If the three giants represent the encounters of the three patriarchs with holiness, this also follows. All the patriarchs had many obstacles placed in their paths before they could reach their goals (see *Shemoth Rabbah* on Exodus, 6:3; Rashi). It was only after they persisted that they were able to reach their goal.

The giants may also represent the tzaddik, who may test a person (Rabbi Rosenfeld, tape).

weep... Since the gate of tears is never closed (Rabbi Rosenfeld, tape). Rabbi Nachman in general taught that through weeping one can break all barriers. This may be the significance of the tears in which the princess's message was written.

It certainly does exist. The viceroy is not dissuaded by the giant. The lesson here is that no matter how great the person trying to discourage one from searching for the princess, one must not be dissuaded (Introduction, p. 23).

since you are so stubborn. In each case when the giant sees that he is not dissuaded, the giant then offers to help him (Introduction, p. 24; see *Biur HaLikutim* 60:17). Once one breaks through the forces of *klipah*, one receives help from the higher spiritual forces.

animals. The first giant represents the lion on the *merkavah* that Ezekiel saw (*Biur HaLikutim* 60:86). The lion is the king of beasts. The *Zohar* also teaches that each of these faces is really a human face, but that the "lion's face" indicates that the owner of the face is like a lion, the king of beasts (*Zohar* 1:71b).

I will summon them. This was a special favor that the giant did for the viceroy (Rabbi Rosenfeld, tape).

they had not seen. "The proud beasts have not trodden it, nor has the lion passed it by" (Job 28:8; see *Biur HaLikutim* 60:67).

stories! Listen to me and go home! It is certain that you will not find it! It simply does not exist!"

[The viceroy] continued to press him, and said, "But it must exist! Definitely!"

[The giant] said, "My brother also lives here in the desert. He is in charge of all the birds. Maybe they know something. They fly high in the air, and it is possible that they have seen such a mountain and castle. Go to him and tell him that I sent you."

[The viceroy] traveled many, many years, searching for him until he finally found him. He encountered another huge giant, just like the first one, and he was also carrying an immense tree.

[This giant] asked the same questions [as his brother had,] and [the viceroy] replied, [telling him] the entire story, and how his brother had sent him here. [The second giant] also discouraged him, [saying,] "This is obviously something that does not exist." But [the viceroy] pressed his convictions to him too.

[The giant] said to him, "I am in charge of all the birds.* I will summon them. Perhaps they know."

He called all the birds, large and small, and asked every one of them. They all replied that they did not know* of any such mountain or castle.

[The giant] said to him, "Don't you see that it certainly does not exist anywhere in the world? Listen to me and go home. Obviously, no such thing exists!"

[The viceroy] pressed him and said, "But it certainly does exist somewhere in the world!"

[The giant] said to him, "Further on in the desert, you will find my brother, who is in charge of all the winds.* They fly all

---

in charge of all the birds. The face of the eagle in the *merkavah*. The eagle is the king of birds (*Biur HaLikutim* 60:86; see *Tikkun* 70, 122b top).

they did not know. "No bird of prey *knows* that path; neither has the falcon's eye seen it" (Job 28:7). (*Biur HaLikutim* 60:67).

Significantly, the animals did not *see* it, but the birds did not *know* of it. There might be a significance in the change here.

in charge of all the winds. This parallels the face of the ox, which is also a human face (*Sukkah* 5b; *Biur HaLikutim* 60:86).

over the world. Perhaps they will know."

[The viceroy] traveled for many years searching, and finally he found another giant* like the first ones. [This giant] was also carrying a huge tree. He asked similar questions, and [the viceroy] answered, [telling] the entire story. [This giant] also tried to discourage him, but [the viceroy] pressed his case on him also.

[The giant] told him that he would assemble all the winds for his sake, and would ask them. He summoned them, and all the winds came. He asked them, but not one of them knew anything about the mountain or the castle.

[The giant] said to him, "Don't you see that people have told you foolish tales?"

[The viceroy] began to weep very bitterly. "I know for certain that it does exist!" he said.

Just then he saw another wind come.* [The giant] was angry at it. "Why did you take so long to come?" [he demanded]. "I decreed for all the winds to come! Why didn't you come with them?"

[The wind] replied, "I was detained* because I had to carry a royal princess to a gold mountain and a pearl castle."

[The viceroy] was very happy.

---

another giant... This third giant would be that of the universe of Beriyah, which is the universe where the princess is to be found.

another wind... This is the fourth *klipah*, which is known as *klipath nogah*. This is the *nogah* (glow) that Ezekiel saw (Ezekiel 1:4), and the still small voice that Elijah heard (1 Kings 19:12). This is the force that mediates between good and evil (*Zohar* 2:203b). It has the power to carry the viceroy from the depths of forgetting the seventy faces of the Torah (*Biur HaLikutim* 60:86).

This wind parallels the face of the man on the throne (*Ibid.*).

This is followed by the "wind of God" which hovered on the face of the water. It is this wind of God (*ruach Elokim*), which transported the princess (*Biur HaLikutim* 60:67, *Rimzey Maasioth, Hashmatoth*).

According to the Midrash, this is the spirit of the Messiah (*Bereshith Rabbah*). Thus the Shekhinah has been transported by the spirit of the Messiah.

I was detained... Thus, if the viceroy had found the golden mountain earlier, the princess would not have been there. He may have been discouraged by the delays, but they really helped him and the princess.

[The giant] asked the wind, "What things are valuable* there?"

"Everything is valuable there,"* replied [the wind].

The one in charge of the winds then said to the viceroy, "You have been seeking [the princess] for such a long time, and you have expended so much effort. You may have difficulty because of [a lack of] money. I am therefore giving you a purse.* Whenever you put your hand into it, you will find money there."

[The giant] then issued an order that this wind carry [the viceroy] there.

The storm wind* came and carried him to that place, bringing him right to the gate. There were soldiers there, who would not let

---

What things are valuable. Since the entire mountain is made of gold, what can possibly be of value there? (Rabbi Rosenfeld, tape).

"One moment of pleasure in the World to Come is worth more than the entire present world" (*Avoth* 3:16).

Everything is valuable there. That is, all the good deeds that we can bring from this world are valuable in the pearl castle, which is the World to Come. "One moment of repentance and good deeds in this world is worth more than the entire World to Come" (*Avoth* 3:16).

purse. *Keli* in both Hebrew and Yiddish (see *Sichoth HaRan* 193). Literally, a vessel or a cup (Rabbi Rosenfeld). Some say that this vessel is trust in God (*bitachon*); if one has such trust, he will be supplied with all his needs (*Oneg Shabbath*, p. 517; see *Likutey Moharan* 76). Others say that it is charity; the more one gives, the more God gives him back (Rabbi Rosenfeld, tape).

However, it seems that the purse here is the Torah in its entirety. One can constantly take merit out of the Torah, and it is never empty. This is the "precious vessel" (*kli chemdah*) that God gave the Israelites (*Avoth* 3:14; *Midrash Shmuel ad. loc.*). This is also the coin which can be used on the mountain of gold, since the Torah "is more precious than gold and fine gold" (Psalms 19:11; see Tosfoth Yom Tov on *Avoth*). From this purse one can get merit and good deeds, which are more valuable than anything on the mountain of gold.

storm wind. *ruach saarah* in Hebrew. The scripture uses the term *ruach saarah* to describe the wind that lifted Elijah up to heaven (2 Kings 2:1, 11). The *ruach saarah* is also seen as the wind of redemption (Zechariah 9:14). We also see that it was in a *ruach saarah* that God answered Job (Job 38:1, 40:6).

The storm wind, however, is the first barrier that Ezekiel had to break through (Ezekiel 1:4), and it is considered the strongest of the *klipoth*. Indeed, it is the force that carried the princess away to the inaccessible golden mountain (see Introduction, p. 23). The greatest force of evil thus becomes the harbinger of good.

him enter the city. But he put his hand into the purse and took some money. He was then able to bribe them and enter the city. *

The city was very beautiful. * He went to a wealthy person * and bought food from him. He would have to remain there a while, since he would have to use his intelligence * and wisdom [to devise a plan] to free [the princess].

[The Rebbe] did not tell * how he freed her. But in the end he did free her.

The *ruach saarah* also represents the suffering that will precede the coming of the Messiah (*chevley mashiach*) (Rabbi Rosenfeld).

If the viceroy is now seen as the personification of David or the Messiah, then this wind (*ruach* is the spirit of the Messiah, regarding which it is written, "The spirit of God shall restore him, a spirit of wisdom and understanding, a spirit of counsel and might, a spirit of knowledge and fear of God" (Isaiah 11:2).

bribe them... The forces of evil do not want to let the Messiah rescue the princess. These are the soldiers. But the Messiah can bribe them with money from the purse, that is, with merit and good deeds that the Israelites have from keeping the Torah.

The city was very beautiful. This is Jerusalem on high (*Taanith* 5a from Hosea 11:9). As mentioned earlier, the Divine Presence is in the Holy of Holies of Jerusalem on high.

went to a wealthy person... This would be a great tzaddik, who has much merit. Such a tzaddik can help sustain the Messiah in his quest for the princess.

he would have to use his intelligence. One needs clever plans to rescue the princess. This is paralleled by Jacob, who had to devise a clever plan to take Rachel (Malkhuth) out of Laban's house (*Biur HaLikutim* 60:69). Similarly, Dinah (Leah's daughter after six sons) could only be taken out of Shechem with trickery (*Biur HaLikutim* 60:62).

[The Rebbe] did not tell... Rabbi Nachman did not tell how he freed her, since this would involve revealing the mystery of the Messiah (*Biur HaLikutim* 60:68; see *Alim LeTerufah* 2). For the same reason, Rabbi Nachman did not reveal the end of the story of the Seven Beggars.

2

THE KING AND THE EMPEROR*

Once there was a [great] emperor* who did not have any children. There was also a [lesser] king* who did not have any children.

The emperor traveled* all over the world, trying to find a

The King and the Emperor. It is not known when this story was told, but it was probably told during the winter of 1806-1807. Rabbi Nathan was away from Rabbi Nachman for quite a while during this winter.

There is also no traditional way of interpreting this story (*Rimzey Maasioth, Zimrath HaAretz*). However, a number of allusions are quite obvious.

Rabbi Nathan repeated this story shortly before his death.

emperor. *Kaiser* in both Hebrew and Yiddish. This also denotes a czar. As we see in a later story (Story #10, p. 206), a kaiser is of a higher rank than a king.

Unlike a king, an emperor has no direct contact with the nations under him.

Kabbalistically, the emperor here denotes the sefirah (emanation) of Chokhmah (Wisdom) (Rabbi Rosenfeld, notes). The Zohar states that a "great king" (*melekh rav*) is Chokhmah (*Tikkuney Zohar Chadash* 109d, from Psalms 48:3). Chokhmah represents the Divine Wisdom that defines the axioms which are the basis of the logic with which God created the universe.

Chokhmah is also reflected in the universe of Atziluth, the universe of the sefiroth. This universe can only be connected with the lower world through the universe of Beriyah, which is the universe of the Throne of Glory (see Ezekiel 1:26). Chokhmah is thus like an emperor who only contacts his subjects through the kings under him.

king. Kabbalistically, this is Binah (Understanding) (Rabbi Rosenfeld; see *Zohar Chadash* 45d). Binah is the logic with which God created the world.

It is true that Binah is usually seen as a feminine force. However, this is only with relation to Chokhmah. In relation to the lower world (Zer Anpin), Binah is considered a masculine force (*Zohar* 2:4a, cf 1:163a).

traveled. This was in the world of *nekudoth* (dots). This is a world where there is no interaction (*Etz Chaim, Shaar HaMelakhim* 8).

remedy and a way to have children. The king also traveled around for the same reason.*

The two of them happened to come to the same inn.* They did not know* anything about each other, but the emperor recognized a certain royal bearing in the king. He inquired, and the other admitted that he was a king. The king also recognized a certain royal manner in the emperor, and [the latter] also admitted [his identity].

The two of them told one another that they were traveling around in order to [find a way to] have children. They made a pact* between them that, when they came home to their wives, if one had a boy and the other a girl, so that they could marry, then the two [children] would marry each other.

The emperor returned home* and fathered a daughter.* The

---

same reason. They lowered themselves so as to create the world (Rabbi Rosenfeld).

the same inn. This is *mazal* that brings father and mother together (*Zohar* 3:292a; *Etz Chaim, Shaar Abba VeImma* 4). This *mazal* is the power of Arikh Anpin that allows *Abba* and *Imma* to have *zivug* (*Etz Chaim, Shaar HaKelalim* 5; *Shaar Abba VeImma* 3).

did not know... Chokhmah is known as Father, while Binah is known as Mother (*Zohar* 3:290). "Knowledge" indicates cohabitation as in "Adam knew his wife" (Genesis 4:1). This is speaking of the time before the supernal Father and Mother consummated their marriage.

They did not know each other at this time, because they were back to back (*Etz Chaim, Shaar HaMelakhim* 8).

made a pact. Hebrew: "bound themselves" (*hithkashru*). This pact itself was the consummation of the marriage between Chokhmah and Binah (see *Etz Chaim, Shaar HaZivugim* 1). Thus it was Chokhmah and Binah together who said, "Let us make man" (*Tikkuney Zohar* 56, 90b). This represents the creation of the Torah 2000 years before the world (*Bereshith Rabbah*). (The 2000 years is Chokhmah and Binah.)

returned home. Nothing more had to be done for them to be able to have children. The meeting and agreement alone were sufficient.

daughter. This is taken to mean the Divine Presence (Kabbalistically, the sefirah of Malkhuth). This is the woman regarding whom it is written "A woman of valor is a crown for her husband" (Proverbs 12:4). This is the mystery of "Abba founded the Daughter," as it is written, "With Wisdom God founded the earth (Malkhuth)" (Proverbs 3:19; *Zohar* 3:258a; *Tikkuney Zohar* 69, 105b, 106b; *Rimzey Maasioth; Zimrath HaAretz*; Rabbi Rosenfeld, notes). This also alludes to the Oral Torah, which comes from the supernal wisdom (see *Tikkuney Zohar* 21, 61b; *Zohar* 3:248). This is the hidden path, that "no bird of prey knows" (Job 28:7; *Zohar* 3:256b). See *Tikkuney Zohar* 17a, that this is "Oral

king [also] returned home and fathered a son.* The pact that they had made, however, was forgotten.*

The emperor sent his daughter away to study, and the king also sent his son away to study. It turned out* that the two of them went to the same tutor.* They fell very deeply in love, and they pledged* that they would marry.

The king's son took a ring* and placed it on her hand,* and they were thus married.

Torah." Also see *Etz Chaim, Shaar Derushey Nekudoth* 6. This is the wisdom of the Torah (see below, p. 55).

son. This is Zer Anpin, the supernal man (Rabbi Rosenfeld; *Zimrath HaAretz*; see *Zohar* 3:258a; *Tikkuney Zohar* 60, 105b). This is reflected in the souls of Israel which were created before the universe (*Bereshith Rabbah* 8; see *Likutey Moharan* 17). Binah (בינה) has the same letters as *ben yod heh*,(בן יה) which means son of "*yod heh*" (Rabbi Rosenfeld; *Zohar* 3:290b). The Talmud teaches that all Israel are the "sons of kings" (*Shabbath* 67a).

was forgotten. Because the angels denounced the creation of man (*Bereshith Rabbah* 8), and also complained that Israel (the son) should not get the Torah (the daughter) (Rabbi Rosenfeld).

In general, memory involves the confluence of Chokhmah and Binah. [Chokhmah is past and Binah is future. To bring something to the present in memory, they must be together. However, when each of them goes back to its own place, they are both in the aspect of "back to back." This aspect results in forgetting (*Etz Chaim, Shaar Shevirath HaKelim* 2).

It turned out. Even though the son and daughter were not aware of the pact that their parents had made, it had become part of their destiny and they were affected by it. "Even if one does not see, one's destiny (*mazal*) sees" (*Megillah* 3a; *Rimzey Maasioth*).

tutor. Arikh Anpin (Long Face) (Rabbi Rosenfeld), the personification of Kether (crown), the Divine Will. The force that draws the son and daughter together is the five loves (*chasadim*), which ultimately come from Arikh Anpin (*Etz Chaim, Shaar HaKelalim* 5).

pledged. This was a renewal of the pledge that their fathers had made (*Rimzey Maasioth*).

ring. The gold ring is seen as the crown of the Torah, which binds Israel to the Torah (*Tikkuney Zohar Chadash* 100b; *Tikkuney Zohar* 10, 25b; also see *Tikkuney Zohar* 5, 19a). Thus the giving of the Torah to Israel is likened to a wedding (*Taanith* 26b; cf *Rimzey Maasioth*).

However, the Hebrew word for ring is *tabaath*, (טבעת), from the root *teva* (טבע), meaning nature. The power to control nature had been given over to the souls of Israel, but now this was given over to the Torah.

It is the forgetting of this ring that ultimately separates the couple.

The ring also refers to the hand tefillin around the finger (*Tikkuney Zohar* 21, 55b). This is the bond that every man has to the Torah.

Then the emperor sent for his daughter* and brought her home. The king also sent for his son and brought him home.

People proposed matches* for the emperor's daughter, but she refused all suitors because of her pledge.* The king's son missed her very much, and the emperor's daughter was also very melancholy.

The emperor brought [his daughter] to his estates and palaces* to make her aware of her high status, but she was still melancholy.

The king's son missed her so much that he became sick. People asked him why he was sick, but he refused to tell them.* They asked his valet,* "Perhaps you can find out the reason."

[The valet] replied that he knew the reason, since he was with [the prince] when he was away studying. He told them the entire story.

Other sources state that the ring represents faith (see Psalms 89:9, *Likutey Moharan* 7:1; *Likutey Halakhoth, Tefillin* 5:42, *Kiddushin* 2:7). Still other sources state that it is the covenant of circumcision (*Tikkuney Zohar* 56, 90b).

on her hand. The finger which is formed like a *vav* (ו), represents the six sefiroth of Zer Anpin, the supernal groom. The ring resembles the *yod* (י), which represents the crown of the Torah. When the ring is placed on the finger, it forms the letter *zayin* (ז), representing Zer Anpin and his bride together, having a numerical value of seven (*Tikkuney Zohar* 10, 25b top).

the emperor sent... There are many obstacles in the path of the young bride and groom (*Rimzey Maasioth*). The very purpose of creation (the two fathers) requires that they be separated. (Therefore both Chokhmah and Binah work to draw them apart.)

matches. The Torah was offered to Ishmael and Esau before it was offered to Israel (Rabbi Rosenfeld).

because of her pledge. The pledge that the Torah had made with the souls of Israel before creation (Rabbi Rosenfeld). The Torah was offered to the souls of other nations before creation (see *Zohar* 1:24b, 25a).

estates and palaces. The supernal worlds. Especially the universe of Atziluth which is a reflection of Chokhmah which is represented by the emperor.

he refused to tell them. So that they would not denounce the match further (Rabbi Rosenfeld).

valet. The angel Metatron (Rabbi Rosenfeld). This is the "genius of the world" (*Yebamoth* 16b). He is also called a "servant" (*Tosafoth, Ibid; Zohar* 1:126a, etc.) Metatron is also seen as a teacher of Torah (*Avodah Zarah* 3b). Metatron is Mishnah (*Likutey Moharan* 79).

This would appear to indicate that he was now in Yetzirah, the domain of Metatron.

The king then remembered that he had agreed to a match with the emperor a long time earlier. He wrote a message to the emperor, telling him to prepare for the wedding because of the pact that they had made a long time ago.

The emperor no longer wanted* the match, but he did not dare refuse. He replied that the king should send his son to him, and he would test him. If he was able to govern the kingdom, he would be able to marry his daughter.

[The king] sent his son to [the emperor]. The emperor placed him in a room, and gave him documents dealing with affairs of state to see if he could govern the country. The king's son had a very great yearning to see [the emperor's daughter], but he was not given a single opportunity to see her.

Once he was walking near a wall of mirrors. He saw her reflection* and fainted. She went over to him and revived him, telling him that she would not accept any match because of her promise to him.

"What shall we do?" he asked. "Your father will not permit it."

"We will go ahead* anyway," she replied.

They decided that they would go out to sea* together. They hired* a ship* and sailed the sea.

The emperor no longer wanted... Chokhmah sees the future. The Talmud thus teaches, "Who is wise? He who sees the future" (*Tamid* 32a). Therefore, he saw that man would sin, and not be worthy of the Torah.

saw her reflection. As the merchant's son later saw her reflection in the sea.

We will go ahead. Literally: Nevertheless...

out to sea. The sea denotes Binah (Rabbi Rosenfeld; *Zohar* 3:279a, 2:42b; *Tikkuney Zohar* 19, 38b, 21, 42a). This consists of the loves (*chasadim*) from the beginning of creation (Rabbi Rosenfeld; see *Zohar* 1:3b). This love is ultimately what brings Zer Anpin and Malkhuth together (*Etz Chaim, Shaar HaKelalim*). The daughter remains at sea throughout most of the story.

It is possible that the sea denotes the lower universes. Thus a soul being born is seen as a ship coming in from the sea (*Shemoth Rabbah* 48:1). The sea is also seen as a place of danger, a place where evil forces and pirates abound (see *Shemoth Rabbah* 17:5).

hired. Since Malkhuth does not have anything of her own.

ship. This ship represents the ability to be considered important (Rabbi Rosenfeld; *Likutey*

After they had traveled at sea for some time, they wanted to rest on shore. They came to a shore where there was a forest,* and they disembarked.

The emperor's daughter took off her ring* and gave it to [the king's son]. She then lay down* [and went to sleep].* Then, when the king's son saw that she was about to wake up, he placed the ring next to her.*

Moharan 1, 4:9). Malkhuth has nothing of its own and therefore must borrow or steal a ship (see *Likutey Moharan* 1). Thus, after this ship is lost, she steals the merchant's ship.

It is thus written, "This is the great sea... there ships go" (Psalms 104:25, 26). The Shekhinah (woman of valor) goes on this sea, as it is written, "She is like merchant ships; from far she brings her merchandise" (Proverbs 31:14; see *Zohar* 2:50b, 3:60a). This is the theme of this entire story. Now she is going in the ship to preserve and consummate her marriage (see *Zohar* 2:50b).

It appears that the sea through which she goes is the universe of Beriyah, which is associated with Binah, where she will encounter all *klipoth*.

forest. A place of hiding and concealment (Rabbi Rosenfeld). This was meant to be a modest place where they could consummate their marriage. But the forest is also the place of wild beasts (Rabbi Rosenfeld, Psalms 104:20). Thus it is the place of the evil forces that eventually separate them.

took off her ring. This is separation for the sake of reaching still higher elevation. This is the concept of "running and returning," where one retreats in order to go still further (Rabbi Rosenfeld; see *Likutey Moharan* on this). If a ring represents *teva* (nature), then when they consummate the marriage, they are totally divorced from nature.

Taking off the ring also seems to indicate a transfer of authority. The Torah was the force with which the world was created. Now she takes off the ring of authority and gives it to the souls of Israel. Henceforth, Israel will have authority over creation. This is a gift of faith given to Israel. Now, in the wilderness, he needs it more.

This seems to refer to the mystery of tefillin, where her *mochin* (mental powers) are transferred to his arm. When he embraces her, he places the ring near her again.

lay down. (See Ruth 3:7) The Hebrew word is *yishkav*, which has the letters *yesh kaf beth* (שׁ כ״ב), meaning "there are twenty-two" (Rabbi Rosenfeld). This is preparation for using the alphabet to unite the couple. The husband must speak to the wife before having marital relations. (cf. *Nedarim* 20b *Orach Chaim* 240:9; also see *Sichoth HaRan* 68, *Wisdom*, p. 200; also see *Likutey Moharan Tinyana* 79; *Tikkuney Zohar* 18, 34a, 70, 132b; *Etz Chaim, Shaar HaYereach* 3). It is the power of the letters that makes marital relations possible (*Etz Chaim, Ibid.*).

This may indicate that the Torah was ready to be put in the form of letters.

[and went to sleep]. This is only in the Yiddish.

placed the ring next to her. Preparing to consummate the marriage (Rabbi Rosenfeld). But

They got up and headed toward the ship, when she remembered that they had forgotten the ring.* She sent him to get the ring,* but when he went back, he could not find the place. He went to another place but could not find the ring. He walked around trying to find it until he got lost,* and could not get back [to the ship]. She went to try to find him, and she also got lost.*

[The king's son] walked further, but he was lost and he was merely blundering around. Then he came upon a path,* and it led him to an inhabited area.* He did not have any occupation,* so

---

it seems as if the marriage was never consummated.

Since she had taken it off, he could not place it back on her finger. The initiative to put the ring back on had to come from her.

Or, he wishes to have Torah, but does not want faith. Let faith remain with the Torah. But then he forgets it, and ultimately loses the Torah.

forgotten the ring. Just as their fathers forgot their bond. Whatever their fathers did had an effect on them (cf *Rimzey Maasioth*).

Or, they totally forgot about the physical world and nature, so great was their ecstasy.

This can also be every man, who forgets his bond to the Torah. If one does not keep his faith strong, then he will ultimately forget it.

sent him to get the ring. He had to go back and get the ring, just as his father had taken the initiative to send to the emperor.

Israel must have some involvement in nature, since without the natural, physical world, it is impossible to keep the Torah.

Regarding "everyman," the Torah sends him back to do repentance, but he gets lost, and does not.

he got lost. She became concealed from him (Rabbi Rosenfeld).

Without faith, Israel and the Torah cannot be kept together.

She also got lost. He became concealed from her (Rabbi Rosenfeld).

path. Repentance (Rabbi Rosenfeld). Even if one has lost the Torah, he can always repent. This path leads him to the land which she will eventually rule, and she will thus be able to get him back, as we see at the end of the story. Thus, even if one loses the Torah, the path of repentance is always open. Nothing can stand before repentance (*Yerushalmi, Peah* 1:1).

inhabited area. *Yishuv* in Hebrew. This denotes calm contemplation (*yishuv ha-daath*) (Rabbi Rosenfeld). Such contemplation can eventually bring a person back to God (*Likutey Moharan Tinyana* 10). Even though he was lost then, he was not in exile (*Ibid*).

From the story itself, however, we see that the land that he found was the land of the elderly king, the King of the Other Side. (He is therefore in this kingdom when the emperor's daughter orders that all aliens come to the wedding.) He is thus in the realm of the *klipath nogah* (see *Tikkuney Zohar* 17b).

He did not have any occupation. A king's son does not learn any trade. Moreover, the son

he became a servant.*

[The emperor's daughter] continued walking [but realized that] she was getting lost.* She made up her mind that she would stay next to the sea.* She went to the shore* where there were fruit trees,* and she remained there. During the day, she would go down to the sea, hoping to come across some travelers.* She survived* by eating the fruit. At night,* she would climb a tree* so that she would be safe from wild animals.

Meanwhile,* there was an extraordinarily great merchant,*

---

cannot do anything without his bride (Malkhuth) (Rabbi Rosenfeld). The klipoth can only be rectified through Malkhuth, this being the mystery of "His Malkhuth rules over all" (Psalms 103:19) (See Etz Chaim, Shaar Klipath Nogah 3 p. 382). Israel's entire occupation is to keep the Torah; without it there is no occupation.

he became a servant. When Israel loses the Torah through a lack of faith, then Israel is no longer a king's son, but a slave (Rabbi Rosenfeld). When we do God's will, we are considered His children; but when we do not, we are considered slaves (Bava Bathra 10a; cf Kethuboth 66b; see Shaarey Zohar on Avoth 1:3). Therefore, without the Torah, Israel is nothing more than a slave.

was getting lost. The Shekhinah cannot find her way on dry land without Israel.

next to the sea. The realm of the spiritual. This is also the sea of wisdom, which is her source (Rabbi Rosenfeld).

shore. The edge of the chasadim (Rabbi Rosenfeld). The Torah (here the Shekhinah) cannot travel on the sea without a ship. She needs a vehicle.

fruit trees. The trees are tzaddikim, and the fruit are their good deeds (Rabbi Rosenfeld).

travelers. In Hebrew, this is ovrim ve-shavim. This can also be translated as "those who sin and repent (Yoma 85b)." Teshuvah is returning the "heh" to the "vav" which comes out teshev vav heh. (ה ו בשת) . The main way that the Shekhinah returns to her husband is through repentance.

She thus encounters the klipoth and rectifies them and gets from them what she needs. This is the concept of "If you return, and I bring you back... and if you bring forth the precious out of the vile, then you will be My Mouth" (Jeremiah 15:19). Malkhuth becomes mouth, which is Torah Shebaal Peh, by bringing the "precious out of the vile."

survived. Malkhuth survives because of the good deeds that people do.

At night. When the forces of evil have power (Rabbi Rosenfeld).

climb a tree. She ascended because of the merit of the great tzaddik. Otherwise, "Her feet go down to death" (Proverbs 5:5). She climbs a tree to protect her feet (Rabbi Rosenfeld).

Meanwhile. Literally, "And it was the day," both in Hebrew and Yiddish. Each section here begins with this expression, VaYehi HaYom, which occurs in Job 1:6, 1:13, and 2:1, when all the children of God came together, and the Satan was with them to denounce

who had business dealings all over the world. He was very old,*
and only had one son.*

One day his son said to him, "You are very old. I am still
young, and your agents do not pay any heed to me. When you die,
I will not know what to do, and I will not have anything.
Therefore, let me have a ship with merchandise, and I will sail the
sea.* This will give me a chance to gain experience* in business."

Job. Therefore, it indicates a time when the forces of evil are functioning.

This expression is used in connection with her encounter with the merchant's son, the
king by the sea, and the elderly king's son.

The Midrash also teaches that *VaYehi* always indicates a time of trouble. (*Vayikra
Rabbah* 11; *Megillah* 10b; also see *Chokhmah U'Tevunah*, p. 116, end,)

The story tells of four encounters that the emperor's daughter experienced: 1) the
merchant's son; 2) the king by the sea; 3) the pirates; 4) the old king's son. This number is
significant, since it parallels the four *klipoth*, that is, the four powers of evil. At the
beginning of his vision, Ezekiel sees a storm wind, a great cloud, flaming fire, and a glow
(Ezekiel 1:4). The *Zohar* explains that these are the four *klipoth* (*Tikkuney Zohar* 19, 36a).
These same *klipoth* were seen by Elijah in the cave: the wind, the earthquake, the fire, and
the small still voice (1 Kings, 19:11-13). At the beginning of creation (Genesis 1:2), they are
described as chaos, void, darkness, and the deep (*Tikkuney Zohar* 26, 71a; *Tikkuney Zohar*
60, 93a). They also parallel the four nations that exiled Israel: Babylon, Persia, Greece and
Rome (*Zohar Chadash* 38b).

Rabbi Nachman writes that Malkhuth must go through the *klipoth* of all four
universes, which parallel the four kingdoms (*Likutey Moharan* 30:6).

merchant. A merchant denotes the Evil One as we see in Story #8.

This is the first *klipah*, which is the "storm wind coming from the North" (Ezekiel 1:4).
The *Zohar* says that this carries the "dregs of gold" (*Zohar* 2:203a); that is, wealth that is
not used for serving God. Indeed, North is the direction of wealth (see Job 37:22; *Bava
Bathra* 25b).

This represents the exile into Babylon (*Zohar Chadash* 38b). Thus, when the Torah is
lost and forgotten, it is restored from Babylon. It is taught that when the Torah was
forgotten, first Ezra and then Hillel restored it from Babylon (*Sukkah* 20a). Babylon is
wealthy because they honor the Torah (*Shabbath* 119a).

Elsewhere, Rabbi Nachman uses a merchant as an allegory for the Evil One (Story #8).

old. One cannot become very wealthy except through old age (*Likutey Moharan* 60).

one son. The *klipah* can produce something positive. It is this son who will begin the rescue
of the emperor's daughter (*Rimzey Maasioth).

I will sail the sea. "Why does Babylon have full granaries? Because they live by the great
sea" (*Taanith* 10a).

to gain experience. His motive was positive. He wanted to learn how to earn an honest
living.

His father gave him a ship with merchandise, and he went from land to land. He sold his merchandise and bought other goods, and was very successful* in his dealings.

While at sea, he saw the trees [where the emperor's daughter was staying]. [He and his men] assumed that it was an inhabited area, and they wanted to go there. However, when they came close, they realized that there was nothing more than trees,* so they decided to leave.

Meanwhile, the [young] merchant looked into the sea. He saw [the reflection of] a tree, and on top of it, the appearance* of a person. He thought that he might be seeing an illusion, so he told the other men who were with him. They looked and also saw what seemed to be the reflection of a person in the tree.

They decided to get closer to it, and sent a man in a small boat [to investigate]. Meanwhile, they looked into the sea [where they could see the reflection], so that they would be able to guide the scout directly to the right tree, so that he would not go the wrong way. When [the scout] got there he saw a person sitting [in the tree], and he reported back to them.

[The merchant's son] went to investigate for himself, and he saw [the emperor's daughter] sitting there. He told her to come down.

She replied that she would not go to his ship unless he promised not to touch her* until they returned to his home, and he would marry her according to the law.

---

very successful... We thus see that a *ruach saarah* spoke to Job, and carried up Elijah. See previous story, p. 52, end.

trees. Tzaddikim, as above. They are of no interest to the merchant, who is only seeking wealth.

reflection. Like the king's son, he sees only a reflection. He is not on a level where he can find her directly. Similarly, Ezekiel in Yetzirah only saw a reflection of the throne and the man on it. He saw in an *ispaklaria* (mirror) that was not shining, as Bachya says (see *Yebamoth* 49b).

promised not to touch her. "It is not over the sea" (Deuteronomy 30:13). The Torah does not remain with those who sail the seas to get wealth. Essentially, this is the one who studies Torah for his own personal profit.

He promised her, * and she went with him to the ship. Soon he discovered that she could play musical instruments * and speak many languages, * and he was very happy to have found her.

When they were beginning to come near his home, she told him that it would be proper for him to go home and tell his father, his relatives, and everyone else who knew him, so they would come out and welcome her, since he was bringing home such an important woman. She would then tell him who she was. (She had earlier made an agreement with him that he would not ask who she was until after the wedding, when he would find out.) He agreed to [go].

She then said to him, "Since you are bringing home a wife like me, it would also be proper that you give all the sailors on this ship something to drink. They will then realize what kind of woman their master is marrying." He also agreed to this.

He had some very excellent wine * on the ship, and he gave

He promised her. Everyone who met the emperor's daughter fell in love with her. He forgot about his business, and went directly home to marry her (see Proverbs 3:14).

musical instruments. The way that Malkhuth communicates with the klipoth (see *Likutey Moharan* 3; see above, referring to the King's Daughter).

speak many languages. This impressed Babylon, since this is where the world was divided into many languages.

wine. This wine is the main weapon of the emperor's daughter. She uses it to get the ship from the young merchant, to take the ladies from the king by the sea and thus bring about his downfall, to kill the pirates, and to obtain the queen of the bald king (see *Rimzey Maasioth*).

In general, wine denotes joy. It is thus written "Wine gladdens the heart of man" (Psalms 104:15).

It is also written that the grapevine said, "Should I then stop producing wine, which gives joy to God and man?" (Judges 9:13). Our sages also teach, "There can be no joy without wine" (*Pesachim* 109a). Rabbi Nachman teaches that with joy one can overcome all the four klipoth (*Likutey Moharan* 24:8, 25:5, 54:6). Rabbi Nachman explicitly writes that wine brings about joy, which can repel the powers of evil (*Likutey Moharan* 41). The klipah is sadness (*Likutey Moharan* 13:1).

Rabbi Nachman also teaches that wine is joy of the Torah, especially, the Oral Torah, which is the emperor's daughter (*Likutey Moharan* 12:4; see *Zohar* 3:95a; *Tanchuma Ekev* 48). Wine (*yayen* יין) also equals seventy, representing the seventy faces of the Torah (*Eruvin* 65a); and *sod,* (סוד) which also equals seventy, the secrets of the Torah (*Ibid.*).

some to [the sailors]. They became very drunk.*

[The young merchant] then went home and told his father and relatives [about his bride]. Meanwhile, the sailors became drunk and left the ship.* They fell asleep and lay on the ground in a drunken stupor.

While [the merchant's] entire family was getting ready to welcome her, [the emperor's daughter] untied the ship from the dock. She unfurled the sails, and sailed the ship.

When [the merchant's family] arrived at the dock, they did not find anything.* The elder merchant was furious at his son.

"Believe me!" cried the son. "I brought home a ship filled with goods!" But they saw nothing.

"Ask the sailors!" he said.

[The father] went to ask them, but they were lying there drunk. When they woke up he asked them, but they had no idea

---

The emperor's daughter gets the wine from the merchant's son. This is the *klipah* of the storm wind, as mentioned earlier. This represents mental confusion, which can be a form of drunkenness. Wine has the same root as this drunkenness and mental confusion, but it can also be used in moderation to produce joy and good.

The four *klipoth* must be passed through before one can have a prophetic experience, as we see from Ezekiel. Since these *klipoth* represent sadness, they can only be overcome with joy. Therefore, it is taught that a person cannot experience prophecy unless he is in a state of joy.

It is taught that the Jews were exiled to Babylon only because of wine (*Bereshith Rabbah* 36). Also, Babylon represents the place where the world was divided into seventy languages, and wine has a value of seventy. Therefore, she got wine from this particular *klipah*. (See above, regarding languages.)

They became very drunk. Babylon had its downfall through wine. It is thus written "Balshazzar the king made a great feast... and drank wine before the thousand" (Daniel 5:1).

left the ship. Thus, "She became like the ship of a merchant, from far she brings her bread" (Proverbs 31:14). She gets the ship from the merchant.

As mentioned earlier, the ship represents the body. The Midrash teaches that, in Aramaic, wine is *chamar,* which has a numerical value of 248. Through wine, one can lose all 248 parts of the body (*Tanchuma, Shemini* 5, *Vayikra Rabbah* 12).

they did not find anything. It is thus taught that wine brings poverty. It is called *tirash*, from the word *rash*, meaning a poor man (*Yoma* 76a). The son thus becomes improverished. The son represents Babylon, and it is taught, "Ten measures of poverty came to the world, and nine were taken by Babylon" (*Kiddushin* 49b).

what had happened to them. They only knew that they had brought a fully laden ship, but now they were completely ignorant of its whereabouts.

The elder merchant was furious with his son, and he banished him from his house. [He told him] that he never wanted to see him again.* [The son] left [his father] and became a vagrant wanderer.*

Meanwhile, [the emperor's daughter] was sailing the sea.

At the same time, there was a king* who had built his palace near the sea. He felt that this was the best place to build a palace because of the sea breezes and the ships that passed by.

When [the emperor's daughter] sailed the sea, she approached this king's palace. The king looked and saw what appeared to be a ship* with no sailors or passengers. He thought that he was seeing an illusion, so he told his men to look, but they also saw the same thing.

As [the emperor's daughter] came closer to the palace, she

---

never wanted... again. The son is thus banished. This is because he had an ulterior motive for rescuing the daughter; he wanted to marry her. It is similarly taught, "The wealthy of Babylon go to Gehenom" (*Betza* 32a). Gehenom is the third *klipah*, namely fire. In the end, however, he gets wealth from the fire (pirates). Gehenom is painful, but it increases a person's reward.

vagrant wanderer. *Na ve-nad* in Hebrew and Yiddish. This expression is found in relation to Cain (*Genesis* 4:12).

king. According to the order, this would be the second *klipah*, which was the great cloud, representing the kingdom of Persia.

This king liked the sea air. A cloud is a mixture of water and air (see *Likutey Moharan* 67:8; also see *Likutey Moharan Tinyana* 8:4; *Likutey Halakhoth, Rosh HaShanah, Roshey Perakim* 6:4).

It also appears that this king represents one who wishes to live a life of pleasure and still have Torah. Even if the Torah does not want him, he will take it against its will. This is worse than the merchant's son, because the merchant's son at least wanted to accomplish something, while this king merely wants pleasure. He wants to enjoy the Torah (sea) without going into it.

Water is also seen as the source of all pleasure (*Tanya* 2).

saw...a ship. While the merchant's son saw her reflection, this king only saw her ship. Even then he thought that it was an illusion.

made up her mind that she had no need for the palace. But when she tried to pull away, the king sent [his men] and made her come back.* They brought her to his palace.

This king was not married.* He could never make up his mind on anyone. Whenever he wanted a woman, she did not want him, and vice versa.

When the emperor's daughter arrived, she demanded that he swear* not to touch her until they were legally married. He made an oath to her.

She then said that it would not be proper for him to open her ship or even touch it. Rather, it must remain untouched on the sea until the wedding. Then everyone would be able to see the vast amount of goods that she had brought with her. Then people would not say that [the king] had taken a woman from the street. [The king] also promised her this.

The king wrote to all the nations, inviting them to his wedding. He also built palaces for her.

[The emperor's daughter] demanded that she be given eleven noblewomen* to accompany her. The king issued an order, and

---

made her come back. She came willingly with the merchant's son, but here she was coerced (*Rimzey Maasioth*).

was not married. The Torah therefore rejected him. Only a married person can have Torah (*Yebamoth* 62b).

Actually, none of the first three is married. It is thus taught that the *klipoth* cannot have a true *zivug* (union) since they do not have Daath (*Etz Chaim, Shaar HaKlipoth* 2). A person cannot have a happy marriage unless he does it with holiness.

swear. She does not trust him as she trusts the merchant's son. In the case of the merchant's son, a promise is enough, but here she requires an oath.

eleven noblewomen. These are the girls that were given to Esther before she went into the king (Esther 2:9). This was done in Persia, which as we have said, was the second *klipah*.

The eleven ladies represent the eleven perfumes used in the incense (*ketoreth*) (*Kerithoth* 6b). Later, these eleven ladies will be used to kill the murderous pirates (see *Likutey Moharan* 35:8). This is the concept that the eleven perfumes have the power to stop the plague (*Shabbath* 89a; Numbers 17:11; see *Zohar* 1:100b, 2:224a; *Etz Chaim, Shaar Klipath Nogah* 3, p. 383).

In general, the eleven perfumes consisted of ten with good fragrances, and galbanum, with a vile odor. The galbanum represented the sinner who joins the minyan of ten good men. It is thus taught, "Every fast that does not include sinners of Israel is not a fast." This

sent her eleven daughters of the greatest nobles, building a special palace for each one. [The emperor's daughter] also had her own special palace, where they all came together. [The women] played musical instruments and they also played games with her.

One day she told [the other women] that she would like to go down to the sea with them. They went with her, and they played games there.

She then offered to serve them some of the very excellent wine* that she had. She gave them from the wine. [The women] became so drunk that they fell asleep and lay there. She then untied the ship, spread the sails, and fled* with the ship.

is derived from the fact that the incense included galbanum (Exodus 30:34). (*Kerithoth* 6b).

The ten good perfumes parallel the ten sayings with which the world was created. The galbanum (*chelbanah*) parallels the eleventh saying, "It is *not good* for man to be alone" (Genesis 2:18). Thus, the eleventh saying is the "not good" (*lo tov*) (see *Shaar HaKavanoth*, pp. 87-88; *Etz Chaim, Shaar HaKlipoth* 1).

In general, the incense also represents joy, as it is written, "Incense makes the heart rejoice" (Proverbs 27:9) (*Likutey Moharan* 13:1, 24:2). As noted earlier, this has the power to break the *klipoth*.

As we have seen, this king represents "cloud," the second *klipah*. From it comes the "cloud" of incense, as it is written, "For in a cloud (of incense) I will appear on the ark cover" (Leviticus 16:2, see Rashi).

It also represents Persia. The leading Jew in Persia was Mordecai, and the Talmud says that Mordecai's name alludes to *mera dakhia* (*Chullin* 139b), which was the first perfume of the *ketoreth* (Exodus 30:34). Thus, the main power of the *ketoreth* comes from this second *klipah*.

Furthermore, Rabbi Nachman teaches that *ketoreth* alludes to the rebuilding of the Temple (see *Likutey Moharan* 35:8). It was Persia who allowed the Israelites to rebuild the Temple after it was destroyed. He writes that "the day of his rejoicing" (Song of Songs 3:11) is speaking of *ketoreth*, but according to the Talmud, it is also speaking of the Temple (*Taanith* 31a). Esther was able to accomplish this through wine (Esther 7:2).

The Talmud also teaches that the mystery of the incense was given by the *klipah*. The Talmud says that when Moses descended from Mount Sinai, the angel of death taught him the mystery of the incense (*Shabbath* 89a) (see *Likutey Halakhoth, Gerim* 3:16).

wine. It is through wine that one can get good from the *klipoth*, as above. Since the wine has its root in a *klipah*, once it is removed from the *klipah*, it can be used for getting other things from the *klipah*. When a person can turn some evil into good, this in turn can transform more evil into good.

fled... Since she had been taken against her will.

When [the king and his men] discovered that the ship was missing, they became very anxious. [The king did not know that the emperor's daughter had fled with the ship; he assumed she was in her chamber.] The king said, "Be careful not to tell her too suddenly. She will be very upset because this precious ship [is gone]. Also, she might think that I gave her ship to someone else. Therefore, send one of her noblewomen to tell her in a subtle way."

[The men] went to one chamber and did not find anyone there. They then went to the second chamber [and the same was true]. They went to all eleven chambers, and did not find anyone.

Finally, they agreed to send an elderly noblewoman at night to tell her. [They all] went to the chamber of [the emperor's daughter] and did not find anyone there. They were very alarmed.

Meanwhile, the fathers of these noblewomen were accustomed to getting letters from their daughters. They usually sent letters back and forth, but now they saw that they were sending letters to their daughters and not getting any replies. The nobles decided to go and investigate, but when they arrived, their daughters were not to be found.

[The nobles] were furious, and they wanted to banish the king [and place him under a death sentence]. As ministers of state, they [had the power to do this]. But then they thought it over. "What did the king do to deserve to be banished? It was really not his fault." Instead, they decided to impeach him and have him exiled. So, they impeached [the king] and exiled him.*

[The king] thus went on his way.

Meanwhile, [the emperor's daughter] sailed away on ner ship [with the eleven noblewomen]. When the noblewomen woke up

---

exiled. *Far-shiken* in Yiddish. She thus caused both the merchant's son and this king to be exiled. Through the wine (joy) she got them out of the realm of the *klipah* into the realm of the *klipath nogah* (which is the land of the old king). We later see that this is where they were.

[they continued playing their games, since they did not know that the ship had left port].

Finally they said to her, "Let's go home."

"No," she replied. "Let's stay here a while longer."

A gale struck. "Let's go home!" they insisted.

[The emperor's daughter] informed them that the ship had already left port.

"Why did you do this?" they demanded.

She answered that she was afraid that the ship would break up in the storm. Her only choice was to untie it and spread sail.

[The emperor's daughter and the eleven noblewomen] sailed the sea and played their musical instruments.* Once they came across a palace, and the ladies said, "Let's go there! Let's see if we can come close!"

[The emperor's daughter], however, did not want to. She said that she still regretted that she had even come close to the palace [of the king who had tried to marry her].

Then they sighted an island, and drew near to it. There were twelve pirates* [on the island] and they wanted to kill* [the women].

"Who is the greatest among you?" asked [the emperor's daughter].

When they pointed him out, she asked him, "What is your occupation?" He told her that they were pirates.

"We are also pirates!" she replied. "You rob with your

---

musical instruments. She taught them all to relate to holiness. As we have seen, through music the *klipah* is raised to holiness.

twelve pirates. This would represent the third *klipah*, which is fire. It would also represent the exile of Edom (*Zohar Chadash loc. cit.*). Even though Edom was the fourth exile, it is represented by the third *klipah*. This is because it is represented by Haman in Persia. Edom is Esau, and this also refers to Amalek, who was a descendant of Esau (Genesis 36:12).

The twelve were the eleven *alufim* (princes) of Esau (Genesis 36), plus Esau himself. These are the eleven *klipoth* (*Etz Chaim, Shaar HaKlipoth* 1) plus Samael himself.

wanted to kill. Esau wanted to kill Jacob (Genesis 27:42). Also Amalek was the first to attack Israel (Exodus 17:8). Fire is totally destructive.

strength, but we rob with cleverness.* We know languages and music.* What will you gain if you kill us? Better marry us. Then in addition to our wealth, you will also have wives."

[The emperor's daughter] showed [the pirates] everything that was on the ship. Taken in by her words, the pirates also showed [the women] all their wealth, taking them to all their hiding places.

They also agreed that they would not all get married at the same time, but one after another. [The pirates would not have a mass wedding, but would get married one after the other.] Also, each one would pick out the lady most suitable for him, with the leaders getting first choice.

She then offered them some of the fantastically good wine* that she had in the ship. [She told them that] she had never used this wine, since she had put it aside until the time came that God would arrange for her to meet her destined husband.*

She served the wine in twelve goblets, and said that each one should drink to all of the twelve [women]. They drank and became so drunk that they fell asleep. "Come," she said to her companions. "Each one of you slit the throat of her destined husband."

[The women] slaughtered* all [the pirates]. They then found

---

we rob with cleverness. Make war with clever tricks (Proverbs 20:18). Jacob also used wisdom to get the birthright and blessing from Esau, which is Edom.

languages and music. Both can be used to cause spiritual harm.

good wine. Through wine, even Amalek can be defeated. Thus, Haman had his downfall through wine.

destined husband. This is the wine from the six days of creation that is destined to be drunk in the Messianic era (*Bereshith Rabbah*). This wine was untainted by the sin of Adam. Now she said that she would give it to the worst *klipah.*

slaughtered. From the pirates, she learned how to kill. The *ketoreth* has the power to destroy Amalek (*Likutey Moharan* 35:8). Also Edom will be destroyed because of the *ketoreth* (*Midrash Lekach Tov, Tzav*). Haman (Amalek) was also destroyed through Mordecai who represents *ketoreth.*

Here, too, what she gained through her previous encounter, she used to be victorious in this one. Each time a person takes something away from one realm of evil, he can use it to conquer a stronger realm of evil.

their treasures,* which were greater than that of any king. They agreed that they would not take any copper or silver,* just gold and precious stones.* They threw everything that was not so valuable off the ship, and loaded it down with the more valuable gold and precious stones that they found there.

[The women] also agreed that they would not dress like women anymore, so they sewed themselves men's clothing,* in the German style.* They then sailed on in their ship.

The pirate captain is not one of the four who is reunited. It seems that his place is taken by the king's son, the emperor's daughter's true husband.

Amalek is evil that cannot be redeemed. "Erase the memory of Amalek, do not forget" (Deut. 25:17). Also this indicates that Gehenom will cease to exist (*Avodah Zarah* 3b). The *klipah* of fire will be no more.

treasures. The *klipah* of fire is also the fire of Gehenom (*Etz Chaim, Shaar Derushey ABYA*). Out of Gehenom comes the ultimate reward, which is the greatest possible treasure.

Also Esther gets control of Haman's house and all his wealth (Esther 8:2).

Iram and Magdiel (Genesis 36:43) will bring treasures to the Messiah (*Bereshith Rabbah* 83).

copper or silver. Extranious strictness (Rabbi Rosenfeld). Rabbi Nachman felt that strictness beyond the law was often harmful.

gold and precious stones. Prayer and Torah study (Rabbi Rosenfeld).

men's clothing. Until now the princess was primarily passive, merely reacting to events that befell her. This is a feminine trait. But now she becomes active, as we see when she kills the bald prince. Thus, she takes on a male aspect.

It seems that when Malkhuth destroys *mochin* and evil in *klipath nogah*, she takes on a male aspect. Malkhuth takes on the male aspect in the person of the Messiah who is a male king. Indeed, she later assumes the role of a male king.

The Zohar teaches that when Malkhuth brings blessings to the world, she is called a male (*Zohar* 1:232a).

Male clothing is also in a sense protection, since now men will not desire her. Kabbalistically, the Hebrew word for *malbush* is the same as that of *chashmal* (*Etz Chaim, Shaar HaChashmal*).

It is thus taught that the *chashmal* (that Ezekiel saw) has the power to repel the forces of evil. Thus, before rectifying the *klipath nogah* she must don a male aspect. Also she will now be killing the male of *nogah* and taking the female queen, as we shall see.

German style. That is, short garments. In Poland and the Ukraine, where Rabbi Nachman lived, people wore long coats.

The *chashmal* is only above the hips of the man on the throne, which is the male aspect (Ezekiel 1:27).

Meanwhile, there was an elderly king* who had an only son.* He married his son off and gave him his kingdom.

The king's son said that he would take a journey by sea with his wife,* so as to accustom her to the sea air. Then, if heaven forbid, they were ever forced to flee by sea, [she would be prepared]. He took his wife and royal ministers, and sailed off on a ship.

They were very happy* and they played games. Then they all decided to take off their clothes.* [The king and royal ministers on the ship were so elated that they decided to undress,] leaving on only their shirts.*

They then had a contest to see who could climb the mast.*

---

elderly king. This is the "old and foolish king" (Ecclesiastes 4:13). This is Malkhuth of the side of evil (*Zimrath HaAretz*; see *Likutey Moharan* 1).

According to the order, this is the *klipath nogah*, the "glow" seen by Ezekiel (1:4). This is seen as the intermediate state between good and evil. If it attaches to the third *klipah*, which is fire, it becomes evil, but as long as it is attached to the *chashmal* (garment), it is good (*Etz Chaim, Klipath Nogah* 4).

Also, this is the fourth kingdom, which is Greece. Greece was known for its wisdom. However, its main wisdom was philosophy, which Rabbi Nachman taught to be mere foolishness (see *Sichoth HaRan* 5). Hence, even though Greece has wisdom, its king is called a "foolish king." Nevertheless, as the *Zohar* states, since Greece is involved with wisdom, it is the closest of the four to Torah (*Zohar Chadash* 38b).

only son. This is the "foolish son," in the verse, "The anger of his father (Chokhmah) is a foolish son" (Proverbs 17:25). It is taught that the male king of *klipath nogah*, is Samael (*Etz Chaim, Shaar Klipath Nogah* 2). This represents the modern world, as we shall see.

wife. This is Lilith (*Ibid.*). (See Isaiah 34:14.) It is the wife of Samael (*Tikkuney Zohar* 69, 100b; see *Pardes, Hekhal HaTemuroth* 5). She is the "foolish woman" (*Likutey Moharan* 23:6.) According to the verse, she is not killed (*Likutey Moharan* 34:15).

There are male and female aspects of nogah (*Etz Chaim, Shaar Klipath Nogah* 3,7).

happy. The *klipath nogah* is not pure sadness. It also contains an element of happiness that can bring them to holiness.

take off their clothes. That is, the *klipath nogah* separated itself from *chashmal* (garment). This removes their protection, and they are now open to becoming totally evil (see *Etz Chaim, Shaar Klipath Nogah* 4).

shirts. Leaving their lower parts completely exposed. "The top of such angels is good, while from the chest down, they are evil" (*Etz Chaim, Shaar Klipath Nogah* 4; also see *Etz Chaim, Shaar Kitzur ABYA* 4, p. 399; *Tikkuney Zohar* 22, 66a).

Secular wisdom often tries to make its point by tempting people with sex.

climb the mast. This is the sin of pride. Like the people at the Tower of Babel, they wanted

The king's son tried to climb [first].

Meanwhile [the emperor's daughter] approached in [her] ship, and she saw the other ship [with the king's son and the ministers]. At first she was afraid to come close, but when [the women] saw that [the men] were playing games, they realized that they were not pirates, so they came closer.

The emperor's daughter said to her companions, "I can knock that bald one into the sea." [This was the king's son, who was climbing the mast.] The king's son had lost all his hair and was bald.*

to go so high that they could fight against God (Genesis 11). Philosophy and secular wisdom often try to fight God Himself.

Kabbalistically, this indicates that the mental powers (*mochin*) of the *klipoth* want to climb to the very top of Atziluth (*Etz Chaim, Shaar HaKlipoth* 2, p. 375). (See Isaiah 33:23, *Targum ad loc.*; also see Story #6.)

bald. According to Rabbi Nachman, hair represents a reflection of what is in the mind (*Likutey Moharan* 29:10, 30:3). Thus, the Hebrew word for a hair is *saar* (שער), which is spelled the same as *shaar* (שער), meaning a gate (*Likutey Moharan* 69). Baldness thus represents the inability to produce anything with one's thoughts. This is Greek philosophy, which may seem intellectually stimulating, but ultimately is fruitless.

On the holy side, hair also represents the ability of the unclean forces to grasp what is on one's mind (*Likutey Moharan* 67:9; *Zohar* 1:217a; *Derekh Emeth* 6). For this reason one must wash one's hands after cutting one's hair.

Conversely, hair on the unclean side indicates that the Holy can grasp the thoughts. But since the Holy cannot in any way grasp the thoughts of philosophy and the *klipath nogah*, it is bald.

The Ari specifically teaches, "*Arikh Anpin*" (the highest level) of *klipath nogah* wants to have hair like *Arikh Anpin* of the Holy. But it cannot, as it is written, 'Though you raise up your nest like an eagle... from there I will bring you down, says God' (Obadiah 1:4, cf. Jeremiah 49:16). (*Shaar HaKlipoth* 3, p. 376)." The eagle represents baldness, as it is written, "Make yourself bald... Enlarge your baldness like the eagle" (Micah 1:16).

Thus, when the "bald one" which is *Arikh Anpin* of the *klipah*, wants to climb high, it is ready to be pushed down. The *Zohar* also applies this same verse to Samael (*Zohar* 3:282a). See below, p. 76.

In Hebrew, bald is *koreach* (קרח). This is also related to Korach. Significantly, the Midrash says, "Among Korach and his group, his sons stood like the *mast* on a ship" (*Midrash Psalms* 1:15; *Yalkut*, Numbers 26; Psalms 614; see *Chayay Moharan* p. 14 #10; *Rimzey Maasioth* of Story #7).

"How is that possible?" they asked. "We are still quite far from them."

She told them that she had a burning glass,* and would use it to knock him down. She explained that she would not knock him down until he had climbed to the very top of the mast. As long as he was climbing the mast, he would fall down to the ship, but when he was on the top, he would fall into the sea.*

She waited until he reached the very top of the mast, and then she aimed her burning glass at this head. His brain was burned* and he fell into the sea.

When [the men on the king's ship] saw him fall, there was great panic. How could they ever return home? The [old] king would die of grief.

They decided to go over to the ship [belonging to the emperor's daughter]. Perhaps there would be a physician* who

---

burning glass. This involves the power of fire, which was represented by the pirates. In each case, she gets a weapon from her previous encounter.

Here, however, she will not use fire but the power of the sun. This is what the Talmud says, "In the future, God will do away with [the fire of] Gehenom, but will take the sun out of its capsule sheath,... and it will heal the righteous and burn the wicked" (*Nedarim* 8b). Now that the *klipah* of fire (Gehenom) is no more, the sun must be used to destroy the evil in *klipath nogah*.

fall into the sea. "Cast in the deep sea all our sins" (Micah 7:19). The Shekhinah (God) will use the power of the sun to destroy all the evil in us, and thus purify us. The evil will not be allowed to be in the body in the World to Come, and the body (ship) will therefore be pure. The two birds in the *Zohar* (see *Likutey Moharan* 3) are cast into the depths of the great deep (*Zohar*); these two birds are the *mochin* of the *klipah* (*Etz Chaim, Shaar Klipath Nogah* 9, p. 391).

brain was burned. The young king represents the present world with its secular wisdom. Actually, the verse in Obadiah is speaking of Edom (*Yerushalmi Nedarim* 3:8). So the old king is Greece and the prince is the rest of Edom, which can be rectified.

The *klipath nogah* is the "tree of knowledge of good and evil" (*Etz Chaim, Shaar Kitzur ABYA* 3). Evil knowledge is philosophy and secular wisdom. Therefore, the brain must be destroyed, to rid Greece and Edom (the modern world) of its evil knowledge.

The *Zohar* speaks of this, saying that Samael is on high, but God says that He will bring him down, quoting the verse (Obadiah 1:4). It says that the Shekhinah (emperor's daughter) is now involved with *nogah*, and she uses the heat of fire to destroy him (*Zohar* 3:282a).

physician. Rabbi Nachman taught that physicians were agents of the Angel of Death

could given them some advice. They came close to the ship [carrying the emperor's daughter and her ladies], and [the men on the dead king's ship] said to [the ladies and the emperor's daughter] that they should not be afraid. They would not do anything to harm them.

[The men] asked them, "Do you have a physician on board? Perhaps he can give us some advice." They told them the whole story about how the king's son had fallen into the sea.

"Fish him out of the sea," said the emperor's daughter.

[The men] located the body, and took him out [of the water]. [The emperor's daughter] felt [the dead king's] pulse* with her hand, and announced that his brain was burned. They opened up [his head, exposing] his brain and they saw that she was right. They were dumbfounded.

[The men] asked her to go home with them where she would be the king's personal physician. She could be very important and have high status. She demurred, saying that she was not really a physician, but merely had certain specialized knowledge. [The men on the king's ship,] however, did not want to return home, so the two ships sailed alongside each other.

The royal ministers decided that it would be a very good thing if their queen would marry* this physician, since they saw that

(*Sichoth HaRan* 50). This represents using secular wisdom rather than prayer for curing. Thus, the ministers were not completely weaned away from their involvement with secular wisdom. But with their king dead, they are won over by the emperor's daughter, the daughter of Wisdom (Chokhmah), hence the wisdom of the Torah.

pulse. The art of using pulse for diagnosis is discussed in the Kabbalah (*Tikkuney Zohar* 69, 109a; *Shaar Ruach HaKodesh*, p. 14; *Likutey Moharan* 56:9; *Likutey Halakhoth, Tefillah* 4:22).

queen would marry. This is Lilith of *klipath nogah*, as above. Lilith is not destroyed in the end, but rectified, as it is written, "The Lilith shall find repose there, and she shall find herself a place of rest" (Isaiah 34:14). This is the rectified realm of *klipath nogah*, the world of gentiles, which will be rectified when the Messiah comes. Still, they cannot return to the land of the king and the emperor. The verse earlier says, "None of her nobles (ministers) shall be called to the kingdom (of the emperor), and all her princes shall be nothing" (Isaiah 34:12). This indicates that the prince (the bald prince) will be destroyed, and the ministers will not come to the kingdom of the emperor, but will eventually be abandoned by the emperor's daughter, as we shall see.

"he" had very great wisdom. [The ministers of the king's son who fell and died thought that the emperor's daughter and her ladies were men, since they were wearing men's clothing. Therefore, they wanted their queen, the wife of the king's son who had just died, to marry the physician, who was really the emperor's daughter. They thought that she was a physician, because she had the wisdom to understand that the brain of the royal prince who fell had been burned.]

[If the "physician" would do this] he would be their king.* They would then kill their [elderly] king. [The royal ministers wanted this very much,] but they found it impossible to say anything to the queen about marrying the "physician." The queen also thought that it would be very good to marry the "physician," but she was afraid that the nation would not want "him" as their king.

[The royal ministers]* decided to make a drinking party, so that when everyone was joyous* at the party, they would be able to speak of [the match]. Each minister made a party, on his day. When the day came for the "physician" [who was actually the emperor's daughter] to give "his" party, "he" gave them some of "his" special wine.* When they were drunk and in a good mood, the ministers declared that it would be nice if the queen would marry the "physician."

---

would be their king. This group wants to be ruled by wisdom. Now that secular wisdom has been killed, they want to be ruled by the wisdom of the Torah, which is the emperor's daughter.

[The royal ministers]. Literally, "they". The subject is not mentioned, but understood. It might also indicate the queen and the emperor's daughter.

joyous. *Chedvah* in Hebrew. This is a word for joy that is not often used. But when Ezra and Nehemiah taught the Torah to the people after it had been forgotten, they said, "Go your way, eat the fat and drink the sweet, for God's joy (*chedvah*) is your strength" (Nehemiah 8:10). This is also joy that is seen as strength (*oz*) as it is written, "Strength (*oz*) and *chedvah* are in His place" (1 Chronicles, 16:27).

Here again, joy is used as a means of reconciling the *klipath nogah* and bringing it under the rule of the *bath melekh*. Rabbi Nachman states that Lilith can be subjugated through joy (*Likutey Moharan* 169; cf. *Likutey Moharan* 226).

wine. It is through the wine that the match is eventually made and the story comes to a happy ending (*Rimzey Maasioth*).

The "physician" said that it would be very nice, but only if it would be declared without a drunken mouth [when everyone was not drunk].

The queen spoke up and said, "How nice it would be to marry the physician. But the nation will have to agree to it."

[The emperor's daughter] replied, "It would be very nice! But only if they would say it without a drunken mouth!"

When the ministers recovered from their drunkenness, they remembered what they had said, and they were ashamed to face the queen because they had made such a statement. [The queen], however, had made a similar declaration, and she was also ashamed to face them. Nevertheless, they had proposed this [first].

They began to discuss this, and agreed that she should marry* the "physician" (that is, the emperor's daughter, whom they still thought to be a physician).

They returned to their own country. When the people saw them coming they were very happy. It had been a long time since the king's son had left, and they did not know where he was. The elderly king had already died, before they came.

Then [the populace] saw that the king's son was not there. "Where is our king?" they asked.

[The royal ministers] told them the whole story about how [the king's son] had died, and how they had accepted a new king, who was now arriving with them. [The people] were very happy that [the ministers] had brought them a new king.*

The "king" (that is, the emperor's daughter, who was now the king) ordered that an announcement* be made throughout each

---

she should marry. Rabbi Nachman taught that the wisdom of the Torah (emperor's daughter, *Gemara*) can overwhelm Lilith since Talmud (תלמוד) has the same numerical value as Lilith (לילית) (*Likutey Moharan* 214).

new king. When Malkhuth wants to sustain the outside forces, which is the mystery of "His kingdom (Malkhuth) rules over all" (Psalms 103:9), she does so through *klipath nogah* (*Etz Chaim, Shaar Klipath Nogah* 3; see *Zohar* 2:139a).

announcement. In the end, Shekhinah rectifies everything. This is, "So that none be cast away" (2 Samuel, 14:14), except for Amalek.

and every country that every foreigner, visitor, fugitive and exile must come to "his" wedding. No one should dare absent himself [and they would receive great gifts.

[The emperor's daughter who was now king] also ordered that wells* be dug all around the city, so that when anyone wanted a drink, he would not have to go anywhere, but would immediately have a well nearby.

[The emperor's daughter who was king] also gave orders that her portrait be placed next to every well. Watches should then be set up, and if anyone stared at the image and made a bad face [looking surprised and grieved], he should be taken prisoner.

It was all set up, and the three people [she had previously encountered] came. They were the first king's son, who was the true husband of the emperor's daughter [who was now king]; the merchant's son, whose father had driven him away after the emperor's daughter had fled with the ship and all the merchandise; and the king who had been impeached [because she had fled from him with the eleven noblewomen].

All three of them recognized her picture. When they looked [at the picture], they remembered her and they grieved. [When they had come to the wells, and saw her picture there, they recognized her and stared at the pictures.] They were arrested and placed in prison.

At the wedding, the [emperor's daughter who was] king ordered that the prisoners be brought before "him," and all three were brought. She immediately recognized them, but, since she was dressed like a man, they did not recognize her.

[Addressing the impeached king,* who was now one of the three prisoners,] the emperor's daughter said, "You, King. You were impeached because eleven noblewomen were lost. Here are

---

wells. Or springs. *Mayan* in Hebrew. In Yiddish, *kvellen*, which can also denote wells. Also from context.

These were like the wells that Abraham dug, which were sources of spiritual flow into the world (Genesis 21, 26).

Addressing the impeached king. The worst *klipah* must be rectified first.

the noblewomen! Return to your land and your kingdom." [The eleven noblewomen were there with her.]

[After addressing the impeached king, she addressed the merchant's son,* and said,] "You, Merchant. Your father drove you away because you lost the ship with merchandise. Here is your ship and all the merchandise. Since your money was tied up so long, the wealth on your ship has been increased manifold." [The ship with the merchandise in which she had fled was still intact. The ship also contained the wealth that she had taken from the pirates. This was enormous wealth, many times the value of what was on the ship previously.]

[Addressing her true bridegroom, she then said,] "And you, Royal Prince,* let us go home."*

With that they both returned home.

Blessed be God forever, Amen and Amen.*

---

merchant's son. Babylon. Babylon is wealthy for honoring the Torah (*Shabbath* 119a).

Also Babylon will not experience the birth pangs of the Messiah (*Kethuboth* 111a).
Royal Prince. The king's son, her true husband.
let us go home. In Yiddish, "Come here let us go home." In Hebrew, "Let's go and be on our way." Once she finds her true husband, she no longer remains in the realm of *klipath nogah*. This is rectified by the Shekhinah, and then she goes back to where she is totally involved with Israel.

The morning of Rabbi Nathan's passing, (Friday, 10 Teveth, 5605 [1845]), these first two stories were read to him (*Alim Leterufah* p.196b). When the words "let us go home" were spoken, Rabbi Nathan nodded, as if to say "it is *my* time to return *home* [to heaven]" (Rabbi Avraham Sternhartz).
Blessed be... Abbreviation (ביל״ו). In Yiddish, just Amen and Amen.

3

THE CRIPPLE*

Once there was a wise man*. Before he died, he summoned his sons and his family and told them that they must water trees.* "You may also earn a living in other ways, but you must also be careful to water trees." With that, the wise man died, leaving behind sons.

He had one son who could not walk.* He could stand,* but

The Cripple. All the standard commentaries note that this story is very deep and opaque (*Rimzey Maasioth, Zimrath HaAretz*). It is said to speak of the mystery of the rectification (*tikkun*), and the destruction of the *klipoth* and the forces of evil (*Zimrath HaAretz*). It is one of the most complex of all the stories.

Psalm 1 is the key to this story (see end of story).

wise man. This is the first wise man. There is also another wise man who escapes from the kingdom of the atheist king.

water trees. It is significant that in no place do we actually find any of the sons watering trees. This may, however, be the motivation of the cripple to seek out the tree mentioned by the moon. This may have been his reason for going to the 2000 mountains. Watering this tree was the concern of the moon, as we shall see (*Rimzey Maasioth*).

The tree also alludes to the Torah, as it is written, "It is a tree of life to all who grasp on to it" (Proverbs 3:18). So the injunction may be to study Torah (*Rimzey Maasioth*).

Every person may also be considered a "tree," as it is written, "For man is a tree of the field" (Deuteronomy 20:19). Man is often likened to a tree in Kabbalistic literature. Therefore, the injunction may be to do good for people, and bring them close to the Torah. The sons may have followed this injunction by supporting their crippled brother.

Kabbalistically, the tree is the array of the sefiroth (see *Zohar* 1:225b; Ari, *Likutey Torah* on "a Tree of Life"). The "water" for that tree is the human mind, when it strives to understand God's Torah (*Tikkuney Zohar* 21, 44a). Also when God's will (Kether) is done, the Tree is watered (*Tikkuney Zohar* 17a).

could not walk. This is alluded to in the verse, "Happy is the man who does not walk in the counsel of the wicked" (Psalms 1:1), as noted by Rabbi Nathan at the end of the story. The Midrash (*Midrash Tehillim* 1:2) states that this relates to King David, as it is written,

he could not walk. His brothers supported him,* giving him enough to live on and to have something left over.* Little by little, [the crippled] son saved up some of the leftover money until he had a considerable sum. He thought it over. "Why should I have [my brothers]* supply my needs? It is better that I start some kind of business [of my own]."

Although he could not walk, he had a plan. He would hire a wagon,* a secretary* and a driver.* He would travel with them to

"David *sat* before God" (2 Samuel, 7:18).

Since this alludes to King David, it may be that this is why he began the Psalms with this verse, as it were, to sign his name at the beginning of his work (*Chokhmah U'Tevunah*). This son witnesses the destruction of the demons, and paralleling this, King David's descendant, the Messiah, will cause all the forces of evil to be destroyed (*Ibid.*). It may also be for this reason that the Psalms are effective in destroying the forces of evil (*Likutey Moharan Tinyana* 92).

The crippled son here is very reminiscent of the seventh beggar in the story of the Seven Beggars, who has no feet.

A major theme of this story is the weakness of the feet. The crippled son parallels the moon, whose feet are weakened by the demons, as we see below. This also alludes to Malkhuth, since the feet of Malkhuth extend down from Atziluth to Beriyah, the realm of the *klipoth*. Malkhuth is thus seen as having weak feet.

He could stand. Later, after he is robbed, he even loses the power to stand (*Rimzey Maasioth*).

Angels and disembodied souls are said to "stand," while a human being is able to "walk" and progress. It is thus written, "I will give you a place to walk among the [angels] standing here" (Zechariah 3:7). The cripple is thus like a soul before it is born. It is supported by others, but not by the work of its own hands. An unborn soul is sustained by God, as a free gift or as charity, and not because it has earned anything on its own.

Some relate this to the soul of the Messiah.

supported him. Following this analogy, the good deeds of people who are already born sustain the unborn soul, which still cannot walk on its own. Some say that other tzaddikim are the ones supporting him.

something left over. The ability to come down into this world and earn merit on one's own. The something left over is the *Yetzer Tov*.

Why should I have [my brothers]... "He who eats that which is not his is ashamed to look in the other's face" (*Yerushalmi, Orlah* 1:3). "A person prefers one measure of his own than ten measures of his fellows" (*Bava Metzia* 38a). This is the concept of "bread of shame" (*nahama de-kesufa*) that a person eats before he earns his own reward (*Magid Yesharim*, p. 10).

wagon. The body.

Leipzig,* and then, even though he could not walk, he would be able to do some kind of business.

When his family heard his plan, they were very pleased. They said, "Why should we continue to support him? It is better that he earn his own living."* They therefore lent* him even more money so that he would have enough to run a business.

[The cripple] hired a wagon, a secretary, and a driver, and he set out. They came to an inn, and his secretary suggested that they spend the night there, but he did not want to. They* implored him, but he was stubborn and continued on his way. Soon they were lost in a forest,* and they were attacked by robbers.*

This band of robbers originated during a time of famine.* A man* had come to the city and announced that whoever wanted food should come to him, thus attracting a number of men.* He

---

secretary. Ne'eman in Hebrew. A man servant. He would take care of his business once he got to his destination. This appears to be the intellect.

driver. The animal soul.

Leipzig. A major city in East Germany. It was the site of a huge fair, held three times a year, where Jews were permitted to attend. However, the Jews were not permitted to have a community in this city at the time this story was told. It was only a place to go and do business, but one would have to return. Thus, it was like the physical world, where one could go to do business, but one could not remain there forever.

better that he earn his own living. It is a general rule in charity, that it is much better to set a poor man up in business than to give him charity (Yad, Matanot L'Aniyim 10:7). Similarly, better than watering the tree every day, one should strive to break down the barriers, so that the tree can constantly receive water, as indeed happens at the end of the story.

lent. This extra was not given, but merely lent.

They. Probably the secretary and driver.

forest. A place of evil forces.

robbers. This was a result of his stubbornness. It may seem that his stubbornness caused his downfall, but this was actually the beginning of his salvation, because as a result of this attack, he discovers the diamond, and eventually cures his legs and gains all the robbers' treasure. The lesson is that at times, one must take chances and be stubborn, even though it may involve danger. If one has faith in God, it can bring about one's salvation.

The robbers represent the forces of evil and klipah.

famine. Tzimtzum, a constriction and holding back of God's power. This resulted in the birth of the forces of evil.

man. The Satan.

attracting a number of men. The forces of evil had their origin in the realm of the holy.

worked with cunning,* and dismissed the men he could not use. To one he said, "You can be a craftsman,"* while to another he said, "You can work in a mill." He thus chose only intelligent youths, bringing them into the woods.* Then he told them that they should become thieves. "From here, people travel to Leipzig, Breslau* and other places. Merchants go by. We will rob them and amass money."

It was these robbers who attacked [the cripple and his men].

The driver and secretary were able to flee,* but [the cripple] remained in the wagon.* When [the robbers] came to take the money chest, they asked him, "Why are you sitting there?"

[The cripple] replied that he could not walk. [The robbers] took the chest and the horses, leaving [the cripple] on the wagon.

The secretary and driver fled [to a town]. They decided that since they had taken out loans* from the wealthy landowners,* it would be foolish for them to return home, since they could be put in chains. It would be better to remain [in the town to which they had fled]. Here they would also be able to work as a secretary and a driver.

The crippled son had provisions he had brought from home,

---

cunning. (See *Rimzey Maasioth*). He did not originally tell the men that he was recruiting them as robbers, but only that he would feed them. That is why he was killed in the end, even though he repented. The Baal Shem Tov teaches that the Satan is destroyed because he misrepresents his intentions to people.

craftsman. *Baal melakhah* in Hebrew and Yiddish.

into the woods. Only after he had them in his domain did he reveal his true intentions.

Breslau. The name sounds very much like Breslov.

Breslau was a city in Eastern Germany which was also the site of major fairs. It had a Jewish community in Rabbi Nachman's time, but they were largely of the *haskalah* and reform persuasion. The same was true of Leipzig (see *Likutey Halakhoth, Tefillah* 4:20).

driver and secretary were able to flee. When a person is born, he loses the intellect that he had as a soul. He also does not have the power to travel through universes.

remained in the wagon. The soul remains helpless in the body.

loans. *Prukladin* in Yiddish.

wealthy landowners. *Peritzim.* Later we find that *peritzim* put chains on the feet of the saints who wish to take suffering upon themselves, thus taking away power from their feet. The secretary and driver were afraid that they would be put in chains by the landowners.

and as long as he had some dry bread in his wagon, he ate it. Then this was used up and he did not have anything to eat. He thought it over, and threw himself down from the wagon* where he would be able to eat grass.* He spent the night alone in the field and was very frightened.

He lost all his strength, until he could not even stand.* He could only crawl,* [pushing himself along]. He ate the grass around him.

As long as he could reach out and eat [the grass around him], he would remain in one place. Then, when the grass was gone, so that he could not reach any more, he would push himself further and eat there. He continued eating grass for some time.

Then, one day, he came across a certain type of grass* that he had never eaten before. The grass looked appealing. He had eaten grass for so long now that he was familiar with the various species, but he had never seen any grass like this. He made up his mind that he would pluck it out, root and all.

Under the root there was a diamond.* The diamond was square, and each side* had a different power.

---

threw himself down from the wagon. Divorced himself from bodily concerns.

grass. This is animal food (Genesis 1:30, 3:18). Rabbi Nachman taught that it is sometimes good to be like an animal (*Sichoth HaRan* 15; see *Likutey Moharan* 47, end).

This is alluded to in the above mentioned first psalm, "Happy is the man.. through the way of sinners, does not stand" (Psalms 1:1).

could not even stand. The robbers had made his feet even weaker. But as a result, he gained a marvelous means of transportation (*Chockhmah U'Tevunah*).

The robbers, representing the forces of evil, attack a person's feet, as we also see in the case of the moon. Feet represent the aspect of faith. Thus, the forces of evil strive to take away a person's faith.

crawl. *Ruken zich.* He was like a spiritual infant.

certain type of grass. There are grasses with great spiritual powers (see *Zohar* 2:80b).

diamond. *Dumit* in Yiddish. In the Talmud we have "if you had not removed the clay, you would not have found the jewel under it" (*Yebamoth* 92b; *Bava Metzia* 17b).

each side... It appeared to have four sides. But actually only two are mentioned as being used. The first side brought him to the place where he could get the information he needed, and the second brought him healing. The two sides may be Torah and prayer, Rabbi Nachman's two foundation stones.

On one side it was written that whoever grasped that side
would be foolish for them to return home, since they could be put
together,* that is, where the sun and moon* meet. When [the
cripple] uprooted the grass concealing the diamond, it turned out
that he was grasping that side [of the stone].

It lifted him up and transported him to the place where day
and night meet. He looked around, and saw that this was the
place where the sun and moon come together. He heard the sun
and moon speaking.

The sun was complaining to the moon, "There is a tree* that
has many branches, [each with] its own fruit and leaves. Every
single branch, fruit, and leaf has its own special power. One has
the power to grant children [to the childless], while another has
the special power to grant livelihood.* One has the power to heal
one's sickness, and the others have the power to heal different
sicknesses. Each one thus has its own different power.

"This tree must be watered.* If it were watered it would have
all these great powers. But not only do I not water it, but when I
shine on it, I am drying it up."*

---

day and night come together. As we have said, this place was the source of his information,
and this is the Torah. The place where day and night come together is the study of the
Torah, as it is written, "He desires God's Torah... day and night" (Psalms 1:2). This is the
psalm which is the key to this story. This is the concept of joining day and night through
Torah (*Rimzey Maasioth; Zimrath HaAretz*).

sun and moon. The sun is wisdom and the moon is Malkhuth (*Likutey Moharan* 1). The
moon represents the power that God gives us to understand the Torah. It also represents
faith, through which the wisdom can be brought to fruition.

tree. This is the "tree planted by the streams of water" (Psalms 1:3) (Rabbi Nathan's notes
at the end of the story). "On the bank of the brook on both sides shall grow the entire fruit
tree. Its leaves shall not wither, and its fruit shall not fail... Its fruit shall be for food, and
its leaves for healing" (Ezekiel 47:12; *Zimrath HaAretz*; and see Hosea 14:9, *Zohar* 1:226b).

grant livelihood. It seems that this tree has the power to grant life, livelihood and children.
These are the three things which do not depend on merit, but on *mazal* (destiny) (*Moed
Katan* 28a). These are said to come from the tree of life (*Zohar* 1:24a) when it is properly
watered (*Zohar* 1:43b).

must be watered. It must be "planted by streams of water" (Psalms 1:3) (*Rimzey Maasioth*).
The cripple thus learns the mystery of his father's command that he water trees.

I am drying it up. The sun cannot do what the father commanded his son to do, that is,
water trees.

The moon replied, "You are worried about the concerns of others. Let me tell you my problem.* I have a thousand mountains,* and around these thousand mountains, there are another thousand mountains. This is the place of the demons.* The demons have feet like chickens,* and they therefore do not have any strength in their feet.* They pull nourishment from my feet,* and because of this, I do not have any strength in my own feet.* I have a powder* which is a remedy for my feet, but a wind

---

The sun represents wisdom. Here we see that wisdom without faith (the moon) can destroy the Torah.

my problem. As we shall see later, if the tree were properly watered, it would also destroy the demons. Therefore, the fact that the sun is drying up the tree is the reason that the moon is suffering (*Zimrath HaAretz*). The moon is the source of water (*Sichoth HaRan* 92).

thousand mountains. These may be the "beasts in a thousand mountains" (Psalms 50:10).

place of the demons. These were the mountains of the East (Numbers 23:7), from which Balaam got his power (*Zohar Chadash* 81b; cf. *Zohar* 3:258b).

In Hebrew, demons are *shedim*. According to tradition, they were created at twilight, just before the Sabbath (*Avoth* 5:61). Since the Sabbath pertains to Malkhuth, the demons have a special attachment to Malkhuth.

feet like chickens. This is a Talmudic teaching (*Berakhoth* 6a; Rashi, *Gittin* 68b s.v.; *Zohar* 3:308b).

do not have any strength in their feet. "Falsehood has no feet" (see *Zohar* 3:229b).

pull nourishment from my feet. The feet of Malkhuth go down to Beriyah, where the forces of evil can draw nourishment. It is therefore written, "Her feet go down to death" (Proverbs 5:5). (See *Likutey Moharan* 54:2; *Chokhmah U'Tevunah*.)

Rabbi Nachman also teaches that "feet" represent worldly involvement and it is from this that the forces of evil can gain nourishment (*Likutey Moharan* 54:2).

The foot represents faith (*Likutey Moharan Tinyana* 80; *Sichoth HaRan* 261).

It is therefore taught that "a person should sell the beams of his house to buy shoes" (*Shabbath* 129a).

I do not have any strength in my own feet. If the trees were watered, the moon's troubles would cease, because the demons would then be destroyed (*Rimzey Maasioth*). It appears that the problem of the moon is reflected in the cripple.

Rabbi Nachman taught that the blemish of the moon is a blemish of faith, which is an aspect of weak feet (*Sichoth HaRan* 261).

Just as the robbers took away the cripple's power to stand, so demons take away the strength in the moon's feet.

powder. *Pil* in Yiddish. "Powder yourselves with the dust of their feet" (*Avoth* 1:4). This may denote the standard prayers, which are often disrupted by the forces of evil (see *Likutey Moharan* 4:10).

comes* and blows it away."

"Is *that* your worry?" answered the sun. "I'll tell you a cure. There is a highway with many roads branching off from it.

"One is the path of the righteous.* When a person is righteous,* some dust from this path is sprinkled under every step he takes. Every time he takes a step, he walks on that powder.

"Then there is the path of the atheist.* If a person is an atheist,* some powder [from this path] is scattered under every step he takes.

"There is also the path of the insane.* If a person is insane, [dust from this path] is sprinkled under him. There are also many [other] paths.

"There is also a path for the righteous persons who accept suffering* upon themselves. The wealthy landowners* lead them

---

wind comes. "The wicked are not so, for it is like the chaff that the wind blows away" (Psalms 1:4; Rabbi Nathan at end of story). The wind mentioned here is the "unclean wind," regarding which God said, "I will remove the unclean wind (spirit) from the earth" (Zechariah 13:2; *Zimrath HaAretz*). This requires water, as the verse opens, "On that day a fountain shall be opened...and I will cut off the names of idols from the land" (Zechariah 13:1,2).

path of the righteous. "God knows the path of the righteous" (Psalms 1:6; Rabbi Nathan at end of story).

person is righteous. "In the way that a person wishes to go, he is led" (*Makkoth* 10a).

path of the atheist. "The path of the wicked shall perish" (Psalms 1:4). Atheism is seen as the root of all evil (*Likutey Moharan Tinyana* 97). This is the path taken by the emperor, from which the wise man flees.

atheist. *Apikores* in Hebrew. An atheist or heretic. From Epicurius, the Greek philosopher, who taught that the main goal in life was the pursuit of pleasure and that religion was the greatest detriment to this goal. Therefore Apikores or Epicurean is one who is opposed to religion.

path of the insane. "The way of a fool is straight in his own eyes, but he who is wise listens to advice" (Proverbs 12:15). Rabbi Nachman teaches that if a person does not listen to advice, he can become insane (*Sichoth HaRan* 67).

who accept suffering. Accepting suffering is one of the forty-eight things through which the Torah is earned (*Avoth* 6). It is an aspect of King David, as the Talmud teaches, God said to David, "Accept suffering upon yourself" (*Sanhedrin* 107a). David is the aspect of weak feet, as we have discussed earlier.

Moreover, this path is the path of the sun, since it is taught regarding the righteous who accept suffering with love, that it is written, "And they who love Him like the sun in its

in chains, and they do not have any strength in their feet. Some powder from this path is scattered under their feet, and this gives their feet strength.

"You must therefore go there. There is plenty of powder,* and it will be a remedy for your feet."

[The cripple] heard all this.* He then looked at the other side of the diamond* and saw written there that if one grasps that side, one will be transported to the highway from which the many paths emanate. He grasped that side, and it immediately transported him there.

He placed his feet on the path containing the powder that was a remedy for the feet, and he was immediately healed.*

He then took powder from all the paths, tying it into bundles. He made one bundle of powder from the path of the righteous by itself. He did the same with the powders from the other paths, and he took them all.

He then decided to go back to the forest* where he had been

---

strength" (Judges 5:31; *Shabbath* 88b).

landowners. *Peritzim.* This may be related to the fact that the secretary and driver were afraid that the landowners would put them in chains. This denotes the weakening of faith.

These landowners have so much wealth and power, that this in itself may weaken faith. "Why do the wicked prosper..." (Jeremiah 12:1).

There is plenty of powder. The fact that saints take suffering upon themselves strengthens the moon, which is Malkhuth.

[The cripple] heard all this. Thus the cripple had a *yeridah le-tzorekh aliyah* "lowering for the sake of elevation." Because he had lost the ability to stand, he learned how to cure his feet, so that he would be able to walk.

other side of the diamond. If he had not grasped the other side first, he would not have known what to do when he came to those paths.

The second side of the diamond apparently relates to prayer. If one does not study Torah, one will not know what to pray for.

immediately healed. Since he is an aspect of the moon. This denotes the Messiah.

back to the forest. Now that he is healed, through the power of faith (feet), he can overcome evil. The same source of power (powder from the paths) which healed his feet can overcome evil.

Eventually, he will see the tree watered, and the demons destroyed; thus, the moon also has the power in its feet restored. The cripple knows that his feet are not completely healed, as long as the robbers exist.

robbed. When he came there, he chose a tall tree* near the path along which the robbers went out to plunder. He took some powder of the righteous and some powder of the insane, mixed them together, and scattered it on the path. He then climbed the tree and sat there, waiting to see what would happen.

A group of robbers, who had been sent out by their leader to plunder, set out. They came to that path, and as soon as they stepped on the powder, they became righteous. They began to cry out for their souls, since they had previously robbed and killed so many people.

However, because [this powder] was mixed with the powder of the insane, they became insane saints.* They began to fight with one another. One said, "It was because of you that we stole," and the other said, "You caused us to steal." This went on until they had all killed each other.*

[The leader] sent out another group,* and the same thing happened. They killed one another just as before.

This happened again, until all [the robbers] were killed.

[The ex-cripple] realized that none [of the robbers] remained except for [the leader] and one other man.* [The ex-cripple]

---

tall tree. Usually a great tzaddik. Or, the power of the Torah.

insane saints. Insane tzaddikim. Rabbi Nachman may have been speaking about his contemporary tzaddikim. He felt that many of their practices were foolish, especially those which went against halakhah.

This teaches that even when a person wishes to be righteous, he must be careful to retain his sanity (*Rimzey Maasioth*). Very often a person becomes religious and begins to behave in a neurotic manner. When a person becomes religious and follows the way of the Torah, he must be very careful to avoid the "dust of the insane."

all killed each other. This is the concept of *tikkun* (rectification). The forces of evil are first rectified, and then they are made so that they destroy each other. This parallels the end of the story, where the various groups of demons cause each other's destruction. Evil thus destroys itself.

sent out another group. This is very reminiscent of what King Saul did to David. David was with Samuel in Nayoth, and Saul sent two delegations to get him. When these were unsuccessful, Saul himself went (1 Samuel, 19:18-24). Here too, as we have mentioned, the ex-cripple is an aspect of David.

one other man. These is no mention as to what happens to this other one. It may be that he climbed down from the tree, and swept away the powder that he had placed on the path. Then he spread pure powder of the righteous, and went back to sit in the tree.

The [head] robber was curious, since he had sent out all his robbers, and not a single one had returned. He therefore set out with the one who remained with him. As soon as he came to the path [where the ex-cripple had scattered the pure powder of the righteous], he became a saint.* He began to cry out for his soul to his companion because he had killed so many people and had robbed so much [property]. He tore out graves* and repented with great remorse.

When the [ex-cripple who was sitting in the tree] heard that the [head robber]. was so remorseful and repentant, he climbed down from the tree. Seeing him, the robber began to cry out, "Woe to my soul! I have committed so many crimes! Give me a way to repent!"*

"Give me back the chest that you stole from me," replied [the ex-cripple].

[The robbers] had kept a record of everything that they had stolen, including the day and the victim. "I will return it to you immediately," said the [chief robber]. "I will even give you all the other wealth* that I stole! But just give me a means of repentance."

survives. This parallels the king of the demons, who survives with one other demon (see below). It may denote Lilith, who survives even when Samael is destroyed (see previous story).

became a saint. Before Satan is destroyed, he must be rectified. The Baal Shem Tov teaches that the "slaughter of the *Yetzer Hara*" indicates that he will be converted into a good angel, just as an animal becomes kosher when it is slaughtered (*Toledoth Yaakov Yosef, Kedoshim* (98d), quoted in *Sefer Baal Shem Tov, Bereshith* 149; see *The Light Beyond*, p. 100). The Satan is actually doing God's will when he tempts people to sin. The *Zohar* says it is like a prostitute hired by the king to test his son. The prostitute is doing the king's will when she tempts the son to sin (*Zohar* 2:163a).

tore out graves. The Talmud speaks about tearing up a headstone from a grave (see *Yerushalmi, Maaser Sheni* 5:1).

At the end of Story #12, p. 348, we find people jumping into graves.

Give me a way to repent. The Messiah must rectify all the forces of evil.

other wealth. Through being robbed, the cripple eventually gains great wealth. The forces

"There is only one way that you can repent," said the [ex-cripple]. "You must go to the city and confess: 'I am the one who made the announcement way back then, and I caused many men to become robbers. I have robbed and killed many people.' This is your repentance."

[The chief robber] gave him all his treasures, and went with him into the city, doing as he had said. Since [the robber] had killed so many people, the people of the city sentenced him to be hanged* as an example.

The ex-cripple then made up his mind to go to the two thousand mountains [that the moon had mentioned] to see what was happening there.

When he got there, he stood at a distance* from the two thousand mountains. He saw thousands and myriads of demon families. They have children* just like human beings, and therefore they are very numerous.

He saw their leader* sitting on a throne. No human being* ever sat on such a throne.

He also saw them joking* [about the mischief they had done].

---

of evil must yield up all their sparks of holiness to Israel. Then the Messiah will be able to rectify the higher worlds. This is the mystery of, "He has swallowed wealth, but he shall vomit it up" (Job 20:15; *Rimzey Maasioth*).

hanged. Like Haman. Because he used trickery, as above (Baal Shem Tov). This is the mystery of the *tikkun* (*Rimzey Maasioth*). We see that the first rectification was to destroy the robbers who had made his feet weak (*Chokhmah U'Tevunah*).

This also alludes to the teaching that reciting psalms can help destroy the forces of evil (*Ibid.; Likutey Moharan* 205; *Likutey Moharan Tinyana* 92).

stood at a distance. Because "He does not sit in the place of jokers" (Psalms 1:1).

They have children. A Talmudic teaching (*Chagigah* 17a).

leader. Malkhuth in Hebrew and Yiddish. This is Malkhuth of the side of evil (*Likutey Moharan* 1). This is the "sitting place of jokers" (Psalms 1:1).

human being. Literally, "one born of woman," *yelud ishah*, both in Hebrew and Yiddish.

The place of demons is hence called a "place of jokers."

joking. All troubles come from this joking and scoffing. It is thus written, "When He deals with jokers, He makes them a joke" (Proverbs 3:34).

In later literature, such demons were called *letzim* (jokers); see story of "The Horse and the Pump." (Also see *Avodah Zarah* 18a; *Likutey Halakhoth, Shabbath* 7:74.)

Also, one can tell the nature of a nation from its jokes (see Story #6).

One said that he had harmed a child; another that he had injured someone's hand; and another that he had injured someone's foot. They also joked in other ways.

Then he saw a father and mother [demon] weeping. "Why are you weeping?" [the demons] asked.

They replied that they had a son who often would take trips, but he would return at a fixed time. But now he had been gone a long time and had not returned.

[The parents] were brought to the king [of the demons], and he commanded that messengers be sent all over the world to find [their lost son]. When the father and mother were returning [from the king], they met [a demon] who had gone together with their son. [He was their son's friend, and they had set out together, but now that they met him, he was alone.]

"Why are you crying?" asked [the friend.]

They told him [that their son was missing]. He replied, "I will tell you:

"We had an island * in the sea, which we had made our base. The king * who owned this island decided to build it up, and he began to lay the foundations.* [Your lost] son said to me, 'Let's hurt [the king]!' With that, we went and took away the king's strength. *

"[The king] went to physicians, * but they could not help him.

---

island. A person isolated from Torah and Judaism. It is therefore a base for the forces of evil.

king. We refer to him as the island king. This might be one who wishes to rule over himself, as it is written, "Therefore the rulers say let us come and make an account" (Numbers 21:27, according to *Bava Bathra* 78b). Thus, this island king wished to repent. This act on his part ultimately led to the downfall of the *shedim*, as we see at the end of the story.

foundations. *Yesod* in Hebrew. This usually refers to the sexual organ. Thus, the king wanted to begin by rectifying himself sexually.

took away the king's strength. Rabbi Nachman taught that when a person wishes to change for the better, he encounters many obstacles (*Sichoth HaRan* 79; *Likutey Moharan Tinyana* 47). As in the case of the moon, they take away strength from Malkhuth.

physicians. Rabbi Nachman taught that physicians do not have the power to actually cure disease. All they can do is remove the symptoms (*Sichoth HaRan* 50).

Then he began to seek advice from sorcerers.* There was one sorcerer who knew [your son's] family. He did not know my family, so he could not do anything to me. But he knew [your son's] family so he was able to capture him. He is now torturing him terribly."

[The parents] brought [their son's friend who had told them this] to the king, and he repeated the entire story. The [demon] king said, "Give [the island king] back his strength."

[The friend] answered and said, "One of [the demons] who was with us did not have any strength. We therefore gave him [the island king's] strength."

The [demon] king said, "Take the strength back from him and give it back to the [island] king."

[The friend] replied to the king, "[The demon to whom we gave the island king's strength] became a cloud."

The [demon] king declared that the cloud should be summoned and brought to him. A messenger was sent to get him.

The [former cripple, who had witnessed all this, said to himself,] "I will go and examine* this phenomenon. I will see how this individual was transformed into a cloud."

He followed the messenger and came to the city where the cloud was. "Why is this city covered by clouds so much?" he asked the citizens.

"Not so," they replied. "There has never been a cloud here. [The city] has been covered by the cloud for only a relatively short time."

Then the messenger came and called the cloud, and it left that place. The [former cripple] decided to follow them and overhear their conversation.

---

sorcerers. It is actually permissible to seek advice from a sorcerer if one thinks one has been harmed by a spell or the like (*Sifethey Cohen, Yoreh Deah* 179:1). In general, however, sorcery is forbidden in the strongest terms.

The power of sorcery is considered to be rooted in a deeper level of evil than that of demons (*Sanhedrin* 67b, Rosh; *Ibid.* 7:8; see *Yoreh Deah* 179:16).

I will go and examine. The very proximity of the cripple seems to have an effect in overcoming the *shedim.* [At first he was the protagonist, but now he is primarily an observer.]

He heard the messenger ask the other, "How did you come to be a cloud here?"

The other replied, I will tell you the story:

Once there was a wise man.* The emperor* of his country was a great atheist,* and he converted the entire land to atheism.

The wise man summoned all the members of his family and said, "Don't you realize that the emperor is a terrible atheist. He has converted the entire land to atheism. He has even made some members of our family into atheists. Therefore, let us leave this place and go into the desert,* so that we will be able to continue to believe in God."

They agreed to this. The wise man pronounced a Divine Name* and brought them to a desert.

[The sage] did not consider this desert good, so he pronounced another Divine Name and transported [his group] to another desert. He did not find this good either, so he pronounced still another Divine Name and transported them to still another desert. This he considered good. This desert was close to the two thousand mountains.* [The wise man] made a circle* around [his

---

wise man. This is the second wise man in the story. The first one was the cripple's father, as we see in the beginning of the story. It is possible that they are identical. This sage is explicitly identified as a Jew, as we see later in the story.

emperor. *Kaiser* in Hebrew. See Story #2. This is a ruler over many lands. It may denote Chokhmah as it did above, and hence atheistic philosophical wisdom.

great atheist. This is the path of atheism mentioned above. He may parallel the robber chief (see *Rimzey Maasioth*). Atheism is the root of all sins (*Ibid*, see *Likutey Moharan Tinyana* 12).

desert. People usually follow their surroundings. If the whole world is bad, one must go to the desert (*Yad, Deyoth* 6:1). This sage is also one "who does not stand in the path of sinners" (Psalms 1:1; *Rimzey Maasioth*). In a way, then, he parallels the cripple. Since this part of the story happened two generations prior to the "present" in the story as a whole (the sage's grandson was a contemporary of the cripple), it is possible that this sage was the one who gave the cripple his spiritual strength.

Divine Name. Divine names can be used to transport a person. This is called *kefitzath haderekh*. This sage was spiritually advanced enough to make use of such divine names. Still, he wouldn't use the demon's book later.

close to the two thousand mountains. It was thus also close to the tree, as we shall see. The

group] so that no one would be able* to come close to them.

There is a tree,* and if this tree were watered, none of us [demons] would survive. We therefore work day and night, digging ditches so that no water can reach that tree.

"Why must you dig continuously, day and night?"* asked [the messenger]. "Once you dig your ditches it should be enough to hold back the water."

"There are talkers* among us," replied [the cloud]. "These talkers go and make strife between one king and another, causing wars. [These wars] cause earthquakes.* The earth around the

---

sage is willing to challenge the forces of evil to be close to the Torah. "One cannot learn Torah unless one stumbles" (*Chagigah* 14a).

circle. Like the circle of Choni HaMaagal (*Taanith* 19a, 23a; see *Zohar* 1:126a). The circle may allude to faith, as it is written, "Your faith all around you"(Psalms 89:9) (see Story #2 regarding the ring).

Rabbi Nachman writes that the righteous sit in a circle (*Likutey Moharan* 183). He also teaches that a circle is an aspect of faith, as it is written, "Your faith all around you" (Psalms 89:9; *Likutey Moharan* 7:1). Faith is protection against the forces of evil.

no one would be able... Nevertheless, even the power of the circle could not protect against the atheistic emperor. Atheism involves an evil much worse than mere demons and the like (see *Likutey Moharan* 64).

There is a tree. This is the same tree mentioned by the moon. It appears that this tree became a much worse problem for the demons after the sage moved there. (Regarding demons and their relationship to trees, see *Pesachim* 111b.)

day and night. The key psalm says, "But God's Torah is his desire, and he meditates on His Torah day and night" (Psalms 1:2). This helps water the tree day and night, even though the demons are constantly digging around it (*Rimzey Maasioth*). In general, the demons work so that the Torah should not flourish.

talkers. *Medabrim* in Hebrew and Yiddish. These are demons who speak to humans (cf. *Gittin* 66a, regarding one who says to write a *get* [divorce]). They also speak to people in dreams (some dreams come through *shedim*) (see *Berakhot* 55b). They often try to entice people to do wrong (see *Likutey Etzoth, Tzaddik* 4), as we see later on.

The Talmud speaks of "talk of demons" (*Sukkah* 28a).

earthquakes. The Talmud says that these come from God's grief that Israel is exiled (*Berakhoth* 59a).

The Talmud (*Yerushalmi, Berakhoth* 9:2) says that earthquakes come because of strife, as it is written, "The valley of the mountains shall be stopped up (see Rashi, *Targum Yonathan ad loc.*), for the valley of the mountains shall reach to nearby" (Zechariah 14:5).

ditches collapses, and water can then get to the tree. Therefore, our people always must stand by to dig."

[The cloud then continued his explanation and story:]

Whenever we appoint a new king, we joke about all the kinds [of mischief that we have done] and we are very happy. One jokes about how he damaged a newborn child, so that his mother mourned him. They joke about all sorts of different things, discussing all their "pranks."

When the [new] king becomes very happy, he strolls around with his royal ministers. He then attempts to uproot the tree. If the tree were no longer there, it would be very good for us. [The new king] therefore gathers up strength to uproot the entire tree.

However, as soon as he comes near it, the tree lets out a very loud scream. The [king] becomes terrified and turns back.

Once, we appointed a new king, and we engaged in tremendous frivolity before him, in the manner I have described. The joy was very great, and this gave him very great courage. He said that he would be the one who would uproot the tree completely.

He went for a walk with his ministers and gathered up great strength. Then he ran to uproot the tree completely. But when he came to it, it gave out a loud scream, and he was overcome with

---

The verse continues, "You shall flee as you fled from the earthquake in the days of Uzziah, king of Judah." The earthquake is alluded to in Isaiah where it says, "The posts of the door trembled" (Isaiah 6:4). (Rashi on Zechariah). The earthquake in Uzziah's time is also mentioned in Amos 1:1. This was a result of strife, since Uzziah had forcibly and illegally burned incense in the Temple, beginning a dispute regarding this (2 Chronicles, 26:16-19; *Peney Moshe* on *Yerushalmi*).

The rest of this section speaks of the reconciliation of the sun and moon, the flowing of water, and the ultimate conquest of evil. The text thus continues, "There shall be one day, known as God's, which is not day and not night... And on that day, living water shall flow from Jerusalem... And God shall be King over all the earth; on that day, God shall be One and His name one" (Zechariah 14:7-9).

Earthquakes also signal the end of a kingdom, as it is written, "The land quakes and suffers, because of what God shall do against Babylon" (Jeremiah 51:29; *Yerushalmi loc cit.*).

terror. He turned back with tremendous frustration.

On the way, he saw a group of human beings sitting.* [This was the group around the wise man, which I mentioned earlier.] He sent some of his men to [harm them] in a fitting manner, as was their way.

When the family of human beings saw [the demons], they were overcome with fear. The sage said to them, "Do not be afraid."

The demons approached, but they could not come near [the humans] because of the circle* [that the wise man had made] around them. [The demon king] sent other messengers, but they also failed. Greatly frustrated, he himself went,* but he could not get close to them. Finally, he asked the old man to let them enter.

"Since you are asking," said [the old man], "I will let you in. But it is not proper that the king come in alone. I will let another individual* come in with you."

With that, [the sage] made an opening and allowed them to come in. Then he closed the circle again.

The [demon] king asked the old man, "Why have you come to settle in our place?"

"Why is this your place?" retorted [the sage]. "It is my place."

"Aren't you afraid of me?" said [the demon king].

"No," replied [the sage].

"Are you still not afraid?" said [the king]. With that he made himself grow larger* until he reached the sky. He threatened to swallow* [the sage].

---

human beings sitting. As King David sits (see above note). This is an aspect of the cripple.

circle. *Shedim* fear God's names (see *Zohar* 1:48b; see *Gittin* 68b).

he himself went. Just like the robber leader who first sent groups, and then went himself. The story of the robbers is now being replayed, but the cripple is now an observer. Chronologically, it seems that this happened long before he killed the robbers.

another individual. Similarly, the robber chief had another survive with him.

grow larger... As Ashmadai, king of the demons, did when Solomon released him. Ashmadai, however, swallowed King Solomon (*Gittin* 68b).

swallow. See Story #8, p. 158. A wicked person is seen as "swallowing" a righteous person (*Berakhoth* 7b from Habakkuk 1:13).

"I'm still not afraid at all," said the old man. "But if you want, I will make you afraid of me!"

With that, [the sage] recited a short prayer. Dark clouds appeared, and there was loud thunder. Thunder* has the power to destroy [demons], and all the royal ministers who had been accompanying [the demon king] were killed. The only survivors were [the king] and the other one* who was with him inside the circle.

[The demon king] begged [the sage] to stop the thunder, and it stopped.

The [demon] king then said, "Since you are such a man, I will give you a book containing all the families of the demons. There are some miracle workers* who only know one family, and do not know even that family completely. But I will give you a book containing all the families, as they are all in the king's records. Every [demon] who is born must be registered by the king."

[The demon king] sent the one who had been with him [inside the circle] to get the book. [It was good that the sage had allowed another demon to survive, since otherwise there would not have been anyone to send to get the book].

[The demon] brought him the book. [The old sage] opened the book, and saw written in it thousands and myriads of families.

The [demon] king also promised that he would never harm the

Thunder. Thunder has the power to destroy the forces of evil, as it is written, "Those who oppose God shall be shattered, He will thunder against them from heaven" (1 Samuel, 2:10). It is also written, "God thunders from heaven. He sends out arrows and scatters them" (Psalms 18:14, 15). Furthermore, "At the sound of Your thunder they flee" (Psalms 104:7).

This is the concept of straightening out the crookedness in the heart. The crookedness in the heart comes from these demons, because they give bad advice. It is taught, "Thunder was created only to straighten out the crookedness in the heart" (*Berakhoth* 59a, *Likutey Moharan* 5:3).

and the other one. As the robber leader survived with one other. Here we see why the other survived, however.

miracle workers. *Baaley Shem*, that is, Masters of the Name. They know how to use divine names, but they also know how to use the names of demons. Thus, coercing demons can involve forbidden sorcery, as above, or it can be done in a sacred manner.

old [sage] or any members of his family. He told [the old man] to bring him portraits of every member of his family. Whenever a child was born, they should immediately bring [the demon king] the child's portrait. In this manner, no harm would ever be done to the old man's family.

Then it came time for the old man to die. He summoned his sons, and as his final testament commanded them saying, "I am leaving you this book. You know that I have the power to make use of this book in holiness.* Nevertheless, I do not make use of it.* The only thing I use is my faith in God. You also must not use [the book]. Even if some of you can use it in holiness, do not use it. Have faith in God alone."

With that, the wise man died, and the book became part of his heritage. Eventually, it was inherited by his grandson, who had the power to use it in holiness. However, he had full faith in God, and did not use it, as the old man had commanded.

The talkers* among [the demons] tried to tempt the old man's grandson. He had mature daughters, and [the talkers told him], "Your daughters are getting older, and you do not have money to support them or marry them off. You should therefore make use of this book."

[The grandson] did not know that [the talkers] were tempting him; he thought that it was his heart* that was giving him this

---

make use of this book in holiness. It is permitted to use holy methods to coerce demons to do one's bidding (*Yoreh Deah* 179). This is very much like King Solomon who coerced Ashmadai to do his bidding by binding him with a chain and ring containing God's name (*Gittin* 68a; see HaGra on *Yoreh Deah* 179).

I do not make use of it. "Although the true tzaddik has the power to use divine names and oaths [binding demons] and the like with great holiness, he does not use it at all. Instead, he has simple faith in God, and God helps him" (*Likutey Etzoth; Mahadurah Bathra, Tzaddik* 84). However, here we see that this sage did make use of names to transport his family to the desert. In order to escape atheism, it is permitted.

talkers. Here we see that the speakers try to tempt people. They even try to make a tzaddik fall (*Rimzey Maasioth*).

his heart. "Sometimes it appears to a tzaddik that he must make use of this, and that it is a great act of virtue and the like. Nevertheless, he must think it over very carefully. Although it seems that his heart is giving him advice, perhaps it is the talkers who are tempting him" (*Likutey Etzoth loc. cit.*).

advice. But he traveled to his grandfather's grave and asked him. "You left orders in your will that we not use this book, that we only have faith in God. But now my heart is tempting me to use it."

The [deceased sage] answered, "Even though you have the power to use it in holiness, it is better for you to have faith in God. Do not make use of it. God will help you." He complied.

[Then one day,]* the king* of the land where the old man's grandson lived, became ill. He went to physicians, but they could not cure him. The land was very hot, so the remedies did not help. The king then decreed that the Israelites* should pray for him.

Our [demon] king said, "This grandson has the power to use this book in holiness, but he refrains from using it. Therefore, we should do something for his benefit."

With that [our king] commanded me to become a cloud there. The [human] king would then be healed by the remedies that he had taken earlier and those he would take later. The [sage's] grandson did not know anything about all this.

This is the story of how I became a cloud here.

(This was the story that the cloud told the messenger. The [former cripple] followed them and listened.)

[The cloud] was brought to the [demon] king. The king ordered that the cloud's strength be taken and given back to the [island] king, and it was done. The demons' son was then able to return to his parents.

[The demons' son] came back worn out and in great pain. He did not have any strength, since he had been tortured very much there. He was very angry at the sorcerer who had tortured him so

---

[Then one day]. *VeYehi HaYom.* See Story #2, p. 62.

king. This appears to be a land not far from the 2000 mountains and the tree.

decreed that the Israelites... The exact opposite of the atheistic emperor. Also unlike the island king who resorted to sorcery. Therefore, the strength of the island king is given to the cloud who helps cure this king.

much, and he left orders to his sons and their families that they should always lie in wait* to trap the sorcerer.

The talkers among [the demons] went and told the sorcerer to watch himself, since [this family] was lying in wait for him. The sorcerer made use of his devices to protect himself from them, and also sought the help of other sorcerers who knew other* families.

The [demon's] son and his family were very furious at the talkers for revealing their secret [plans for revenge] to the sorcerer.

Once, this son's family and some talkers were going to serve a term of duty* for the [demon] king. The family fabricated a false accusation against the talkers, and the king killed them.

The surviving talkers were very angry, and they incited rebellion against all the kings. The demons were stricken with hunger, weakness, sword and plague. There were wars among all the kings, and this caused earthquakes.* The ditches fell in and the tree was completely watered. All the [demons] were then destroyed* and nothing remained of them. Amen.

"Happy* is the man who does not walk... does not stand, and in the

---

always lie in wait. Thus the forces of evil (demons and sorcery) are pitted against each other. This is a "dispute not for the sake of heaven, and it is therefore doomed" (*Avoth* 5:17). It is like the robbers, again, who killed one another.

At this point it is not clear that the cripple is even an observer.

other. Only in Yiddish.

term of duty. *Mishmar.* Like the terms of duty of priests. *Vartu* in Yiddish, which is *wartung* in German, denotes attending or duty.

this caused earthquakes. "[He] looks at the earth and it trembles...sinners shall cease to exist in the earth, and the wicked will be no more" (Psalms 104:32, 35).

destroyed. Evil thus destroys itself.

Happy. This is a translation of the Yiddish. In the Hebrew, Rabbi Nathan expands this:

The following notes are found in the original at the end of the story: The mystery of this story is alluded to in the first verse of the psalm, "Happy is the man..." (Psalms 1:1). [It speaks of] "the way of the wicked;" "the way of the righteous..." (Psalms 1:6). This is the concept of the paths which have the powder spread...as mentioned above.

It says, "He shall be like a tree planted on streams of water, which gives its fruit in its

place of jokers [does not sit]. He shall be like a tree planted on streams of water..." (Psalms 1:1,2). This entire story is alluded to in this Psalm.

He who has eyes should see, and he who has a heart should understand what is happening in this world.

time and its leaf does not wither... and in whatever he does he prospers" (Psalms 1:3). This is the tree mentioned above. All its fruit and trees have great power, as mentioned above. Look carefully and you will find other allusions.

"Happy is the man who does not walk..." (Psalms 1:1) for at first he cannot walk, and does not stand. Later he also could not stand.

"And in the sitting place of jokers..." This is the sitting of the aforementioned individuals who engage in scoffing...

"Like the chaff which the wind drives away" (Psalms 1:4). This is the wind that carries the above mentioned powder.

All this is only an illusion which enlightens our eyes a little so that we will understand and be somewhat intelligent (*maskil*) to whatever extent the words reach. However, the words are still hidden with the ultimate concealment. All these stories that he told are very high. They are very much higher than human intellect and hidden from the eye of all life...

4

THE BULL AND THE RAM *

Once there was a king* who issued an edict to exile his subjects* through religious persecution. Anyone wishing to remain in the land, would have to give up his religion. Otherwise, he would be exiled.

Some people gave up all their property and wealth, and departed in poverty. They wanted to keep their faith and remain

---

the Bull and the Ram. This is the name that Rabbi Nathan gives this story in his writings (*Likutey Halakhoth, Rosh Chodesh* 7:46; *Genevah* 4:5, 5:15). In most editions of the stories, it is called, "The king who decreed apostasy." Rabbi Nathan also refers to this story simply by the first words, "The king who issued an edict to exile his subjects through religious persecution" (*Likutey Halakhoth, Hekhsher Kelim* 2:5, *Nedarim* 3:13). In the first edition, the story is referred to as "The Story of Miracles" (*Maaseh Nissim*) (see *Rimzey Maasioth; Zimrath HaAretz*).

On its simplest level, this story speaks about how an ordinary Jew cherishes the commandments, and how important the commandments are (*Rimzey Maasioth*). However, it also has a much deeper meaning.

The theme of this story is astrology. Its key is Psalm 2.

king. There are four generations of kings in this story (see end of story). They most probably denote the four kingdoms which had power over the Israelites: Babylon, Persia, Greece and Rome. These have already been discussed to some degree in Story #2.

This first king therefore denotes Babylon. Babylon destroyed the Holy Temple, and exiled the Jews for the first time. This is the religious persecution in this story.

exile his subjects. This is a description of the choice given to people during the expulsion from Spain during the reign of King Ferdinand and Queen Isabella in 1492. They could give up Judaism or leave.

Rabbi Nachman may also be alluding to the choice that many Jews in his time felt they had to make. If they wanted to live among the gentiles and prosper, they felt that they had either to give up their Judaism or hide it.

Rabbi Nachman said that this decree is alluded to in the verse, "Why are nations in an uproar...? The kings of the earth stand up, and the rulers take counsel together, against God and His anointed one" (Psalms 2:1,2).

Jews. Others however were more concerned with their property and wealth, and they remained, becoming Marranos.* Secretly, they kept their Jewish faith, but publicly they were not able to.

Then this king died and his son became king.* He began to rule his kingdom with a very firm hand.* He conquered many lands and was very wise.

Since he held the royal ministers with such a firm hand, they plotted against him. They agreed to attack him, and to kill him and his children.

Among these ministers, however, there was a Marrano. He thought over the situation. "Why did I become a Marrano? I did it because I was concerned with my wealth and property. But if the land will now be without a king, people will swallow* each other alive. It it impossible for a country to be without a king." He therefore decided to tell the king* of their plot without letting [the other ministers] know that [their plan had been compromised].

[The Marrano] went and told the king that [the other ministers] were plotting against him. The king investigated to see if [the accusation] was true. When he discovered that it was true, he stationed guards.

Marranos. *Anusim* in Hebrew. Literally, "forced ones." In the time of the Spanish inquisition, such people were known as marranos, which meant "pigs."

his son became king. The second king. This would parallel Persia, the second of the four kingdoms.

The four kings parallel (on the Other Side) the four letters of the Tetragrammaton. The "*yod*" is what is given; the first "*heh*" is the hand that gives; the "*vav*" is the arm that reaches out; and the final "*heh*" is the hand that takes (*Zera Berakh, Terumah; Sefer Baal Shem Tov, Ekev* 8). Here, the second king is the hand that gives, while the fourth is the hand that takes. The second king gives the Marrano permission to put on tefillin, while the fourth king takes it away. Similarly, Persia let the Jews build the Temple, while the fourth kingdom, Rome, destroyed it.

firm hand. As in the case of the emperor's daughter, the second kingdom is harsher than the first.

swallow... "Pray for the welfare of the government, since if not for fear of the government, people would swallow each other alive" (*Avoth* 3:2).

tell the king. Very much like Mordecai (Esther 2:22). Significantly, Mordecai lived during the Persian rule.

That night, the ministers made their move. [The king] had them arrested and gave each one an appropriate sentence.

The king then addressed the Marrano minister: "How can I reward you for this? You have saved me and my children. I could make you a minister, but you are a minister already. I could give you wealth, but that, too, you have. Tell me what reward you want, and I will give it to you."

"Will you really grant my request?" replied the Marrano.

"Certainly," replied the king.

"Swear to me by your crown and kingdom,"* said [the Marrano].

The king made the oath.

"The only honor I want," said [the Marrano], "is to be able to be a Jew openly.* I want to be able to wear my tallith* and tefillin* publicly."

---

crown and kingdom. Kabbalistically, the highest and lowest sefiroth. Also, Kabbalistically, the crown is the head tefillin, and the kingdom (Malkhuth) is the hand tefillin. (See *Berakhoth* 6a).

to be a Jew openly. Even though the Marrano had originally given up Judaism because of his wealth, the *pintele yid* remained in him. He was therefore willing to risk the wrath of the king to make this request (*Rimzey Maasioth*).

tallith. A four-cornered garment containing the tzitzith or tassles prescribed in Numbers 15:38.

One of the main themes of this story is fours, and the tallith has four corners.

This shows the dominance of the Jews over the gentiles. "Ten from each nation shall grab the corner" (Zechariah 8:23; see *Shabbath* 32b).

Tzitzith on the tallith are a protection against apostasy and disbelief. It is written, "You shall see them and not stray after your heart" (Numbers 16:39), and the Talmud says that "your heart" denotes atheism and apostasy (*Berakhoth* 12b; *Likutey Halakhot, Genevah* 4:5). Tzitzith are thus seen to represent the light of truth (*Likutey Halakhoth, Genevah* 5:15). They thus represent accepting the yoke of God's kingdom (*Berakhoth* 12b; *Likutey Etzoth, Tzitzith* 1).

tefillin. Worn in accordance with the commandment, "You shall bind them as a sign on your arm and an insignia in the middle of your head" (Deuteronomy 6:8).

The tefillin are also a concept of four, since they contain four different readings.

Tefillin also show the dominance of the Jews. This is the theme of the story, namely that the gentile world is dependent upon the Jews.

Tefillin contain a knot, and this also has the symbolic power to bind a Jew to his faith

The king became very angry.* Throughout his land it was forbidden to practice Judaism. But he did not have any choice because of his oath.

The next morning* the Marrano publicly wore his tallith and tefillin.

Then the king died and his son became king.* Realizing why people had plotted to kill his father, he ruled benevolently. He also conquered many lands.

He was a very wise* man, and he summoned all his astrologers to tell him what could destroy his children, so that they would be able to safeguard themselves against it. They told him that as long as he is careful with regard to a bull and a ram, his children would not be killed. He had this written in the book of chronicles. He also commanded his sons that they should rule in a benevolent manner as he did.

However, when his son became king,* he began to rule with a firm hand* and an autocratic manner like his grandfather. He

---

(cf. *Likutey Halakhoth, Genevah* 4:5). One of the main writings in the tefillin is the Sh'ma, which is the Jewish creed. Putting on the tefillin literally brings this to a person's body. The tefillin are also the light of the truth (*Likutey Halakhoth, Genevah* 4:15), and accepting the yoke of God's kingdom (*Likutey Etzoth loc. cit*).

In Rabbi Nathan's notes at the end of the story, the verse, "Serve God with fear" (Psalms 2:11) is said to relate to the tallith and tefillin. "Serve God" denotes the tallith, and "with fear" denotes the tefillin.

angry. This anger may have created the angel. Although the king granted the Jew permission, it was with anger. This caused his grandson to take away the privilege.

The next morning. This denotes the building of the Temple, which was permitted by the Persian empire.

The Jews also had the mitzvah of tefillin, as the Talmud interprets the verse, "The Jews had light, joy, happiness, and beauty" (Esther 8:16); beauty, this is tefillin (*Megillah* 16a). Mordecai also wore the blue wool (*techeleth*) of tzitzith (Esther 8:15).

his son became king. This is the third king. He represents the Greek empire. The Greek empire was initially benevolent toward the Jews. As we have seen, it represents the *klipath nogah*.

very wise. Greece personified wisdom.

his son became king. This is the fourth king. He represents Rome. This parallels the *klipah* (destructive force) of fire (*Zohar Chadash* 38b), and hence he is destroyed by fire.

firm hand. Kabbalistically, the second and fourth kingdoms are closely related, and both of them relate to (feminine) harsh judgment.

also conquered many lands.

Then he thought up a clever plan. So that his children would not be killed, he ordered that no bulls or rams* be allowed in his land. He would then have nothing to fear, and he continued to rule as an autocrat.

He became very wise, and devised a plan to conquer the entire world without war. Since the world is divided into seven areas,* it contains seven parts. There are also seven planets;* each planet shines on one part of the world. Likewise, there are seven metals,* and one planet shines* on each type of metal.

---

no bulls or rams. He assumed that the astrologers had been speaking of physical animals.

seven areas. This may relate to the seven latitudes, from the equator to the polar areas (Rabbi Chaim Vital, *Sefer Tekhunah*; explicit in *Likutey Halakhoth, Hekhsher Kelim* 2:5).

These may be the "seven earths" mentioned in various sources (*Sefer Yetzirah* 4:15; *Avoth DeRabbi Nathan* 37; *Vayikra Rabbah* 29:11; *Bamidbar Rabbah* 3:8; *Pirkey DeRabbi Eliezer* 18, 43a).

In a modern sense, they may parallel the seven continents: Europe, Asia, Africa, Australia, North America, South America, Antarctica.

seven planets. More correctly, seven astronomical bodies. These are Saturn, Jupiter, Mars, Sun, Venus, Mercury, Moon (*Sefer Yetzirah* 4:7; *Pirkey DeRabbi Eliezer* 6; Rashi, *Berakhoth* 59b s.v. *Shabatai*).

The seven planets parallel faith in the sages (*Likutey Halakhoth, Hekhsher Kelim* 2:5).

seven metals. They are (along with associated sefiroth): silver (Chesed), gold (Gevurah), copper (Tifereth), tin (Netzach), lead (Hod), mercury (Yesod) and iron (Malkhuth) (Rabbi Moshe Chaim Luzatto, *Daath Chokhmah*, p. 32b; *Likutey Torah HaAri* on Psalm 84, p. 342).

Of these, six are mentioned in the verse, "The gold, silver, copper, iron, tin and lead" (Numbers 31:22). Mercury was known in ancient times and is mentioned in other ancient sources as *kesef chai* (quick [live] silver) (Rashi, *Shabbath* 78b; *Kedey Ramban* on Genesis 41:33).

The seven metals parallel the seven aborigine nations that lived in the land of Canaan. Hence, metals have an affinity for the forces of darkness. This is why, when a Jew purchases a metal pot or eating utensil from a gentile, he must immerse it in a mikvah (*Likutey Halakhoth, Hekhsher Kelim* 2:5,6).

Of the metals, four of them also allude to the four empires that subjugated Israel: gold is Babylon, silver is Persia, copper is Greece and iron is Rome (*Shemoth Rabbah* 35:5). The other metals are secondary to these (*Likutey Halakhoth, Ibid.* 2:7; see below).

one planet shines... The planets symbolize faith in our sages, since only the sages were able to make astronomical calculations and determine the calendar. This faith can remove the power of evil from the type of metal associated with it (*Likutey Halakhoth, Hekhsher Kelim* 2:5)

[The king] gathered together all seven types of metal. He also ordered that he be brought the golden portraits* of the kings, which hung in their palaces. Out of these he made a man.* The head was made of gold, the body of silver, and the other parts of the body of other metals. The man thus contained all seven types of metal.

[The king] placed [the figure] on top of a high mountain,* so that all seven planets would shine on it.

Whenever a person needed advice as to whether to engage in a venture or not, he would stand in front of the part of the body made of the metal paralleling the part of the world from which he came. He would then meditate on his question. If it was something that he should do, that part of [the statue's] body would glow and shine.* If not, that part of the body would remain dark.

With [this statue], the [king] conquered the entire world.* He

On the other side of this, the seven stars also parallel grammar, rhetoric, logic, arithmetic, music, geometry, and astronomy, seven branches of secular wisdom. The wicked king was thus able to have all wisdom reflecting in his statue.

golden portraits. The reference is most probably to portraits made like the golden icons common in Russia and the Ukraine. By including these portraits, all the powers of these kings and all their wisdom became included in the statue. The head was made of gold, so its "mind" consisted of the wisdom of all the kings.

made a man. This is reminiscent of the statue that Nebuchadnezzar saw in a dream, "Its head was gold, its breasts and arms were silver, its belly and thighs were copper, and its feet were iron" (Daniel 2:33,34; *Likutey Halakhoth, Hekhsher Kelim* 2:7). The four types of metal in the statue explicitly symbolize the four kingdoms: Babylon, Persia, Greece and Rome (Daniel 2:39,40; *Shemoth Rabbah* 25:5).

high mountain. It is written in the key psalm, "I have established My king, on Zion, My holy mountain" (Psalms 2:6). This statue is the counterpart on the side of darkness of God's Messiah (Rabbi Nathan at end of story; *Zimrath HaAretz*). Hence, it probably parallels Armalis, the magical leader of Rome (*Targum* on Isaiah 11:4; *Sefer Zerubavel* in *Batey Midrashoth* 2:500). Armalis is said to emerge from a statue (Rabbi Makhir, *Avkath Rokhel*).

glow and shine. Very much like *urim* and *thumim* (*Yoma* 73a). The twelve stones corresponded to the twelve tribes. These oppose the seven nations, which are represented by the seven metals of this man.

conquered the entire world. Regarding the Messiah, God says in the key psalm, "Ask of Me

also amassed much wealth.

However, the human statue only had its power if the king would lower the haughty* and lift the lowly.

The king issued a royal decree* that all his generals* and ministers who had rank and special privileges* should come. When they appeared before him, he took away their rank and privileges. Even if they had had privileges from the time of his great-great-grandfather,* these privileges were taken away.

[The king] also raised up the lowly. He raised them up and gave them the positions of [the elite].

Among [the ministers whose privileges the king had taken away] was the Marrano minister. "What is your rank and what are your privileges?" asked the king.

"My privilege," replied [the Marrano], "is that I have the right to practice publicly as a Jew. [I got this] because of the favor I did for your grandfather."

[The king] took away* [this privilege],* and once again [the

and I will give you nations for an inheritance, and the ends of the earth for your possession" (Psalms 2:8). Here, this statue accomplishes this on the side of darkness (see Rabbi Nathan at end of story).

lower the haughty... This is God's attribute, as it is written, "God lifts up the lowly; He lowers the wicked to the ground" (Psalms 147:6). Right before this the verse says, "He counts the number of the stars; He calls them all by name" (Psalms 147:4). Thus, using the powers of the stars is very closely related to lifting the humble and humbling the haughty.

Rabbi Nachman also points out that in Hebrew, "lowers the wicked to the ground" is *Mashpil Reshaim Adey Aretz,* and this has the same initial letters as *Mayim, Ruach, Afar, Aesh*; water, air, dust, fire, which are the four elements. Thus by lowering the proud, one has dominance over the elements (*Likutey Moharan* 8:5).

Of course, what the message really meant was that he should humble himself.

royal decree. *Ukase, ukaz* in Russian and Yiddish. This was an imperial order having the force of law.

generals. *Yedniralin* in Yiddish.

privileges. *Ordirsh* in Yiddish.

great-great-grandfather. The king who ruled before the one who initially made the decree against the Jews.

took away. As mentioned earlier, the fourth king is the hand that takes. It took away this privilege, just as Rome destroyed the Temple.

[this privilege]. That is, of wearing tallith and tefillin. This is alluded to in the key psalm,

Marrano] had to become a secret Jew.*

Once, when the king was sleeping, he had a dream. The heavens were clear, and he could see all twelve constellations of the zodiac. Among the signs of the zodiac, the bull* (Taurus) and the ram* (Aries) were laughing at him.*

When the king woke up, he was very angry* and frightened. He ordered that the book of chronicles be brought, and there he read that his children would be destroyed by a bull and a ram. He became terrified. When he told the queen, she and her children were also terror-stricken. [The king's] heart pounded in fear.*

He summoned his dream interpreters, and each one gave the dream his own interpretation, but the king did not find them acceptable. He remained very fearful.

Finally, a wise man came to him and said that he had a tradition from his father that the sun travels in 365 paths.* There

"Let us break their straps, and cast away from us their strings" (Psalms 2:3). The straps are the straps of tefillin, while the strings are the tzitzith (tassles) of the tallith (*Yerushalmi, Avodah Zarah* 2:1, 9a; *Tosafoth, Avodah Zarah* 3b; s.v. *U'menichin*; notes at end of story).
had to become a secret Jew. Israel was once again exiled.
bull. This is the constellation associated with the Hebrew month of Iyar (see *Sefer Yetzirah* 5:2). Rabbi Nachman writes that *Iyar* (אייר) can be read as an acrostic of (אויבי ישובו יבושו רגע) *Oyvay Yashuvu Yevoshu Raga*, "My enemies shall return [and] be humiliated in an instant" (Psalms 6:11; *Likutey Moharan* 277). (Also see *Megaleh Amukoth* 121; *Dan Yadin* 7; *Karnayim* p. 4b.)
ram. The constellation of *Nissan* (see *Sefer Yetzirah* 5:2), the month that the Israelites were redeemed from Egypt.
laughing at him. After, "Let us break their straps, and cast away from us their strings" (Psalms 2:3) in the key psalm, it says, "That which sits in heaven laughs; God has them in derision" (Psalms 2:4). The Talmud also says that God laughs at the gentiles for casting away tefillin and tzitzith (*Avodah Zarah* 3b).
angry. As the verse continues, "He then speaks to them with His anger" (Psalms 2:5; notes at end). This anger is a reflection of the anger that his grandfather had when he granted the privilege. He now has similar anger when he takes it away. This anger helps create the angel that destroys him.
pounded in fear. "He frightens them with His displeasure" (*Ibid.*). Rabbi Nachman thus taught that fear comes from anger (*Sefer HaMiddoth, Kaas* 41).
sun travels in 365 paths. That is, every day of the year, it travels along a different path (see *Pirkey DeRabbi Eliezer* 6; *Zohar Chadash* 15c; also see *Yerushalmi, Rosh HaShanah* 2:4 12b; *Shemoth Rabbah* 15:22; *Midrash Psalms* 19:11; *Yalkut* 2:186; *Sefer HaPeliah* 32c,d; *Megaleh Amukoth* 100,101).

is also a place where all of the sun's 365 paths shine, and in this place an iron rod* grows. If a person has any fear, he can come to this rod and have his fear dispelled.

The king was satisfied [with this statement]. Taking along the wise man, he set out to this place together with his wife, his children, and all his offspring.

Along the way stands an angel that oversees anger.* Through anger, a destructive angel is created,* and this angel is in charge of all destructive forces. One must ask [the angel] the way* [to the iron rod].

There is a straight path* before a person. There is also a path that is full of quicksand. There is a path that is full of holes and pits, and there are also other paths. Finally, there is a path where

---

iron rod. Rabbi Nachman says that this is the iron rod mentioned in the key psalm, "You shall break them with an iron rod" (Psalms 2:9). It is through the quest for this iron rod that the king is killed.

As we have seen, the fourth kingdom is alluded to by iron (Daniel 2:33,35,40, *Shemoth Rabbah* 25:5). Therefore, it is fitting that it be destroyed by iron.

The Hebrew word for iron is *barzel* (ברזל). This is an acrostic for Jacob's four wives, Bilhah, Rachel, Zilpah, Leah (*Etz Chaim, Shaar Klipath Nogah* 9, p. 392). [Incidentally, this is also a mneumonic to remember that Bilhah was Rachel's maid, and Zilpah was Leah's.] The sun, on the other hand, alludes to Jacob (*Likutey Moharan* 1). Thus, just as Jacob comes together with his wives, the sun shines on this iron rod.

Also, the Hebrew word for rod is *shevet*. This also means tribe. Thus the iron rod may also be read "the tribe of Bilhah," etc. That is, the Israelites, when they have the power to destroy.

As we have seen, iron is Malkhuth. Therefore, God's Malkhuth, the Messiah, will destroy the fourth kingdom.

angel that oversees anger. This is mentioned in the *Zohar* (2:263b) (see *Likutey Etzoth, Kaas* 3).

Through anger ... had been created. This was created by the king's grandfather when he got angry and gave permission for the Jew to wear tallith and tefillin. This king was also angry when he awakened from his dream.

one must ask... the way. And thus were destroyed in fire. It is thus written in the key psalm, "You will perish, for his anger will burn" (Psalms 2:12; *Chokhmah U'Tevunah*).

The king's anger was therefore his downfall. In general, anger is a very bad trait and can be a person's downfall (*Likutey Etzoth, Kaas* 3).

there is a straight path. "There is a path that seems right to man, but at its ends are the paths of death" (Proverbs 14:12, 16:25).

there is a fire* [which is so hot that] when one comes within four miles* of it, one is burned.

[When they asked the angel the way, he directed them to the path of fire.] This is the way they went.

The wise man looked ahead, on constant watch for the fire. He had a tradition from his father that there was such a fire.

Then he saw the fire. Walking through the fire were kings, along with Jews wearing the tallith and tefillin.* The kings were able to walk through the fire because Jews lived in their lands.

The wise man said to the king, "I have a tradition from my father that if one comes within four miles of this fire, one is consumed. I therefore do not want to go any further."

The king, however, saw all the other kings walking through the fire. He assumed that he would also be able to do so.

The sage was insistent. "I have a tradition from my father, and I do not want to go any further. If you want to, go ahead."

The king and his family went into the fire. The fire consumed them,* so that he and his family were burned and destroyed.

---

fire. This is a reflection of the fire on high, as it is written, "God is a consuming fire" (Deuteronomy 9:13) (*Likutey Halakhoth, Nedarim* 3:13).

four miles. Yiddish. In Hebrew, four leagues. This is the concept of four again, which is the theme of this story.

tallith and tefillin. The power of the tallith and tefillin allow one to walk through the fire unharmed. Both the tallith and the tefillin are concepts of constricting and reducing the Divine light; the tefillin through its knots and straps, and the tallith through its knots and strings (*Likutey Moharan* 49; *Likutey Halakhoth, Nedarim* 3:12). Therefore, the tallith and tefillin reduce the heat of this fire and make it possible to walk through it (*Likutey Halakhoth, Nedarim* 3:13).

Here we see that the tallith and tefillin can even protect kings who allow Jews to wear them. How much more so does it protect the Jews themselves (*Likutey Etzoth, Tzitzith* 1). Indeed, the Talmud teaches that if a person wears tefillin, he cannot be destroyed by the fires of Gehenom (*Rosh HaShanah* 16a).

fire consumed them. This fire seems to be associated with the sun, since the iron rod is in the place where all the paths of the sun come together. The Talmud teaches that there will be no Gehenom in the World to Come but God will take the sun out of its sheath, and it will destroy the wicked (*Nedarim* 8b).

When the wise man returned home [and related what had happened], the ministers were amazed. [The king] had very carefully avoided any bull or ram. How did it happen that he and his children were destroyed?

The Marrano then spoke up. "They were destroyed because of me. The astrologers saw something, but they did not know what they saw. From the skin of the bull,* tefillin are made. From the wool of the ram,* the tzitzith-tassels of the tallith are made. Therefore, because [of the tallith and tefillin,] the king and his family were destroyed.

"The kings who walked through the fire unharmed have in their lands Jews who wear the tallith and tefillin. But [this king] did not allow the Jews in his land to wear the tallith and tefillin, and therefore, he was destroyed.

"This was the reason that the bull and the ram in the zodiac laughed at him. The astrologers saw this, but they did not understand what they saw. It was for this reason that he and his children were killed."

Amen. So shall all Your enemies be destroyed, O God.*

"The house of Jacob shall be fire and the house of Joseph shall be flame, and Esau shall be straw" (Obadiah 1:18).

This king was destroyed by fire, since he represents the fourth *klipah*, which is fire.

In general, we also see here that evil destroys itself. The king went into the fire of his own free will. Beyond that, he destroys himself through his own attribute.

From the skin of the bull. Tefillin are made of leather. It is for this reason that when one steals a bull, one must pay back five times as much (Exodus 21:37). The tefillin contain five boxes, four in the head part and one in the arm part. Since the bull (or ox) has this special status, in holiness, one must repay more when one steals it (*Likutey Halakhoth, Genevah* 4:5).

The bull represents *Iyar*, and according to *Sefer Yetzirah,* this represents the left arm, where tefillin are worn (*Sefer Yetzirah* 5:2).

From the wool of the ram. Tzitzith are made of wool. Therefore, when a person steals a sheep, he must pay back four times as much (Exodus 21:37). Since there are four tzitzith on the tallith, the tzitzith are a concept of four (*Likutey Halakhoth, Ibid.*).

So shall all Your enemies be destroyed... Judges 5:31.

"Why* are the nations in an uproar" (Psalms 2:1)

"You shall break them with an iron rod" (Psalms 2:9). This is the iron rod in the story.

"Let us break their straps and cast away their strings" (Psalms 2:3). This denotes the tefillin and tzitzith.*

The entire story is alluded to in this psalm. Fortunate is he who knows something of these stories, which are very great mysteries of the Torah.

Why. In Hebrew Rabbi Nathan elaborates on this.

This denotes the tefillin... *Yerushalmi, Avodah Zarah* 2:1, see above.

5

THE PRINCE OF GEMS*

Once there was a king* who did not have any children.* He

The Prince of Gems. Rabbi Nathan relates that he had heard that before telling this story, Rabbi Nachman said, "I know a tale that contains the entire forty-two letter name of God." However, he was not sure that this was the story involved. Rabbi Nachman had also asked Rabbi Nathan to find an explanation for the two letters *vav* and *tzadi* appearing in the last line of that name. It was obvious that the Rebbe knew the secret of the Name but wanted to disguise it, and could not include these two in the story. The forty-two letter name of God consists of the initial words of the prayer, *Ana Bekoach* (*Sichoth HaRan* 147; See below p. 124).

It appears that Rabbi Nathan was not in Breslov when this, and a number of the previous stories were told. During the year that Rabbi Nachman told these stories, Rabbi Nathan was away from Breslov from the day after Yom Kippur (September 25, 1806) until Chanukah (December 10) (*Yemey Moharnat* 12b-14a).

The story revolves around Moses and the exodus from Egypt. The Midrash says "one woman gave birth in Egypt to 600,000 souls. This was Yocheved who gave birth to Moses who was equal to all the Jews." (*Shir Hashirim Rabbah* 1). The numerical value of the word Yocheved is 42 (יוכבד), representing the Name of forty-two. Moses represents the prince, and the precious stones the Jewish nation. Jeremiah referred to the Jews as precious stones (Lamentations 4:1) (Rabbi Rosenfeld).

There is also a Breslov tradition that this story is speaking of "the 'known one' who fell into the water several times and was almost drowned" (*Rimzey Maasioth*). The known one was Rabbi Aryeh Leib of Shpola (1725-1812), popularly known as The Shpoler Zeida (the Grandfather of Shpola). Once he bitterly denounced the *Likutey Moharan*, and then set out on a journey over a bridge. The wagon veered off the bridge, into the river, and the Shpoler was almost drowned (Rabbi Chaim Kahana and Rabbi Chaim Yissachar Gross, *Evven Shethiyah*, "Chaim of Kosos" 2:5; *Nevey Tzaddikim*, p. 44).

The general theme of this story is jealousy and sorcery.

king. This may relate to God. He wanted to have a nation who could be called His children. Of course, the nation of Israel is called God's children, as it is written, "My son, my firstborn, Israel" (Exodus 4:32). It is also written, "You are children of God your Lord" (Deuteronomy 14:1).

who did not have any children... At the time of creation *Bereshith Rabbah* 8:4) the angels did not want his kingdom* to be inherited by strangers, so he went to physicians,* but they could not help him.

Then he made a decree that the Jews* should pray that he should have children. The Jews sought out a tzaddik* whose prayers would be effective in granting the king children. They searched and found a hidden tzaddik,* and told him to pray that the king should have children.

[The tzaddik] answered that he did not know anything.*

[The Jews] told this to the king. The king issued a royal edict and had [the tzaddik] brought to him.

The king began to speak to him in a pleasant manner. "Don't you realize that the Jews are in my hands? I can do anything I wish to them. But I am asking you in a nice way to pray for me that I have children."

---

argued against the creation of man. God revealed that tzaddikim will come forth and withheld the knowledge that evil will be born. Otherwise, the attribute of Justice would not have allowed man to be created (Rabbi Nachman Burshtyn).

kingdom. The World to Come. God created the world in order to do good for others, and had Israel not been created, there would have been no one for whom to do good.

physicians... The angels were divided. *Chesed* (kindness) and *Tzedek* (righteousness) said to create him, as he will engage in these acts. *Emeth* (truth) and *Shalom* (peace) were against his creation as he would be full of falsehood and strife (*Bereshith Rabbah* 8:5) (Rabbi Nachman Burshtyn).

Jews. The souls of the Jews which existed before creation (*Likutey Moharan,* 21:9; *Bereshith Rabbah* 1:4)

tzaddik. This is Yesod. It is the sefirah of Yesod which existed before the shattering of the vessels.

Go to a tzaddik (*chakham*) to pray (*Bava Bathra* 116a; *Yoreh Deah* 335:10 in *Hagah*).

hidden tzaddik. Although he was hidden, they found him because it was decreed.

he did not know anything. In contrast to the sorcerer, who immediately says that he can cast the spell.

The tzaddik could not have said that he could pray since this would have been lying. For until he met the king, he did not know if it would be possible for the king to have a child.

Kabbalistically, this indicates that Yesod does not have any Daath. He knew that he had been given light to give the princess, but if he received the light, he would be shattered. Yesod was given two portions of light, one for himself and one for Malkhuth (the princess).

[The tzaddik] promised him that he would have a child.* He then left and returned home.

The queen gave birth to a daughter.* The queen's daughter* was very beautiful. When she was four years old,* she knew all types of wisdom. She could play musical instruments and she knew all languages.* From all lands, kings came to see her. The king was very happy.*

Afterwards, the king still yearned very much for a son, so that his kingdom would not be passed on to a stranger. Again he decreed that the Jews should pray that he have a son. They searched for the tzaddik [who had prayed for the king the first

---

a child. The tzaddik did not designate the gender of the child, and it turned out to be a daughter, not a son as the king wanted. This teaches that when one prays, one must be specific (see *The Torah Anthology* 2:396).

daughter. This daughter is important; if not for her, the true nature of the son would not have been revealed.

It is taught that, "If a daughter is born first, it is a good sign for sons" (*Bava Bathra* 141a). The *Zohar* teaches that this relates to precious stones, since in the son (Zer), these lights do not have any color, until it is revealed by the daughter (Malkhuth) (*Tikkuney Zohar* 10a). The true precious stone, however, is the son (*Tikkuney Zohar* 19, 41b). This is also related to the name of forty-two letters (*Tikkuney Zohar Chadash* 116c), since it was through the name of forty-two letters that the stones in the breastplate shone (*Zohar* 2:234b).

The son and daughter also parallel the sun and moon. Darkness and night, the domain of the moon (see Genesis 1:16), were created before light and day, the domain of the sun (see *Pardes Rimonim* 18:3).

Rabbi Nachman teaches that the son is the higher, relaxed state of consciousness, while the daughter is the lower, analytic consciousness. When the lower consciousness comes first, it is a good sign for sons, the higher state of consciousness (*Likutey Moharan* 30:3).

queen's daughter. Throughout the story she is called this. She is not seen as related to her father. She does not have her father's interests at heart.

four years old. During the first four days of creation, until she complained, the moon was preeminent (*Pardes Rimonim* 18:3).

The four years may also allude to coming through the four universes to the universe of action.

musical instruments and... languages. See Story #2. She can communicate with the forces of evil. This is a theme that has been discussed in many places.

king was very happy. Even though his goal was not accomplished, he was still proud of his daughter.

time], but they could not find him, since he was already dead.*

[The Jews] continued searching until they found another hidden tzaddik.* They told him that he must provide the king with a son.

[The tzaddik] replied that he did not know anything.

[When the Jews] told this to the king [he did as before]. He similarly told the tzaddik, "The Jews are in my hands...."

The sage* [as this tzaddik was called] asked the king, "Will you be able to do* what I order?"

"Yes,"* replied the king.

The sage said, "You must bring me every type of precious gem. Every precious stone has its own specific property. Kings have a book in which all precious stones* are listed."

---

was already dead. This is the concept of the *shevirath ha-kelim*. After the tzaddik had accomplished his goal, he no longer had to live.

There are many hidden tzaddikim in the world, such as the thirty-six hidden tzaddikim in every generation (cf. *Succah* 45b) who can only accomplish their purpose if they remain concealed. If they were to be revealed, their effectiveness in helping to protect the world would cease. Here the tzaddik performed a miracle, thereby revealing himself. Accordingly he passed away. The second tzaddik hid his miracle, because he said that the king would have a son made of precious stones, and when the son was born, he was not. By hiding his miracle, the tzaddik survived (Rabbi Nachman Burshtyn).

another hidden tzaddik. This tzaddik is associated with Chokhmah, as we shall see.

sage. *Chakhham* in Hebrew, the concept of Chokhmah. Binah is separation, while Chokhmah is involvement.

will you be able to do... The second tzaddik involves the king and queen, while the first tzaddik only prayed for them. Here there is also "awaking from below."

This is the mystery of *tikkun* (rectification). When light is given to the sefiroth without any participation on their part, they shatter. It is only when the sefiroth are rebuilt in the image of man (as *partzufim*) that they can endure. As *partzufim*, just like man, they must *earn* whatever they are given.

Yes... When a tzaddik says something one must accept to do so immediately. This causes success (see *Sefer Hamiddoth, Hatzlachah* 19). Through belief in the tzaddik one succeeds (Rabbi Rosenfeld).

precious stones. This alludes to the stones of the breastplate worn on the chest of the High Priest. This contained twelve stones, one for each of the twelve tribes (*Zimrath HaAretz*).

Furthermore, the stone upon which the ark stood, was called the Foundation Stone (*evven shethiyah*) (*Yoma* 54b). It consisted of the twelve stones that Jacob had placed under

The king said, "I am willing to give half my kingdom* in order to have a son!" He brought forth all types of precious stones.

The sage took [these gems] and ground them into a powder. He then placed [the powder] in a cup of wine.* He gave half the cup to the king to drink, and half to the queen. He told them that they would have a son who consisted entirely of precious stones, and he would thus have the powers of every gem. With that, [the sage] returned home.

[The queen] gave birth to a son,* and the king was very joyous. However, when the son was born, he was not made of precious stones. Nevertheless, by the time he was four years old,* he was very beautiful and well versed in all types of wisdom. He knew all the languages,* and kings came to see him.

---

his head when he had the dream of the ladder. These stones came together to form a single stone. which was the Foundation Stone. The Foundation Stone had the power of all the twelve stones in the breastplace (*Zimrath HaAretz*). It was called by Jacob, "the gate of heaven" (Genesis 28:17), since it was the channel for all spiritual forces.

It is therefore said that this story might contain the mystery of the name of forty-two. This name is in the breastplate (*Zohar* 2:234b), and it is also on the Foundation Stone (*Targum Yonathan* on Exodus 28:30).

Rabbi Nachman taught that all the forces of *tzimtzum* were concentrated on the Foundation Stone (*evven shethiyah*) (*Likutey Moharan* 61:6).

Also, precious stone is hard, but it reflects light (*tzimtzum*).

This also refers to the soul who learns the entire Torah prior to birth (*Niddah* 30b). The Torah is the light reflected through Moses (Rabbi Rosenfeld).

half my kingdom. Just as Achashverosh had told Esther (Esther 5:3, 7:2). When Achashverosh said, "half my kingdom," he meant up to halfway of his kingdom, referring to the Holy Temple. This was where the Foundation Stone was (*Megillah* 15b) (Rabbi Chaim Kramer).

wine. When wine goes in, mystery goes out.This brought forth the hidden mystery of the son. Wine also alludes to joy (see Stories #1 and #2).

son. Zer Anpin. This is in the world of *tikkun*. Moses is referred to as Zer Anpin (*Tikkuney Zohar* 69).

four years old. Like the queen's daughter.

knew all the languages. But does not mention that he played music. This is the feminine concept, which nourishes the *klipoth*. The son is Zer, which is the Torah, which was translated into seventy languages.

The queen's daughter realized that her status had diminished, and she was jealous.* Her only consolation was that the tzaddik had said that [the boy] would be made completely out of precious stones, [and this had not been fulfilled]. She was glad that [her brother] was not made of precious stones.*

Then one day the king's son was carving wood and injured*

---

jealous. This is the jealousy that the moon had for the sun (*Chullin* 60a). As a result the moon was reduced.

The princess was accorded great honor by the kings of the world. Yet she was still very jealous of the prince. This jealousy ultimately caused her downfall (Rabbi Nachman Burshtyn).

Rabbi Nachman once said, "When a person holds to this, *it is also very great.*" He was speaking about someone who is happy to see his friend succeed in his efforts at becoming a good Jew and a tzaddik even if he himself is not successful (*Sichoth HaRan* 119).

Rabbi Nathan writes that when he first heard this thought, it seemed obvious. "Of course I want my friend to succeed, because it is the essence of loving your fellow Jew to want to see him succeed." But in fact, he continues, there are many people who have tried serving God only to fall from their aims later on. When they see others making sincere efforts to serve God, their jealousy causes them to sneer and laugh at them. (*Ibid.*)

Rabbi Akiva said: "When I was an *am ha-aretz* (a boor) I used to say, give me a Torah scholar and I'll bite him like a mule bites." His students said, "Rabbi, say as a dog bites." R. Akiva replied, "A mule bites and breaks the bone, a dog bites and does not break the bone" (*Pesachim* 49b). The *Maharshah* (*loc.cit.*) explains that the biting referred to here is not literal. It means grinding one's teeth and seeking to do harm — as the princess intended to do.

The Talmud (*Ibid.*) continues: "The hatred of the *amey ha-aretz* for the scholars is greater than that of the heathens for Israel. And the hatred of their wives is greater than theirs. And the hatred of one who has abandoned the Torah is greater than everyone else's." This hatred stems from their jealousy (Rabbi Chaim Kramer).

This also relates to the Jews in Egypt. The Egyptians were very jealous of the Jews (Exodus 1:9; see Rashi *ad. loc.*). Pharaoh decreed that all infant boys were to be killed, while infant girls were to be permitted to live (Exodus 1:16). This corresponds to the jealousy of the princess in the story.

not made of precious stones. The son's true nature can only be revealed by the daughter. Zer Anpin is only known through Malkhuth (*Tikkuney Zohar* 10a).

injured. In order for the precious stones to be revealed the prince had to injure his finger.

Rabbi Nachman taught that it is impossible to come to genuine truth unless one first cleanses one's blood of impurities (*Likutey Moharan*, 51). Truth is likened to a precious stone (*Ibid.* 9, 112). Thus when the prince cut himself — i.e. he let blood — the precious stones were revealed.

his finger. When the queen's daughter ran to bandage the finger, she noticed a precious stone* there. She was very jealous, and she made believe that she was sick.*

Many physicians came, but they were not able to cure her. Then sorcerers were summoned.* Finally she told one sorcerer the truth, that she was merely acting as if she was sick.

She asked this [sorcerer] if he could cast a spell on a person to make him into a leper.*

"Yes,"* he replied.

Once the Rebbe took hold of R. Shmuel Isaac, one of his closest followers, right by his heart, and said to him, "For a little bit of blood in the chamber of your heart, will you lose this world and the world to come? You should sigh and sigh until you *purify* it and subdue the evil in your heart" (*Shevachey Moharan*, 23a #5).

made believe that she was sick. This is the reduction of the moon. God told the moon, "Go diminish yourself." Therefore she had to do it herself. This in itself may have created the sorcery that the king consulted.

sorcerers were summoned. Originally the king did not consult sorcerers. When he wanted children, and the doctors did not help him, he immediately asked the Jews to pray for him. But now, with the reduction of the moon, the realm of evil exists, and it even affects the king. Therefore, he summons sorcerers, who draw their power from the power of the dark forces.

Once the moon is diminished, the dark forces have access to Malkhuth. They can even be thought to try to "cure" her. Night is the time when the dark forces have power.

leper. Leprosy comes from the birds, which are the *mochin* of the *klipah* which derive nourishment from Malkhuth (*Likutey Moharan* 3). Therefore, it represents the relationship that Malkhuth has with the *klipah*.

Also, leprosy comes from *lashon hara.* Speech is Malkhuth, and evil speech is Malkhuth that has fallen into the *klipah*.

In general, leprosy is considered a high degree of uncleanness (Leviticus 13). Instead of having a skin of jewels, he would have unclean, leprous skin.

But "many thoughts are in man's heart, but God's council will stand" (Proverbs 19:21). Although the daughter meant bad, she ultimately brought forth the son's full glory (*Rimzey Maasioth*).

When Moses was born it is written, "and she saw that he was *good (TOV)*" (Exodus 2:2). The story alludes to this in the figure of the prince. The Hebrew for precious stones is *avanim TOVim.* Moses was *TOV.* Just as Moses was smitten with leprosy and then healed (Exodus 4:6) so too, the prince was afflicted with leprosy and eventually healed. The princess used sorcery in an attempt to harm the prince. Egypt was a land of sorcerers (see Exodus 7,8). Just as the princess was drowned, so the Egyptians were drowned in the Red Sea (Rabbi Shmuel Moshe Kramer).

Yes. Unlike the tzaddik who demurs, he immediately says he can do it.

"But what if he finds another sorcerer who can cancel this spell?" she asked. "Then he will be healed."

The sorcerer said, "If the charm is thrown into water,* it cannot be annulled."

She did this, [casting a spell on her brother]. Then she threw the charm into the water.

The king's son became very leprous.* The leprosy broke out

If the charm is thrown into water. This concept is found in the Talmud, where a sorceress cast a spell on the mother of ben Bethirah that she not have any children. She cast it into the sea, so that when the sages threatened her, she said that it could no longer be annulled once it had been cast into the sea (*Yerushalmi Sanhedrin* 7:13, 41a; see *Sefer Chasidim* 1144). The reason for this is that as far as sorcery is concerned, dry land and water are two different domains, and magic done on one cannot affect that done on the other (*Sefer Chasidim* 475). Therefore, if magic is done on dry land, it is usually annulled when it comes in contact with water (*Sanhedrin* 67b, Rashi s.v. *Pashar*). But if the charm itself is placed in water, then as long as the sorcerer is on dry land, he has no power over it. However, if he is in the water, as below, then he is in the same domain again.

became very leprous. As we shall see, this is a lowering for the sake of reaching a higher level (*Rimzey Maasioth*). This is very much like the Jews, who first suffer in order to reach their true high level.

This is very much like the houses in the Holy Land, which became leprous (Leviticus 14:34). Then, when they were torn down, jewels were found hidden in their walls (Rashi; *Zimrath HaAretz*).

The Midrash relates the tearing down of a leprous house to the destruction of the Temple. God said, when the Temple was rebuilt, "I will lay in Zion for a foundation, a stone, a tested stone, a precious corner stone of firm foundation..." (Isaiah 28:16) (*Vayikra Rabbah* 17:7). This alludes to the Foundation Stone, which was made from the twelve stones which Jacob placed under his head (see *Bereshith Rabbah* 16). Thus, the Temple had to be destroyed in order for the full potential of the Foundation Stone to be realized (*Zimrath HaAretz*).

This is also related to the name of forty-two. The *Zohar* states that the Israelites took twelve journeys to Sinai. They had to take an additional thirty moves after the Golden Calf, to make a total of forty-two moves (Numbers 33). Before they entered the Holy Land, they had to journey in forty-two stages, paralleling the letters in the name of forty-two letters (*Zohar Chadash* 60b; *Zimrath HaAretz*).

To reveal the greatness of the tzaddik, Moses, there must first be the lowering before the ascent. The prince cut his finger and then became a leper. Only afterwards was he healed and revealed to be of precious stones. So too, Moses was a leper and then healed to reveal his greatness (Rabbi Rosenfeld).

on his nose,* and on his face* and the rest of his body. The king had physicians and sorcerers* try to cure the boy, but to no avail. Finally, he decreed that the Jews should pray. [The Jews] searched for the tzaddik [who had given the king this son], and brought him to the king.

This tzaddik had been constantly praying to God since he had told the king that the prince would consist completely of precious stones, and this prediction had not been fulfilled. He argued before God, "Did I do this to enhance my own prestige? I only did this for *Your* glory! But now what I predicted did not come true."

The tzaddik came to the king and prayed [for the boy] but to no avail. He was then told* that a spell had been cast [on the boy].

This tzaddik [had powers that were] much higher* than all types of sorcery. He informed the king that a spell had been cast, and that the charm had been thrown into water. The king's son could not be cured unless the sorcerer who had cast the spell was also thrown into the water.

The king said, "I will give you all the sorcerers to throw into the water, so as to heal my son."

The queen's daughter was very frightened. She knew where she had placed the charm, and she ran to the water to take it out. [While she was trying to fish it out,] she fell into the water.* The fact that the queen's daughter had fallen into the water caused a great panic.

---

nose. Rabbi Nachman relates nose to prayer (*Likutey Moharan* 2). First the power of prayer was taken away from him.

face. Then the wisdom was taken away from him (*Likutey Moharan* 1).

sorcerers. Again.

was then told. From on high.

much higher. The true tzaddik can overpower all types of evil (*Berachoth* 7b). Rabbi Nachman teaches (*Likutey Moharan* 8), that one who is attached to the true tzaddik can also overpower the evil forces (Rabbi Rosenfeld).

fell into the water. She fell into the place of the *klipoth*. As mentioned earlier, this is said to relate to the Shpoler (see above). This also alludes to water washing away evil in the end of days.

The tzaddik then came and told [the people] that the king's son would be healed. [The king's son] recovered, and the leprosy dried up and fell away. All his skin peeled off, and [it was revealed that] he consisted entirely of precious stones* [just as the tzaddik had predicted]. [The king's son] had the power of every precious stone.*

he consisted entirely of precious stones. It is thus through the evil and jealousy that she had that he reached his full potential (see *Rimzey Maasioth*). It is like Joseph's brothers, who sold him as a slave, but he ended up as king. "You thought to do bad, but God made it come out good" (Genesis 50:20).

As we have said, this is the concept of the *evven shethiyah*. Rabbi Nachman writes that the *evven shethiyah* includes the concept of all *tzimtzumim* (*Likutey Moharan* 61:6). He also writes that *SheTHiYah* (שתיה) spells out *Hen Tavey Shadai Yaaneni* (הן תוי שדי יענני) (Job 31:35), "Here is my signature, let God answer me, and that I had the indictment that my adversary has written" (*Ibid.*). The concept of *evven shethiyah* is revealed through dispute. This alludes to the strife and jealousy between the daughter and the son.

power of every precious stone. The Name of forty-two consists of the six initial letters in *Ana Bekoach*. There are seven verses, totalling forty-two. Each letter refers to a sefirah, Chesed, Gevurah, Tifereth, Netzach, Hod, Yesod. The group of six letters itself is Malkhuth.

The Name of forty-two is known as *Mem Beth*. This Name was the name used in the creation of the world. MB are the initial letters of Ma'aseh Bereshith (the Work of Creation). Each day represents a sefirah. Every thousand years also represents a sefirah. "For a thousand years in Your eyes is a day" (Psalms 90:4).

The last name in this group of forty-two is SHKU-TZYT (שקוציית) referring to the reign of Malkhuth. The third letter is *vav*, relating to Tifereth of Malkhuth. The fourth letter is *tzadi*, relating to Netzach of Malkhuth. Moses is Tifereth (the *vav*) (*Tikkuney Zohar* 69). Rabbi Nachman is Netzach (the *tzadi*). NaCHMaN numerically is 148. NeTZaCH numerically is 148 (Rabbi Rosenfeld).

The *Zohar* states that Moses' soul is present in every generation in the form of the tzaddikim. This is what Rabbi Nachman was referring to, when he said that he did not know how to fit in the letters *vav* and *tzadi*. The mystery will be revealed when the Messiah will come to complete the *tikkun* of the Malkhuth. Then Moses will be here together with the tzaddik (Rabbi Rosenfeld).

The Midrash tells the story of someone who came upon a friend of his while the latter was making a crown. "Who is this for?" he asked. "For the King!" "If so, if it is for the King, then every precious stone that you find you should place in the crown" (*Vayikra Rabba* 2).

Each precious stone has a mystical quality which is a correlate of the spiritual qualities of the soul. Thus, it was found that the prince possessed all the precious qualities which were in the precious stones. The Hebrew word for a precious, mystical quality is *segulah*. The Jewish Nation is called *am segulah*, "a precious people" (Deut. 7:6). Rabbi Nachman explains (*Likutey Moharan* 21) we are called "a precious people" in the same sense that there are special remedies, for whose curative powers there is no natural explanation, but whose powers are beyond nature and beyond the power of the human mind to understand.

Similarly in our case God took us to be His precious people even though the human mind cannot understand at all how God could have taken one people from all the nations. All the special qualities (*seguloth*) possessed by precious stones are found in every Jew, and all these qualities together make up a crown, because each Jew is a crown for God. All that is necessary is for us to search out these qualities (*Likutey Moharan* 6).

6

THE HUMBLE KING *

Once there was a king* who had a wise advisor.* The king said to the wise man, "There is a king* who signs himself, 'the mighty warrior,* man of truth* and humble* person.'

"I know that he is a mighty warrior,* because his land is surrounded by the sea.* [He has] a navy of ships* with cannons;*

The Humble King. This is the name given in the first edition. The story is also known as "The King and the Sage" (*Zimrath HaAretz*).

king. This is the sefirah of Malkhuth, the lower king.

wise advisor. This is the Yesod of Chokhmah which comes down to Malkhuth, this being the mystery of, "With wisdom (Chokhmah) God laid the foundation (Yesod) of the earth (Malkhuth)" (Proverbs 3:19). It also alludes to the saints and sages in every generation (*Rimzey Maasioth*).

king. This is Binah (*Rimzey Maasioth*), the higher king. (See Story #2)

mighty warrior. *Gibbor* in Hebrew, denoting a "mighty man of strength." It is thus written, "I am understanding (Binah), I have strength (Gevurah)" (Proverbs 8:14). This is the left side.

man of truth. The middle line.

humble. (See *Tikkuney Zohar* 5b) This is the right side, known as *gedulah* (God's greatness) in the verse, "Wherever you find *gedulah*, there you find *anavah* (humility)" (*Megillah* 31a).

I...mighty warrior. Since Binah is on the side of Gevurah, to the left (*Zimrath HaAretz*).

　　Binah is the concept of concealing, like a garment, separating and holding back, which is also the concept of Gevurah (*Rimzey Maasioth*). This is the mystery of "Behold the bed of Solomon, sixty mighty men (*gibborim*) are around it" (Song of Songs 3:7; *Zimrath HaAretz*).

his land is surrounded by the sea. It is thus written, "The land and everything in it belongs to God, for He founded it on the seas" (Psalms 24:1).

navy of ships. It is thus written, "With the east wind, You break the ships of Tarshish" (Psalms 48:8). Earlier, this psalm says, "Great is God, and highly praised in the city of our God...Mount Zion...the city of the great King. God has made Himself known as a stronghold in its palaces. For kings assemble, they come together" (Psalms 48:2-5). This

they do not let anyone come close [to the land]. On the side away from the sea, there is a quicksand bog* surrounding his land. There is only one small path,* upon which only one man at a time can go. This [path] is also defended with cannons, and if anyone attacks, they fire the cannons. It is impossible even to come close to [his land].

"However, when he signs himself, 'man of truth and humble person,' I do not know [if he is telling the truth]. I therefore want you to bring me a portrait* of that king."

The king [who was speaking] had portraits* of every single [other] king with the exception* of the one [he was now

---

seems to contain the entire theme of the story, the assembly of portraits, Mount Zion (alluded to at the end of the story), being praised and revealing Himself.

with cannons. *Hormates* in Yiddish. This may be alluded to in the verse, "He shall dwell on high, his place of defense shall be munitions of rocks" (Isaiah 33:16). This is part of a key chapter, as we shall see at the end of the story.

bog. *Zump* in Yiddish, a swamp.

one small path. This appears to be the narrow path leading from the lower sefiroth to Binah. In man it corresponds to the throat between the body and the head. The Ari says that this is the concept of constriction and constricted consciousness (*mochin de-katnuth*), and it is an aspect of *Mitzraim* (Egypt) which comes from the root *tzar*, meaning narrow.

portrait. It was possible to discern a person's personality from his physical appearance (See *Zohar* 2:78a; *Tikkuney Zohar* 70 121b). There is a story in the Midrash of a person who analyzed a portrait of Moses.

had portraits. In a sense, he was a king who included all other kings, just as there is a land that includes all other lands, etc., later in the story.

At the end of the story, Rabbi Nachman speaks of Zion as being the place where all monuments (*tzionim*) are gathered together. This is very ambiguous. It seems to indicate the portraits, but later, Rabbi Nachman says, "See Zion the city of our gatherings." It is the place where one goes if one needs to know how to do business. Therefore, Zion relates to the "city that includes all cities." However, from this we see that bringing together all the portraits, was making him include all other kings (see *Rimzey Maasioth*).

Kabbalistically, the first king is Malkhuth. All the other sefiroth shine on Malkhuth, and are seen through Malkhuth. Therefore, the "portraits of all the other kings" which are the lights of the other sefiroth, are found in Malkhuth (*Rimzey Maasioth*). The sefiroth are known as "kings" from Genesis 36.

with the exception. Binah is high above Malkhuth, which hides its face (*Rimzey Maasioth*). Zion, mentioned earlier, is the concept of Binah coming down to Malkhuth. Therefore, the only way to get this portrait is to go to Zion, the city that includes all other cities.

discussing]. No king had that king's portrait, since he kept himself hidden* from all people. He kept himself at a distance from his subjects, and sat behind a canopy.*

The wise man traveled to that land. He decided that he must [first] know the essential nature of that land. One can understand the nature of a land by knowing its humor.* In order to

---

kept himself hidden. As we see later, because he cannot tolerate the falsehood of his nation. This is alluded to in the teaching, "Jerusalem was not destroyed until it lost men of truth" (*Shabbath* 119b; *Rimzey Maasioth*). It is also the concept of the verse, "He who speaks falsehood shall not be established before My face" (Psalms 101:7; *Rimzey Maasioth*). Jerusalem is therefore called the city of truth (Zechariah 8:3; *Rimzey Maasioth*).

God thus says, "When you come to see My face, Who needs this from your hands?" (Isaiah 1:12). To rectify this, God told the prophet, "Seek justice, and relief for the oppressed" (Isaiah 1:17; *Rimzey Maasioth*).

The Holy Land itself is the concept of the concealed king. It is therefore taught that Abraham understood the concept of every nation in the world, but not that of the land of Israel (*Zohar* 1:78; *Zimrath HaAretz*).

canopy. Or curtain, *kulah* in Yiddish. This is like the Divine Presence behind the *parokheth*, veil, in the Tabernacle and Temple.

humor. Or jokes, *kataves* in Yiddish. The concept of humor is one of the main themes of this story.

The Talmud explicitly says that a person can be known through "his cup, his purse and his anger — and also through his humor" (*Eruvin* 65b).

This is taken as a general lesson. If a person wants to know the inner nature of a place, he should analyze its jokes (*Likutey Etzoth, Letzanoth* 1). People will often tell jokes about things that they are too inhibited to discuss openly. Therefore, their jokes may tell more about their inner essence than their serious speech.

Humor also requires a certain objectivity. When a person can laugh at something, it indicates that he is not too involved in it. In order to understand something, one must be able to examine it objectively.

This contains an important lesson for the world. Thus, if we were to see a person trying desperately to convince people to do something, but we knew that he really did not want them to do it, we would find it very humorous. This is true of the Evil Urge. The *Zohar* says that the Evil Urge is like a harlot that the king hires to test his son. The harlot is really also working for the king, and genuinely does not want the prince to succumb to her wiles (*Zohar* 2:163a). Therefore, on a very deep level, the actions of the *Yetzer Hara* are really very funny (*Rimzey Maasioth*). The Talmud therefore teaches that a person cannot sin unless he has in him "a spirit of foolishness" (*Sotah* 3a).

Humor also involves incongruities. One such incongruity involves the most basic forces of creation, the forces through which God gives (*chasadim*) and the forces through which

understand something, one must know the jokes related to it.

There are many types of jokes.

Sometimes a person wants to hurt another with his words. When the other shows that he is annoyed, he says, "I was only joking." It is thus written, "One exerts oneself [casting firebrands, arrows and deadly weapons...] and then says, 'I am only joking'*" (Proverbs 26:18,19).

There are also cases where someone really is only joking, but nevertheless, the other person is hurt by his words. There are also other types of humor.

There is a land* that includes all other lands.* In the land that

---

He holds back (gevuroth). Ultimately, of course, even the gevuroth are given by God, and therefore, even the gevuroth have their roots in the chasadim. The curtain that hides the King consists of nothing other than the King's essence. This is humor and incongruity on the highest levels (Rimzey Maasioth).

The Zohar speaks about this in the context of the verse, "I have seen that the advantage of wisdom is from foolishness, just as the advantage of light is from darkness" (Ecclesiastes 2:13, according to the Zohar). The Zohar says that one can only gain true wisdom through foolishness and humor, which come from a much higher source (Zohar 3:47a,b).

A joke cannot be understood logically, but only with a level of consciousness that is higher than logic. A person laughs at a joke, but he does not know why. Therefore, it appears that jokes have their origin in Kether, and this seems to be the case from the Zohar. This is the level that is higher than wisdom.

Also, foolishness and evil must exist in the world, so that man will have free will, which enables him to come to higher levels of wisdom.

I am only joking. We find that King Yehu said, "Ahab served the Baal a little, but Yehu will serve him much" (2 Kings, 10:18). Even though he only said it as a joke, it was like an arrow and a firebrand (Rimzey Maasioth; see Sichoth HaRan 237).

The Rambam says that this verse is speaking specifically of one who speaks lashon hara as a joke. One may be destroying the other, but saying that it is a joke (Yad, Deayos 7:4).

The Talmud states that this verse is speaking of Ishmael who shot arrows at Isaac, and then said that it was only a joke (Tosefta, Sotah 6:3; Bereshith Rabbah 53:11). Yitzchak means laughter, and he, Isaac, is the paradigm of holy laughter. Ishmael tried to destroy the holy laughter with harmful jokes.

There is a land. Although the story is speaking about a particular land where the concealed king lives, it says that the wise ma 1 went to the land that includes all lands. This indicates that this story is speaking of the entire world. The Holy Land is referred to as a "princess among nations" (Lamentations 1:1). The Midrash says that it is called this because it includes all other nations (Rimzey Maasioth).

includes all lands, there is a city that includes all the cities* of that
land. In the city that includes all cities, in the land that includes all
lands, there is a building that includes all buildings.* Here, there
is a man who includes everything in that entire building*... Here,
there is the one who composes all the humor* and jokes in the
entire land.

Kabbalistically, the land that includes all other lands is the universe of Asiyah.

Obviously, the land that includes all lands is the Holy Land. This is called Zion, as
alluded to at the end of the story. It is also written, "Out of Zion, the perfect of beauty,
God shone forth" (Psalms 50:2). Our sages derive from this that, from the *evven shethiyah*,
veins go forth to the entire world, and that King Solomon was expert in it (*Koheleth
Rabbah* 2:7; *Rimzey Maasioth*; see *Sichoth HaRan* 60). Everything, even bad traits, have
their root in the Temple in the Holy Land.

The concept of making jokes out of everything is one of constriction and *tzimtzum*.
One takes the wisdom of the world and constricts it into foolishness. Rabbi Nachman
teaches that the *evven shethiyah* is the source of all the *tzimtzumim* in the world (*Likutey
Moharan* 61; *Rimzey Maasioth*).

that includes all other lands. The Yiddish adds, "That is, it is the main thing and general
rule of all lands." This means that it is a paradigm of all other lands.

city that includes all the cities. This is Jerusalem (*Rimzey Maasioth*). It denotes the universe
of Yetzirah.

building that includes all buildings. The Temple (*Rimzey Maasioth*). This parallels the
universe of Beriyah. The Temple was thus like the throne of God, and Beriyah is the
universe of the throne.

a man... This is the man on the throne (Ezekiel 1:26). It alludes to the High Priest, who
could go into the Holy of Holies once a year. Of course, the *evven shethiyah*, mentioned
earlier, was in the Holy of Holies.

the one who composes... In general, the origin of folk humor is a mystery. Here we see that
it comes from the genius of that particular land. This genius has his root in the man on the
throne, who is over all lands.

It is taught that there are seventy geniuses (*sarim*) for all the seventy nations. The *sar* or
genius for each nation is the root of its humor.

Ultimately, however, humor comes from Zion, as mentioned above. This is where
"kings assemble" (Psalms 48:5). Rabbi Nachman therefore gives us the meaning of this
story in the verse, "look upon Zion, the city of our gatherings" (Isaiah 33:20), which spells
out in its initial letters *metzachek*, meaning laughing (see *Rimzey Maasioth*).

This entire thing is alluded to in the verse, "When God brings back the return (*shivath*)
of Zion... our mouths shall be filled with laughter" (Psalms 126:1,2). This indicates that
Zion has a strong relationship to laughter.

The concept of laughter thus ultimately comes from the Holy of Holies. This may be
related to the teaching that when the Men of the Great Assembly nullified the *Yetzer Hara*

The wise man* took a large sum of money* and went there. He saw many types of jokes and humor being composed.

From the jokes, he understood that the land was totally filled with falsehood, from the beginning to the end. He saw that jokes were being made about how people were cheated and deceived in business, and how when people took a case to court, it was all decided on the basis of falsehood and bribery. Even when someone went to the Supreme Court,* there was nothing but falsehood. Humorous skits were made of all these cases.

From this humor, the wise man understood* that the land was totally full of falsehood and dishonesty, and that there was no truth at all there.

He then bought and sold merchandise, allowing himself to be cheated. He took his case to court,* and saw that they operated

---

of idolatry, they saw it coming out of the Holy of Holies (*Yoma* 69). Even harmful humor has its origin in the Temple, from the *evven shethiyah*. The Evil Urge in its highest root is a concept of holiness, and therefore it is all a joke. It is only in this world that it becomes harmful (*Rimzey Maasioth;* see *Likutey Moharan* 72; *Parparoth LeChokhmah, ad. loc.*).

In general, this teaches that in order to compose satire, one must be in a position to see the entire country.

Since the man on the throne represents God, this may be related to the concept of God laughing (Psalms 2:4; *Avodah Zarah* 3b). The Talmud also says that God laughs with the wicked in this world, and with the righteous in the World to Come (*Shabbath* 30b). A person can therefore also be brought to God through humor (*Taanith* 22a).

The wise man. The tzaddikim and sages in each generation work to rectify the falsehood in the world, so that the king can be seen (*Rimzey Maasioth*).

large sum of money. To do business, so that he would eventually be able to appeal his case to the king and thus see him (see Story #1).

Supreme Court. *Sanad* in Yiddish, the senate. The Sanhedrin was both the Supreme Court and the senate of the Jews.

The senate may be the court of seventy *sarim* (princes).

the wise man understood. Regarding this wise man, it is written, "He walks righteously and speaks uprightly... shaking his hands to avoid bribes" (Isaiah 33:15). He is the one who can approach the king, since "He shall dwell on high, his place of defense shall be the munitions of rocks... Your eyes shall see the king in His beauty" (Isaiah 33:16,17). The verse concludes, "Look upon Zion, the city of our gatherings" (33:20), which spells out laughter, as we see at the end of this story (*Rimzey Maasioth*).

court. Asiyah.

with falsehood and bribery. One day he could give a bribe, and the next day they would not recognize him.

He took his case to a higher court,* and this was also full of falsehood. Finally he came to the Supreme Court,* and this, too, was full of falsehood and bribery.

Finally, he brought his case before the king.* When he came to the king, he said, "Over whom are you king?* The land is completely full of falsehood, from beginning to end. There is no truth at all in it." He then began to describe all the falsehood in the land.

Hearing this, the king inclined his ear* toward the curtain to listen to [the wise man's] words. The king was very surprised that there was a man who was aware of all the falsehood in the land.

When the ministers of state heard [the wise man's] words, they were very angry with him. However, he continued describing the falsehood in the land.

[The wise man] then said, "It would be logical to say that [since you are] king, [you] are just like the rest — that you like falsehood, just like everyone else in the kingdom. But there is one thing that shows me that you are a man of truth. Since you cannot tolerate the land's falsehood, you keep yourself at a distance* from your [subjects]." With that, [the wise man] began to praise the king* very, very highly.

---

higher court. Yetzirah.

Supreme Court. Beriyah.

king. In Atziluth.

Over whom are you king. One may complain to God in one's personal prayers.

Abraham also said, "Shall He who judges the entire world not do judgment?" (Genesis 18:25). It was actually Abraham who revealed God to the entire world.

inclined his ear. *Hirkhin* in Hebrew.

keep yourself at a distance. Therefore, the king was never seen, as at the beginning of the story.

"Sometimes when a land is full of falsehood, and the king is a man of truth, he hides himself so that no one can see his face. 'He who speaks falsely shall not be established before My face' (Psalms 101:7)' " (*Likutey Etzoth, Emeth VeEmunah* 27).

he began to praise the king. He tested the king to see whether or not he was a man of truth. Now he tests him to see if he is humble, as he signs himself. The King is God and through praising Him, we make Him reveal Himself (*Rimzey Maasioth*).

The king was very humble. Wherever he had greatness, he had humility.* When a person is truly humble, the more he is praised and made great, the smaller and more humble he becomes.* Therefore, when the wise man praised him and spoke of his greatness, the king became very small and humble, until he literally became nothing.*

[The king] then could not hold himself back. He threw aside the curtain* so as to see the wise man. [He had to see] who knew and understood all this. In doing so, however, the king revealed his face, and the sage saw him.* The wise man was then able to paint his portrait* and bring it to his king.*

Wherever he had greatness... A paraphrase of the Talmudic statement, "Wherever you find God's greatness, you find His humility" (*Megillah* 31a).

more humble he becomes. Rabbi Nathan writes that counting increases the Israelites, and it is therefore dangerous. However, if it is done with charity, which diminishes a person, it is not harmful. It is a virtuous deed to make Israel great, since this makes them recognize God more, and this makes them smaller. Israel reduces itself, as it is written, "For you are the least of all nations" (Deuteronomy 7:7; *Chullin* 89; *Likutey Halakhoth, Tefillin* 6:24; also see *Likutey Moharan* 4:7).

literally became nothing. The highest levels of the Divine are referred to as *ayin* (nothing). They are called nothing, because man has no categories in his mind with which to grasp them. Since there is nothing that a person can grasp with his mind, his entire perception is that of nothingness.

The more one praises God the closer one comes to this ideal. It is thus written, "To You praise is silence" (Psalms 65:2). The highest praise of God is silence, since there is really nothing that we can say about Him. God is infinitely higher than any praise that we can offer Him (also see *Likutey Moharan Tinyana* 48, 72).

It is only when a person has this perception of God that he can "see." God can reveal Himself to that person.

threw aside the curtain. "Three times each year all your males shall see My face" (Exodus 23:17, 34:23; Deuteronomy 16:16). Our sages teach that just as we come to see God, so He wants to see us (*Rimzey Maasioth*).

We can only see God when He wants to see us.

the sage saw him. As it is written in the key chapter, "Your eyes shall see the King in His glory, they shall behold a land far off" (Isaiah 33:17) (*Rimzey Maasioth*). The land at a distance is the land that was far from God. Through the king revealing himself, his land could also be rectified (*Rimzey Maasioth*).

able to paint his portrait. Only in Yiddish. This is alluded to at the end of the story, "One shall see a man and make a portrait next to him" (Ezekiel 39:15).

bring it to his king. This is the rectification of the world. Therefore, the story ends, "May it be Your will to rebuild Your Temple."

"The ways of Zion (*tzion*) are mourning"* (Lamentations 1:4). "Zion," *tzion* in Hebrew alludes to monuments of all the lands that came together. It is thus written, "One shall see a man and build a monument (*tzion*) next to him" (Ezekiel 39:15).

This is the significance of the verse, "See Zion (*tzion*), the city of our gatherings" (Isaiah 33:20). In Hebrew, this is *chazeh Tzion kiryat moadenu* (חֲזֵה צִיּוֹן קִרְיַת מוֹעֲדֵנוּ).] The initial letters of this verse spell out *metzachek* (מְצַחֵק), which means to tell a joke. This is the place where all the monuments come together. If a person needs to know if he should engage in a certain type of business, he can know it there.

May it be [God's] will that He rebuild His Temple. Amen.

Look, see and understand the extent of these concepts. Happy is he who waits and reaches the point where he can know and perceive even a small degree of the mysteries of these stories. Nothing like this has been heard since ancient times.

All the verses and allusions that are cited after some of the stories are only hints so that people will realize that [the story] is not something devoid of meaning,* heaven forbid. [Rabbi Nachman] expressedly said that he was revealing some hints and verses alluding to the mysteries in

---

The ways of Zion are mourning. The verse ends, "Without anyone coming for a *moed* (appointed time)" (Lamentations 1:4). This is the concept of "Three times each year shall all your males be seen by God." This is when they are seen and they see (see *Likutey Moharan* 30). This is when the face of the King shines forth, especially on festivals, which are a concept of Binah and humility (*Likutey Moharan* 135; *Rimzey Maasioth*). Jerusalem is therefore called the city of truth (Zechariah 8:3; *Rimzey Maasioth*). On the Sabbath and festivals, Malkhuth rises up to Binah, this being the concept of bringing the portrait to the king.

But when the ways of Zion are in mourning, there are no correct jokes or laughter, and then there is no festival and no time that God can be seen (see *Rimzey Maasioth*).

Furthermore, Zion is the place on high where even the worst evil can be see as a joke. But the "ways of Zion," when they are manifested in the lower worlds, are seen as the evil that separates man from God and causes Him to hide His face (*Rimzey Maasioth*). This causes the nations to have power over Israel, reducing the ways of Zion to mourning in a literal sense (*Rimzey Maasioth*).

devoid of meaning. See Deuteronomy 32:47.

the stories, so that people will realize that he was not merely engaging in idle chatter, heaven forbid.

However, the mysteries of these stories extend far beyond the grasp of our knowledge. "It is deep, deep; who will find it."*

It is deep, deep... See Ecclesiastes 7:24.

7

THE SPIDER AND THE FLY

[Rabbi Nachman introduced this story by saying,] "I will tell you about the journey that I took*.... But do not think* that I will tell you everything, or that you will be able to understand."

the journey that I took. Rabbi Nachman was speaking of the journey to Navritch that he took during the spring and summer of 1807 (*Chayay Moharan*, p. 15c #59, p. 35a,b #10). Rabbi Nathan was not there at the time (*Yemey Moharnat* 20b).

Rabbi Nachman began his trip shortly before Purim of that year (*Chayay Moharan* 34b #3). Rabbi Nachman traveled disguised as a businessman (*Sippurim Niflaim* 150, *Chayay Moharan* 29a #15). He took along two of his followers, R. Shmuel of Teplik and Rabbi Naftali. Rabbi Naftali became ill, however, in Lipovetz, and was replaced by R. Isaac Yosef of Lipovetz (*Sippurim Niflaim* 150; see *Kochavay Or* 33 #30). Rabbi Nachman arrived in Navritch shortly before Purim (which that year occurred on March 24).

Shortly before Passover, Rabbi Nachman left Navritch for Ostrog (*Alim Leterufah*). He then sent for his wife, who was suffering from tuberculosis, to be treated by Dr. Gordon (Rabbi Aaron ben Shimon), who was a disciple of the Mezricher Maggid (*Chayay Moharan* 34b #3). They all traveled to Zaslov, where they spent Passover (*Yemey Moharnat* 17a). His wife died there on the day before Shavuoth (June 11; *Yemey Moharnat* 19b; *Chayay Moharan* 34b #3).

In Tammuz (July), Rabbi Nachman traveled to Dubno and Brody. In Brody, he became engaged to the daughter of Rabbi Yechezkiel Trachtenberg (*Yemey Moharnat* 20b; *Chayay Moharan* 35a #10). Right after the engagement, Rabbi Nachman contracted the tuberculosis that would kill him (*Chayay Moharan* 29b #15, 35b,#14). He then returned to Breslov, and on the first Sabbath, told this story (*Chayay Moharan* 35a #10,12; *Yemey Moharnat* 20b). Thus, this story was told on the Sabbath of *Mattoth-Massai* (August 1, 1807). The story was recorded by Rabbi Naftali, since Rabbi Nathan was not there at the time (*Chayay Moharan* 35b #12).

This story is usually interpreted as speaking of the dispute between Rabbi Nachman and Rabbi Aryeh Leib, known as the Shpoler Zeida. The dispute began after Sukkoth of 1800, soon after Rabbi Nachman moved to Zlatipolia, which was a short distance from Shpola. The Shpoler was one of the most famous Chasidic leaders of his time, and this dispute caused Rabbi Nachman and his followers to be severely persecuted.

but do not think... Actually, this was told after the first paragraph in the original.

There was once a king.* He was attacked and had to fight many wars,* but in the end he was victorious.* He took many prisoners.*

The king would hold an annual ball* on the anniversary of his victory. In the royal manner, all his royal counselors* and all his ministers would attend the ball.

All sorts of comedy* acts would be performed. They would

---

king. From the context of this story it appears that the king is Rabbi Nachman himself (*Chokhmah U'Tevunah* #7). Of course, it can speak of any person who wishes to overcome evil, both in himself and in others.

From the story, it appears that the king is presented as being a gentile, since he later wishes to convert to Judaism. However, even if he is a Jew, after the dream, he wants to be a true Jew, serving God in truth. He also wants to bring everyone else back to God.

many wars. Rabbi Nachman himself says that this is alluded to in Psalm 3, which is the key to this story. The wars are alluded to in the verse, "O God, how many are my enemies, many rise up against me" (Psalms 3:2).

Rabbi Nachman was speaking of the great opposition and many troubles that he had encountered. His wife had just died, and he had caught tuberculosis. Before telling this story he wept, and said that he would soon die. He wanted to have "sixty warriors" (see Song of Songs), just as the Baal Shem Tov had had (*Chayay Moharan* 35b #12).

The theme of persecution is repeated four more times throughout the story. It is represented in the fly, which is attacked by the spider; the attack on the king in his dream by the men from the diamond; the attack on the mountain; and the opposition to this soul being born into the world.

One of the main themes of this story is Rabbi Aryeh Leib, the Shpoler Zeida, who was the Rebbe's main adversary (see *Chokhmah U'Tevunah* #10).

was victorious. Although, as we see in the end of the story, the Evil One had a plan against him, the king is still victorious and eventually sets forth to rectify the world (*Likutey Etzoth* B, *tzaddik* 85).

Some say that this victory implied his overcoming the barriers, and arriving in the Holy Land. This occurred just before Rosh HaShanah. Rabbi Nachman therefore made Rosh HaShanah his special day when all his followers came together (*Chokhmah U'Tevunah* #6).

In general, a person's final victory occurs when he dies and leaves the world unconquered by evil. It is therefore a custom especially among Chasidim to make a celebration on the anniversay of a tzaddik's death.

prisoners. Expanded upon at the end of the story. See "spider."

ball... *Bal* in Yiddish.

all his royal counselors. Just as Rabbi Nachman required all his followers to be there on Rosh HaShanah.

comedy. Through which one can tell the true nature of things, as we saw in the previous story.

parody and tell jokes about all the nations, including the Turks. *
They would mock and parody the customs and ways of every
single nation. Most probably they also mocked Israel. *

The king then gave an order that he be brought the book
containing the customs and ways of every nation. Wherever he
opened the book, he saw that the customs and ways of each
nation were exactly as had been parodied by the comedians. It
could be assumed that the ones making the jokes and parodies
had all consulted this book. *

The annual ball may also denote Purim, which represents Israel's victory over Amalek,
as personified by Haman. Later we find that the spider also represents Amalek. Purim is a
time of humor.

In general, Rabbi Nachman taught that the tzaddik of each generation was an aspect of
Moses (*Likutey Moharan* 2). The main opposition that Moses faced was Korach (Numbers
16). Rabbi Nachman taught that Purim was a rectification of Korach's rebellion. He based
this on the verse, "If from the edge of his face his head becomes bald" (Leviticus 13:41),
which in Hebrew is: *Veim Mip'ath Panav Yi'maret Rosh-o* (ואם מפאת פניו ימרט ראשו). The initial
letters of this verse spell out Purim (פורים) (*Chayay Moharan* 21a # 10; *Rimzey Maasioth*). As
the *Zohar* explains, this "bald one" denotes Korach, Moses' adversary (*Zohar* 3:49a).
Rashi indicates that "baldness" denotes old age (Rashi on Leviticus 13:55; see *Rimzey
Maasioth*). Therefore, making jokes and humor as is done on Purim is seen as countering
the Shpoler Zeida, the "old one."

This may also be significant, because Rabbi Nachman left on his journey to Navritch
just before Purim.

This laughter, however, is seen as not entirely good, since there was a possibility that
they were laughing at Jews. This represents the *klipah* trying to emulate the holy, just as a
monkey tries to emulate a human being (*Chokhmah U'Tevunah* 9).

If the annual ball represents Rosh HaShanah, then the laughter may represent
Yitzchak, who was born on Rosh HaShanah. The name Yitzchak denotes laughter in
Hebrew (*Chokhmah U'Tevunah* #6). Also the merit of the binding of Isaac is recalled on
Rosh HaShanah, and this is one of the themes of the shofar sounded on Rosh HaShanah.
the Turks. (Yiddish). In Hebrew, this is Yishmael, denoting Ishmael. Of course, Ishmael
was the antithesis of Isaac (*Ibid.*).

The allusion may also be to the Turk with whom Rabbi Nachman had an encounter
when he first arrived in the Holy Land (*Rabbi Nachman's Wisdom,* p. 56, Journey to Israel
#18).

Israel. This seems to represent the *klipath nogah*, which is not definitely against Israel, but
very probably so. The laughter was therefore not from the side of the Holy.

consulted this book. Torah is first seen in parodies, like on Purim, and then the Torah itself,
which is this book, as we shall see, can be revealed in truth (*Chayay Moharan* 21b # 10; see

While the king was looking at the book, he saw a spider*
crawling along the edge of the pages.* On top of the [open]
page,* there stood a fly.* Where does a spider go? To a fly!

Rimzey Maasioth). This is very much like after the joy of Purim, the Jews accepted the
Torah as it is written, "The Jews kept and accepted for themselves and their children"
(Esther 9:21; *Shabbath* 88a).

spider. The spider represents the king's enemies, against whom he had battled. Just as the
spider was destroyed in the end, so were the king's enemies.

In general, the spider is the concept of evil trying to swallow up the good (*Chokhmah
U'Tevunah* 11). In the end this was reversed, since the king took captives from his enemies
(*Ibid.* 12).

The concept here is alluded to in the verse, "The spider grasps with its hand (or 'is
grasped with the hand'), but it sits in the king's palace" (Proverbs 30:28). In the story, the
spider is in the king's palace.

The Midrash (*Shocher Tov ad loc.*) says that the spider represents Edom, since no
creature is hated as much as it is. It is "found in the king's palace," because Edom
destroyed the Temple. The spider also represents Amalek, the archenemy of Israel
(*Shocher Tov, Zimrath HaAretz;* see *Bereshith Rabbah* 66:7). It therefore may represent
Haman, the personification of Amalek, and hence the concept of Purim and jokes, as
above.

Rashi notes that the Hebrew word for spider here is *shemamith* (שממית), which has the
connotation of destruction *shamam,* (שמם). It also denotes *sam maveth* (סם מות), indicating
poison (Rashi on *Bereshith Rabbah* 66:7).

Rabbi Nachman also taught that a spider's web represents the last barrier that a
warrior must overcome before his final victory (*Sichoth HaRan* 232). This is the lack of
faith. It is thus written that those who forget God "have faith that is like a spider's web"
(Job 8:14).

edge of the pages. It was involved with all the other pages, which described the customs of
the other nations. From them, the spider got its power.

[open] page. As we shall see, this is the page that involved the customs of Israel.

fly. The fly here obviously represents the king himself, who is being pursued by his
enemies. In more general terms, it applies to Malkhuth which is pursued by Edom and
Amalek (*Chokhmah U'Tevunah* 8). Although flies are usually considered evil, this fly is
good. Indeed, the Hebrew word for fly, *zevuv* (זבוב), has a numerical value of seventeen,
which is the value of *tov* (טוב), meaning good (Rabbi Shimshon Ostropoli, *Sefer Karnayim*
13:22, 16a).

In general terms, the fly represents the nation Israel (*Zimrath HaAretz*).

It is also quoted from Rabbi Shimshon Ostropoli (*Karnayim* 13:21, 16a) that *zevuv* can
be seen as an acrostic of the verse *Zikharon Besefer Vesim Beozney* (זכרון בספר ושים באזני).
"[Write this] for a remembrance in a book and place it in the ears [of Joshua]" (Exodus
17:14). This is the power that we have to battle against Amalek, which is very weak. This is

While the spider was crawling toward the fly, a wind came and blew the page of the book,* [lifting it] so that the spider could not get to the fly. [The spider] turned around and made believe that it was going the other way, and no longer wanted to go toward the fly.

The page then fell back to its place, and the spider started crawling toward the fly again. The page lifted up again, and prevented it, so the spider turned back again. This happened a number of times.

Finally, the spider crawled toward the fly, but this time it got

---

especially true on Rosh HaShanah, when the power of the imagination becomes strong, and one does not know "what is written in the book" (*Chokhmah U'Tevunah* 6; see *Likutey Moharan* 54).

The fact that a fly (*zevuv*) represents that which is "written in a book" is also significant, because, in the story, the fly is actually on the book (*Chokhmah U'Tevunah* 7).

If this is speaking of Rosh HaShanah, it was the time that Pharaoh had his dream, which was interpreted by Joseph (see *Likutey Moharan* 54). Joshua, who fought against Amalek, and who is also alluded to in the verse "place it in the ears of Joshua," was a descendant of Joseph. The chief steward was put in a position to help Joseph in prison because Pharaoh had found a *fly* in his cup.

It is also taught that the fly is associated with the destruction of a marriage. The Talmud thus teaches that the concubine in the story of *pilegesh beGivah* (see Judges 19), was distrusted because her husband found a fly in his food (*Gittin* 6b; *Sefer Karnayim* 17:21, 15b).

page of the book. The Torah is seen as the main protection that the Israelites have against their enemies. When Moses wants to defeat Amalek, he says, "Write this... in a book" (Exodus 17:14).

This part of the story is reflected in the key psalm, "And You God are a protector for me."

In general, the Torah is the main protection for the Jew. As we shall see, this is the page containing the Jewish practices, that is, the Torah. It is taught that "When the voice is the voice of Jacob" (Genesis 27:22), then power is taken away from "the hands of Esau." It is also written, "Why was the land destroyed, because they abandoned My Torah" (Jeremiah 9:12). Our sages say, "If only they had abandoned Me, but kept My Torah" — the land would have been protected (*PeSichta d'Eichah Rabbatai; Zimrath HaAretz*). Rabbi Akiba also taught that when the Jews are away from the Torah, they are as vulnerable as fish out of water (*Berakhoth* 61a).

The king's destiny is to become a Jew and bring the world back to God and His Torah. Thus, the page protecting the fly represents the king's Torah destiny, protecting him.

one of its legs slightly on the page.* The page lifted itself up again with the spider partially on it. Then the page went down all the way, so that the spider was caught between this page and the next. It crawled around but it remained there, [going] lower and lower, until nothing at all was left of it.

([Rabbi Nachman interjected,] "I will not tell you what happened to the fly."*)

When the king saw this, he was astonished, and he realized that this was not something trivial. He understood that he was being shown something important. (All the ministers watched the king staring, astonished.)

[The king] began to ponder the matter. What was it, and what was its meaning? He fell asleep* over the book, and began to dream:

In his dream, he had a diamond* in his hand. As he stared at it, a huge number of people* began to come out of it. He threw the diamond from his hand.

---

one of its legs... Thus, when it seemed that there was no longer any hope for the fly (since for some reason it could not fly away), the spider was destroyed (*Chokhmah U'Tevunah* 6).

It is written that when Jacob was born, "his hand was grasping the foot of Esau" (Genesis 25:26). Rashi explains that this means that Esau will not complete his task until Jacob drags him down. That is, as soon as the foot of Esau (Amalek, was a descendant of Esau) begins to get the upper hand, it is grasped by Jacob, through the power of the Torah, and Esau is destroyed (*Chokhmah U'Tevunah* 1,6,7; *Sichoth VeSippurim* 5:4).

what happened to the fly. This involves the Messianic promise (see end of Story #1). Also the fly may represent Rabbi Nachman himself, and he did not want to reveal his own destiny.

fell asleep. Alluded to in the verse, "I lay down and sleep" (Psalms 3:6). Very much like Pharaoh dreamed on Rosh HaShanah (*Chokhmah U'Tevunah* 11).

diamond. *Dumit* in Yiddish. In Story #3, a diamond represents the ability to travel. At the end of the story, the diamond is what gives his captive woman the element of grace. The captive woman may represent the fact that Rabbi Nachman totally overcame the desire for women (*Shevachey HaRan* 16). Now, however, the enemies were coming out of it. The king had to do battle with his desires, and they were threatening to destroy him.

So the diamond may also be related to the woman to whom Rabbi Nachman was now engaged.

huge number of people. In the key psalm, "I am not afraid of myriads of people who have set themselves around me" (Psalms 3:7).

Kings usually hang a portrait* over their throne, and on top of this portrait, they hang the crown. The men coming out of the diamond cut off the head of [the king's] portrait.* Then they took the crown* and threw it into the mud. (All this occurred in his dream.)

The men then ran toward [the king] to kill him.* However, a page* from the book upon which he was lying lifted itself up to protect him, so they were not able to do anything to him. They went away [from him]. Then the page returned to its place, and they attacked him again. The page lifted itself up again. This happened a number of times.

[The king] very much wanted to see which page was protecting him, and which nation's customs it contained, but he was afraid to look. He began to scream, "Help! Help!"*

---

portrait. Or icon. See above p. 110.

cut off the head... They wanted to take away the king's wisdom. This is related to grace (*chen*) (*Likutey Moharan* 1).

crown. This is the king's importance (*chashivuth*). Rabbi Nachman teaches that grace (*chen*) comes from wisdom. The wisdom and importance of Israel are taken away from them and are in the hands of their enemies (*Likutey Moharan* 1). The stone had false grace, and thus, it took away the true grace of the king. It is thus written, "False is grace, and vain is beauty" (Proverbs 31:30).

to kill him. Just as the spider wanted to kill the fly (Rabbi Nachman). Esau and Amalek (represented by the spider) want to take away the grace and importance of the Israelites, and ultimately destroy them (*Likutey Moharan* 1).

page. Obviously the same page that protected the fly. The king sees that the Torah can protect him from his adversaries. Torah protects a person from sexual temptations, because it is a "beloved gazelle" (Proverbs 5:19; see *Eruvin* 54b). Also regarding evil, it is said, "If this disgusting one approaches you, draw him to the house of study" (*Kiddushin* 30b).

Regarding the Torah it is said, "A beloved gazelle and a graceful doe, let her breasts satisfy you at all times, and always be ravished with her love" (Proverbs 5:19; see *Kethuboth* 77b; *Yad, Issurey Biyah* 21:19, 22:21; *Evven HaEzer* 23:3).

These desires can kill a person spiritually.

This is actually alluded to in the key verse, "Many say of my soul, 'He has no salvation in God' (Psalms 3:3)." The Midrash interprets this to refer to King David, who was told by many that after sinning with Bathsheva, he had no more hope (*Midrash Psalms, Yalkut*). The enemies are thus seen as sexual desires.

Help! Help! *Chaval chaval* in Hebrew; *gevalt gevalt* in Yiddish. This is alluded to in the key psalm, "With my voice I call out to God" (Psalms 3:5).

All the ministers sitting nearby heard [him scream] and they wanted to wake him up. However, since it is not proper to awaken the king, they began banging all around him to arouse him. [The king, however,] did not hear* anything.

Meanwhile [in the dream] a tall mountain* appeared to him and asked, "Why are you screaming so much? I have been sleeping* for a long time now, and nothing ever woke me at all. But now you woke me up."

did not hear. Since on Rosh Hashanah the power of the imagination is strong (*Chokhmah U'Tevunah* 6; *Likutey Moharan* 54).

mountain. In the key psalm, "With my voice I call out to God, and He answers me from His holy mountain" (Psalms 3:5). After the king calls "help! help!," the mountain answers.

Obviously, the mountain denotes deep mysteries (*Rimzey Maasioth*). It also denotes the mountain upon which the Temple was built. Even after the Temple was destroyed, the mountain was a place from which prayers could be answered, as the Midrash says on the verse, "He answers me from His holy mountain" (*Midrash Psalms, Shemoth Rabbah* 2:2; *Zimrath HaAretz*).

As we saw earlier, the "spider" in "the king's house" denoted that Edom wanted to destroy the Temple (*Shochar Tov*). Here too the nations want to destroy the Temple, represented by the mountain. In a number of places, Rabbi Nachman taught that a mountain represented the Temple (*Likutey Moharan* 10:3, 15:6). For the nations, destroying the Temple represented destroying the Jewish people as well.

Rabbi Nachman also taught that a mountain denotes greatness (*Likutey Moharan* 58:9). This means that the enemies wanted to take away the king's stature.

Rabbi Nachman also taught that a mountain represents intelligence (Daath) which is also an aspect of the Temple (*Likutey Moharan* 81). Thus, the attack on the mountain can represent the cutting off of the head in the portrait.

The Hebrew word for mountain is *har* (הר), which is related to the word for pregnancy (*harah*, הרה) (see *Yerioth Shlomo*). Hence, mountains are often seen as the Patriarchs, or one's ancestors (*Rosh HaShanah* 11a; *Makkoth* 24b; *Bereshith Rabbah* 68; see Psalms 121:1). Therefore, the mountain here may denote the merit of Rabbi Nachman's ancestors, especially the Baal Shem Tov. This is what may have defeated the Shpoler, as we shall see.

It is also taught that "mountain" denotes the Messiah (*Tanchuma, Toledoth* 14). It is thus written, "Who are you O great mountain before Zerubbabel?" (Zechariah 4:7).

Note that "fly," "king" and "mountain" are all the same. Each time he gets larger with respect to his enemies.

I have been sleeping... The mountain's sleep seems to parallel the king's sleep. The king is now sleeping. Thus the mountain may be speaking in the key psalm, "I lay down and sleep, and I awaken, for God sustains me. I am not afraid of myriads of people who have set themselves around me... Arise God... You have broken the teeth of the wicked" (Psalms 3:6-8).

"How can I not scream?" replied [the king]. "People are attacking me to kill me. The only thing protecting me is this page."

"If this page is protecting you," replied the mountain, "then you have nothing to fear. I also have many enemies attacking me, and this page alone protects me.* Come, I will show you."

[The mountain] showed [the king] that thousands and myriads of enemies stood around it.* They were making feasts and celebrations, playing musical instruments and dancing. The reason for this celebration was that one group had devised a clever plan how to climb the mountain,* and they were celebrating it with feast and song....

"This is true whenever any of these groups [devise such a plan," explained the mountain]. "The only thing that protects me is this same page of customs that protects you."

At the top of this mountain there was a tablet.* On it were written the same customs that were on the page that protected him, as well as the nation to which it pertained. However, since the mountain was so tall, it was impossible to read the script.*

At the bottom of the mountain, there was [another] tablet. Written on it were the words, "Only one who has all his teeth* can climb the mountain."

---

this page alone protects me: So the page protects the fly, the king, and now the mountain. However, later we see that the grass is protecting the mountain, so it must be related to the page.

thousands and myriads of enemies stood around it. "I am not afraid of myriads of people who have set themselves around me" (Psalms 3:7).

to climb the mountain. Nevertheless, the mountain slept as usual during this.

tablet. This may represent the tablets that were in the ark in the Holy of Holies of the Temple, which is represented by the mountain here. It may also pertain to the teachings of the Baal Shem Tov, which no one could understand.

it was impossible to read the script. It is impossible to understand the Torah of a tzaddik from a previous generation.

teeth. Which are later broken (see Psalms 3:8). See below.

It is thus written, "Who shall ascend to God's mountain... He who has a pure heart" (Psalms 24:4). The Hebrew word for heart here is *levav* (לבב), which can be read as *be-lamed beth* (בל"ב), that is, "with 32." One can only climb the mountain if one has all 32 teeth (*Chokhmah U'Tevunah* 6).

However, God had arranged things so that a certain type of grass* grew on the approach where one could climb the grass* grew on the approach where one must climb the This would happen whether one went by foot, rode, or went in a wagon drawn by animals; all his teeth would fall out. Piles of teeth lay there, like mountains.

In general, a person has 32 teeth, and these parallel the 32 paths of wisdom (Raavad on *Sefer Yetzirah* 1:1). Thus, one can overcome the teachings of the mountain only if one has full wisdom.

The 32 paths of wisdom also spell out *lev*, denoting heart. Also *"lamed"* is the last letter of the Torah, and *"beth"* is the first letter; thus, *"lamed beth."* Only one who has the entire Torah at his grasp can climb the mountain.

The teeth also represent Netzach and Hod, the source of prophecy (*Maaver Ya'avak* 2:20, p. 79a).

grass. It is taught that just as a mountain grows grass, so the righteous have good deeds (*Vayikra Rabbah* 17).

Grass may denote humility, as in the case of the Cripple (Story #3, p. 84), who eats grass. The humility of the tzaddik takes away the weapons of his enemies.

would lose all his teeth. This is in the key psalm, "Arise O God,... You have struck all my enemies on the cheek, You have broken the teeth of the wicked" (Psalms 3:8).

The *Zohar* relates this verse to Esau (*Zohar* 1:171b). It is said that when Esau met Jacob after his return from Laban (Genesis 33:4), Esau bit him in the neck, but God hardened Jacob's neck so that Esau's teeth broke (*Bereshith Rabbah* 78:9). Thus, the destruction of the spider and the breaking of the teeth are both the same concept.

This may also relate to the opposition to the Baal Shem Tov or of rabbis to the chassidic tzaddikim in general. Those who opposed him lost their complete wisdom (teeth), and therefore could not "chew" their lesson and make them readily understood.

There is a Breslover tradition that this pertains particularly to the Shpoler Zeida. Rabbi Nachman said that he was not afraid of the Shpoler since he knew that the Shpoler had lost all his teeth.

Once Rabbi Nachman was with the Shpoler. The Shpoler was rationalizing his opposition, saying that he really did not want to make a fight, since how could an old man like him, who no longer had teeth, really fight? He then took Rabbi Nachman's finger and placed it in his mouth, to show him that he did not have any teeth (*Rimzey Maasioth*).

The Shpoler Zeida's name was Rabbi Leib or Leibish, which means lion. A lion without teeth is not particularly dangerous. Thus, "The lion roars, the fierce lion howls, but the lion's teeth are broken" (Job 4:10; also see Joel 1:6).

Also, "Break their teeth in their mouths, O God, break out the teeth of the young lions" (Psalms 58:7).

It is written, "Many thoughts are in the heart of man, but God's counsel will stand (Proverbs 19:21). "The heart of man" in Hebrew is *lev ish* (לב איש), which Rabbi Nachman

Then the people* [who had come out of the diamond] took the portrait, put it together, and restored the portrait* as it was originally. Then they took the crown and washed it off. They hung [both the portrait and the crown] in their proper places.

With that, the king woke up.*

He immediately looked at the page that had protected him to see which nation's customs it contained. He saw that it had the customs of Israel written on it. He began to look [at the page] in a sincere manner* and he understood the real truth.*

He made up his mind that he would have to become an Israelite.* However, he also wanted to know what could be done to return everyone to goodness and bring them to truth.*

---

punned to make Leibish, the Shpoler's name. The verse would then say, "There are many thoughts in Leibish..." This may denote the many plans that the enemies made against the mountain (see *Chokhmah U'Tevunah* 10).

But the words *lev ish* can also denote the 32 teeth of a person. Leibish is only dangerous when he is a man of 32 — with all 32 teeth. Now that his teeth are gone, "God's counsel will stand." This is God's plan to put the grass on the mountain to make teeth come out.

The teeth indicate wisdom, as above ("wisdom teeth"). The people from the diamond wanted to take away his wisdom by cutting the head off the portrait. In return, they had their teeth, which represent their wisdom, taken away.

people. After the mountain showed him that his enemies could not hurt him, the king's enemies no longer opposed him. This is very much like the case of the giants, who try to discourage the viceroy (in Story #1), but after they cannot do so, they help him.

Also, from the mountain he learns that the enemies are really helpless against him. They only have power because he thinks they do. Once he is reassured, they do not have any power. It is again like Story #1, where the viceroy sees the soldiers around the first palace, but when he decides to walk past them, they do not stop him.

restored the portrait. "But You, God, are a shield around me, my glory and the one who lifts my head" (Psalms 3:4). The "one who lifts my head" denotes lifting up the decapitated head from the portrait. "My glory" may indicate the restoration of the crown.

Once Israel realizes that their enemies really cannot harm them, the world will be rectified.

woke up. "and I will awaken" (Psalms 3:6). "For God will support me."

sincere manner. Literally, "way of truth."

real truth. He understood the true meaning of the Torah.

to become an Israelite. As mentioned above, this seems to indicate that the king was a gentile. Also, we see from this the fact that his people made fun of Jewish customs. However, in the parable, it may mean that he would want to become a true Jew.

to goodness and truth. Rabbi Nachman thus interpreted the verse in the key psalm, which

[The king] made up his mind that he would travel* about to find a wise man who would be able to interpret his dream* accurately. He took along two men,* and began traveling around the world. He did not go as a king, but as a simple person.* He went from city to city, from country to country, asking, "Where is there a wise man who can accurately interpret a dream?" Finally he was told where he could find such a wise man.

[The king] journeyed there and came to the sage. He revealed that he was actually a king who had won many battles and then related the entire story. He asked [the sage] to interpret the dream.

---

literally can be translated, "O God, how many are my enemies many stand up through me" (Psalms 3:2) to indicate that when a person has many adversaries and much suffering, then he can eventually bring many people to "stand up through him." That is, he can bring many people to recognize the truth (*Likutey Moharan* 170).

he would travel. This is the mystery of Rabbi Nachman's journey to Navritch.

Rabbi Nathan ties this in with the concept that all of Israel's journeys are because of a lack of faith. People must travel from place to place because they do not have faith in sages and saints, just as the Israelites traveled through the desert because they didn't have faith in Moses. Through traveling, one can repent, and can then uplift the place to which he comes (*Likutey Halakhoth, Choshen Mishpat, Pikadon* 5:19, see *Likutey Moharan* 40).

Here, too, the king saw that the people from the diamond were only able to attack him because he lacked faith. When his faith was restored by the mountain, these same people became his friends. Because of his lack of faith, he had to take a journey.

to interpret his dream. Just as Pharaoh had to have his dream interpreted (Genesis 41:8; *Chokhmah U'Tevunah* 6). This also happened on Rosh HaShanah (*Ibid.*).

Before the king could rectify the world, the dream would have to be interpreted. As long as it remains in the realm of the imagination, it cannot give him the power and confidence to fulfill his task (*Chokhmah U'Tevunah* 6, and 8).

This is also related to the verse, "Many thoughts are in the heart of man, (*lev ish*), but God's counsel will stand" (Proverbs 19:21). Therefore, the king wanted to go and find God's counsel and advice (*Chokhmah U'Tevunah* 10).

two men. See note at the beginning of the story. The two men that Rabbi Nachman took on his journey were R. Shmuel of Teplik and R. Isaac Yosef of Lipovetz (*Chokhmah U'Tevunah* 2). When Abraham went to the mountain to sacrifice Isaac, he also took two men (Genesis 22:3; see Rashi *ad loc*; also *Bereshith Rabbah* 55).

simple person. On his trip to Navritch, Rabbi Nachman did not go as a rabbi, but like a common merchant (see beginning of story). A rabbi is a king, as our sages teach, "Who are kings? the rabbis" (*Gittin* 62a).

"I myself cannot interpret it," replied [the sage]. "But there is a certain time, on a certain day of a certain month,* when I gather together all the incense* fragrances, and I blend them into a mixture. I allow a person to inhale the smoke of these incenses. The person thinks of what he wants to see and know, and then he knows everything."

The king decided that since he had spent so much time already on his quest, he would wait a while longer until that day and month. [When the time came,] the sage did as he had described, and he had [the king] inhale the smoke of the fragrant incense.

The king began to see even what had happened to him before he was born, when he was a soul in the upper universe. He saw that his soul was being led through all the [spiritual] worlds, and an announcement* was being made, asking that anyone who had anything to say against this soul should come forth. No one had anything to say against him.*

Suddenly, someone came running and screaming, "Lord of the Universe! Listen to my petition! If this soul comes to the world, I will not have anything more to do. For what did You create me?"*

---

day of a certain month. Perhaps Purim, since this is when Rabbi Nachman was in Navritch. Purim represents the time of overcoming the *klipah* of Amalek, which is done through eleven spices of incense *(Likutey Moharan*, see above).

incense. Incense has the power to break the power of the *klipoth* (see Story #2; *Chokhmah U'Tevunah* 9). Once one breaks the *klipoth*, one can see into one's soul, and know the complete truth. The main day that incense was burned in the Holy of Holies was Yom Kippur. This is Yom HaKippurim, which is interpreted to be "Yom, the day which is like Purim." Hence the main time for this is Purim.

announcement. In general, such an announcement is made whenever a great tzaddik is about to be born *(Likutey Etzoth B, Tzaddik* 85).

No one had... The *Tikkuney Zohar* gives an example of a king who had a trusted messenger, whom he wanted to put in charge of his nation. But first he wanted to make sure that no one would oppose him, so he said, "Let us make man..." (Genesis 1:26). *(Tikkuney Zohar* 70, 137b; *Rimzey Maasioth).*

   In general, the tzaddik is the one whom God puts in charge of His world.

For what did You create me? The Baal Shem Tov similarly taught that before a great tzaddik is to be born, the Evil One argues, "This tzaddik will bring everyone to repent. Therefore, why did You create me?" *(Toledoth Yaakov Yosef, Shoftim* 184b).

[The one who was screaming] was the Evil One* himself. He was answered, "This soul must certainly go down to the world. You must devise your own plan."

[The Evil One] left. The soul was then led further through the [spiritual] worlds, until it was brought to the Tribunal on high so that it could be bound by an oath* in order to be born into the world.

Meanwhile, [the Evil One] had not returned. A messenger was sent to fetch him, and he finally came. [The Evil One] brought with him an old man,* who was bent over like the very aged. He was acquainted [with this old man] from previous experiences.* [The Evil One] laughed and said, "I have already devised a plan. [The soul] can go down into the world."

The soul was then released, and it went down to the world.

[The king] then saw everything that happened to him, from the beginning to the end. [He saw] how he had become king and fought many wars.

(He took prisoners, and among them was a beautiful

---

the Evil One... Identified here as Samael, or "the *samekh mem*."

bound by an oath. The oath that a person must take before birth. Before a soul is born, it is bound by an oath, "Be a righteous person, and not wicked. Even if the entire world says to you that you are righteous, consider yourself wicked" (*Niddah* 30b).

old man. The soul of the tzaddik is the concept of Moses, and hence, the "old man" is the concept of Korach, which denotes old age (see Rashi on Leviticus 13:55; *Rimzey Maasioth*).

It also may denote the "old and foolish king" (Ecclesiastes 4:13), who is the incarnation of evil (see Story #2).

Commenting on the verse, "For what vanity have you created the sons of man" (Psalms 89:48), the Baal Shem Tov taught that Moses was destined to perform many miracles, so the Evil One complained that people would never be foolish enough to sin and take the Evil One's advice. Therefore, an evil person had to be sent down who would appear to be a tzaddik, and this person would be able to trick people (*Toledoth Yaakov Yosef, Shoftim,* 184b; *Rimzey Maasioth*).

It is thus taught that whenever a great tzaddik is to be born, the Evil One produces a famous person who will oppose him and hide his light (*Likutey Etzoth* B, 85).

It is assumed that this old man was the Shpoler. Thus, when Rabbi Nachman's dispute with the Shpoler began, he said, "I knew that the Evil One would stand up against me. But I am very surprised that he placed this in the hand of [the Shpoler]" (*Chayay Moharan* 29b #21).

previous experiences. Since incarnations of this "old man" were opposed to tzaddikim in previous generations.

woman,* who had every possible type of grace.* However, the grace was not hers intrinsically, but came because of a diamond* that she wore as a pendant. This diamond had every type of grace, and because of it, it seemed as if she had all types of grace.)

(Only those who were wise and wealthy could climb the mountain*....)

([Rabbi Nachman] did not tell any more than this,) but there is very much more.

(The section from, "He took prisoners," to the end was not written exactly as he told it.)

beautiful woman. In another place, Rabbi Nathan said that this woman had children (*Chayay Moharan* 35b #10).

The captives, and especially the woman, represent the side of good taking back what evil has swallowed up (*Chokhmah U'Tevunah* 12). This is the concept of, "He swallows up wealth, but he shall vomit it up" (Job 20:15).

In Hebrew, the "beautiful girl" here is a *yefath toar*. This is usually used to denote a captive taken in accordance with the Torah's strictures (Deuteronomy 21:11). She is taken from gentile captives.

The Talmud states that King David married such a gentile captive girl (*Sanhedrin* 21a). It was from her that his son Absalom was born. This is significant, because the key psalm begins, "A Psalm of David when he fled before Absalom his son" (3:1). We find that Absalom rebelled against David and wanted to usurp his throne (*Chokhmah U'Tevunah* 46, 12; see *Likutey Moharan* 54).

grace. *Chen* in Hebrew (also used in the Yiddish). Rabbi Nachman taught that *chen* (חן) comes from a conjunction of Wisdom (of Zer Anpin) and Malkhuth, the sun and the moon (*Likutey Moharan* 1). This is the proper paradigm of the relationship of a man and woman.

However, there is also false *chen*, as it is written, "False is *chen*, and vain is beauty" (Proverbs 31:30). When the *chen* is intrinsic to the person it is true, but when it is outside only, it can be false.

diamond. This is the diamond discussed earlier in the story. Rabbi Nachman taught that precious stones represent an aspect of *tzimtzum* (constriction) (see The Prince of Jewels). The *chen* here was not spiritual, or even from flesh and blood, but from a cold, hard stone.

This may be related to the teaching that Abraham had a daughter as well as a precious stone that hung as a pendant (*Bava Bathra* 16b). If so, it may be related to Story #1, which also has this theme.

could climb the mountain. Therefore, this mountain may be related to the golden mountain in Story #1.

"A Psalm of David when he fled.... God, how many are my enemies, many rise up against me. But You God are a Shield to me, my glory and the One who lifts my head" (Psalm 3:1-4). Translate the entire psalm, and understand it well, and you will see that it alludes to this entire story. *

this entire story.

The following material is found at the end of the story;

"A Psalm of David when he fled... God, how many are my enemies. Many rise up against me.. but You, God, are a shield for me. My glory and the one who lifts up my head. With my voice I call out to God, and He answers me from His holy mountain" (Psalms 3:1-5). The mountain is that mentioned above.

"I lay down and sleep" (Psalms 3:6) as mentioned above, and "I awaken... I am not afraid of myriads of people... for You have struck all my enemies on the cheek, You have broken the teeth of the wicked" (Psalms 3:6-8). Their teeth fell out when they wanted to climb the mountain.

"Your blessing is upon Your people selah" (Psalms 3:9).

"Stand up and contemplate these wonders if you are a master of your soul, you will lift up your flesh in your teeth, and your soul you will place in your hands. You will stand trembling and astounded. The hairs of your head will stand on end and you will return amazed at these words which stand in the highest places."

8

THE RABBI'S SON*

Once there was a rabbi who did not have any children. Finally, he had an only son. He raised him and married him off.

[The son] would sit in an upstairs room and study, as was customary with the wealthy. He would constantly study and pray. However, he felt that something was lacking, although he did not know what. Somehow, he did not feel any inspiration* in his study or prayer. When he confided this to two of his friends, they advised that he visit a certain tzaddik.

This young man had done a good deed* that had caused him to become an aspect of the Lesser Light.*

The only son told his father that he did not feel any inspiration in his religious devotion. Since he felt a lack and did not know what it was, he wanted to visit this tzaddik.*

The Rabbi's Son. This story was told during the week of August 1, 1807, soon after the previous story. The next week, Rabbi Nachman traveled to Tchehrin and Medvedevka, in the eastern Ukraine (*Yemey Moharnat* 20b; *Chayay Moharan* 15b).

The theme of this story is how the Evil One tries to prevent a person from traveling to a true tzaddik (*Rimzey Maasioth*). It also shows the dangers of trying to be too sophisticated, and thus shares the theme of the next story. This is the last of the short stories. The following ones are much longer and more complex.

inspiration. Literally "taste."

good deed. He did not gain this through his intense learning or family, but because he did an act of virtue. Everything depends on what one does (*Rimzey Maasioth*).

the Lesser Light. This is the moon, as the Torah says explicitly (Genesis 1:16). Kabbalistically, it is Malkhuth, which is the power to receive, the vessel. Since the son had now become a vessel, he felt that he was empty, and lacked something.

Rabbi Nachman taught that the small light is an aspect of faith (*Likutey Moharan* 35:5). The son got a tremendous new ability to have faith, and therefore, he needed a tzaddik, as an object of his faith.

this tzaddik. It is thus taught that if a person does not feel any enthusiasm and inspiration

"Why should you go to him?"* replied the father. "You are a more accomplished scholar than he is. Your family background is better than his. It is not at all fitting that you go to him. Give up this idea."* [The father] continued in this manner until he stopped [his son] from going.

[The young man] returned to his studies, but he felt this lack again. This time he also sought advice from his two friends, and again they advised him to visit this tzaddik. Again he went to his father, and his father dissuaded him and prevented him from going. This happened a number of times.

The son continued to feel this lack, and he had a great yearning to fill it, not knowing what it was. This time he came to his father and kept on urging him until his father was forced to go with him. He did not want [his son] to travel alone, since he was an only son.

"See!" said the father. "I'm even going with you! I will show you that there is nothing to this tzaddik." With that, they harnessed the carriage and set off.

"I will make a test,"* declared the father. "If everything goes smoothly, then it is from Heaven. If not, then it is not from Heaven, and we will return home."

in his worship and religious practice, he should visit a tzaddik (*Likutey Etzoth* B, *Tzaddik* 86). No matter how much spiritual progress a person has made on his own, he needs the help of another to perfect himself. It is thus taught, "A prisoner cannot free himself from the dungeon" (*Berakhoth* 5b).

Why should you... A main lesson of this story is how important it is to avoid pride. It was primarily because of the father's pride that he was opposed to his son's going to the tzaddik. This caused him to lose his son in the end.

Give up... Literally, "Get yourself away from this path."

Let us make a test. The father wanted to demonstrate his righteousness. However, this teaches that it is dangerous to make such tests, since the Evil One can intervene. If a person knows that something is right, he should not let any sign or portent dissuade him (see *Rimzey Maasioth*).

Moreover, according to many authorities, it is actually forbidden to make such a test, since it touches upon superstition. In the Torah, we find that Abraham's servant, Eliezer, made a test when he met Rebecca. He said that if a girl offers to draw water, it should be a sign that God had sent her (Genesis 24:14; see *Taanith* 4a; *Bereshith Rabbah* 60)). However,

They continued traveling until they came to a small bridge. One horse slipped and the carriage turned over, so that they almost drowned.

"See," said the father. "Things did not go smoothly. This journey is not [approved] by Heaven." With that, they returned home.

The son returned to his studies. Again, he recognized something missing in himself, even though he could not pinpoint exactly what it was. He urged his father, and his father went with him again. While they were traveling, his father made a test as he had done the first time, that if everything went smoothly, [they would know that it was God's will].

As they were proceeding, both of the carriage's axles broke.

His father said, "See! We are being directed not to continue! Is it natural for both axles to break at the same time? We have ridden in this carriage many times before, and nothing like this has ever happened." Again they returned home.

The son went back to his old study habits, but he felt the same lack again. His friends advised him to make the pilgrimage. He went to his father and urged him as before, and he had to go with him again.

The son said that they should not make a test as before. It was natural that a horse should occasionally fall, or that an axle should break. This time, they would continue unless the sign was very obvious.

They traveled until they came to an inn to rest. They encountered a merchant.* They began to converse with him as merchants do, not telling him where they were going. The rabbi was ashamed* to admit that he was going to this tzaddik.*

---

many authorities maintain that he did wrongly, and that such a test is forbidden (*Yoreh Deah* 179:4 in *Hagah*).

merchant. The Evil One, as we shall see. See Story #2.

was ashamed. When a person is ashamed that he is doing something good, it gives the Evil One an opportunity to trap him. This is the first step in being trapped by evil (*Rimzey Maasioth*).

tzaddik. "*Guter Yid*" (good Jew) in the Yiddish.

They continued to discuss wordly affairs,* until the conversation began to touch upon tzaddikim, and where they can be found. [The merchant] told [the rabbi] about a tzaddik in a certain place, and others elsewhere and they began to discuss the tzaddik to whom they were traveling.

"Him? But he is worthless!"* said [the merchant]. "I am coming from him now. I was there when he committed a sin!"

"My son," said the rabbi. "Don't you see what this merchant is telling us* in all innocence?* And he has just come from there!"

With that, they went home.* Soon afterward, the son died.* Then he came to his father, the rabbi, in a dream, appearing in great anger.

[His father] asked him why he was so angry.

"Go to the tzaddik [that I wanted to visit,]" replied [the son], "and he will tell you why I am angry."

When [the father] woke up, he said, "It was merely a chance occurrence."* When he had the same dream again, he still said

---

worldly affairs. They did not speak of Torah. They could not, since Torah is the main weapon against the Evil One. Even though the rabbi prided himself on his learning, now he did not speak of Torah.

worthless. *Kal* in Hebrew. Here we see the power of slander. It is thus written, "Let the lying lips be speechless, since they speak arrogantly against the tzaddik, with pride and contempt" (Psalms 31:19; *Rimzey Maasioth*). This is the main power that the Evil One has against the tzaddik (*Likutey Etzoth* B, *Tzaddik* 86).

is telling us. The father now had committed another sin in listening to malicious speech (*lashon hara*). Not only was the Evil One keeping him from the tzaddik, but he was also causing him to sin. Malicious speech is considered among the very worst of all sins (see *Erchin* 15b; *Yad, Deayoth* 7:3).

in all innocence. *Lefi tumo* in Hebrew. But they did not consider that he might have had an ulterior motive or might have been an opponent of the tzaddik (*Rimzey Maasioth*).

they went home. Although they had overcome the physical barriers, such as the falling of the horse and the breaking of the axles, they could not overcome the mental barriers (*Rimzey Maasioth*).

son died. The Evil One blemished his faith with his slander. Now he was not a perfect vessel of faith, as he had been originally. The son was therefore no longer an aspect of the Lesser Light. Therefore, he could no longer fulfill his mission, and he died.

chance occurrence. The father was not willing to dismiss the falling of the horse or the that it was a meaningless dream. However, when this happened a third time, he realized that it was significant, so he set out [toward the ·tzaddik].

On the way, he met the merchant whom he had encountered while traveling with his son. He recognized him, and said, "Aren't you the one I met in the inn?"

"You certainly did see me," replied the other. Then he opened his mouth and said, "If you want,* I will swallow* you!"

"What are you saying?" asked [the rabbi].

"Do you remember," replied the merchant, "when you were traveling with your son? First the horse slipped on the bridge and you turned back. Then the axles broke. Finally you met me and I told you that the [tzaddik] was worthless. Since I put your son aside, you may now make the journey.

"[Your son] was an aspect of the Lesser Light. The tzaddik was an aspect of the Great Light.* If the two had come together, the Messiah would have come. But now that I caused him to die, you may make the pilgrimage."

---

breaking of the axles as chance occurrences, but he was now willing to dismiss this dream. When a person is prejudiced, it does not bother him when his thoughts are self-contradictory.

If you want. The Evil One can only destroy a person if a person wants to let him. Ultimately the person himself has free choice whether or not to allow himself to be destroyed (*Rimzey Maasioth*).

swallow you. See Story #3, where the demon threatens to swallow the wise man.

It is thus written, "A wicked person can swallow up one who is more righteous than he" (Habakkuk 1:13). The Talmud comments, however, that if a person is totally righteous, then evil cannot swallow him up (*Berakhoth* 7b; *Bava Metzia* 71a; *Megillah* 6b; *Rimzey Maasioth*). This was a sign that the rabbi was not perfectly righteous.

When a person is depressed, evil has all the more power over him. Now that the rabbi was discouraged because of his son's death, he was in even more spiritual danger (*Rimzey Maasioth*).

Great Light. The sun (Genesis 1:16). In every generation there is one tzaddik who is an aspect of the Great Light (the sun), and another who is an aspect of the Lesser Light (the moon). Thus, the Baal Shem Tov says that if he had come together with Rabbi Chaim ibn Atar (author of *Or HaChaim*), they could have brought the Messiah.

This was the meeting of Moses and Joshua, as our sages teach, "Moses' face was like the sun, while Joshua's face was like the moon" (*Bava Bathra* 75a).

While speaking, [the merchant] vanished. [The rabbi] did not have anyone* with whom to speak.

When [the rabbi] finally got to the tzaddik, he screamed, "Woe! Woe!* Woe is to those who are lost and can no longer be found!"*

May God return our lost ones. Amen.

The merchant in this story was the Evil One* himself. He had disguised himself as a merchant in order to fool [the rabbi]. When he met [the rabbi] a second time, he tormented him for taking his advice. This is his way, as is known.* May God only protect us!

---

did not have anyone... The Evil One opens his hand in the end, and it is empty (*Sichoth HaRan* 6).

Woe! Woe! *Chaval chaval* in Hebrew; *gevalt gevalt* in Yiddish.

woe is to those who are lost... See Rashi on *VaEra* (Exodus 6:9).

Evil One. Samael.

as is known. The Yiddish adds, "For he urges on the person, but if the person follows him, heaven forbid, he himself provokes and punishes the person for listening to him." It is taught, "The Evil Urge, the Satan and the Angel of Death are all the same" (*Bava Bathra* 16a).

9

THE SOPHISTICATE AND THE SIMPLETON*

There were once two homeowners* who lived in the same city. They were very, very wealthy,* and they had large mansions.* Each one had one son, both of whom studied in the same school. *

The Sophisticate... This is the ninth story. However, some sources list it as the eighth story (*Chayay Moharan* 15c).

This story was told before Purim, during the winter of 1809 (*Chayay Moharan* 15c #59, 15d #1). Over a year had passed since the last story was told. Meanwhile, Rabbi Nachman had spent eight months in Lemberg (Lvov) from the fall of 1807 until the summer of 1808. During this period, his first work, *Likutey Moharan*, had also been published, shortly before Rosh HaShanah of 1808.

This story is unique insofar that it can be understood in its most simple sense from the beginning to the end (*Chokhmah U'Tevunah* 1). Perhaps this is most fitting, since the hero of the story is the Simpleton, who took everything at face value, without probing beneath the surface.

homeowners. *Baaley batim* in Hebrew and Yiddish. In the literal sense, *baaley batim* means "masters of homes," or homeowners, or householders. In a more general sense, however, a *baal habayith* (in the singular) is a substantial citizen.

As we shall see the houses denote faith. Therefore, the *baaley batim* may denote people who had mastered the faith.

wealthy. "Who is wealthy? He who is satisfied with his lot" (*Avoth* 4:1). Since they were "masters of faith," they were automatically wealthy. This also denotes wealth in Torah knowledge.

mansions. The mansions or houses denote faith (*Likutey Etzoth* B, *Temimuth* 5). It is thus written, "[God] remembers His love and faith to the *house* of Israel" (Psalms 98:3; see *Likutey Moharan* 94).

same school. *Cheder* in text. The Talmud refers to the womb of a woman as a *cheder* (*Niddah* 17b). Elsewhere, the Talmud teaches, "When a child is in the mother's womb he learns the entire Torah" (*Niddah* 30b). In this sense, Jacob and Esau "went to the same school," because they were twins who grew in the womb together (Genesis 25:22). Until they were fifteen years of age, they were together. After Abraham's passing, Esau "went out" (cf. *Bava Bathra* 16) (Rabbi Nachman Burstyn).

One of these sons had deep understanding and was quite sophisticated.* The other one was simple;* he was not lacking in intelligence, but had a straightforward, humble approach, without any sophistication.

sophisticated. In the Hebrew, it merely says, "He was a master of understanding (*bar havanah*)," while the Yiddish says "he was a *chakham.*" Throughout the story, this son is referred to as the Chakham, which we translate as the Sophisticate.

Of course, wisdom is usually considered a positive trait. However, wisdom must always be accompanied by humility and piety. Thus, the sages of the Talmud referred to themselves by the term *talmid chakham* which means "a student of the wise." The Sophisticate in this story, on the other hand, was arrogant and skeptical. He would let his curiosity get the better of him; he was never satisfied with the surface meaning of things, but always probed and analyzed to find the "true" meaning. This often led him to conclusions that were totally wrong.

Rabbi Nachman had contact with *maskilim* in Lemberg. The Sophisticate is the archetype of the *maskil* who left tradition to seek worldly sophistication.

The main path to true wisdom, on the other hand, is reverence for God. It is thus written, "Behold the fear of God; that is what wisdom is" (Job 28:28). It is thus taught, "If a person's wisdom is greater than his good deeds, then he is like a tree with more branches than roots; even the slightest breeze can blow it down" (*Avoth* 3:17; *Likutey Moharan Tinyana* 5:15; *Likutey Halakhoth, Tefillah* 4:9). This is even true of Torah wisdom; without fear and reverence of God, it can sometimes be more harmful than good (see *Likutey Moharan Tinyana* 5:18; also see *Shabbath* 31a).

One of the problems with wisdom is its great light. Rabbi Nachman taught that wisdom is like the sea (*Likutey Moharan* 5:4). The sea might have curative powers, but if one does not learn how to swim properly, and goes in too deep, he can drown (*Chokhmah U'Tevunah* 1).

Rabbi Nachman taught that such sophistication is associated with Amalek (end of story in Hebrew; *Likutey Moharan Tinyana* 19: *Rimzey Maasioth*). Amalek was the nation that attacked the Israelites just before they received the Torah (Exodus 17:10), and is the subject of God's wrath for all time (Deuteronomy 25:17). This nation is seen as evil incarnate.

However, Amalek was a direct descendant of Esau (Genesis 36:12). Esau was the opposite of his brother Jacob, whom the Torah describes as a *tam* (Genesis 25:25), the very word Rabbi Nachman uses here for the Simpleton (*Chokhmah U'Tevunah* 2).

The Torah also describes the serpent as being clever and subtle (Genesis 3:1). He made Eve go beneath the simple meaning of God's commandment, telling her that she could become Godlike if she disobeyed the commandment (Genesis 3:5). Therefore, the root of such sophistication and subtlety is the serpent.

It is significant that the first example of Amalek is Haman. The Talmud teaches that the name Haman (המן) is alluded to in the words, "Is it true that from the tree that I commanded you, 'do not eat from it' you ate?" (Genesis 3:11). In Hebrew, the expression, "Is it true that from" is *ha-min* (הֲמִן), which can also be read as Haman (הָמָן) (*Chullin* 139b). Rashi comments on this, "If the master says something, and the student says something, to whom must one listen?"

Here God was refuting the sophistication of the serpent, who was later embodied in Amalek and Haman. He was saying that one must obey His commandments simply and literally, without looking for any deeper hidden meanings and motivations.

Among the religious too there are those who are wise in the sense that they take on a heavy burden of extra-strict practices. This leaves them devitalized and unhappy (*Likutey Moharan Tinyana*, 44).

simple. The term *tam* is used in both the Hebrew and the Yiddish. This does not mean that this son lacked intelligence, but that he was without guile, and shunned casuistry and roundabout reasoning. He always accepted things at their face value.

Rabbi Nachman taught that the main goal of a Jew was to serve God with simplicity and without sophistication (*Likutey Moharan Tinyana* 19; see *Likutey Moharan* 123). He taught that it is better to be so unsophisticated as to believe false superstitions, than to be sophisticated and deny important beliefs (*Sichoth HaRan* 103). Simplicity can be the greatest wisdom (*Rimzey Maasioth*).

The paradigm of the simple man is Jacob, whom the Torah explicitly refers to as a *tam* (Genesis 25:27). Israel as a whole is also called by God, "My dove, My simple one" (Song of Songs 5:2, 6:9). God told us that we should "be simple with God your Lord" (Deuteronomy 18:13; *Zimrath HaAretz*).

The word *tamim*, as used in the Torah, can thus denote this trait of simplicity. Thus, Noah was called, "a simple righteous man" (Genesis 6:9). Also God told Abraham, "walk before Me and be simple" (Genesis 17:1). The word has the connotation of completeness, but completeness may also denote simplicity. Rabbi Nachman thus taught that simplicity is the highest possible trait, since God is higher than everything, and God is ultimately simple (*Sichoth HaRan* 101). It is thus written that, "God's task is simplicity" (Deuteronomy 32:4; see *Oneg Shabbath*, p. 37).

The *chakham* and the *tam* are two of the four sons mentioned in the Haggadah. Here we see that the *tam* is not unintelligent, but simple and straightforward. Thus, his question is "What is this?" It is not a foolish question, but an unsophisticated and extremely straightforward question. The answer given to him is also simple, "With a strong hand God brought us out of Egypt" (Exodus 13:14).

Actually, this is very closely related to Rabbi Nachman's teaching that the goal of wisdom and knowledge is to realize one's lack of knowledge and understanding (*Sichoth HaRan* 3). This is obvious, since God is ultimately beyond all understanding. The highest perception of God is seen as Nothingness (*Ayin*), since the human mind cannot perceive or understand or grasp anything at all at this level. However, the level of Nothingness is also the level of God's ultimate simplicity. In this deeper sense, then, simplicity is also much higher than wisdom.

Rabbi Nachman also spoke at length of the greatness of simplicity in all walks of life (see *Likutey Moharan Tinyana* 78; *Sichoth HaRan* 153).

These two sons loved each other very much, even though one was sophisticated, while the other was simple, with a very humble mind. Nevertheless, they loved each other very much.

In the course of time, the two homeowners began to decline. They went lower and lower until they lost everything and became poor.* The only thing they managed to keep was their mansions.*

Meanwhile the sons were beginning to get older, so their fathers said to them, "We do not have the means to support you. Do whatever you will be able to."

The Simpleton went and learned the trade of a shoemaker.*

The Sophisticate, however, felt that he had deep understanding, and did not want to occupy himself with such simple work. He made up his mind that he would go out into the

---

poor. The poverty of Torah and observance in Rabbi Nachman's generation. It thus refers to the decline of traditional Judaism that was occurring at the time.

keep was their mansions. No matter how spiritually poor a man becomes, he should not give up his faith.

shoemaker. A shoemaker is usually seen as the lowliest of occupations. Shoes are considered something unclean, so much so, that the law requires that one wash one's hands after touching them (*Orach Chaim* 4:18).

On the other hand, there were great people who were shoemakers. One of the great masters of the Talmud was Rabbi Yochanan HaSandler, literally, "Rabbi Yochanan the Shoemaker."

The Talmud also teaches, "A person should sell the beams of his house (faith) and buy shoes for his feet" (*Shabbath* 129a). As we saw in the third story, the forces of evil have the power to gain nourishment from the feet of the moon (see above, p. 88), which also denotes faith and Malkhuth. It is thus written, "Her feet go down to death" (Proverbs 5:5). The concept of shoes is therefore protecting the feet, alluded to in the verse, "He protects the feet of His pious ones" (1 Samuel, 2:9).

In general, then, the simpleton remains home, and does whatever he can to protect his faith.

From the allusion at the end of the story, however, it appears that the shoe denotes prayer. Rabbi Nachman said that an incomplete prayer is a triangular shoe. Prayer protects faith as a shoe protects the foot.

Rabbi Nachman thus taught that prayer is an aspect of the foot (*Likutey Moharan* 9:2; also see *Likutey Moharan* 38:4). It is written, "Watch your feet when you go to the house of God" (Ecclesiastes 4:17). It is also taught that the angel that brings the prayers to God is called Sandelphon (*Zohar* 1:167b), which has the connotation of a sandal or shoe.

world and see what he could do.*

He went to the marketplace and strolled around. He saw a large wagon* with four horses in harness* rushing through. He called out to the merchants, "From where are you?"

"From Warsaw,"* they replied.

"Where are you heading?"

"To Warsaw."

He asked them, "Maybe you could use a helper?"

They saw that he was bright and diligent, and found this pleasing. They took him on, and he went with them, serving them very well on the road.

However, he considered himself quite sophisticated, and when they came to Warsaw, he decided, "Now that I am in Warsaw, why should I be bound to them?* Maybe there is some better

---

see what he could do. The Sophisticate is not rebelling at this point, only using this as an opportunity to make a better start. He does not know what is in the world outside, but wants to probe beneath the obvious. He leaves the small town to seek the excitement and opportunities of the city.

There are two types of "*Ashrei*" (Happy is he) that allude to the different fates of the Sophisticate and the Simpleton. "*Ashrei yoshvey beitecha*" (Happy are those who dwell in Your house), ends with the words, "Let my mouth express the praise of God" (Daily Liturgy). This denotes the Simpleton who stayed home. "*Ashrei t'mimey derekh*" (Happy are those who follow the path of purity), concludes with "I have strayed like a lost sheep" (Psalm 119), referring to the Sophisticate who strayed very far from the true path (Rabbi Nachman Burshtyn).

Worms found in fruits are permitted to be eaten, as long as they have not moved from their place in the fruit, but forbidden if they have moved (*Yoreh Deah* 84). Rabbi Nathan explains, that as long as impurity is contained in its place there is hope that it can return to its source of holiness. But if it begins to leave its place of containment it loses hope. The analogy is drawn with those who have left, or seek to leave, the realms of Torah, in search of the corruption of the temporal world. Having "gone out," they have abandoned themselves in a place which is devoid of holiness (*Likutey Halachot, Yoreh Deah, Tolaim* 3).

large wagon. *Broki* in Yiddish.

harness. *Chamitch* in Yiddish.

Warsaw. Warsaw was a major metropolis in that time, having a population of around 70,000, of whom around 12,000 were Jews. To Jews in Rabbi Nachman's town, it represented the utmost in a cosmopolitan city within the borders of Eastern Europe.

why should I be bound to them. Here we see the Sophisticate's restlessness begin to manifest itself. He is never satisfied with what he has; he is always looking for something better over the horizon.

place. I will go and see what I can find."

He went to the marketplace, and began to seek information. He asked about the people who had brought him there, and at the same time, looked to see if he could find a better situation.

He was told that the people [who had brought him] were honest men, and it would be good to stay with them. However, one might find it difficult, since their business takes them to very distant places.

He went further, and saw the shop clerks going to market. They seemed very elegant as they went about their affairs with their hats, and long pointed shoes,* and other elegant mannerisms in dress and bearing. This refinement appealed to his sense of sophistication and intelligence, and also does not involve leaving one's home.

He went to the men who had brought him there and thanked them, but told them that he no longer felt comfortable remaining with them. His work for them along the journey would be in exchange for having brought him there.

He then took a job with a shopkeeper. It was customary that new employees receive very low wages and do very hard work. Only then could they be promoted to higher positions.

The employer made him do hard work. He was sent to lords carrying merchandise. He would strain himself carrying large bolts of cloth under his arms. The work was burdensome for him. Sometimes he would have to carry his load up many flights.

The work was very hard for him. Being a philosopher, he made up his mind, "Why do I need such work?* The main reason [a man works] is so that he will be able to get married and earn a

---

long pointed shoes. Here we see the shallowness of the things that attract the Sophisticate. In a deeper sense, however, Rabbi Nachman is using shoes here as a symbol, in a Kabbalistic sense, as a protection of faith through prayer. The Sophisticate felt that these "clerks" might have a better means of prayer. It might be an allusion to the changes in the prayer service that the first reformers were considering at the time.

Why do I need such work. Here we see an example of his pragmatism. He can always use it as a justification for moving on and changing his position.

living. But this is not my concern now. I will have plenty of time for this in the future. The best thing for me now would be to travel all over the world. I can go to different lands, and enjoy the sights."

He went to the market, and saw merchants traveling on a large coach. He asked them where they were going.

"To Lagorna."*

"Would you take me there?"

"Sure."

They took him along and went there. From there they traveled to Italy* and then to Spain.*

Years passed. Since he had visited so many countries, he became all the more sophisticated.

Finally, he made up his mind, "Now is the time to set a goal for myself." He began to philosophize about what sort of occupation to pursue. He decided that it would be very good to learn the trade of a goldsmith.* It was pleasant, prestigious work, and required great skill. It was also very lucrative work.

With his intelligence and philosophical inclination, it did not take him many years to master this craft. At the end of a quarter of a year, he had mastered everything in this craft, and had become very highly skilled. He was more expert even than the master who had taught him.

Then he began thinking about it. Even though I have this skill, it is not enough. It might be prestigious now, but at another time, some other skill might be more prestigious.

Lagorna. Usually referred to as Leghorn or Livorno, the main port of Tuscany in central Italy. In Rabbi Nachman's time, it had a Jewish population of around 5,000, many of whom were engaged in making coral jewelry. It was also an important center of Hebrew printing.

Italy. That is, to Italy proper.

Spain. A land where no Jews had lived since the expulsion of 1492. This indicates that the Sophisticate was becoming totally involved in gentile, non-Jewish values.

goldsmith. Working with the most precious metal, demanding very great skill. Moreover, as we saw in Story #1, the Lost Princess was ultimately held on a golden mountain.

Therefore, he apprenticed himself to a gem cutter.* As a result of his great intelligence, he mastered this craft in a relatively short time, in a quarter of a year.

Still, he philosophized about his situation. Although I have mastered two skills, it is possible that there would come a time when neither one of them would be valuable. "The best thing would be for me to learn a profession that is always valuable." Pondering this with his intelligence and philosophy, he concluded that he should study medicine.* This was something always necessary and important.

In order to study medicine, one had to study Latin and know how to write it. One also had to study philosophy formally. With his intellect, he mastered all this in a quarter of a year. He thus became a great physician and philosopher, expert in all areas of wisdom.

But then the world began to seem like nothing to him. Through his wisdom, he had become a great craftsman, intellectual and physician, and everyone in the world seemed like nothing.

He made up his mind that the time had come for him to seek his goal in life and get married. But he said to himself, "If I marry a woman here, who will know what I have accomplished? I must return home.* Then they will see what I have accomplished. I left

---

gem cutter. Even more exacting than the work of the goldsmith. A single misstroke can destroy a gem, and it cannot be repaired. Later, he makes a small mistake while cutting a gem, and it devastates him. This may also be related to the "pearl castle" where the king's daughter was held in Story #1. This shows a lack of faith in himself — he needs a trade that will always insure his success.

medicine. Here one is dealing with the most valuable commodity of all, human life. Of course, as we shall see, even the best physician cannot cure everyone since some diseases are incurable. Rabbi Nachman, in general, taught that medicine was often ineffective, and even dangerous (*Sichoth HaRan* 50). He had recently been to Lemberg, where he sought a cure for his tuberculosis.

return home. Even though he had become so great, he still felt he needed approval from his own people. From this we see that, to a large extent, his motivation was insecurity, or as Rabbi Nachman would put it, a lack of faith in himself (cf. *Likutey Moharan* 61).

as a young lad, and now I have attained such greatness."

He therefore headed home. However, he was very miserable along the way, since he was so sophisticated that he could not find anyone with whom to speak.* He was also very unhappy* because he could not find the kind of lodging* he desired, and he suffered greatly.

Now let us set aside the story of the Sophisticate and tell the story of the Simpleton.*

The Simpleton had learned the trade of a shoemaker. Since he was simple, he had to study very much to master it, and even then he was not very expert in the craft. He got married and earned a living from his work. However, he was simple and not expert in his craft, so his livelihood was very meager and limited.

Since he had limited skill, he had to work constantly,* and did not even have time to eat. As he ate, he would make a hole with his awl. He would then draw the thick sewing thread used by shoemakers in and out, and then he would bite off a piece of bread and eat it.

Throughout this, he was always very happy.* He was filled

---

with whom to speak. The Sophisticate's lack of self-confidence did not allow him to speak to those whom he considered his inferiors, since this would tend to reduce his own status. But since he could not speak to anyone, he was miserable (*Chokhmah U'Tevunah* 8). If one cannot share one's success, one cannot enjoy it. Elsewhere, Rabbi Nachman writes that the faithless skeptic has nowhere to turn when troubles strike (*Sichoth HaRan* 32).

unhappy. Rabbi Nachman taught that when a person tends to be overly sophisticated and philosophical, his life will be filled with unhappiness. Rabbi Nachman speaks of this at length (*Sichoth HaRan* 102).

lodging. He had given up his own mansion, which symbolized his faith. As he traveled from place to place, he could not find a satisfactory faith (lodging) with which to replace it.

now let...Simpleton. This teaches us how one *must* set aside one's sophistication before one can achieve simplicity.

had to work constantly. The Simpleton was aware of his lowly status, and felt that he had to work constantly, serving God. He did not even have time to eat a regular meal, or take care of his wordly needs. (*Likutey Etzoth* B, *Temimuth* 9).

very happy. It is thus taught, "Who is wealthy? He who is satisfied with his lot" (*Avoth* 4:1). Although the Simpleton was very poor, he was satisfied with his lot, and therefore could with joy at all times.

He had every type of food, drink and clothing.

He would say to his wife, "My wife,* give me something to eat." She would give him a piece of bread, and he would eat it.

Then he would say, "Give me some soup with groats,"* and she would cut him another slice of bread. He would eat it and speak highly of it, saying, "How nice and delicious this soup is!"

He would then ask her for some meat and other good food, and each time he asked, she would give him a piece of bread. He would enjoy it very much and praise the food very highly, saying how well prepared and delicious it was. It was as if he were actually eating the food he had asked for.

Actually, when he ate the bread, he would taste in it any kind of food he wanted.* This was because of his simplicity and great happiness.

He would also ask his wife, "My wife, bring me a drink of beer." She would bring him some water,* but he would praise it and say, "How delicious this beer is."

"Give me some honey wine."* She would give him water, and

---

always be happy (*Rimzey Maasioth*). If a person stays in the house (faith) of his fathers, and has strong faith, he can be happy even if he only has bread and water (*Likutey Etzoth B, Temimuth* 4).

wife. *Ishah*, a wife, is a concept of prayer. We see that the simple one asked his wife for whatever he wanted — his food, drink and clothing. Thus he used prayer to accomplish whatever he needed (Rabbi Nachman Burshtyn).

groats. *Kashah* in Yiddish. However, in Hebrew it is *kitnioth*, which would denote beans.

any kind of food he wanted. In this respect, his bread was like the manna, which had any flavor the eater desired (*Chokhmah U'Tevunah* 2, *Yoma* 75a). The manna had every possible taste only when people had absolute faith in God (*Zohar* 2:62b). Since the Simpleton had absolute faith, he could taste everything he desired in his bread.

This was also the level of Jacob, who only asked God for "bread to eat and a garment to wear" (Genesis 28:20). This was because Jacob was a simple person, a *tam* (Genesis 25:27), and he could taste anything he wanted in this bread (*Oneg Shabbath,* p. 100, 108). His faith gave him expanded consciousness (*mochin de-gadluth*), which could bring any taste he wanted into the bread (*Ibid.*).

water. Like Miriam's well, which had every taste a person desired (*Chokhmah U'Tevunah* 2).

honey wine. *Me'ed* in the Yiddish. In the Hebrew it is simply "honey."

he would speak highly of it.

"Give me some wine" — or other beverages. Each time, she would give him water, but he would enjoy it, and praise the beverage as if he were actually drinking it.

The same was true of clothing.* Between them, the only outer garment he and his wife had was a sheepskin coat.* Whenever he wanted to go to the market, he would say to his wife, "Give me the sheepskin," and she would give it to him.

When he wanted to wear a fur coat* to visit people, he would say, "My wife, give me my fur coat." She would give him the sheepskin, but he would enjoy it and praise it, saying, "What a nice coat this is."

When he needed a caftan* to go to synagogue, he would ask her, "My wife, give me the caftan." She would give him the sheepskin, and he would praise it, "What a nice, beautiful caftan this is."

Similarly, when he needed a silk coat,* she would also give him the sheepskin. He would enjoy it and praise it, "What a nice, comfortable silk coat!"

This was true no matter what happened. He was always filled with happiness and joy.

---

clothing. Like in the 'desert, as it is written, "Your garment did not wear out" (Deuteronomy 8:4). The Midrash teaches that the garments that the Israelites wore in the desert actually grew with them, so they never had to change them (*Devarim Rabbah* 7).

Rabbi Nachman teaches that through true knowledge, one can have all the food, drink and clothing that one needs (*Likutey Moharan* 58:5). He says that this comes from destroying the concept of Amalek (*Likutey Moharan* 58:4), which as we have seen here is the concept of false sophistication.

sheepskin coat. *Peltz* in Yiddish and Hebrew. Often this denotes a coat with the fur on the inside, with a cloth exterior.

fur coat. *Tulip* in Yiddish and Hebrew. This was a fancy coat with a fine fur on the inside, with the fur rolled over onto the collar, so that it appeared to have a fur collar.

caftan. A silk garment worn to synagogue, very much like a *bekeshe*.

silk coat. *Yupa* in the original. Like the *jepetza*, a long, unlined silken robe. It would be a dress-up garment. This is the garment that he puts on to meet the Sophisticate when he returns.

Since he had not completely mastered his trade, when he finished a shoe, it was usually triangular in shape.* But he would take the shoe in his hand and speak very highly of it, deriving much enjoyment from his handiwork.* He would say, "My wife, what a beautiful, wonderful shoe this is! How sweet this shoe is! This shoe is as sweet as honey and sugar!"

Sometimes she would answer him, "If that's true, why can other shoemakers get three gulden* for a pair of shoes, while you only get a gulden and a half?"*

He would then answer, "What do I care about that? That is their work, and this is my work!"*

---

triangular in shape. Most probably, something like the shape of a duck's foot. After presenting this lesson, Rabbi Nachman taught that "Incorrect prayer is like a triangular shoe" (see *Likutey Halakhoth, Pesach* 9:22). Thus, even if his prayers were not perfect, he still would be happy. It is thus taught that once Rabbi Nathan did not pray very well on Yom Kippur. He therefore asked God that his prayer should be better the next day (*Oneg Shabbath*, p. 469).

It is taught that there are four levels of prayer, paralleling the four supernal universes. These correspond to the four major parts of the service, the Sacrificial Readings, the Introductory Psalms (*Pesukey DeZimra*), the Sh'ma and its blessings, and the Amidah. If any one of these is deficient, the prayer is "three-sided."

much enjoyment from his handiwork. This is Rabbi Nachman's most basic teaching, that one should always look for good points in oneself (*Likutey Moharan* 282; *Oneg Shabbath*, p. 37).

In this way one can emulate God, who, as we have seen, is called "simple in His ways" (Deuteronomy 32:4). Even though the physical world is small and imperfect compared to God and His spiritual domain, the Torah states that after creating the world, "God saw all that He did and behold it was very good" (Genesis 1:31). It is thus taught that God, "Looks for good and not for evil; He is wealthy, rejoicing in his portion" (*Tana De Bei Eliahu Rabbah; Oneg Shabbath, Ibid.*).

gulden. Or guilden or guilder. A small gold coin in use at that time. *Zehuvim* in Hebrew.

gulden and a half. In the original, this is defined as a half-thaler. Thus a thaler was three gulden. It is significant that, earlier, the price was given as three gulden rather than a thaler.

that is their work, and this is my work. From this we see the tremendous self-confidence (belief in himself) that the Simpleton had. He was totally unconcerned if other people did a better job than he did (*Likutey Etzoth* B, *Temimuth* 4).

It is precisely this self-confidence that keeps him from sophistication. He is satisfied with understanding things the way he sees them, precisely because he has confidence in his powers of perception and understanding.

"Why must we speak about others?" [he would continue].
"Let's think about how much clear profit* I make on this shoe.
The leather costs so much, the glue* and thread... so much, and

The lesson also applies to serving God. Even though one does not do it perfectly, one still enjoys it very much. One might know that others may get more reward for their service, but one does not pay attention to that. If God has some pleasure from this imperfect work, it is better than any treasure, and it is something worth devoting one's life to (*Likutey Etzoth* B, *Temimuth* 9).

Rabbi Nathan picks up on this theme, and says that if a person becomes depressed because others are better and more God-fearing than he is, this is not humility, but pride. He feels that it is not fitting that he serve God when he is so far from Him, while others are so near. But it is written that, "Abraham was one" (Ezekiel 33:24). He acted as if there was no one else in the world.

This is also the concept of counting the Omer, where each individual must count for himself. One person cannot have another count for him. The Omer represents the progress that the Israelites made from the degradation of Egyptian slavery to the exaltation of the revelation at Sinai. Each person must count his own progress without paying attention to others.

The Simpleton worked very hard to make a shoe, but in the end it was still inferior. Nevertheless, since it was his work and accomplishment, he was very happy with it (*Likutey Halakhoth, Pesach* 9:22; *Choshen Mishpat, Genevah* 5:8).

Rabbi Nathan writes further that when a person sees that another is more pious and learned than himself, he can become discouraged. It is considered good to be jealous of another person's accomplishments in Torah, prayer and reverence, as it is taught, "Jealousy among scribes increases wisdom" (*Bava Bathra* 21a). However, this can be good or bad, depending on the situation, as it is said, "The righteous walk in them, while sinners stumble in them" (Hosea 14:10).

Many people fall because of such jealousy. When a person is jealous of others, thinking that they are more pious and righteous than he, it is very easy for him to become depressed. One can thus lose one's way completely. It is impossible to explain the extent to which the Evil One tries to discourage a person. Therefore, one should not be foolish; he should be sure that his jealousy benefits him and does not harm him, that it brings him closer to God and not further away. One must emulate the Simpleton, who could cheerfully say, "That is their work, and this is my work" (*Likutey Halakhoth, Shabbath* 7:74). See Story #5, p. 122.

Rabbi Shmuel Isaac had a brother whom the Rebbe told to concentrate on study. The brother saw that the Rebbe spent a lot of time with R. Shmuel but very little with himself. He went and fasted, and when he came to the Rebbe, the Rebbe said to him "I wanted to do away you. What does it have to do with you, what I have to do with R. Shmuel Isaac? Your task is learning" (*Biur HaLikutim* p. 8b).

clear profit. "From hand to hand" in the original.

glue. Or pitch. *Zefeth* (pitch) in Hebrew. *Zivitze* in Yiddish.

the other things so much. I also have to pay a certain amount for the tongues.* Therefore, I have a clear profit of ten groschen. As long as.I make such a clear profit, what do I care?" He was thus always filled with joy and happiness.

For most people, this was a big joke. They would enjoy themselves making fun of him, since they considered him insane. *

People would come to him especially to engage him in conversation so that they would be able to ridicule him. But the Simpleton would merely say, "Just don't make a joke of it."

If the other person would assure him that he was not making a joke of it, the [Simpleton] would listen to what he had to say and engage in conversation. He did not probe the other person's motives more deeply to see if this in itself might be a means of mocking him, since he was a very simple person, and he avoided such sophisticated ideas.

However, if he saw that the other's intention was clearly to mock him, he would say, "So what if you prove yourself smarter than I? You will still be a fool. What am I that it is such a great thing to be smarter than I am? Even if you are, you will first be a fool." *

(All these were the ways of the Simpleton. Now we will return to our story.)

---

tongues. *Lapkes* in Yiddish.

insane. Because they doubted their own values.

People thought the Simple One was mad. The Talmud (*Sanhedrin* 97a) teaches that in the era preceding the coming of the Messiah "he that departs from evil *mishtolel*" (Isaiah 59:15). Rashi explains that *mishtolel* is an expression meaning to be mad. The Talmud says that the one who departs from evil will be considered mad by other people (Rabbi Nachman Burshtyn).

you will first be a fool. We thus see that the Simpleton was self-confident enough even to remain unimpressed when people tried to make fun of him (*Likutey Etzoth* B, *Temimuth* 4).

This may explain why the same word, *tamim*, is used for simplicity and wholeness. If a person is really whole, then he has enough self-confidence to be simple. He does not find it necessary to impress others with his sophistication.

The difference between wisdom and sophistication is that wisdom comes from an inner desire to know the truth, while sophistication here comes from the desire to impress others.

One day, there was a great commotion. The Sophisticate was returning* with great status and wisdom.

The Simpleton was overjoyed. He rushed to join the crowd that was greeting [the Sophisticate], saying to his wife, "Quick! Give me the silk coat! I want to meet my friend! I want to see my old buddy!" She gave him the sheepskin, and he ran to greet [his old friend].

The Sophisticate was traveling with great pomp, in a huge coach. The Simpleton greeted him with love and joy, "My brother! My best friend! How have you been doing? Thanks to God who brought you back, and I am able to see you!"

The Sophisticate considered even the whole world to be nothing, as we have seen. Someone like the Simpleton appeared to him like a madman. However, because of their friendship in their youth, he was friendly to him, and rode with him into the city.

While the Sophisticate had been abroad, the two homeowners had died, leaving behind their mansions.

The Simpleton had remained home, so that when he inherited his father's mansion, he lived in it. The Sophisticate, however, was abroad, so there was no one to care for the mansion. The Sophisticate's mansion therefore was neglected and in ruins, so that nothing remained of it.*

Thus, when the Sophisticate returned, he had no place to live, and he had to stay in an inn.* However, the inn was not to his

---

The Sophisticate was returning. Right after we learn how the Simpleton could taste anything he wanted in his bread, and how self-confident he was, the Sophisticate returned. This is very much like the account in the Torah, where right after the manna, and the water from the rock, Amalek appears on the scene (Exodus 17:8; *Chokhmah U'Tevunah* 2).

nothing remained of it. As a result of the Sophisticate's straying away from home, the faith of his fathers was completely destroyed (*Likutey Etzoth, Temimuth* 5).

We find that even when Jacob left his father's home, all his yearning was to return. Jacob prayed "that I come back to my father's house in peace" (cf. Genesis 28:21) (Rabbi Nachman Burshtyn).

in an inn. He could only find a temporary lodging. Since he did not have a firm faith, he had to live by the pragmatic decisions of the moment (see *Ibid.*). At best, his home was now a temporary rest stop.

liking, and he was very miserable.

The Simpleton now had something new to do. Whenever he had a chance, he would leave his house and run to the Sophisticate with love and joy. He noticed how unhappy the Sophisticate was with his quarters.

The Simpleton said to the Sophisticate, "My brother, come to my house. You can stay with me. I will move all my belongings into one corner, and you can have full use of the rest of my house."*

The Sophisticate liked this idea, so he moved into the [Simpleton's] house and stayed with him.*

The Sophisticate was always very miserable because it became known that he was very brilliant, as well as a fine craftsman and a highly skilled physician.

One day a nobleman came and commissioned him to make him a gold ring. He made a very exquisite ring, engraving it with detailed images. The pattern engraved on the ring was a very exquisite tree. However, when the nobleman came for it, he was not pleased at all with the ring. [The Sophisticate] was very miserable since he knew that if he had made such a ring with a tree in Spain, it would be very precious and highly regarded.*

---

the rest of my house. The Simpleton would not press his faith on him. But, he invited the Sophisticate to share his "house" of faith. The Sophisticate felt that since he had no other alternative, he would, at least for the time being, abide by the faith of his fathers.

This teaches us how important it is to have good friends. Even though the Sophisticate did not want to recognize the Simpleton, the Simpleton let him have full use of his house because they had been friends (*Rimzey Maasioth*).

stayed with him. However, the friendship of the Sophisticate was for the Simpleton worse than hatred; he always derided him. Thus, the moving in of the Sophisticate can be likened to Amalek's attack (*Chokhmah U'Tevunah* 2).

Once, with regard to a certain person, Rabbi Nachman said, "I suffered more from his friendship than from his hatred and anger" (*Shevachay HaRan, Nesiya LeEretz Yisroel* 17, *Rabbi Nachman's Wisdom*, p. 56).

Although the Wise One had wanted to travel far from his roots, when he was in need he came back immediately and moved into the house of the Simple One. Similarly Esau went out hunting, but when he was hungry he went to Jacob for pottage (Genesis 25:30) (Rabbi Nachman Burshtyn).

highly regarded. Thus, even when he does perfect work, there is no one in his home town to

Another time, an important landowner came and brought him a valuable gem from a distant land. He brought another gem that had an image engraved on it, and commissioned him to reproduce the image on the gem he had brought. [The Sophisticate] was able to reproduce the image exactly, with the exception of one very minor detail that no one but himself would ever notice. When the landowner returned and took his gem, he was very pleased. The Sophisticate, however, was very miserable because of his mistake. "What good is my skill,"* he said, "if I can make such an error?"

His medical practice also brought him misery. Often, he came to a sick person and gave him remedies. He knew that if the patient were to survive, he would be healed through these remedies. Yet, there were cases where the patient died, and people would blame him. This made him very miserable.

On the other hand, there were cases where the remedies that he gave his patients were effective, and they recovered. In such cases, however, people would say that it was a chance occurrence [and the patient would have recovered without his treatment]. [The Sophisticate] thus was always full of misery.*

The same happened when he needed clothing. He summoned a tailor, and struggled to teach him how to make the type of garment with which he was familiar. The tailor finally got the point, and made the garment exactly as he wanted. The only flaw

---

appreciate it. His work has become so sophisticated, it can only be appreciated in Spain, a country where there are no Jews.

What good is my skill. The Simpleton could be happy even though his shoes came out triangular, but the Sophisticate was upset even when he made an error that no one would notice (*Oneg Shabbath*, p. 37, p. 469). This is a measure of his insecurity — he does not "believe in himself."

This is reminiscent of the *maskilim* who made a fetish of studying Hebrew grammar, and were unhappy if they mispronounced a word in worship (see *Sichoth HaRan* 235). They were perfectionists, and if everything was not perfect, they could not tolerate it (see *Chokhmah U'Tevunah* 3).

always full of misery. The Sophisticate needs public approval. This is in contrast to the Simpleton, who can be ridiculed and not have it bother him. But the Sophisticate did not have faith in himself, so he needed others to have faith in him.

was that one of the lapels was not lined up exactly right.

[The Sophisticate] was very upset. Here the garment may be considered nice, since people do not know better. "But," he said, "if I were in Spain with such a lapel, it would be a joke.* People would consider it ridiculous." This only added to his misery.

The Simpleton would constantly run to the Sophisticate in joy. When he found him miserable and full of grief, he would ask, "Why should a brilliant, wealthy person like you always be so miserable. Here I am always full of joy!"

The Sophisticate considered the question ridiculous, and thought [the Simpleton] to be a madman. But the Simpleton said to him, "Even if ordinary people mock me they are fools, since since even if they are smarter than I am, they are first fools. This is even more true of a brilliant person like you. If you are smarter than I am, so what?"

The Simpleton then spoke up and said to the Sophisticate, "If only you could reach my level [of intelligence]."

The Sophisticate replied, "It is very possible that I can reach your level. Heaven forbid, I could lose my intelligence. I could become ill, heaven forbid, or I could become mad. After all, what are you? A madman! But for you to attain what I have is truly impossible. You could never be as intelligent as I am."

"For God everything is possible," answered the Simpleton. "In the wink of an eye I can attain everything that you have."

The Sophisticate laughed at this very much.

People had given the two sons surnames. One was called "the Sophisticate," while the other was called "the Simpleton."

Of course, there are many people in the world who are sophisticated or simple. However, in their case, these traits were very obvious, since both of them came from the same place and

---

it would be a joke. Here, too, he was worried about what things would be like in Spain, where, as a Jew, he could never live. This presents a sharp contrast to the Simpleton, who could wear a sheepskin and feel as comfortable and secure as if he were wearing the finest clothes.

had studied together. Then, one had become a very sophisticated person, while the other had become very, very simple.

There is a royal registry* where everyone is registered by his family name. Here, one son is registered as "the Sophisticate," while the other is registered as "the Simpleton."

Once, the king* was reading the royal registry, and saw the names of the two sons, one recorded as "the Sophisticate," and the other as "the Simpleton." He found it very remarkable that these two should be called "the Sophisticate" and "the Simpleton," and he wanted very much to see them.*

The king considered the situation. "If I send an unexpected message that they should come to me, they will be terrified. The Sophisticate may not be able even to answer my questions. The Simpleton may be so terrified he might lose his mind."

The king therefore decided to send a sophisticated messenger* to the Sophisticate and a simple messenger* to the Simpleton.

There was, however, a problem in finding a simple person in the capital city, where most people are very sophisticated. But there was one person who was especially simple — the man in charge of the treasuries.* It is not desirable to put a sophisticated person in charge of the treasuries, since he could

---

royal registry. In the Torah we find Jacob described as an *ish tam* — "Mr. Simple" while Esau is called *ish sadeh* ("a man of the field") — "Mr. Field" (Genesis 25:27) (Rabbi Nachman Burshtyn).

king. Allegorically denoting God (*Likutey Etzoth* B, *Temimuth* 4).

to see them. In this allegory, this appears to denote the revelation at Sinai, where God appeared to Israel. This occurred after the battle against Amalek (see *Chokhmah U'Tevunah* 2).

sophisticated messenger. Samael, the genius of Esau (see *Zohar* 1:170a).

simple messenger. Moses.

in charge of the treasuries. "He is trusted in all My house" (Numbers 12:7).

Rabbi Nachman taught in general, that if a person relinquishes his entire intellect, and only does as God desires, he can enter into areas of the king's treasury where even a son cannot go (*Likutey Moharan Tinyana* 5:15; see *Likutey Etzoth* B, *Temimuth* 7).

Thus, if God entrusted his deepest mysteries to a Sophisticate, the latter might pervert them and use them for his own desires. Therefore, the only one to whom such mysteries are entrusted is one who has no other motive than to serve the king with perfect simplicity.

use his sophistication and shrewdness to embezzle. Therefore, a particularly simple man was placed in charge of the treasuries.

The king summoned a sophisticated man and the simple man [who was treasurer] and sent them to the two sons. He gave each one a letter.

He also gave them letters to the governor* of the district where these two sons resided. In his letter, he ordered that the governor send notes* to the Sophisticate and the Simpleton in his name, so that they not be afraid. [The governor] should write them that it was not a particularly important affair, and the king was not actually ordering them to come. It was up to them, and if they wanted they could come. However, the king wished to see them.

The sophisticated messenger and the simple one both set off, and they came to the governor, giving him the letters. The governor asked them about these two sons, and they told him that they had been informed that the Sophisticate was extraordinarily brilliant and very wealthy. The Simpleton, on the other hand, was extremely simple, and he used a sheepskin for whatever garment he needed.

The governor decided that it would certainly not be proper to bring [the Simpleton] to the king wearing a sheepskin. He therefore had proper clothes* made for him, and placed them in

---

governor. In this allegory, apparently Mount Sinai.

notes. The Torah, or the "book of the covenant" (Exodus 24:7; see *Chokhmah U'Tevunah* 2). According to Rashi, Moses read the book of the covenant to the Israelites before the revelation at Sinai (Rashi on Exodus 24:7).

Some say that the "book of the covenant" is the entire Torah until the revelation at Sinai.

The letter may also have been God's promise, "If you listen to My voice, and keep My covenant, then you shall be My own treasure among all nations, for the whole world is Mine. You shall be to Me a kingdom of priests and a holy nation" (Exodus 19:5,6).

proper clothes. The crowns that were given to the Israelites at Mount Sinai (*Shabbath* 88a). Also, they were given new bodies, which would be free of death (*Avodah Zarah* 22b; *Shabbath* 146a). This might also have included garments of the soul, which they would wear in the World to Come (see *Zohar, Pardes Rimonim*). It would have also implied a greater intelligence, as we shall see.

the simple messenger's coach. He gave [the messengers] the letters [that the king had ordered].

The messengers continued on their journey and arrived. The sophisticated [messenger] gave his letter to the Sophisticate, while the simple [messenger] gave his to the Simpleton.

As soon as the Simpleton got the letter, he said to the messenger who delivered it, "I don't know what the letter says. Read it for me."

"I will tell you what it says," replied [the messenger]. "The king wants you to come to him."

"You're not playing a joke on me," said [the Simpleton].

"It's absolutely true," answered the messenger. "I'm not joking at all."

[The Simpleton] was overjoyed. He ran and told his wife, "My wife! The king has sent for me!"

"Why?" asked the wife. "What reason* could he possibly have to send for you?"

But [the Simpleton] did not have any time to answer. He joyfully rushed out and immediately left* with the messenger. When he got on the coach, he found the clothing there, and this made him all the more happy.

Meanwhile, the governor was accused* of a crime, and the king had him removed from his position. The king thought it over, and decided that it would be best if the governor were a

---

What reason... See Yiddish. In the Hebrew it is simply, "For what and why."

immediately left. Just as the Israelites did not ask any question, but as soon as they were offered the Torah (after the book of the covenant was read), they said, "We will do and we will listen" (Exodus 24:7) (*Chokhmah U'Tevunah* 2).

governor was accused... This might denote the sin of the Golden Calf, which took place at Sinai. As a result, Mount Sinai lost its status as a holy place, and was replaced by Mount Moriah or Mount Zion where the Holy Temple was built. Mount Moriah was in the Holy Land, and was associated with the people of Israel. In one sense, the Simpleton also denotes the Holy Land (*Zimrath HaAretz*).

Actually, the two sons, the Simpleton and the Sophisticate, can be alluded to by two mountains, Mount Zion and Mount Seir.

simple person, who would not know of sophistication and deceit, and would therefore run the country truthfully and honestly.

The king decided that the Simpleton should be appointed governor. He sent orders that the Simpleton for whom he had sent should be the new governor. Since he had to travel through the governor's capital, [the king ordered] that people be stationed at the city gates, and as soon as he arrived, he should be stopped and crowned as governor.

The people did this. They stood at the gates, and as soon as [the Simpleton] passed through, they stopped him and told him that he had been appointed governor.

"You're not playing a joke on me," said the [Simpleton].

"Of course we are not joking," they replied.

The Simpleton immediately accepted the position of governor with full authority and power.*

Now his fortune was on the rise, and good fortune adds to one's intelligence.* He therefore achieved some additional understanding. Nevertheless, he did not make use of this sophistication, but behaved with simplicity as he always had. He ruled the land with simplicity, truth, and honesty, without any corruption whatever.

Ruling a nation does not require great intelligence or sophistication. All that is needed is honesty and simplicity.

When two people came before him to seek justice, he would declare, "You are innocent and you are guilty." It would be a simple verdict, without any ulterior designs or motives.

He thus governed honestly, and the people loved him very much. He also had advisors who truly loved him.

Out of love, one of the advisors reminded him that he would

---

with full authority and power. The Simpleton had the confidence to accept his position, whether lowly or high. When he is given a high position, he can accept and use his power without questioning it.

good fortune adds to one's intelligence. The source (both in Yiddish and Hebrew) uses the term *mazal machkim* (מזל מחכים), which also occurs in the Talmud (*Shabbath* 156a).

It is also taught, "Even the least of the least, when he becomes a leader over the community, becomes like the greatest of the great" (*Rosh HaShanah* 25b).

eventually be summoned before the king. "After all," he said, "the king has already sent for you. Furthermore, the governor must customarily present himself to the king. Although you are very honest, and you are ruling the land without corruption, the king usually steers the conversation away from these issues and begins to discuss intellectual ideas and foreign languages. It would be only proper and respectful if you were able to reply to him. Therefore, it would be very good if I would teach you intellectual ideas and foreign languages."

The Simpleton found this idea acceptable. "What harm can there be* in learning intellectual ideas and languages?" he said.

It then crossed his mind that his friend, the Sophisticate, had told him that it would be utterly impossible for him to attain his achievements. But, here, he had already attained his knowledge.

Nevertheless, even though he already knew all sorts of

What harm can there be. Rabbi Nachman was very much against the study of secular subjects and foreign languages, but nevertheless, he taught that a great tzaddik may study these subjects. There are seven sciences of the ancients: grammar, rhetoric, logic, arithmetic, music, geometry, and astronomy (Rabbi Moshe Butril, Introduction to *Sefer Yetzirah*). These can be a stumbling block through which one can fall and be spiritually injured.

Rabbi Nachman thus interpreted the verse quoted in the Hebrew at the end of the story. "The tzaddik can fall seven, but he will get up again" (Proverbs 24:16). He said that this means that the tzaddik can fall into the seven sciences, but he can rise up again. He also notes that the final letters of this verse (see end of notes) spell out Amalek (עמלק) (*Likutey Moharan Tinyana* 19). If a person has the faith of Moses, he can even overcome the disbelief of Amalek (*Likutey Moharan Tinyana* 19).

We see that many great tzaddikim were expert in secular subjects. However, they could accomplish this without spiritual harm only after they had spent many years serving God with truth and simplicity, no matter how much sacrifice it entailed. Then, when they reached a level where their fear of God came even before their Torah wisdom, they were able to study secular subjects to benefit the world. Even in such cases, they did not spend very much time on such studies, but learned them quickly and returned to their simple path. Their faith and simplicity were so great that these subjects could not harm them.

However, if one has not attained the path of simplicity, these studies can be very harmful. Regarding secular studies, it is then written, "Whoever comes to her will not return, he will never attain the paths of life" (Proverbs 2:19) (*Avodah Zarah* 17a; see *Likutey Moharan* 64). The path of life is simplicity, where "the tzaddik lives by his faith" (Habakkuk 2:4; *Rimzey Maasioth*).

intellectual ideas, he did not make use of any of this sophistication. Rather, he ruled with simplicity, just as he had originally.

Afterwards, the king sent a message for the simple governor to come to him, and [the Simpleton] went to him. The king began by discussing running the government, and he was extremely pleased. He saw that [the Simpleton] was ruling with truth and honesty, without any falseness or corruption.

Then the king directed the conversation to intellectual ideas and languages, and the Simpleton was able to respond properly. The king was then all the more pleased. "He is indeed a very intelligent man," he said, "but he still rules with great simplicity." The king was so pleased with this that he made [the Simpleton] his prime minister, putting him in charge of all his other ministers. *

[The king] ordered that a special city* be given to [the Simpleton] as his official residence. The walls around this city were to be fine and beautiful, as appropriate [for such] a residence. [The king] also gave a letter* of appointment, stating that he would be prime minister.

This was carried out, and the city the king had ordered was built. [The Simpleton] went there and accepted his position with full authority. *

Meanwhile, when the Sophisticate received his letter from the king, he replied to the sophisticated messenger who delivered it, "Wait. Spend the night here.* We will discuss the matter and

---

in charge of all his other ministers. Israel is thus higher than all the other angels and nations. All the angels are subservant to Israel's destiny.

"He that walks in the *simple* path, he shall serve Me" (Psalms 101:6).

special city. First the Tabernacle, which was erected after the revelation at Sinai. Later, Jerusalem.

letter. The Tablets, or the Torah.

full authority. Thus, through his humility and simplicity, the Simpleton becomes the most powerful person in the land. Now the career of the Sophisticate is contrasted to his.

Spend the night here. Like Balaam (Numbers 22:8). The Sophisticate has to sleep on it and see if there is a deeper meaning.

make up our minds."*

That evening, the Sophisticate made a great feast [for the messenger]. During the meal, the Sophisticate used his intelligence and philosophical discipline to analyze the message. He spoke up and said, "What does this really mean? Why should such a king send for an insignificant person like me?* Who am I that the king should send for me? The king has his power and prestige. Compared to such a great, awe-inspiring king, I am lowly and despicable. How can the mind reconcile the fact that such a king would send for an insignificant person like me. I may be intelligent, but what am I compared to the king? Doesn't the king have other wise men? Besides, the king himself is certainly also very wise. For what possible reason could the king send for me?" He found this all very puzzling.

The Sophisticate, who was the Simpleton's friend, thought it over in this manner. At first, he was very puzzled and confused, but soon he thought he had a reasonable answer.

He said to the messenger, "I declare that, in my opinion, it is absolutely certain and logical that the king does not exist* at all!"

---

make up our minds. Thus, when Esau was offered the Torah, he first asked, what is written in it. When he was told, he said that he could not possibly keep it (*Avodah Zarah* 2b; *Chokhmah U'Tevunah* 2).

an insignificant person like me. Just as the Sophisticate had false pride, now he had false humility. He felt that God was so great that He had absolutely no need for him. He did not realize that every person has his own unique good points (*Likutey Moharan* 282), which no one else has. No matter how great God is, He created us to do His will and He wants our service. God can receive pleasure even from the lowliest Jew, and even from a gentile (*Likutey Moharan* 33; *Likutey Etzoth* B, *Temimuth* 8).

There are thus two types of disbelief. One is atheism, where one denies God completely. However, the other is deism, where one thinks that God is too lofty to be concerned with the world. As we see from the story, the second can often lead to the first.

Here we see how dangerous the Sophisticate's lack of faith in himself can be. It can lead to a loss of faith in God. Moreover, the false modesty, where he questions the king's need for him, can lead to false pride, where he wants to convince the whole world that there really is no king.

the king does not exist. Since the Sophisticate could not reconcile the letter with a king who logically should be indifferent to him, his only solution was to deny the king's existence completely (*Likutey Etzoth* B, *Temimuth* 8).

[He explained], "The entire world is mistaken, since they foolishly believe that there really is a king. Think it over! How is it possible that all the people in the world would submit to one man as their king? Obviously, no such thing as a king exists!"

The messenger, who was also very intelligent, replied, "But I brought you a letter from the king."

"Did you yourself actually receive the letter from the king in person?" asked the Sophisticate.

"No," replied the messenger. "Another man gave me the letter in the king's name."

"Now -see with your own eyes that I am right," said [the Sophisticate]. "There is no king at all." *

[The Sophisticate] queried him further. "Tell me. Aren't you from the capital? Didn't you grow up there and live there all your life? Tell me, did you ever see the king?"

"No," replied [the messenger]. (Of course, this was true. The king would only appear on rare occasions * and not everyone would get to see him.).

Here, too, sophisticates may deny the veracity of the Torah, since why would an infinite God want to communicate with such a lowly creature as mankind? From denying the Torah, the next step is to deny God Himself.

Thus, many people say that they believe in God, but they do not have to keep all the commandments of the Torah. Either these people themselves, or their children, ultimately end up denying God completely.

Even though God is infinite, this in itself makes it possible for Him to care for us. An infinite intellect can be concerned with every detail in the universe, no matter how minor. Only a finite intellect would be restricted to major concerns. Our sages thus teach, "Wherever you find God's greatness, you also find His humilty" (*Megillah* 31a; see above story #6).

It is also written, "High above [the conceptions] of nations in God, [since they say] 'His glory is over the heavens.' But who is like our God, who dwells so high, but looks down to see both heaven and earth" (Psalms 113:5,6).

Thus, the Sophisticate begins as a rational philosopher, but he ends up an atheist. **There is no king at all.** Since he cannot be seen. The Sophisticate does not realize that God is so different from anything in His creation, that man does not possess the senses to see Him. We must believe in God even though He is hidden and even our thoughts cannot grasp Him (*Zimrath HaAretz*).

rare occasions. God only appears to the greatest prophets, and then, only in a vision.

"Now you see," said the Sophisticate. "What I am saying is obvious and very logical. It is certain that there is no king at all. Even you have never seen the king."

"So who rules the land?"* asked the messenger.

The Sophisticate replied, "I can answer this very simply, since you are asking an expert. I have traveled to many lands, and I was once in Italy. There, it is the custom to elect seventy advisory ministers* who serve as representatives.* Each one serves for a set time. Thus, everyone in the land has a turn to rule, one after the other."

His argument began to convince the messenger. Finally, they came to an agreement, and announced that it was certain that no king existed.

The Sophisticate then said, "Wait until morning. I will show you further proof that no such thing as a king exists."

The Sophisticate got up early in the morning. He woke up his friend, the sophisticated messenger, and said to him, "Come outside with me. I will clearly show you what a great mistake the world is making. The truth is that there is no king at all. Everyone is making a great mistake."

They went out to the market and saw a soldier. They took hold of him and asked, "Whom do you serve?"

"The king," he replied.

"As long as you have lived, have you ever seen the king?"

"No."

They declared, "See! Is there anything more foolish?"

Then they approached an army officer. They entered into conversation with him, until they finally asked him, "Whom do you serve?"

---

who rules the land? The argument from design. We see an element of order in the world, and it must have an author.

seventy advisory ministers. The seventy geniuses (*sarim*) of the nations (*Zimrath HaAretz*). Or, the Sophisticate may believe in the destinies of the seventy nations, even without a divine foundation. This would be very much like Marxism; Marx believed in a kind of supernatural, historic destiny, even though he denied God.

representatives. *Ratheiren* in the text.

"The king."

"Have you ever seen the king?"

"No."

"You can see it with your eyes!" declared [the Sophisticate]. "Everyone is clearly in error. In all the world, there is no king at all!"

They thus both agreed that the king did not exist.

The Sophisticate then spoke up and said, "Come! Let us travel around the world. I want to show* you how the entire world is caught up in this great error."

They set out and traveled around the world. Wherever they came, they found people in error. They used the idea of a king as an example. Wherever they found people in error, they took the king as a paradigm: "This idea of yours is as true as the idea that a king exists."

They continued traveling until they had used up all their wealth.* First they sold one horse, then another, until they had sold them all, and had to travel by foot.

They were always analyzing people's beliefs, and they found people to be in error. But they had become poor and they had to go on foot, so they lost all their status. They did not have any status at all, since people would not pay any attention to paupers like them.

As things turned out, they traveled all over, until they finally came to the city* where the prime minister lived. He was the

---

I want to show. The atheist and *maskil* (secularist) are not satisfied with their own disbelief; they must bring everyone to deny the truth. Moreover, by showing that the world is in error, they can enhance their own importance. Meanwhile, they feel that, of all the people in the world, only they have the key to the truth, and they are therefore greater than anyone else. Thus, the Sophisticate finds his atheism a defense against his own feelings of insecurity and inferiority.

used up all their wealth. Their sophistication and denial of the king thus led them to lose everything, both spiritually and materially (*Likutey Etzoth* B, *Temimuth* 4). While the Simpleton became the most powerful man in the kingdom, the Sophisticate is now an impoverished outcast.

the city. "Saviors shall climb up Mount Zion to judge Mount Seir" (Obadiah 1:21). It is in the Simpleton's city that the Sophisticate has his final judgment and his downfall.

Simpleton, who had been the Sophisticate's friend.

In that city, there lived a true miracle worker.* He was considered very important because of the miracles that he performed. He was important and famous even among the ministers.

The Sophisticate and his companion came to the city. They wandered around until they came to the miracle worker's house. They saw many wagons there, forty or fifty, with sick people. The Sophisticate assumed that a physician lived there. Since [the Sophisticate] was also a skilled physician, he wanted to go in and become acquainted with the other.

"Who lives here?" asked [the Sophisticate].

"A miracle worker," answered the people.

[The Sophisticate] began to laugh. He said to his companion, "What a tremendous falsehood* and error! This is even more foolish than belief in the king! My friend, let me tell you about this falsehood, and to what an extent the world falls for this chicanery."

Meanwhile, they became hungry, and they discovered that they still had three or four groschen. They went to a public

---

miracle worker. *Baal Shem* in the text, literally, "master of the name." This is a person who was able to use God's names to bring about miracles (see Story #3). This concept is often discussed in the Talmud. This might be an allusion to the Baal Shem Tov, the founder of Chasidism, and a great-grandfather of Rabbi Nachman. This might also be an allusion to the concept of miracles in general, which the Sophisticate dismissed as superstition. Since this city is Jerusalem, it is taught that ten miracles occurred there (in the time of the Temple) (*Avoth* 5:5).

The Midrash teaches that God's name is not complete as long as Amalek exists in the world (see Rashi on Exodus 17:16). Therefore, the Sophisticate, who is an aspect of Amalek, pits himself against the "Master of the Name," who strives to make God's name whole (*Rimzey Maasioth*).

From this we see that we must believe in tzaddikim who know how to use divine names when necessary to destroy the forces of evil (*Zimrath HaAretz*).

tremendous falsehood. If he denied the existence of God, he certainly denied the possibility that anyone could produce miracles with His name (*Likutey Etzoth* B, *Temimuth* 8).

It is true, however, that Rabbi Nachman said that in many places people gullibly accept miracle workers, while in other places they do not (*Sichoth HaRan* 63).

kitchen where food can be bought for even as little as three or four groschen. They ordered food and were served.

While they were eating, they spoke about the miracle worker, and made fun of the concept, saying how false and foolish it was. The restaurant owner overheard their words, and he became very angry. The miracle worker was very highly esteemed in that area.

"Eat what you have in front of you," he said to them, "and then get out of here!"

Then the miracle worker's son came in. They continued to make fun of the miracle worker in his son's presence. The restaurant owner rebuked them for making fun of the miracle worker while his son was there. Finally, he beat them soundly and threw them out.

They were very angry, and wanted to sue the restaurateur for beating them. They decided to go to the innkeeper, where they had left their luggage, to seek advice as to how to obtain justice for what had happened. They came and told him that the owner of the public kitchen had beaten them very severely.

When the innkeeper asked them why, they told him that it was because they had spoken against the miracle worker.

"It is certainly not right to beat up people," said [the innkeeper], "but you also did not act properly in speaking against the miracle worker. The miracle worker is very highly respected in these parts."

They concluded that there was nothing to [the innkeeper either]. He was also deluded by this superstition. They went to the town clerk.

The town clerk was a gentile. They told him the story of how they had been beaten.

When [the town clerk] asked them why it had happened, they replied that it was because they had spoken against the miracle worker. The town clerk beat them soundly and had them thrown out of his office.

They went from place to place, from one official to a higher official, until they finally came to the prime minister.

Guards were stationed in front of the prime minister's

residence. They told the prime minister that people wanted to see him, and he bid them enter.

The Sophisticate came in before the prime minister. As soon as they entered, the prime minister recognized that this was his old friend, the Sophisticate. The Sophisticate, however, did not recognize him, since he was now such a great person.

The prime minister immediately said to him, "Look at my simplicity. It brought me such greatness. But what did your sophistication bring you?"

"That you are my old friend the Simpleton," replied the Sophisticate "can be discussed later. Now I want justice for having been beaten."

"Why did it happen?" asked [the prime minister].

"Because I spoke against the miracle worker," replied [the Sophisticate]. "I said that it was superstition and a great fraud."

The Simpleton, who was prime minister, spoke up and said, "You still hold by your sophistication! See! You said that you could achieve what I have very easily, but I would never be able to attain what you have. But I have attained what you have, and you have not yet attained what I have. I see that it is more difficult for you to achieve my simplicity." *

Nevertheless, since the [Simpleton] knew him * from a long time ago when he was great, he ordered that [the Sophisticate] be given clothing. He then invited him to eat with him.

During the meal, they began to converse. The Sophisticate began to argue his case that there is no king.

The simple prime minister rebuked him. "I myself have seen the king!"

---

difficult for you to achieve my simplicity. We thus see that it is more difficult to attain simplicity and straightforwardness than it is to attain sophistication (*Rimzey Maasioth*). If a person is simple and straightforward, he can reach a higher level of wisdom than one who is casuistic and sophisticated. Once a person tries to be sophisticated and complex, it is very hard later on for him to attain the path of simplicity (*Likutey Etzoth* B, *Temimuth* 6).

knew him. Here again, we see how important it is to be close to a tzaddik (*Rimzey Maasioth*).

The Sophisticate laughed and asked, "Are you really certain *
that he was the king? Did you really recognize him? Do you know
if his father and grandfather were kings? How do you know that
he was really the king? People only told you that he was the king.
They fooled you with their lies."

The Simpleton was very, very angry about what the other was
saying, denying the king's existence.

In the middle of all this, someone came and said, "The Devil *
has sent for you."

The Simpleton began to tremble * very, very much. He ran
and told his wife that he was very much afraid, since the Devil had
sent for him. His wife advised him to send for the miracle worker.
When they sent for him, the miracle worker came and gave him
amulets * and other means of protection. He said, "Now you have
nothing to fear." He had great faith in this.

Later, the Sophisticate and the Simpleton were sitting together
again. "Why were you so frightened?" asked the Sophisticate.

"Because [the Devil] sent for us," replied [the Simpleton].

---

are you really certain... At first his argument was that no one had ever seen the king. Then,
when he discovered someone who had seen the king, he questioned whether this was really
the king (*Likutey Etzoth* B, *Temimuth* 8). He has made the step from skepticism to
dogmatic atheism. He ends up even more irrational than the believer.

It is a historical fact that the Israelites received the Torah at Sinai; this was witnessed
by the entire nation of Israel. Yet the nonbeliever tries to find some rational "explanation"
to dismiss this.

Devil. *Teivel* in Yiddish; *azazel* in Hebrew. The term *azazel* is found in the Torah, relating
to the place where the Yom Kippur scapegoat was sent (Leviticus 16:10). In general, it
denotes the forces of evil (*Rimzey Maasioth*).

began to tremble. He was frightened by the devil because he had entered into a debate with
the atheistic Sophisticate. He was frightened even though he rebuked the Sophisticate.
This teaches how important it is to avoid nonbelievers, and not even to debate with them
(*Rimzey Maasioth*).

amulets. *Kemea.* Such charms are mentioned in the Talmud in a number of places. There is
even a distinction made, where one is allowed to wear an amulet on the Sabbath if it has
been proved effective, but not if it has not (*Shabbath* 61a).

The only protection the Simpleton had after associating with the atheist was to
associate with the tzaddik (see *Rimzey Maasioth*).

[The Sophisticate] laughed and said, "Do you really believe in the Devil?"*

"Who then sent for us?" asked [the Simpleton].

The Sophisticate spoke up and said, "It was most probably my brother,* who is trying to see me. He sent for me with that pretense."

"And how did he get through the guards?"* asked the Simpleton.

"He must have bribed them," said the Sophisticate. "They purposely lied and said that they did not see him."

In the middle of this conversation, someone again came and said, "The Devil has sent for you."

The Simpleton was not afraid at all, since he had the protection that the miracle worker had given him. "Now what do you say?" he declared to the Sophisticate.

"I have a brother who is angry with me," the other answered. "He is pulling this trick in order to frighten me."

He stood up and asked the one who had come for them, "What does the one who sent for us look like? What is his face like? What color hair does he have?" He asked a few more, similar questions.

The messenger gave a description.

"But this is an exact description of my brother," declared the Sophisticate.

"Will you go with him?" asked the Simpleton.

---

really believe in the Devil. Just as we believe in God, we must also believe that evil exists. The denial of evil comes from evil itself (*Zimrath HaAretz*).

my brother. This is the first mention of such a brother. In the beginning of the story, it specifically states that each homeowner had one son. However, he is inadvertently admitting that the Devil is his brother. This is not his companion, since as we see, his companion was with him.

"Save me, please, from *my brother*, from Esau" (Genesis 32:9). From my brother who acts towards me with love, and from Esau who acts towards me with hate, save me from them both (*Beth HaLevi ad. loc.*). This indicates how much one must be distant from these intellectuals (Rabbi Chaim Kramer).

guards. *Vartish* in the text.

"Sure," replied the other. "Just give me a few soldiers as an escort,* so he won't harass me."

[The Simpleton] provided him with an escort. The Sophisticate and his companion went with the messenger who had come for them. Soon the soldiers returned.

"Where are the Sophisticate and his companion?" asked the prime minister.

[The soldiers] replied that they did not know, since the two had vanished.

[The Devil] had captured the Sophisticate and his companion, and had brought them to a quicksand bog.* The Devil sat on a throne in the middle of this bog, and he threw the Sophisticate and his companion into the mud. The bog was thick and sticky like glue, and they could not move at all in it.

[When the Devil and his cohorts began to torture these two sophisticates,] they screamed out, "Fiends! Why are you torturing us? Does such a thing as the Devil really exist? You are fiends, and you are torturing us for nothing!"

(These two sophisticates still did not believe in the Devil.* They thought that these were wicked people, who were torturing them for no reason.)

The two sophisticates remained in the bog, and they tried to analyze their situation. "What does this mean?" [they said]. "These are common hooligans.* We argued with them once, and now they are torturing us so much."

The two were tortured, and they suffered for many years.

One day, the Simpleton was walking in front of the miracle worker's house. He remembered his friend,* the Sophisticate, and

---

escort. *Zlaga* in the text.

bog. Symbolic of their disbelief. It is like glue trapping them and not letting them move. This is symbolic of purgatory.

did not believe in the Devil. No matter what happens, the Sophisticate clings to his disbelief. Even supernatural events do not change his mind (*Likutey Etzoth* B, *Temimuth* 4). Therefore, even though he was thrown into the bog, his heart was so twisted he could not admit to the truth. It is thus taught, "The wicked do not repent even at the door to Gehenom" (*Eruvin* 19a; *Zimrath HaAretz*).

hooligans. *Hultiyas* in Yiddish; *puchazim* in Hebrew.

He remembered his friend. The fact that the Sophisticate had once been the Simpleton's

went in to the miracle worker. He bowed to him, as nobles do, and asked if it would be possible to see the [Sophisticate] and free him.

"Do you remember the Sophisticate?" he asked the miracle worker. "The Devil sent for him and carried him away. Since that day, I never saw him again."

"Yes," replied the other. ["I remember him."]

[The Simpleton] asked him to show him where [the Sophisticate] was, and to free him.

"Certainly," replied the miracle worker. "I can show you where he is, and I can free him. But no one can go* except you and me."

They went together.* The miracle worker did what he had to do, and they came to the place. They saw the [two sophisticates] lying in the thick mud and quicksand.

When the Sophisticate saw the prime minister, he screamed to him, "My brother! Look! These fiends are beating me and torturing me for no reason!"

The prime minister rebuked him. "You are still immersed in your sophisticated ways. You do not believe anything. You are trying to tell me that these are human beings! But here is the miracle worker whom you denied. He is the only one who can free you, [and he will show you the truth]."

The Simpleton, who was prime minister, asked the miracle

friend saved him in the end. This teaches us the importance of being close to the righteous (*Rimzey Maasioth*).

no one can go. There are realms of evil into which only the greatest tzaddikim can go (*Likutey Moharan* 64).

They went together. Atheists are punished in the next world, and they can only be rescued by the tzaddik and the simple person (*Likutey Etzoth* B, *Temimuth* 4). The true tzaddik has the power to extricate the wicked even from the lowest levels of Gehenom (*Zimrath HaAretz*; see *Zohar* 3:220b; also *Sotah* 10b, *Tosafoth* s.v. *d'eisay l'almah d'asi*).

Thus, even the lowest sparks can be elevated by the tzaddik. It is thus taught that Haman's descendants taught Torah publicly (*Sanhedrin* 96b). Nevertheless, there is also an evil that cannot be rectified, and must ultimately be obliterated (*Chokhmah U'Tevunah* 2).

worker to free them, and show them that this was really the Devil and not a human being.

The miracle worker did what he had to do, and they were suddenly standing on dry land. The bog simply vanished, and the evil spirits* turned to dust.

The Sophisticate saw it all, and he was forced to admit to the truth, that there was a king....*

The Rebbe's lesson,* which discusses simplicity, is a commentary on this story. It teaches that the object of Judaism is not sophistication, but simplicity and straightforwardness.

After telling this story, [Rabbi Nachman] declared, "If a prayer is not said properly, it is a triangular shoe."*

Think about the story itself. A person can have bread, water, and a sheepskin, and have a better and happier life than the most sophisticated and wealthiest person, since the latter always tends to be miserable. In the end, things turned out best for the Simpleton, who was always satisfied with what he had and was constantly cheerful.

---

evil spirits. *Mazikim* in the text, literally "destroyers."

that there was a king. The fact that he was a childhood friend of the Simpleton eventually led the Sophisticate back to the truth (*Rimzey Maasioth, Zimrath HaAretz*).

lesson... *Likutey Moharan Tinyana* 19.

triangular shoe. Like the one the Simpleton made, (see above, p. 171). The following material is found in the Hebrew, but not in the Yiddish:

This story told a lesson about sophistication and simplicity. The main perfection is only simplicity and straightforwardness.

Also the concept of Amalek, who was sophisticated and denied the main thing...

We see in the verse, "Seven times fall the righteous and he rises (*sheva yipol tzaddik ve-kam* — שבע יפול צדיק וקם) that the final letters spell out Amalek (עמלק). The main reason for falling is sophistication... See there.

Also, Agog was a descendant of Amalek. Even though he saw his downfall when Samuel came to Saul to kill him, he did not believe. It is thus written, "Agog went with luxury" (1 Samuel, 15:32). The *Targum Yonathan* translates it *mefanka*, which means "luxury," for he still did not believe in his downfall until he saw with his own eyes the end of his downfall. Then he said, "Aha, take away the bitterness of death" (1 Samuel, 15:32). Until then he did not believe. (Place your eyes on the story and you will understand wonders of wonders.)

But one who is sophisticated, and thinks too much, is always troubled. He is constantly miserable and never enjoys life, and in the end, he can be totally destroyed. His only hope is that the Simpleton will have pity on him and help him.

Besides this, this story also contains very deep mysteries. Throughout these stories are great mysteries of the Torah.

And if a prayer is not correct, it is a shoe with three corners, and understand.

Also, look at the end of the book in the commentary of the rabbi and you will see wondrous explanations.

10

THE BURGHER AND THE PAUPER *

Once there was a burgher,* [that is a great merchant]* who

The Burgher and the Pauper. This story was told after Purim in 1809 (*Chayay Moharan* 15c
#59). Rabbi Nachman had been told about something written in golden letters, and related
it to this story, where the pauper is given a document in golden letters (*Chayay Moharan*
15d #1). After the story, the people said, "For God will console Zion" (*ki nicham Hashem
Tzion*) (Isaiah 51:3) (*Rimzey Maasioth, Hashmatoth*).
    This is a very complex story and it is very difficult to interpret. In general, it speaks
about the redemption and the Messiah (*Rimzey Maasioth*). The theme is closely related to
"The Lost Princess" and "The King and the Emperor"
burgher. A member of the middle class, the bourgeoisie. He was not a member of the
peasant class, nor of the aristocratic class.
    At the end of the story, Rabbi Nachman states that the burgher is alluded to in the
instructions given to Lot when Sodom and Gomorrah were destroyed, "flee to the
mountain" (Genesis 19:17). The Yiddish for mountain is *burg*. Actually, Lot did not end
up in the mountain, but in Tzoar (Genesis 19:22). The mountain denotes Abraham's merit,
as it is written, "When God destroyed...he remembered Abraham, and took out Lot..."
19:29). Lot then lived in a cave, and as a result, fathered Moab through his daughter
(Genesis 19:37). Ruth was a descendant of Moab, and King David, the ancestor of the
Messiah, was her descendant (*Rimzey Maasioth*). Thus, Lot's fleeing and escaping in
Abraham's merit began the process that would lead to the Messianic goal.
    The Patriarchs are often alluded to by mountains in such verses as, "jumping over the
mountains" (Song of Songs 2:9), and "Listen, you mountains" (Micah 6:2) (*Zimrath
HaAretz*). Therefore, the burgher can represent the archetype of the Patriarchs, especially
Abraham. A mountain is something huge, and the burgher is seen as a spiritual giant. A
mountain is used in a very similar imagery in "The Spider and the Fly." Here, we indeed
see the burgher as wealthy in both money and spirit.
    The term mountain also is often used to denote Jerusalem, which is called "God's
mountain." Jerusalem is a place where the merit and spiritual essence of the Patriarchs is
concentrated, as it is written, "Jerusalem has mountains around it" (Psalms 125:2)
(*Zimrath HaAretz*).
    Thus, in general, the burgher in this story can be seen as the spiritual nature and merit
of the Patriarchs, most notably, of Abraham.
great merchant. This is in the Yiddish only.

was extremely wealthy. He was involved with many types of merchandise, and his notes* and letters* were accepted* all over the world. He had the best of everything.

Below him lived a pauper.* He was extremely poor and the opposite of the wealthy burgher in every respect.

Both of them were childless.* In this respect the two were alike.

Once, the burgher dreamed* that people had come [to his house] and were packing bundles.

"What are you doing?" he asked.

"We are bringing everything to the pauper," they replied.

When he discovered that they wanted to take all his wealth and bring it to the pauper, he was very upset. However, since there were so many people involved, he could not dissuade them with his anger. The strangers made bundles of everything, including all his merchandise, his wealth and his inheritance. They carried everything to the pauper's house, not leaving anything in his house except the bare walls.

He was very upset, but then he woke up and realized that it had all been a dream. However, even after he realized that it had been nothing but a dream, and thank God, everything was still in his possession, his heart beat with great apprehension. The dream upset him very much, and he could not get it out of his mind.

---

notes. *Vekslin* in Yiddish, "exchange notes."

letters. *Briev* in Yiddish.

accepted. Expressed idiomatically by "went out."

pauper. As we see from the story, the pauper was poor in spirit. Unlike the burgher, who was willing to risk his life for others, the pauper was willing to kill for the sake of his pride.

   From the context, it appears that the pauper here represents the gentile world. In particular, he may symbolize Lot, as indicated at the end of the story. It is the Pauper who gives birth to the beautiful daughter, who might be a representation of Lot's descendant Ruth.

childless. Abraham was originally childless. He had Ishmael, but he was only the son of the slave. Lot also only had daughters, but no sons.

dreamed. This may be the vision that Abraham had, that his children would be exiled (Genesis 15). Power and wealth in the spiritual realm would be taken from him and given to the gentile world (see *Bereshith Rabbah loc. cit.*).

Before this he would also care for the pauper and his wife, giving them whatever he could. Now, after the dream, he began giving them even more care than before. However, whenever the poor man or his wife came to his house, his expression would change, and, recalling the dream, he would be very frightened.

The pauper and his wife were frequent visiters of his and would go in to him often. Once the pauper's wife* came to him, and he gave her his gift. His expression changed, and he appeared very frightened and confused.

"I beg your pardon," the woman said, "but could you tell me what's wrong. Whenever we come to you, your expression changes very much."

He told her the whole story about his dream, and how, ever since, he had been extremely apprehensive.

She mentioned a certain date, and asked, "Did the dream take place on that night?"

"Yes!" he replied. "What does it mean?"

"On that night I also had a dream," she said. "I dreamed that I was very wealthy, and that people came to my house, making many packages. I asked them where they were carrying them, and they replied, 'To the pauper!' (They were referring to the burgher, but now they call him the pauper.) Why are you so worried about a dream? I also had a dream."

Hearing her dream, [the burgher] was all the more frightened and confused. It seemed that his wealth and property were destined to be brought to the pauper, and that the pauper's poverty was to be brought to him. He was extremely frightened.

One day* the burgher's wife took a trip by coach. She invited her friends to join her, and among them was the pauper's wife.

---

pauper's wife. Significantly, she has the complement of the burgher's dream, and not her husband. She is modest, innocent and loyal, having many of the qualities that are lacking in the pauper himself.
One day. Literally, "And it was the day." See Story #2, p.62.

On the journey, they encountered a general* and his army. They turned off the road to avoid him, but as the army passed, he noticed that women were traveling, and he gave orders that one of them should be taken. [His men] went and took the pauper's wife, forcing her into the general's coach. They then left with her.

They were soon far away and there was no way that she could be rescued. Besides, the general had his whole army with him. So he took her and brought her back to his land.

The woman was very God-fearing,* and ignored [the general's] entreaties, weeping very much. They implored her and wooed her, but she remained very God-fearing.

Meanwhile, [the women] returned home from their journey, and reported that the pauper's wife had been snatched away. The pauper wept and mourned for his wife incessantly.

One day the burgher passed by the pauper's house and heard him weeping and lamenting. He went in and asked, "Why are you lamenting and weeping so bitterly?"

"Why shouldn't I weep?" replied the pauper. "What do I have left? Some people may have wealth or children, but I have nothing. Now my wife was also taken from me. So what do I have left?"

The burgher's heart melted and he had great pity on the pauper, seeing his great bitterness.

Then [the burgher] did something reckless.* It was really utter madness. He made inquiry as to where the general lived, and went there.

---

general. *Jedniral* in Yiddish. This may represent Lot being captured in Sodom, where he was a captive of the forces of evil. He was saved through the merit of Abraham.

Moab was born through an incestuous liaison between Lot and his eldest daughter. Thus, the soul of the offspring was symbolically taken captive by the forces of evil. It would not be released until the birth of Ruth.

God-fearing. She had every opportunity and temptation to sin, but she did not. Therefore, she was worthy of having such a wonderful daughter (*Rimzey Maasioth*).

reckless. Our entire service is to take the Holy out of the realm of evil. Sometimes a person has great motivation to do something holy, and as a result does something so reckless that it seems mad. No one would ever think that he could succeed, but because of his great motivation, he overcomes all barriers and succeeds. He can then free the holy essence.

But when a person does this, he must be able to "run and return" (Ezekiel 1:14). After

When he got there, he again did something highly reckless. He marched right into the general's house. There were guards around the house, but [the burgher] was behaving so recklessly that he was oblivious to them. He was in such a state of recklessness that he did not pay any attention to the guards.

When they saw a person approaching them in such a wild manner, the guards were also confused and frightened. They were too confused to understand how he had arrived there. Almost in panic, the guards did not challenge, and he was able to pass through all the guards until he got into the general's house where [the pauper's] wife was lying.

He went over to her and woke her up. "Come!" he said.

When she saw him, she was confused and frightened. "Come with me immediately!" he urged her.

She went with him, and again they passed all the guards, until they were outside. Only then did he realize what he had done. He realized that there would soon be an alarm sounded.

And so it was. There was a great outcry in the general's house.

[The burgher] hid himself in a pit full of rainwater* until the

---

such an act, he must be able to regain full mastery of his mind (*Likutey Etzoth* B, *Yirah VeAvodah* 38).

A great Breslover leader, Rabbi Avraham ben Rabbi Nachman of Tulchin, taught, "Sometimes, when a person is involved in a holy mission, he must dig a hole, jump in, and then worry about how to get out."

Here, it appears that the reckless thing that Abraham did was to use his merit to bring out a descendant, namely Ruth. This was done physically, when Lot was rescued from Sodom through his merit, as we have seen. It may have also involved rescuing Ruth's soul from the realm of evil. The reckless deed may have thus been the event of Judah and Tamar, as we shall see.

In general, it appears as if the pauper's wife is the spiritual essence of the gentiles. Abraham is known as "the father of all proselytes" (see Rashi on Genesis 17:5). Abraham recklessly allowed his merit to be used to free these souls from the realm of evil and *klipah*.

pit full of rainwater. This has the status of a mikvah, and can be used for ritual immersions. This was true of all the bodies of water in which they hid.

This is significant, since the only way a person can become a proselyte is by immersion in a mikvah. If we see this escape as Abraham's merit bringing gentile souls, especially that of Ruth, from the *klipah*, then he literally caused her to immerse.

outcry died down. He remained in this pit with [the pauper's wife] for two days.

The woman saw the great self-sacrifice that he had made for her, as well as the great suffering he had endured for her sake. She realized that it might one day be possible that she would have some good fortune, greatness and success, so she made an oath * before God that if she ever had any good fortune, she would not withhold it from [the burgher]. Even if he wanted to take all her fortune and greatness, so that she would be just as she was originally, she would not stop him at all.

But how could witnesses be found in such a place? She took the pit as a witness. *

After two days, he left with her. They went further, but as they continued their escape, they realized that people were still searching for them in that area. This time, he hid himself in a mikvah * with her.

Again, she thought about the great sacrifice and suffering that he had endured for her. She made the same oath as before, this time making the mikvah her witness. They remained there approximately two days.

They then left and went further. Upon a number of occasions, he had to hide with her in similar places, so that all together, they hid in seven places of water. * There were the pit and mikvah

---

On a very simple level, mikvah is seen as a means of purification. Since they were fleeing the forces of evil, they had to make every effort to purify themselves. This is especially true when they were close to being caught. Through immersing in such water, they were worthy of the Torah, which is also likened to water (*Biur HaLikutim* 61:68; *Chokhmah U'Tevunah* 2).

made an oath. This was an unbreakable bond that the spiritual essence of the gentiles would help the Israelites reach their goal (see *Zimrath HaAretz*).

pit as a witness. There is a famous story of a girl who took a pit and a weasel as witnesses to an oath when a boy saved her from a pit (Rashi, *Tosafoth Taanith* 8a, s.v. *MeChuldah; HaShulchan Arukh* s.v. *Chalad; The Torah Anthology,* Volume 3, p. 106).

mikvah. A specially made pool, used for ritual immersion.

seven places of water. Kabbalistically, the seven bodies of water here represent the seven lower sefiroth (cf. *Rimzey Maasioth*). This alludes to the seven bodies of water surrounding the Holy Land (*Zimrath HaAretz*). It also represents the seven voices through which the

mentioned above, a pool, * a spring, a stream, a river, and a lake. In every place they hid, she remembered his self-sacrifice and suffering, and made the same oath she had made earlier, taking the place as a witness. They continued traveling, hiding in these places, until they finally came to the sea.

Since he was a great merchant, as soon as they reached the sea,* he knew what to do,* and was able to make arrangements to reach his homeland. He finally came home with the pauper's wife, and returned her to the pauper. The joy was tremendous.

Torah was given (*Chokhmah U'Tevunah* 1).

However, it seems to me that this may also represent the seven generations from Judah's son Peretz, to Boaz, who married Ruth: Peretz, Chetzron, Ram, Aminadav, Nachshon, Salmon, Boaz (Ruth 4:18-21). The spiritual essence had to be purified through all these levels.

The places of water also represent tests, since he spent the night in them with another man's wife. But when evil is pursuing, a mikvah is a place of purification and it is a good place to hide (*Likutey Etzoth* B, *Yirah VeAvodah* 38). The seven bodies of water thus represent seven tests. This also seems to be hinted in the princess' later words to her suitors, "The waters have not passed over you."

Water also alludes to love and kindness. The water of kindness that impelled the burgher to do this daring deed was what protected him from the pursuing evil.

Rabbi Nathan explains this in terms of the verse, "Truth was cast down to the earth" (Daniel 8:12). The Midrash states that when God was about to create man, Truth spoke up against it, and said that in truth, man would sin and be unworthy and false. But God did not listen, and cast Truth down to the earth (*Bereshith Rabbah* 8:5). This is because God is even higher than Truth, and Truth cannot conceive of God's will until it is cast down to the realm of the physical — "to the earth." Thus, being cast down to the earth was Truth's rectification. Then, "Truth springs forth from the earth" (Psalms 85:12).

This was just like the pauper's wife, who could not have any children until she had been taken captive. Furthermore, because the burgher had passed through the seven waters, his son was the only one who could marry the daughter of the pauper's wife (*Likutey Halakhoth, Ribbith* 5:20,21).

It is significant that the Talmud relates this same verse, "Truth springs forth from the earth," to the story of the oath on the pit, mentioned above.

pool. *Agam* in Hebrew; *gemozukhtz* in Yiddish.

sea. Perhaps the Sea of Wisdom.

knew what to do. After a reckless act, one must be able to return to one's normal intelligence and faculties (*Likutey Etzoth* B, *Yirah VeAvodah* 38). One cannot remain constantly in a state of recklessness.

The burgher was rewarded for this, as well as for resisting temptation with her. He was granted a special providence* by God, and that year he had a son.*

The pauper's wife had also resisted temptation, both with the general and with [the burgher]. As a result, she was worthy, and she gave birth to a daughter.*

[The daughter] was extremely beautiful. It was a beauty that totally set her apart from the rest of humanity. Such beauty is never found among human beings. People would say, "She should only reach maturity!" [When a person is so unique,* it is difficult for him to survive to maturity.] Her beauty and loveliness* were very extraordinary, the likes of which had never before been seen in the world.

---

special providence... *Pakad* in Hebrew. The sign of the Messiah will be *pakod pakad-ti.* The first words that Moses was to say in God's name to the sages of Israel were, " *pakod pakad-ti eth-chem* (פקד פקדתי אתכם), "I have definitely kept you in mind." There was a tradition that when a person came before the Israelites and said in God's name the words " *pakod pakad-ti,*" he would be the true redeemer (*The Torah Anthology*, Volume 4, p. 93). (*Rimzey Maasioth, Rimzey Maasioth Hashmatoth*).

son. This is the soul of the Messiah. He thus had to have all the proper signs. At the end of the story, Rabbi Nachman says,"The Messiah will tell Israel everything that happened" (see *Chayay Nefesh* 21, p. 33,34).

Rabbi Nachman states at the end of the story that Tamar also had signs (see Genesis 38:25), and that the Messiah would be her descendant. Tamar was Judah's daughter-in-law, but she had relations with him, and bore him Peretz, who was King David's ancestor.

Thus, just as Lot's spiritual essence entered the realm of evil when he had relations with his daughters, so did Abraham's when Judah was with Tamar. Abraham's essence had to enter the realm of evil in order to rescue Lot's, this being the "reckless act" mentioned earlier. It was only Boaz, a descendant of Judah's liaison, who could rescue Ruth from the domain of evil, and eventually give rise to the soul of the Messiah (see *Zohar* 1:187b).

daughter. She is the Shekhinah, the root of holiness of Israel (*Likutey Etzoth* B, *Yirah VeAvodah* 39), also known as "the Congregation of Israel" (*Rimzey Maasioth, Hashmatoth*). She was personified by Ruth, who was the ancestress of David, and hence of the Messiah. She could only be born after the pauper's wife had been taken captive

unique. A *chidush* in the original; literally "something new," or "something that was never before seen." It would be difficult for her to grow to maturity, because unusual individuals are subject to the evil eye.

loveliness. *Tifereth,* also the name of a sefirah.

All the world came to see her, and they were astonished at her extraordinary beauty. Out of their love for her, they gave her many gifts. She was given so many gifts that the pauper soon became very wealthy.

Meanwhile, the burgher got the idea that he would have his son marry the poor man's daughter, since the girl was such a unique beauty. He said to himself, that this might be the significance of the dreams, where that which was his was brought to the pauper, and that which was the pauper's was brought to him. The dream might mean that they should make a match between their children, and, as a result, what was theirs would be exchanged.

One day, when the pauper's wife visited him, he told her of his idea that their children marry each other. He suggested that through such a match the dreams might come true.

"I have also thought about this," she replied, "but I could never be so bold as to propose such a match to you. If you want it, I am certainly prepared to go along with it, and I will do nothing to stop you. I have already sworn that I will never withhold from you any good or success that I have."

The [burgher's] son and the [pauper's] daughter went to school together,* learning foreign languages and the like. Meanwhile, people would come to see the daughter because of her unusual beauty, and they gave her so many gifts that the pauper became quite wealthy.

Royal ministers also came to see the girl, and they were very pleased with what they saw. They realized that her beauty was unique and extraordinary, beyond normal human bounds.

Then some of the ministers got the idea of making a match with the pauper. Ministers who had sons very much wanted their sons to marry her. However, it would not be proper for them to marry someone of such low station. They therefore made an effort to raise the pauper's status.

---

went to school together. Like the emperor's daughter and king's son in "The Emperor and the King."

They arranged for the pauper to get an appointment in the emperor's service as a lieutenant.* They then worked to have him promoted, and he quickly rose from one rank to the next, until he became a general. At this point, the ministers proposed matches to him, but it was difficult for him to decide, since many were rushing to propose matches, and many had worked to secure his promotions. Besides, he could not make a match with them, since he had already promised his daughter to the burgher.

Once the pauper became a general, his success continued. The emperor sent him to lead battles, and he was constantly victorious. He was promoted still higher, and his success continued.

Then the emperor died. All the citizens decided that the pauper should be the new emperor. When the ministers met, they all agreed that he would be the emperor.*

[The man who had previously been the pauper] thus became emperor. He fought battles and was victorious, conquering many lands. He was victorious in battle, and continued making conquests, until all the other lands decided that they would willingly subjugate themselves to him. They saw his great success, since he had all the beauty in the world,* as well as every possible good fortune. All the kings therefore decided that he would be emperor over the entire world, and they gave him a document written in golden letters.*

The emperor now refused to make a match* with the burgher. He was an emperor now, and it was beneath his station to make a

---

lieutenant. *Prapirchik* in Yiddish. This might denote Moab becoming a powerful nation.

emperor. Denoting that the gentile nations gained world dominance. The term used here is *kaiser,* the same as in Story #2, p.55.

all the beauty in the world. His daughter.

written in golden letters. The event that prompted this story was when Rabbi Nachman had been told about a document written in golden letters (*Chayay Moharan* 15d #1).

refused to make a match. Although he had been raised to a high position, the pauper remained poor in spirit. Rabbi Nachman taught that the poor are distant from mercy, and can be very cruel (*Sichoth HaRan* 89; see *Zohar* 1:13b).

match with a mere burgher. However, his wife, the empress, refused to abandon the burgher, and the emperor therefore saw that he could not make another match if it meant denying the burgher. He felt totally stymied, since his wife supported [the burgher] very strongly.

He therefore began to devise plans against the burgher. His first plan was to lower [the burgher's] status. He carried out these plans, as if it were not through him that [the burgher] suffered losses. A world emperor certainly has this power. He caused [the burgher] to suffer losses and lowered his status, until [the burgher] was impoverished and totally penniless. *

Nevertheless, the empress continued to support [the burgher]. The emperor realized that as long as [the burgher's] son was alive, it would be impossible to make another match, and he began working to remove the burgher's son. * He devised a plan to be rid of him, setting up false charges, and appointing judges to try the case. The judges understood that the emperor wanted to be totally rid of [the young man], so they sentenced him to be placed in a sack * and thrown into the sea.

In her heart, the empress was very grieved because of this. However, even the empress could do nothing to oppose the emperor.

Then she had an idea. She went to the men whose job it was to throw [the young man] into the sea. When she came to them, she fell at their feet, * pleading very much that they spare him for her

---

totally penniless. This represents the exile of the Israelites from their land and their subjugation and persecution by the gentiles.

to remove the burgher's son. The nations tried to pervert the concept of the Messiah. However, the exile of the son eventually led him to be reunited with his bride (*Rimzey Maasioth*). We learn from this that apparently evil happenings can have long-term good benefits.

placed in a sack. Just like the emperor's daughter is later placed in a sack (*Rimzey Maasioth*). Earlier we saw that the burgher and the pauper were exactly the same. Now their children share very much the same destiny.

fell at their feet. First the burgher had risked his life to save the pauper's wife. Now she is willing to take a risk to save the burgher's son.

sake. After all, why did he deserve to be put to death? She pleaded that they take a prisoner* who had been sentenced to death anyway and throw him into the sea, sparing the young man.

Her pleading was effective, and they swore to her that they would spare him. They threw another man into the sea and spared [the burgher's son]. "Get away from here!" they told him, and he went.

The boy was quite intelligent already, so he went on his way.

Before this had happened, the empress summoned her daughter. "My daughter," she said, "you must realize that this burgher's son is your destined bridegroom."

She then told [her daughter] her entire story. "The burgher risked his life for me, and was with me together in seven places. I swore to God that I would never withhold my good from him, and took these seven places as my witnesses. (These were the pit, the mikvah, and the other places mentioned earlier.) Now, you are all my good, my fortune, and my success. Certainly, you belong to him, and his son shall be your husband. But because of his pride, your father wants to kill him for no reason. I have already made an effort to save him, and I have been successful. But you must realize that he is your true bridegroom, and you must never agree to marry anyone else."

The [daughter] accepted her mother's words, because she also feared Heaven.* She replied that she would certainly abide by her [mother's] words.

The daughter then sent a letter* to the burgher's son, who was

---

take a prisoner. Later, a sailor was substituted for the emperor's daughter in a very similar fashion.

feared Heaven. And wanted to fulfill her mother's oath.

letter. Although the burgher's son and the princess had gone to school together as children, she had never seen him as an adult. Therefore, the letter would be her only sure way of recognizing him. Later, we find that when he lost the letter, she would not believe who he was.

This letter thus denotes the signs that the Messiah will have, through which he will gain acceptance among the Israelites (see end of story; also see *Rimzey Maasioth; Likutey Etzoth B, Yirah VeAvodah* 39).

still in prison at the time. She wrote that she considered herself promised to him, and that he was her destined bridegroom. She sent him a fragment of a map, drawing on it all the places where her mother had hidden with his father, the pit, the mikvah and the other places which had been the seven witnesses. On it, she drew pictures of a pit, a mikvah, and the other places. She warned him very, very strongly that he should be very, very careful to keep this letter. Then she signed her name at the bottom.

It was after this that the ones in charge substituted another man and let [the burgher's son] go free, so that he was able to escape.

[The young man] traveled until he reached the sea, where he embarked on a ship and set out to sea. A gale then arose, carrying the ship to a desert shore. The wind was so strong that its impetus* broke the ship up. The passengers, however, survived, and they reached dry land.

Each one went on his own way to find food to sustain himself. Since it was a desert area, ships did not usually pass by.* Since they could not anticipate a ship coming and bringing them home, they went into the desert to seek food. Thus, the entire group scattered and separated.

The young man went into the desert, and he continued until he was very far from the shore. When he decided to return, he could not. The harder he tried to get back, the further he went, until he himself realized that it was impossible for him to return. He therefore continued moving on in the desert. He had a bow* to protect himself against the wild animals* in the desert.

Since the letter included part of a map with the seven bodies of water, it may contain the mystery of how Abraham rescued Ruth's soul from the *klipah*. The Messiah would use a similar means to rescue all the other souls that are trapped in the realm of evil.

impetus. *Umpit* in the original.

ships did not usually pass by. So it later would not be a coincidence when the princess and emperor landed on that island.

The Messiah's soul is on a desert, where no one ever goes.

bow. A bow usually denotes prayer (see Rashi on Genesis 48:22). The pirate did not have this weapon, and he was devoured by wild animals.

wild animals. The minions of evil (see *Likutey Etzoth, loc. cit. 39*).

Wherever he went, he was able to find something to eat. He continued walking until he came out of the desert, and found himself in an uninhabited area* where there was water surrounded by fruit trees. He thus had fruit to eat and water to drink.*

He decided that he would settle in this area and remain there for the rest of his life. He realized that it would be difficult for him to return to civilization, and if he went on, he could not be sure that he would find another place as good as this.* Therefore, he decided that he would remain there and live there for the rest of his life.

He found the place very good. He had the fruit to eat, and water to drink. Sometimes he would use his bow* and shoot a rabbit* or deer, and he would have meat to eat. There were also very good fish in the water, and he would catch them. He therefore felt that it would be quite good for him to spend the rest of his life there.

Meanwhile, the emperor assumed that the sentence had been carried out against the burgher's son, and that he was totally rid of him and could now make a match for his daughter. He therefore began to discuss matches with various kings.

The emperor established an appropriate estate for his daughter, and she remained there. While she was there, she took the daughters of noblemen* to be her companions. She would play musical instruments* and engage in similar pastimes, as was the custom.

---

uninhabited area. An area of the Garden of Eden.

fruit... and water... Good deeds and Torah.

as good as this. Like the world of souls, where one can enjoy the radiance of the Divine. He was like Jacob, who "wanted to live in tranquility" (see Rashi, *Vayeshev* Genesis 37:1).

bow. Prayer. He could get anything he needed with prayer.

rabbit. Surprisingly, a non-kosher animal (Leviticus 11:6); *arneveth* in the original. This shows that he was not a Jew. Or that the Messiah is nourished by the unclean as well as the clean.

daughters of noblemen. Possibly the souls of the righteous. In "The King and the Emperor," the emperor's daughter asks for eleven noblemen's daughters.

play musical instruments. Like the emperor's daughter in "The King and the Emperor."

Whenever a match was proposed to her, she would respond that she would not discuss any match unless the suitor came to her in person. She was very expert in the art of lyrics.*. She skillfully arranged a place where her suitors could come. He would then stand facing her and recite his lyrics. These consisted of love poems,* such as the words of passion that a person in love uses towards his beloved.

Kings would come to court her. They would go to the place and each one would recite his poem.*

[The daughter] would answer some of them through her ladies, also with a love poem. To others, whom she favored more, she would raise her voice and reply lovingly in a poem. To those whom she favored still more, she would actually show her face, and respond to him with poetry and affection. However, in the end, she would say to all of them, "But the waters did not pass* over you." No one understood what she meant by this.

Whenever she showed her face, [her suitors] would fall to the ground* upon seeing her great beauty. Some remained unconscious. Others lost their minds because of the lovesickness brought on by her very extraordinary beauty. Although people

---

lyrics. *Shir.* Can denote either song or poetry.

love poems. *Shir shel cheshek* in Hebrew and Yiddish. Many people can compose love poems, but only one will be her destined bridegroom and will be chosen (see end of story). her suitors sang to her (*Sichoth HaRan* 256).

each one would recite his poem. Such songs or poems were used to enter the realm of the spiritual, which was known as *Pardes* (*Kochavey Or* p. 125, p. 160; *Chokhmah U'Tevunah* 1).

But the waters did not pass... There are many tzaddikim who come to woo the Divine Presence, but they cannot enter, since they did not emulate the burgher, going into the realm of evil to rescue the sparks of holiness. Only the true tzaddik who is on the level of Moses or the Messiah can do this (*Likutey Halakhoth, Ribbith* 5:20; see *Likutey Moharan* 64).

would fall to the ground. Like the four who entered *Pardes,* where Ben Azzai died, Ben Zomah went mad, and Elisha ben Abuyah became an apostate (*Chagigah 14b; Rimzey Maasioth, Hashmatoth*).

went mad and were left unconscious, kings still came to woo her. But in the end, she gave them all the same answer.

Meanwhile, the burgher's son remained in that desolate place, and he made himself a place to live. He dwelled there, and he was also able to play music.* He was skilled in the art of lyrics. He looked for trees out of which musical instruments could be made, and he made himself instruments. Out of the veins of wild animals,* he made the strings. Thus, he was able to play and sing to himself.

He would take the letter that the emperor's daughter had sent him, and he would sing and play his instruments. He would remember all that happened to him, how his father had been a burgher, and how he had arrived here.

He took the letter and made a mark on a tree. There, inside the tree, he hollowed out a place, and hid the letter.

After he had been there a while, one day, there was a hurricane* that blew down all the trees. He could not recognize the tree where he had hidden the letter. As long as the trees were standing, he could recognize his sign,* but now that the trees had fallen, this tree was among the very many other trees there, and he had no way of recognizing that particular tree. There were so many trees that it was impossible for him to split them all open to find the letter. This caused him to weep and grieve very, very much.

---

play music. Like the princess.

veins of wild animals. He can take the forces of destruction, and use them for harmony. Of course, this is the concept of the Messiah.

hurricane. As if he was not far enough from the princess, now he is shunted still further, since he loses his letter (*Likutey Etzoth* 39; *Rimzey Maasioth, Hashmatoth*). However, this event moves him out of his complacency, so that they are eventually reunited. When a person becomes too complacent, sometimes a hurricane is necessary to motivate him to move again.

he could recognize his sign. At the end of the story, Rabbi Nachman mentions that Tamar also lost the signs that she had been given by Judah. They were taken away by the Satan, or Samael, the force of evil (*Sotah* 10b). This would be replayed by the Messiah, her descendant, who loses the signs that he was given to prove his identity.

He realized that the situation had become very difficult for him, and that if he remained there, his great anguish would cause him to go mad. He decided that no matter what happened to him, he would have to move on. If he did not, he would be in danger because of his great grief.

Taking some meat and fruit, he set off, clearly marking the place that he had left. He continued until he reached a civilized area. "What land is this?" he asked.

When they replied, he asked if they had ever heard of the world emperor. When they answered that they had, he asked if they had heard about his beautiful daughter. They said that they had, but it was impossible to marry her.

He decided that it would be impossible* for him to travel there, so he went to the king* of that land, and poured out his heart to him. He told him that he was her true bridegroom, and that because of him, she did not want to marry anyone else. Since it was impossible for him to go there in person, he was giving the king all the signs she had provided him, that is, the seven waters she had described. He asked that the king go there and woo her, and that [the king] should pay him for this [information].

The king realized that he was telling the truth, since it would be impossible to make up a story like this, and the idea pleased him. However, he decided that if he brought [the princess] here and the young man was also still here, it would not turn out very well. He did not have the heart to kill [the young man], since it would amount to killing him for doing a favor. Therefore, he decided to send [the burgher's son] two hundred miles* away.

---

it would be impossible. Even the Messiah gives up hope (*Zimrath HaAretz*). A tzaddik must fight constantly against this feeling of hopelessness. How much more so an ordinary person!

king. Some interpret these three kings to be false messiahs (*Rimzey Maasioth, Hashmatoth*). However, it does not seem likely that the Messiah would give his secrets to charlatans. The three kings could have been Rabbi Shimeon bar Yochai, the Ari and the Baal Shem Tov. They did not consciously cast the Messiah away, but they had so much to accomplish, that they delayed his coming in their generations. Perhaps they rectified the world so much that the Messiah did not have to come in their times.

two hundred miles. Yiddish. In Hebrew, 200 *parsaoth* or leagues.

The son was very upset by this turn of events, since he had been exiled for doing the king a favor. So he went to another king, and told him the same story. He related the signs to the second king, and also added an additional detail. He told the king that he should make haste and set out immediately, so that he would get there before the first king. But even if this king did not get there first, he still would have a more compelling sign than the other.

The second king had the same thought as the first, and he also sent the son two hundred miles away. He was very upset, so he went to a third king, and he gave this king signs that were clearer than the others.

The first king immediately set out on the journey, and came to the place where the emperor's daughter was. He composed a lyric, and skillfully included in it all the seven places that had served as witnesses. However, the rules of lyrics led him to speak of the places in a different order than the story really happened. He came to the place [set aside for wooers] and recited his lyric.

When the emperor's daughter heard the mention of these places, she was very surprised. She was positive that this was her destined husband.* However, she still had some questions, since the places were not in correct order. But she decided that he had had to change the order to make the poem rhyme, and she made up her mind that he must be the one. She wrote to him that she agreed to marry him.

There was great joy and a great shout because she had found her destined one. Plans were made for the wedding.

Meanwhile, the second king arrived in a hurry. When he was told that she had already agreed to marry another, he said that he still had something to tell her that would affect the entire situation. He got to her and recited his poem, placing all the places in correct order, and also adding an additional sign.

"Then how did the first one know all this?" she asked.

He did not think it advisable to tell the truth, so he said that he

---

her destined husband. Since the Messiah would tell Israel the entire story of their exile (see end of story).

did not know. She found this very surprising and did not know what to think. The first one had also recited all the places. How could everyone know these signs?

Still, it seemed logical that the second king was her destined one, since he had given her the signs in order. It was possible that the first one had mentioned these places merely because they had come to him while making up the poem. Meanwhile, she decided to do nothing.

After the second king had sent the young man away, the young man was very upset. He went to a third king, and told him the same story as before, and gave him signs that were even more compelling. He poured out his whole heart, telling him that he had a letter on which all these places were drawn. He told the king to draw all these places on a piece of paper and bring it to her.

Like the others, the third king decided that it would not be good if this young man were here when he brought her back. He therefore had the young man sent two hundred miles away.

The third king also rushed off to claim the beautiful princess. When he arrived, he was told that two other suitors had come earlier. He said that he would try anyway, since he had something that would change the situation. The people did not know why she wanted these kings more than the others.

The third king recited his lyric with even more obvious signs. Then he showed her his picture with all the places.

She was very confused, but she would not do anything. It had appeared that the first king was the one, and also the second king. Therefore, she said that she would not believe anything until someone brought the letter written in her own hand.

Meanwhile, the burgher's son thought, How many times will he be sent away? He therefore made up his mind that he would go there himself, since there was a chance that he would be able to accomplish something. He wandered around until he finally got there. He said that he had something to tell... and he came and recited his lyric. His signs were even more obvious. He told her how they had gone to school together, and similar personal details. He also told her how he had sent the other kings, how he had hidden the letter in a tree, and everything else that had happened to him.

Still, she refused to accept his word.* [The other kings had also some excuse for not having the letter.] Such a long time had passed that it was totally impossible to recognize him. She refused to pay heed to any signs at all until he actually brought her letter. She had already thought that the first one was surely him, and similarly the second [and then the third]. Therefore, nothing else would do.

The young man decided that it would be impossible for him to remain there too long, since the emperor might discover his presence and kill him.* He therefore made up his mind that he would go back to where he had been in the desert, and spend the rest of his life there. He walked and walked to come to this desert, and finally he arrived there.

While all this was happening, many years went by. The young man made up his mind that he would live in the desert and spend the rest of his life there. He had thought about a persons entire life in this world, and concluded that it would be best for him to spend the rest of his life there in the desert. There he lived and ate the fruits, just as before.

Meanwhile, on the sea, there was a pirate.* He heard that

---

she refused to accept his word. Since false suitors had come, she would now not accept the true one. This explains the opposition that Rabbi Nachman and the Baal Shem Tov had (*Rimzey Maasioth, Hashmatoth*). Rabbi Nachman believed that he was the tzaddik of the generation, and as such, had the soul of the Messiah. In every generation there is a tzaddik who could be the Messiah, but there is a special spirit (*ruach*) that he must be given before he can actually become the Messiah (see *Arba Meoth Shekel Kesef*, p. 68c).

and kill him. Only in the Yiddish.

pirate. Here he is called a *rotzeach*, a murderer. Later he is called a *gazlan*, a thief.

This represents the forces of evil. The side of evil tries to capture the holy. However, as we shall see, it is through this alone that the princess is uplifted and reunited with her destined one (*Rimzey Maasioth*). This is reminiscent of the princess in Story #1 who was trapped in the domain of Evil. It is significant that the pirate can capture the princess only after she rejects her true bridegroom.

The pirate may denote Edom. See Story #2, p. 69.

such a beautiful woman existed, and got the idea to take her prisoner. He himself could not do anything with her, because he was a eunuch.* However, he felt that if he could kidnap her, he could sell her to a king for a huge sum of money.* He began to set a plan in motion.

The pirate was a person who normally took risks.* He would now take a gamble. If he was successful, he would win; and if not, what would he lose? Like all pirates, he was a gambler.

The pirate went and bought a huge amount of merchandise. He also made golden birds,* and they were made with such great skill that they actually appeared to be alive. He also made golden stalks, upon which the birds stood. This itself was remarkable: although the birds were quite large, they were able to stand on the stalks without the stalks breaking.

He also made mechanisms so that the birds appeared to sing. One clicked its tongue,* one chirped,* and one sang. It was skillfully arranged that men would be in the room on the ship behind the birds, and they would manipulate invisible wires* with great skill, so that the birds would appear to be singing on their own.

Taking all this, the pirate set off to the land where the emperor's daughter was. When he came to her city, he docked his

---

eunuch. The forces of evil are sterile, and the Evil One is thus called a eunuch (*Etz Chaim, Shaar HaKlipoth* 1; cf. *Likutey Moharan* 23).

huge sum of money... Rather than contribute to civilization, he is a parasite.

took risks. *Mufkar* in the original. Literally, he had "made himself public." That is, he did not care at all about his own life or wellbeing, as long as he fulfilled his goal. In this respect, he is a parody of the burgher. We shall see that in many ways, the pirate parodies the burgher. The forces of evil always try to imitate the good.

golden birds. These may be the mentalities of the evil forces (*mochin* of the *klipah*), which are represented by birds in the Kabbalah (see *Etz Chaim, Shaar HaKlipoth* 2; *Likutey Moharan* 3). But the birds are not really alive; they are merely activated by invisible strings and wires.

clicked its tongue. *Geknakt.*

chirped. *Geshvishtshit.*

wires. *Drutten.*

ship and cast anchor.* He presented himself as a great
merchant,* and people came to buy all kinds of precious goods.*
He remained there for somewhat more than a quarter of a year,*
while people brought home the beautiful merchandise they had
bought from him.

The emperor's daughter also wanted to buy from him, and she
sent a message, asking him to send his wares to her. He replied
with a message that he has no need to bring his wares to a buyer's
house, even if she is the emperor's daughter. Whoever wants his
goods must come to him. A merchant cannot be compelled to do
otherwise.

The emperor's daughter decided to go to him. Whenever she
went out, she would place a veil over her face, so that people
would not be able to see her; otherwise they would faint because
of her beauty. She therefore covered her face.*

The emperor's daughter went out, with her face covered, and
she took her companions* with her. A troop of guards* escorted
her. She went to the "merchant" (who was actually the pirate),
bought some of his wares, and [was ready to] go on her way.

"If you come back," said the merchant, "I will show you even
more beautiful articles.* They are truly amazing." With that, she
went home.

She came again, bought some things, and went on her way.
[The pirate] remained there for a while, and she became

---

cast anchor. *Ge-ankert.*
great merchant... Like the burgher.
precious goods. Everything that evil tries to sell the world seems precious.
quarter of a year. Like the amount of time it took the Sophisticate to learn a trade in "The
Sophisticate and the Simpleton."
covered her face. Like Moses (Exodus 34:33). The Shekhinah covers her face (*Sichoth
HaRan* 86).
companions. The daughters of the noblemen, mentioned earlier.
troop of guards. *Vach.*
even more beautiful articles. The Evil Urge constantly promises a person greater and more
beautiful pleasures.

accustomed to visiting him. She would come and go.

Then one day she came to [the merchant] and he went and opened the door to the cabin where the golden birds were.* She was able to see them, and it was an amazing sight. Her bodyguards also wanted to come in.

"No no!" he said, "I don't show this to anyone except you because you are the emperor's daughter. But I don't want the others at all."

She went in alone. He also went into the room, locking the door behind them. Then he did a vulgar* thing; he forced her into a sack,* and took off all her clothing.*

He then dressed one of his sailors* with her clothing, covered his face, and pushed him out. "Go!" he said.

The sailor did not know what was happening to him. As soon as he emerged with his face covered, the guards began to escort him, not realizing who he was. They assumed that he was the emperor's daughter.

[The sailor] went along with the troop which was accompanying him, not realizing where he was until he came to the emperor's daughter's room. When he then uncovered his face, they realized that he was a sailor. There was a great uproar. They slapped him in the face* very hard and threw him out, realizing that he was ignorant, and not responsible for what had happened.

---

where the golden birds were. The birds represent the mental powers of the side of evil. Therefore, this can represent the Israelites as a whole being enticed by secular studies. Thus, the pirate may represent the *haskalah*.

vulgar. *Peshut* in Hebrew; *prust* in Yiddish.

sack. Just as the burgher's son had been placed in a sack (*Rimzey Maasioth*). Sackcloth denotes mourning and loss of status.

took off all her clothing. Took away all her spiritual garments. Adam saw that he was naked — of all good.

one of his sailors. The Evil One presents one of his minions as the Divine. People are not even aware of the holiness that they have lost, because they are given a ridiculous substitute.

slapped him in the face. This is repeated at the end of the story. Somehow it appears to relate to the false tzaddik or the *maskil*.

Having captured the emperor's daughter, the pirate knew for certain that he would be pursued. He left the ship, and hid himself together with her in a pit full of rainwater until the outcry would subside. He ordered his sailors to cut anchor and flee immediately, since they would certainly be pursued. They would surely not fire at the ship, since it would be assumed that the emperor's daughter was on board. "Therefore, flee immediately," [he said]. "If they catch you, they catch you. What will happen?" Like all pirates, they were not concerned with their own welfare. own welfare.

It happened as [he predicted]. There was a great outcry, and [the emperor's men] immediately set out after [the ship], but they did not find [the princess] there. He had hidden himself along with [the princess] in a pit of rainwater, and they remained there.

He threatened her so that she should not cry out so that people would hear her. "I have risked my life to capture you," he said. "Now that you are in my hands, if I lose my life, it is not worth anything anyway. If I lose you now, I will not be able to capture you again, and my life won't be worth living. Therefore, as soon as you scream out, I will immediately strangle you. It does not matter what will happen to me, since I do not consider my life worth anything."

She was mortally afraid. * [The emperor's daughter was afraid to scream out because of the pirate's threat.]

He finally left his hiding place, and brought her to a city. They continued traveling, until he came to a place where he realized that people were searching for him. He hid himself together with her again, this time in a mikvah.

They continued traveling, and they had to hide in other places, until they had hidden in all the seven places * in which the burgher had hidden with [the princess'] mother. [These were the seven

---

She was mortally afraid. False fear is one of the favorite weapons of the Evil One. Actually, as she realizes later, he cannot kill her, since unless she is alive, his quest is in vain.
in all the seven places. The burgher had to pass through these seven stages to escape evil. The pirate passes through them to go back to the realm of evil (See *Rimzey Maasioth*).

waters, the pit, the mikvah, the spring, and the others.]

When they finally reached the sea, he tried to find at least a fisherman's boat so that he could sail off with her. He finally found a ship, and escaped with the emperor's daughter.

He had no personal need for her, since he was a eunuch. But he wanted to sell her to a king, and was apprehensive that someone might try and take her from him by force. He therefore dressed her in sailor's clothes, so that she looked like a man.*

A storm* arose, carrying the ship to a strange shore, and smashing it to pieces. It was the shore of the same desert where the burgher's son was staying.* This is where they were carried.

The pirate* had the usual expertise in ships' routes and knew that ships never came to this desert. Therefore, he realized that he had no one to fear, and he let her go off by herself. He went one way, and she went another, as they foraged for food. She went further and further from him.

When the pirate realized that she was not in his vicinity, he began to call out for her, but she decided not to reply. "He intends to sell me," [she said to herself]. "Why should I answer him? If he finds me again, I will say that I did not hear him. Since he intends to sell me, he can't kill me in any case."

She did not answer him, and went further away. The pirate looked all over, but could not find her. In the end, he was most probably eaten by wild animals.* Meanwhile, she continued walking.

---

she looked like a man. Like the emperor's daughter in Story #2, p. 79. Here, like there, she gets her clothing from a pirate.

storm. The same as that which brought the burgher's son there originally. The storm wind indicates that they were brought there against their will.

where the burgher's son was staying. Here again, her destiny parallels his. This is not coincidence, since, as we saw earlier, this was a shore to which ships usually did not come.

pirate. Here he is called a *gazlan* rather than a *rotzeach*.

eaten by wild animals. The burgher's son had a bow, which denoted prayer. The Evil One does not have this power, and therefore does not have a defense against the higher forces of destruction. This is the concept of evil being destroyed in the ultimate future, as God said, "I will remove the unclean spirit from the earth" (Zechariah 13:2).

She foraged for food and walked until she found the place where the young man was living. Since her hair had grown and she was dressed like a man in a sailor's outfit, they did not recognize one another.

As soon as she arrived, he became very happy that another person had come there. "How did you get here?" he asked.

"I was with a merchant on the sea," she replied. "How did you get here?"

"Also through a merchant..." he replied.

The two of them remained together.*

After the emperor's daughter was taken, the empress mourned and grieved bitterly* for her daughter. She berated the emperor since, as a result of his pride, he had lost the young man, and now he had lost their daughter. "She was all our fortune and success," [she said]. "Now we have lost her! What do I have left now?" She continued berating him very harshly.

[The emperor] also grieved very much for the loss of his daughter. When the empress berated him and troubled him so much, it brought about arguments and strife between them. She said so many evil things to him, and angered him so much, that he decided to banish her. He appointed judges, and they sentenced her to be banished. She was thus exiled.*

Soon after this, the emperor fought a battle and was defeated. He blamed it on an error made by one of his generals, and exiled him.

The next war that the emperor fought also ended in defeat,

The two of them remained together. However, they did not recognize each other. The young man still hated the emperor, and as long as there is hatred in the world, the Messiah cannot be united with the Shekhinah.

grieved bitterly. Expressed idiomatically, "She hit her head against the wall."

exiled. This apparently does not denote mere exile, but also imprisonment as we see from the context later, where the emperor begs for his freedom. In an earlier story (#2, The King and the Emperor, p. 68), this can denote imprisonment until one is sentenced to death. There we see that *far-shiken* denotes being sent to a place of the condemned. The same expression *far-shiked* is used here. However, we see that she was not killed.

and the general was also exiled. A number of generals were thus banished.

The citizens realized that he was behaving in a bizarre fashion. First he had exiled the empress, and now the generals. They decided to reverse the situation, recalling the empress and exiling [the emperor].* The empress could rule the land.

This was accomplished. The emperor was exiled, and the empress was given the throne to rule the land.

The empress* immediately sent messengers to have the burgher and his wife restored. She brought them into her palace.

When the emperor was exiled, he asked those who were taking him to spare him. "I was your emperor," he said, "and I did good for you. Now have pity on me and let me go. I will certainly not return to this land anymore. You have nothing to fear. Let me go, and I will leave. At least let me be free for the rest of my life."

They let him go, and he went on his way. In the course of a few years, the emperor continued walking until he reached the sea, [where he took a ship].

A wind carried away his boat, and he also came to the desert. He finally came to the place* where the other two were living. [These were the young man who was the burgher's son, and his own beautiful daughter, who was now wearing men's clothes.] They did not recognize each other, since during the many years that had passed, the emperor's hair had grown very long. Their hair had also grown long.

"How did you get here?" they asked him.

---

exiling [the emperor]. This was because he refused to honor the pledge his wife had made, and also for his sentencing the burgher's son to death (*Chokhmah U'Tevunah* 3, *Sichoth U'Sippurim* 20, p. 42). Once the princess had rejected the burgher's son, the responsibility was his. When they came together on the island, events had to be set in motion to bring him there as well. He would have to be reconciled with the young man, since she could not be married without her father's consent.

The empresss. Since she was virtuous, loyal, and God-fearing, she was given full power.

finally came to the place. Only after the emperor arrives there, and the three are united, can the redemption come about (*Rimzey Maasioth*).

"Through a merchant..."* he replied.

They gave similar answers to his questions, and they all remained together, eating and drinking as before. All of them knew music, and they played musical instruments.* The emperor knew how to play, and they did also.

Among them, the young man was the most resourceful,* since he had been there the longest. He brought them meat, and they ate. They burned wood* that in civilized areas would be more precious than gold.

[The young man] argued with them that this would be a good place for them to spend the rest of their lives. Based on the benefits that people usually have in civilized areas, it would be better for them to spend the rest of their lives here.*

They asked him, "What good did you have before you came here that you say that it is better here?"

He answered them, telling them his whole story, how he had been a burgher's son, how he had eventually come to this spot, and what benefits he had had as a burgher's son. As a burgher's son he had had a good life, and here he also had a perfectly good life. He showed them that it would be good to spend their lives in this place.

"Did you every hear of the [world] emperor?" asked the emperor.

[The burgher's son] replied that he had.

[The emperor] then asked if he had heard of his beautiful daughter.

"Yes," replied the other.

The young man began to get upset. "He's a murderer!"* he

---

through a merchant. There is no mention of a merchant bringing him there. Since he lost his daughter through a merchant, he was now exiled here.

musical instruments. They thus have the beginnings of harmony. See Story #2.

resourceful. *Beriyah* in Hebrew, *Beryah* in Yiddish. It has the idiomatic meaning of a resourceful person. It can also mean the most healthy or the most robust.

They burned wood. This was very much like the golden mountain in Story #1.

spend the rest of their lives here. The savior has totally despaired of his task. Still, he looks for the letter.

murderer. The same term used for the pirate earlier in the story — *rotzeach.*

said. [He did not know that the man he was speaking to was the emperor, and he spoke in anger, grinding his teeth and declaring that the emperor was a murderer.]

"Why is he a murderer?" asked the emperor.

"I am now here because of his cruelty and pride!" replied the other.

"How did that happen?" asked [the emperor].

The young man decided that he had no one to fear, so he told him the entire story. [Originally, he had merely told them that he was the burgher's son, but he had not told the rest of the story.]

The emperor asked him, "If you had the emperor in your hands, would you exact revenge from him now?"

[The young man was merciful,* and] he replied, "No. Quite to the contrary. I would take care of him just as I am taking care of you."

The emperor then began to sigh and groan. "What a bitter old age this emperor must be having!" He had heard that his beautiful daughter had been lost and he himself had been exiled.

The young man replied, "This was because of his cruelty and pride. He destroyed both himself and his daughter. He also caused me to come here. It was all because of him."

The emperor repeated his question, "If you got him in your hands, would you take revenge against him?"

"No," replied the other. "Quite to the contrary. I would take care of him just as I am taking care of you."

The emperor then revealed his identity. He told [the young man] that he himself was the emperor, and then related what had happened to him. [The young man] fell on him, hugging and kissing him.* [The beautiful girl who was disguised as a man] overheard everything* that they had said to each other.

---

was merciful. Like his father.

hugging and kissing him. Although they had originally been enemies, they were now reconciled. When the true Messiah is reconciled with the nations, the redemption can occur.

overheard everything. Thus, she knew that the young man was her bridegroom, and that the other was her father. She also knew now that they had been reconciled.

The young man had made it his practice* to go each day to make a mark on three trees.* There were thousands and thousands of trees, and he was still looking for the [princess'] letter. He would examine [three trees each day], and mark those trees so that he would not search them again. He did this in the hope of eventually finding the letter. When he returned from his search, he would come with tears in his eyes. He wept* because he had searched, but he had not found it.

"Why are you searching* in these trees?" they asked. "And why do you return with tears in your eyes?"

He answered them, telling them the entire story how the emperor's daughter had sent him a letter, how he had hidden it in one of the trees, and how the hurricane had come. Now he was looking for it with the hope of eventually finding it.

They said to him, "Tomorrow when you go to look, we will also go with you. Maybe we will find the letter."

The next day they went with him, and the emperor's daughter found the letter* in a tree. When she opened it, she recognized her own handwriting.

---

had made it his practice. Although he had reconciled himself to remaining there for the rest of his life, he still had the goal of finding the letter. As we see later, he was not sure what he would do with it, especially since he had now heard that the princess was taken prisoner. Still, he felt that some effort was in order (*Rimzey Maasioth*). When a person has a goal, no matter how hopeless, he should put aside some time each day to work on it (*Likutey Etzoth* B, *Yirah VeAvodah* 39).

three trees. This denotes the three daily prayers (an oral Breslover tradition). Now that the hurricane has confused everything, he must pray to find the true way.

He wept. Like the viceroy in Story #1, this is his main weapon. Even if a person cannot reach his goal for many years, he should not give up hope, but should weep and beg God to let him reach it (*Rimzey Maasioth*).

Why are you searching. Only after they are reconciled are they interested in what he is doing.

emperor's daughter found the letter. Once the three of them had come together, and the young man and the emperor had been reconciled, the Princess herself found the letter (*Rimzey Maasioth*). This is very much like Story #1, where the lost princess tells the viceroy where she can be found. Also in Story #2, the emperor's daughter arranges for her husband to come back to her. The Divine Presence always does everything possible to hasten the redemption.

She thought about the situation. If she immediately revealed her identity to him, she would have to put aside her disguise. However, when she revealed her original beauty, he could collapse and die. She wanted everything done correctly, so she could lawfully marry him. She therefore merely brought back the letter and told him that she had found it.

He immediately fell unconscious.* They revived him and nursed him back to health, and they were all very happy. But the young man said, "What use do I have for the letter?* Where will I ever find her? Surely she is now with some king? Why do I need all this? Let me spend the rest of my life here."

He gave her back the letter, [and since he thought that she was a man], said, "Here is the letter. Go marry her yourself."

She agreed to go, but asked him to accompany her. [She said,]* "I will certainly win the [beautiful princess'] hand. But I want to share with you any good that I get out of it."

The young man realized that "he" (the emperor's daughter, whom he assumed to be a man) was very clever, and he would certainly be successful in getting her. He therefore agreed to go with her.

Significantly, it was because of the pirate that both she and her father were on the island. The father was there because he had been exiled, since his fortune had gone down with her loss. Therefore, both of them said that they came through a merchant. Thus, because she was kidnaped, she was able to find the letter and eventually be restored to her bridegroom (*Likutey Etzoth* B, *Yirah VeAvodah* 39). This is very much like the beginning of the story, where the pauper's wife can have a child only after she is kidnaped by the general. In a sense, her daughter is repeating her life.

Furthermore, although the burgher's son did not find the letter, his effort helped. If he had not been looking for it, they never would have questioned him, and she would not have searched for it.

fell unconscious. Since he had put in so much effort to find it.

What use do I have for the letter. He had given up hope so completely, and was satisfied to remain where he was (*Likutey Etzoth* B, *loc. cit.*).

[She said]. This is in the first person in the original, but it is difficult to express it accurately and clearly in translation. We have therefore translated it in the first person.

Here we see that Holiness itself is consoling him. Now the emperor's daughter is the decisive one. This has been symbolized by her wearing men's clothing, very much like Story #2.

This, however, would leave the emperor alone, since he was afraid to return to his land. She asked him to come along, [saying], "Once I get back to civilization, I will trace the beautiful girl. [Your good fortune will have been restored,] and I will be able to bring you back."

The three set out together. They hired a ship, and came to the land where the empress lived, heading toward her capital where they left the ship. [The emperor's daughter] realized, that if she revealed her identity immediately, and told her mother that she was back, [her mother] might die. She therefore sent a message that a man had been found who had some information about the [missing] daughter.

She herself then went, and told the empress everything that had happened to [the missing] daughter, relating the entire story. When she had ended she said, "She is also here." She then revealed the truth. "It is I," [she said]. "I am she."

She then related that her bridegroom, the burgher's son, was also here. However, she insisted that her father, the emperor, be returned to his place. Her mother did not want to do this, since she was still very angry with him, because everything had been his fault. Still, she had to fulfill her daughter's request. They wanted to bring him back, but when they looked, discovered that the emperor was missing.*

The daughter then told her that [the emperor] was there [with them].*

The wedding took place, and the joy was complete. The couple took over the kingdom and the majesty, and reigned supreme over the entire world.*

---

was missing. From the prison colony to which he had been sentenced.

the emperor was there [with them]. The gentiles will also be rectified in the Messianic age.

This story was told after Purim, as mentioned earlier. This teaches that even though the wicked will be redeemed, they will lose their position. The same was true of the miracle of Purim. All the people were redeemed, but there were still some who were punished (*Chokhmah U'Tevunah* 3, *Sichoth U'Sippurim* 20, p. 42).

the entire world. Ruled *be-kipah* in Hebrew; in Yiddish, "over the entire world." They were given the power rather than the emperor. This is the concept of, "God will be king over all the world; on that day, God will be One and His name One" (Zechariah 14:9) (*Likutey Etzoth loc. cit.* 39).

Subsequently, the old emperor had no true greatness, since everything had been his fault. The burgher, on the other hand, had very much greatness, [since he was the father of the new emperor, who had the main power].

The sailor had been beaten, slapped in the face, and thrown out.

Lot was told, "flee to the mountain" (Genesis 19:17). [In Yiddish, mountain is *berg*. Therefore,] this is the burgher, [*berger* in Yiddish]. From him the Messiah was born* (May he come quickly in our days).

In Egypt, the Israelites had a [secret] sign,* "Remember, I have remembered."* The one who said these words would be the redeemer. This is somewhat difficult to understand; if all the Israelites knew it, how could it be the sign? It was therefore probably known only by the elders. *

The final redeemer also has certain signs.

The Messiah will tell Israel everything that happened* to Israel every single day, to each and every Israelite in particular.

Tamar also had signs* and lost them, as discussed in the Midrash. When she was being taken out to be burned,* Samael took away her

---

the Messiah was born. Since Lot's daughter gave birth to a child from him on the mountain. This child was Moab, of whom Ruth was a descendant. Ruth was the ancestress of David, from whom the Messiah will be descended.

a [secret] sign. This is mentioned in the Midrash (*Shemoth Rabbah* 3:11).

Remember, I have remembered. *Pakod pakad-ti* (Exo. 3:16). These words had been used by Joseph (Genesis 50:24) and by Jacob also (Genesis 50:24; *The Torah Anthology* 4:93).

known only by the elders. See Ramban.

everything that happened. Just as the burgher's son had to tell his whole story to her.

Rabbi Nachman writes that the Messiah understands every concept perfectly (*Sichoth HaRan* 93). Since he will know everything that ever happened he will be able to rectify everything (*Chayay Nefesh* 21, pp. 33,34).

Tamar also had signs. Judah's staff, seal and cord (Genesis 38:25).

taken out to be burned. (Genesis 38:24).

signs, and then Gabriel brought them back, as discussed in the Midrash.* From her the Messiah will be descended* (May he come quickly in our days, Amen).

The story relates how each one came with a love song, and how she behaved with each one. The parallel is obvious. There were many great people who did what they had to do, and made poems, trying to reach the desired goal. However, no one was worthy of attaining the main goal perfectly other than the one who was truly worthy. Some are answered through a messenger, or from the other side of the wall, while others are shown a face... as the story relates. However, in the end, they die and have accomplished nothing, receiving the same answer that the beauty gave, "But the waters* have still not passed over you."

This will happen until the proper leader comes...

Midrash. *Targum Yonathan; Sotah* 10b.

From her the Messiah... Since she gave birth to Peretz, who was the ancestor of David (Ruth 4:18-22).

but the waters... As she told her suitors. This is in the Yiddish but not the Hebrew.

11

THE EXCHANGED CHILDREN *

Once there was a king* who had a slave woman* to serve the

The Exchanged Children. This story was told on Saturday night of the Portion of *Noah*, 5570 (October 14, 1809) (*Chayay Moharan* 15c #59).

Rabbi Nathan and his friend, Rabbi Naftali, had gone in to visit Rabbi Nachman on Saturday night, but he had gestured that they should leave. They were taken aback, since they would usually converse with him on Saturday night. They visited Rabbi Aaron, the official rabbi of Breslov, for several hours, and then Rabbi Nachman summoned them back, asking them to tell him the current news. Rabbi Naftali told him about Napoleon's current battles, and how surprising Napoleon's career was. He had been born a simple slave, and had then become emperor.

Rabbi Nachman said, "Who knows what sort of soul he has? It is possible that it was exchanged. There is a Chamber of Exchanges (*Hekhal Ha-Temuroth*), where souls are sometimes exchanged." He then told the story of "The Exchanged Children" (*Chayay Moharan* 15d #2; see *Yemey Moharnat* 30b).

It is significant to note that on October 14, 1809, the same day that this story was told, the Treaty of Schönbrun was signed, giving Napoleon control of Austria's share of Poland, including the Warsaw area. Napoleon had defeated Austria, and negotiations had been going on since August 11 (Baron C.F. de Meneval, *Memoirs of Napoleon Bonaparte*, Collier, New York 1910, p. 585). This brought Napoleon's influence into Eastern Europe, not too far from Rabbi Nachman's domain.

This story speaks of the World of Rectification and the refinement of the souls and sparks of holiness that have fallen into the realm of the unclean (*Rimzey Maasioth*). Rabbi Nathan wrote that it contains the entire Torah (*Likutey Halakhoth, Birkath HaShachar* 3:8).

The last three stories, which began Rabbi Nachman's series of longer stories, dealt with two contrasting personalities. He told of "The Sophisticate and the Simpleton," and of "The Burgher and the Pauper." Here the personalities are not necessarily contrasting; they are two people whose destinies were reversed.

king. This is not God, since he later dies. Rather, the king here represents the Sefiroth of the Universe of Chaos (*Olam HaTohu*).

slave woman. The realm of evil. The *Zohar* states that the realm of evil is a woman whom the king hires to tempt his son, and hence, she is considered the king's servant (*Zohar*

queen in the palace. (Obviously, a simple cook would not have access to the king. But this slave woman was a servant of low status.)

The time came when the queen gave birth. This slave woman also gave birth at the same time. The midwife* exchanged the

2:163a). She was not an ordinary servant, but one who had access to the king. We also see later in the story, that her husband had money. Thus, instead of being a mere slave, she was probably a leading servant in the palace.

midwife. Before telling this story, Rabbi Nachman spoke of the Chamber of Exchanges (*Hekhal HaTemuroth*) where souls are occasionally exchanged (*Chayay Moharan* 15d #2). This Chamber of Exchanges is normally seen as a place of evil (cf. *Likutey Moharan* 24:8 end, 245). The midwife is seen as a representation of this Chamber (*Likutey Halakhoth, Birkath HaShachar* 3:2).

In general, the Chamber of Exchanges confuses good and evil, causing people to be far from God (*Likutey Etzoth* B, *Daath* 17).

Rabbi Nathan writes that the Chamber of Exchanges came into existence when Adam ate from the Tree of Knowledge. It is alluded to in the Torah by the "revolving sword" (Genesis 3:24), which would more accurately be translated as the "sword of transformations" or "the sword of reversals." This sword is thus the power that exchanges good and evil. The *Zohar* thus teaches that it is called "the transforming sword," because it transforms from one side to the other, from good to evil and from evil to good (*Zohar* 1:221b) (see *Likutey Halakhoth, Ibid.* 3:9).

It is also represented by Moses' staff, which was transformed into a serpent and then back into a staff (*Zohar* 2:28a). As a result of this exchange, the order of creation is reversed, so that evil has power, whne Israel is exiled (*Likutey Halakhoth, Birkath HaShachar* 3:20).

If Adam had not sinned, the body would have been able to become totally spiritual without dying (*Ibid.* 3:20). But death came about because the body (the slave's son) gained power over the soul (the king's true son) (*Ibid.* 3:21) as a result of this sin.

Laban is also an aspect of the Chamber of Exchanges, since he exchanged Jacob's two wives, giving him Leah instead of Rachel (Genesis 29:25). If Jacob had married Rachel first, then Joseph would have been the firstborn, and his brothers would not have been jealous of him. He then would not have been sold as a slave and exiled to Egypt (which is an aspect of the king's true son being raised as a slave and exiled).

The dispute between the Kingdoms of Ephraim (Israel) and Judah also resulted from the dispute regarding Joseph's status. This dissension in Israel then resulted in the destruction of the Temple (*Likutey Halakhoth* 3:31).

The midwife in this story is very much like the king's anger in the story of the lost princess. In this story, the midwife seems to be seen again as the wise king, who changes things around in the garden and the throne.

The story itself represents an aspect of this Chamber of Exchanges, since, as Rabbi Nachman said at the end of the story, in this tale, things are sometimes given one name, and sometimes another.

babies, to see what would happen and how the situation would develop. She exchanged the infants by placing the king's son* next to the slave and the slave's son* next to the queen.*

king's son. This represents the power of Holiness in general, and the nation of Israel in particular.

Rabbi Nathan cites the Talmud, which teaches that "all Israelites are the sons of kings" (*Shabbath* 67a). The Israelites are the true "son of the King," because the entire world was created for Israel's sake. The Torah begins with the words, "In the beginning," and Rashi states that the word "beginning" here alludes to Israel, so that the first verse of the Torah can be interpreted, "For the sake of Israel, God created the heaven and the earth." Thus, everything belongs to Israel, and all the world should be subjugated to them. The Israelites had a taste of this in the time of King David and Solomon when Israel had a great kingdom, and it will be totally fulfilled in the Messianic age (*Likutey Halakhoth, Birkath HaShachar* 3:2).

slave's son. The slave's son is falsehood in general, and the gentile world in particular (*Likutey Halakhoth, Ibid.* 3:39). See below.

next to the queen. Rabbi Nathan writes that this exchange alludes to the status of Israel; they are in a dependent position, like slaves, while the gentile nations are the kings and rulers. This was the result of Adam's sin, as well as the sins of subsequent generations.

Regarding this exchange it is written, "Three things make the earth tremble...a slave who rules...and a handmaid who becomes heir to her mistress" (Proverbs 30:21,22). King Solomon also said, "I have seen slaves riding horses, while princes walk on the ground like slaves" (Ecclesiastes 10:7) (*Likutey Halakhoth, Birkath HaShachar* 3:2).

This is also the mystery of Isaac and Ishmael. Abraham could not have any children from Sarah, and had to marry her slave, Hagar, who gave birth to Ishmael (Genesis 16). This was to rid himself of the taint of Adam's sin, since this taint was completely taken by Ishmael. The true princess, however, was Sarah, whose name actually means "princess." Ishmael thus represents the slave's son in this story.

Ishmael, however, claimed to be the king's true son. It is thus written, "Sarah saw Ishmael...making sport" (Genesis 21:9). Rashi notes that Sarah's response to Abraham was, "The son of this slave woman shall not have inheritance with my son Isaac" (Genesis 21:10). This teaches that Ishmael was claiming to be Abraham's true firstborn, and, thus, his primary heir. Ishmael wanted to usurp Isaac's status as the king's true son.

This is also the mystery of Jacob and Esau. Here the two were exchanged in Rebecca's womb, so that Esau emerged first instead of Jacob. Rebecca was thus told, "There are two nations in your womb...but the older will be a slave to the younger" (Genesis 25:23). In this case, the results of the Chamber of Exchanges were manifested in the womb; this Chamber has many manifestations in each generation.

The Chamber of Exchanges also has effects on every person in each generation, causing a person to rise and fall spiritually. A person often must be reincarnated a number of times in order to cleanse himself of the taint of Adam's sin, which causes all other sin. It is because of this that a saint sometimes falls from his spiritual level, and may even actually commit serious sins, and become a wicked person. Thus, Jeroboam son of Navat, who is counted as one of the most evil kings of Israel (see *Sanhedrin* 101b), was originally a great saint. The same is true of other saints. All this comes from the exchange and incarnation of souls, where a wicked soul may be given to a righteous person. As a result, a person can instantly be transformed into a totally different person.

The opposite can also be true, where a wicked person can be given the soul of a saint, and as a result, he can suddenly repent and change his ways completely. All this is the mystery of the verse, "There are righteous men who are reached according to the deeds of the wicked, and wicked persons who are reached according to the deeds of the righteous" (Ecclesiastes 8:14; see *Likutey Moharan* 31). However, despite all this, what a person does ultimately depends on his own free will. Every person has free choice whether to be the greatest saint or the worst fiend (*Likutey Halakhoth, Ibid.* 3:3).

King David prayed for this more than any other person. The main rectification of the Chamber of Exchanges is through King David and it will be completed through his descendant, who will be the Messiah.

Because of the Chamber of Exchanges, many souls were captured in wicked families. Thus, Abraham was a descendant of Terach, who was a manufacturer of idols. Similarly, King David himself was born as the result of a sin (see *Shaar HaGilgulim*, p. 162). It is for this reason that King David's soul had to emerge through the daughters of Lot (as discussed in our notes to the previous story; also see *Chokhmah U'Tevunah*), as well as through Judah and Tamar (see previous story). All this had to happen in order to "sneak" his soul out of the realm of evil (see *Likutey Torah* on Job).

It is for this reason that King David was destined to die at birth, but he was given seventy years by Adam. King David was thus in mortal danger all his life, as he said, "If God had not helped me, I would have dwelt in the Darkness" (Psalms 94:17; *Likutey Halakhoth, Ibid.* 3:41). Since the Messiah will descend from David, this also applies to the soul of the Messiah (see *Chokhmah U'Tevunah* 3).

This exchange thus has many manifestations in all generations. One of the first such manifestations was through Abraham, who was the first one to try to rectify Adam's sin. He had many battles with Nimrod and others in his generation who claimed that Abraham was a nonbeliever, for worshiping an invisible God. Nimrod, a descendant of Ham, and hence a slave, was king, while Abraham appeared to be a slave. Abraham suffered very much at Nimrod's hands, being thrown into the fiery furnace (*Bereshith Rabbah* 38). All this was the result of the original exchange (*Likutey Halakhoth, Ibid.* 3:8).

Among the Jews themselves this concept of exchange also has an effect, since things are the opposite of what they should be. Long ago, the prophet said, "The child shall behave insolently against the aged, and the base against the honorable" (Isaiah 3:5). We thus see that religious Jews are often looked down upon, while those who are far from Torah are in positions of leadership. This was even true in Talmudic times, as one sage said, "I have seen an upside-down world; those above are below and those below are above" (*Bava Bathra* 10b; *Pesachim* 50a).

Nowadays, this is manifested in the strengthening of falsehood. This is alluded to in the

The two boys grew. The one who was [assumed to be] the king's son was given greater and greater status, until he continued to advance, becoming highly talented.* The one who was [assumed to be] the slave's son [but was the king's true son] grew up in [the slave's] house. The two of them studied together in the same school.*

verse, "Truth was cast down to the earth" (Daniel 8:12). Our sages teach us, "In the time before the Messiah, arrogance will increase, and the truth will be hidden... There will be many groups, each one claiming to have the truth" (*Sanhedrin* 97a).

All this comes from the slave's son, who took the kingdom for himself and exiled the king's true son. This causes the gentiles to have the upper hand, while the Jews are downcast in exile and subjugation. Similarly, even among the Jews, nonbelievers have great wealth and power while faithful Jews are poor and downtrodden.

Furthermore, even among religious Jews, there is much confusion and dissension, so that no one knows where the truth is (see *Likutey Moharan Tinyana* 71). There are therefore disputes among saints (tzaddikim) as well as many religious celebrities who are utterly false. Even among tzaddikim there are so many disputes that no one can know where the truth lies (*Likutey Halakhoth, Ibid.* 3:9).

Rabbi Nathan cites the Ari, that this is the reason that every morning we recite the blessing, thanking God "for not making me a slave." We thank God that our souls were not exchanged for those of slaves. The main purpose of this blessing is then to thank God for sparing us from the effects of the Chamber of Exchanges (*Likutey Halakhoth, Ibid.* 3:10).

Another thing that resulted from the concept of exchange mentioned in this story was the selling of Joseph as a slave. Moreover, the dispute between Joseph and his brothers is reflected in all the disputes among saints and sages (*Ibid.* 3:17).

Sickness also comes from this exchange. The king's son represents the soul, while the slave's son represents the body. As long as the soul is stronger than the body, the body remains healthy. But when the body tries to dominate the soul, then the body itself also becomes weak and sick (*Ibid.* 3:18).

Another aspect of the exchange involved the Land of Israel, which was originally under the dominance of the wicked Canaanites, and later, after the exile, was also dominated by other nations (*Zimrath HaAretz*).

In the end, of course, the king's son benefits from the exchange. Instead of merely being a king in an ordinary country, he becomes the king of the "Foolish Land with the Wise King," which is actually a land of very wise people.

talented. An idiomatic use of the word *beriyah* (בריה), similar to that in the previous story.

in the same school. A motif that we find in "The King and the Emperor," "The Sophisticate and the Simpleton," and "The Burgher and the Pauper."

We see that during their childhood, the distinction is obscured. Similarly, during the early generations of the human race, there was no real distinction between Jew and gentile.

The king's true son was called "the slave's son."* Nevertheless, by nature he was drawn to the ways of royalty,* even though he was raised in the slave's house.

Conversely, the slave's son was known as "the king's son." He was drawn by his nature to different ways, not the ways of royalty. However, since he was growing up in the king's palace, he was raised in the royal manner, and learned to behave accordingly.

Having a weak character,* the midwife told someone the secret* of how the boys were exchanged. One friend has another,* and in the usual manner, the secret was passed from one person to another until everyone was speaking about how the king's son had been exchanged.

Of course, people did not speak about it openly, since they did not want the king to hear about it. They did not want the king to know about it, since the king could not do anything. There was no remedy. He could not believe the rumor, since it might have been false, and he could not exchange the boys again. Therefore, the

---

was called "the slave's son." Actually, of course, the individuals themselves were not changed. They remained the same. The only thing that was changed was their names. This in itself is an aspect of the dominance of the slave's son, who as mentioned earlier, denotes the concept of falsehood (*Likutey Halakhoth, Ibid.* 3:39). This is related to the concept discussed later in the story, where the moon says that it does not have a name when the sun is present.

drawn to the ways of royalty. Even though the soul is a prisoner, it is still drawn to serve God (*Likutey Halakhoth, Birkath HaShachar* 3:19). Similarly, although the Israelites have lost their status, they are still drawn to Godly ways (see *Zimrath HaAretz*).

weak character. Actually quoting the Talmudic teaching (נשים דעתן קלות — *nashim daatan kaloth*), which means, "Women have light knowledge" (*Shabbath* 33b; *Kiddushin* 80b; *Tanchuma Vayera* 22; *Zohar* 2:218a). This dictum is specifically related to Eve and it was the reason why the serpent tried to tempt her rather than Adam (Rashi on Genesis 3:15). Thus, we see that the "midwife" in this story may very well have represented Eve.

told someone the secret. The immediate effect of this was that the king's true son would be persecuted. But in the end, this brought the king's son to his true destiny.

One friend has another. *Chavra, chavra ith lei,* a Talmudic expression (see *Kethuboth* 109b; *Bava Bathra* 28b).

report could not be revealed to the king. Still, the people spoke about it* among themselves.

Then one day* someone* revealed the secret to the "king's son," telling him that people were saying that he had been exchanged. "However," [he said], "it is impossible for you to investigate this, since it would be beneath your dignity. Besides, there is no way to ascertain the truth. However, I feel that it is my duty to inform you of this, since there may be a rebellion against the king some day, and the rebels' hand could be strengthened if they could claim that they are making the king's true son the king. I am speaking of the one whom they claim is the king's son in their rumors. Therefore, you must devise some sort of plan to do away with him."*

The "king's son"* began to persecute the father of the "slave's son," [not realizing that he was really his own father].*

---

people spoke about it. Although the gentile world will not openly admit that the Israelites are the true sons of God, they whisper about it among themselves. On a personal level, people realize that the body is not the true son, but they will not "speak about it with the king." They will not tell God about it. Still, this "murmuring" is responsible for the vague discontent that each person has with the rewards of the material world.

Then one day. Literally, "A day came." See Story #2, p. 62.

someone. This was a second revelation, the first being that of the midwife. It is as if the truth cannot be held down.

As we have seen earlier, in one aspect the king's son represents truth, while the slave's son represents falsehood. Just as the king's son cannot be held down, so truth cannot be held down.

We see that this "someone" is an evil person, because he advises that the king's true son be killed. However, this is but another process in the king's son's realization of his destiny.

do away with him. In the story there is additional text: "All these were the words of the man who revealed the secret to the slave's son, who was called 'the king's son.' "

The king's son. The text adds: "The one who was called 'the king's son.' " In general, wherever we mention 'the king's son' here without comment, we are referring to the exchanged one, that is, the one who was actually the slave's son, who was called 'the king's son' because he grew up with the king. The same is true of 'the slave's son.' However, when we speak of 'the king's true son' or 'the slave's true son' then we are speaking literally.

his own father. On the basis of the rumor, he should have thought of the possibility that

He was always looking for ways to do him harm. He caused him one evil after the other, trying to get him to emigrate together with his son.

As long as the king was alive, he did not have much power. Still, he caused him evil. But then the king grew old and died,* and this slave's son inherited the kingdom. He then did much greater evil to the father of the other son, causing him one evil after another. He would do it in secret ways, so that people would not trace the evil back to him, since it would not be proper for the masses to realize what he was doing. Nevertheless, in his secret ways, he was able to cause [the father] much evil.

The father of the other son understood that [the new king] was doing him evil because of the [rumors]. He told his "son" [who was actually the king's true son] the entire story. He told him, "No matter what the truth is, I have great pity on you. If you are my son, I certainly have great pity on you. If you are really the king's son, the pity is even greater. He wants to destroy you* completely, heaven forbid! Therefore, you must get yourself far away from here."

The [son]* thought this was terrible. But [he did not have any choice] since the king continued directing persecutions,* one after another. The son therefore made up his mind to leave. His father gave him very much money, and he went on his way.*

---

this man might have been his father. But the forces of Exchange (which are the forces that exchange good and evil) led him to discount this possibility to the extent that he ended up persecuting his own father (*Rimzey Maasioth*).

the king ... died. Here we see that the king is not God. Rather, the king here denotes the array of the Sefiroth as they were first created, before the shattering of the vessels. The original vessels are referred to as "the Kings of Edom" (Genesis 36). When the "king" died, and the vessels were shattered, the "slave's son" was able to take over.

He wants to destroy you. "Let us destroy him as a nation, so that the name of Israel shall no longer be recalled" (Psalms 83:5) (*Rimzey Maasioth*).

The [son]. Literally, "It was evil in his eyes." It is not obvious that "his" refers to the son; it can possibly refer to the father. The ambiguity may be intentional.

directing persecutions. Literally, "would constantly fire his evil arrows." Compare Genesis 49:23, where Jacob said of Joseph, "Masters of arrows attacked him."

he went on his way. This is the mystery of the exile of the Israelites, where we were exiled

The [king's true] son was extremely upset at having been exiled from his land for no reason. He thought about his situation and tried to understand why he was being exiled. "If I am really the king's son, I do not deserve this to happen to me. And if I am not the king's son, I also do not deserve to have to flee for no reason. What have I done wrong?"*

He felt that a terrible tragedy had happened to him, and he began to drink and visit brothels.* He wanted to spend his life doing nothing else but getting drunk and following his heart's desires,* since he had been exiled without reason.

from our homeland (*Likutey Halakhoth, Birkath HaShachar* 3:2). It also denotes the exile and suffering of the soul. When the Israelites are exiled from the land they inherited from their ancestors, they are considered like slaves. People mock them, and they are like sheep going to the slaughter (*Rimzey Maasioth; Zimrath HaAretz*).

In a sense, the land of Israel parallels the Garden of Eden; hence, the exile from the land of Israel parallels Adam's exile from Eden (*Zimrath HaAretz*). This, in turn, is paralleled in the end of the story, where there is something in the garden that does not allow anyone to enter.

In another sense, this represents the exile of Holiness in general with the breaking of the vessels, where the sparks of holiness fell down from Atziluth to Beriyah.

What have I done wrong? Very often a person despairs because he has been wronged through no fault of his own. The Israelites as a whole also despaired after they were exiled from their land (*Zimrath HaAretz*).

drink and visit brothels. As a result of this despair, one does not care what one does, and one sins and leads a dissolute life. Similarly, when the Israelites as a whole are exiled, they despair, and this causes them to become immersed in material desires and sin. The exile is therefore primarily spiritual rather than physical (*Likutey Halakhoth, Birkath HaShachar* 3:2).

Furthermore, Jews do not fully realize their status. They think that they can never be as great as the tzaddikim, and therefore there is no real hope for them. As a result, they become spiritually drunk and end up committing sins (*Ibid.* 3:6).

This despair itself was the power that the Exchange (*temuroth*) had over the king's true son. Within him as well, the "slave" was now master. This led him to drink (*Rimzey Maasioth*). Since the powers of Exchange interchange good and bad, people are far from God (*Likutey Etzoth* B, *Daath* 17).

following his heart's desires. The main pain of the exile is the fact that the powers of evil can defile the holy souls and cause them to become blemished. This is the concept, that the Israelites "were intermingled with the nations and learned from their deeds" (Psalms 106:35). The Israelites naturally would want to avoid sin, but the exile makes it very difficult (cf. *Likutey Moharan Tinyana* 7). Thus, all our sins in exile come from the

The new king took over the kingdom with a firm hand. Whenever he heard people speaking and spreading rumors of the exchange, he would punish them harshly.* He ruled with strength and arrogance.*

Then one day,* the king went hunting* with his royal ministers. They came to a pleasant area where a river was flowing, and stopped there to rest and stroll about.

The king lay down and began thinking about how he had exiled the other son for no reason. No matter what the truth was, it was not fair. If the other were actually the prince, then not only had he lost his position because of the exchange, but he had been exiled without reason. And if he was not the king's son, he also did not deserve to be exiled, since he had done nothing wrong.

The king thought about it, and regretted the great wrong* that he had done. But he did not know what to do for himself or what advice to follow. He could not speak to anyone* to get advice. Worrying about this, he became quite depressed.

Chamber of Exchanges (*Likutey Halakhoth, Birkath HaShachar* 3:2). One of the Talmudic sages thus prayed, "Lord of the World, we want to do Your will, but we are prevented by the subjugation of foreign governments and the leaven in the dough" (*Berakhoth* 17a).

The lesson is then, that one should never consider oneself wicked (*Likutey Halakhoth, Ibid.* 3:5).

He tried to get out of slavery by doing anything he wanted. But the only truly free man is one who is immersed in Torah.

punish them harshly. Thus his fear of exposure leads him to stifle any real thought. No one can say anything favorable about the Jews.

with strength and arrogance. Gentile values completely dominate the world. The slave's son now has total power (*Likutey Etzoth* B, *Daath* 17).

Then one day. Literally, "it was the day" (see Story #2).

hunting. *Navlavi* in Yiddish-Russian.

regretted the great wrong. The king only wanted to exile the king's true son, so that he wouldn't compete with him. But once the king's son began to fall spiritually, it had gone beyond what he wanted. Therefore, now that the king's true son has begun to live a dissolute life, the slave's son has regrets. "The wicked are full of regrets" (*Shevet Mussar* 25, cf. *Nedarim* 9b).

could not speak to anyone. When a person is in a situation of falsehood, he is on his own, and cannot seek advice from anyone.

He told his ministers to go back; he had this concern and he did not feel like being on an outing. [The entire group] returned home.

When the king got back, he obviously had many other interests and concerns. He became involved with his affairs, and soon forgot about the entire matter.*

Meanwhile, the king's true son continued his activities and squandered his money. One day he took a stroll by himself, and then lay down to rest. He started thinking about what had happened to him. "What has God done to me?"* he thought. "If I am the king's son then it is certainly not right. And if I am not the king's son, I still don't deserve to be an exiled fugitive."*

Then he began to look at the matter in a different light. "On the contrary. If it is so, if God can do such a thing, to exchange a king's son and all this should happen to him, is it right what I have done? Was it proper for me to act as I did?" He began to grieve and regret* very much the evil deeds that he had done.

Afterwards, he returned home and began getting drunk again. But since he had already begun to have thoughts of regret and repentance, these thoughts constantly bothered him.*

---

forgot about the entire matter. Unlike the king's true son who is constantly plagued by guilt. Later in the story, however, we see that his regret led him to abdicate his kingdom.
What has God done... "What is this that God has done to us?" (Genesis 42:28). But this time, he puts God into the question.
I still don't deserve... He begins by complaining as before, but this leads him to think about repenting (cf. *Likutey Halakhoth* 3:6). This is because he has begun to think of this as God's deed, rather than as a mere accident.
regret. It appears that once the slave's son had begun to repent, it had an effect on the king's true son (cf. *Rimzey Maasioth*). This is because the destinies of the two were linked together so that they would eventually come together in the woods. It appears that around the same time that the king's son left home, the slave's son abdicated as well.

As a result of his regret, he eventually rectified the throne, and as a result the entire world was rectified (*Likutey Etzoth* B, *Daath* 17).

This may allude to Abraham, who began the *tikkun* by opposing Nimrod and the Tower of Babel (*Likutey Halakhoth, Birkath HaShachar* 3:8). After that, man fell down again, with the building of the Tower of Babel.
constantly bothered him. If a person regrets leading a bad life, then even if he cannot give it

One night he went to sleep and dreamed* that there was a fair
in a certain place on a certain day. He was told to go there and
take the first job he was offered,* even if he felt that it was
beneath his dignity. When he woke up the dream was imbedded

up immediately, his thoughts of repentance will constantly motivate him to improve, and
in the end he will change his ways. Thus, both the true prince and the slave's son repented,
and in the end, they both came to give up their evil ways (*Likutey Etzoth* B, *Teshuvah* 8).
dreamed. "If one comes to purify oneself, one is helped from on high" (*Yoma* 38b). These
are reminiscent of the dreams that Joseph's fellow prisoners had, as well as Pharaoh's
dreams. Although Joseph did not have these dreams, in the end, he was freed through
them (Genesis 40,41).

first job he was offered. When a person has to break out of evil, he must do something, no
matter what, as long as he does not maintain the status quo. A person must do the first
thing that he can to serve God, and the rest will follow.

Rabbi Nathan notes that sleep is an aspect of slavery. Thus, in the morning we recite
the blessing, "Who moves aside sleep from our eyes," to remove this concept of slavery
(*Likutey Halakhoth, Birkath HaShachar* 3:13). This therefore begins to show how the
concept of prayer freed him. Thus, the king's son had to enter the concept of sleep and
dream in order to be freed. Similarly, he had to take a job and enter a sort of voluntary
slavery before he could be freed.

By entering into slavery voluntarily, he was able to annul the concept of slavery at its
root.

Rabbi Nathan notes that King David was the soul of the king's son, and hence, evil had
its strongest hold on him. Therefore, he had to annul the concept of slavery at its root by
making himself a slave or servant of God. He thus said, "I am your slave, son of your slave
woman" (Psalms 116:16), and many similar expressions (*Likutey Halakhoth, Birkath
HaShachar* 3:7).

Jacob also tried to rectify the concept of slavery at its root, and for this reason, he was
an indentured servant for Laban for twenty years. Moreover, the concept of slavery began
with the woman, namely the midwife, who was personified in Eve. It was for this reason
that Eve, and woman, was punished with a form of slavery, as she was cursed that "Your
husband...will rule over you" (Genesis 3:16). The relationship between slavery and
womanhood is also alluded to in the juxtaposition of the two blessings, "Who has not
made me a slave," and "Who has not made me a woman" (Daily Liturgy see *Menakhoth*
44b).

One of the things that Jacob tried to rectify by his voluntary slavery was the concept of
slavery in his wives, where it was the strongest. It is thus written, "Israel slaved for a
woman" (Hosea 12:13). Jacob did this to rectify his wives, so that the children they would
bear would be free of the taint of slavery (*Likutey Halakhoth, Birkath HaShachar* 3:31).

Jacob worked for Leah before he married her, but he did not work the seven years for
Rachel until after he married her. This is why, during the first seven years of their

firmly in his thoughts. Sometimes the thought is immediately forgotten, but this dream was constantly on his mind. However, he felt that it was something very difficult to do, so he just got all the more drunk.

The dream, however, recurred a number of times, and it disturbed him very much. Once, he was told in the dream, "If you want to have any pity on yourself, do as you have been told." He then realized that he had to obey the dream.

He went and gave all the rest of his money to his host.* He also left all his fine clothing* with his host, wearing only a simple merchant's robe.* Thus, he went to the fair.

He arrived there, and got up early to attend the fair. When he

---

marriage, Rachel did not have any children. It was only after Jacob's period of service was almost over that she gave birth to Joseph.

to his host. Rabbi Nathan writes that after Rabbi Nachman told this story, he had a debate with his friend Rabbi Naftali. One said that he had left his money with his host to pay for what he owed for his lodging, while the other said that he had just abandoned it. After debating it, they went to ask Rabbi Nachman himself. The Rebbe was involved in his devotions, and was walking back and forth. Finally he said that the second interpretation was correct, and that the king's son had simply given his host the money and left it there, not in payment of any debt.

Later, one of the important followers was there, and Rabbi Nachman spoke to him. He said that in these stories, if even one detail is changed from the way he himself told it, the story would be lacking very much. He mentioned that two men were debating what they thought to be a minor, unimportant detail, but actually, very much depended on it (*Chayay Moharan* 15d #2).

This was then a concept of the king's true son abandoning all his worldly goods to start anew.

left all his fine clothing. He took off all the spiritual garments that he had soiled and left them behind. This is very similar to what God told Zechariah regarding Joshua the High Priest, "Take the filthy garments off him." Then God said to Joshua, "I will take your sin away from you, and I will clothe you in fine robes" (Zechariah 3:4).

The new song that the animals sang relates to a new providence over the world, as Rabbi Nachman himself teaches (*Likutey Moharan Tinyana* 8:10). This is because Rosh Chodesh is the joy of the moon, and denotes the renewal of the world, when the effects of the Exchange are nullified (*Likutey Halakhoth, Keriyath HaTorah* 6:5).

merchant's robe. *Pinche* in Yiddish.

merchant. This merchant was the first element of his rectification. Therefore, it appears that this merchant represents the conscience of the king's true son. He is seen as cruel,

got there, he met a merchant * who asked him, "Would you like a job?"

"Yes," he replied.

"I am driving some cattle,"* said [the merchant]. "You can work for me."

Because of the dream, he did not take any time to think the

---

because, as Rabbi Nathan writes, when the "slave's son" (the body, as discussed earlier) is dominant in a person, then anything good that a person wishes to do is very difficult, and seems like slave labor (*Likutey Halakhoth, Birkath HaShachar* 3:19; *Likutey Moharan* 14:12).

driving some cattle. As we see later in the story, these cattle are seen to be sins. Through hiring people to drive cattle, the merchant is getting them to control their sins.

Rabbi Nathan notes that in general it is the animal spirit in man that brings man to sin. The Talmud thus says of an adulterous woman, "She acted like an animal, and therefore, her offering is animal food" (*Sotah* 15b).

From the context, we can also say that the merchant is the tzaddik, or perhaps even the angel of Asiyah.

However, in one place, Rabbi Nachman himself says that a "merchant" is the concept of prayer. He notes that the Rashbam says (*Bava Bathra* 73b) that a merchant denotes Ishmael. Ishmael is prayer. He was named *Yishma-el* in Hebrew, which means "God will hear," because "God has heard your prayer" (Genesis 16:11; see *Targum*). This is also the concept of faith (*Likutey Moharan* 7:5). Rabbi Nathan therefore explains this entire episode in terms of the morning service.

The merchant is therefore seen as a man riding a horse. As we saw earlier, Ishmael is an aspect of the slave's son. When a person wishes to elevate the slave's son in himself, he must take control of his body — this being the concept of riding a horse, as we shall see.

The concept of an animal is an aspect of slavery. Abraham thus told his slaves, "remain here with the donkey" (Genesis 22:5), and the Talmud notes that this indicates that an animal is an aspect of slavery (*Yebamoth* 62b). The exchange between the king's son and the slave's son is therefore also an exchange between the human spirit and the animal spirit (*Likutey Halakhoth, Birkath HaShachar* 3:27).

In becoming a driver, the king's true son was to a degree following in the footsteps of King David and the Patriarchs, who were all shepherds. They did this to go into the very root of the concept of slavery, not only to work as slaves, but to work with animals, which are the epitome of the concept of slavery. Only then would they be able to refine the exchange of animal and man, and thus rectify the exchange in general (*Likutey Halakhoth, Ibid.* 3:30).

In general, driving animals means being in control of them. This indicates that the king's true son was hired by his conscience (the merchant) to take control of his animal passions.

matter over. He immediately said that he would.

The merchant took him on and immediately gave him work to do. He ordered him around as a master would order his servants.

[The young man] began to appraise his situation. This type of work was certainly not befitting his station. He was a gentleman,* and now he had to drive animals, walking on foot* alongside them. Still, he could not change his mind.

The merchant was ordering him around like a master.*

The young man asked him, "How can I drive the animals all by myself?"*

"I have other drovers for my animals," replied [the merchant]. "You can work alongside them."*

With that, [the merchant] gave him some animals to drive, and he brought them outside of the city.* There the other drovers were gathered,* and they all set out together.

[The young man] helped drive the animals, while the merchant rode alongside on his horse.* The merchant rode the horse

---

gentleman. A delicate person. That is, one who is very concerned with his body. He sees this as a sign of freedom, but as we saw earlier, the body is an aspect of "the slave's son." Also, he feels like a gentleman, since deep down, he knows that he is the king's son.

walking on foot. This is an aspect of "princes walking on the ground" (Ecclesiastes 10:16). This is a further sign of his present voluntary servitude.

like a master. When one submits to one's conscience, it eventually takes control. This was as before; even though he tried to put his thoughts of repentance out of mind, they constantly came back to trouble him.

all by myself. It is very difficult to control one's animal passions if one is doing so all alone.

You can work alongside them. There are other people who are also working to control their passions. In a group it is much easier.

out of the city. Here the city represents the place where the king's true son had lived a degenerate life.

other drovers were gathered. This is the place where those who are trying to control their passions come together. It appears that this may be the gathering around a tzaddik. Jacob also had to come to a place where all the shepherds were gathered before he met Rachel (Genesis 29:3; see *Zohar* 1:152a; *Likutey Halakhot, Choshen Mishhpat, Matanah* 4:12,13).

rode alongside on his horse. The horse represents the body (see Story #1), and riding a horse indicates that a person is in control of his body. It is thus taught, "The horse is secondary to the rider" (*Bereshith Rabbah* 68:9; *Tikkuney Zohar* 47, 84b; 70, 134a; see *Rimzey Maasioth*). Later in the story, the man who teaches the king's true son how to "understand

cruelly, [with anger and arrogance] and treated [the young man] even more cruelly.

Seeing how cruel the merchant was, [the young man] was very frightened. He was afraid that [the merchant] would strike him * with his staff — he was so gentle that such a blow would surely kill him. He thus drove the animals with the merchant alongside them.

Finally they came to a place, and they took the sack of bread * that [the merchant] had given the drivers to eat. They also gave [the young man] from this bread, and he ate it. Afterwards, they passed close to a very thick forest, * [where trees were very close to each other].

Two of the animals * that the young man was driving for the

---

one thing from another" is also riding on a horse. In contrast, the slave's true son is seen as chasing his horse, and not being able to catch him.

Thus, the merchant can be seen either as a tzaddik who has complete control of his bodily passions, or as the conscience, which is the element in man that controls the bodily passions.

would strike him. This is the fear that a person has of his conscience (or of the tzaddik). It is very difficult to begin doing good. He is afraid that all sorts of bad things will happen to him. However, Rabbi Nachman taught that one should not assume that doing good causes one to become sick and weak, but that any bodily harm is the result of one's bad deeds (*Sichoth HaRan* 298; see *Likutey Moharan Tinyana* 123).

bread. "This is the way of Torah, eat bread in salt" (*Avoth* 6:4). The merchant is now giving the son spiritual nourishment and wisdom that he needs.

This may also be symbolic of the sack of bread that the king's true son later finds in the forest. It is with this sack of bread that he buys the slave's true son (who had become king) as his slave.

Bread also denotes truth (see below, p. 251).

forest. This represents Asiyah, the lowest of the four universes in the spiritual realm. There are four such universes: Asiyah (making), Yetzirah (formation), Beriyah (creation), and Atziluth (nearness). These parallel the four main parts of the morning service, the sacrificial readings (*korbanoth*) paralleling the universe of Asiyah; the introductory psalms (*Pesukey DeZimra*) paralleling the universe of Yetzirah; the Sh'ma paralleling Beriyah; and the Amidah paralleling Atziluth. Rabbi Nathan said that the story speaks of these four parts of the morning service (*Likutey Halakhoth, Birkath HaShachar* 3:27f).

Two of the animals. These represent the two animals that were sacrificed in the Temple as part of the daily *tamid* offering (*Likutey Halakhoth* 3:27).

In general, the concept of sacrifice is to separate the human spirit from the animal

merchant strayed away. The merchant screamed at him* so he followed them to catch them. They ran further away, while he ran after them.

The forest was so dense and thick that as soon as [he] entered the forest, they could not see each other. He immediately became hidden from his companions. The more he chased the animals, the farther they fled.* He continued chasing them until he was deep in the forest.*

spirit. It is thus written, "Who knows the soul of an animal if it goes up, or the soul of man if it goes down" (Ecclesiastes 3:21). Since it is the animal in man that causes him to sin, an animal must be sacrificed as an atonement. The slaughtering and sacrifice of the animal represents the destruction of the animal spirit in the individual.

This part of the story represents the first part of the morning service. The prince's first learning that he may actually not be a slave's son is represented by the blessing, "who did not make me a slave." The dream is represented by "who removes sleep from my eyes." His stirring of conscience afterwards is the "yehi ratzon" said after this, where we ask God to protect us from all evil desires. Now come the sacrifical readings (korbanoth) which parallel the world of Asiyah.

The king's true son is punished by having to chase the animals because he followed his animal nature and sinned (Likutey Halakhoth 3:27; Rimzey Maasioth).

Now, he must rectify this in its root, and be totally subjugated to the animal. He is bound to chase the animals, and must follow wherever they lead. Thus, in a sense, he is totally under their control. But since the animals now belong to the merchant, they lead him into the "forest," the spiritual realm. Once he has been nourished by the "bread" of the merchant he can enter the spiritual realm. Sacrifice is also called "bread," as it is written, "my sacrifice, my bread" (Numbers 28:2).

This is very much like the concept of sacrifice, where a person vicariously identifies with the animal being sacrificed (Ramban). Then, by "following the animals," he can enter the spiritual realm.

merchant screamed at him. The conscience (or tzaddik) forces the person to enter the spiritual realm to rectify his sins.

the farther they fled. The more a person pursues the material, the farther it flees from him. A person can run after money and the like all his life, but he never really gets it (Likutey Etzoth B, Parnasah 23). "Whoever pursues honor, honor runs away from him."

In a way, the king's true son chasing the animals is reminiscent of King Saul, who had to look for his father's donkeys, and ended up coming to the prophet Samuel and thus becoming king of Israel (1 Samuel, 9).

deep in the forest. He was getting lost in the forest, and this in itself is a concept of Exchange. Because he had sinned and allowed himself to become involved in the concept of Exchange, he was now punished by getting lost. Moreover, because he did not control his desires, he now could not gain control of the animals (Rimzey Maasioth).

He thought over his situation. "No matter what I do, I will die. If I go back without the animals, the merchant will kill me." He really thought that this was true; he was so afraid of the merchant that he was sure that he would be killed if he returned without the animals.* "But if I stay here," [he thought,] "I will be killed by the wild beasts in the forest. Why should I go back to the merchant? How can I confront him without the animals?" He was deathly afraid [of his employer].

He continued chasing the animals, but the more he chased them, the more they fled.*

Meanwhile, it became night.* He had never before spent the night deep in the forest like this. He heard wild animals* growling and decided, "I will climb a tree,* and spend the night there." [All night], he heard the sound of wild animals roaring.*

In the morning, he looked and saw his cattle standing right next to him.* He climbed down from the tree, but when he tried to catch them, they ran further away. The more he chased them,

---

returned without the animals. Since this would indicate that he had totally lost control of his animal desires.

the more they fled. A person's desires lead him from one thing to the other, and he runs after vanity (*Likutey Etzoth* B, *Parnasah*).

night. When the forces of evil are especially prevalent in the world of Asiyah. This denotes the reading "*Abayah hayah mesader*," which is one complete day (Daily Liturgy from *Yoma* 33a).

wild animals. The forces of evil that abound in Asiyah at night. "You make darkness, and it is night; then all the beasts of the forest creep forth" (Psalms 104:20). See Story #2 and the story of "The Burgher and the Pauper."

climb a tree. See Story #2. A tree is always seen as a place that the forces of evil cannot reach. It is interesting to note that the word tree in Hebrew is *etz*, having the same root as *etzah*, meaning good advice. This may denote a person seeking good advice so as to escape evil. We thus say in the evening prayer, "rectify us with good advice from before You" (see *Sichoth HaRan* 238). The tree also represents the Torah and the tzaddik.

wild animals roaring. On this level, he cannot yet hear it as a song, as he does later.

right next to him. As long as he is on the tree (Torah, tzaddik), the animals are to some degree under his control. But as soon as he gets down from the tree and tries to catch them, they run away again. If animals represent one's animal nature, the Torah helps one keep it under control. God said, "I have created the Evil Urge; I have created the Torah as its remedy" (*Kiddushin* 30b). Also "if the disgusting [Evil Urge] is encountered, bring him to the house of study" (*Kiddushin* 30b).

the more they ran. The animals then found some grass,* and began to graze, but when he tried to catch them, they ran away again. He kept on chasing them, and they kept on running away.

He continued chasing them, and they continued fleeing, until they got deeper and deeper into the forest. They were so deep in the forest, and so far from civilization, that the wild beasts there were not afraid of man at all.*

Night fell again, and when he heard the beasts roaring, he was very much afraid. Then he saw an immense tree.* He climbed the tree, and when he got up in the tree, he found another person* lying there. He was very frightened. At the same time, however, he was somewhat comforted, since he had found another person there.

They began questioning one another. "Who are you?" [he asked].

"A human being. Who are you?"

"A human being."

"How did you get here?"

[The young man] did not want to tell him what had happened, so he said, "Because of the cattle. I was tending cattle, and two animals strayed. This is how I got here."

He then asked the stranger he found in the tree, "How did you get here?"

"I came here because of a horse," replied the other. "I was out riding,* and when I stopped to rest,* the horse strayed into the

---

grass. See Story #3. Also see *Likutey Moharan* 47, end.

not afraid of man at all. God had told Noah, "I will place fear of you and dread of you upon all the beasts of the earth" (Genesis 9:2). Thus, normally, the beasts are afraid of man. However, away from civilized areas, such fear does not exist.

This denotes an area deep in the realm of the *klipoth*.

immense tree. See Story #1.

another person. As we shall see, the slave's son, who had become king. He had gotten there first. "God brings the remedy before the sickness." God had now brought them together (*Rimzey Maasioth*).

riding. "I have seen slaves riding horses" (Ecclesiastes 10; see *Rimzey Maasioth, Hashmatoth*). As we shall see later, he had abdicated his kingdom and was determined to repent.

to rest. Yiddish. *Push* in Hebrew, which would mean to stretch. As soon as one rests and

forest. I tried to catch it, but it fled further and further, until I came here."

They decided to join forces and remain together. They spoke about how they would remain together even after they got to civilization.

The two of them spent the night [in the tree]. They heard the wild beasts roaring and making a great noise.

In the morning, he heard the sound of loud laughter,* "Ha ha ha!"* passing over the entire forest. The laughter seemed to spread all over the forest.* It was such loud laughter that the sound made the tree tremble and shake. [The young man] was very confused and terrified by the sound.

The [stranger he had discovered in the tree] said, "I am not afraid* of this any more. I spent a number of nights here already, and just before each day I hear this sound* of laughter, making all the trees tremble and shake."

---

stops controlling the body, it can run away (cf. *Rimzey Maasioth*). As a result, the slave's true son was "cast down" from his horse, this being the concept, "I will sing to God, for He has been very high; the horse and rider He cast in the sea" (Exodus 15:1; *Rimzey Maasioth, Hashmatoth*).

It is significant to note that the king's true son was pursuing cattle, which are kosher animals, while the slave's true son was pursuing a horse, which is a non-kosher animal.

laughter. As we shall see, this is the day laughing at the night. This will be discussed later.

It is significant that the king's true son does not hear this laughter the first night; only now that he has met the slave's true son. Of course, day represents the king's true son, while night represents the slave's true son (*Likutey Halakhoth, Birkath HaShachar* 3:10). Day laughs at night only when they come together, since the night then does not have a name, as we will see later. Similarly, now that the false "king's son" has met the king's true son, he has lost the name of "king's son."

Ha ha ha. *Cha Cha Cha* in the original. *Cha* is spelled *cheth alef* (חא) and can be seen as an abbreviation of *Chayay Emunah* (חיי אמונה), "A life of faith." It is repeated three times, since one must have faith in three things: God, Moses and the Torah (*Oneg Shabbath*, p. 475).

the forest. "Then all the trees of the forest will sing forth" (Psalms 96:12).

I am not afraid. Even though the laughter is directed at him, he has become inured to it. Nevertheless, the laughter portends his downfall.

I hear this sound. We thus see that the slave's true son heard the laughter even before he met the king's true son. This was because the laughter was directed at him. When the king's true son meets him, the king's true son can also hear it.

[The young man] was still very upset, and he said to his companion, "This seems to be a place of the dark forces.* Such laughter is never heard in civilized areas. Who has ever heard laughter all over the world?"

It was then daybreak, and they saw their animals standing nearby. [The young man's] cattle were there alongside the [stranger's] horse. They climbed down and began to give chase, one after the cattle, and the other after the horse.

The cattle fled further away, and [the young man] ran after them as before. The stranger also ran after the horse, which ran further away. Eventually they were far from each other.

Meanwhile, [the young man] found a bag of bread.* This is surely very precious in the wilderness. He took the sack on his shoulders and continued after the cattle.

Suddenly he encountered another stranger.* He was very frightened, but he was also comforted for having found another human being here.

"How did you come here?" asked the stranger.

He responded by asking the stranger, "How did *you* come here?"

"I?" replied the stranger. "My father and my father's fathers grew up here. But you? How did you come here? No one from a civilized area* ever comes here."

---

dark forces. "Known ones" in Hebrew; *shedim* in Yiddish.

bag of bread. Reminiscent of the bag of bread that the merchant gave his workers.

Bread also alludes to truth (cf. *Likutey Moharan* 47). Through the power of truth the king's true son is able to gain the upper hand over the slave's true son, who represents falsehood.

another stranger. The forest man, as we shall see.

It is significant that the king's true son only finds the forest man after he has met the slave's true son and has separated from him again. But after he has encountered falsehood and separated from it to follow his own path (after the animals), he can find "bread." After he has had access to the truth, he can meet the forest man, who will uncover even deeper truths for him.

It seems that the forest man is the angel of Yetzirah (Metatron), who leads him out of Asiyah.

No one from a civilized area. See Story #1, p. 46, regarding the "giants."

[The young man] was very confused. He realized that the stranger was not a human being. He had said that no one from a civilized area ever comes here, and that his fathers had grown up here. He was obviously not a human being. Still, this stranger [from the forest] was behaving in a friendly manner and did nothing to harm him.

"What are you doing here?" asked [the forest man of the king's true son].

He replied that he was chasing his animals.

"Stop chasing your sins," * said the stranger. "These are not animals at all. They are your sins, and they are leading you around. But it is now sufficient. You have already received your punishment. Now you can stop chasing. * Come with me, and you will attain what is coming to you."

[The king's true son] went with him, but he was afraid to speak to him and ask him any questions. [He realized that the other was not a human being.] Perhaps he would open his mouth and swallow him. *

While he was walking after the [forest man], he encountered his companion who was chasing his horse. As soon as he saw him, he signalled him, "This [stranger with me] is not a human being. Don't talk to him. [Don't have any dealings with him,] since he is not human."

---

your sins. Since sin comes from man's animal nature (*Likutey Halakhoth, Birkath HaShachar* 3:27). A person tries to get many things in the world, but if he realized what was the truth, he would understand that he was merely pursuing his own sins (*Likutey Etzoth, Parnasah* 23).

Now you can stop chasing. Since the entire goal of chasing the animals was for him to meet the forest man and learn the truth.

Chasing the animals represents the sacrificial offerings (*korbanoth*) in Asiyah. In meeting the forest man, he had come to the gates of Yetzirah. Here, the main thing will be song.

In Asiyah, all he hears are the roars of animals; in Yetzirah, he can make out that they are a song. This is because Yetzirah is the world of voice — and also the world of anthropomorphisms — where even animal sounds take on a human aspect.

open his mouth and swallow him. As a demonic being would do. See Story #3, p. 99; and "The Rabbi's Son," p. 158.

[His companion] joined them. He then whispered in [his companion's] ear, "This stranger is not human...," telling him everything he knew.

His companion, [the man with the horse], stared at him and saw the sack of bread on his shoulder. He began to plead, "My brother! I have not eaten for days! Give me bread."

He replied, "Here in the desert, [such pleas] are of no avail. My life comes first.* I need the bread for myself."

[The other] began to plead and beg. "I will give you anything I have."

[The king's true son, however, realized that here in the wilderness no gift or bribe is worth as much as bread.] He replied, "What can you give me? Here in the wilderness, what can you trade for bread?"

[The man with the horse] said to [the man with the cattle, who was the king's true son], "I will give you my entire self. I will sell myself to you* for bread!"

[The man with the cattle] decided to buy this stranger. He made up his mind that it would be a good bargain to buy a person for some bread. He bought [the other] as an eternal slave. [The other] made an oath, and swore that he would be his eternal slave when they came to civilization. [The king's son] would give him bread, and they would eat together from the sack until the bread was used up.

My life comes first. A Talmudic teaching. If there is only enough for one person to survive, he need not share it (*Bava Metzia* 62a).

I will sell myself to you. This is very much like Esau selling his birthright for the bowl of pottage (Genesis 25:33). The birthright is an aspect of royalty (cf. *Likutey Moharan* 56). Thus, when Esau sold the birthright, he became in a certain aspect, a slave (*Likutey Halakhoth, Birkath HaShachar* 3:8). This was very much like Haman selling himself to Mordechai for bread (*Midrash*). The false prince thus exchanges eternal life for temporary life. He has become totally dependent on the king's true son.

Also, as mentioned above, the bread represents truth. Even the king's son has a need for the truth, as we shall see. But the truth is that he is a slave's son, and therefore, through the bread, he becomes a slave.

They followed the forest man. [The man with the horse, who was now] his slave followed [the man with the cattle] and the two of them walked behind the forest man.

Things were now somewhat easier for [the king's son]. If he had to lift something, or needed something else done, he would order his slave* to do it for him.

They followed the forest man until they came to a place of serpents and scorpions.* [The king's son] was very much afraid. Out of fear, he asked the forest man, "How can we get across?"

"You think that's hard?" replied the other. "How can you get to my house?"

[With that,] he pointed to his house, which was standing in midair.* "How can you get to my house?" [he asked]

They went with the forest man, and he brought them safely across, and then brought them into his house. He gave them food and drink, and then went on his way.

[The king's true son, who had been with the cattle,] made use of his slave for all his needs.

Meanwhile the slave was very upset. He had sold himself as a slave because he needed bread. He had only needed that bread for one hour, since he had plenty of food to eat. For an hour's worth

---

he would order his slave. Thus, he is beginning to act like a king's son.

serpents and scorpions. These represent spiritual dangers. They are the evil forces (*klipoth*) between the worlds of Asiyah and Yetzirah. In a sense, this is very much like the giant in Story #1. This may also represent the chasm between *korbanoth* and *Pesukey DeZimra*, which is bridged by the rabbinical Kaddish.

standing in midair. This is the concept of "a tower floating in air" (*migdal haporeach be-avir* — מגדל הפורח באויר; *Chagigah* 15b; *Sanhedrin* 106b). It is also related to the request that the sages of Athens asked Rabbi Yehoshua, "Build us a building in the air, between heaven and earth." He replied, "Bring me bricks and mortar there" (*Bekhoroth* 8b).

The Kabbalists explain that the "tower floating in air" denotes Yesod. Yesod is alluded to in the verse, "For all in heaven and earth" (2 Chronicles, 29:11). Yesod connects Zer Anpin and Malkhuth. Since Zer Anpin is heaven, and Malkhuth is earth, Yesod is seen as floating in the air between heaven and earth (*Likutey Moharan* 28:3).

However, Zer Anpin also parallels Yetzirah, while Malkhuth parallels Asiyah. Therefore, there would be an aspect of Yesod between Asiyah and Yetzirah as well. This is represented by the forest man's house, which floats in the air.

Once they enter the forest man's house, they are able to perceive the truth.

of food,* he would now be a slave for the rest of his life. He moaned and sighed, "How did I come to such a state — to be a slave?"

[The king's true son, who was his master,] asked him, "What great status did you have before, that you are groaning for having come to this state?"

He answered, telling him the whole story of how he had been a king, and that people had spread rumors* that he had been exchanged as an infant. (The man with the horse was actually the king, who had been the son of the slave woman.) He related how he had exiled his friend. Then, one time, he realized that it was an evil thing, and he had regretted it. After that, he constantly regretted the evil deed and the great wrong that he had done to his friend.

Then one night he had had a dream* that he could make up this wrong by abdicating his kingdom and going wherever his eyes would lead him. This would be an atonement for his sin, but he did not want to do it. However, the dreams continued to disturb him and urge that he do it, until he finally decided to. He abdicated his kingdom, and wandered around until he came here. Now he had become a slave.

[The king's true son, who was the man with the cattle] listened to everything that [the man with the horse, who was now his slave] said, and he remained silent. He said to himself, "I will see what happens. Then I will make up my mind how to deal with him."

For an hour's worth of food. Like the physical world, where one gives up eternal bliss for temporal enjoyment.

people had spread rumors. This was the first time that he had been able to discuss this with anyone. But since he had eaten the bread of truth, and was now in a place of truth, he could admit the truth.

dream. Paralleling the dream of the king's true son, described earlier. Similarly, both Joseph and Pharaoh had dreams.

The destinies of the two are exactly the same. Both begin to have regrets, then have a dream, then go into voluntary exile, and end up chasing animals in the woods, until they come together. Rabbi Nachman thus taught that for every story that can be told about a tzaddik, there is a similar story that can be told about a wicked person (*Likutey Moharan* 234; *Likutey Halakhoth, Birkath HaShachar* 3:10).

That night, the forest man came and gave them food and drink. They spent the night there. Before morning they heard the sound of the loud laughter, which made all the trees shake and tremble.

[The slave] persuaded* [the king's true son, who was his master] to ask the forest man the meaning of this.

[The king's son] asked [the forest man], "What is this loud sound of laughter [every day] before morning?"

He replied, "This is the sound of the day laughing at the night.* The night asks the day, 'Why is it when you come, I do not have a name?'* Then the day laughs with this loud laughter and then it becomes day. This is the significance of the sound of laughter."

The slave persuaded. Just as the slave's true son did not see the forest man at first, so he cannot question him on his own. The forest man represents the truth, and the slave's true son, who represents falsehood, cannot confront him.

day laughing at the night. The night represents falsehood, and hence, is an aspect of the slave's true son. This comes from the dimunition of the moon. If the moon had not been reduced, the night would also have been light (*Likutey Halakhoth, Birkath HaShachar* 3:41)

Thus, the day represents the king's true son and the night represents the slave's true son. Now that the slave's true son has sold himself to the king's true son, it can be revealed that the day is laughing at the night (*Chokhmah U'Tevunah* 39).

I do not have a name. After telling the story, Rabbi Nachman explained that the significance of this is that "the moon held a lamp in its hand, but when the day came, the lamp could not shine, since a lamp in broad daylight is of no avail" (*Chullin* 60).

Rabbi Nachman also says that names are also very important in the story; in one place things have one name, and elsewhere they have different names. The actual persons of the two sons had not been exchanged, but only their names.

From Rabbi Nachman's statement, we see that a name parallels the concept of a lamp. When a thing's true name is known, the truth can be revealed. The concept of a lamp is thus the revelation of truth, and the rectification of the Exchange. This is the concept of the Chanukah lamp, which represented the victory of the Israelites over the Greeks (slave's true son) (*Likutey Halakhoth, Birkath HaShachar* 3:38,39). It also represents the Sabbath lamp. Later, we shall also see that the Sabbath is the man in the garden (*Likutey Halakhoth, Ibid.* 3:40).

In a sense, day represents Zer Anpin, while night represents Malkhuth. [Evil has a hold on Malkhuth, which is the moon, as we have discussed in Story #3.] Therefore, the house floating in the air also represents the connection between day and night. Therefore, in this house, the mystery can be revealed.

[The king's son] found this very astonishing. It is a very wonderous thing that the day laughs at the night.

In the morning, the forest man once again went on his way, while they remained there, eating and drinking. At night he came back, and they ate, drank, and spent the night.

That night, they heard the sounds of the beasts. All of them were making noise and roaring with different sounds. The lion roared,* while the leopard growled with a different sound, and the birds chirped and whistled with their own sounds. All of them made loud sounds, and at first, they trembled in fear. They were so afraid* that they could not concentrate on the sounds.

However, they then began to concentrate, and they heard that it was the sound of music, an awesomely beautiful song.* They

---

The lion roared. The lion and the leopard here appear to be parallel to those that were on the paths coming from the throne. Rabbi Nachman said that the animals, the garden and the throne were all one (end of story). Every universe is a reflection of the one above it. Therefore (as we shall see), the throne is in Atziluth, the garden in Beriyah, and the animals in Yetzirah.

The animals in the forest paralleled the animals that were carved on the throne. Both sets of animals sang when they were rectified.

They were so afraid. This is very much like the fear that the people experienced when they tried to enter the garden, below. There is song and harmony in the world, but people are usually too afraid to hear it.

song. The song of the animals is a great mystery (*Rimzey Maasioth*). It is the song of faith, and is related to the song that Moses will sing in the ultimate future (*Rimzey Maasioth, Hashmatoth*). The Talmud states that the song of the Red Sea begins with the words, *az yashir* (אז ישיר), which should literally be translated, "Then Moses will sing," (Exodus 15:1). Hence, it relates to the song that Moses will sing at the resurrection (*Sanhedrin* 91b).

In general, the song of the Red Sea denotes the concept of freedom from slavery. Now that the king's true son is about to be freed from his status as the slave's son, he can hear this song.

The same is true of the resurrection. As we have seen earlier, one aspect of the slave's true son is the body. At the resurrection, however, body and soul will be together, but the soul (the king's true son) will dominate. Then they will be able to hear Moses' song.

Rabbi Nathan writes that in the order of prayer, this song of the animals represents the *Pesukey DeZimra* (literally: "verses of song") which comprise the second part of the morning service. Song is what refines the human spirit and separates it from the animal in man (cf. *Likutey Moharan Tinyana* 63). Later he also gets an instrument which can make every animal sing — this is very much the same concept, as we shall see. The *Pesukey* listened more intently, and heard that it was a very wondrous chant. It was a tremendous joy to hear it. All the joys in the world were like nothing — like absolute nothingness — compared to the wondrous enjoyment of listening to this song.

They discussed the situation, and agreed that they would remain there forever.* They had enough to eat and drink, and they could enjoy this wonderful delight, compared to which all other enjoyments were nothing.

The slave persuaded his master,* [the king's true son,] to ask

---

DeZimra are read after the *korbanoth*, just as the Levites would sing their song when the sacrifices were offered (*Likutey Halakhoth, Birkath HaShachar* 3:28).

We therefore see that at this point the prince is entering the world of Yetzirah, this being the universe that parallels the *Pesukey DeZimra*. This is the universe of the *chayoth* — the beasts that Ezekiel saw in his vision (Ezekiel 1:5). The prophets, however, heard the *chayoth* singing — and this is the song of the animals (*Chagigah* 12b; *Chokhmah U'Tevunah* 50).

The Talmud teaches that *chayoth* sing primarily at night, as it is written, "At night his song is with him" (Psalms 42:9) (*Chagigah* 12b).

The song of the animals parallels the song of the throne, as we shall see. Since the concept of song refines the human spirit from the animal, it is a means of rectifying the exchange. For this reason, the king's true son can hear it only after he has made the slave's true son his servant. Similarly, after he adjusts the throne and makes it sing, he knows for certain that he is the king's true son (*Chokhmah U'Tevunah* 6).

On a somewhat deeper level, since song is the resolution of the exchange (between animal and man), then in order for the song to exist, the initial exchange had to come into being. It is for this reason that man also has to have an element of the animal in him (and on a deeper level, why man must have an Evil Urge). Thus, the fact that the Prince fell into a state of drunkenness and dissolution may have been a result of God's song not being correct as long as the sons were still exchanged (*Chokhmah U'Tevunah* 11,12).

In general, the animals also represent the forces of evil and destruction. Their sound is fearsome and frightening, but if one can rectify the exchange in oneself, then one can hear the harmony in all things.

Rabbi Nachman also writes that song is finding the good points in all things, including other people and oneself (*Likutey Moharan* 282). Thus, when the king's true son realized that he was really not a bad person, and should not spend his life drinking and womanizing, he heard this song.

remain there forever. Very much like the burgher's son in the previous story, who wanted to remain on his island. Even though this is an inferior level compared to what one can reach, it is serene and blissful.

slave persuaded his master. Again he cannot confront him with the truth directly.

[the forest man] the meaning of this song, and he asked.
[The forest man] replied that the sun had made a garment for
the moon.* The animals of the forest realize that the moon

garment for the moon. Rabbi Nachman says at the end of the story that this is the joy of the
moon (*chedvatha de-lavanah*) when it receives any new concepts from the sun.

The Ari explains that *Hodu* (which the Sefardim say before *Barukh Sheamar*) relates to
Asiyah, even though it is normally part of the *Pesukey DeZimra*. This is the concept of the
"joy of the matron" — *chedvah de-matranutha*, the Yesod of Yetzirah, which comes down
to Asiyah (*Pri Etz Chaim, Shaar HaZemiroth* 1). In the story, this is the house standing in
the air. It is also related to the "joy of the moon." The moon is related to Malkhuth and
Asiyah, and when Yesod of Yetzirah penetrates into Asiyah (in *Hodu*), then the moon
receives a new garment.

Rabbi Nathan also writes that this is the concept of the blessing, "Who clothes the
naked." The concept of the garment that the sun gives the moon is the root of all garments
(*Likutey Halakhoth, Birkath HaShachar* 3:14).

A garment is a concept of a name. In the exchange, the bodies were not exchanged, but
only the names and "garments" as we mentioned earlier.

Now that the prince has gotten his status back, in a sense, the garment has been
rectified.

Rabbi Nathan furthermore writes that all evil comes from the blemish of the moon. As
we have seen earlier (Story #3), evil attaches itself primarily to the moon and draws its
strength from it. As a result of the reduction of the moon, God's name cannot be
pronounced as it is written — the pronounced name is necessary to overcome evil.

The moon has joy when it gets a new garment. This denotes the removal of its blemish,
and its being rectified so that the forces of evil can no longer attach themselves to it. As
long as the moon is blemished, the forces of evil have power, and they (the slave's true son)
have dominion. But when the moon is rectified, the slave's true son is subjugated.

Moreover, as long as the moon is blemished, God's name is not pronounced as it is
written and is therefore also in a sense blemished. When the moon is rectified, then God's
name is rectified. However, since all other names in the world are dependent on God's
name, when God's name is rectified, then all other names in the world are rectified. The
exchange, as we have seen, primarily involves names, and the rectification of names is a
rectification of the exchange itself. The new garment is the rectification of the blemish of
the moon (*Likutey Halakhoth, Birkath HaShachar* 3:41).

The joy of the moon is also an aspect of Rosh Chodesh. Essentially, Rosh Chodesh (the
New Moon festival) does not come automatically, but must be declared by the Israelites
(see *Zimrath HaAretz*). Therefore, the main joy of the moon comes from the rectification
down below. Moreover, this is accomplished only through the Jews, who parallel God's
throne on high. Thus, the rectification of the moon parallels the rectification of the throne
later in the story (*Parparoth LeChokhmah* on *Likutey Moharan Tinyana* 1, end; see *Zohar*
2:238).

does them a great service. [Animals] dominate the night,* because sometimes they must enter an inhabited area. They cannot do this by day, so their main time is the night. By shining for them then, the moon provides for them a great benefit.

[The wild animals] therefore agreed that they would compose a new melody* in honor of the moon. This is the melody that they

In general, the sun represents the light of Torah, while the moon represents the Jew (*Knesseth Yisroel*) and the Shekhinah. The new garment given to the moon thus represents the raising up of the Jew from his subjugated status. We thus say in *Lekhah Dodi*: "Put on your clothes of glory (Tifereth, which denotes the sun), My people;" (cf. Isaiah 52:1). The people Israel will then be renewed just like the moon, as we say in the blessing of the moon: "They will be renewed just like it (the moon)."

[Animals] dominate the night. The night is seen as the time when the forces of evil abound. As we have seen in story #3, the forces of evil have their power primarily from the moon.

new melody. Rabbi Nachman, at the end of the story, says that this is the psalm, "Sing to God a new song, because He has done wonders" (Psalms 98). The Midrash states that this is the song that will be sung for Israel's redemption (*Midrash Tehillim ad loc.*).

Rabbi Nachman also points out that this was the song that the cows sang as they carried the ark back to Beth Shemesh (see *Avodah Zarah* 24b; *Zohar* 1:123a). The holy ark had been captured by the Philistines in battle, but when they were struck with a plague, they decided to send the ark back to the Israelites. The Philistines placed the ark on a cart, and had two milk cows draw it to Beth Shemesh. The scripture states that the "cows sang on the way" (1 Samuel, 6:12; see Rashi).

Beth Shemesh literally means "house of the sun." The song is therefore related to the sun, and comes because of the new garment that the sun gives the moon.

The Philistines represent the forces of evil; hence, the slave's son. The ark, on the other hand, contained the tablets of the Ten Commandments and the original Torah, so that it represents the king's true son. Thus, when the Philistines captured the ark, it was a concept of the Exchange.

The Philistines were struck with a plague, and on their own, decided to return the ark. This is very much like the slave's true son, who on his own decided to abdicate his throne. Then the Philistines sent the ark to Beth Shemesh — the house of the sun. Evil draws its power from the blemished moon, but this blemish can be rectified by the sun. When the ark was sent back, this was a rectification of the Exchange, and that is the significance of the song the cows sang. This was also the significance of the song that was being sung now by the animals in the forest.

The *Zohar* speaks of this song, and states explicitly that the song sung by the cows is the same as that sung by the *chayoth* when they lift up the Throne of Glory. This occurs on Rosh Chodesh, when the moon receives new light from the sun (*Zohar* 2:138a; cf. *Zimrath HaAretz*).

In the Talmud, there is an opinion that the song that the cows sang was the song that

were now hearing. [All the animals and birds are singing a new song in honor of the moon's receiving a garment from the sun.]

When they heard that this was a melody, they paid even more attention to it. They heard that it was a very wonderful and beautiful song.

The forest man said to them, "Why do you find this so novel? I have an instrument* that I received from my ancestors, who in

---

Moses and the Israelites sang at the Red Sea. As we have seen, this song also denotes a rectification of the Exchange.

There is still another opinion that the song the cows sang was, "On that day you will say, 'Give thanks to God, proclaim His name...' " (Isaiah 12:4) (*Avodah Zarah* 24b).

This is significant, since the verse obviously seems to be referring to the song, "Give thanks to God, proclaim His name..." (1 Chronicles, 16;8-36), which was the song that King David sang when the ark was brought to Jerusalem. This is the *Hodu* prayer, and that according to the Sefardic rite is said before *Barukh Sheamar*, as discussed earlier. They were in the forest, which denotes Asiyah, and as we have seen, this prayer denotes the transition from Asiyah to Yetzirah.

In general, song denotes joy. Thus, this song is a reflection of the moon's joy (*chedvatha de-lavanah*). Moreover, as we have seen, the night denotes falsehood, which is an aspect of the slave's true son. However, when the moon receives its new garment, it is rectified, and the night is no longer dark and false. The song denotes this rectification (*Likutey Halakhoth, Birkath HaShachar* 3:41).

Rabbi Nathan also writes that, in general, the Torah is a fourfold song, which comes from the four letters of the Tetragrammaton. This is related to the new song that the animals sang when the moon received its garment. This is also why four men are called to the Torah reading on Rosh Chodesh — the four men represent the fourfold nature of this song. This, in turn, is related to the restoration of the throne to the king's true son, which is an aspect of King David. On blessing the new moon we therefore say, "David King of Israel lives and endures." King David is also the fourth leg of the throne (the Patriarchs being the other three). Therefore, the rectification of the moon is related to the rectification of the throne later in the story.

The new song that the animals sang relates to a new providence over the world, as Rabbi Nachman himself teaches (*Likutey Moharan Tinyana* 8:10). This is because Rosh Chodesh is the joy of the moon, and denotes the renewal of the world, when the effects of the Exchange are nullified (*Likutey Halakhoth, Keriyath HaTorah* 6:5).

In general, we see then that the reduction of the moon is very closely related to the Exchange. Thus, when the Exchange is rectified the moon receives its new garment. Out of the resolution of the Exchange comes this song (*Chokhmah U'Tevunah* 38).

instrument. *Keli* (כלי) in Hebrew. It was a box, as we see later in the story. In the first story, *keli* denotes a purse.

turn inherited it from their fathers' fathers. The instrument is made with special leaves and colors.* When this instrument is placed on any animal* or bird, [the creature] immediately begins to sing this song."

The laughter was then heard, and it was day.

The forest man went on his way, and [the king's true son] went to search for the instrument. He searched the entire room, but could not find it, and he was afraid to go any further. The area. [The king's true son and his slave] were afraid to ask * the forest man to bring them back to civilization.

The forest man then returned and told them that he would bring them back to civilization. When he had brought them to a civilized area, he gave the instrument to the king's true son, and said, "I am giving you this instrument." [Then referring to the slave's son, who had become king, and was now a slave again, he said,] "You will know how to deal with him."

"Where shall we go?" they asked.

[The forest man] told them that they should ask around, and

---

special leaves and colors. Or leaves and colors. Actually, as we shall see, the instrument was made of the same wood as the throne. This might be significant, since, as we shall see, the instrument is representative of the ark. The ark contained the tablets, and they were made of sapphire, the same material out of which the Throne of Glory is made. It is thus written, "They saw under [God's] feet a brickwork of sapphire" (Exodus 24:10). This is the sapphire out of which the tablets would be made.

placed on any animal. Just as the cows who brought the ark to Beth Shemesh sang when the ark was placed on them (*Zohar* 1:123a). In a similar manner, when the *chayoth* — the heavenly beasts that Ezekiel saw — lift the throne, they also begin to sing (*Zohar* 2:138a).

Rabbi Nathan writes that the king's true son's getting this instrument parallels the part of the service known as *Pesukey DeZimra* — the "verses of song" (*Likutey Halakhoth, Birkath HaShachar* 3:28). This parallels the world of Yetzirah, which is the world of the *chayoth* which support the throne. These *chayoth* sing when they lift the throne.

In general, this instrument is then seen as the Torah. The Torah has the power to refine the animal element in every person. It is also seen as the power of the tzaddik, which can refine the animal in every person and make him "sing" (*Oneg Shabbath*, p. 297).

There is also a Breslover tradition that this instrument is the advice given by a tzaddik.

afraid to ask. They were even more afraid to ask for the instrument. But in the end, the forest man gave it to them. Sometimes we are afraid to ask for what we need, but our fears are groundless. We are given what we want without even having to ask for it.

seek a land known as "The Foolish Land with the Wise King." *
"In which direction shall we begin asking about this land?"
they asked.

The forest man pointed out the direction and said to the king's
true son, "Go to the king there, and you will attain your
greatness."

They set out and began their journey. They wanted very much
to find a wild or domestic animal so as to try out the instrument,
to see if it would produce the wondrous song, but they did not
encounter any animals.

Then, when they had come closer to an inhabited area, * they
came across an animal. They placed the instrument on it, and it
began to sing * [the song of the forest].

They continued traveling until they came to the land [the
forest man had described]. There was a wall * all around the land,
with no means of getting in except through one gate. They had to
walk several miles until they came to the gate where they could
enter the land. They walked around [along the wall] until they
finally came to the gate.

When they came to the gate, [the guards] did not want to let
them come in, since the king of the land had died, and his son was
now the new king. The king had left a will declaring that although
the land had previously been called 'The Foolish Land with the
Wise King', [after his death] it would be called 'The Wise Land
with the Foolish King.'* If a man came and was successful in

The Foolish Land... Rabbi Nachman used the words in Yiddish: "*Das naarishe land un der
kluger malkhuth.*" This kingdom alludes to all creation as well as to the divine attributes
(*Chokhmah U'Tevunah* 8). This is a great mystery (*Rimzey Maasioth*).

inhabited area. Yetzirah.

began to sing. *Pesukey DeZimra.*

wall. The firmament over the heads of the *chayoth* (Ezekiel 1:22).

Wise Land with the Foolish King. This is also an aspect of the Exchange. Just as the prince
and the slave's son had been exchanged, so had the land's name. Regarding the land now,
it is written, "Woe is to you, land, when your king is a fool (*naar*)" (Ecclesiastes 10:16)
(*Rimzey Maasioth, Hashmatoth*).

It might be that when the slave's son became king over his kingdom, this kingdom got

restoring the land's name to 'The Foolish Land with the Wise King,' that man would be king.*

No one was being allowed to enter the land unless he was prepared to undertake this. They therefore did not want [the king's son] to enter. They said to him, "Can you undertake the task of restoring the land's original name?" It was certainly impossible for him to attempt it. They therefore could not go in.

The slave urged [the king's son] to return home, but he did not want to, since the forest man had told him to go to this land, and here he would come to his greatness.

Just then, another man* arrived. He was riding a horse,* and he wanted to enter [the gate]. However, [the guards] would not let him in for the same reason as before.

Seeing the stranger's horse standing there, he placed the instrument on it. It began to play the wonderful melody [of the forest].

The horse's owner asked very strongly that he sell him this instrument, but he refused to sell it. "What can you give me for such a wonderful instrument?" asked [the king's son].

The horse's owner said, "What can you really do with this instrument? [It has no real use. At best] you can make a show and get a gulden.* I have knowledge that is better than your

---

the name, "the Wise Land with the Foolish King." Later, when the king's true son was restored, the land's name was also restored (*Chokhmah U'Tevunah* p. 107).

This was a reversal; normally people respect their leaders. Now, however, they would not.

that man would be king. To restore the land's name would involve rectifying the garden and the throne, as we shall see. As long as things in the garden and throne were not in their rightful places, the land could not have its right name.

another man. Possibly the angel of Beriyah. Or Metatron, who serves as the conduit between Yetzirah and Beriyah.

riding a horse. Like the merchant.

gulden. In Yiddish; *diner* in Hebrew. Although the song was very beautiful, it has its limits. Truth is on a higher level. Yetzirah is the world of beauty, while Beriyah is the world of understanding of truth. He now must go to the higher level.

instrument. From my father's father,* I have inherited the knowledge of how to understand one thing from another thing. * [What I have from my father's fathers is the knowledge of how to understand one thing from another thing.] No matter what someone says, through the tradition that I have, I can understand one thing from another. I have never revealed this to anyone in the world. But if you give me your instrument, I will teach you this knowledge."

[The king's son, who had this instrument,] decided that it would be very wonderful to understand one thing from another. He gave [the horse's owner] the instrument,* and the other taught him the method through which he could understand one thing from another.

Now that the king's true son could understand one thing from another, when he went to the land's gate, he understood that it would be possible* for him to make an effort to restore the land's

---

From my father's father. Like the forest man and the instrument.

understand one thing from another thing. *Mevin davar mitokh davar*, the Talmudic definition of understanding (Binah) (*Chagigah* 14a, *Sanhedrin* 93b, Rashi on Exodus 31:3).

Rabbi Nathan writes that when the prince received this information, this parallels the third part of the morning service, the Sh'ma. When we recite the Sh'ma, we receive new insight and a new state of consciousness (*mochin*) (*Likutey Halakhoth, Birkath HaShachar* 3:29).

In general, Binah (understanding) parallels the world of Beriyah. This is also the universe that parallels the Sh'ma.

gave...the instrument. He was actually trading something tangible for something very intangible.

The instrument is called a *keli*, which is usually something with which one receives. A person has to rid himself of the intangible means he has to accumulate truth and beauty, and take the tangible way of understanding one thing from another (*Yagel Yaakov*, p. 43).

The prince realized that he was in a kingdom where wisdom was valued. Therefore, he wanted the ability to understand one thing from another.

This kingdom is the universe of Beriyah. As long as Malkhuth, which is the Shekhinah, was in its place, in Atziluth, the king was wise. This is because Atziluth parallels Chokhmah. But when the king died, and Malkhuth went down into Beriyah, then the king was no longer wise, and the land was "the Wise Land with the Foolish King."

understood that it would be possible. This is because he now had understanding. He did not

original name. Since he understood one thing from another, he understood that it would be possible, even though he did not know how, or by what means. Nevertheless, understanding one thing from another, he understood that it would be possible.

He therefore made up his mind that he would tell them to let him enter, since he would make an effort [to restore the land's original name]. After all, what could he lose?*

He spoke to the men who would not let anyone enter without making the effort, and told them to let him in. He would make the effort to restore the land's original name.

They let him enter and informed the ruling ministers that a man had been found who was willing to make an effort to restore the land's original name. He was brought to the ministers of the land, and they told him, "You must realize that we are not fools, heaven forbid. However, the late king was so extraordinarily wise that compared to him we were all considered fools. It was for this reason that the land was called. 'The Foolish Land with the Wise King.' When the king died, his son* took his place. He is also wise, but compared to us, he is not wise at all. The land is therefore now called the opposite, 'The Wise Land with the Foolish King.'

"The king left a will stating that when a wise person was found who could restore the original name to the kingdom, that person would be king. He ordered his son that when such a person was found, [the son] should abdicate the throne, and let the wise person be king. This person would have to be so extraordinarily wise that compared to him everyone else would be foolish. This

---

have wisdom (Chokhmah), which is higher than Binah, but he knew he could attain it. Moreover, Binah denotes repentance, and with repentance he would be able to restore the name (*Likutey Halakhoth, Shabbath* 4).

what could he lose? When a person has a chance to do something great, he should not allow his own insecurity to stop him. He may fail, but what can he lose?

his son. The king could not tell the secret to his son nor could he leave the kingdom to him. The prince, who was now trying to rectify the kingdom, was actually an incarnation of the king who had died (*Chokhmah U'Tevunah* 20,49). The king therefore would let a more intelligent person take over the kingdom from his son (*Ibid.* 48).

man would be king, and then the name of the land would once again be 'The Foolish Land with the Wise King,' since compared to him everyone else would be fools. Now you know what you are getting yourself into."

The ministers continued, "We have a test to see if you are so wise. There is a garden* here which was left by the late king,* who was an extremely wise man. This garden is a great wonder. All sorts of metal instruments grow in it, gold instruments and silver instruments.* It is an awesome wonder. However, it is impossible to enter the garden. As soon as anyone enters it, he is pursued, and he begins to scream. He does not know who is chasing him, and he sees nothing. Still, he is pursued until he is chased out of the garden.* Let us see if you are wise enough to enter this garden."*

---

garden. At the end of the story, Rabbi Nachman himself said that this garden parallels the Garden of Eden. He also said that the animals in the forest, the garden, and the throne were all one. The garden also parallels the Land of Israel, which is an aspect of Eden (*Zimrath HaAretz*).

The garden can also allude to the Torah, since there are fifty-three portions in the Torah, and this adds up to *gan* (גן) (*Tikkuney Zohar* 13, 29b).

left by the late king. The king had purposely put the garden out of order, so that no one would be able to enter it. This act of the king paralleled the midwife's exchanging the two sons (*Chokhmah U'Tevunah* 1). He had also exchanged things in the throne (*Rimzey Maasioth, Hashmatoth*).

gold instruments and silver... Perhaps the souls that are in Beriyah. The son then takes on an aspect of the "master of the field" (*Likutey Moharan* 65:1).

chased out of the garden. When a person wants to enter holiness and do good, it is like entering the Garden of Eden. However, there are then many things that chase him away and prevent him from doing good (*Likutey Halakhoth, Shabbath* 4).

This fear of the garden is very much like the fear that the prince and the slave's son had of the animals in the forest.

But here there is actually nothing to fear — it is all in the mind.

Being chased out of the garden is very much like Adam being chased out of the Garden of Eden (*Likutey Halakhoth, Shabbath* 4). This is also reflected by the Israelites being exiled from the Holy Land (*Zimrath HaAretz*).

Thus, just as the king's true son was exiled as a result of the Exchange, so the garden ejects those who come into it for the same reason.

to enter this garden. Entering the garden is also like entering *Pardes*. The Talmud tells of the four who entered *Pardes*, where only Rabbi Akiva entered in peace and left in peace. Of

[The king's son] asked them if the person who enters the garden is beaten in any way.

They answered, "Primarily, he is chased, and he does not know who is chasing him. But he flees in great terror.* This is what they had been told by people who had entered the garden."

[The king's true son] went to the garden. He saw that there was a wall around it and an open gate. There were no guards there, since such a garden obviously did not need guards.

He went up to the garden and looked. Next to the garden, he saw a statue of a man. He looked more closely, and saw a tablet* above the man. The inscription on it said that this man had been a king many centuries ago, and during this king's reign there had been peace.* Before this king's reign there had been wars, and

the others, Ben Zoma went mad, Ben Azzai died, and Elisha ben Abuya became an apostate (*Chagigah* 14b).

The Talmud also teaches that the only one who can be taught the mysteries of the *merkavah* is one who "is wise, understanding from his knowledge." He must therefore have the concept of "understanding one thing from another" (*Chagigah* 11b). Hence, only after the prince was able to understand one thing from another was he able to enter the garden (*Rimzey Maasioth, Hashmatoth*).

flees in great terror. This is in itself an aspect of the Exchange. Although the garden was harmless and beautiful, people would flee from an unexplained terror (*Chokhmah U'Tevunah* 15).

Thus, there is no true obstacle in the garden. The only obstacle is fear.

tablet. See "the tablet on the mountain" in the story of "The Spider and the Fly," p. 146.

there had been peace. The king is obviously "the king to whom peace belongs" (*melekh she-hashalom shelo*), which is an obvious reference to God (*Shavuoth* 35b). It is thus taught that wherever the name Solomon (*Shlomo* — man of peace) occurs in the Songs of Songs, it refers to "the king to whom all peace belongs," that is, God (*Ibid.*).

At the end of the story, Rabbi Nachman himself said that this king was the Sabbath. Sabbath is a concept of peace.

Rabbi Nathan writes that the weekdays are an aspect of foolishness. The Torah states that the people "spread out" to gather the manna (Numbers 11:8). The word for "spread out" is *shatu*, which also has the connotation of foolishness (*shotah*). This is the aspect of the forest, where they had to chase their animals.

The Sabbath, on the other hand, is an aspect of understanding, and hence, since he was able to understand one thing from the other, the prince was able to comprehend the concept of this man (*Likutey Halakhoth, Shabbath* 4).

The man therefore reflects Solomon, who was the wisest of all men. He is a reflection of

afterward there had also been wars, but during his reign there had been peace.

He contemplated the situation. He already could understand one thing from another, and understood that everything depended on this man. When a person entered the garden and was pursued, he did not have to run out at all. He only had to stand next to this man,* and he would be saved. Furthermore, if this

---

the prince, who now understands one thing from the other. It therefore also seems that the man who gave the secret to the prince was a descendant of this king. Thus, one could not enter the garden unless one was wise, like Solomon (see *Chokhmah U'Tevunah*, p. 106).

The man in the garden parallels the man on the throne that Ezekiel saw (*Rimzey Maasioth, Hashmatoth; Chokhmah U'Tevunah,* p. 106).

The main rectification of the garden, and hence the world, thus depends on the Sabbath. It is taught that if the Israelites kept two Sabbaths, they would immediately be redeemed (*Zimrath HaAretz*).

Also, the concept of peace is very important, since the Exchange is the opposite of harmony and peace. Peace exists when all things are in their proper places. Therefore, the rectification of the garden comes through the king who had peace in his days (*Chokhmah U'Tevunah* 66).

Also, from here we see that from wisdom one can gain courage.

stand next to this man. Rabbi Nathan writes that this man represents the Sabbath, which is an aspect of faith. When a person is afraid to enter the garden and do something good, he must stand firmly next to the concept of faith. Then he will believe in repentance, and will realize that he can rectify everything. Only then will he be able to place the man back in his right place in the garden. Moreover, the Sabbath is an aspect of the rectification of the Shekhinah, which is the rectification of the garden (*Likutey Halakhoth, Shabbath* 4).

The Sabbath is also the concept of nullifying oneself for one's goals. Thus, standing next to the garden rids him of all thoughts which prevent him from serving God and entering the garden (*Ibid.* 6:5).

Rabbi Nathan also notes that in the Torah, the Sabbath is mentioned (Exodus 31:12-17) just before the Torah describes the sin of the Golden Calf (Exodus 32). The sin of the Golden Calf is a reflection of Adam's sin, and the Sabbath essentially protected the Israelites from destruction. Similarly, after Adam sinned, he sang, "A psalm a song for the Sabbath day" (Psalms 92, *Midrash*). It is also taught that after Adam sinned, the Sabbath protected him and prevented him from being ejected from the Garden of Eden immediately. Therefore, when a person is in danger of being thrown out of the "garden," he must stand next to the Sabbath (*Likutey Halakhoth, Shabbath* 7:41).

As we have said, the man in the garden parallels the man on the throne, seen by Ezekiel. Just as the prince was protected by standing next to the man, when Moses went to get the Torah and the angels wanted to attack him, he was protected by grasping onto the Throne of Glory (*Rimzey Maasioth, Hashmatoth*; see *Likutey Moharan Tinyana* 1).

man were stood in the middle of the garden* [instead of next to it], then anyone would be able to enter the garden safely. [The king's son understood all this since he was able to understand one thing from another.]

[The king's son] went and entered the garden. As soon as he was pursued, he walked over and stood next to this man, who stood just outside the garden. He was thus able to leave safely,* without being harmed. Others who had entered the garden had fled in such terror when they were pursued that they had been injured. However, [the king's son], had emerged safely and calmly since he had stood next to the statue. The ministers were amazed to see him come out safely.

[The king's true son] then ordered that the statue be placed in the middle of the garden. When this was done, all the ministers were able to enter the garden. They entered the garden and went out in peace, without being harmed in any way.

The ministers said, "Nevertheless! Even though we have seen such a thing from you. Nevertheless, for one thing you do not deserve to get you the kingdom. We shall give you one more test."

They explained, "The late king had a throne.* The throne is

---

in the middle of the garden. Thus, once he was able to enter the garden, he was also able to rectify it, so that everyone would be able to enter.

In a way, the man in the garden was "exchanged" so that he was not in his proper place. This parallels the exchange of the two sons. Rectifying the place of the man is the first main step in rectifying the Exchange, since through it the king's true son will once again become a royal personage (*Chokhmah U'Tevunah* 5).

As we have seen, Rabbi Nathan teaches that the man represents faith (the Sabbath), while the garden represents the Torah. Originally, faith was to the side of the Torah, so that people were frightened of its mysteries. But when faith is made central to the Torah, then anyone can enter in peace.

leave safely. Literally, "left in peace." This parallels Rabbi Akiva, whom the Talmud says, "entered in peace and left in peace" (*Chagigah* 15a). Since he could understand one thing from another, which is the true aspect of Beriyah, he could enter and leave Beriyah in peace (see *Rimzey Maasioth, Hashmatoth*).

throne. Rabbi Nachman himself says that the throne is merely another aspect of the garden (end of story). The animals, the garden, and the throne are all one.

He also says that the song of the animals is the same as the song of the throne at the end of the story.

very tall,* and next to it stand all kinds of animals and birds* carved out of wood. In front of the throne stands a bed. * There is a table* near the bed, and on the table stands a lamp.*

"From the throne, well-trodden walled paths go forth. These paths go forth from all sides of the throne, but no one knows the relationship of the throne to these paths.

This is why the prince must rectify both the throne and the garden. As long as one is not rectified, the other is not.

The throne, of course, represents the throne that Ezekiel saw in his vision (Ezekiel 1:26). It was also seen by Isaiah, who said that he saw "God sitting on a high and exalted throne" (Isaiah 6:1).

The throne had animals and birds carved on it. In this respect, it resembled King Solomon's throne, which was said to be made in this manner. Since the man in the garden was an aspect of Solomon, this was an aspect of his throne. (Regarding Solomon's throne, see *Targum Sheni* on Esther 1:2).

The throne is also an aspect of Jerusalem as well as the Temple. Regarding the Temple, it is said, "You throne of glory on high from the beginning, You place of our sanctuary" (Jeremiah 17:12).

This throne is the epitome of the concept of understanding one thing from another, since the Throne of Glory is in Beriyah as taught by the Kabbalists. As we have mentioned a number of times, Beriyah is an aspect of Binah (*Chokhmah U'Tevunah*, p. 106;*Chokhmah U'Binah*, p. 30).

very tall. The "high and exalted throne" (Isaiah 6:1).

animals and birds. The throne is the throne of judgment. Therefore, if it is not correct, then judgment is also incorrect and is reversed. It is for this reason that the sons can be exchanged. The animals on the throne are the angels that direct providence (*Chokhmah U'Tevunah* 10).

The animals on the throne represent the animal nature in man; hence, they are an aspect of the slave's son. When the true prince sits on the throne, he has dominion over the slave's son. Then judgment is correct, and the soul has power over the body (*Chokhmah U'Tevunah* 34).

bed. The bed represents the ark that stood in the Holy of Holies. It was called this because it was the "resting place" of the Divine Presence. We thus find that the Holy of Holies is known as the "chamber of beds" (2 Kings, 11:2; Rashi *ad loc*; cf. *Shir HaShirim Rabbah* on 1:16).

Or, a couch upon which one reclines to eat (see Ezekiel 23:41).

table. In the Tabernacle (Exodus 25:23).

lamp. Paralleling the lamp in the Tabernacle (Exodus 25:31).

This is the concept of the lamp of Chanukah, which is an important element in bringing out the truth and rectifying the Exchange. The lamp is thus the last thing to be rectified in the story (see *Likutey Halakhoth, Birkath HaShachar* 3:39). This is also the concept of the

"After the paths spread out for a certain distance, there is a golden lion standing by the [first one]. If a person comes near to it, it opens its mouth to swallow him.* However, the path extends far beyond the lion. The same is true of the other paths extending from the throne. Thus, the second path extending from the throne is very much the same. Standing there is another type of wild beast, such as a leopard, made of a different metal. It is also impossible to come close to it. The path then extends beyond where it is standing. This is true of all the paths.

"These paths extend throughout the entire land. No one understands the meaning of the throne with all its details and the paths. This, then, will be your test. See if you can understand the significance of the throne and everything associated with it."

They showed him the throne and he saw that it was extremely tall*.... He went over to the throne and gazed at it. As he contemplated the throne, he realized that it was made of the same type of wood as the box* [or instrument, that the forest man had given him]. He gazed further, and saw that a rose* was missing

---

Sabbath lamp (*Ibid.* 3:40). The lamp also denotes faith (*Likutey Halakhoth, Shabbath* 4).

There are thus four things mentioned here: the throne, the bed, the table, and the lamp. The throne can be seen as the ark cover containing the Cherubs, from which God's voice emanated. Thus, these four things were the four primary things in the Tabernacle: the ark, the ark cover, the table, and the menorah-lamp. The *Zohar* also states that these four objects represent the Shekhinah (*Zohar* 2:133a; also see *Tikkuney Zohar* 47, 84a; 2 Kings, 4:10).

At the end of the story, Rabbi Nachman presents these four items in this order: bed, table, throne, lamp. In Hebrew they are *mittah, shulchan, kissey, ner* (מטה, שלחן, כסא, נר). As Rabbi Nathan points out, the initial letters of these words spell out *Mishkan* (משכן) while the final letters (rearranged) spell out Aaron (אהרן). The four objects thus represent the *Mishkan* or Tabernacle, which is rectified by the High Priest, represented by Aaron (*Likutey Halakhoth, Shabbath* 4).

to swallow him. Like the demons (see above and Story #3).

extremely tall. Just as the garden had been changed slightly, so had the throne (*Rimzey Maasioth, Hashmatoth*). The king knew that someone would come who could rectify it (see *Chokhmah U'Tevunah* 1).

wood as the box. From here we see that the instrument was a box made of wood. The ark was made of wood covered with gold.

rose. This rose is alluded to in the verse, "I am the rose of Sharon, the lily of the depths"

from the top of the throne. If the rose were in the throne, then the throne would have the same power as the box,* [which would produce music whenever it was placed on any animal or bird]. Then he gazed even more and noticed that the rose missing from the top of the throne was lying at the bottom of the throne.* He would have to take it and place it on top, and then the throne would have the same power as the box. The late king had devised* each detail with such wisdom that no person could

(Song of Songs 2:1). The rose alludes to the Israelites, and is now fallen, and is hence called "the lily of the depths." However, it has the power to make the throne sing, and is therefore called "Sharon," which comes from the root *shir*, meaning song. When it is put in its correct place, the throne will sing (*Zohar* 1:221a).

The *Zohar* also teaches that the rose had thirteen petals, paralleling the Thirteen Attributes of Mercy. These come from Arikh Anpin, the highest personna in Atziluth, paralleling Kether (see *Zohar* 1:1a).

Kether is usually represented by the letter *alef.* God said that "the hand is on the throne of YH a war against Amalek for all generations" (Exodus 17:16). Since the word throne is spelled *kis* (כס), instead of *kissey* (כסא), the *alef* is missing, and our sages teach that the throne is not complete. The letter *alef*, representing Kether and the rose, is missing.

same power as the box. The box represented the ark, containing the Torah, as Rabbi Nachman says explicitly at the end of the story. The *Zohar* states that, just as the cows sang when the box was placed on them, so the *chayoth* (the beasts on high) sing when they lift the Throne of Glory (*Zohar* 2:138a). Rabbi Nachman also states explicitly that this is the concept of the throne. In the story, things are sometimes called by one name, and sometimes by another.

When the upper worlds and the Throne of Glory are correct, then all judgment follows the Torah, and the "throne has the power of the box."

Rabbi Nathan expands the teaching that "God's name and throne are not complete as long as Amalek exists. Amalek is a descendant of Esau (see Genesis 36:12), and is hence an aspect of the slave's son. Thus, as long as Amalek has power, and the effects of the Exchange remain, God's throne cannot be whole (*Likutey Halakhoth, Birkath HaShachar* 3:41).

As we have seen, the Exchange came from the serpent. This also led to the concept of Amalek, which prevents the throne from being whole (*Likutey Halakhoth, Shabbath* 4).

Thus, the exchange of the two sons was like the exchange of the throne (*Chokhmah U'Tevunah* 5). Rectifying the throne is very much like fixing the garden. Just as one can then enter the garden, when the throne is rectified, one can then sit on it (*Ibid.* 19).

at the bottom of the throne. Since the rose represents the congregation of Israel, the fact that it is at the bottom of the throne denotes Israel's lowly state. Israel is the king's true son; hence, the rose being at the bottom shows the effects of the Exchange explicitly.

had devised. The plan of the king here is very much like the anger of the king in Story #1.

understand its significance until an extraordinarily wise person came along, who would understand the concept. He would then know how to exchange and arrange all things correctly.*

[He then saw that] the same was true of the bed. He understood that it had to be moved slightly from the place where it stood. The table also had to be moved somewhat, and the lamp likewise had to have its position adjusted.* The birds and animals also had to be moved to different places. Thus, a bird would have to be taken from one place and set in another place. The same was true of all the animals. The king had cleverly disguised everything so that only a very wise person would be able to contemplate it and then rearrange it correctly.

The same was true of the lion which stood [where the path emerged]. It had to be stood in a different place. This was true of all [the beasts on the paths].

[The king's son] gave instructions that everything be rearranged properly: to take the rose from the bottom, and insert it on top. Everything else was also rearranged in proper order.

[All the animals and birds] then began to sing a very wonderful melody.* Each one functioned properly.*

He had deliberately altered the throne, so that the true prince would be able to rectify it and become king. Similarly, God created evil in the world, so that the Israelites would be able to rectify it and thus become the rulers of creation.

What the king had done to the throne actually caused the Exchange.

arrange all things correctly. When the throne is corrected, all souls will know where their true roots are (*Likutey Halakhoth, Birkath HaShachar* 3:41). Therefore, after the prince did this, he knew that he was the king's true son. Moreover, the rectification of the throne parallels the giving of the new garment to the moon on a lower level (*Parparoth LeChokhmah* on *Likutey Moharan Tinyana* 1, end).

adjusted. This is the rectification of the Shekhinah (*Likutey Moharan* 2:6; *Likutey Halakhoth, Shabbath* 4; see *Zimrath HaAretz*).

wonderful melody. Just as the rectification of the moon brought forth a melody, so does the rectification of the throne. This is the concept of the rectification of the Exchange, "Happy are you, land, whose king is a free man" (Ecclesiastes 10:17). The melody parallels the song of the Levites (*Zimrath HaAretz*).

In general, song is a means of resolving an exchange. Therefore, after hearing this song, the prince said, "Now I know that I am the king's true son" (*Chokhmah U'Tevunah* 6).

[The king's son] was then given the kingdom.*

The king's son, who had by now been crowned king, then said to the actual son of the slave woman, "Now I understand * that I am actually the king's son, and you are actually the slave woman's son."

After telling the story, the Rebbe (may his light shine) said the following:

In early generations,* when Kabbalah was discussed, it was discussed in the manner [of this story], since until the time of Rabbi

---

Since the throne parallels the man who, in turn, represents the Sabbath, the song that was sung may be "A Psalm, a song for the Sabbath day" (Psalms 92), which is the song of the Future World (*Tamid* 7:4). This psalm ends, "To tell that God is straight" (Psalms 92:16), indicating that everything had been rectified (*Chokhmah U'Tevunah* 17). When the king's true son was able to sit on the throne, the song was complete (*Ibid.* 31).

Significantly, it is taught that the Throne of Glory sings every day, especially when a person is successful in entering into the *merkavah* (*Hekhaloth Rabathai* 25:1 in *Batey Midrashoth*).

functioned properly. Some say that the instrument and the throne were reflections of the prince's soul. When they functioned correctly, he could also find his true destiny (*Chokhmah U'Tevunah* 7). The rectification of the throne and all its components reflects the rectification of the world and everything in it in the ultimate future (*Chayay Nefesh* 29, p. 43).

given the kingdom. This is Atziluth. Rabbi Nathan thus writes that this is the Amidah. The Amidah rectifies all worlds, and gives one power over them (*Likutey Halakhoth, Birkath HaShachar* 3:29). When the prince sat on the throne, the rectification was complete (*Chokhmah U'Tevunah* 31).

Thus, when the Messiah comes, Israel will have dominion over the world. It is thus written, "Kings will be your servants, and their nobles your nurses, they will bow face down to you" (Isaiah 49:23; *Likutey Halakhoth, Birkath HaShachar* 3:2).

This will be reflected in God's rule over all the world, as it is written, "God will be king over all the world; on that day, God will be One and His name One" (Zechariah 14:9). It is also written, "God will rule forever, your God, Zion, for all generations" (Psalms 146:10; *Zimrath HaAretz*).

Now I know. Once the throne was rectified, the prince's own mind and belief were rectified, and he no longer had any doubts about his status.

In early generations. This is quoted in the Introduction.

Shimon bar Yochai,* Kabbalah was not discussed openly. Only Rabbi Shimon bar Yochai revealed Kabbalah explicitly. Earlier, when the initiates discussed Kabbalah, they would use veiled expressions.

"When they placed the ark on the cattle,* they began to sing." Understand this.

This involves the Renewal of the Moon, which exists when the moon receives new concepts from the sun. Thus, when the ark was carried to the House of the Sun (Beth Shemesh),* all the animals (chayoth)* which carry the throne began to make a new melody. This is the concept of, "A Psalm: Sing to God a new song" (Psalms 98:1). This is the song that the cattle of Bashan sang.*

This is also the idea of the bed, table, throne and lamp.* They are the rectification of the Divine Presence.

This is also the concept of the garden. Adam was exiled from the garden, but the Sabbath protected him, as discussed [in the sacred literature].

The Sabbath is the concept of "the King who has Peace." This relates to the king who had peace in his days. Therefore, [the king's son] stood next to the Sabbath. Further, he did not explain.

After telling the story, [the Rebbe also] said these words:

This story is a great wonder.* It is all one. The animals...the throne...

Rabbi Shimon bar Yochai. In the Zohar, which was written around 140 c.e.

When they placed the ark on the cattle. The explanation of the story is like the ark being placed on the cattle, where its true meaning or "song" comes forth (Chokhmah U'Tevunah 2).

Beth Shemesh. See 1 Samuel, 6:12.

chayoth. Actually, the cows were behemoth, not chayoth. But this alludes to the chayoth that carry the Throne of Glory.

cattle of Bashan sang. According to the Zohar (see above; Avodah Zarah 24b). In Samuel 1, there is no mention of the cows of Bashan. The cows of Bashan, however, are mentioned in the verse, "Hear this word, you cows of the Bashan" (Amos 4:1).

bed, table, throne and lamp. See Kings 2, 4:10; Zohar 2:133a.

This story is a great wonder. Quoted in Likutey Halakhoth, Birkath HaShachar 3:1.

and the garden, are all one. Sometimes [a concept alluded to in the story] is given one name, and sometimes another, according to the context of the concept.

These ideas are a very deep, awesome wonder.

(The Rebbe then said:)

There is also much more, but it is not necessary to reveal it to you. The king in the above-mentioned land had done something representing the sun and something representing the moon. [That is, the things he did alluded to the sun and the moon.] The moon held a lamp in its hand, but when day came, the lamp could not shine, since "[Of what avail is] a lamp in broad daylight?"* This is the significance of what the night said to the day, "Why is it that when you arrive I do not have a name?" During the day, the lamp is of no avail.

The explanation of the story is like the throne the king made. The main knowledge lies in understanding how to arrange each thing. So too, one who knows the sacred texts and has an unblemished heart, then one will be able to understand the explanation. However, one must know how to arrange the components well, since sometimes they are given one name and sometimes another. The same is true of the other aspects of the story. Sometimes a character in the story is given one name, and sometimes another. This is true of all the story's components. Happy is he who is worthy of understanding these concepts correctly.

Blessed be God forever Amen and Amen.*

(All these are the words of our holy Rebbe, may he rest in peace; may the memory of a Tzaddik be a blessing.)

---

lamp in broad daylight. *Chullin* 60.
Blessed be God... This is an abbreviation.

12

THE MASTER OF PRAYER *

Once there was a Master of Prayer.* He was constantly engaged in prayer, and in singing songs and praises to God.

Master of Prayer. This story was told on Saturday night, at the end of Rosh Chodesh Shevat, 5570 (January 6, 1810) (*Chayay Moharan* 15c, #59).

Rabbi Yosef, the cantor (*baal tefillah*) of Breslov, was with Rabbi Nachman, along with his other followers. The cantor had a torn caftan, and Rabbi Nachman said, "You are the cantor, through which everything comes about. Why don't you have a decent caftan?" He then began, "There was once a story about a prayer leader (*baal tefillah*)..."

He told the entire story that night. At first those present thought that he was relating a true anecdote, and did not realize that he was telling a story. However, as the story unfolded, they realized that he was telling one of his stories from "ancient times" (*Chayay Moharan* 16a #3; see *Tovoth Zikhronoth*, p. 25).

During that winter, Rabbi Nathan had been in Berdichev to collect a debt from Rabbi Nachman's brother-in-law (*Yemey Moharnat* 27b). When he returned from Berdichev after Chanukah, Rabbi Nachman said, "I know a story that was told prior to the time of the First Temple, and only the Prophet who told the story and I, know its secret." It was shortly after this that he told "The Master of Prayer." However, he said that this was not the story to which he was referring (*Sichoth HaRan* 198). During this winter, Rabbi Nachman told three stories, "The Exchanged Children," "The Master of Prayer," and "The Seven Beggars" (*Yemey Moharnat* 30b).

Rabbi Nachman himself said that this story is related to the 31st chapter in Isaiah (end of story).

There are ten characters in the story, relating to the Ten Sefiroth (end of story), as well as the Ten Commandments (*Parparoth LeChokhmah* on *Mekhilta, Yithro*). The ten characters are also the ten people of a minyan, who are led by the *baal tefillah* (*Likutey Halakhoth, Tefillah* 4:1).

It is also possible that the ten characters in the story parallel the ten men in Rabbi Shimon bar Yochai's circle (*Idra*). It is also told that the Ari had a similar circle of ten men (*Vayakhel Moshe,* introduction). As we shall see, Rabbi Nachman himself also sometimes identified with certain characters in this story.

Master of Prayer. *Baal Tefillah* (בעל תפילה) in Hebrew, a word that is usually used to denote a cantor or "prayer leader." Although he had many other good traits, and was a great

He lived away from civilization.* However, he would visit

saint, he is called the Master of Prayer, or the prayer leader (*Likutey Etzoth, Tefillah* 24). This is because prayer is the main rectification of all the fallen attributes (*Likutey Halakhoth, Tefillah* 4:12). Through prayer one can achieve the highest levels and accomplish all one's desires (*Likutey Moharan Tinyana* 111). The Baal Tefillah is thus the first character introduced in the book (end of story), and the leader of the king's group of ten in rectification (*Likutev Halakhoth. Tefillah* 4:1).

The Baal Tefillah is seen as the paradigm of the tzaddik, the righteous man or saint (*Likutey Etzoth, Tokhachah* 8). In some ways, he is modeled after the Baal Shem Tov, or Rabbi Nachman himself.

In a deeper sense, all the characters in the story relate to the Sefiroth, which are aspects through which we can understand God. The Talmud thus teaches that God Himself prays (*Berakhoth* 7a). Similarly, at the beginning of creation, after the chaos and void, which allude to the breaking of vessels, God said, "Let there be light" (Genesis 1:3), and this can be considered the first prayer. Hence, God Himself can be seen as a Master of Prayer (*Chokhmah U'Tevunah* 10).

The Master of Prayer is said to parallel the last of the Ten Commandments, "Do not covet" (Exodus 20:14), which according to the *Zohar* includes all the other commandments (*Zohar Chadash* 44c; *Parparoth LeChokhmah, Mekhilta, Yithro*).

Among the Sefiroth, the Master of Prayer most probably relates to Malkhuth. Hence, the Master of Prayer "passes through the places" of all the characters in his descent, while the others do not pass through his place. Malkhuth is usually personified by King David, who was indeed the paradigm of a Master of Prayer.

away from civilization. Before the *tikkun*, civilized areas are far from the true goal. We thus say in the morning service, "All their deeds are chaos."

The Master of Prayer was also far from civilization conceptually. He did not concern himself with the things that people do. For him, fasting and prayer were the greatest enjoyments, the opposite of ordinary people.

This teaches that if a person truly wishes to serve God on the highest level, he must separate himself from people. If he cannot do so physically he should do so mentally. This is the concept of *hithbodeduth* — secluded meditation — that Rabbi Nachman taught.

Actually, we see that the great hurricane transformed desert into civilized areas and civilized areas into desert. Therefore, by remaining in the deserts, the Baal Tefillah was in what was a civilized area before the time of confusion (*Rimzey Maasioth*).

This teaches a general lesson that a tzaddik who wants to bring people close to God must keep away from civilization, if not physically, then conceptually (*Likutey Etzoth* B, *Tzaddik* 80).

In general, there is a dispute as to whether it is better to reject the world or to try to elevate it. The Baal Tefillah held that the best thing to do at such a time was to reject the world. This same dispute may have been the one that existed between Cain and Abel. After God cursed the earth (Genesis 3:17), Abel disassociated himself from the earth by becoming a shepherd (Genesis 4:2, Rashi *ad loc.*). Cain, on the other hand, became a

inhabited areas* on a regular basis. When he came, he would spend time with the people, usually those of low status, such as the poor.* He would have heart to heart discussions with them, speaking about the goal.* He would explain that the only true goal was to serve God all the days of one's life, spending one's days praying to God and singing His praise...

He would speak to an individual at great length, motivating him, so that his words entered the other's heart, and the individual would join him. As soon as a person agreed with him, he would take him and bring him to his place away from civilization.

For this purpose, the Master of Prayer had chosen for himself a place far from civilization. There was a river flowing there, as well as fruit trees, whose fruit [he and his followers] would eat.* He was not at all concerned about clothing.*

---

farmer, trying to rectify the curse. In a time of great upheaval, however, Cain's approach may not be successful (*Oneg Shabbath*, p. 40).

Since, as we shall see later, the world had fallen into errors, and each land was inhabited by a group with a different error, the Master of Prayer kept away from settled areas. It also seems that the faction that chose prayer as its goal (later in the story) did not settle any place. In the case of all the other factions, the story says that they settled in a land, but not this group. Later in the story we also see that they are traveling, rather than settled.

visit inhabited areas. Although the tzaddik must keep away from the ways of ordinary people, there are times he must behave like an ordinary person in order to bring others close to God. In this respect, he is entering "inhabited areas" (*Likutey Etzoth* B, *Tzaddik* 80).

the poor. It is best to bring great, intelligent people close to God, since these people have greater souls. Furthermore, when the great are attracted, others will automatically come. However, the Evil One makes this task very difficult; therefore, the tzaddik must begin working with the humble masses (*Likutey Etzoth, Tokhachah* 7).

the goal. As we shall see later, various factions in the world had chosen all sorts of false and warped goals for themselves.

would eat. They were thus not very concerned with eating and drinking, and needed no money to buy their necessities (cf. *Rimzey Maasioth*). In a sense, they were like Rabbi Shimon bar Yochai, who lived in a cave, nourished by a stream and a carob tree (*Shabbath* 33b). Earlier, we noted that the Baal Tefillah is like Rabbi Shimon bar Yochai because he was the leader of a group of ten as well.

clothing. Rabbi Nachman added this remark because the Breslover cantor's robe was torn,

It was the custom of [the Master of Prayer] to visit inhabited areas, and spread his ideas, convincing people to emulate him, serving God and constantly praying. Whenever people wanted to join him, he would take them to his place away from civilization, where their only activities would be praying, singing praise to God, confession,* fasting, self-mortification,* repentance, and similar occupations. He would give them his books* of prayers, songs, praises, and confessions, and they would occupy themselves with them at all times.

Among the people he brought there, he would find individuals who had the ability to lead others to serve God. He would allow such individuals* to visit inhabited places, and also bring people to serve God.

In this manner, the Master of Prayer constantly spread his teachings. He would constantly attract people and bring them away from civilization.*

Eventually, his teachings began to make an impression, and his activities became well known. People would suddenly vanish without a trace; no one knew where they were. A person might

---

and he, the cantor, was not concerned about it (*Chayay Moharan* 16a #3).

Rabbi Nachman generally taught that the desire for good clothing can lead a person to sin (*Sichoth HaRan* 100). Furthermore, the lust for wealth, which is the most difficult to rectify (as we see in the story) can be rectified by not being concerned with clothing (*Likutey Halakhoth, Genevah* 2:9, *Rimzey Maasioth*).

confession. Confessing their sins to God, the first stage of repentance.

fasting, self-mortification. Also used by the Kabbalists as a means of repentance and self-purification.

books. The Baal Tefillah himself wrote many of these prayer books, as we see later in the story (cf. *Likutey Etzoth* B, *Tefillah* 24).

allow such individuals. After the tzaddik's disciples have followed his regime of prayer and other practices, he can let them mingle with people to bring others close to God (*Likutey Etzoth* B, *Tokhachah* 7).

away from civilization. This involves *hithbodeduth* (isolated meditation), which is the only way to the goal (*Rimzey Maasioth*). Therefore, the Master of Prayer insisted that prayer be in isolated places (see *Likutey Moharan* 52 regarding *hithbodeduth* away from the city). Furthermore, when they are among other people, they are subject to adverse influences and cannot reach their full potential (*Likutey Etzoth* B, *Tokhachah* 7).

lose a son or a son-in-law, and not have any idea of his whereabouts. But finally people began to realize that all this was due to the Master of Prayer, who was attracting people to serve God.

People tried to capture him,* but it was impossible to recognize him. The Master of Prayer devised clever plans,* and he would constantly disguise himself* in different ways. Every time he visited a person, he would be disguised differently. With one person, he would be a pauper; with another a merchant; while with others, he would have different disguises.

On many occasions when he spoke to the people, he saw that he could not make any impression on them, and could not draw them to his goal. He would then engage in subterfuges, so they would not be aware of his intention. It would appear that his intent was not at all to bring people to God; it was totally impossible to recognize that this was his purpose. Although his main intent was only to draw people close to God, and this was his entire motivation, whenever he saw that he was not making any impression, he would use roundabout ways so that the person would not recognize his true intent.

The Master of Prayer kept this up until he began to make a major impression on the world. He also became quite famous. People tried to capture him, but it was not possible.

The Master of Prayer and his men lived far away from civilization. They would spend their time engaged only in prayer, song, praise to God, confession, fasting, self-mortification and repentance.

---

to capture him. Because the world is in confusion, people try to take the Baal Tefillah captive, rather than to emulate him. When a person is close to the goal, and tries to bring others to serve God, the forces of evil try to take him prisoner. However, a person must continually strive to bring others close to God, even if it means that others will try to capture him (*Rimzey Maasioth*).

clever plans. Or more literally, "conducted himself with wisdom." Since evil tries to trap the tzaddik who tries to bring others close to God, he must act with great wisdom (*Rimzey Maasioth*).

disguise himself. The tzaddik who wants to bring others to God must behave intelligently and occasionally use various disguises. If people recognize him, they might not listen to him at all, and they might even try to harm him (*Likutey Etzoth* B, *Tokhachah* 8).

The system of the Master of Prayer was to provide each [of his followers] with what he needed. * If he realized that one of his followers, according to [that follower's] mentality, needed to wear golden robes, * in order to serve God, then he would provide them for him. On the other hand, occasionally he would attract a wealthy person and bring him away from civilization. If he understood that he needed to wear torn, humble clothing, he would instruct him to do so.

This was his general custom. He would provide each one with what he understood to be necessary for him.

For the people he attracted to God, fasting and self-mortification were better and more precious than all wordly enjoyment. They would have greater pleasure* from fasting or self-mortification than from all worldly pleasures.

Meanwhile,* there was a land that had great wealth.* Everyone there was wealthy.

what he needed. The tzaddik gives all those who are close to him what each one needs (*Likutey Etzoth* B, *Tzaddik* 87). Thus, Rabbi Nachman gave each of his followers particular practices to do, each according to his needs (*Sichoth HaRan* 185).

golden robes. *Golden geshtik* in Yiddish. For special people (*anshei segulah*), he might give very fine clothing, even though in general he was not concerned with clothing (*Rimzey Maasioth*). For some people, he would understand that such things would help them serve God (*Likutey Etzoth* B, *Tzaddik* 87). Sometimes people must also wear "religious garments" to help them serve God better, while for others this can be detrimental.

greater pleasure. In this respect, he and his followers were very far from the ways of the civilized world (*Rimzey Maasioth*). Thus, the tzaddik took his people away from other people conceptually if not physically (*Likutey Etzoth* B, *Tzaddik* 80). Again, as we have seen, the great hurricane transformed desert into populated area and vice versa. Therefore, it also transformed pain into pleasure and vice versa. In suffering and fasting, if one brings it back to the time before the turnover, there is genuine pleasure of the highest sort.

Meanwhile. *VaYehi HaYom,* "and the day came." See Story #2, p. 62. The expression denotes evil.

great wealth. Every person needs money, but some people develop a lust for wealth and money and begin to think of it as a goal in life. This, as we shall see in the story, can lead to idolatry. People must realize that all wealth ultimately comes from God (see Psalms 75:7,8); *Likutey Halakhoth, Tefillah* 4:11).

Actually, the concept of wealth and its rectification forms one of the primary themes of this story (*Ibid.* 4:15).

It is significant to realize that the Hebrew word for wealth is *ashiruth* (עשירות), which is spelled very much like *asiruth* (עשירות), denoting the concept of ten. This is because the lust for wealth goes diametrically against the good traits of the ten characters in this story, and conversely can only be rectified after all the ten come together (cf. *Ibid.* 4:20).

One reason for this is that wealth is now in the hands of the forces of evil (see *Sichoth HaRan* 4). People must earn a living, but the Evil One makes it very difficult; therefore earning a living can serve as a great hindrance to serving God (*Likutey Halakhoth, Keriyath Sh'ma* 5:15).

Actually, the concept of wealth began to fall into the realm of Evil after the sin of Adam. When God cursed Adam, "By the sweat of your brow you will eat bread" (Genesis 3:17), the concept of earning a living fell into the realm of Evil (*Likutey Halakhoth, Purim* 6:9).

This curse was then reflected in Abraham's career. As soon as he came to the Holy Land (which parallels the Garden of Eden), he experienced a famine (Genesis 12:10). Thus, Abraham had to leave the Holy Land, very much like Adam had to leave the Garden of Eden.

Abraham then went down to Egypt (Genesis 12:10), which, as we see in the notes at the end of the story, represents the lust for wealth. Abraham had to go there to rectify this concept at its very root. When Abraham left Egypt, however, he left with great wealth (Genesis 13:2). This represents the refinement of the holy sparks of wealth (*Likutey Halakhoth, Shabbath* 7:75).

The Israelites as a nation also had to rectify the lust for wealth at its root; they therefore had to spend years of slavery in Egypt. They would then bring out great wealth and thus rectify the holy sparks, as God promised Abraham, "After that they will leave with great wealth" (Genesis 15:14). Nevertheless, the Israelites had too much lust for wealth. From an overabundance of unrefined wealth, they were led to make the Golden Calf (see Rashi on Deuteronomy 1:1). Thus, the lust for wealth had not yet been rectified (*Likutey Halakhoth, Purim* 6:9).

Before the Israelites went to Egypt, Joseph (possibly representing the King's Treasurer) went to Egypt to rectify the concept of wealth. Joseph was the one who was in charge of all the wealth of Egypt, as it is written, "Joseph gathered up grain like the sand of the sea..." (Genesis 41:49). Later, Joseph took over all the wealth in the land, as it is written, "Joseph gathered up all the money that was in the land of Egypt" (Genesis 47:14) (*Parparoth LeChokhmah, Mekhilta, Yithro*).

The land of wealth was rectified by the King's Treasurer. It parallels the Commandment, "Do not steal" (Exodus 20:13). Alternatively, it parallels the commandment, "Remember the Sabbath" (Exodus 20:8), since the Sabbath provides the world with all bounty and wealth (*Parparoth LeChokhmah* B, *Ibid.*).

It is significant that when the different factions are mentioned later, that of wealth is not listed among them. This is discussed below, where the various sects are listed.

Kabbalistically, from the context, it appears that this kingdom represents the sefirah of Hod. Hod is the sefirah to which Evil is particularly attached. It represents the left foot. Just as the feet tread in filth, so Hod and Netzach touch upon the forces of Evil. This is particularly true of the left foot, since Evil has a stronger grasp on the left. That is why the angel which wrestled with Jacob, Samael, the angel of Evil, struck him in the left thigh (Genesis 32:26), which represents Hod (see *Zohar loc. cit.*).

This land, however, had very strange and unusual customs, since everything was made dependent on wealth. Thus, a person's status and worth were determined solely on the basis of his wealth. One who had thousands or ten thousands in cash had a certain rank, while others who had different amounts had a different rank. The entire order of social rank was thus determined by the amount of money that each one had. According to their constitution, the one with the [most] money was king.*

The people there had banners.* There was one banner that denoted a certain amount of money, and a certain rank associated with that banner. For a different sum of money, there would be a different banner, with a different rank associated with it. Thus, a person with one degree of wealth would have a banner conferring one rank, and one with a different degree of wealth would have a different banner, conferring a different rank. Each person's rank and status was thus determined by how much wealth he had.

Rank was determined in the following manner: If a person had a certain amount of money, he was considered an ordinary human being. If he had less than this, then he would be

---

This angel of Evil, Samael, is the angel of Esau. The source of this land of wealth is Esau who was immersed very deeply in the desire for wealth. He was very greedy (Genesis 33:11; *Bereshith Rabbah* loc. cit.), and murdered and plundered for the sake of money (cf. *Bava Bathra* 16b). His firstborn son, Eliphaz, was named for money. Eli-Phaz in Hebrew means my god-gold (Rabbi Rosenfeld).

Rabbi Nachman taught that the Malkhuth of evil is one that collects wealth, for money contains the holy sparks. Haman, who was a descendant of Esau, also sought much wealth (*Megillah* 10b; see *Likutey Moharan* 56).

The sefirah of Hod is personified by Aaron. It was Aaron who served in the Tabernacle, which was built of gold. Thus, in a sense, Aaron parallels the King's Treasurer, who works to rectify wealth. On the other hand, it was the other side of Aaron that built the Golden Calf, which represents unrectified wealth and the idolatry that follows it. Hod is thus related to the lust for wealth and its worship.

king. Therefore, unlike the other factions, they did not choose a king from outside their land.

banners. Very much like the ancient Romans, who had pennants displaying their social rank.

considered a bird or a beast. Some people even had the status of harmful animals and birds. If a person had only a small amount of wealth, he might be considered a human lion   or the like. Thus, the poorest among them were considered no better than birds or beasts, since money was the most important thing to them, and status was decided solely on the basis of wealth.

News of this land began to spread. The Master of Prayer sighed* because of this and said, "Who knows how far they will go because of this and what great errors they will make!"

Some of the Master of Prayer's men visited that land without even seeking his advice. They wanted to bring the people back to the good way, since they had great pity on them for having fallen into such great error through their desire for wealth. They were all the more concerned since the Master of Prayer had said that [the people of that land] could fall into even greater error. These men therefore went to the land, hoping to be able to get them to improve their ways.

When they came to that land, they approached an individual. Most probably they approached a "wild beast," [that is, a person who had so little wealth and such low rank that he was considered a wild animal]. They began to speak to him in their way, telling him that [wealth] is no goal at all, and the only true goal is to serve God.

Master of Prayer sighed. One of the main themes of this story is how the Master of Prayer works to rectify this land. Prayer denotes faith, as it is written, "[Moses'] hands were faithful" (Exodus 17:12). Faith is the opposite of idolatry and the lust for wealth (see *Likutey Moharan* 23), and this is why it is a custom to give charity before worshiping. Charity is a means of breaking the lust for wealth and even of obtaining it in a holy manner (*Likutey Moharan* 13; cf. *Likutey Halakhoth, Tefillah* 4:14).

The Talmud compares one who has diminishing wealth to a sheep who has to cross the river. If he crosses laden with wool, he will absorb the water and drown. If however, the sheep is shorn prior to crossing, then he will be able to reach the other side. So too, giving charity enables one to overcome one's difficulties (*Gittin* 7a). Charity also opens up new opportunities. Therefore, one should give to charity before one begins any new venture (*Likutey Moharan Tinyana* 4).

The individual, however, would not listen to them at all. The belief that money was the main thing in life was too deeply rooted in the people there. They went to another individual and he too would not listen.

Finally, [one of the Master of Prayer's men] engaged a man in conversation, speaking to him at great length. The man eventually said, "I don't have any more time to speak to you."

"Why?" asked the other.

[The man] replied, "Because we are all preparing to move away from this land. We are migrating to another area. Since we realize that the main goal in life is only wealth, we have decided to move to a land where we can amass wealth. It is a place where gold and silver can be taken from the ground. We are all prepared to migrate to that land."

[Around this time] the people agreed that they wanted to establish [the rank of] stars and constellations.* If a person had a certain agreed-upon amount of wealth, he would be a star.

The logic was that one who had that much wealth had the power of a star, since a star can increase the amount of gold in the world. Wherever gold ore* exists, it is because the star made gold dust grow in that area. Therefore, gold is derived from the stars; hence, one who had a certain amount of wealth was considered to have the power of a star. Therefore, he himself was also a "star."

They also conferred the rank of "constellation." If a person had a certain determined amount of wealth, he would be a "constellation."

Eventually, they also established the rank of "angel."* This too depended on a person's wealth.

Finally, they also agreed to confer the rank of "gods."* If a

---

constellations. *Mazaloth.* Generally denoting signs of the zodiac.

gold ore. For the relationship between planets and metals, see Story #4.

Now that they were going to a land of gold ore, they wanted to give special status to the "stars" who produced wealth.

angel. This is important to our story, because they later find a land where the horses have as much wealth on them as an angel.

rank of "gods." The key verse thus speaks of "gods of gold and gods of silver" (Isaiah

person had a huge amount of wealth as set up in their rules, then he would be a "god." Since God had granted him such great wealth, that person would also be a "god."

Once this had been established, they agreed that it was not fitting for them to remain in the atmosphere of this world.* Moreover, it was not considered fitting for them to mix with other people in the world, since this would defile them. They considered all other people in the world to be unclean.

They therefore decided that they would search for the highest mountains in the world and live there. Then they would be higher than all the air in the world.

They sent out explorers to find the highest mountains. They explored and found very high mountains, and all the people of that land migrated to these mountains. On every mountain there was a group of people from that land.

Around each mountain they erected great fortifications.* They also made deep trenches around the mountain, so that it would be utterly impossible for anyone to approach them. The only approach was through a hidden path* to the mountain, so that no strangers would be able to come to them. Similar fortifications were also erected around all the other mountains.

Guards were stationed far from the mountains so that no strangers would be allowed to approach them. They lived there in the mountains and abided by their customs.

These people worshiped many gods. They were appointed on the basis of wealth. Since wealth was the main thing to these people, through a great amount of wealth, one could become a god.

30:22, see Isaiah 2:20,21; end of story).

If a person does not realize that wealth comes from God, he can end up worshiping wealth (cf. *Likutey Halakhoth, Tefillah* 4:11). The lust for money in itself is often seen as a form of idolatry (*Ibid.* 4:14; also see *Zimrath HaAretz; Likutey Moharan* 23).

atmosphere of this world. "Gods" could not breathe the same air as ordinary humans.

fortifications. *Chazakoth* in Hebrew.

hidden path. As in the story of The Humble King #6, p. 129.

This, however, brought about great concern about murder and robbery.* People would be very ready to kill and steal, since they could become gods with the stolen money. [They were afraid to, however,] because [the wealthy were considered gods]. They were thus considered to be able to protect themselves from robbery and assassination.

They set up a system of services and sacrifices to their "gods." They would also offer human sacrifices.* Many people would also voluntarily offer themselves as sacrifices to their "gods," believing that they would then become incorporated into them, and later be reincarnated as wealthy men.

They thus institutionalized their belief in wealth. They had services, sacrifice and incense* which were used to serve [the extremely wealthy people who were] their gods.

Nevertheless, there was much killing and robbery in the land. People who did not believe in their religion became murderers and thieves in order to amass wealth. Their main thing in life was money. With money, one could buy anything, whether it be food or clothing. According to their belief system, human existence was based on money.

Wealth was therefore the focus of their belief. Every effort was made that there not be any lack of money since it was their main object of faith and the focus of their gods. They made every effort to bring wealth from other places to their land. Merchants were therefore sent out to do business in other lands so as to earn money and bring it back to their homeland.

According to their religion charity was a very great sin.* They

---

robbery. Since this land paralleled, "Do not steal" (Exodus 20:13; *Parparoth LeChokhmah* on *Mekhilta*).

human sacrifices. As many people indeed sacrifice their lives to the worship of money (*Likutey Etzoth* B, *Yirah VeAvodah* 40). Rabbi Nachman once said: "Man and his money cannot remain together. Either the money is taken from the man, or the man from the money" (*Sichot HaRan* 51) (Rabbi Rosenfeld).

sacrifice and incense. Later we shall see that these are aspects of the "kitchen" that rectifies these people.

charity was a very great sin. It is told that in France, it was forbidden to beg for alms.

believed that if a person gave charity, it would diminish* the influx of wealth that God had given him. The main goal was to have as much wealth as possible, and if one gave charity, it would blemish and diminish one's wealth. It was therefore forbidden in the strongest terms to give charity.

They also had officers. These officers were in charge of determining whether or not each person had as much wealth as he claimed. Each individual would have to be able constantly to demonstrate his wealth in order to retain his wealth-status.

Sometimes an animal would become a human being, and at other times, a human would become an animal. If a person lost his wealth, then he would become an animal, who did not have to have so much money. Similarly, if an "animal" amassed wealth, he could become a human being. This was true of all ranks; rank could be [gained or lost] depending on one's wealth.

Rather, one would have to sell some trinket, and the donor could pay as much as he wanted to donate (*B'Ibey HaNachal* 29).

The basic law of charity is to give one tenth (*ma'aser*) of the income. A higher level is *chomesh* or one-fifth (*Yoreh Deah* 249:1). The *chomesh* relates to the King and Master of Prayer, because through them comes about the complete rectification of all the different groups (Rabbi Rosenfeld).

The Talmud teaches that one should give tithes in order that one become wealthy (*Taanith* 9a). There was a wealthy man who commanded his son to give tithes. The field yielded one thousand *kurim* a year. After his passing, the son felt that one hundred *kurim* was too much to give away so he did not tithe that year.

The following year, the yield was one hundred *kurim*. When confronted with the poor yield, his family said, "Last year you gave tithes, the field was yours and the tithes God's. This year the field is God's and the tithe yours (*Tosafoth, ad loc.*) .

diminish. The Talmud further states, that one is permitted to test God in giving tithes, to see whether one's income will increase (*Ibid.*). Conversely, any loss of income a person will sustain is decreed on Rosh HaShanah. If he merits, it will go to charity (*Bava Bathra* 10a). "The door that does not open for charity, will open for the doctor" (*Yerushalmi*).

"You shall tithe what comes from *your fields*" (Deuteronomy 15:25). "If you tithe *your fields* it shall be yours. If not, the *field man*, Esau, will tithe it for you" (*Tosafoth Ibid.*) (Rabbi Rosenfeld).

Though wealth is a derivitive of the charity one gives, here they sought to wipe out charitable acts.

No one ever became poor by giving charity (cf. *Gittin* 7a; *Yoreh Deah* 249).

These people also had images and icons of [the wealthy people who were] their gods. They would embrace these images and kiss them. This was part of their religious service.

The Master of Prayer's virtuous followers [who had visited the land of wealth] returned home and told the Master of Prayer about the foolishness and great error of the land. They related how these people had become confused because of their lust for wealth, and how they wanted to move to another land and set up the rank of stars and constellations.

The Master of Prayer replied that he was afraid that these people would become involved in even greater error.

Then he heard that they had made themselves into gods. The Master of Prayer said that this had been his original concern. He had great pity on these people and decided that he himself would go there, since he might be able to make them abandon their error.

When the Master of Prayer arrived in that land, he approached the guards who stood around the mountain. These watchmen were probably insignificant individuals of low rank, since they were allowed to breathe the atmosphere of the world. Citizens who had rank as a result of their wealth would not breathe the atmosphere of the world and could not mingle with other people, since they believed that this would defile them. They could not even speak to foreigners, since they believed that they would become defiled by their breath. [Therefore, the guards who stood outside the city must have been of very low rank.]

Nevertheless, the guards had images which they would constantly embrace and kiss. Belief in wealth was also their religion.

The Master of Prayer approached one guard, and began to discuss the goal of life. He explained that the main goal is only to serve God through Torah, prayer and good deeds. Wealth is mere foolishness, and is not the goal at all....

The guard would not listen to him at all. All his life he had been imbued with the belief that the main thing is wealth.

When the Master of Prayer went to a second guard and spoke to him, this guard also would not listen to him. He went to all the guards in this manner, but none of them* would pay any attention to him.

The Master of Prayer finally made up his mind that he would go into the city on the mountain.* When he arrived, the people considered it a great wonder. "How did you get here?" they asked. "It is impossible for any outsider to come here."

"I have already got in," he replied. "It does not matter how I did it. Why bother asking me about it?"

The Master of Prayer began to speak to one of the people about the goal of life, but the other refused to listen. He went to a second, and the same thing happened. None of them would listen to him, since they were totally immersed in their false belief.

The citizens of the city found it very surprising that someone would speak to them in this manner, which was directly opposed to their faith. Soon, however, people began to realize that this stranger might be the Master of Prayer. They had already heard that such a Master of Prayer existed.

The existence of the Master of Prayer was already well known in the world. Throughout the world, he was called, "The religious Master of Prayer."* However, it was [known that it was] impossible to recognize or capture him, since he would always appear in a different disguise. He would appear to one person as a merchant, and to another as a pauper.

[When the Master of Prayer realized that his identity had been discovered,] he immediately fled from the land.

Meanwhile,   there   was   a Mighty Warrior.* Many other

---

none of them. Now there was no threat from the Warrior; he did not make any impression whatsoever. Fear helps to awaken one's perception.
into the city... As we shall see later, he did so with the power of the King's Hand.
The religious Master of Prayer. *Der frumer Baal Tefillah* in Yiddish. Also, "the devout prayer leader," or "the devout cantor."
Mighty Warrior. *Gibbor* in the original. In Hebrew, this has two connotations, both a

warriors* had joined him. The Mighty Warrior and his men were conquering one land after another.

The [Mighty Warrior] only demanded subjugation.* If the citizens of a land subjugated themselves to him, he would spare them; but if not, he would destroy them. He went and conquered. He did not want any wealth, only that the people subjugate themselves to him.

It was the custom of the Mighty Warrior to send soldiers to a land when he was still far away, some fifty miles distant. The message was that the populace must subjugate themselves to him. In this manner, he conquered many lands.

---

mighty person and a warrior. We therefore translate it as "mighty warrior."

Most commentaries state that the *gibbor* parallels the sefirah of Gevurah (strength), which would be the simplest interpretation (*Rimzey Maasioth, Hashmatoth; Chokhmah U'Tevunah* 3).

In a more general sense, he is seen as the Attribute of Justice (*Chokhmah U'Tevunah* 4; *Sichoth U'Sippurim*, p. 8). The Attribute of Justice is seen as the left hand, as is the sefirah of Gevurah. This is the opposite of the King's Hand. The storm came from the left hand, and the punishment for its results also comes from the left hand (*Chokhmah U'Tevunah* 13:56).

However, from the order of appearance, the Warrior is the second character. This would seem to indicate that he is the sefirah of Yesod, the second to last sefirah, since the story appears to go in an upward direction. Yesod parallels Joseph. Hence, the *gibbor* might represent the Messiah, son of Joseph, who will battle to rectify the world before it is rectified by the Messiah, son of David. Joshua, who was the first warrior and conquerer among the Israelites, was, similarly, from the tribe of Joseph. Likewise, the symbol of the Warrior later in the story is the bow, which always represents Yesod.

The Warrior is said to parallel the commandment, "Honor your father and mother" (Exodus 20:12). He becomes king over the body builders, and the body is the product of one's parents (*Parparoth LeChokhmah, Mekhilta, Yithro*).

other warriors. The faction of body builders, as we shall see.

demanded subjugation. This is the concept of the Attribute of Justice, that wants nothing except that we subjugate ourselves to God. It thus gives the world the choice, be subjugated or be destroyed.

Rabbi Nathan once said that for this reason, after the curses in Leviticus, the Torah says, "Then their uncircumcised heart will be subjugated" (Leviticus 26:41; *Rimzey Maasioth, Hashmatoth*).

The Attribute of Justice comes particularly to destroy the lust for wealth (*Chokhmah U'Tevunah* 4; *Sicoth Ve'Sippurim*, p. 8). That is why the curses in Leviticus deal primarily with the loss of wealth and sustenance.

When traders from the land [of wealth] returned home from doing business in other lands, they brought back reports of this Mighty Warrior. All the people were terrified.

Initially, they wanted to subjugate themselves to him. However, they then heard that he despised wealth, and did not want any wealth at all. This was diametrically opposed to their faith, and it was therefore impossible for them to subjugate themselves to him. To do so would be apostasy, since he did not at all believe in their faith, which was wealth.

Because of their great fear of him, they began to worship and bring sacrifice to their "gods." They took [people of lesser wealth whom they considered] "animals" and sacrificed them to their gods. They also engaged in other similar acts of worship.

Meanwhile, the Mighty Warrior was constantly coming closer to them. He began to send soldiers asking if they were willing to submit to his way, and they became terrified. They did not know what to do.

Their traders came forth with advice. They told them of a land where all the people were gods* who rode on angels.* All the

---

were gods. Egypt is seen as a paradigm of this land, since it was a land of great wealth. Egypt was therefore also filled with idolatry. Rabbi Nachman at the end of the story therefore says that this is alluded to in the verses, "Woe is to those who go down to Egypt for wealth and rely on horses...The Egyptians are men and not gods, and their horses are flesh and not spirit" (Isaiah 31:1,3).

The Exodus was thus seen as the breaking of the lust for wealth (cf. *Likutey Moharan Tinyana* 1). This is why the Paschal Lamb consisted of a sheep. The sheep was the god of Egypt (*Shemoth Rabbah* 11). Sheep also denote wealth, as it is taught, "Sheep make their owners wealthy" (*Chullin* 84). Since the Egyptians worshiped wealth, they made sheep their gods. The sacrifice of a sheep therefore annuls the lust for wealth.

For the same reason two sheep were sacrificed daily as the *tamid* offering (Numbers 28:3). The lust for wealth must be broken every day (*Likutey Halakhoth, Tefillah* 4:17).

Later, this land of wealth is represented by the Greeks. The lust for money is seen as quicksand, which is *yaven* (יון) in Hebrew (see Psalms 40:3). Rabbi Nachman taught that the lust for wealth is like apostasy, which was decreed by the Greeks (*Likutey Moharan* 23). Just as the Greeks wanted us to forget the Torah, so the lust for wealth makes one forget the Torah.

We were rescued from this by the Hasmonean (*Chashmonai*) priests, who denote the element of charity. The Hasmoneans are said to have come out of Egypt, as it is written,

people of that land, great and small alike, were so wealthy that according to the standards of the land of wealth, they would all be gods. [Even the lowliest among the people in that land was so wealthy that in the land of wealth he would be a god.]

The people of that land used "angels" for transportation. Their horses were bedecked with so much gold and treasure, that their ornamentation alone would be enough to confer the status of "angel" upon a person [in the land of wealth]. They therefore used "angels" for transportation. They would harness three pairs of "angels" to their coaches, and this would be their means of transportation.

"Therefore," [the trader said] "You must send messengers to this land. Since all the people in this land were gods, they would certainly be able to help you."

They believed that they would surely be helped by that land, since everyone there was a god.

Meanwhile, the Master of Prayer decided to return* to the [land of wealth], hoping to wean them away from their erroneous belief. When he arrived, he approached the guards and began to speak to them. He spoke to one guard in his normal manner, but the guard began to tell him about the Mighty Warrior, relating how terrified they were of him.

"What are you going to do?" asked the Master of Prayer.

"Chashmonim come up out of Egypt" (Psalms 68:32). Thus the lust for wealth was rectified by those who had "come out of Egypt" and had abandoned this lust (*Likutey Halakhoth, Avedah U-Metziah* 3:6).

It is significant that this land is not mentioned among the lands that were divided after the hurricane. From Rabbi Nachman's comments, it seems to represent a particularly strong power of evil. It may thus represent the galbanum (*chelbanah*), the eleventh of the incense spices, which had a vile odor. This is only rectified together with the other ten, as discussed earlier. Thus, there is nothing in the story that speaks about the rectification of this land.

on angels. As the verse concludes, "Their horses are flesh and not spirit" (Isaiah 31:3). "Spirit" in this verse denotes angel.

decided to return. Now that they are desperate, they might be more likely to repent. When people are afraid, they are more accessible to the truth.

The guard told him that they were planning to send a delegation to the land where all the people were gods.

The Master of Prayer laughed at him very much. "What great foolishness!' he said. "The people in that land are human beings, just like us. The same is true of you. Your gods are just human beings, not deities. There is only one God in the world, and that is the Creator, may His name be blessed. He alone deserves our worship, and to Him alone must we pray. This is the main goal."

The Master of Prayer spoke to the guard in this manner at some length, but the guard would not listen to him, since he had been immersed in his erroneous beliefs for a long time. Nevertheless, the Master of Prayer spoke to him for a long time, until the guard finally replied, "Besides, what can I do? I am only one [and they are many]!"

To some degree, these words were a consolation to the Master of Prayer. He understood that his words had begun to make an impression on the guard. The words that the Master of Prayer had spoken to this guard the previous time, combined with the words he spoke this time began to make a bit of an impression on his heart. The guard now had begun to have doubts* and to lean toward [the Master of Prayer's teachings] somewhat, as was evident from his reply.

The Master of Prayer went to the second guard, and spoke to him in the same manner, but this one would also not listen. However, in the end, he finally said, "But I am only a single person opposing all the people in the land..." In the end, all the guards gave him a similar reply.

The Master of Prayer then entered the city and began to speak to the people in his way. He told them that they were in great error, and theirs was not the true goal at all, since the main goal

---

to have doubts. When a person tries to correct others, even if his words do not have an immediate effect, they can cause people to have doubts. If he continues doing this, he can weaken their false beliefs, and eventually bring them back to God (*Rimzey Maasioth*).

We thus find in the previous story, that when the true prince began to have thoughts of repentance, even though he did not act upon them, they began to haunt him.

was to engage in Torah and prayer. However, since all the people had been immersed in [their beliefs] for a very long time, they would not listen to him.

When they told him about the Mighty Warrior and their plan to send to the land where everyone was a god, he laughed at them. "This is foolishness," he said. "They are all mere human beings... and they will not be able to help you at all. They are not gods at all. You are human beings and they are human beings and not gods at all. There is only one God, may His name be blessed."

About the Mighty Warrior he said, "Can this be *the* Mighty Warrior?" [From the tone of his voice, it seemed as if he knew the Warrior.]

The people did not understand what he was getting at.

He also went to other people and spoke to them. Whenever the Warrior was mentioned, he would say, "Can this be *the* Mighty Warrior?" No one understood what his point was.

There was a great stir in the city, since there was someone there mocking their faith and preaching that there was only one God. He was also saying strange remarks about the Mighty Warrior. They understood that this was the Master of Prayer, since he was quite well known by this time.

Orders were given that he be found and captured. Although he was constantly disguising himself, [sometimes appearing as a merchant and at other times as a pauper,] they were already aware of his disguises. They gave orders that he be found and taken prisoner.

They searched for him, and when they captured him, they brought him before the ministers of state. When they began to speak to him, he told them that all of them had very foolish beliefs and were in error. "[Wealth] is not the goal of life at all," [he said]. "The only [goal] is the Creator, may His name be blessed... You may think the people of that land are gods, but they will not be able to help you at all, since they are only human beings..."

He was considered mad. The people in that land were so immersed in their belief in wealth that anyone who spoke against them was considered a madman.

They they asked him, "Whenever the Mighty Warrior is mentioned you ask, 'Can this be *the* Mighty Warrior?' What is the meaning of your words?"

"I was once with a king," he replied, "and he had a Mighty Warrior who was lost. If the warrior is this Mighty Warrior, then I know him. Furthermore, your faith in the land where you consider all the people gods, is mere foolishness. They will not be able to help you. In my opinion, if you trust in them, it will be your downfall." *

"How do you know that?" they asked.

He replied: *

The king with whom I was had a Hand. * That is, he had an

---

it will be your downfall. The key verse thus says, "The Egyptians are men and not gods, and their horses are flesh and not spirit, so when God shall stretch out His hand, the helper shall stumble, and the one being helped shall fall, and they shall perish together" (Isaiah 31:3).

He replied. Prayer reveals the concept of God's hand. It is for this reason that the first one to reveal the concept of the Hand was the Master of Prayer.

The Baal Tefillah parallels the Amidah, while the Hand is the Priestly Blessing. The Amidah "reveals" the Priestly Blessing, insofar as the Priestly Blessing is part of the Amidah (*Likutey Halakhoth, Tefillah* 4:24).

Hand. Rabbi Nachman said that this is the hand alluded to in the verse, "God shall stretch forth His hand, and the helper shall stumble, and the one being helped shall fall" (Isaiah 31:3).

The Zoharic literature also states that the Hand, which in Hebrew is *yad*, represents the letter *yod* in the Divine Name (*Tikkuney Zohar* 7b, 21, 46b; *Likutey Moharan* 66:2, from Psalms 145:16). The *yod* is the power of Chokhmah. However, *yod* also has a numerical value of ten, which represents the ten characters in this story (*Chokhmah U'Tevunah* 6).

Thus, the hand in general represents the constriction of God's infinite power. All the world thus came from God's hand, as it is written, "Also His hand founded the earth" (Isaiah 48:13) (*Chokhmah U'Tevunah* 5).

The Master of Prayer and the other men of the King knew everything from the Hand. The Hand is thus an aspect of prophecy. Thus, when Ezekiel had a prophetic vision, it is written, "God's hand came upon him" (Ezekiel 1:3).

Insofar as the Hand represents Wisdom, it represents the basis of all creation. It is thus written, "All of them were made with Wisdom" (*Chokhmah U'Tevunah* 16). It is through the Hand that the world is rectified (*Ibid.* 15).

As we have seen, the Hand represents faith and prayer. After the Exodus, which represents emerging from the desire of wealth, the Israelites saw, "the great Hand that

image of a Hand with five fingers.* The lines on the Hand*

God had set against Egypt, and they believed in God and in His servant Moses" (Exodus 14:31). They were then⁴worthy of song, which is the way of the Master of Prayer (*Likutey Halakhoth, Tefillah* 4:21).

The Hand can thus be seen as an aspect of the Introductory Psalms (*Pesukey deZimra*) in the morning service. This is the power through which we elevate the sparks of holiness (*Likutey Halakhoth, Tefillah* 4:19, 20; see previous story).

Thus, the rectification of all groups is through the Hand. The Introductory Psalms have all the paths in the entire world. The reason for this is because the psalms were composed on King David's harp, which had ten strings (Psalms 92:4), paralleling the ten characters in the story. This is also an aspect of the Hand, as it is written, "David played with his *hand*, like every day" (1 Samuel, 18:10; see *Likutey Moharan* 54:6). In the Introductory Psalms we praise God for all creation on all levels (*Likutey Halakhoth, Tefillah* 4:20).

The Hand also represents the Temple, as it is written, "Your hand established a sanctuary" (Exodus 15:17). The center of the Temple was the Foundation Stone (*evven shethiyah*), which had channels leading all over the world. Similarly, the hand has channels leading to the entire body, and for this reason, from the pulse beat, one can know about the condition of the entire body (see Story # 2). The pulse beat is also reflected in the lines on the hand (*Likutey Moharan* 56:9).

The lines on the hand come from the pulse beat, and are therefore very closely related to the effects of the heart on the hand. In this manner, the Hand is related to the breastplate of the High Priest, which was worn over his heart. The breastplate represents judgement, which is the rectification of the lust for wealth (*Likutey Halakhoth, Tefillah* 4:22).

The rectification of money-lust relates to the Hand in another way. Through the Hand, the Master of Prayer enters their city, and the Hand reveals the path of the Mighty Warrior, which is the rectification of this lust. The lust for wealth is a blemish in the Hand, since it involves the claim, "My strength and the power of my hand attained this wealth for me" (Deuteronomy 8:17) which is a denial of God's providence. This must be rectified by the Hand, which is an aspect of faith, and song. This is the concept of the Introductory Psalms (*Likutey Halakhoth, Tefillah* 4:23).

The lifting of the hands in the Priestly Blessing denotes the elevation of the concept of the "Hand" to rectify wealth. The Priestly Blessing comes from the Hand, as it is written, "Aaron lifted up his hands and blessed the people" (Leviticus 9:22; cf. *Likutey Moharan* 24). The Priestly Blessing therefore begins, "May God bless you" — with money — "and keep you" - from harmful forces. This means that one should have wealth, but that it should not be blemished by the forces of evil. Wealth can then be something holy, as it is written, "God's blessing gives wealth" (Proverbs 10:22).

The Priestly Blessing was first uttered by Aaron, who represents the Treasurer in this story. It is he who becomes king over the land of wealth, and initially tries to rectify it.

Some say that the Hand represents the Tetragrammaton, YHVH. Through this name, all can be known (*Chayay Nefesh* 26, p. 39).

five fingers. The Hand appears to represent the power of the Torah, with the five fingers formed a map of the world.*

Everything that existed from the time Heaven and Earth were created until the end, and even what will exist after that, was inscribed on that Hand. The lines in the hand provided a picture of the structure of every universe with all its details, just like a map. The lines also formed letters,* like the inscriptions on a map, so that one can know what each thing is.

Thus, one can know that in one place there is a city, and elsewhere a river and the like. The lines in the Hand were like captions on a map, inscribed next to each detail on the Hand, so that one could know what it was. Inscribed with the lines on the Hand were the details of all the lands, cities, rivers, bridges, mountains* and other details, [in this world* and in other worlds]. Next to each detail there were letters describing it.

Also on the Hand were inscribed the names of all the people traveling in each land, as well as everything that happened to them. It also had inscribed all the paths* from one land to

---

representing the five books.

Also, the concept of the Hand is seen as the first *heh* in the Divine Name (*Sefer Baal Shem Tov*). This is the hand that gives. This *heh* represents Binah, the Divine Understanding. *Heh* has a numerical value of five, paralleling the five fingers.

lines on the Hand. The *Zohar* teaches that all the secrets of a person's entire body can be seen in the lines of his hand (*Zohar* 2:74b; *Sefer Chasidim* 162). These are said to be in the form of letters (*Ibid.*). Since man is a microcosm, the Divine "Hand" would contain all the secrets of creation (also see *Chayay Nefesh* 22, p. 34.). So secret was this science that the Ari would not teach it to Rabbi Chaim Vital (*Midbar Kadmuth, Chokhmah* 13).

map of the world. *Land kart* in Yiddish. Not only of the physical world, but of all worlds, as we later see (*Likutey Halakhoth, Tefillah* 4:20).

formed letters. *Zohar* 2:74b. These paralleled the letters on the *urim* and *thumim*, which would light up, revealing paths (*Likutey Halakhoth, Tefillah* 4:22). Some say that the *urim* and *thumim* actually contained a map (see *The Living Torah* on Exodus 28:30).

cities, rivers, bridges, mountains. On Tuesday, May 8, 1810, Rabbi Nachman left Breslov for Uman. He said, "There is a path like this outside the house, and from there to the mountain. From there it goes to a small river, and the bridge. From there it goes to Reb Shimon's house, and from there to Reb Zelig's house, and from there to Uman." He then said that this is the Hand that the King had, where all the paths were inscribed (*Chayay Moharan* p. #26).

in this world... Only in the Yiddish.

all the paths. Since the paths between places unify the world, the Hand thus contains the mystery of the Unity of all creation. Furthermore, people bring merchandise and produce

another, and from one place to another.

This is how I knew how to get into the city,* even though it would be impossible for anyone else to get in here. Also if you wished to send me to any other city, I would also know the way. Everything through this Hand.

Also inscribed on this Hand is the path from one world to another. There is a road and a path* upon which one can travel from earth to heaven.* [The only reason that it is impossible to go up to heaven is because people do not know the path; but on the Hand is inscribed the path to heaven.]

On it are written all the paths from one universe to another. Elijah went up to heaven* on one path, and that path is

---

along the paths. Thus, the Hand contains the secret of all divine influx.

Paths also contain the element of rectification. If a person does not know the right path to a place, he can be lost and injured. But if he knows the correct path, he will be successful and will reach his goal. This Hand therefore contained the secret of rectification.

In the morning psalms, we say, "For He commanded and they were created" (Psalms 148:5). In this aspect, the Introductory Psalms reveal the aspect of Unity in the Hand (*Likutey Halakhoth, Tefillah* 4:20).

Rabbi Nathan suggests that the lines on the Hand lit up to reveal the paths, just as the letters on the *urim* and *thumim* lit up to reveal a message. This detail, however, is not found in the story (*Likutey Halakhoth, Tefillah* 4:22).

I knew how... As we saw earlier.

One may ask, since the Master of Prayer could use the Hand for this purpose, why could he not use it to find the others? However, it appears that the Hand could not be used to sort out the effects of the storm. The Hand represents the power of prophecy, and they could see all that was decreed before creation, but they could not see what Evil would cause man to do through his free will.

This is very much like the case of Isaac, who was a great prophet, but still could not recognize the evil in Esau, nor the greatness of Jacob.

In Hebrew, the hurricane is a *sa'arah* (סערה), which is related to the word Seir (שעיר), denoting hair and Esau. The power of Esau is the hurricane, and this prevents one from using the Hand of prophecy to ascertain the truth (*Chokhmah U'Tevunah* 8).

road and a path. *Derekh* and *nethiv* in Hebrew. This is the "path (*nethiv*) which no bird of prey knows" (Job 28:7) (See above).

from earth to heaven. This is the "gate of heaven" (Genesis 28:17) that Jacob saw. Through the gate of heaven, there is the "ladder" (Genesis 28:12) which leads from earth to heaven (*Likutey Halakhoth, Tefillah* 4:22).

Elijah went up to heaven. "While they were still talking, there appeared a chariot of fire and horses of fire, which separated the two of them [Elijah and Elisha], and Elijah was carried up to heaven in a storm wind" (2 Kings, 2:11).

inscribed* on [the Hand]. Moses went up* on a different path, and that path is also inscribed. Enoch went up* to heaven in still another way, and that is also inscribed there. The paths from one world to another are also inscribed in the lines of the Hand.

Also inscribed on the Hand is everything as it existed at the time of creation, the way it exists now, and the way it will exist later. Thus, Sodom is inscribed as it was when it was inhabited, before it was destroyed. The destruction and upheaval of Sodom* is then inscribed, as well as the way Sodom exists after it was destroyed. Thus, inscribed on the Hand is what was, what is, and what will be.*

On the Hand I also saw the land which you described, where you claim that the people are gods, as well as all the men who are going to seek help from them. All of them will be annihilated* and destroyed.

---

that path is inscribed. Space comes from the constriction (*tzimtzum*), but the connection that transcends space comes from the Hand. This is why the Master of Prayer speaks at length of the various people who used the paths to go up to heaven (*Chokhmah U'Tevunah* 14).

It is also for this reason that prophecy is called God's Hand as mentioned earlier. Prophecy also involves traveling the path from earth to the spiritual dimension.

Moses went up. "And Moses went up to God" (Exodus 19:3). Moses went up to God to get the Torah, and remained there for forty days and forty nights.

Enoch went up. "Enoch walked with God, and he was no more, for God took him" (Genesis 5:24). It is taught that Enoch went up to heaven while he was still alive, and never died.

the destruction... of Sodom. Genesis 19:25.

what was, what is, and what will be. This is the meaning of the Tetragrammaton (*Orach Chaim* 5). Thus, the Hand represents the power of the Tetragrammaton (see *Chayay Nefesh* 26, p. 39).

Rabbi Nachman said that learned men should be able to know the future from the Torah. "*Kedem, yadati me-eydotechah,*" I knew beforehand (what will be), from Your Torah (the Hand) (Psalms 119:152) (*Likutey Moharan Tinyana* 35).

The Hand thus had the mystery of rectifying all the groups that had fallen into error (*Likutey Halakhoth, Tefillah* 4:20).

will be annihilated. "God shall stretch out His hand, the helper shall stumble, and the one being helped shall fall" (Isaiah 31:3) (see end of story).

The Hand therefore teaches that the road to salvation for these people, to save them from the Warrior, is not to go to the land of the money-gods but instead to go along the

(All the above was the answer that the Master of Prayer gave them.)

This was a great wonder to them. They realized that he was speaking the truth, since they were aware that everything could be drawn on maps. They also recognized his words as being true, because they saw that it was possible to bring together and connect two lines on the hand and form a letter. [They realized that it would have been impossible for him to make up such an account. It was therefore a great wonder to them.]

"Where is your king?" they asked. "Maybe he can tell us how to gain more wealth."

"You still want wealth!" he replied. "I don't want you to mention wealth at all!"

"Still," they insisted, "where is the king?"

"Actually, I don't know where the king is," he answered. "This is what happened."

[The Master of Prayer then related the following story:]

There was* a King* and Queen,* and they had an only

___

path of the Warrior himself. This path is known only through the Hand (*Likutey Halakhoth, Tefillah* 4:23).

This is somewhat difficult to understand. Later in the story, they do go to the land of the money-gods, and they are not destroyed. Rather, they end up meeting the Treasurer, who takes them to the path of the Warrior. Through this the entire group of the King is once again reunited.

However, it is possible to say that when the "gods" of the land of wealth threw themselves into graves, as we see at the end of the story, this represents death (*Chokhmah U'Tevunah* 12). It is thus taught in the Talmud that humiliation is equivalent to death (*Bava Metzia* 58b).

Moreover, although there is no mention of the downfall of the land of the money-gods, it may be that the unification of the King's group leads to the rectification, and this itself was the downfall of this land.

There was. Now the Master of Prayer begins to describe the rest of the characters in the story. As Rabbi Nachman points out at the end of the story, the characters in the story, in the order of appearance, are: [1] The Master of Prayer; [2] the Mighty Warrior; [3] the Treasurer; [4] the Wise Man; [5] the Bard; [6] the Faithful Friend; [7] the Queen's Daughter; [8] her Son; [9] the Queen; and [10] the King. This is the order in which the characters are discovered by the Master of Prayer and reunited. Rabbi Nachman says that this represents the order of the World of Rectification (*Olam HaTikkun*).

Daughter.* When she came of age, they sought advice from their counselors as to who would be fit to marry her. I was among the advisors, since the King was very fond of me.

My advice was that she should marry the Mighty Warrior.* The Mighty Warrior had captured many lands, and brought great

---

There are ten characters, because prayer must have a quorum (minyan) of ten, all led by the Prayer Leader (Baal Tefillah) (*Likutey Halakhoth, Tefillah* 4:1). These parallel the ten sefiroth (*Ibid.* 4:2). They also parallel the ten types of songs that are found in the Psalms. These ten types of songs are the universal rectification (*tikkun hakellali*) (*Likutey Moharan* 205, *Likutey Moharan Tinyana 92; Sichoth HaRan* 141; *Likutey Halakhoth, Tefillah* 4:20).

The King and his men also represent the ten times the word praise (*hallel*) appears in Psalm 150 (*Likutey Halakhoth, Ibid.* 4:20).

King. The first person mentioned by the Master of Prayer. The King represents the first of the Ten Commandments, "I am God your Lord, who brought you up out of the land of Egypt" (Exodus 20:2). He eventually became king of the group who thought that the goal of existence was honor (*Parparoth LeChokhmah, Mekhilta, Yithro*).

Kabbalistically, the King represents the sefirah of Kether, the Crown. Therefore, the Master of Prayer sees a crown as the symbol of the King, later in the story.

Queen. The second person mentioned. The Queen represents the sixth commandment, the first on the second tablet. This is the commandment, "Do not kill" (Exodus 20:13). She eventually became queen over the group that maintained that murder was the purpose of existence (*Parparoth LeChokhmah, Mekhilta, Yithro*).

Kabbalistically, the Queen appears to represent Chokhmah, the second of the sefiroth.

The symbol of the Queen was a pool of blood, which was made by her tears. Tears come from the eyes, and hence represent Chokhmah, because the eyes are Chokhmah. Blood also comes from Chokhmah and Binah (*Shaar HaMitzvoth, Bereshith*). But since the blood comes from tears, it is related primarily to Chokhmah.

There is also a Wise Man, who may be related to Chokhmah, but as we shall see, the Wise Man is actually Netzach. There is some confusion because of this.

Daughter. The Daughter is the third one mentioned. She parallels the commandment, "Do not commit adultery" (Exodus 20:13). She eventually becomes queen over the group that takes female beauty as the goal of existence (*Parparoth LeChokhmah, Ibid.*).

Following the order, she would represent the sefirah of Binah. Since she gives birth to the infant, she is the "mother," and Binah is called a mother, as it is written, "And to Binah call a mother" (Proverbs 2:3). She is also the paradigm of the mother, since her breasts form the pool of milk (cf. *Zohar* 2:122b).

marry the Mighty Warrior. "I am Binah; Might is mine" (Proverbs 8:14). The *Zohar* teaches that, "Binah reaches down to Hod" (*Zohar* 3:223b). Thus, she must connect with the next sefirah, which is Yesod, represented by the Warrior, as above. It is also taught that "Binah takes Hod and Gevurah" (*Tikkuney Zohar* 69, 107a).

benefits [to the kingdom], and therefore, it would be proper to have him marry the Queen's Daughter. My advice was well taken and everyone agreed to it. There was a great joy, since a husband had been found for the Queen's Daughter. She married the Mighty Warrior.

The Queen's Daughter gave birth to a Child,* and the infant was extremely beautiful. His beauty was beyond all human bounds.* His hair was gold with all colors* in it, and his face was as bright as the sun. His eyes were like stars.*

The Child was born with a fully developed intellect. [As soon as he was born] it was recognized that he was fully intelligent. When people said something humorous, he would laugh. They recognized that he had a great intellect, except that he did not yet have the coordination of an adult enough to speak, etc.

The King had a Bard,* an orator who was a master of rhetoric

Child. The fourth one mentioned. The child represents the commandment, "Do not have any other gods besides Me" (Exodus 20:3), the second of the Ten Commandments (*Parparoth LeChokhmah*). He became king over the land that felt that fine food was the goal of existence.

. Kabbalistically, the Child would represent Chesed. Since Chesed is the first day of creation, it is seen as a newborn child. Chesed also represents Abraham, who also involved the birth of a new concept in the world.

The symbol of the Child was the pool of milk. Milk also represents Chesed (*Pardes Rimonim* 23:8).

beyond all human bounds. Literally, "Was not human beauty at all."

gold with all colors. See below, regarding the seven hairs which the Warrior found.

like stars. Literally, "other lights."

Bard. *Melitz* in Hebrew. The fifth character described by the Master of Prayer. A Bard was a person who sang, recited, and composed verses in honor of the achievements of warriors and kings, and accompanied such recital with music.

The word *melitz* can also denote an interpreter or translator.

The Bard paralleled the ninth commandment, "Do not bear false witness" (Exodus 20:13). This commandment on the tablets was opposite the commandment, "Remember the Sabbath" (Exodus 20:8), because one's speech on the Sabbath should not be like one's weekday speech.

It is also possible to say that the Bard represents the commandment, "Do not steal" (Exodus 20:13). With his speech, the Bard can swindle people and steal their wealth. The *Zohar* states that this commandment represents Binah (*Zohar Chadash* 44d), as it is

and poetry. He could speak and compose wonderful poems, as well as songs and praise to the King. Although the Bard was very skillful in his art in his own right, the King showed him a path* through which he could ascend and receive poetic skills. As a result he became an extremely skilled bard.

The King also had a Wise Man.* The Wise Man was very intelligent in his own right, but the King showed him a path through which he could ascend and receive wisdom. Through this, he became an extraordinarily wise man.

The Mighty Warrior* was also a warrior in his own right. But

---

written, "To understand parable and *melitzah*" (Proverbs 1:6) (*Parparoth LeChokhmah, Mekhilta, Yithro*).

The Bard eventually becomes king over the group that maintains that the goal of existence is speech.

The Bard appears to represent the sefirah of Tifereth in the order of rectification. This represents Jacob, who was the perfection of speech, as it is written, "The voice is the voice of Jacob."

After having published the *Likutey Tefilloth*, someone remarked to Rabbi Nathan that he must be the *Baal Tefillah*. Rabbi Nathan said: "The Rebbe (Rabbi Nachman) is the *Baal Tefillah. If I am considered to be among the men of the King I am the Meilitz*" (*Chokhmah U'Tevunah* 1; *Sichoth MeInyaney Rabbeinu zal; Likutey Moharan* 3 #5, pp. 23,24).

showed him a path. The King knew this path through the Hand. The same was true of all the other men of the King. They all received their power through the paths that the King knew from the Hand (*Likutey Halakhoth, Tefillah* 4:20).

Wise Man. The sixth one described by the Master of Prayer. He represents the third commandment, "Do not take God's name in vain" (Exodus 20:7). God's name is an aspect of Wisdom (*Zohar Chadash* 3d). It is also written, "Better a good name than good oil" (Ecclesiastes 7:1), and oil is an aspect of Wisdom. Secular wisdom is thus an aspect of taking God's name in vain.

Alternatively, it can be said that he represents the commandment, "Do not bear false witness" (Exodus 20:13) because testimony involves Wisdom (*Parparoth LeChokhmah, Mekhilta, Yithro*).

The Wise Man becomes king over the faction that maintains that the goal of existence is wisdom.

Kaballistically, the Wise Man refers to the sefirah of Netzach (and not Chokhmah). Netzach is the sefirah of Moses, who was God's sage and lawgiver. Also Netzach parallels the fourth day, when the stars were created, and astronomy is an aspect of wisdom, as it is written, "The children of Issachar who know wisdom of the times" (1 Chronicles, 12:32).

The Mighty Warrior. The seventh one mentioned. He is discussed earlier in the story.

the King showed him a path* through which he could ascend and receive great strength. Through this he became an extraordinarily fearsome warrior.

There is a sword* that is suspended in midair. This sword has three powers. When the sword is lifted, all the enemy's officers flee in panic,* and the enemy is automatically defeated. Without any leadership, they cannot do battle.

Still, it is possible for the survivors to get together and do battle. But the sword has two edges, and these have two additional powers. One edge makes the entire [enemy army] fall.* The other edge causes them to become emaciated,* with their flesh falling away.

One need only stand still and swing the sword toward the enemy, and each edge has this effect.

---

a path. As we shall see, this is the path through which the desire for wealth is rectified (see *Likutey Halakhoth, Tefillah* 4:20-4:23). It may be because the Warrior has this power that he was chosen to be the King's son-in-law.

sword. This is the sword alluded to in the key verse, "Then Assyria shall fall by the sword, not by man" (Isaiah 31:8). The Midrash states that the sword of Eden is circumcision (*Bereshith Rabbah* 21:9). Hence it is related to Yesod, which is the aspect of the Warrior.

The Midrash also states that the sword is the Torah (*Bereshith Rabbah* 21:5). To some degree, this sword might represent the power of prayer, as it is written, "High praise of God in their lips, a two-edged sword in their hand" (Psalms 149:6). Jacob also said that he conquered Shechem with "my sword and my bow" (Genesis 48:22), and this sword is interpreted as prayer (Rashi).

The sword may also be the sword at the entrance to the Garden of Eden (Genesis 3:24). This sword represents purgatory-Gehenom (Bachya). The Warrior (tzaddik-Yesod) conquers with the fear of Gehenom.

The *Zohar* states that the sword is God's name, the Tetragrammaton, which has the power to destroy all His enemies (*Zohar* 3:274b).

officers flee in panic. The first power. This is denoted in the key verse, "He shall flee from the sword, and his young men shall become captives" (Isaiah 31:8) (Rabbi Nachman, end of story).

fall. The second power alluded to in the verse, "Assyria shall fall by the sword, not by man" (Isaiah 31:8).

emaciated. This is the sickness known as *dar,* which means emaciation. It is alluded to in the verse, "His rock shall pass away from terror" (Isaiah 31:9) (see end of story). It may also be alluded to in the verse, "The sword, not of man, shall devour him" (Isaiah 31:8). In this verse alone, the word "sword" is mentioned three times.

The King showed the Mighty Warrior the path to that sword. It is from there that he received his great strength in battle.

The same was true of me.* The King showed me the path to my occupation. From there I received what I needed.*

The King also had a Faithful Friend.* The bond of friendship between him and the King was wonderful and awesome, so that it was impossible for them to go without seeing each other for any length of time. Nevertheless, there were times when they had to be separated to some extent. Therefore, they had portraits * made of themselves together. Whenever they were separated from each other, they would have great pleasure from these pictures.

The pictures showed the great friendship between the King and his Friend, how they hugged and kissed each other with great affection. These images had the power that anyone looking at

---

me. The Master of Prayer mentions himself eighth.

I received what I needed. Maybe this is how the Master of Prayer knew the path to the land of wealth through the Hand.

Faithful Friend. The ninth one mentioned. The Faithful Friend parallels the commandment, "Remember the Sabbath..." (Exodus 20:8). It is thus written, "How fair and how pleasant are you, friend, for delights" (Song of Songs 7:7). Delight refers to the delight of the Sabbath. The Sabbath is also love, as we say in Kiddush, "Your holy Sabbath, with love and desire You gave us."

The Faithful Friend, later in the story, sits in a sea of wine and becomes king over the group which maintains that joy is the goal of existence. It is taught that the commandment, "Remember the Sabbath," denotes "remembering it over wine" (*Pesachim* 106a).

Alternatively, the Faithful Friend represents, "Do not take God's name in vain" (Exodus 20:7). The Talmud states that this commandment parallels the commandment, "You shall love God your Lord with all your heart" (Deuteronomy 6:5) in the Sh'ma, since one who loves the King does not swear falsely by his name (*Parparoth LeChokhmah, Mekhilta, Yithro*).

The Friend represents Gevurah in the order of rectification.

portraits. If the Faithful Friend represents the Sabbath, then this is the concept that one must do things to remember the Sabbath all week long (*Betzah* 16b; *Parparoth LeChokhmah, Ibid.*).

Significantly, the Treasurer is not mentioned by the Master of Prayer. This may have been because he was speaking to the group involved in money, and the Treasurer was destined to become their king. However, later, when the soldier tells of the groups, he does not mention the group that took money as the goal of existence. Again, this may have been because they were about to attack the land of wealth.

them would have feelings of extremely deep love. [That is, the attribute of love would come to whoever gazed at these images.] The Faithful Friend also received love from the place that the King showed him.

There came a time when each of [the King's men] went to the place where he would receive his power. The Bard, the Mighty Warrior, and all the other King's men went to their places to renew their powers.

At that time, there was a powerful hurricane,* which threw the whole world into confusion. It transformed* sea into dry

---

hurricane. In general, the hurricane represents the breaking of the vessels (see Story #1), when the original sefiroth were shattered, and their light left its proper place (*Likutey Halakhoth, Tefillah* 4:1,3).

This is alluded to in the verse, "The earth was chaos and void, with darkness on the face of the deep, and God's *wind* blew on the face of the earth" (Genesis 1:2). After this, God began the ten sayings through which He created the world, and these parallel the ten characters in the story (*Chokhmah U'Tevunah* 7). Thus, although the breaking of vessels created evil, it also brought about the physical world, which resulted in an even greater rectification (*Chokhmah U'Tevunah* p. 115).

The storm wind also represents the sin of Adam, which was a reflection of the breaking of the vessels. This caused the sparks to fall still more (*Likutey Halakhoth, Purim* 6:9).

The storm also represents the power of Esau. In Hebrew, hurricane is a *saarah*, which is related to *sa'arah*, meaning hair. Esau was a "hairy man" (Genesis 27:11), and was referred to as *se'ir* (Genesis 32:4) (*Chokhmah U'Tevunah* 8). The verse, "And the earth was emptiness and void" also denotes the four exiles (*Bereshith Rabbah* 1). Thus the storm represents the exiles, particularly, the Roman Exile (*Chokhmah U'Tevunah* 10).

Historically, if we assume that the King and his men represent Rabbi Shimon bar Yochai and his group, then the storm wind could represent the Roman persecutions that made him hide in the cave (*Shabbath* 33b). It might also be reflected by the Spanish expulsion before the time of the Ari, and Chmelnitzky massacres, Shabbethai Tzvi, and the Haidemak pogroms, before the time of the Baal Shem Tov.

There is a Breslover tradition that this also represents false accusations that were leveled against Rabbi Nachman during the summer of 1806. Rabbi Nachman taught that false accusations and the blemish of speech create a storm wind (*Likutey Moharan* 38:2; *Chokhmah U'Tevunah* 1).

transformed. Thus, what people think to be civilized territory is really desert and vice versa. When the Master of Prayer went out to the desert, he was in a truly civilized area (*Rimzey Maasioth*). Therefore, everyone's values are confused (*Likutey Etzoth* B, *Yirah VeAvodah* 40).

This transformation is very much like the exchange of the children in the previous story.

land, and dry land into sea; desert into inhabited land, and inhabited land into desert. The entire world was thus turned upside-down.

When this hurricane struck the King's palace, it did not do any damage. However, when the storm struck, it carried away the Child* of the Queen's Daughter. In the middle of the panic caused when the beautiful child was carried away, the Queen's Daughter ran after it. The King and Queen [also pursued].* They became scattered, and no one knows where they are.*

The rest of us were not there at the time, since each of us had gone up to his place to renew his power. When we returned, we could not find them. The Hand was also lost* at that time. Since that time, we became scattered, and none of us can go to his place to renew his power. The whole world was turned upside-down and thrown into confusion, where all the places were exchanged, the sea becoming dry land [and the like]. It is certainly impossible

---

carried away the Child. Some say that the Child represents Malkhuth, which is an aspect of the moon. The loss of the Child therefore parallels the reduction of the moon. The upper three sefiroth (the King, Queen and Princess) thus scattered voluntarily to find the Child, while the rest of the group were scattered involuntarily. In the breaking of vessels, only the lower seven were shattered, while the upper three were merely reduced (*Chokhmah U'Tevunah* 9).

According to our contention, however, that the Child is Chesed, this would refer to the "chaos and void" and "darkness" on the first day of creation. The main blemish was in Chesed, making it even a word for incest (Leviticus 20:17).

King and Queen [also pursued]. There is a Breslover tradition that the child in the story represents Rabbi Nachman's child, Shlomo Ephraim, who died in Sivan 1806 of tuberculosis. After that Rabbi Nachman traveled to Navritch, and just before Shavuoth of 1807, his wife, Sasha (the Queen), died. Then, on the way back, Rabbi Nachman himself (the King) contracted tuberculosis, which he said would kill him. Thus, the King and Queen pursuing the Child represent Rabbi Nachman and his wife dying after Shlomo Ephraim. This was caused by the denunciation of the Shpoler in the summer of 1806 (*Chokhmah U'Tevunah* 1).

no one knows where they are. Although only the lowest seven sefiroth were shattered, the upper three (the King, Queen, and Princess) were also blemished (*Likutey Halakhoth, Tefillah* 4:2).

Hand was also lost. Hence the Master of Prayer had to know the way to the land of wealth from before the storm.

now to go up on the original paths; now that places have been altered and exchanged, we need different paths.

Therefore, we are no longer able to return to the places where we renew our powers. Nevertheless, the trace* that remains with each of us is still very great.

Now if this warrior is the King's Mighty Warrior, he is certainly a very great warrior.*

[All this was the Master of Prayer's reply to the men.] When they heard what he was saying, they were very astounded. They kept the Master of Prayer with them and did not allow him to leave. [They realized that the Mighty Warrior advancing on them might just be the warrior whom the Master of Prayer knew.]

Meanwhile, the Mighty Warrior was coming closer and closer, constantly sending messengers. Finally he arrived and camped right outside the city. When he sent his emissaries, [the people] were terrified.

They asked the Master of Prayer for some advice. He told them to investigate the ways and customs of this warrior, so as to determine whether or not he was the Mighty Warrior [of the King].

The Master of Prayer left and went out to the Mighty Warrior. When he came to the Mighty Warrior's camp, he began to speak to one of the Warrior's guards, [to determine if he was the King's Warrior]. The Master of Prayer asked him, "What is your occupation? How did you join up with this Warrior?"

[The soldier]* replied to the Master of Prayer, [telling him this story]:

It all happened in this manner:

---

trace. *Reshimah.* As the Ari taught, after the *tzimtzum,* even though the sefiroth were not in the vacated space, there was a trace of them (*Etz Chaim, Drush Egolim Veyoasher* 2).
very great warrior. In the text, Rabbi Nathan adds, "It appears to me that something is missing." See below.
[The soldier]. After telling this story, Rabbi Nachman asked those present, "Who told the

In our chronicles* it is written that there was a great hurricane* in the world. This hurricane turned the whole world upside-down. Sea was transformed into dry land, and dry land into sea. Desolate areas became inhabited, [while inhabited areas became desolate]. It threw the whole world into confusion.*

After this period of panic and confusion, where all the world was disoriented, the people of the world decided to elect a king.* They then delved into the question as to who would be most fit to be elected king. Upon deliberation, they finally said, "The most important consideration is the goal of life. Therefore the person who strives the most toward this goal is the most fit to be king."*

But then they had to determine the goal of life. Regarding this question, there were many factions.

---

story written in their chronicles about the groups formed as a result of the storm?" Those present answered that one of the Mighty Warrior's soldiers told it to the Master of Prayer. Rabbi Nachman then nodded, as if to say that they had it right. From this they understood that every word in the story teaches a great lesson (*Sichoth HaRan* 148).

chronicles. *Kroinikesh* in Yiddish.

great hurricane. The same one mentioned above. The groups that existed later were the broken vessels that formed the evil husks (*klipoth*) (*Likutey Halakhoth, Tefillah* 4:2).

confusion. Just as dry land was transformed into sea, etc., all good traits were transformed into evil ones. All false beliefs come from this breaking of the vessels (*Likutey Halakhoth, Tefillah* 4:2).

Thus, all the evil traits in the world are fallen attributes. All types of false ideologies come from the broken sefiroth. Every person has a trait that is worst in him (*Likutey Halakhoth, Tefillah* 4:13).

Thus, there are many groups in different times and places, which have different ideologies that take them away from God. These ideologies can also make it very difficult for the individual to serve God (*Rimzey Maasioth*). However, ultimately, every evil ideology and bad trait has its root in the realm of Holiness (*Zimrath HaAretz*).

elect a king. Since the true king had been lost.

fit to be king. Although many of the people chosen were certainly not fit to rule, as Rabbi Nachman himself says in the stories.

The idea that the person closest to the goal is fittest to be ruler is a true concept. Everyone agrees that the main thing is the goal. However, from this time, the goals had been confused (*Likutey Etzoth B, Yirah VeAvodah* 40).

At the beginning of the story, we thus find the Master of Prayer urging people to seek the true goal.

One faction said that the main goal is honor.* In the world, the main consideration is honor. If a person is not given proper honor, or if people say something that impinges on his honor, he can even commit murder. He is *mortally* offended, because honor is most important among people.

Even after death the main consideration is honor. People are careful to honor the dead, burying him with honor. [They even say to him, "Whatever is being done is being done for your sake, for your honor."] The dead have nothing more to do with wealth or pleasure, but still, people are very careful to honor the dead. Therefore honor is the main goal of life. They also had other [confused, foolish] "logical" reasons.

(The same was true of all the other groups,* which shall be discussed

---

honor. *Kavod* in Hebrew. This is the first group. The King became their leader. Thus, we find some people devoting their lives to the pursuit of honor. This is why people want wealth. People even become rabbis and teachers in order to attain honor (*Likutey Halakhoth, Tefillah* 4:13).

This concept fell from the holy concept of honor, where we must honor God and His Torah. The whole world was created for honor — the honor of God, as it is taught, "Everything that God created, He created for no other reason than for His honor" (*Avoth* 6:11).

Therefore, the main concept of honor is that a person must minimize his own honor so as to honor God. It is thus written, "God said, 'I will honor those who honor Me' " (1 Samuel, 2:30) (*Likutey Halakhoth, Tefillah* 4:31) (see *Likutey Moharan* 6).

Honor is therefore like the King's scepter, and no commoner may use it. This was the worst of all the groups, since it could only be rectified by the King himself. Therefore, at the end of the story, the King himself becomes king over this group (*Zimrath HaAretz*).

This group represents the first commandment, "I am God your Lord" (Exodus 20:2; *Parparoth LeChokhmah, Mekhilta*).

The Midrash also mentions that when the Israelites were in the desert they had ten things: [1] the manna; [2] the quail; [3] the well; [4] the Torah; [5] the Tabernacle; [6] the Divine Presence; [7] priests; [8] Levites; [9] a king; [10] clouds of glory (*Shir HaShirim Rabbah* on 3:6; cf. *Tanchuma Shemoth* 14). These represent the ten men of the King and the ten groups here.

Of these, the Divine Presence (Shekhinah) represents the land of honor (*Parparoth LeChokhmah, Mekhilta*).

all the other groups. This was because all the factions were based on true concepts, but the truth was reversed. Therefore some of these arguments are so logical that people could actually be misled by them even today (*Likutey Halakhoth, Tefillah* 4:2).

presently. They also had logical arguments for their confused, foolish opinions. Some of them are discussed, but the Rebbe, of blessed memory, did not want to present all the confused logic for these opinions. Some of the logic is so twisted that it would be possible for people to take it seriously and fall into error.)

They were thus led to agree that the main goal is honor. They therefore felt that they would have to seek an honored man who also pursued honor.* [Such an "honored man"] would be one who pursued honor and also gained honor. If he was an honored man who already had honor, then when he pursued honor, and desired it, his nature would help him attain it. Since the goal is honor, such a man would be striving for the goal and also attaining it. [In their foolish and confused opinion] such a man would be most fitting as king.

They went out to find such a man. They finally discovered an old gypsy beggar who was being carried and followed by some five hundred gypsies. The beggar was blind, crippled and mute, and the people following him were all members of his clan. They were his brothers and sisters, as well as the children that he had sired. These were the people who followed him and carried him.

This beggar was very particular about his honor. He had a nasty temper and was always angry at them and scolding them. He constantly ordered different people to carry him, and then became angry with them.

Obviously, this old beggar was a highly honored person. He also pursued honor, since he was so particular about it. This faction therefore felt that it would be best to accept him as their king.

The land itself also had influence. Some lands had an influence that was particularly conducive to honor, while other lands were conducive to other traits. Therefore, the group [which had determined that the main goal was honor] sought a land

---

pursued honor. *Rodef kavod.* The expression *rodef kavod* is reminiscent of the teaching, "Whoever runs after honor, honor runs away from him."

conducive to honor. They found a land which was particularly good in this respect, and settled there.

Another faction decided that honor was not the main goal. Instead, they concluded that the main goal was murder. *

It is obvious that all things come to an end and decay. Everything in the world, whether herbs, plants, or people, deteriorates and decays. Therefore, the final goal of everything is decay and destruction.

Hence, a murderer who kills people and destroys lives is doing very much to bring the world to its goal. [This group] therefore concluded that the goal of life is murder. The man who would be most qualified to be king would be a murderer who was easily provoked and was fiercely jealous. [According to their warped opinion] such a person would be qualified to be king.

---

murder. This is the second group. Eventually the Queen became their leader.

Rabbi Nachman once said that he found in a book that people exist who consider murder a virtue. This is the other side of the concept that there is anger and vengeance that is holy. It is thus written, "God is jealous and vengeful" (Nahum 1:2). It is also considered an act of virtue for the courts to administer the death penalty. This is a rectification of all worlds, insofar as the four modes of execution rectify the four letters of the Tetragrammaton. This group, however, had transformed this concept into actual murder (*Likutey Halakhoth, Tefillah* 4:4).

This group ultimately took the Queen as its ruler, because she was sitting in a sea of blood. The *Zohar* states that the Queen is "the law of the land is the law" (*Zohar* 2:118a; see *Nedarim* 28a), which is the death penalties given over to the courts. This is the virtue of the Levites, who even killed their brothers when it was demanded of them (Exodus 32:28,29) (*Zimrath HaAretz*).

We find this concept among people. Some are literally murderers, fighting, hating, and taking away the livelihood of others (*Likutey Halakhoth, Tefillah* 4:13). They found death more powerful than wealth, because when a person dies, he cannot take his wealth with him (*Likutey Halakhoth, Ibid.* 4:14).

Also, death is a rectification of all sins (end of story, "They dig themselves graves").

This group parallels the sixth commandment, "Do not kill" (Exodus 20:13). Among the ten things the Israelites had in the desert, it paralleled the Tabernacle. This rectified the concept of murder, as it is written, "Whoever comes to the Tabernacle shall die" (Numbers 17:28). However, the Tabernacle cannot rectify wanton murder, as it is written, "If a person purposely kills another, you shall take him even from My altar to put him to death" (Exodus 21:14; *Parparoth LeChokhmah, Mekhilta*).

While seeking such a person, they heard an outcry. "What is this loud outcry?" they asked.

They were told, "The reason for this outcry is that a man just slit the throats of his father and mother!"

"Could there be a murderer with a harder heart or a fiercer temper than this?" they exclaimed. "Here is a man who killed his own father and mother!"

According to their opinion, this man had attained the goal of life, and it was good in their eyes. They accepted him to be their king.

They then chose a land that was conducive to murder. It was a hilly, mountainous land, where murderers lived. They settled there with their king.

Another faction maintained that the person best qualified to be king was one who had a great abundance of food,* but who

---

food. This is the third group. The Child eventually becomes their ruler.

Here too, eating is very important. The true tzaddikim break their desire for food, eating only a little, so that it seems that they are not eating human food. This is the concept of, "A man ate the food of the mighty [angels]" (Psalms 78:25). It is also taught, "The Torah was only given to those who ate the manna" (*Mekhilta*). If a person has a pure mind, the food he eats is the food of angels (*Sefer HaMiddoth, Akhilah* 5; *Likutey Halakhoth* 4:6).

There are, of course, times when it is a virtue to eat, as it is on the Sabbath and festivals. It is thus written, "A tzaddik eats to satisfy his soul" (Proverbs 13:25), since there are people who derive purely spiritual benefits from their eating. It is also written, "You shall eat and be satiated, and bless God your Lord for the good land He gave you" (Deuteronomy 8:10). On the other side, Esau is seen as a glutton, selling his birthright for a bowl of pottage. He represents this group, which saw eating as the main goal of existence (*Zimrath HaAretz*).

The group parallels the commandment, "Do not have any other gods besides Me" (Exodus 20:3). Idolatry began because people thought that God's influence was too intangible, and therefore they needed other gods to make it palatable for humans.

Among the ten things in the desert, this is represented by the manna (*Parparoth LeChokhmah, Mekhilta, Yithro*).

It is significant that, at the end of the story, the nation of wealth is rectified by special food.

It also appears that these last two groups tried to raise up the curses of Adam to virtues. Thus the group of murderers took the decree of death, "On the day you eat of it,

did not eat the food of ordinary people, but highly refined food [such as milk, which does not make the mind too physical]. Such a person would be qualified to be king.

They could not, however, immediately find a person who was nourished in such a manner. They therefore chose as a temporary king a wealthy man who had a great abundance of food. He would rule until they could find the kind of person whom they desired, who did not eat like other men. Meanwhile, until they found a person with the full qualifications, this wealthy man would be king, after which he would resign.

They accepted this man as king and chose a land that was conducive toward their goal, settling there.

Another faction maintained that a beautiful woman* was most qualified to rule. They held that the main goal was that the land be populated, since it was for this reason that the world was

---

you will die," as a virtue, making murder their prime virtue. This group took the curse, "By the sweat of your brow you will eat bread" (Genesis 3:19) and made it their prime virtue. It is taught that Adam was cursed with ten curses, and they may all be represented among these ten groups.

beautiful woman. This is the fourth group, and the Queen's Daughter eventually became their ruler. Not only was she the paradigm of beauty, but also of motherhood, which was important for this group.

These people felt that feminine beauty was conducive to sex, and sex can be a virtue. In some cases it is, since the first commandment in the Torah is to "be fruitful and multiply" (Genesis 1:28). It is also written, "It was not created for emptiness, but it was formed to be inhabited" (Isaiah 45:18). God wanted the world to be populated and it is a virtue to have sex to bear children, but these people turned it upside-down (*Likutey Halakhoth, Tefillah* 4:5).

Besides the commandment to have children, there is also a commandment to have conjugal relations (Exodus 21:10) to strengthen the love bond between husband and wife.

We also see that feminine beauty is extolled in the Torah, as in the case of Rachel (Genesis 29:17). Beauty comes from a holy light on high (*Likutey Moharan* 27). It is thus taught that ten measures of beauty were given to the world, and that Jerusalem took nine of them (*Kiddushin* 49b). The Holy Land is also seen as a center of beauty (*Zimrath HaAretz*).

This group parallels the commandment, "Do not commit adultery" (Exodus 20:13). Among the ten things that the Israelites had in the desert, this parallels the King; one who guards the covenant is worthy of royalty (*Parparoth LeChokhmah, Mekhilta, Yithro*).

created. Since a beautiful woman arouses the desire to populate the world, she brings about the goal, and such a beautiful woman is best qualified to rule.

They chose a beautiful woman and she became their queen. They then sought out a land conducive to this, and settled there.

Another group maintained that the main goal was speech.* The primary advantage that man has over other animals is that he is able to speak. They accordingly sought an orator who was expert in language, who knew many languages, and spoke them all the time. Such a person would be closest to the goal.

They went and found a crazy Frenchman* who was

---

speech. Language has the power of good and evil. A person who writes a novel, for example, can influence people for both good and bad. Rabbi Nachman said that there are masters of language who are sinners, as it is written, God said that "Your masters of language (*melitzim*) sinned against Me" (Isaiah 43:27). Most atheistic philosophers were linguists.

On the holy side, however, the power of speech can do very much to draw a person to God. Language can have this power as well. One who speaks good for a person is called a *melitz*, since he must know the right language in which to frame his pleas. Similarly, when one prays to God, the right words are very helpful. But this group took the other side of it. Similarly, today, there are many poets and writers who use this power to draw people away from Torah (*Likutey Halakhoth, Tefillah* 4:7).

In addition, saints are able to rectify worlds with their speech. It is thus written, "I have placed my word in your mouth...to spread out the heavens..." (Isaiah 51:16) (*Zohar* 1:4b). The Hebrew language is the perfection of speech (*Likutey Moharan* 19; *Zimrath HaAretz*).

This group represents the perversion of the commandment, "Do not bear false witness" (Exodus 20:13). Among the ten things in the desert, it represents the Levites, who sang praises to God (*Parparoth LeChokhmah*).

This is the fifth group, which eventually took the Bard as its ruler.

Frenchman. Rabbi Nachman was concerned with France, because Napoleonic conquests were going on at the time (see beginning of previous story). On Shavuoth, 1806, Rabbi Nachman spoke about France, which is *Frank* in Yiddish. He said that *Frank* (פראנק), is spelled out by the final letters of the verse: (כסף נבחר לשון צדיק) *kesef nivchar leshon tzaddik —* "Chosen silver is the tongue of the righteous" (Proverbs 10:20). Thus the rectification of speech is the praise of the tzaddik (*Chayay Moharan* 7c #20).

France is a country where there is sexual immorality and a lack of charity; therefore, its speech is attached to the side of Evil. Begging is not allowed in France, and therefore they are involved in sexual immorality. Therefore, the king chosen by the group that had perverted speech was a Frenchman.

constantly talking to himself. They asked him if he knew languages, and he did.

[According to their foolish, confused opinion] he had reached the goal. He was a master of language and knew many languages. Moreover, he spoke very much, since he was constantly talking to himself. He was very good in their opinion, and they accepted him as king. They also chose for themselves a land that was conducive to their concept, and they settled there with their king. One can be sure that he led them in a straight path!

Another faction maintained that the main goal was joy.* When a child is born, people are joyous. When there is a wedding,

---

Speech is only rectified by praising the tzaddik. Therefore, this land was rectified by the Bard, who would constantly praise the King, who is the true tzaddik (*B'Ibey HaNachal* 29).

joy. This is the sixth group. They eventually took the King's Faithful Friend as their ruler.

Here again, their goal has a root in holiness, since the joy of holiness is very great. God thus said that the Israelites would be punished, "Because you did not serve God with joy..." (Deuteronomy 29:47). Similarly, it is written, "God's teachings are upright, they give joy to the heart" (Psalms 19:9), and "I will rejoice in God" (Psalms 104:34). There are many such passages.

But there is also joy that is wrong. It is thus written, "What point is there in joy?" (Ecclesiastes 2:2), and the Talmud says that this is joy which is not associated with a good deed (*Shabbath* 30b; *Likutey Halakhoth, Tefillah* 4:8).

Joy is associated with the King's Faithful Friend. Joy and love are closely associated on the side of holiness, as it is written, "Those who love Your name shall rejoice" (Psalms 5:12). They made the Faithful Friend king because he was sitting in a sea of wine. The wine came from consoling the King, which was a good deed, and it therefore represented the joy of a good deed (*Zimrath HaAretz*).

This group represents a perversion of the commandment, "Remember the Sabbath" (Exodus 20:8). The Sabbath is a day of delight and joy, this being the concept of "joy of the Sabbath." "The day of your rejoicing" (Numbers 10:10) is said to denote the Sabbath and the *Zohar* teaches that the Sabbath brings joy to all worlds. The sea of wine represents the wine of the Kiddush recited on the Sabbath, which is the joy of a good deed.

Alternatively, this group can be seen as a perversion of the commandment, "Do not take God's name in vain" (Exodus 20:7).

Among the ten things that the Israelites had in the desert, this parallels the well. The water of the well had the taste of all beverages (see "The Sophisticate and the Simpleton"), and thus rectified the false joy of drunkenness. It is also written, "You shall draw water in joy" (Isaiah 12:3) (*Parparoth LeChokhmah, Mekhilta, Yithro*).

they are joyous. When they conquer a land, they are joyous. Therefore, the goal of everything is joy, They therefore sought a man who was always happy. He would be closest to the goal, and was best qualified to be king.

They went and found a heathen* wearing a filthy shirt [and carrying a bottle of whisky]. A number of heathens were following him. [Since he was very drunk,] this heathen was very happy. When they saw that this heathen was very happy and had no worries, he was very good in their opinion, since he had attained the goal of joy. They accepted him as their king. One can be sure that he led them in the straight path!

They also chose a land which was conducive to their concept. It was a place of vineyards [and the like], which they could use to make wine. Out of the seeds* they made brandy, so that nothing would go to waste. Their main goal was to become drunk and thus always be happy. Actually, of course, this had nothing to do with their concept of joy,* since they had nothing for which to be happy. Still, they felt that they were attaining their goal by being happy even though they had no reason. They therefore chose a land conducive to this, and they went and settled there.

Another faction maintained that the most important thing was wisdom.* They sought for themselves a very wise man and

---

heathen. *Arel* in Hebrew, denoting one who is uncircumcised. In Yiddish, *goy,* a gentile.

seeds. Thus, grape seeds are forbidden to a Nazirite (Numbers 6:4).

nothing...joy. Such false joy actually brings no satisfaction.

wisdom. This is the seventh group. They eventually were rectified by the King's Wise Man.

Wisdom, of course, is very great in the service of holiness. We say to God, "How great are Your works; You made them all with wisdom" (Psalms 104:24). Wisdom is the life force of all things, as it is written, "Wisdom gives life" (Ecclesiastes 7:12). But wisdom is mainly to fear God, as it is written, "The beginning of wisdom is the fear of God" (Psalms 111:10) (*Likutey Halakhoth, Tefillah* 4:9). Otherwise, wisdom can be perverted, as we see in the story of the Sophisticate and the Simpleton.

Moreover, at times, some of these traits are needed to reach the highest levels of holiness. It is thus taught that the Divine Presence (prophecy) can only rest on one who is wise, strong and wealthy (*Shabbath* 92a). These represent the next three groups, those of wisdom, body builders, and wealth (*Zimrath HaAretz*). However, when wisdom is used for

made him their king. They also sought a land which was conducive to wisdom and they settled there.

Another faction maintained that the main goal was to pamper* oneself with food and drink,* and thus develop large muscles. They therefore sought a man who had large muscles, and who exercised to enlarge them, since such a person would have large limbs, thus having a greater portion in the world, [taking up more space in the world]. The person with the largest limbs would therefore be closest to the goal, and should be king.

They went and found a very tall athlete,* and he was good in their opinion. He was a person with large limbs, and close to the goal, so they accepted him as king. They also sought a land that

secular subjects, it can be perverted (*Chokhmah U'Tevunah* 10).

This is a perversion of Netzach.

This group parallels the commandment, "Do not take G-d's name in vain" (Exodus 20:7). Alternatively, it parallels the commandment, "Do not bear false witness" (Exodus 20:13).

Among the ten things in the desert, it parallels the Torah (*Parparoth LeChokhmah; Mekhilta, Yithro*).

pamper. *Piliven* in Yiddish.

food and drink. This is the eighth group mentioned, and it was eventually rectified by the Mighty Warrior.

On the side of holiness, a person should eat so as to be able to serve God. Sometimes it is a virtue to eat, such as on the Sabbath and on festivals. It is also a virtuous deed to eat matzah on Passover. From this, however, can come the error that eating a lot is generally good. Before telling this story, Rabbi Nachman once said that there was a king who said, "Give me a belly so that I will be able to eat a lot" (*Likutey Halakhoth, Tefillah* 4:10).

Also, the concept of body building and having a large body has its place in holiness. Thus, the members of the great Sanhedrin had to be tall (*Sanhedrin* 17a). Moses was also very tall, as was Abraham, who was called, "The man great among giants" (Joshua 14:15). It is taught that Jacob had two hands like two pillars of marble (*Bereshith Rabbah* 65:17); while regarding King Saul it is written that "he was head and shoulders higher than all the other men" (1 Samuel, 9:2). It is also taught that Rabbi Eliezer, the son of Rabbi Shimon bar Yochai was an extremely large person (*Zimrath HaAretz; Bava Metzia* 86a).

This group is a perversion of the commandment, "Honor your father and your mother" (Exodus 20:12), because a person's body comes from his parents. Among the ten things in the desert, it parallels the quail, since a person's body is enlarged when he eats meat (*Parparoth LeChokhmah; Mekhilta*).

athlete. *Vinger* in Yiddish.

was conducive to this, and they went and settled there.

There was another faction who maintained that none of this could be the goal of life. The main goal was to pray to God* and to be humble and lowly.... They sought for themselves a prayer leader* and made him their king.*

(If one examines this, one will understand that each of these factions was greatly in error except for this last group. Their goal was a true one; happy are they.)

All this was what one of the soldiers told the Master of Prayer.

[The soldier] explained that [the soldiers who had joined the Mighty Warrior] belonged to the faction of body builders, who took as their king a man with a large body.

One day,* a group of these men were following the main group with the supply wagons* carrying food, drink and the like.

---

to pray to God. This is the ninth group mentioned, and they eventually made the Master of Prayer their ruler.

This parallels the commandment, "Do not covet" (Exodus 20:14). Through prayer one can have what one needs, and one will not covet that which belongs to others. Among the ten things in the desert, it parallels the priests, who led the prayers and the divine service (*Parparoth LeChokhmah, Mekhilta*).

prayer leader. *Baal Tefillah*, the same word which we usually translate as Master of Prayer.

Significantly, although the story stresses that each of the other groups chose themselves a land, it does not say that about this group.

their king. The one group not mentioned here is the group which had made wealth the goal of existence. The soldier may not have mentioned it, since they were outside the city of this group. Alternatively, the Rebbe may not have mentioned it because he had already discussed it at length.

The faction of wealth was a perversion of the commandment, "Do not steal" (Exodus 20:13). Alternatively, it is a perversion of the commandment to remember the Sabbath, since the Sabbath is one day on which one must refrain from amassing wealth. Indeed, we see that the prime motivation people have in violating the Sabbath is to increase their wealth.

Among the ten things in the desert, the faction of wealth parallels the Clouds of Glory. This is discussed further when the Treasurer is introduced.

There is a significant parallel here. Just as the group of money is not mentioned among the others, so is the Treasurer not mentioned earlier among the King's men.

One day. Literally, "A day came." "And it was the day." See Story #2, p. 62.

supply wagons. *Ibaz* in Yiddish. See story #1, p. 44.

In general, people were very much afraid of these body builders, since they were large, powerful men. Whoever encountered them would turn aside from the road to avoid them.

As this camp was traveling, they encountered a warrior. When he encountered the camp, he did not turn aside from the road. Instead, he went right into the middle of the camp, and scattered the men in all directions. The men of the camp were very much afraid of him.

He then went into the wagons that were following the camp, and ate all their provisions. This was all a great wonder in their eyes. [He was so strong that he was not afraid of the entire camp. He went right into the middle of them and ate all their provisions.]

[The men] immediately fell before him and exclaimed, "Long live the king!" They knew that this Mighty Warrior was certainly qualified as king, since in their opinion, the main goal was to be a body builder. Therefore, the king would relinquish the kingdom, since they had found a Mighty Warrior who was such a body builder to rule them.

[The Mighty Warrior] whom they encountered was thus accepted as the king* of the group [who had concluded that the main thing was to be a body builder].

[The soldier concluded,] "He is the Mighty Warrior with whom we are now conquering the world. But he said that he had an ulterior motive for wanting to conquer the world. His intent is not that the world be subject to him. Rather he has a completely different motive."

"This Mighty Warrior who is your king," asked the Master of Prayer, "what sort of power does he have?"

He replied to him, "There was one land that did not want to surrender to him. The Mighty Warrior took his sword, and it has three powers. When he lifted it, all the enemy officers fled...." [He

---

the king. The Warrior was thus the first one of the King's men whom we learned became a king. Each of the King's men became king over one of the ten factions into which the world divided, so that each of them would be able to rectify his group.

then described the three powers of the Mighty Warrior's sword, as discussed earlier.]

When the Master of Prayer heard this, he realized that this was certainly the Mighty Warrior who had been with his king.

The Master of Prayer asked if it would be possible for him to meet with the Mighty Warrior who was their king. They replied that they would have to speak to the Mighty Warrior and ask if he would grant an audience. When they asked, he granted the audience.

When the Master of Prayer came* to the Mighty Warrior, they immediately recognized each other. They were both very happy at being reunited. Their joy, however, was intermingled with tears; when they remembered the king and his men, they wept. Therefore, the two of them rejoiced and wept.

The Master of Prayer and the Mighty Warrior then discussed how they had come to be where they were.

The Mighty Warrior told the Master of Prayer that at the time of the great hurricane, they had all been scattered. When he came back from the place he had gone to renew his power, he did not find the king or any of his men. However, as he traveled he passed by [the King and] all his men. [Although he could not actually find them there,] he understood that these were the places of each of the men.

Thus, when he passed by one place, he understood that the King was certainly there, but he could not search for him* so as to find him. When he passed by another place, he understood that the Queen had been there, but he could not find her. Similarly, he passed by the places of all [the King's] men. "However," he concluded [to the Master of Prayer], "I did not pass near your place."*

Master of Prayer came. This meeting was the beginning of the rectification. As we said, the Master of Prayer is Malkhuth and the Warrior is Yesod. The unification of Yesod and Malkhuth is the beginning of the rectification.

search for him. Literally, "He could not seek him and find him." From the wording, not only could he not find him, but he could not even look for him.

The Master of Prayer replied [to the Mighty Warrior], "I also passed by the places of all of them, as well as your place.*

"I passed by one place and saw the King's crown* there. I understood that the King was certainly there. However, I had no way of seeking him or finding him.

"I went further and passed a sea of blood.* I understood that this was certainly made from the tears of the Queen,* who had wept because of all that had happened. The Queen was certainly there, but it was not possible to seek and find her.

"Similarly, I passed a sea of milk.* I understood that this was certainly made from the milk of the Queen's Daughter,* whose son was lost. She was strained by her abundance of milk, and this produced the sea of milk. The Queen's Daughter was certainly there, but it was not possible to seek and find her.

"I went further and saw some of the infant's golden hairs* lying on the ground. I did not take any of them. I knew for certain that the infant* was there, but it was not possible to seek and find him.

"I traveled further and passed a sea of wine.* I knew for

I did not pass near your place. We thus see that in his descent from the King (Kether), the Warrior passed by all the places except that of the Master of Prayer. We therefore see that the Warrior's place is directly above the Master of Prayer. Since the Master of Prayer is Malkhuth, as we shall see, the Warrior must be Yesod.

as well as your place. Since only prayer can rectify eveything, only the Master of Prayer can pass by all the places of the King's men (*Likutey Etzoth* B, *Tefillah* 24).

From here we see that the Master of Prayer alludes to Malkhuth. Malkhuth is the lowest of the sefiroth, and must therefore pass through the places of all in its descent.

crown. From here we see that the King represents Kether. He was the first one that the Master of Prayer encountered in his descent.

sea of blood. See above.

Queen. Here we see that the Queen is the second sefirah, which is Chokhmah.

milk. See above.

Queen's Daughter. She is thus the third sefirah, which is Binah.

golden hairs. See below.

infant. The fourth sefirah, Chesed.

sea of wine. This also pertains to the True Friend. See above. Just as the Queen's Daughter and the Child are related, so are the Friend and the Bard. The Friend is the fifth sefirah, Gevurah.

certain that this was made from the words of the Bard,* who consoled the King and Queen, and then consoled the Queen's Daughter. These words produced the sea of wine [as it is written, 'The roof of your mouth is like the finest wine' (Song of Songs 7:10)]. However, I could not find him.*

"I traveled further and saw standing, a stone upon which was engraved an image of the King's Hand,* with all its lines. I realized that [the King's] Wise Man* was there, and that he had engraved an image of the Hand on a stone for himself. However, it was impossible to find him.

"I also traveled further, and saw, arranged on a mountain, golden tables* and credenzas* and other treasures* of the King. I understood that the [King's] Treasurer* was certainly there, but it was not possible to find him."

The Mighty Warrior replied, "I also passed by all these places. I took some of the child's golden hairs. I took* seven hairs,* each of a different color, and they are very precious to me. I remained in my place, and nourished myself with grass and the like as much as possible. Finally, when I did not have anything else to eat, I went on my way. However, when I left my place, I forgot my bow."*

Bard. The sixth sefirah, Tifereth.

I could not find him. Here it does not say that he could not seek him.

image of the King's Hand. This was the one that the Wise Man made. See below.

Wise Man. The seventh sefirah, Netzach.

golden tables. Like in the Temple.

credenzas. Show cupboards. *Krudentzin* in Yiddish. Perhaps alluding to the Holy Ark, which held the tablets, which were the greatest treasure.

other treasures. The golden vessels of the Temple.

Treasurer. The eighth sefirah, Hod. This parallels Aaron, who was in charge of the Temple's vessels.

Significantly, this is the first mention of the Treasurer. He is not listed among the other King's men. Similarly, the land of wealth is not listed with the other groups.

I took. The Warrior took them because, as the Queen's Daughter's husband, he was the father of the Child.

seven hairs. The *Tikkuney Zohar* (70, 123b, end) states that King David had seven colors of gold in his hair. These are the seven hairs that the Mighty Warrior took (*Rimzey Maasioth, Hashmatoth*).

bow. The bow is a sign of Yesod. We thus see that the Warrior had two weapons, the bow

"I saw the bow," replied the Master of Prayer, "and I knew for certain that it was your bow. But I could not find you."

The Mighty Warrior told the Master of Prayer what happened after he left there. "I was traveling continuously until I came to the camp [of the body builders]. When I entered the camp, I was ravenously hungry, and I had to eat something. But as soon as I came in, they made me their king. I am now conquering the world. In doing so, I hope that I will be able to find the King and his men."

The Master of Prayer spoke to the Mighty Warrior about what could be done* with the people [of the land which had fallen into the desire for money to such an extent that they made the wealthiest citizens into gods. He told him about all their foolish beliefs.]

The Mighty Warrior told the Master of Prayer that he had heard from the King* that when a person becomes entrapped by any desire, it is possible to pull him out. However, if somebody becomes trapped by the lust for wealth,* it is totally impossible to get him out of it. Therefore nothing can be done for these people. It is totally impossible to get them away from [their error].

---

and the sword, just as Jacob did (Genesis 48:22, Rashi *ad loc.*).

It is interesting to note that the Master of Prayer does not mention passing the place of the Faithful Friend. However, we see that the Faithful Friend is associated with joy. This would indicate that a person must never be without joy. If one cannot find a reason to be happy, then one must force oneself, even with foolish means (*Sichoth HaRan*). "One does not stand to pray, except with happiness" (*Berakhoth* 24b) (Rabbi Chaim Kramer).

what could be done. The rectification involves the land of wealth. This is Hod, to which evil is particularly attached, as discussed earlier.

heard from the King. Ultimately all rectification comes from the King (Kether).

lust for wealth. It is possible to escape from any desire, except for the desire for wealth (*Likutey Halakhoth, Tefillah* 4:11).

One may raise a question here. There are two very strong desires, that for money and that for sex. In most places, however, Rabbi Nachman speaks of sex as being the stronger desire. Therefore, why does he indicate here that the desire for money is the worst?

From childhood on, a person's main test in life involves sexual desire. However, if a person succumbs to sexual desire, he also begins to want money. Once he falls into the lust

However, he had also heard from the King that [the one remedy] is the path to the sword, * from which he received his

for money, he cannot get out (*Likutey Halakhoth, Kiddushin* 3:3, p. 45; also see *Likutey Moharan* 23).

Thus, even though a person may be immersed in sexual desire, one can speak to him about religion. However, when a person falls into the lust for money, he will not listen to any discussion of holiness (*Likutey Halakhoth, Kiddushin* 3:4).

The three watches of the night are divided into various analogies. A mule braying, a dog barking and a woman speaking with her husband (*Berakhoth* 3a). Rabbi Nachman relates these to the three major desires of man. A mule braying to the desire for money, the dog barking to the desire for food, and the woman speaking — to man's lust for woman (*Likutey Moharan Tinyana* 1). The *Parparoth LeChokhmah* (*ad. loc.*) explains that the lust for money is always present even in old age. Not only that, but a person who desires money will boast and brag about his desires as a mule brays (Rabbi Rosenfeld).

For this reason, the rectification of the lust for money also involves the rectification of one's sexual desires (*Likutey Halakhoth, Genevah* 2:9).

Thus, other desires can be sublimated or raised, but the lust for money must be broken from without.

path to the sword. This was known only from the Hand, so that the main rectification was from the King's Hand (*Likutey Halakhoth, Tefillah* 4:20).

As we saw earlier, the Mighty Warrior represents the sefirah of Yesod. This is also the path to the sword.

Therefore, the rectification of the lust for money is only through the subjugation of one's sexual desires, this being the path of the sword (*Likutey Halakhoth, Genevah* 2:9). This is an aspect of the Mighty Warrior (*gibbor*), since it is taught, "Who is a Mighty Warrior (*gibbor*)? He who controls his lust" (*Avoth* 4:1).

This is alluded to in the verse, "It is in vain for you who rise up early and stay up late, you who eat the bread of toil... Children are God's heritage, the fruit of the womb is a reward. Like arrows in the hand of a Mighty Warrior, so are the children of one's youth" (Psalms 127:2-4; *Likutey Halakhoth, Kiddushin* 3:3).

Another aspect of Yesod is the tzaddik, as it is written, "The tzaddik is the foundation (Yesod) of the universe" (Proverbs 10:25). Hence, this path is the advice of the tzaddik, which began to be revealed from the time of the Ari (Rabbi Yitzchak Luria, 1534-1572). (*Likutey Halakhoth, Keriyath Sh'ma* 5:15).

Another aspect of Yesod is charity, which is *tzedakah* (coming from the same root as tzaddik). Rabbi Nachman thus taught that the lust for money could be cured by charity (*Likutey Moharan* 13). This is also the path of the Mighty Warrior (*Likutey Halakhoth, Kiddushin* 3:4).

This is alluded to in the Exodus, which was the rectification for the lust for money, as we have seen. The Exodus was only accomplished by the sword which killed the firstborn. We thus say in the Passover Haggadah, "With an outstretched arm (Deuteronomy 26:8) —

power. Through this [path] he could get a person out of the desire for wealth, even though he has fallen into it and is immersed in it.

The Mighty Warrior then sat together with the Master of Prayer for a while. Regarding the respite that the citizens had asked the Master of Prayer to gain for them, he got the Mighty Warrior to grant it, * and to spare the citizens for a period of time. The Master of Prayer and the Mighty Warrior then established a code with which they could communicate with each other, and the Master of Prayer went on his way.

Along the way, * the Master of Prayer saw people walking * and praying. They were carrying prayer books. He was afraid of them, and they were afraid of him.

He stood up and prayed. They also prayed. Then he asked them, "Who are you?"

They replied, "At the time of the great hurricane, all the people of the world were divided into different factions, each with its own ideology. (These were the various groups mentioned earlier.) We chose for ourselves to pray constantly to God. We found ourselves a prayer leader and made him king."

When the Master of Prayer heard this, it was very good in his

---

this is the sword." Thus, the lust for money can only be rectified through the sword (cf. *Shabbath*).

The sword also represents Gehenom, as we have seen. From the story itself, we see that the path of the Mighty Warrior (*gibbor*) branched off to Gehenom. Since a person cannot take his money with him when he dies, purgatory is the true rectification for money-lust.

grant it. Through prayer, one can ameliorate justice, and gain a respite from divine retribution (*Rimzey Maasioth*). The attribute of prayer always stands up for a person to gain time for him to rectify his deeds (*Chokhmah U'Tevunah* 4).

This is alluded to in the last verse in the prophets, where God says, "Behold, I will send you Elijah the prophet before the coming of the great and terrible day of God. And he will turn the hearts of the fathers to the children and the hearts of the children to the fathers, lest I come and smite the land with utter destruction" (Malachi 3:23,24).

Along the way. It seems that the Master of Prayer had to travel a distance to the Warrior.

It also appears that the Master of Prayer could not become a king in his own right until after he had come together with the Warrior. Kabbalistically, Malkhuth (the Master of Prayer) is not complete until it is rectified by Yesod (the Warrior).

walking. As mentioned earlier, the group of prayers did not have a homeland.

eyes, since this was also what he desired. He began to speak to them, and revealed to them the way he prayed, as well his works and ideas. When they heard his words, their eyes were opened, and they realized the greatness of the Master of Prayer. Their king abdicated, and they immediately made [the Master of Prayer] their king,* since they realized that he was a very great person.

The Master of Prayer taught them and enlightened them, making them into very great saints. They were righteous people before, [since they engaged only in prayer,] but the Master of Prayer enlightened them so that they became awesome saints.

The Master of Prayer sent a note to the Mighty Warrior informing him how he had discovered this group and had become their king.

Meanwhile, the people of the Land of Wealth became even more devout in their practices and modes of worship. The deadline that the Mighty Warrior had set was coming closer and closer, and they were extremely frightened. They performed their services, offered sacrifice, incense and prayers, worshipping their gods.

They agreed among themselves that they had no other choice but to [carry out their original plan and] send to the land of extraordinary wealth, where they considered all the people gods. Since all these people were gods, they would certainly be able to help them. They sent emissaries to that land.

On the way, the emissaries got lost.* As they traveled, they

---

their king. It is only after the Master of Prayer becomes king that the process of rectification begins (cf. *Likutey Etzoth* B, *Yirah VeAvodah* 40). Although the *Gibbor*-Warrior had to become king first, the process of rectification began only after the Master of Prayer became king. Only then could they begin to find the others.

The reason for this is that prayer includes all ten concepts of holiness embodied by the King and his men (*Zimrath HaAretz*). The Master of Prayer brings them together, just as a prayer leader brings together the congregation.

Breslover tradition states that the beginning of the rectification was Rabbi Nachman's return from Lemberg, in the summer of 1808, when he re-married (*Chokhmah U'Tevunah* 1ᵃ).

got lost. The Master of Prayer had told them that if they sought help they would be

encountered a stranger, walking with a staff.* The staff was worth more than all of their gods' wealth. It contained precious stones that were worth more than the wealth of all of their gods [both in their homeland, and the gods to whom they were going. This staff was worth more than the wealth of all of them].

[The stranger] was also wearing a hat* set with precious stones that was also worth an enormous amount.

[The emissaries] immediately fell before him, bowing and prostrating themselves. This stranger had such extraordinary wealth that in their opinion he could be the god over all their gods.

[Actually, the stranger that they met was the Treasurer* of the Master of Prayer's King.]

"Do you find this surprising?" remarked the stranger. "Come with me. I will show you real wealth!"

He took them to the mountain where he had set out the King's treasures, and he showed them to [the emissaries]. They immediately fell down, bowing and prostrating themselves. According to their beliefs, this was the god over all gods. [This

---

destroyed. This, however, occurs later, when they come to the path of the Mighty Warrior. Meanwhile, the seeds of this are planted when they now meet the Treasurer (*Chokhmah U'Tevunah* 12).

staff. Since the Treasurer is Aaron, this might represent Aaron's staff, which is the sign of his position. Aaron's staff grows buds and leaves (Numbers 17:23).

hat. *Kapulish.* The hat may be represent the Clouds of Glory which rained down precious stones to the Israelites in the desert (*Parparoth LeChokhmah; Mekhilta, Yithro*).

Treasurer. He is the third character (see end of story), and hence represents Hod, the third to last sefirah. He is represented by Aaron. He eventually becomes king over the land of wealth.

He parallels the commandment, "Do not steal" (Exodus 20:13). Alternatively he parallels the commandment, "Remember the Sabbath" (Exodus 20:8).

Among the ten things in the desert, he parallels the Clouds of Glory. Rain is from clouds, and God said, "God will open His good treasury, and give you rain in its time" (Deuteronomy 28:12). The Clouds of Glory also provided the Israelites with precious stones (*Parparoth LeChokhmah; Mekhilta, Yithro*)

Furthermore, Israel is considered God's treasure, as He said, "You will be My treasure from among all nations" (Exodus 19:5). Hence, the Clouds of Glory were actually protecting God's treasure.

was their false belief in money and wealth, discussed earlier.]

Nevertheless, they did not offer sacrifice to him there. [Although they considered him the god of gods, and would have sacrificed themselves to him,] these emissaries had been warned before leaving that they should not offer sacrifice. There was concern that if they offered sacrifice on their journey, none of them would survive. Perhaps they will find some treasure on the way. One of them might go to the bathroom and find a treasure there, [and he would be considered a god]. If they began to sacrifice themselves to it, not one of them would survive. Therefore [the people of the land] warned the emissaries that they should not offer any sacrifice at all along the way. This is why the emissaries did not offer sacrifice to the Treasurer.

Nevertheless, because of his tremendous wealth, it seemed obvious to them that he was the god of all gods. The emissaries therefore decided that it would be unnecessary for them to go to the "gods," that is, to the land of extraordinary wealth where they considered everyone to be gods. This stranger could certainly help them, since he was the greatest god of them all [according to their twisted belief. After all, he had more wealth than all of them]. They therefore asked him to accompany them back to their land. He agreed and went with them.*

When they arrived home, the citizens were very happy to have found such a god. They were certain that he would bring them great salvation, since [with such tremendous wealth] he was obviously a most powerful god.

[The King's Treasurer, whom the people took for a god] issued orders that prior to the carrying out of certain reforms in the land, they should not offer sacrifices at all. [Actually, the Treasurer was an extremely righteous person, since he was one of the King's men, who were all great saints. He detested all the evil and foolish customs of this land, but was not able to make them

---

went with them. The land of wealth thus subjugated itself totally to the Treasurer, and made him their king. This was the beginning of their rectification (*Parparoth LeChokhmah, Mekhilta, Yithro*).

change their evil ways. But the least he could do at the time was to stop them from bringing sacrifices.]

The citizens began to ask him about the Mighty Warrior who was threatening them. The Treasurer also answered, "It is possible that this is the Mighty Warrior [whom I know]."

The Treasurer went out to the Mighty Warrior. He asked the Warrior's men if it would be possible to meet with him.

They said that they would inform him, and when they asked him, he gave permission. When the Treasurer came to the Mighty Warrior, they recognized each other, and there was great joy and weeping. The Mighty Warrior told the Treasurer, "I have also seen our saintly Master of Prayer, and he has become a king."

The Treasurer told the Mighty Warrior that he had passed by the places of the King and all his people, but he had not passed by* the places of the Master of Prayer or the Mighty Warrior. He had not passed near either of these two places.

The Treasurer and the Mighty Warrior discussed the Land [of Wealth] and spoke about how they had become so confused until they believed in utter nonsense.

The Mighty Warrior gave the Treasurer the same reply that he had given the Master of Prayer, telling him that the King had said that if a person is immersed in such a lust for wealth, it is impossible to bring him out except through the path to the sword [where he got his power for battle]. This was the only way to get people out of it.

[The Mighty Warrior] extended the deadline.* The Treasurer spoke to the Mighty Warrior, asking him to extend the deadline,

---

had not passed by. From this we see that the Treasurer is the third from the last sefirah, that is, Hod.

extended the deadline. Giving them further respite. Together with the Master of Prayer, he is able to increase the respite and give them further time to repent (*Rimzey Maasioth, Hashmatoth*).

The Treasurer may represent charity. The Master of Prayer (prayer) and the Treasurer (charity) together have the power to grant a respite from the evil decree (*Chokhmah U'Tevunah* 4). Through giving *ma'aser*, tithes, one is saved from one's enemies (*Likutey Moharan* 221) (Rabbi Chaim Kramer).

and the Mighty Warrior did so.

The Treasurer and the Mighty Warrior then set up a code between them. The Treasurer then left the Mighty Warrior and returned to the Land [of Wealth].

[The Treasurer admonished them for their evil ways, telling them that they were in error and totally confused in their lust for wealth, but it did not help at all. They were already too deeply immersed in it. However, since both the Master of Prayer and the Treasurer had admonished them so much, they became perplexed.* Even though they maintained their beliefs very strongly and did not want to turn away from their error, they would say, "If this is true, please get us out of our mistaken beliefs." Whenever they were admonished, they would reply, "If it is as you say, and we are in such great error, do something to change our beliefs."]

[The Treasurer] was able to give them advice,* telling them that he knew the source of the Mighty Warrior's power, and the place from which he received his power to wage war. He told them about the sword from which the Mighty Warrior had the power to be victorious, concluding, "Therefore, let us all go — all of you and myself — to the place of the sword. We will then be able to gain power against him."

The Treasurer's intent was that if he could bring them there, he would be able to release them from their erroneous beliefs. [He knew that the path to the sword was the only remedy for the lust for wealth.]

[The citizens] accepted his advice and agreed to [go with him to the sword]. The Treasurer thus set off, along with the greatest people of the land, who were considered gods. [These "gods" were bedecked with gold and silver jewelry] as they traveled together.

---

they became perplexed. Since both prayer and charity are rectifications for the lust for money (*Likutey Halakhoth, Tefillah* 4:20; *Kiddushin* 3:1).

give them advice. Again, charity is what leads them to the true path. Also, since *klipoth* are attached to Hod, he can lead them. Aaron brought people to Torah (*Avoth* 1:12).

The Treasurer informed the Mighty Warrior that he was taking the people to the place of the sword, and that his intent was that along the way they might be successful in finding the King and his men.

"I will go with you," declared the Mighty Warrior.

The Mighty Warrior disguised himself so that the people accompanying the Treasurer would not recognize that he was the Warrior. He disguised himself and accompanied the Treasurer.

They then decided that they would inform the Master of Prayer. When they informed him, he said that he would also go with them. The Master of Prayer went to them, instructing his men to pray * to God to make their mission successful so that they would be worthy of finding the King and his men. This had always been the supplication of the Master of Prayer, and he had instructed his men to pray for this and had composed appropriate prayers. But now that he was setting out with the Treasurer and the Mighty Warrior, he told them that they must pray even more at all times that he should be worthy of finding [the King].

When the Master of Prayer came to the Treasurer and the Warrior there was great joy and weeping. The three of them, the Treasurer, the Mighty Warrior, and the Master of Prayer, set off * along with the wealthiest people of the land, who were considered gods.

They continued traveling until they came to a land surrounded by guards. They asked the guards about the affairs of the land as well as the identity of their king.

The guards replied that when there was the great hurricane that divided the human race into different factions, the people of their land concluded that the main thing in life was wisdom. They

---

to pray. Since prayer is the main rectification of the fallen attributes. It is eventually these prayers that help the King's men become reunited (*Likutey Halakhoth, Tefillah* 4:12).

set off. Although the "gods," which represent the *klipoth*, are attached to Hod (the Treasurer), he cannot bring them up to the other higher sefiroth without Yesod and Malkhuth. Hod is the priest, Elijah, while Yesod is *Moshiach ben Yoseph*, and Malkhuth is *Moshiach ben David*. All of them are necessary for the final redemption and rectification.

had originally accepted upon themselves a great sage as king. However, recently, they had discovered a great Wise Man,* who had extraordinary intelligence. Their king had abdicated his throne, and they had accepted this Wise Man as their king. For them the main thing in life was wisdom, and therefore, since they had discovered such an extraordinary Wise Man, they accepted him as their king.

The three of them, [the Treasurer, the Mighty Warrior and the Master of Prayer] observed, "It seems that this is our Wise Man." [It seemed that this was the Wise Man of their King.] They asked if it would be possible to meet with him.

[The guards] replied that they would inform him and seek his permission. They went, and when they asked, he granted an audience.

[The three] went to the Wise Man who was king of that land, and they immediately recognized each other. This sage was the Wise Man of their King. There was obviously great joy and weeping. They wept since they did not know how they would be able to find the King and his other men.

They asked the Wise Man if he knew where the King's Hand was.

He answered that he had the Hand with him. However, since the time that they had been scattered by the great hurricane and the King had been concealed from them,... he no longer looked at the Hand, since it was only meant to be used by the King. But he had engraved an image of the Hand* on a stone, so that to some degree he would be able to use it for his own purposes. He would not gaze at the Hand itself at all.

Wise Man. He is the fourth one to be found. Hence, the Wise Man is Netzach, personified by Moses. See above. Among the festivals, this denotes Chanukah, because of Greek wisdom. The Mighty Warrior is Rosh HaShanah; the Master of Prayer is Yom Kippur; and the Treasurer is Sukkoth.

image of the Hand. If the Hand is the Torah, as above, then Moses had the entire Torah. But now, he did not have the Torah, as it was in heaven, but only stone tablets. This denotes the restoration of the Tablets which have been lost since the destruction of the First Temple.

They spoke to the Wise Man and asked him how he had come to this land. He told them that at the time of the great hurricane, he traveled on his way. [As he traveled, he passed by the entire group, except for the places of those three,* the Master of Prayer, the Mighty Warrior, and the Treasurer, whom he did not pass.] Finally, the people of this land found him and took him as their king. Now he must lead them according to their way, which is the way of wisdom, until after a long time he would be able to bring them back to the truth.

They spoke to the Wise Man about the people of the land which had erred and had become confused by the worship of wealth. They said, "If all of us had been isolated and scattered only to make that land good again, it would be enough for us, since they have become so foolish and imbued with their error."

Actually, all the factions were in error and confused, and needed to be brought back to the true goal. This was true even of the group that had chosen wisdom as a goal. Even this group had not attained the true goal and still needed rectification and repentance, since they had chosen for themselves secular wisdom and heresy.* Nevertheless, all the other groups were relatively easy to bring back from their errors. The group of money worshippers, however, were so immersed in it that it would be virtually impossible to get them out of it.

[The Wise Man also told them that he had heard from the King that it was possible to get a person out of any desire except for the desire for wealth. If one has fallen into that desire, one can only be brought out through the path to the sword.]

It is asked, that since the Wise Man did not look at the King's Hand, how could he have made a copy of it? However, this is likened to the light of the sun, which a person cannot see. However, one can see the light of the sun reflected in the moon. The Wise Man saw the Hand reflected in all creation, and with his wisdom, was able to reproduce it (*Chokhmah U'Tevunah* 13).

The stone copy of the Hand may also be reflected in the Foundation Stone (*evven shethiyah*), which contains all the paths in the world (*Ibid.*).

the places of those three. From here we see that he was the fourth from the lowest sefirah.

heresy. *Apikorsus.*

The Wise Man also wanted to go with them, so all four set out together. The foolish "gods" also went with them.

They traveled on until they came to another land. There they also asked about the land and the identity of its king. The people replied, "Ever since the great hurricane, the people of this land concluded that the main thing in life is speech and therefore they sought a master of language as king. Finally, they found a master of language and poetry who was an extraordinary speaker, and appointed him as king. Since this man was such a great speaker, the [previous] king abdicated his throne for him."

The four observed, "This is our Bard."* [They realized that this was their King's Bard,] and they asked if it would be possible for them to meet with this king. The people said that they would inform him and seek permission; when they asked, he granted an audience.

The four went to the king of this land, and they saw that he was their King's Bard. They recognized one another, and there was great joy and weeping among them.

The Bard joined them, and they traveled on, hoping to find the rest of the King's men. They saw that God had granted them success, and that they had already been successful in finding some of their companions. They realized that this was due to the merit of their saintly Master of Prayer, who was always praying for this; through his prayers they had been worthy of finding their companions. They thus traveled on, hoping that they would also be worthy of finding the others.

Eventually they came to a land, and they inquired about the land and the identity of its king. They were answered that this was the group that had chosen for themselves joy and drink as their goal. Their king therefore had been a drunkard who was always happy. They had then found a man sitting in a sea of wine. This

---

Bard. He was the fifth one to be reunited (see end of story). Hence he is the fifth from the bottom sefirah, that is, Tifereth.

He represents Pesach, which is *peh sach* (פה סח), "a mouth speaking."

was very good in their opinion, since this man must be an extraordinary drunkard, so they accepted him as their king.

They asked to meet with him, and were granted an audience. [The five companions] went to this king, and discovered that he was their King's Faithful Friend.* He was sitting in the sea of wine* made from the words of consolation* spoken by the Bard. [The people of that land had seen him in the sea of wine, and had thought him to be an unusual drunkard; therefore they appointed him king.]

They recognized one another and there was great joy and weeping.

The Faithful Friend joined the others and they continued their journey, and came to another land. They asked the guards, "Who is your king?"

[The guards] replied that their ruler was a beautiful woman. She brought people closer to the goal, since the goal was to populate the world. At first they had chosen a beautiful woman as queen, but they had later found a very extraordinarily beautiful

---

Faithful Friend. He was the sixth one to be reunited (see end of story). Hence he is the next sefirah in an upward direction, Gevurah. This might seem surprising, but the *Zohar* teaches that love begins with Gevurah, as it is written, "His left hand (Gevurah) is under my head, and with his right hand he embraces me" (Song of Songs 2:6, 8:3; *Zohar* 1:244a, 245a). Therefore, tefillin, which are a sign of this love, are worn on the left hand.

The group that chose joy as their goal took him as their leader, since joy is an aspect of true friendship, as it is written, "All those who love Your name shall rejoice" (Psalms 5:12) (*Kedushath Shabbath* 18d). However, it is supreme irony that they exchanged a common drunkard as king for the King's Faithful Friend. The Friend denotes the festival of Shemini Atzereth.

sea of wine. Wine is related to love, as it is written, "Remember your love from wine" (Song of Songs 1:4; *Kedushath Shabbath* 18d).

Furthermore, wine represents secrets, since both the Hebrew word for wine, *yayin* (יין), and word for secret, *sod* (סוד), have numerical values of seventy. One's faithful friend is a person to whom one tells all one's secrets. Wine is also Gevurah (*Zohar* 3:41a), the attribute of the Faithful Friend.

According to those who say that the Friend represents the Sabbath, the wine represents the wine of Kiddush (*Parparoth LeChokhmah, Mekhilta, Yithro*).

Alternatively, he represents the festival of Purim.

words of consolation. This is the joy of doing a good deed (*Zimrath HaAretz*).

woman to be queen. [The companions] understood that this must be the Queen's Daughter,* so they asked to meet with her and were granted an audience.

When they came to the queen, they recognized that she was the Queen's Daughter. Their great joy was beyond estimation. "How did you get here?" they asked her.

She answered, that when the hurricane came that snatched away the precious infant [from its crib], she had gone out after the infant in the panic, but she could not find him. Her breasts were engorged with milk, and this created the sea of milk. Then the people of this land found her, and accepted her as their ruler.

There was great joy [at the reunion], but they also wept very much because the precious infant was lost, and because she did not know the whereabouts of her father and mother.

The Mighty Warrior, who was this queen's husband, had now arrived, and the land now had a king.

The Queen's Daughter [who was queen of this land] asked the Master of Prayer to cleanse this land of its lasciviousness. Since their main goal involved beautiful women, they were very much immersed in sexual desire. She therefore asked the Master of Prayer to cleanse them at least temporarily, so that they not become engrossed in lust; it was a matter of faith to them that this was the goal of existence.

[Each of the factions had chosen a bad trait as their goal, and each one treated their trait as a matter of faith.] Therefore, they were very much immersed in it. [The queen] therefore asked [the Master of Prayer] to cleanse them of their trait to some degree at this time.

After this, they all set out to seek the King and the other ones.

They traveled and finally came to a land, asking, "Who is your king?"

[The people] answered that their king was a "yearling." This

Queen's Daughter. She is the seventh to be reunited. Significantly, she is found before her Child. However, it appears that she is Binah rather than Chesed.

was the faction that had chosen for themselves as king a person who had an abundance of food, and who did not eat the food of other people. They had temporarily accepted a wealthy man as king, but later they had discovered a person sitting in a sea of milk, and this was very good in their eyes. All his life, this person had been nourished by the milk, and therefore, he was not sustained by the food of the rest of the world. The people therefore accepted him as king. They called him "the yearling," since he was nourished by milk like a one year old child.

They understood that this was the lost Child,* and they asked to meet with him. He was asked, and they were granted an audience. When they went in, they recognized one another. [The infant who had become king] recognized them even though he had been a tiny infant when he was separated from them. Still, he had possessed a high intelligence from the time of his birth, having been born with a fully developed intellect. He therefore was able to recognize them. They certainly recognized him and there was awesome joy. But they still wept, since they still did not know anything about the King and Queen.

"How did you get here?" they asked him.

He replied that the great hurricane had snatched him up and carried him someplace. He sustained himself with whatever he could find, in any way possible. Finally, he came to a sea of milk, and he understood that this milk was certainly from his mother. She had become engorged with this milk, and it had produced this sea. He had sat in that sea of milk, and had sustained himself with it, until the people of this land had come and taken him as their king.

They continued traveling until they came to another land. When they asked, "Who is your king," the people answered that they had chosen murder as their goal, and had set a murderer as their king. Then, they had found a woman sitting in a sea of

---

Child. He is the eighth to be reunited and is Chesed. He was called the yearling, *ben shanah* in the original, which means "son of a year." Year, however, denotes Binah (*Zohar* 3:253a), and as the son of Binah (the Queen's Daughter), he was literally, "son of a year."

blood, and had accepted her as their ruler. Since she was sitting in a sea of blood, she must have been a very fierce murderess.

They also asked to meet her, and were granted an audience. When they went to her, they saw that she was the Queen.* She was constantly weeping, and out of her tears the sea of blood was formed. When they recognized one another there was very great joy, but they still wept, since they still did not know anything about the King.

The went further, and came to another land. They asked, "Who is your king?" and the people replied that they had chosen for themselves an honored man as king, since for them, the main goal was honor. Then they had found in a field an old man sitting with a crown on his head. Such a man appeared very honored, and he was good in their eyes, since he wore his crown even in a field, so they accepted him as king.

The companions realized that this was certainly their King.* They asked if it would be possible to meet him, and they were granted an audience. When they went in, they recognized that it was the King. The joy that they experienced is impossible to imagine.

The [wealthy leaders of the Land of Wealth, who were gods in their land], who were accompanying them, did not have any idea* of what was happening and the reason for this joy.

Now the entire holy gathering* had come together. They sent* the Master of Prayer* to all lands [which had chosen evil

---

Queen. The ninth one to be found. She is Chokhmah.

King. The tenth and final one to be reunited. He is Kether. Once he is found, everything can be rectified (*Likutey Halakhoth, Tefillah* 4:24).

did not have any idea. Those immersed in evil have no idea of the joy of holiness.

holy gathering. That is, all ten characters in the story. Everything is rectified by a minyan of ten men who come together to pray. Whenever ten people come together to pray, they also bring together the ten men of the King, who are then with them (*Likutey Halakhoth, Tefillah* 4:12). Moreover, the entire group came together because of the prayers of the Master of Prayer (*Parparoth LeChokhmah; Mekhilta, Yithro*).

They sent. Although all the King's men were very great, they all agreed that the rectification had to be accomplished by the Master of Prayer (*Likutey Etzoth* B, *Tefillah* 24).

traits as their goals in life] so that he would rectify and purify them, and get them to repent their foolishness. Each land had its own foolishness and error, but the Master of Prayer had the power* to go to them and bring them to repent. He had power and permission from all the kings of these lands, since their kings* were all members of [the Holy Gathering of the King. The King had now been restored and had assembled his men, who were kings over all the factions].

The Master of Prayer left with their authority to cleanse their lands and bring them to repent.

The Mighty Warrior spoke to the King about the people in the land which had fallen into the worship of wealth. The Warrior said to the King, "I heard from you that the only way to release those who are immersed in the worship of the lust for wealth is through the path that I have to the sword."

"That is true," replied the King. The King then told the Mighty Warrior that on the road to the sword there is a path to the side. That path leads to a Mountain of Fire* upon which

---

the Master of Prayer. The main rectification of all the groups is through the Master of Prayer, who leads the ten in prayer. When ten men worship together, led by a proper *baal tefillah* (prayer leader), they can rectify all worlds (*Likutey Halakhoth, Tefillah* 4:12). Ultimately, everything is accomplished through the King and the Master of Prayer, the first and last characters in the story (*Parparoth LeChokhmah, Mekhilta, Yithro*).

This also stresses the importance of praying with a minyan (Rabbi Rosenfeld).

had the power. First the Master of Prayer had brought the King's household together; now he could rectify everything else. All the attributes had fallen, and this was a reflection of the scattering of the King and his household. But now that the King and his men had been reunited, the fallen attributes could also be re-elevated (*Likutey Halakhoth, Tefillah* 4:12). Through prayer, one can break all bad traits (*Ibid.* 4:13).

their kings. Each of the King's men had become king over one of the fallen factions. Therefore, each one had the power to rectify one fallen attribute (*Likutey Halakhoth, Tefillah* 4:12).

Mountain of Fire. Rabbi Nachman also speaks of a mountain of fire elsewhere, in terms of a barrier to be overcome (*Sichoth HaRan* 191).

At the end of the story, Rabbi Nachman said that God has a fire in one place and an oven in another place, as it is written, "The word of God whose fire is in Zion and whose oven is in Jerusalem" (Isaiah 31:9) (end of story).

crouches a lion.*

Moreover, the Talmud states that the "fire" in this verse denotes purgatory, while the "oven" represents the entrance to purgatory (*Eruvin* 19a). Some say that this is a purgatory that will even exist in the World to Come (*Bereshith Rabbah* 6:6; 26:6).

The fire is on the path of the sword. As we noted earlier, the sword also represents purgatory (cf. *Targum Yonathan* on Genesis 3:24). The mountain here may be the mountain in the verse, "God of Hosts will come down to fight on Mount Zion and on its *mountain*" (Isaiah 31:4). This is the mountain associated with the lion, and hence the fire in the verse, "God whose fire is in Zion" (Isaiah 31:9). Thus, it is a mountain of fire.

In general, Rabbi Nachman taught that fire is a revelation of all colors, which is a revelation of God's greatness (*Likutey Moharan* 25, *Likutey Halakhoth, Maakheley Akum* 3:1,2). Actually, the Baal Shem Tov taught that purgatory is the shame that a sinner feels when he becomes aware of God's greatness (see *Likutey Moharan* 10).

[The colors of the fire may be related to the colors of the Child's hair, which the Mighty Warrior took. Both pertain to the path of the Warrior.]

Sexual passion is also likened to fire (cf. *Kiddushin* 81a). It is therefore quenched by the fire that represents God's greatness. This fire is the rectification of sexual desire, which in turn rectifies the lust for wealth (*Likutey Halakhoth, Genevah* 2:9). The Evil Urge is also likened to a mountain (*Sukkah* 52a).

The fire also represents the fire of charity, which cools the heart of the lust for money (*Likutey Moharan* 13, *Likutey Halakhoth, Kiddushin* 3:1).

This concept is also reflected in the Paschal Lamb. As we discussed earlier, the lamb represents wealth, and hence was the god of Egypt, which was the land of the "gods of wealth." God commanded that the Paschal Lamb (*korban Pesach*) be roasted over fire. The idolatry of money worship is very strong, and can only be broken by fire (*Likutey Halakhoth, Tefillah* 4:17).

The fire is also reflected in the *charoseth* into which the *maror* is dipped (*Pesachim* 114b; *Orach Chaim* 473:4). The *charoseth* is made of fruits, which have all the colors of fire. The bitter herb (*maror*) represents the bitterness of Egypt, which is the lust for money. This is rectified through the *charoseth* (*Likutey Halakhoth, Choshen Mishpat; Harshaah* 4:18, p. 106).

lion. Rabbi Nachman said that this is alluded to in the key chapter, "A lion growls over its prey; even though many shepherds are called against it, it will not be frightened of their voices nor humble himself because of their noise. So will the God of Hosts come down to fight on Mount Zion and on its mountain" (Isaiah 31:4). Zion is the place of the fire, as it is written, "whose fire is in Zion" (31:9). Therefore the fire and the lion are together.

The reference to the lion may be to the fire on the altar, which had the form of a lion (*Yoma* 21b). The *Zohar* says that this lion appeared to eat the sacrifices (*Zohar* 3:211a). This was also in Jerusalem. The name "God of Hosts" in this verse denotes Netzach and Hod.

The root of the word *korban* (sacrifice) is *karev* to draw close the Jews to their Father in heaven. This is accomplished through repentance. Therefore every sacrifice must be

When the lion wants to eat, he attacks the flocks taking the sheep and cattle and eating them. The herdsmen* know this, and watch their sheep very carefully because of him. The lion, however, does not pay any attention whatsoever to this. Whenever he wants to eat, he attacks the flocks, and even though the herdsmen strike him and shout at him, the lion does not pay any attention. He takes whatever sheep and cattle he wants, roars and eats them.

The Mountain of Fire is totally invisible.

There is another path off to the side leading to a Kitchen.*

---

accompanied with confession and repentance (Rabbi Rosenfeld).

Rabbi Nachman explains that there are six parts of the *nefesh* (*Likutey Moharan* 13). The lion represents the desires of the soul, that are drawn together and collected by the lion, as the lion on the altar accepts the sacrifice. The lion collects the bitterness and the blemishes of the soul and elevates it to give forth a good fragrance.

This also represents the angel Michael, the guardian of Israel, who is represented by the lion in the heavenly chariot (Rabbi Rosenfeld).

herdsmen. Literally, shepherds. These may refer to the Patriarchs, or the Seven Shepherds, who try to protect their "sheep" from the lion of purgatory. But even the merit of the Patriarchs does not help.

This may be related to the teaching that Abraham sits at the entrance to purgatory, and does not allow anyone in who is circumcised. But if a person has sinned, he removes the mark of circumcision from him (*Eruvin* 19a).

Kitchen. *Kech* in Yiddish; *beth habishul* in Hebrew. This is the "oven in Jerusalem" (Isaiah 31:9) in the key chapter (end of story). The Midrash states explicitly that the "oven" in this verse is the type of oven used for baking bread (*Tanchuma, Bamidbar* 2). The Talmud says that this is the entrance to purgatory (*Eruvin* 19a).

The concept of fire is that of consuming evil. When the fire is directed toward a kitchen, however, it turns bitter into sweet, and inedible into edible. This is the concept of Gehenom, which turns the wicked into righteous.

As discussed earlier, the desire for money comes from the curse, "By the sweat of your brow you will eat bread" (Genesis 3:19). Therefore, the desire for money is very closely related to food. It can thus be rectified by the food from the holy kitchen.

The holy kitchen also refers to charity. Rabbi Chiya once told his wife to run to a poor person and bring him sustenance, so that people will do so to her children. She asked, "Are you cursing us that our children should be poor?" He answered, "The wheel of fortune constantly turns" (*Shabbath* 151b).

Giving tithes assures one of increasing one's income, even to the point of saturation. "I will give.... until you say enough" (*Taanith* 9a). When one is satiated, one says enough. This breaks the desire for money (Rabbi Rosenfeld).

There are all kinds of food* in that Kitchen, but no fire. The food is cooked by the Mountain of Fire, and although the Mountain of Fire is very far away, there are channels and pipes* from the Mountain of Fire to the Kitchen, and these cook the food.

The Kitchen is also invisible. However, there is a sign of where the Kitchen is; birds* hover over it, and one can thus know the location of the Kitchen. By flapping their wings, the birds make the fire burn more fiercely or bank it so that it will not burn more fiercely than necessary. They thus make the fire burn as required by the food. One type of food may need one heat, while another needs a different heat, depending on the food. They make the fire burn accordingly.

[All this was what the King told the Mighty Warrior. Speaking of the "gods" of the Land of Wealth who had accompanied the

---

food. This food may be the food alluded to in the verse, "They saw the God of Israel, and they ate and drank" (Exodus 24:11). The *Zohar* speaks about this as the level of being nourished by the radiance of the divine (*Zohar* 1:135b). Rabbi Nachman also said that there are spiritual joys so great that they can nourish a person like food. When a person eats this spiritual "food" he no longer has any desire for the physical, especially not of material wealth.

This food is reflected in the sacrifices, which the *Zohar* calls "food of the king." The main point of the sacrifices is their fragrance, as it is written, "a fire offering, a pleasant fragrance to God" (Numbers 28:6). In the service, it represents the sacrificial readings (*Likutey Halakhoth, Tefillah* 4:15).

The Paschal Lamb also was to be roasted over an open fire, so as to provide a pleasant fragrance (*Likutey Halakhoth, Tefillah* 4:17; *Purim* 6:9).

The idea of this food is also, "Taste and see that God is good" (Psalms 34:9).

channels and pipes. Like the heat of the heart that is brought to the stomach to "cook" the food.

The *chayoth* sweat in fear, and this sweat makes the river Dinur (*Chagigah* 13b).

birds. In the key chapter these are alluded to in the verse, "As birds hovering, so will God of Hosts protect Jerusalem. He will deliver it as He protects it, and He will rescue it as He passes over it" (Isaiah 31:5).

Jerusalem is the place of the oven, as it is written, "Whose oven is in Jerusalem" (Isaiah 31:9). The birds protect Jerusalem. That is, they make sure that the fire is hot enough, but not so hot as to burn the food. Thus, purgatory is hot enough to atone and cleanse a person of sin, but not hot enough to destroy the sinners.

Also see "The Seven Beggars," the third day, p. 387; *Likutey Halakhoth, Melamdim* 4:13.

others, the King said,] "You must bring them in this manner. First bring them downwind [from the Kitchen] so that the fragrance* of the food will reach them. Then, when you give them the food, they will denounce the lust for wealth."

The Mighty Warrior* did as he had been bidden. He took the leaders of the Land of Wealth, who were gods in their land. These "gods" were there because they had accompanied the Treasurer. When they had left their land with the Treasurer, the citizens had given them authority to do anything necessary, and the people of the land would abide by anything these emissaries did. These emissaries [were the most important people in their land, as well as their gods,] and no one would refute whatever they did.

The Mighty Warrior took these men who were considered gods in their land because of their wealth, and brought them along his path. When they came near the food Kitchen, he brought them downwind so that the fragrance of the food reached

---

fragrance. This is the "pleasant fragrance" of the sacrifice. A sacrifice was like a fine, since it involved a major monetary expenditure in ancient times (see *Sifra,* Rashi on Leviticus 6:1). However, in spending money for sacrifices, one also breaks the desire for money (*Likutey Halakhoth, Tefillah* 4:15).

The fragrance also represents the incense that was burned in the Temple (Exodus 30:34). Incense is a concept of joy, as it is written, "Incense makes joy" (Proverbs 27:9). This is diametrically opposed to money, which leads to sadness, as it is written, "In sadness (*itzavon*) you will eat" (Genesis 3:18). Thus, the lust for money can be broken by the joy of the incense (cf. *Likutey Moharan* 13).

The incense also rectifies wealth and brings it to holiness, as it is taught, "The incense brings wealth" (*Yoma* 26). As long as a person has a lust for money, he is never wealthy; he is always in debt to his desires. It is thus taught, "The more money, the more worry" (*Avoth* 2:7). The only time one is wealthy is when one has broken this desire, as it is taught, "Who is wealthy? He who has joy in his portion" (*Avoth* 4:1). This joy comes from the incense (*Likutey Halakhoth, Tefillah* 4:16).

Thus, when the Messiah comes and the Temple is rebuilt so that sacrifices and incense are offered once again, the lust for money will be totally rectified (*Likutey Halakhoth, Genevah* 2:9).

It is significant that the people of the land of wealth also brought sacrifices and incense to their gods, as we see earlier. It seems that they were trying to pervert this concept.

Mighty Warrior. The concept of Yesod. This is because Gehenom is also related to Yesod (see *Kehillath Yaakov,* s.v. Gehenom).

their nostrils. They began to beg that he give them some of these delicious foods.

Then he brought them away from the wind. They began to cry out that there is a horrible stench. He once again brought them in the path of the wind, and when they smelled the delicious fragrance of the food, they again asked that he give them some. He again took them away from the wind, and they cried out that there was a very awful stench.

"Don't you see that there is nothing here with a vile odor?" exclaimed the Mighty Warrior. "The vile odor is coming from you yourselves. There is nothing else here that has a foul odor."

He then gave them some of the food. * As soon as they ate * it, they began to throw away all their gold and silver. * Each one dug himself a hole.

Each person then buried himself* in the hole out of great

---

food. Rabbi Nathan states that this is why we recite the Sh'ma as part of the *Korbanoth* in the morning service. The concept of the *Korbanoth* is to break the idolatry of money worship, and this is enhanced by reciting the Sh'ma (*Likutey Halakhoth, Tefillah* 4:18). Afterward, we recite the Introductory Psalms (*Pesukey deZimra*), since the psalms and songs separate the good from the bad. After we break the lust for money we can elevate the sparks of holiness in the wealth (*Likutey Halakhoth, Tefillah* 4:19).

As soon as they ate. There are some forms of spiritual nourishment that, when tasted, cause a person to cast away his entire desire for money (*Likutey Etzoth B, Mamon U'Parnassah* 22).

gold and silver. This is alluded to in the key chapter in the verse, "For on that day, each man shall cast away his idols of silver and his idols of gold, which your own hands have made for you as a sin" (Isaiah 31:7) (end of story).

This happens on the Mighty Warrior's way to the sword, since the very next verse states, "Assyria shall fall by the sword, not by man..." (Isaiah 31:8), which, as we have seen, speaks of the Mighty Warrior's sword.

Another allusion to this is the verse, "They shall cast their silver in the streets, and their gold shall be like an unclean thing; their silver and gold shall not be able to deliver them in the day of God's wrath; neither shall it fill their insides" (Ezekiel 7:19; *Likutey Halakhoth, Genevah* 2:9). Now that the food fills their insides, the silver and gold have no room.

buried himself. "Then men shall go into the caves of rocks, and into holes in the earth, before the terror of God... On that day, each person shall cast away his idols of silver and his idols of gold... and leave them to the moles and the bats. To go into the clefts of the rocks and into the crevices of the crags..." (Isaiah 2:19-21) (see end of story).

shame. As a result of tasting the food, the money smelled as vile [as excrement].* They tore at their faces and buried themselves, and could not lift their faces at all.

Each one was ashamed of the other. In that place, wealth is the greatest shame. If someone wants to insult another, he says that the other has money. Money is so great a shame, that the more money a person has, the greater his shame. Because of their great shame, they buried themselves. They could not bear to face even their friends, and much more so, the Mighty Warrior.

Each one who had a gulden* or a grush* immediately got rid of it and threw it away as fast as he could.

The Mighty Warrior then came and took them out* [of their holes and graves]. He said to them, "Come with me. Now you no longer have to be afraid of the Mighty Warrior. I myself am the Mighty Warrior."

They asked the Mighty Warrior to give them some of the food to bring back to their land. They themselves now totally rejected wealth, but they also wanted all the people of their land to abandon the lust for wealth.

The burial is also symbolic of the fact that wealth cannot follow a person beyond death. Death and burial are thus the ultimate rejection of wealth (*Likutey Halakhoth, Tefillah* 4:14). Jumping into the holes was a sort of symbolic death (see *Rimzey Maasioth, Hashmatoth; Chokhmah U'Tevunah* 12). The only true wealth that can be taken with a person is Torah and good deeds (*Avoth* 6) (Rabbi Rosenfeld).

excrement. "You shall defile your graven images overlaid with silver, and your molten images plated with gold; you shall reject them like something unclean, and say to them, 'get away from here' " (Isaiah 30:22) (see end of story). It is also written, "They shall all be ashamed of a people that cannot profit them, that are neither a help nor a profit, but a shame and a reproach" (Isaiah 30:5).

The reason that it stank so much is because they had money as a form of idolatry. However, it is taught that idolatry is just like excrement; hence, for them, money was like excrement (*Parparoth LeChokhmah, Pesachim* 118).

gulden. Yiddish. *Dinar* in Hebrew.

grush. Yiddish. *Gadol* in Hebrew.

took them out. The Mighty Warrior, *Gibbor* in Hebrew, took them out. In the Amidah, we say to God, "You are a *Gibbor* forever, O God... You bring the dead to life." Bringing the people out of the holes is an aspect of the resurrection, and this is done through the attribute of the *Gibbor* (*Rimzey Maasioth, Hashmatoth*).

He gave them the food, and they brought it back to their land. As soon as the people were given this food, they began to throw away their gold and silver. Out of great shame they hid themselves in dirt caves.*

The wealthiest ones, who were their gods, were all the more ashamed.* The inferior ones who were considered beasts were also ashamed for feeling inferior because of their lack of wealth. Now it was revealed that wealth is the main thing of which to be ashamed. This was because the foods had the special power that anyone who ate them would become extremely repulsed by money, and to him it would have a stench like excrement and filth.

They then "cast away their gods of silver and their gods of gold" (Isaiah 2:20).*

[The Mighty Warrior] then sent for the Master of Prayer,* who gave them a means of repentance and rectification, and thus purified them.

The King ruled over the entire world. The whole world returned to God, and occupied itself only with Torah, prayer,* repentance and good deeds.

Amen, may this be His will. Blessed be God forever, Amen and Amen.

The Scripture states that God has an oven in one place and that the fire is in another place, far from the oven. It is thus written, "The word of God, whose fire is in Zion and whose oven is in Jerusalem" (Isaiah 31:9).

---

dirt caves. *Mechiloth* (מחילות) in Hebrew. The Talmud uses this expression for the caves through which people outside the Holy Land will crawl to the land (*Kethuboth* 111a).
ashamed. The Baal Shem Tov thus taught that the main punishment of the wicked in the next world is shame (see *Likutey Moharan 10*).
Isaiah 2:20. Also see Isaiah 31:7. See end of story.
Master of Prayer. In the morning service, the food represents the sacrificial reading. Then the Master of Prayer must rectify them completely through the rest of the service (see *Likutey Halakhoth, Tefillah* 4:19).
Torah, prayer. Once the lust for money is rectified, then everything else is rectified (*Zimrath HaAretz*).

One should consult this entire chapter, since it relates to the concept of this story.

It is written, "Woe is to those who go down to Egypt for help, and rely on horses" (Isaiah 31:1). "The Egyptians are humans, and not gods, and their horses are flesh, and not spirit" (Isaiah 31:3). This is speaking of the land which the Land of Wealth thought would help them. They assumed that all the people were gods and their horses were angels, as we see in the story. This is why the verse concludes, "The Egyptians are humans, and not gods, and their horses are flesh..." Understand this.

"God shall stretch out His Hand, and the helper shall stumble, and the one being helped shall fall, and they shall perish together" (Isaiah 31:3). This relates to the Hand in the story. On the Hand, [the Master of Prayer] saw that both the helper and the ones seeking help would be destroyed, as mentioned in the story.

"A lion growls over its prey, even though many shepherds are called against it..." (Isaiah 31:4). "As birds fly..." (Isaiah 31:5). [This relates to the lion and the birds in the story.] Look at the story well and you will understand it. "On that day, each man shall cast away his gods of silver and his gods of gold..." (Isaiah 31:7).

"Assyria shall fall by the sword not by man...and she shall flee from the sword... and his rock shall pass away in terror" (Isaiah 31:8,9). This relates to the three powers of the sword in the story. [The expressions, "shall fall" and "shall flee" denote these powers. "His rock shall pass away in terror" denotes the emaciation, where one loses one's strength and power.] The expression "rock" here denotes strength. [This is the third power of the sword.] Look at this carefully, and you will understand.

The section then concludes, "The word of God, whose fire is in Zion and whose oven is in Jerusalem" (Isaiah 31:9). This is the oven and fire in the story. If you look, see and understand, you will find that this chapter explains the entire story.

[All these are the words of the Rebbe, of blessed memory.]

The Rebbe, of blessed memory, said explicitly that the entire story, from beginning to end, is alluded to in this chapter (Isaiah 31). He said everything in the story can be found in various other verses, but the main story is from the above mentioned chapter. However, no one knows how this is true except where he revealed it explicitly.

There are also other concepts in the story that are alluded to in this chapter, but we were not worthy of comprehending them. However, he said explicitly that the entire story is alluded to there.

The order* of the King and his men in the story is: The Master of

---

order. The ten characters in this story parallel the ten sayings with which the world was created (*Chokhmah U'Tevunah* 7). They also parallel the Ten Commandments, as well as the ten things that the Israelites had in the desert (*Parparoth LeChokhmah; Mekhilta, Yithro*). They furthermore parallel the ten levels of holiness in the Holy Land (*Zimrath HaAretz*).

The following material is found at the end of the story in Hebrew:

Many concepts in the story are alluded to in verses such as, "You shall defile your graven images overlaid with silver, and your molten images plated with gold, you shall reject them like something unclean" (Isaiah 30:22). And, as it is written, "On that day, each person shall cast away his idols of silver and his idols of gold... to the digger of fruits... to go into the clefts of the rocks..." (Isaiah 2:20,21). That is, they will throw away the desire for money, which is literally idolatry. They will hide themselves in holes that were dug... as mentioned above, for money stinks, literally, like excrement. It is thus written, "They will make it strange like uncleanness. They will say to it 'Get out' " (Isaiah 30, above) and the like. One can find all the words of this above story in verses, etc.

The order of the King with his men, mentioned above, is this: The Master of Prayer and the Warrior, the Treasurer and the Wise Man, the Bard and the Faithful Friend, the Queen's Daughter with her Child, the King and the Queen.

This is their order. This is the concept of the World of Rectification (*Olam HaTikkun*).

They are ten things and they are not set in order, that is, that they are not set (the above mentioned ten) according to the order mentioned in the books of Kabbalah. However, there is a hidden meaning.

The sacred texts also teach that when the influx (*shefa*) of one attribute passes through a second attribute, and the first influx remains there, then the second attribute sometimes takes on the name of the first one. It is because of this that the order of the characters in this story [is not necessarily the same as the order of the Sefiroth].

There are also other concepts in this that are clear to those who are very expert in the sacred texts. All this our Rabbi, of blessed memory, said explicitly.

I also understood from his words that this story alludes to the death of the "Kings" and their rectification.

Prayer and the Mighty Warrior, the Treasurer and the Wise Man, the Bard and the Faithful Friend, the Queen's Daughter and her Child and the King and Queen.

This is their order. It is related to the World of Rectification (*Olam HaTikkun*).

Both the concept of the destruction and the concept of the rectification are related so that the destruction and rectification are depicted as they are on high. This involves the reasons discussed earlier.

Still, the words are hidden and sealed up. He did not reveal the mystery of this story at all. He only enlightened our eyes with verses and the above mentioned concepts so that we would know that in this story there are great, hidden, awesome mysteries. There is none among us who understands why. Happy is he who is worthy to understand something of the mysteries of these stories mentioned in this book. All of them are wondrous new concepts, very, very awesome; deep, deep, who can find them. What shall we say and what shall we speak? Who heard such as this and who saw such as these?

13

THE SEVEN BEGGARS *

I will tell you how people once rejoiced. *

There was once a king* who had an only son.* The king

The Seven Beggars. This story was begun on a Friday night (March 30, 1810), and was told in parts during the following week (*Chayay Moharan* 15c #49; *Yemey Moharnat* 31b). See next note.

That Friday night, Rabbi Nachman told the first part of the story until the end of the first day after the wedding, where the blind beggar tells his story. Rabbi Nathan was home in Nemerov when the story was told. However, the next Tuesday, his friend, Reb Naftali (see *Yemey Moharnat* 31b), came to his house and repeated the story. Rabbi Nathan was so astounded that he just stood there trembling. He had heard many stories from Rabbi Nachman, but he had never heard anything like that. He went to Breslov that evening, but Rabbi Nachman was already sleeping. The next day, Wednesday (April 4), Rabbi Nachman outlined the entire story, and explained the subplot where each one remembers back as far as he can. This was interrupted when Rabbi Nachman's attendant, Reb Michel (see *Yemey Moharnat* 21b), came in and told them it was time for his meal (*Sichoth HaRan* 149).

As with many lessons and stories, this one began with a mundane discussion, "an awakening from below." Rabbi Nathan reviewed the story with others, but Rabbi Nachman's introductory remarks to the story were lost (*Sichoth HaRan* 151).

Rabbi Nachman himself held that this story was very great. He said, "If I only told the world this one story, I would still be truly great" (*Likutey Halakhoth, Tefillin* 5:1; see end of story). He said that this story could be used as a sermon in synagogue (*Chayay Moharan* 16b #4).

I will tell you... The story happened to be told because one of Rabbi Nachman's followers had sent him a snuff box. Rabbi Nathan wrote one of his friends about it, and told him to remain happy. When Rabbi Nachman saw this letter, he said, "I will tell you how people once rejoiced," and with that, he began the story (*Sichoth HaRan* 149).

According to some sources, Rabbi Nachman's actual words here were, "Since you are so depressed, what do you know about being happy? I will tell you how people once rejoiced" (*Chayay Moharan* 16b #4). According to another source, he said, "I will tell you how, out of depression, people were able to rejoice" (*Chokhmah U'Tevunah* 15:1).

king. God.

wanted to give over his kingdom* to his son during his lifetime.

[On the day of his son's coronation, the king] made a great ball.* Whenever the king makes a ball, there is great rejoicing. But now, when the king was giving over the kingdom to his son during his lifetime, the rejoicing was immense. All the royal ministers, dukes* and officials were there, and they rejoiced greatly at this feast.

[Everyone in] the land was also pleased* by this. It was a great historic event* that the king was giving the kingdom over to his son during his lifetime, and there was great rejoicing. There were all sorts of entertainment at the ball, such as bands,* comedians,* and the like; everything to make people rejoice.*

---

only son. Israel. It is thus written, "My son, my firstborn, is Israel" (Exodus 4:22). In a more general sense, however, this refers to mankind as a whole.

give over his kingdom. God thus gave all dominance to Israel and the righteous. It is thus written that God said, "[I] will say to Zion, you are My people (*ami*, עַמִּי)" (Isaiah 51:16). The *Zohar* says, "Do not read *ami* — "My people" — but *imi* (עִמִּי) — "with Me" so that the verse would read, "[I] will say to Zion, you are with Me." This indicates that the Israelites are God's partners in sustaining and directing the world (*Zohar* 1:5a).

It is possible to say that this occurred with the giving of the Torah, where God promised the Israelites that they would be a "Kingdom of Priests" (Exodus 19:6). This was a time of great rejoicing, as we say in the *Piut* for Shavuoth, "Those on high rejoiced, and those below exulted, when the Torah was received at Sinai."

If we say that the son is mankind as a whole, then this "giving over of power" denotes the creation of the physical world.

The concept of a king giving his son his kingdom during his lifetime is paralleled by King David, who gave his throne to Solomon (see 1 Kings, 2; *Oneg Shabbath*, p. 31).

ball. The Yiddish word "*bal*" is used. Rabbi Nachman taught that there was a concept of dancing when the Torah was given (see *Sichoth HaRan* 86).

dukes. *Dukhsin* in Yiddish.

pleased. The word here is *hana'eh*, which denotes pleasure, but also denotes benefit. It can be translated either way.

historic event. Literally, "honor."

bands. *Kapelesh.*

comedians. *Kamediesh.* See Story #6, p. 132; Story #7, p. 140.

rejoice. There is always rejoicing in God's presence, especially when He is being honored. It is thus written, "Honor and majesty are before Him, strength and joy are in His place" (1 Chronicles, 16:27).

This great, lavish ball at the beginning of the story is to be contrasted with the poor

When the rejoicing reached its peak, the king stood up and said to his son, "I am an expert in astrology, and I see that you are destined to lose your kingdom. When you lose power, be careful not to become depressed; you must remain joyful.* If you are happy, then I will also be happy. But if you become sad, then I will still be happy — because you are no longer king. If you are not able to remain happy when you lose your royal power, then you are not fit to be a king. But if you remain happy, then I will be extremely happy."

The king's son took over the kingdom with a firm hand.* He appointed his own ministers, dukes and officials, and set up his own army.*

The king's son was very wise, and he loved wisdom* very much. He surrounded himself with great sages. Whenever anyone presented him with a wise thought, he cherished it, and gave the person whatever he wanted, whether honor or wealth.* If the

---

conditions of the children's wedding later. Nevertheless, the joy was the same on both occasions.

remain joyful. The lesson is that even if one falls, one must remain happy. If a person allows himself to become depressed, then he deserves his downfall (*Rimzey Maasioth*).

Furthermore, whenever a person falls, it is for the sake of ultimately elevating him further (*Oneg Shabbath*, p. 301). Therefore, when a person remains happy even when he falls, he will eventually reach this higher level (*Ibid.* p. 31).

Here the king told his son to be happy. Later in the story, the beggars make the children happy at their wedding.

firm hand. *Yad ramah* in Hebrew. This means "high-handedly" (see Exodus 14:9). In Yiddish, the expression used is *zehr sharf*, which literally means "very sharp," but idiomatically means "in a very strong manner."

army. He had all the symbols of power, but he became so engrossed in sophistry that he forgot how to use them.

wisdom. Sophistry rather than true wisdom. *Chokhmoth* in Hebrew, which often denotes secular wisdom or mental gymnastics. This was very much like the "wisdom" in the story of "The Sophisticate and the Simpleton."

This might be an allegory of Adam, who "loved wisdom" and hence ate from the Tree of Knowledge. As a result, he forgot the art of war — against evil (see below p. 357).

honor or wealth. The secular world promises honor and wealth. Actually, however, honor and wealth come from God (1 Chronicles, 29:12). The main source of honor and wealth is the Torah (Proverbs 3:16, 8:18, 22:4; cf. Ecclesiastes 6:2).

person wanted wealth he would be given wealth; if he wanted honor, he would be given honor. The [king's son] valued wisdom so much, he would give anything for it.

All the people therefore became involved in academic studies. Soon the entire land was involved with wise thoughts. Those who desired wealth did so to receive wealth [from the king's son], while others did it to gain importance and honor.

Since everyone was immersed in theoretical studies, the land forgot the art of war.* The people became so totally involved in mental gymnastics, that they all became very intelligent, even the least of them. The people developed such high intelligence that the least of them would be the most intelligent people in other lands. The wise men of that land were therefore extremely intelligent.

As a result of their secular studies, the wise men of that land became atheists.* They convinced the king's son of their ideas, and he also became an atheist.

The common people, however, did not become atheists. The arguments of the wise men were so deep and subtle* that the common people could not grasp them, and therefore they were not harmed [by these ideas]. But the king's son and the wise men all became atheists.

Nevertheless, the king's son had a spark of good in him. He had been born with good, and he had a good nature. Whenever he contemplated his situation, and realized what he was doing... he would moan and sigh* because he had fallen into such confused

---

forgot the art of war. The people forgot how to fight against evil (*Likutey Etzoth* B, *Chakirah* 4).

atheists. *Nithpaker* in Hebrew, but "became *apikorsim*" in the Yiddish.

The lesson is that even a great person must be very careful not to be led astray by his intellect. In this land, the people became atheists because of their highly developed intellects (*Rimzey Maasioth*). Secular studies often lead a person away from true belief (*Likutey Etzoth* B, *Chakirah* 4).

deep and subtle. *Dakuth* in Hebrew.

moan and sigh. Even when a person falls away from faith, sometimes he remembers who he is (*Rimzey Maasioth*). In general, a Jew might become weak in belief, but there are times when he doubts his own disbelief.

beliefs. Realizing that he had fallen into error, he would moan and sigh very much. But then he would try to think logically,* and he would once again become immersed in his atheistic ideas.

This happened many times. When he contemplated, he would moan and sigh, but as soon as he began to think logically, his atheistic ideas would overwhelm him.*

One day* there was a mass flight* from a certain country. All the people fled, and in the course of their flight, they passed through a forest. There, a boy and girl* were lost.* One person lost a little boy, and another lost a little girl. They were [both] small children, around four or five years old.*

[The children] did not have any food.* They began to scream and weep because they did not have anything to eat.

Suddenly a beggar* appeared. He had a sack* in which he

---

try to think logically. This is because there are systems of thought that can totally confuse a person's logic. One's logic depends completely on the system of axioms that one accepts initially.

Regarding such use of the intellect it is written, "Do not be overly wise" (Ecclesiastes 7:16) (*Rimzey Maasioth*).

would overwhelm him. This part of the story seems to break off abruptly, and it is not brought to a conclusion (*Rimzey Maasioth*; also see end of story). However, it may be related to the story of the beggar without feet (see below; *Chokhmah U'Tevunah* 15:1). Then, just as the handless beggar healed the king's daughter, the footless one healed the king's son who had lost his faith (*Ibid.*).

One day. Literally, "A day came." See Story #2, p. 62. This may also indicate that this is a continuation of the previous part of the story (*Chokhmah U'Tevunah* 15:1).

mass flight. *Berichah* in Hebrew. Some say that this relates to the king's land. They were exiled because they could not fight (Rabbi Rosenfeld).

This mass flight may refer to the Great Flood, the scattering of people after the Tower of Babel, or the exile of Israel. It may also denote the breaking of the vessels.

boy and girl. *Zakhar* and *nekevah*; literally, "a male and a female." The two children can represent Israel and the Shekhinah, or alternatively, the body and the soul.

were lost. When people flee from the true purpose in life, sensitive people are lost.

four or five years old. Above this, a child is considered to have enough intellect to engage in monetary transactions (*Gittin* 59a).

did not have any food. Perhaps they were as hungry for spiritual food as for material food.

beggar. The beggars are the main characters in the story. The great tzaddikim are called

was carrying bread. The children approached him and began to follow him. He gave them [some bread] and they ate.

"How did you come to be here?" he asked them.

"We don't know," they replied. The were only little children.

When he began to leave, they asked him to take them along. "I do not want* you to go with me," he replied.

Meanwhile they got a better look at him, and they realized that he was blind.* They found this very surprising. If he was blind, how did he find his way? [Actually, it might seem strange that they were surprised at this, since they were still little children. But they were very intelligent children, and therefore found this surprising.]

[The blind beggar] blessed them* that they should be like him, saying that they should be old like him. He left them some bread to eat and he went on his way. The children realized that God was watching over them, and had brought them this blind beggar to give them food.

When the bread was used up, they began to cry for food again. Night fell and they slept. In the morning, they did not have anything to eat, and they cried out and wept.

---

beggars, since they seem very insignificant in the eyes of the world. The light of great tzaddikim is hidden so much that they appear to be totally disabled (*Likutey Etzoth* B, *Tzaddik* 97). Furthermore, they are called beggars because they were worthy of this great level only because they begged God to help them. Rabbi Nachman thus taught that all tzaddikim attained their achievements primarily through prayer (*Rimzey Maasioth*, note at end).

The Yiddish word used for beggar is *betler,* which also means "seeker."

sack. *Tarbas* in Yiddish.

I do not want. Perhaps because they had to meet the other six beggars. Moreover, they would not be worthy of following in his path until they were married.

blind. The seven beggars represent the seven leaders of Israel; Abraham, Isaac, Jacob, Moses, Aaron, Joseph and David. Some say that the blind one represented Isaac, who was blind (Genesis 27:1). The blind beggar also represents the first day of creation, when light was made.

blessed them. Each day a beggar gave them a different blessing. The concept of a different blessing each day is related to the verse, "Bless God each day" (Psalms 68:20) (*Nachath HaShulchan, Yoreh Deah* 242, p. 47a).

Meanwhile, another beggar came. They realized that he was deaf.* As soon as they began to speak to him, he made gestures with his hands indicating that he did not hear. He also gave them some bread. When he was about to leave, they asked him to take them along, but he refused. He also blessed them that they should be like him. With that, he left them some bread and went on his way.

When the bread was used up, they cried out again. Another beggar appeared, and he had a speech defect.* When they began to speak to him, he stammered* so badly that they could not understand what he was saying. He could understand them, but because of his stammering, they could not make out what he was saying. He also gave them bread, and before he left, blessed them that they should be like him. He then went on his way, just as the previous ones had.

Later, another beggar came. He had a crooked neck.* The same thing happened as before.

Then another beggar came, and he was a hunchback.*

Later, a beggar without hands* came.

Finally, they encountered a beggar without feet.*

---

deaf. Some say that he represents Abraham. There is a Midrash that speaks of Abraham as "God's deaf servant."

speech defect. *Kaved peh* in Hebrew. Literally, "heavy of mouth." The Torah speaks of Moses as being *kevad peh* (Exodus 4:10).

stammered. *Megamgem* in Hebrew; *Geshamperet* in Yiddish.

crooked neck. Some say that this is Aaron, who was able to enter the Holy of Holies.

hunchback. *Hokir* in Yiddish. Some say that this is Jacob. He is the pillar who supports the world.

without hands. Some say that this is Joseph, representing the tzaddik, who can rectify the *brit.*

without feet. Some say that this is David. Regarding Malkhuth it is written, David is Malkhuth, and "Her feet go down to death" (Proverbs 5:5).

There is no definite tradition as to which beggar may represent which leader. At the end of the story, however, Rabbi Nachman himself relates King David to the third day.

The seven beggars represent the entire human structure, from head to foot. As we shall see, these beggars were so perfect that, to an imperfect world, they appeared to be disabled (*Rimzey Maasioth*).

As mentioned earlier, the seven beggars, in a sense, denote the "seven shepherds."

Each one of these beggars gave them bread, and blessed them that they should be like him. Each one behaved in the same manner.

When all their bread was used up, they began to walk, [hoping to come] to an inhabited area. They came to a path and followed it until they came to a small town. The children came to a house, and the people had pity on them, and gave them some bread. They went to another house, and the people also gave them food. They thus began to go from door to door. The children realized that things were going well for them, [and that people were giving them bread].*

The children promised each other that they would always remain together. They made themselves large beggars' sacks,* and continued going from door to door.* They also attended all celebrations, such as circumcision ceremonies and weddings.

They then decided to move on, and they went to the larger cities, where they also begged from door to door. They went to the fairs, where they sat together with the other beggars by the fences,* holding their alms plate.

Eventually, these children became well known to all the beggars. They all knew them, and were aware that they were the children who had been lost in the forest.

Once there was a huge fair in one of the large cities. All the beggars went there, and these children were also there. Suddenly the beggars got the idea that these two children would be a perfect match for one another, and that they should be married. As soon as a few of the beggars began to discuss it, they all agreed that it was an excellent idea, and the match was made. The only problem was how to make a wedding.

When they discussed the problem, they realized that soon it

However, Rabbi Nathan said, that since Rabbi Nachman knew these praises, he must have attained these levels himself (*Yemey Moharnat* 44b, 45a).

and that people... In Yiddish but not in Hebrew.

beggars' sacks. *Tarbas* in Yiddish.

from door to door. The beggars all blessed the children that they should be like them, and one benefit that the children derived from this was that they learned to be beggars.

fences. *Prezbes* in Yiddish.

would be the king's birthday, and that he was making a public feast.* All the beggars decided to go there, and any meat and bread that they could beg would be used to make the wedding.

[The beggars] carried out their plan and went to the public feast. All the beggars went to the feast, and they begged meat and bread. They also gathered the meat and fine white bread* that was left over from the feast.

They then went and dug a huge pit, large enough to hold one hundred men. They covered it with reeds, earth and dung.* All of them then entered the pit, and they made a wedding* for the children. [The beggars] brought them under the marriage canopy* and were very, very joyous.*

The bridegroom and bride were also extremely joyous. They

---

public feast. *Minyanes* in Yiddish.

fine white bread. *Kolitch* in Yiddish.

reeds, earth, and dung. The reeds are reminiscent of the covering on a sukkah. However, the dirt and dung are to camouflage the place. When something very holy is done, it sometimes must be camouflaged so that the forces of evil will not deter it. The dirt and dung covering the hole might represent the physical world. It is also possible that the reeds, dirt, and dung represent the three *klipoth*.

It is significant that the beggars only reveal themselves in this pit covered with dung. The true greatness of a tzaddik can only be seen in the physical world (*Likutey Etzoth* B, *Tzaddik* 97).

wedding. The wedding refers to the Messianic age, when there will be a full joining between God (the Bridegroom) and the Shekhinah (the Bride). Alternatively, this can be an allusion to the Giving of the Torah, which the Talmud likens to a wedding (*Taanith* 31a). Actually, if the Israelites had not sinned with the Golden Calf, the Giving of the Torah would have been the final rectification (*Avodah Zarah* 3a).

The lowly state of this wedding can be contrasted with the great pomp in the hall at the beginning of the story. In both cases there was great joy. But the ball at the beginning denoted the joy at creation, while here the joy is because of the rectification of a very imperfect world.

marriage canopy. *Chupah* in Hebrew. This symbolizes the bride and groom entering into one household. The Midrash states that at the Giving of the Torah, God held Mount Sinai over the Israelites like a marriage canopy (*Rokeach* 353).

joyous. Just as the king told his son to be happy, so the beggars now made the couple happy. The first was a case of "awakening from above," while this may be a case of "awakening from below."

began to remember the kindness* that God had shown them when they were in the forest. They wept and yearned* very much, [saying], "If only the first beggar — the blind one — who had brought us bread in the forest — could be here."

[The First Day]

Suddenly, while they were yearning very greatly for the blind beggar,* he spoke up and said: Here I am! I've come to be at your wedding. I am giving you a wedding present* that you should be old like me. I originally gave you this as a blessing,* but now I am giving this as a full gift for your wedding present — that you should have a long life like mine.

You think that I am blind. Actually, I am not blind at all.* But the entire duration* of the world's existence is not considered

---

remember the kindness. When a person experiences a time of joy, he should remember all the good that God has done for him and thank God for it (*Rimzey Maasioth*).

yearned. Because of their yearning for the blind beggar, he came to the wedding. From here we see the power of yearning and longing (see *Likutey Moharan* 31). We also see the level of these children, who could bring about things through their yearning alone (*Rimzey Maasioth*).

Furthermore, they actually mentioned the blind beggar. When a person mentions the name of a tzaddik, he becomes bound to that tzaddik (see *Sefer HaMiddoth, Tzaddik* II, 20). It is for this reason that, when the children mentioned the blind beggar, he came to them (*Chayay Nefesh* 48).

blind beggar. See above.

wedding present. *Matanah liDerashah* in Hebrew; *drasha geshank* in Yiddish. It is a custom for the bridegroom to give a discourse (*derashah*) at his wedding, and the gifts are seen as being given, not for the wedding, but for the discourse. Therefore, they are called *drasha geshank*, or "discourse gifts" (see *Sichoth HaRan*)

blessing. Marriage is an extremely high concept. When a couple is married, they can produce a child, thus bringing down a soul from the highest realms. The source of souls is the Divine itself, higher than all four supernal universes (see *Likutey Moharan* 17). It is for this reason that the seven beggars blessed the couple when they became married (*Likutey Halakhoth, Tefillath Minchah* 7:93).

I am not blind... Both he and the deaf beggar are alluded to in the Messianic prophecy, "Who is blind, except for My servant, and deaf like the messenger I send? Who is blind like the perfect one, blind like God's servant? Seeing many things, you do not watch it, and opening the ears of the deaf, he will not hear" (Isaiah 42:19,20).

the entire duration. This phrase is only in the Hebrew, but not in the Yiddish. Therefore,

by me to be even like the blink of an eye.

(It was for this reason that he appeared to be blind; he did not look at the world* at all. Since the entire duration of the world's existence was not considered by him to be even like the blink of an eye,* the entire concept of looking* at anything in the world or seeing it did not apply to him at all.)

I am extremely old,* but I am completely young.* I have not yet begun to live, but nevertheless, I am very old.

the Yiddish would be translated, "All the world's existence is not considered to be like the blink of an eye." The beggar is saying that he has such an extended concept of time, that the entire duration of the universe's existence is like no more than an eyeblink to him.

did not look at the world. The true tzaddik does not derive any enjoyment whatsoever from the world. On the highest level, he only wants to please God, and does not want even the rewards of the Future World. This is the level of the blind beggar, who did not want even to look at the world (*Likutey Halakhoth, Yoreh Deah, Shiluach HaKen* 4:11, p. 134a).

like the blink of an eye. The blind beggar boasts of his long life. Here we see that his life is so long, that even the duration of the world's existence is like nothing compared to it. Since the duration of the world's existence is like nothing to him, he does not look at the world, and therefore appears to be blind (*Likutey Etzoth* B, *Tzaddik* 88).

In many ways, the blind beggar is like a person who is sleeping. All of time is for him like an instant, and he does not see (*Parparoth LeChokhmah, Eruvin* 65; see *Likutey Moharan Tinyana* 7; see *Chokhmah U'Tevunah* 16).

concept of looking. If a person watches his sight, then he is not susceptible to the Evil Eye, and will have an unusually good memory (see *Likutey Moharan* 54:1). Furthermore, if a person does not look at this world, and always keeps the World to Come in mind, he will also have a great memory. This was the level of the blind beggar (*Likutey Halakhoth, Birkath HaRiyah* 5:8). The blind beggar is thus blind primarily because he is aware that the entire world is nothing more than an illusion.

I am extremely old. This was the level of Isaac, regarding whom it is written, "When Isaac was old, his eyes were dim, so that he could not see" (Genesis 27:1).

Once Rabbi Nachman said, "I am the oldest of the old." It was understood that he was referring to the level of the blind beggar (*Shevachey Moharan* 7a #32).

completely young. On a simple level, this means that he is always beginning to serve God anew. Since one is always making a new beginning, it is as if one's life were just starting. God thus speaks of the commandments "that I command you today" (Deuteronomy 6:6), and the sages teach, "The Torah should always be like something brand new" (*Sifri*). Likewise, Moses told the Israelites, "Listen, Israel, today you are becoming a people to God your Lord" (Deuteronomy 27:9). Rashi comments that this means that one's serving God should always be as if one were starting "today" (*Likutey Halakhoth, Tefillin* 5:5).

Furthermore, God is constantly renewing creation. According to the creation of this instant, then, one has actually not yet begun to serve God. Furthermore, the Ari teaches that every second is completely different, and no one second is like any one that ever existed (*Etz Chaim, Drush Egolim VeYosher* 5). Moreover, when a person makes each day holier than the previous one, he is accomplishing more on that day, and the day thus becomes "longer." This is the mystery of "length of days" (*Likutey Moharan* 60). In order to accomplish this, one must forget everything that he did in previously serving God, and begin anew (*Likutey Halakhoth, loc. cit.; Likutey Etzoth* B, *Tzaddik* 88).

The Evil One is called an "old and foolish king" (Ecclesiastes 4, see *Likutey Moharan* 1). He is given this name because the foolishness that he teaches people is that one is old and weak, and cannot change any more. But here we see that true old age is being able to look at life as if it were just beginning (*Likutey Halakhoth, Tefillin* 5:6).

Thus, we can learn from the blind beggar the power of this continuous renewal. One must be blind when it comes to looking at obstacles in one's path to serving God (*Likutey Halakhoth, Tefillin* 5:9).

God said to the Messiah, "I have given birth to you today" (Psalms 2:7). The Messiah will thus be seen as a newborn babe. Yet at the same time, it is taught that the soul of the Messiah existed from the very beginning of creation (*Likutey Halakhoth, Tefillin* 5:15).

King David, the ancestor of the Messiah, was therefore likened to the moon. The moon is the paradigm of this concept, since it is very old, yet constantly being renewed. The Israelites are also likened to the moon (Song of Songs 7:3). Likewise, the Israelites establish their calendar according to the moon. This is because we must be constantly renewed like the moon (*Likutey Halakhoth, Tefillin* 5:18,19).

This is also the basic concept of the cycles of the month and the year (see *Likutey Moharan Tinyana* 1). Rosh HaShanah is therefore called the "Day of Remembrance" (*Yom HaZikaron*). The blind one, who had perfected the concept of renewal, also had the greatest memory. He was able to reach the highest level of renewal, which is the root of memory (*Likutey Halakhoth, Tefillin* 5:23,24).

Moses thus told the Israelites, "You, who are attached to God, are all alive *today*" (Deuteronomy 4:4). When a person is truly attached to God, then he is in a constant state of renewal, just as God is constantly renewing creation. Then his life is just beginning "today" (*Likutey Halakhoth, Tefillin* 5:25).

If Adam had not sinned, he would have been included, to the greatest possible extent, in the Infinite Being (*Ain Sof*). Of course, he could not have kept contact with *Ain Sof*, but he would have touched it for the most infinitesimal instant, this being the concept of "running and returning" (Ezekiel 1:14). He would then have been infinitely old and infinitely young, just like the blind beggar (*Likutey Halakhoth, Tefillin* 5:18).

Kabbalistically, this is the level of Kether. Kether is the first and oldest of the sefiroth, yet it is before time, and thus, has not yet begun to exist. Thus, the Divine Name associated with Kether is *Ehyeh*, (אהיה) which means, "I will be" (Exodus 3:14). This is the level where being has not yet begun. It is the concept of being in a state of pregnancy, where one can only say, "I will be," and not "I am." God revealed this name to Moses just before the Exodus, which was the birth of Israel (*Likutey Halakhoth, Tefillin* 5:26; cf. *Likutey Moharan* 6).

The Exodus is seen as a concept of birth (Ezekiel 16:5). Similarly, the final

This is not merely my own opinion; I also have the word* of the Great Eagle.* Let me tell you the story·*

redemption is also a concept of birth, as it is written, "Zion shall give birth to her children" (Isaiah 66:8) (*Likutey Halakhoth, Tefillin* 5:29).

The redemption, again, can only be brought about through repentance. This is the concept of beginning anew, and particularly, a new start each day. This is the concept of the youth of the blind beggar (*Likutey Halakhoth, Tefillin* 5:32).

If the seven beggars are seen as paralleling the seven lower sefiroth, then the blind beggar would parallel the sefirah of Chesed, as well as the first day of creation. This is logical, because on the first day light was created, but it was a light that was stored away for the righteous in the World to Come, and not a worldly light. Hence, one who saw with this light would be blind to everything worldly.

It is significant to note that in the story of the Master of Prayer, the sefirah of Chesed is also apparently represented by a child.

word. *Haskamah* in Hebrew. The word means agreement or approbation.

Great Eagle. The obvious allusion here is to the verse, "[God] satisfied your old age with good things, so that your youth is renewed like the eagle" (Psalms 103:5). Rashi comments on this that an eagle becomes younger the older it gets. As we shall see, just like the blind beggar, the Eagle is also very old, yet very young (*Likutey Halakhoth, Tefillin* 5:5).

The Eagle, of course, was one of the animals that Ezekiel saw in the *merkavah* (Ezekiel 1:10). It is taught that of these animals, the lion represents the Messiah son of David, the ox represents the Messiah son of Joseph, and the eagle represents Elijah (*Reshith Chokhmah, Chupath Eliahu*). Thus the animals in the *merkavah* represent the personages involved in the redemption. It is also taught that Divine Inspiration (*ruach hakodesh*) brings Elijah. Elijah brings the resurrection (*Avodah Zarah* 20b). Thus, it is Elijah who tells the people to go back to their bodies (*Chokhmah U'Tevunah* 16).

Others, however, say that the Eagle here represents God Himself, as it is written, "As an eagle stirs up its nest...so God led them..." (Deuteronomy 32:11,12). It is also taught that one of the keys that God never gave to another is the key to resurrection (*Taanith* 2a) (*Chokhmah U'Tevunah* 16, in note).

Other sources say that the Great Eagle is the angel in charge of the resurrection. This is also apparent later from the story (*Rimzey Maasioth*).

Later we see that the Eagle also said that it "was very old but very young." This might be alluded to in the verse, "I was young, and I have also become old" (Psalms 37:25). The Talmud states that this verse was said by the angel Metatron (*Yebamoth* 16a). The *Zohar*, however, also says that Metatron is the angel in charge of the resurrection (*Zohar* 1:181b; *Rimzey Maasioth*).

the story. The story of the elders is a story from "ancient times," that is, from another plane of reality (cf. *Likutey Moharan* 60; *Likutey Halakhoth, Tefillin* 5:18). The first generations after Adam were an aspect of Arikh Anpin, and all the events that happened then were stories from "ancient times" (*Likutey Halakhoth, Tefillin* 5:21).

Once upon a time, people took to the sea* in many ships.* A great storm came, and shattered the ships.* The people, however, survived, and they came to a tower. They went up into the tower,* and there they found food, drink, clothing,* and everything else that they needed. All good things, and every pleasure in the world was there.

The people began to converse, and they decided that each one should tell an ancient story involving his earliest memory.* Each one would tell what he remembered from the time that his memory began.

There were old and young people present. They honored the oldest man among them to tell his story first.

---

people took to the sea. These were the souls of the righteous, who came down to the world (*Rimzey Maasioth*).

ships. The story later states explicitly that these ships are the bodies. The *Zohar* also speaks of the ship that carried Jonah as being an allusion to the body that serves as a vehicle for the soul (*Zohar* 2:199a; *Rimzey Maasioth*).

shattered the ships. This is death, where the body is shattered (*Rimzey Maasioth*; cf. *Zohar* 2:199a).

tower. This is the world of souls, where souls remain until the time of the resurrection (*Rimzey Maasioth* see *Derekh HaShem* 1:3,11,12). The tower is reminiscent of the Pearl Castle in "The Lost Princess."

food, drink, clothing. Food in the Future World is Torah, while clothing is good deeds (*Sichoth HaRan* 23).

earliest memory. This is not simple memory, but the memory of souls involving the highest levels of creation (cf. *Rimzey Maasioth*). All of these tzaddikim were boasting about the supernal worlds. Each one boasted about what he had gained in an upper world (*Likutey Halakhoth, Tefillin* 5:1).

Rabbi Nathan teaches that this entire episode involves tefillin, since tefillin are an aspect of memory, as it is written, "They shall be a sign on your hand, and a memory device (*zikaron*) between your eyes" (Exodus 13:9). The Torah specifically says, "between your eyes," because as we see in this story, memory depends on the rectification of the eyes. Thus, the blind beggar ended up having the best memory of all. Elsewhere, Rabbi Nachman also teaches that memory depends on the eyes (*Likutey Moharan* 54; *Likutey Halakhoth, Tefillin* 5:3).

Thus, the eight old men here represent the eight sections (*parshioth*) in the tefillin, four in the head tefillin, and four in the hand tefillin (*Ibid.*).

Tefillin are related to the eight sections of Aaron's beard. These are the source of the eight writings. This is the holiness ôf old age (*Ibid.*).

"What shall I tell you?" he said. "I can even remember when they cut the apple from the branch."*

No one understood what he meant. However, there were wise men there, and they said, "This is obviously a very ancient story."

They then honored the second one to tell his story. The second one, who was not as old as the first, said, "Is that then an old story?* That story I also remember! But I can also remember when the lamp* was lit!"

"This story is even older than the first!" said [the wise men]. But they were quite surprised, since the second one was not quite as old as the first, but still, he could remember an older event.

They then honored the third one to tell his story. The third one, who was younger [than the first two], said, "I remember when the fruit began to have a structure — that is, when the fruit began to be put together."*

Memories such as these are also found in the Talmud. A number of Talmudic sages remembered events surrounding their births (*Yerushalmi, Kethuboth* 5; *Likutey Halakhoth, Tefillin* 5:45, end; *Rimzey Maasioth*).

In general, these saints were able to annul time; therefore, they had good memories. The higher a man's level, the more time is annulled for him (*Likutey Halakhoth, Milah* 4:5).

One can transcend time by closing one's eyes in pain (cf. *Likutey Moharan* 65). Then, even though he does not see, his destiny (*mazal*) sees (*Megillah* 3a). A child experiences this when it closes its eyes in pain at the time of circumcision. That is why the beggar who was above time appeared to be totally blind (*Likutey Halakhoth, Milah* 4:7).

apple from the branch. As we shall see, this is the cutting of the umbilical cord. All the allegories here are later explained by the Eagle (see *Likutey Halakhoth, Tefillin* 5:2).

an old story. From this we can understand the level of this second old man. To him, the first one's accomplishment was a joke. This is what the *Zohar* says, "each universe is like a point compared to the one above it" (*Tikkuney Zohar* 70, 123a; *Likutey Halakhoth, Tefillin* 5:1).

Thus, even though each of these elders was very high, he was like nothing compared to the one above him. This is true in every category. From each spiritual level, there is another which is infinitely higher (*Likutey Halakhoth, Yoreh Deah, Shiluach HaKen* 4:11, p. 134a).

lamp. see below.

put together. *Rakam* in Hebrew; that is, when it was "knit" or "embroidered" together. This usage is found in the verse, "I was knit together in the lowest places of the earth" (*Psalms* 139:15, cf. Rashi, *Metzudoth ad loc.*). In Yiddish it is, "I remember the beginning

"That story is even older," they responded.

The fourth one, who was still younger, spoke up, "I also remember when the seed was brought to plant the fruit."

The fifth one, who was younger yet, said, "I also remember when the wise men invented* the seed."

The sixth one, who was younger still,* said, "I remember the taste of the fruit before it entered the fruit."

The seventh one spoke up, "I remember the fragrance of the fruit before it entered the fruit."

The eighth one said, "I remember the appearance of the fruit before it was drawn* onto the fruit."

I was also there at the time, and I was still an infant. I spoke up and said to them, "I remember all these events, and I remember *absolutely nothing*."*

"This is a very ancient story," said [the wise men], "more so than all the others." They were very surprised that a child remembered more than any of them.

In the midst of this, the Great Eagle came and knocked on the tower. "Stop being poor!* Return to your treasures! Make use of your treasures!"

He then told them to leave the tower in order of their age, with the oldest going out first.

As he brought them out of the tower, he brought [me], the infant, out first, since I* was actually older than all the rest, and

---

of the structure of the fruit, when the fruit began to become a fruit."

invented. *Mamtzi* in Hebrew, which can mean invent or bring into existence.

In Yiddish the word is *ois getracht,* which means "thought up."

who was younger still. Only in the Yiddish, represented by ellipses in the Hebrew.

drawn. In Yiddish it is, "I remember the appearance of the fruit before the appearance was on the fruit."

I remember absolutely nothing. *Un ich gedenk gar nisht* in Yiddish. This means that he could remember back to the time when absolutely nothing existed (*Sichoth HaRan* 149; cf. *Likutey Halakhoth, Milah* 4:5).

Stop being poor. In the world of souls, people only have a glimmer of the perception that they will have in the World to Come, which is the world that will exist after the resurrection.

I. The text uses the third person "he."

he was bringing us out in order of age. Actually, the youngest was the oldest, and the oldest of them was the youngest.*

[The Great Eagle] then said, "I will explain the stories that each one told.

"The [first] one said that he remembered when they cut the apple from the branch. He was saying that he remembered* when they cut his umbilical cord.* [He was saying that he remembered when he was born, and they cut his navel cord.]

---

the oldest ... was the youngest. Thus, the blind beggar, who was the youngest, was really the oldest. Moses was both old and young. He is described as "a child weeping" (Exodus 2:6), even though he already had every perfection. Regarding him the verse states, "I was young, but I have also become old" (Psalms 37:25). Moses also attained the same perfection of vision as the blind beggar, as it is written, "his eyes were not dimmed" (Deuteronomy 34:7).

Moses was also on the level of constantly beginning anew. He thus said to God, "You have begun to show Your servant" (Deuteronomy 3:24). Even though he had received the Torah and had led the Israelites for forty years in the desert, he felt as if he had just begun.

Since Moses felt as if he had not yet begun to serve God, he was always very humble. The *Zohar* also says that with the young, Moses was young, while with the old, he was very old (*Likutey Halakhoth, Tefillin* 5:36).

remembered. The Talmud relates that Shmuel remembered the pain of his circumcision (*Yerushalmi Kethuboth* 5).

cut his umbilical cord. This was his final detachment from his mother's body. We see that this is speaking of something above the common realm, since there is no one alive who can remember having his umbilical cord cut.

This old man is alluded to in the straps of the tefillin, which must extend as far as the navel. The final stage of birth is the cutting of the umbilical cord. The Exodus from Egypt was also like the cutting of the umbilical cord. God therefore told the Israelites that before the Exodus, "Your umbilical cord was not cut" (Ezekiel 16:4). Tefillin recall the Exodus, which is the cutting of the umbilical cord, and hence, the straps must extend as far as the navel.

It is true that the other elders remembered more, but their memories are hidden in the parchments inside the tefillin boxes. The only one to whom we can relate is the first one, and he is also represented by the *retzuah*-strap which extends outside the tefillin (*Likutey Halakhoth, Tefillin* 5:16).

With the cutting of the umbilical cord, a child becomes independent of his mother. It is from the cutting of the umbilical cord that the seventy years of human life come. This is the level of stories of "ancient times." This is received from this first elder, since the others are not revealed to the external world (*Likutey Halakhoth, Tefillin* 5:20).

On a deeper Kabbalistic level, there are four levels in the human body: bone, sinews,

"The second one said that he remembered when the lamp was burning. He could also remember when he was in his mother's womb, with a lamp burning over his head.*

"The [third] one said that he remembered when the fruit began to form. He could remember when his body began to knit together as the fetus took its form.

"The [fourth] one said that he remembered when the seed was brought to be planted. He remembered how the drop was emitted at the time of conception.*

---

flesh, and skin. Skin is therefore an aspect of Malkhuth, the lowest of the four levels. The cutting of the navel cord thus represents the rectification of the skin, the outermost level of the body. The bones, sinews and flesh are rectified within the body, but the skin is not rectified until the umbilical cord is cut.

The *partzufim* (Divine personae) stand in such a way that each one ends at the level of the navel of the one above it. Hence, when the first elder remembers his navel cord, he is actually speaking of the link between the supernal *partzufim* and universes. This process begins when the world of *nekudim* (dots) comes out under the navel of Adam Kadmon (*Likutey Halakhoth, Tefillin* 5:34).

This is also related to the concept of the Holy Land. Jerusalem is thus called "the navel of the earth" (*Zimrath HaAretz*).

lamp burning over his head. The Talmud teaches that before a child is born, while it is in the womb, it has a lamp over its head with which it looks from one end of the universe to the other (*Niddah* 30b). This is based on Job's words, "Oh, that I was as in the months of old, in the days when God watched over me, when *His lamp shone above my head,* and I walked through darkness by His light" (Job 29:2,3). The light with which one can see from one end of the earth to the other is the light that God created at the very beginning, and then put aside for the righteous in the World to Come. The Midrash states explicitly that with this light one can see from one end of the universe to the other (Rashi on Genesis 1:4; *Likutey Halakhoth, Tefillin* 5:1). An unborn child can have such perception, since evil has no grasp on a child before he is born (*Anaf Yosef,* on *Eyn Yaakov, Niddah* 30b).

Death can be seen as a birth into a new dimension. Therefore, it is customary to light a lamp for the death anniversary (*yahrzeit*) of a close relative. The *yahrzeit* lamp parallels the lamp that burns over a child's head before he is born (*Likutey Halakhoth, Tefillin* 5:43).

of conception. It is significant to note that among these eight elders, the first four remember events that occurred in the womb, while the last four remember events that preceded the womb. Thus, in a sense, the first four have a feminine memory, while the second four have a male memory (that pertains to their fathers).

This is related to the eight readings in the tefillin, of which four are in the head tefillin and four are in the hand tefillin. The hand tefillin is a female aspect, so its four readings pertain to the first four elders. The head tefillin, on the other hand, represents the male

"The [fifth] one remembered the wise men who discovered the seed. He remembered when the seed was still in the brain.* [The brain's mental power gives rise to the drop.]

"The [sixth] one remembered the taste. This is the *nefesh*-soul.*

---

aspect, and hence, the second four elders (*Likutey Halakhoth Tefillin* 5:3). The significance of this is discussed somewhat.

The four readings in the tefillin are Sh'ma (Deuteronomy 6:4-9), *Vahaya im shamoa* (Deuteronomy 11:13-21), *Kadesh* Exodus 13:2-10), and *Vahaya ki yaviakha* (Exodus 13:11-16). Respectively, they speak of faith in God, keeping the commandments, sanctification of the firstborn, and entering the promised land.

The Sh'ma, which speaks of our relationship to God, parallels the first elder, who remembers conception and intercourse. Sh'ma speaks of unity, and in a sense, this unity is like a joining of Israel and God. Indeed, the *Zohar* states that the seven blessings surrounding the Sh'ma (three in the morning, and four in the evening) are the *Sheva Berakhoth* (seven marital blessings) for this union.

Vahaya im shamoa, which speaks of our obligation to keep the commandments, parallels the second elder, who remembered when his body began to form. There are 613 commandments, 248 positive, and 365 negative, paralleling the 248 limbs and 365 nerves in the body. Hence, the perfection of the body's formation is the keeping of the commandments.

Kadesh, the third reading, parallels the one who remembered the light over his head. *Kadesh* speaks of the miracles surrounding the Exodus, when God's glory was revealed to the Israelites. This revelation parallels the light over the child's head. The ten plagues, of which the killing of the firstborn was the last, marked the end of the "pregnancy" of the Israelites. The "lamp over their head" may also allude to the giving of the Torah, which was the end of the "pregnancy" of the Jewish people.

VaHaya ki yaviakha relates to entering the Holy Land. This is the cutting of the umbilical cord of the Israelites. As long as they were in the desert, they were nourished by the manna, food which came directly from God, very much as a child is nourished through its navel cord. But when they entered the Holy Land, the manna stopped, and they had to provide their own food. This parallels the cutting of the navel cord in a child (cf. *Likutey Halakhoth, Tefillin* 5:12, 5:15).

seed was still in the brain. It is a Kabbalistic teaching that the sperm has its origin in the father's brain. This might mean that the main thing that the father imparts in the sperm is information, on the level of Chokhmah. In any case, we see that the fifth elder has a memory that transcends the womb and goes back to his father.

nefesh-soul. The Torah uses three words for the soul: *nefesh* (meaning rest), *ruach* (meaning wind), and *neshamah* (meaning breath). The Kabbalists liken it to a glassblower, where the process begins with his breath, extends through his blowing tube as wind, and then comes to rest in the vessel being formed.

"[The seventh one remembered] the fragrance. This is the *ruach*-spirit.*

"[The eighth one remembered] the appearance. This is the *neshamah*-essence.*

When this elder said that he remembers when the taste was placed in the fruit, he was indicating that he remembered when his *nefesh*-soul was drawn from on high (*Likutey Halakhoth, Tefillin; Likutey Halakhoth, Tefillath Minchah* 7:93).

Taste requires actual contact with the thing being tasted. In a similar manner, the *nefesh*-soul is in direct contact with the body.

The three parts of the soul, *nefesh, ruach* and *neshamah*, represent the three inner lights of the person, enclosed within the form of his body. Similarly, the body has three inner parts, bone, sinew and flesh, enclosed within the skin. The first elders recalled the beginnings of bone, sinew, flesh, and skin, while the second group recalled the *nefesh, ruach, neshamah* and form (*Likutey Halakhoth, Tefillin* 5:34).

ruach-spirit. *Ruach* means wind, and fragrance is carried by the wind.

Furthermore, taste involves the mouth, which represents the sefirah of Malkhuth and parallels the *nefesh*. Smell involves the nose, which represents Zer Anpin, and parallels the *ruach*.

neshamah-essence. Thus, there are eight elders, four with a feminine memory (involving their relationships with their mothers), and four with a masculine memory (involving their existence before conception).

As mentioned earlier, these represent the eight readings in the tefillin. The four in the head tefillin represent the four elders with masculine memories, while the four in the hand tefillin represent the four with feminine memories (*Likutey Halakhoth, Tefillin* 5:3).

The eight elders also parallel the eight "rectifications" (*tikkunim*) of Aaron's beard. These parallel the eight priestly vestments. The blind beggar, the ninth one, then represents Moses. It is thus written, "The midwives feared God, and He made for them houses" (Exodus 1:21). Our sages say that one of these midwives was Yocheved, and the "houses" speak of Moses and Aaron. It is also taught that the "houses" represent the tefillin, since the boxes are called *batim*, which literally means "houses." Thus, Moses and Aaron in a sense represent the tefillin, as well as the nine elders here (*Likutey Halakhoth, Tefillin* 5:36).

It is also taught that in the Makhpelah Cave, four pairs were buried: Adam and Eve, Abraham and Sarah, Isaac and Rebecca, and Jacob and Leah (*Eruvin* 53a). These eight individuals also parallel the eight portions in the tefillin, and hence, the eight elders. Thus, again, four of the elders have masculine memories, and four have feminine memories (*Likutey Halakhoth, Tefillin* 5:39).

The eight elders can also be seen as paralleling the eight days preceding circumcision. The Kabbalistic texts teach that cutting off the foreskin (*chitukh*) annuls the three *klipoth*, while the uncovering of the glans (*periyah*) annuls the *klipath nogah*, which is a mixture of good and bad. The *chitukh* is represented by the eight elders, while the *periyah* is represented by the blind beggar, who is higher than all of them (*Likutey Halakhoth, Milah* 4:5, 4:9; cf. *Likutey Moharan* 72).

"Finally, there was the child who said that he remembered absolutely nothing. He is higher than all the rest, since he remembered even what was before the *nefesh*-soul, the *ruach*-spirit, and the *neshamah*-essence. This is the concept of Nothingness."*

Nothingness. This is the level which no thought can grasp. Therefore it is experienced as Nothingness.

If the eight elders represent the eight readings in the tefillin, the blind beggar would represent the source of their holiness. He is so high that his concept cannot be included in any of the readings. He is on a level that touches the Infinite (*Ain Sof*). He cannot remember anything because his mind is above the concept of memory. He remembers everything that the other elders do, but in his case, this cannot be called memory at all. He is the root of memory, much higher than memory (*Likutey Halakhoth, Tefillin* 5:3; see *Chokhmah U'Tevunah* 16).

This beggar was blind, because he had rectified his eyes completely. Since the tefillin are worn "between the eyes," this is the source of the light of the eight readings in the tefillin. From there it extends to the strap that comes down to the navel, which represents the first elder, who gives the light to the world (*Likutey Halakhoth, Tefillin* 5:34).

In Kabbalah, it is taught that the light from the eyes of Adam Kadmon is revealed as the world of *nekudim* (dots) below his navel (*Etz Chaim, Shaar HaNekudim*). This light of *nekudim* is taken from his eyes, and then channeled through the eight "rectifications" of his beard. The breaking of vessels comes from his eyes, and it is for this reason that in warning us to keep from sin, the Torah says, "Do not stray after your eyes" (Numbers 15:39). The blind beggar purifies his eyes and rectifies both this concept and the breaking of vessels (*Ibid.*).

Marriage is a very high concept. The union of man and woman can bring down a soul from the highest reaches. This is why the first beggar came and told them about memories of birth, and even before conception. He is telling them the levels they will have to reach to bring down a soul to the world. The blind beggar himself then tells them that they must even reach up to the level of Nothingness to bring down a soul (*Likutey Halakhoth, Tefillath Minchah* 7:93).

In one way, the blind beggar doesn't remember anything because he remembers what the soul was like even before the *tzimtzum*. Since the Messiah comes from the highest level, he can rectify even the lowest (*Ibid.*).

When a person is sexually pure, he is connected to the source of souls. This is the concept of circumcision, which relates to the elders, as mentioned earlier. When a person commits sexual misdeeds, the penalty is *kareth* (כרה), being cut off before one's time, which is the opposite of old age. The old men in the story were on a level of Kether (כתר) which has the same letters as *kareth*, but is its rectification. Kether is related to Arikh Anpin, whose beard has thirteen rectifications. These parallel the thirteen covenants that were made with regard to circumcision (*Nedarim* 31b).

He then said to them, "Return to your ships, which are your bodies.* They were shattered, but they will be rebuilt. Now go back to them." With that, he blessed them.

The Great Eagle then said to me, "You come with me, since you are just like me. You are very old, and at the same time very young; you have not yet begun to live, but you are extremely old. I am the same, since I am old and at the same time, I am young..."

Therefore, I have the word of the Great Eagle [that I have lived a very long life].

Now, I am giving you my long life as a wedding present.*

[When the beggar said this,] there was tremendous joy and rejoicing there.*

[The Second Day]*

On the second of the seven days of celebration,* the couple

Thus, a true tzaddik, who is sexually pure and keeps the covenant of Abraham, is considered old. He gets his power from the blind beggar who is the highest of these old men (*Likutey Halakhoth, Milah* 4:8).

The Talmud teaches that the commandment, "Do not stray after your eyes" is a commandment specifically related to sexual chastity. The blind beggar perfected this to its highest degree, and therefore also attained the highest level of sexual chastity. Thus, he could see into the highest reaches from where the soul was drawn.

which are your bodies. Here we see explicitly that the ships represent the body. This is speaking of the resurrection of the dead (*Rimzey Maasioth*).

wedding present. *Drasha geshank*, see above. The beggars gave these gifts at the wedding, because a wedding is the first stage of the coupling of man and woman that brings souls down to the world. To bring down a soul requires all the powers of the seven sefiroth (*Likutey Halakhoth, Tefillath Minchah* 7:93).

there. At this point, Rabbi Nachman's attendant, Reb Michel (*Yemey Moharnat*, p. 21b) came in and told Rabbi Nathan to leave, since it was time for the Rebbe's meal (*Sichoth HaRan* 149).

The Second Day. On Wednesday, April 4, after Rabbi Nachman had eaten and taken a short nap, Rabbi Nathan returned, telling the Rebbe how the wealthy people in Berdichev are constantly in debt. He quoted the verse, "[God] has set the world in their heart, so that men cannot find out God's deeds from the beginning to the end" (Ecclesiastes 3:11). Rabbi Nachman said, "Is this not our tale? Where are we holding now?" He then began to tell the story of the second day (*Sichoth HaRan* 149; *Likutey Halakhoth, Evven HaEzer, P'ru U'R'vu* 3:32).

seven days of celebration. It is customary to make a feast for the first seven days after a

began to remember the second beggar, the deaf one, who had sustained them and given them bread. They wept and yearned, "How can we bring here the deaf beggar who sustained us?"

While they were yearning for him, he suddenly appeared and said, "Here I am!" He fell on them and kissed them.

He then said to them: Now I will give you a gift that you should be like me. You should live a good life* like mine. I originally gave you this as a blessing, but now, as your wedding present, I am giving you this as an unrestricted gift.

You think that I am deaf. I am not deaf at all. But the whole world does not amount to anything to me that I should listen* to its shortcomings.

All sounds come from deficiencies,* since everyone cries out because of what he is lacking. Even all the joys of the world are the result of lacks, since it is only because one has a lack that one

---

wedding, during which the seven nuptial blessings (*Sheva Berakhoth*) are recited. We find this at the weddings of Jacob (Genesis 29:27) and Samson (Judges 14:12). The seven days of celebration parallel the seven days of creation.

good life. This is a life that reflects the life in the World to Come, living on a high spiritual plane. The Israelites were worthy of a good life in the Land of Israel, since it was a "land that has no lack" (Deuteronomy 8:9; *Zimrath HaAretz*),

that I should listen. The deaf beggar did not want to derive any enjoyment from hearing the sounds of the world (*Likutey Halakhoth, Choshen Mishpat, HaOseh Sheliach LiG'both Chovo* 2:10, p. 82a).

deficiencies. *Chasronoth.* All worldly sounds are an echo of the True Voice (*Likutey Moharan Tinyana* 23). This echo is the source of all the deficiencies in the world. It is the sound of worldly foolishness that results from the constriction (*tzimtzum*).

The Torah is the direct sound that was the power of all creation. An echo is a direct sound that strikes a barrier and is reflected. In the original *tzimtzum*, there was a thin line of Light that entered the Vacated Space. This was the light of the Torah. It struck the central point, and produced the reflected light, or the echo.

The ring of Light was the direct voice with which all things were created, as it is written, "With God's Word the heavens were made" (Psalms 33:6). When this voice hits the central point, which is the final barrier of the *tzimtzum*, it creates an echo. This is so much like the direct Voice, that one can be mistaken and think it to be the True Voice. This is the source of Free Will (*Likutey Halakhoth, Evven HaEzer, P'ru U'R'vu* 3:32).

The Echo is lacking in Divine Power and good. Since this echo is the source of all worldly sounds, they are not holy; they have some worldly desire in them (*Ibid.* 3:34).

rejoices when this lack is filled. But the entire world does not amount to anything for me that I should allow its deficiencies to enter my ears.*

I have a good life where nothing is lacking. I have the word* of the Land of Wealth* that I live the good life. (His good life was that he had bread to eat* and water to drink.)

[He then told them the story]:

There was a land that had lots of wealth and great treasures.* Once, the people got together, and each one began to boast about how he lived the good life. Each one related exactly what kind of good life he had.

I spoke up and said, "I am living a good life that is better than your good life. If you want proof, [let me tell you about a certain land]. If you are truly living a good life, let's see if you can save this land.*

"This land had a garden.* This garden had fruit which had every taste in the world. It also had every fragrance in the world. It also had every sight in the world — every color and every kind

---

to enter my ears. A true tzaddik lacks nothing, and therefore does not have any need to hear any worldly sounds. He therefore appears to be deaf (*Likutey Etzoth* B, *Tzaddik* 99).

word. *Haskamah*, see above p. 366.

Land of Wealth. The wealthy people in this land were the great tzaddikim, who were wealthy in good deeds (*Rimzey Maasioth*). This is in contrast to the Land of Wealth in the story of "The Master of Prayer."

bread to eat... A true tzaddik can find all tastes in bread and water (*Rimzey Maasioth*). It is also taught, "This is the way of Torah, eat bread and salt, and drink water by measure" (*Avoth* 6:4). The Mishnah concludes, "If you do this, happy are you, and it shall be good for you — happy are you in this world, and it shall be good for you in the World to Come."

The deaf beggar is to be compared in this respect to the Simpleton in "The Sophisticate and the Simpleton," who also tasted all foods in his bread.

great treasures. Tzaddikim have great spiritual treasures (*Rimzey Maasioth*). These are the treasures of good life that they have stored in the World to Come (*Likutey Etzoth* B, *Tzaddik* 90). King Monvoz thus said, "My ancestors amassed treasures in this world, but I will amass treasures in the World to Come" (*Bava Bathra* 11a).

save this land. There are levels that can only be helped by the greatest possible tzaddik (*Likutey Etzoth* B, *Tzaddik* 90).

garden. The world of the spiritual.

of flower.* Everything was in that garden.

"There was a gardener* in charge of this garden. Because of that garden, the people of that land lived a good life.*

"The gardener then vanished.* With no one tending the garden, everything in the garden naturally withered and died. Nevertheless, the people were still able to live from the wild plants* that grew in the garden.

"A cruel king* then attacked the land, but he was not able to do anything to the people. He therefore decided to ruin the good life that the land had from the garden. However, he did not ruin the garden itself. Instead, he left three groups of servants.*

"He ordered them to follow his instructions, and thus ruin the people's sense of taste. As a result of what they did, whenever anyone tasted anything, it had the taste of a rotten carcass.*

"They also ruined the sense of smell. Every fragrance that the people smelled had the stench of galbanum.*

"They also destroyed the sense of sight. They dimmed the people's eyes, as if they were covered with clouds and mists.*

"[All this was done at the cruel king's command.] Now if you

---

flower. *Kviyatin* in Yiddish.

gardener. *Gradnik* in Yiddish. The *Zohar* states that the gardener is the tzaddik who tends the spiritual world and distributes its power (*Zohar* 2:166b; *Likutey Moharan* 65; *Rimzey Maasioth*; cf. *Kedushath Shabbath*; *Sichoth HaRan* 252).

lived a good life. Everyone in the world can have a good life from the spiritual world (*Likutey Etzoth* B, *Tzaddik* 90).

vanished. The gardener vanished because of our sins (*Ibid.*).

wild plants. The spiritual realm has enough to nourish the world even without the tzaddik (cf. *Ibid.*).

cruel king. The Evil One (*Likutey Etzoth* B, *Tzaddik* 90).

three groups of servants. They were to ruin the taste, sight, and fragrance. In a sense, they were to ruin the concept of the Sabbath. The preparations for the Sabbath include setting the table (taste), lighting a lamp (sight), and making the bed (fragrance, see below) (*Kedushath Shabbath*).

rotten carcass. *Nevelah.*

galbanum. *Chelbanah* in Hebrew. This was one of the ingredients of the Temple incense (Exodus 30:34).

clouds and mists. These are the clouds that cover the eye (*Likutey Etzoth* B, *Tzaddik* 90).

are truly living the good life, let's see if you can save them. I am telling you this because, if you do not save them, then the damage that has stricken this land can also harm you."*

The wealthy people set off toward that land, and I also went with them. While travelling, each of them lived the good life in his way, since each one had taken along his treasures.

However, as soon as they came near that land, their sense of taste began to go bad. They also began to feel that other things were also being spoiled for them.

I said to them, "You have not even entered the land yet, and your sense of taste etc. is ruined... What will happen once you actually get there? How will you be able to save them?"

I then took my bread and water and gave some to them. As soon as they tasted* my bread and water, their sense of taste was remedied.* [The same was true of their sense of smell and the like...]

Meanwhile, the people of the land [that had the garden] began to look for ways to remedy their senses that had been ruined... Their conclusion involved the Land of Wealth [from which I was now coming]. It seemed that their lost gardener [who had provided them with the good life] had the same roots as the people of the Land of Wealth, who also had a good life. Therefore, their plan was to send a delegation to the Land of Wealth, who would certainly be able to help them.

They sent messengers to the Land of Wealth. Along the way, the messengers met [the people from the Land of Wealth, with whom I had gone].

---

can also harm you. The Talmud thus teaches that an incomplete tzaddik can be "swallowed" by evil. Only a complete tzaddik is not touched by it (*Berakhoth* 7b; Rabbi Rosenfeld).

tasted. "Taste and see that God is good..." (Psalms 34:9).

remedied. When people want to remedy things, they go to the great tzaddikim. But in the end, even these tzaddikim need the power of the greatest tzaddik, who here is represented by the deaf beggar (*Likutey Etzoth* B, *Tzaddik* 91).

The true tzaddik shares his good life with others, and he can then undo any spiritual damage that they may have experienced.

"Where are you going?" they asked the messengers.

"We are going to the Land of Wealth," they replied. "We want them to help us."

"We ourselves are from the Land of Wealth," said the others. "We are on our way to you."

I said to the others, "Actually, you need me. You cannot go there yourselves,* as you have already seen. You stay here. I will go with the messengers, and help the land."

I went with them, and we came to a city in the land. When I arrived, I saw a few people come and begin to tell jokes.* Then other people gathered around, and they told jokes, giggling and laughing.

When I listened more carefully,* I realized that they were telling obscene jokes.* One made an obscene remark, and another would repeat it in a more subtle fashion. Some would laugh, another would enjoy it.

I then went to another city, and saw two people arguing about a business deal. They went to court to settle the affair, and the court ruled that one was liable and the other innocent. However, as soon as they left the court, they once again began to argue. They said that they did not like the decision of this court, and wanted another court. [Since both of them wanted to try the case in another court, they chose another one.] But after the case was tried, one of the people began arguing with someone else, and these two chose another court.* The place was thus full of strife and argument. The people needed so many courts that the entire city was full of courts.

You cannot go there yourselves. In order to rectify the world, all tzaddikim need the help of the greatest tzaddik. There are places where other tzaddikim cannot go to rectify things (*Chayay Nefesh* 34; see *Likutey Moharan* 64).

jokes. *Halatzah* in Hebrew; *vertil* in Yiddish.

listened more carefully. Literally, "inclined my ear."

obscene jokes. *Nivul peh,* which means profanity. The word *nivul* (ניבול) shares the same root as *nevelah* (נבלה), which denotes a rotten carcass. Since they spoke *nivul,* all food tasted like *nevelah,* as we shall see.

chose another court. Rabbi Nachman is referring to a system such as exists in Jewish

I observed all this, and realized that there was no truth there. Today a judge might decide in one person's favor and show him special consideration, and tomorrow the other would return the favor. Everything was based on bribery, with no sense of the truth. *

I also noticed that the people were totally immoral sexually. Sexual immorality was so prevalent, that everything seemed permissible* to them.

I said to them, "This is the reason that the taste, the fragrance, and the appearance have been spoiled for you. This cruel king left with you three groups of his servants, and they ruined the land.

"[These servants] began by speaking in a profane manner among themselves, and this brought profanity to the land. As a result of the profanity, * the sense of taste became ruined, and everything tastes like a rotten carcass.

"They also brought bribery into the land. As a result, the eyes were dimmed, and the sense of sight was ruined, since 'Bribery blinds the eyes of the wise' (Deuteronomy 16:19).

"Also, they brought sexual immorality into the land. This caused the sense of smell to be ruined. *

---

jurisprudence, where in addition to standing courts, people can set up *ad hoc* courts to judge their cases. Each party in litigation chooses one judge, and then the two judges decide on a third, thus making a three judge *ad hoc* court.

no sense of the truth. From here we see how important a true system of justice is (*Rimzey Maasioth*).

everything seemed permissible. Literally, "became like permissible." This is based on the Talmudic teaching, "When a person sins, and repeats the act, it becomes to him as if it were permissible" (*Yoma* 86b).

as a result of the profanity. See above p. 380. The first step in the downfall of the people was listening to profanity. Since the deaf beggar could not "hear" it, he was not affected. The story says that he heard it, but he did not hear any of the worldly evil in it.

The perfection of the Hebrew language is the rectification for the profanity. It is thus taught that there are no profane words in Hebrew, and for this reason it is called "the Holy Tongue" (*Kedushath Shabbath*).

smell...ruined. This teaches that one must be very careful regarding sexual immorality, since it destroys one's sense of smell (*Rimzey Maasioth*).

It is thus taught that the prophet Elisha had a bed that had the fragrance of the Garden

"Therefore, you must correct these three wrongs in your land. Find out who [the king's servants] are, and drive them away.* When you correct these three wrongs, then not only will you restore the taste, fragrance and appearance, but the missing gardener will also be able to be found."

The people did this, and began to rid the land of these three wrongs. They investigated [the king's agents] and when they captured them, they asked, "Where do you come from?" When they determined that they were the cruel king's agents, they banished them. The land was thus rectified of the three wrongs.

While this was going on, there was sudden excitement. [People began to say,] "There is a crazy man who is going around, saying that he is the gardener.* Everyone thought that he was crazy, so they threw stones at him and drove him away. But somehow, it is possible that he is the one! Maybe he is actually the gardener!"

[The men who were trying to remedy the land] went and brought him before them. I said, "Certainly this is really the gardener!"

Therefore, I have the word of the Land of Wealth that I live the good life, since I was able to rectify this land.*

Now my gift to you is my good life.

[When he finished speaking], there was great joy and tremendous rejoicing.

[Similarly, all the beggars were to return and come to the wedding, giving the couple wedding presents that they should be

of Eden because he always kept himself sexually pure (*Zohar* 2:44a; *Kedushath Shabbath*). The Talmud also teaches that the young men of Israel have a beautiful fragrance when they are sexually pure (*Berakhoth* 43b; *Parparoth LeChokhmah ad loc.*).

drive them away. The good life involves spiritual sight, taste and fragrance. In order to be worthy of it, one must keep away from people who are involved in the sins that destroy these spiritual senses (*Rimzey Maasioth*).

saying that he is the gardener. When someone claims to be the true tzaddik, people laugh and throw stones at him (*Likutey Etzoth* B, *Tzaddik* 90). People who have lost their senses of taste, smell and sight cannot recognize the true gardener.

rectify this land. The reason that he could rectify the land was because he himself did not lack anything. Therefore, nothing of the land could affect him (*Rimzey Maasioth*).

like them. What they had originally given as a blessing, they gave
as a wedding present.] The first one thus gave them a gift of long
life, while the second one gave them a gift of a good life.

[The Third Day]*

On the third day, the couple once again began to reminisce,
and they wept and yearned, "How can we bring the third beggar
who had a speech defect?" All of a sudden he appeared and said,
"Here I am!" He fell on them and kissed them.

He then said: At first I blessed you that you should be like me.
Now I am giving you as a wedding present that you should be like
me.

You think that I have a speech defect. I do not have a speech
defect at all. Rather, all the words in the world which do not
praise God do not have any perfection* in them. [I therefore seem
to have a speech defect, since I cannot speak words which lack
perfection.] But actually, I do not have a speech defect at all.
Quite the contrary, I am a wonderful orator* and speaker. I can
speak in parables* and lyric* that are so wonderful that there is

---

The Third Day. The stories of the third and fourth days were told on the subsequent Friday
night (April 6) (*Sichoth HaRan* 149). At that time, Rabbi Nachman's grandson was very
sick (*Yemey Moharnat* 32b). Rabbi Nachman discussed how the heart is pursued. He then
asked, "Where are we holding?" Then he began the story of the third day (*Sichoth HaRan*
151).

The 61st psalm pertains to the story of the third day, as we shall see (end of story).
Rabbi Nachman told this part of the story with great longing, tremendous reverence, and a
wonderful attachment to God. From this, everyone present could understand that this part
of the story contained many wondrous concepts (*Rimzey Maasioth*).

do not have any perfection. This teaches the importance of being careful about what one
says. The mute beggar felt that any words that did not praise God were imperfect, and he
could not pronounce them (*Rimzey Maasioth*). This was also a manifestation of his not
wanting to have anything to do with the worldly (*Likutey Halakhoth, Choshen Mishpat,
HaOseh Sheliach LiG'both Chovo* 2:10, p. 82a).

wonderful orator. Like Moses, who was a stutterer, but said the greatest things in the world.
Since God created the world with speech, this power is among the greatest in the world.

parables. *Chidoth.*

lyric. In Hebrew it is "*shirim* which are *luder,*" but in Yiddish it is "*shirim* and *luder.*"

no created thing* in the world that does not want to hear me.

The parables and lyrics that I know contain all wisdom.* Regarding this, I have the word* of a great man, who is called the True Man of Kindness.* There is an entire story about this.

Once all the wise men were sitting together, and each one boasted of his wisdom.

One boasted that with his wisdom he had discovered how to make iron.

One boasted that he had discovered another type of metal.

One boasted that with his wisdom he had discovered how to make silver, which is more valuable.

One boasted that he had discovered how to make gold.

One boasted that he had discovered how to make weapons.

One boasted that he had invented ways of making metals from ingredients out of which metals are not usually made.

One boasted about other sciences, since with these sciences such things as saltpeter* and gunpowder* were invented.

Thus, each one boasted about his wisdom.

Finally, one of them spoke up and said, "I am wiser than all of you; I am wise like the day."

The others did not understand what he meant when he said that he was wise like the day.

He explained to them, "If all your wisdom was put together, it would only amount to a single hour. It is true that each science is derived from a particular day, depending on what was created on that day. Nevertheless, all the sciences merely involve combining* things in different ways. [Therefore, each science is only derived

---

created thing. Including even the highest spiritual beings (*Rimzey Maasioth*).

all wisdom. Since all creation was accomplished through words, words contain all wisdom. One who has perfected the power of speech thus has access to all wisdom.

word. *Haskamah.* See above p. 366.

True Man of Kindness. In Yiddish, "*der groiser man, der emes-er ish chesed.*" This is the exact wording of our Rabbi of blessed memory.

saltpeter. *Salitra.*

gunpowder. *Pilver.*

combining. Literally, "combinations," *harkavoth* in Hebrew.

from combinations of things created on that day.] With true wisdom, one can gather all these sciences into a single hour. But I am wise like a full day."

This was the boast of the last wise man.

I spoke up and said to him, "Like which day?"*

[Speaking of me, this wise man] replied, "This man is even wiser than I am, since he can ask, 'Like which day?' However, I am wise like any day you prefer."

Now you might ask why a person who can ask, "Like which day?" is wiser than one who is as wise as any day he desires. This, however, involves a story. It concerns the True Man of Kindness,* who is actually a very great man.

I go around and gather all true kindness and bring it to the True Man of Kindness. [Time itself is something that was created,] and time exists primarily* as a result of true kindness. I therefore go around gathering all true kindness, and bring it to the True Man of Kindness.

There is a mountain. On the mountain there is a stone. From this stone, flows a Spring.*

Like Which Day. The text adds, "That is, like which day are you wise?"

True Man of Kindness. This is alluded to in the key psalm, "May he be enthroned before God forever, appoint mercy and truth so that they will preserve him" (Psalms 61:8).

The main trait of this man was kindness, Chesed in Hebrew. It is taught that charity is not perfect except when it is given with kindness, as it is written, "Sow charity for yourselves, and reap according to Chesed" (Hosea 10:12; *Sukkah* 49b; *Likutey Halakhoth, Melamdim* 4:13).

time exists primarily... Time comes into existence primarily through charity and kindness (*Likutey Halakhoth, Melamdim* 4:13). This teaching is based on the verse, "To tell Your Chesed in the morning, and Your faith by night" (Psalms 92:3; *Zimrath HaAretz*). In order to have a share in this process, one must do charity and kind deeds (*Likutey Etzoth B, Tzedakah* 8).

Kabbalistically, time comes into existence as a result of the actions of the lower sefiroth (*Pardes Rimonim*). These sefiroth begin with Chesed, and hence, Chesed is the source of time.

Spring. This Spring is the point which is the source of the rectification of all worlds. It is the source of all good points that a person can find in himself (*Likutey Halakhoth, Melamdim* 4:13; see *Likutey Moharan* 282). This point is Chokhmah (*Likutey Moharan* 34:5). Hence, the Spring in the story is Chokhmah (*Zohar* 2:42b). In this sense, the Spring can also be seen as the brain (*Kedushath Shabbath*).

Everything has a heart.* Therefore the world as a whole also has a heart.* The Heart of the World has a complete body,* with face, hands, and feet... However, a toenail of the Heart of the World has more of the essential nature of a heart* than the heart of anything else.

The mountain with the stone and the spring stands at one end of the world. The Heart of the World stands at the opposite end of the world. The Heart of the World faces the Spring and constantly longs and yearns* to come to the Spring. It has a very, very great longing, and it cries out* very much that it should be able to come to the Spring.

The Spring also yearns for the [Heart].

The Heart has two things* that make it weak.

First, the sun* pursues it* and burns it.* [This is because it

---

heart. Kabbalistically, the heart always represents Binah. Hence, the relationship between the heart and the Spring is basically the relationship between Chokhmah and Binah.

also has a heart. This heart is the root of all Jewish hearts (*Rimzey Maasioth*). In another sense, the Temple was the heart of the world (*Zimrath HaAretz*).

complete body. The sefirah of Binah becomes the *partzuf* of *imma* (mother), which is a spiritual entity having the form of a human body.

essential nature of a heart. More concisely, "hearty," *meluvav* in Hebrew; *hartziker* in Yiddish.

longs and yearns. The existence of the universal Heart does not depend on its getting to the Spring, but only on its yearning for the Spring.

cries out. King David identified with the Heart of the World, and in the key psalm, he cried out, "From the ends of the earth I call to You. When my heart is faint, lead me to a rock that is too high for me" (Psalms 61:3). Rabbi Nachman states this allusion explicitly (end of story).

From the yearning and crying out of this Heart comes the yearning and crying out in all prayer and in all *hithbodeduth*-meditation (*Likutey Halakhoth, Melamdim* 4:13).

two things. The two things that make it weak are the sun, and its yearning for the Spring. The sun represents worldly desire, while the Spring represents spiritual desire. But worldly desire and unfulfilled spiritual desire weaken the Heart (*Likutey Halakhoth, Melamdim* 4:13).

sun. All worldly desires are considered "under the sun," as it is written, "What profit does a man have of all his labor which he does under the sun" (Ecclesiastes 1:3). All evil is "under the sun," that is under the realm of time. Above time, there is no evil. But time is related to the sun, for time is counted by the solar day. Although the Heart is pure and holy, it is sick because of what is done "under the sun" (*Likutey Halakhoth, Melamdim* 4:13).

has such a desire, yearning to go and be close to the Spring.]

The second thing that weakens the Heart is the great longing and yearning that it constantly has toward the Spring. It longs and yearns so much that its soul goes out, and it cries out. It constantly stands facing the Spring, and cries out, "Help!"* desiring it so very much.

When [the Heart] wants to rest a bit and catch its breath, a great bird* comes and spreads its wings over it, protecting it* from the sun. It then can relax a bit. However, even when it is resting, it looks toward the Spring and yearns for it.

One may wonder, since it yearns for it so much, why does it not go to the Spring?

However, if it were to come close to the mountain, then it would no longer see the peak.* It then could not gaze at the

---

pursues it. This part of the story began with Rabbi Nachman discussing "the Heart that is pursued" (*Sichoth HaRan* 151).

burns it. This is the "heat" of the Evil Urge, the concept of fallen love. The Heart's love is directed toward the Spring, but the "sun" wants to annul this love, and make it involved in worldly love and lust. The Evil Urge thus pursues the heart of the Jew and tries to burn it (*Likutey Halakhoth, Melamdim* 4:13).

Help. *Na Gevalt.*

great bird. The wings of this bird are alluded to in the key psalm, "I will take refuge in the cover of Your wings" (Psalms 61:5) (end of story).

The wings protecting the Heart are very much like the wings of the cherubim which protected the holy ark (Exodus 25:20; *Zimrath HaAretz*). The bird's wings also represent the lungs, which protect the Heart and nourish it (*Likutey Halakhoth, Melamdim* 4:17; *Kedushath Shabbath*).

protecting it. The bird's wings represent the lungs. It is taught that, if not for the wings of the lungs that blow on the heart, the heat of the heart would burn the entire body (*Tikkuney Zohar* 13, 27b). Rabbi Nachman teaches that the power of speech involving prayer and Torah study cools down the desires of the heart and allows a person to survive (*Likutey Moharan* 78). The heart may burn for worldly things, but the power of the "wings" of prayer and Torah study protect it from consuming the body.

The bird also protects the Heart from weakness due to its yearning for the Spring. If a person does not have too much worldly desire, he is not weakened by his spiritual desire. Because of the bird, the Heart can look at the Spring with proper measure, so that it is not weakened by it (*Likutey Halakhoth, Melamdim* 4:13).

peak. *Shpitz* in Yiddish. *Shipua* in Hebrew, which has the connotation of inclination.

Spring, and if it stopped looking at the Spring, it would die, since its main·source of life is the Spring. When it stands facing the mountain, it can see the peak upon which the Spring is, but as soon as it comes close to the mountain, the peak is hidden from its eyes. [This is clearly demonstrable.] If it could not see the Spring, then it would die. *

If the Heart died, then the entire world would cease to exist. The Heart is the life-force of all things, and nothing can exist without a heart.

It is for this reason that it cannot go to the Spring. It therefore stands facing it, yearning and crying out. *

Time does not exist for the Spring. The Spring is not inside of time * at all. The Spring only has time because the Heart gives it as a gift for one day.

However, when the time comes for the day to come to a close, then at the end of the day, the Spring will not have any more time, and it will therefore die. This in turn would cause the Heart to die. The entire world would then cease to exist. *

Toward the end of the day, * they begin to take leave * of each

---

would die. Expressed idiomatically, "Its soul would leave it."

yearning and crying out. When the Heart gazes at the Spring, the breaking of vessels is rectified, and as a result, everything else is also rectified (*Likutey Halakhoth, Melamdim* 4:13). In general, this teaches that the world exists primarily because of the longing and desire for the holy on the part of people's hearts. Although the Heart cannot approach the Spring, its longing is enough for it to accomplish this purpose (*Likutey Etzoth* B, *Ratzon* 5).

not inside of time. The Yiddish adds, "That is, the Spring does not have any time whatsoever. That is, it has no day, and no time in the world. This is because it is very much higher than the time of the world."

The Spring is very much like God, who is the Creator of time, and is hence above time (cf. *Likutey Halakhoth, Tzitzith* 3:15). It is significant to note that the third beggar was able to transcend time, while the fifth one was able to transcend space.

cease to exist. This is prevented by the True Man of Kindness. The key psalm thus says, "Appoint mercy and truth that they may preserve it" (Psalms 61:8).

Toward the end of the day. At the end of the day, a person must be highly motivated, thinking of how the Heart and the Spring take leave of each other and sing to each other. The creation of that day is over, and who knows what the next day will bring? Therefore, at this time, one must prepare oneself to accept the holiness of the next day (*Likutey Etzoth* B, *Tefillah* 25).

other. At that time, they begin to speak to one another in wonderful parables and lyrics* [with great love and tremendous desire].

The True Man of Kindness watches very carefully over this. At the exact end of the day, the True Man of Kindness gives the Heart a gift of one day.* The Heart gives the day to the Spring, and the Spring then once again has time.

When this day comes from the place from which it comes, it also comes with very wonderful parables and lyrics [containing all types of wisdom].*

There are differences between the various days.* There is

---

take leave... *Gezegen.*

lyrics. *Luder*, in Yiddish. This is alluded to in the key psalm, "I will sing praise to Your name forever, so that I will daily keep my vows" (Psalms 61:9). The days that the Heart gives the Spring come from these songs and hymns (end of story).

Time is produced by song. Thus, the seven voices in Psalm 29 parallel the seven days of creation. The voices of song are the source of time (*Likutey Halakhoth, Rosh HaShanah* 5:9). In this story, the third, fourth and sixth beggars have their power through song (*Likutey Halakhoth, Apitropos* 3:4).

The daily song of the Heart and Spring parallel the song of the Levites sung in the Holy Temple. These songs contain great wisdom, as it is written, "Sing O wise one" (Psalms 47:8). It is also written, "Hezekiah spoke to the Levites who have good intelligence toward God" (2 Chronicles, 30:22). Rashi comments that the song of the Levites is referred to as intelligence and wisdom (*Zimrath HaAretz*).

gift of one day. It is therefore written in the key psalm, "May You add to the days of the King" (Psalms 61:7).

all types of wisdom. Thus, the third beggar had access to all sorts of wisdom. The wisdom of all the other men involved something from something, while the wisdom of the Torah involves something from nothing. The others could find metals in the ground, and combine various substances, but this is all something from something. But "Wisdom comes from Nothingness, and where is the place of Understanding?" (Job 28:12). Wisdom and understanding of the Torah come from Nothingness, and from it, one can understand how God brought the creation forth from Nothingness.

The third beggar was on the level of perceiving this. The other men knew how to find various metals, but he knew the songs which were the source of time, and hence the source of all wisdom (*Likutey Halakhoth, Keriyath HaTorah* 6:36).

between the various days. This is discussed in detail in the writings of the Ari (see *Etz Chaim, Drush Egolim VeYoshar* 5, p. 43). Since every day is different, one must praise God with different songs, and with an entirely new mentality, each day (*Likutey Etzoth* B, *Tefillah* 25). It goes without saying that during the month of Elul and on Rosh HaShanah one must worship God with new praise (*Rimzey Maasioth*).

Sunday, Monday, etc... Besides this, there are New Moon days and festivals.

All the time that the True Man of Kindness has comes from my hand. It is I who go forth and gather all the true kindness, from which time comes into existence.*

(It is for this reason that he is wiser even than the wise man who is as wise as any day one prefers. This is because time and days come into existence primarily through the beggar with a speech defect, who gathers true kindness, which is the basis of time, and brings [this kindness] to the True Man of Kindness. The latter gives a day to the Heart, who in turn gives it to the Spring, and as a result, the entire world is sustained. Therefore, time is brought into existence with parables and lyrics that contain all wisdom, through the beggar with the speech defect.)

Therefore, I have the word of the True Man of Kindness that I can recite parables and lyrics that contain all wisdom. [All time, along with parables and lyrics, comes into existence through my hand.]

And now, I am giving you this as a wedding present. You should be just like me.

[After he gave them this blessing] there was great joy and rejoicing.

[The Fourth Day]*

They completed the celebration of that day, and went to sleep. The next morning, the couple began to yearn for the beggar with the crooked neck.

---

existence. Thus the Heart only exists because it can look at the Spring, and because of the Heart, the rest of the world can exist. But both the Heart and Spring only exist because of the stutterer (who perfected the concept of speech), who gathers all Chesed-kindness, and weaves it into time (*Likutey Halakhoth, Melamdim* 4:13).

The Fourth Day. Rabbi Nachman told this part of the story on the same Friday night as he told about the third day. He finished telling the story of the fourth day, and then quickly left the table (*Sichoth HaRan* 151).

All at once, he appeared and said: Here I am... Originally, I blessed you that you should be like me. Now I am giving you this as a wedding present.

You think I have a crooked neck.* Actually, my neck is not crooked at all. Quite the contrary, I have a very straight neck. I have a very beautiful neck.*

However, there are vapors* in the world. I do not want to exhale and add to the vain vapors* of the world. [It is for this reason that my neck appears to be crooked. I made my neck crooked to avoid exhaling into the vapors of the world.] But actually, I have a very beautiful, wonderful neck, since I have a wonderful voice.* There are many sounds in the world that do

---

crooked neck. The neck involves the sefiroth of Binah and Tifereth (*Kedushath Shabbath*).

In the writings of the Ari, however, the neck is not seen as a sefirah, but as a manifestation of "immature mentality" (*mochin de-katnuth*).

In order to produce the perfect sound, his neck had to be crooked, just as a shofar must be bent (see *Rosh HaShanah* 16b).

beautiful neck. This is alluded to in the verse, "Your neck is like the tower of David, built with turrets, upon which hang a thousand shields, the armor of mighty warriors" (Song of Songs 4:4).

The tzaddik thus has a wonderful neck (*Likutey Etzoth* B, *Tzaddik* 93). The neck also alludes to the Temple. We thus find that when Joseph fell on Benjamin's neck, our sages state that this alluded to the destruction of the two Temples (*Zimrath HaAretz*).

vapors. The Hebrew word is *hevel*, which denotes both vapor or breath and vanity (see Ecclesiastes 1:2). *Dukh* in Yiddish. Here too the beggar was so removed from the wordly that he did not want to leave any breath in this physical world (*Likutey Halakhoth, Choshen Mishpat, HaOseh Sheliach LiGboth Chovo* 2:10, p. 82a).

add to the vain vapors. This beggar boasted that he would not let any worldly vapor come into his throat; therefore, his neck appeared crooked. As a result, he had perfection. This is like the shofar, which is crooked and is the root of all sound. The shofar is related to the Future World, and the sefirah of Binah. It is thus written, "On that day, the great shofar will be sounded" (Isaiah 27:13). When this beggar makes his neck crooked so that no worldly vanities can enter his body, he exists totally in the World to Come.

The "vapors" or *hevel* of the shofar is that which is mentioned in the verse, "Vapor of vapors, says Koheleth, vapor of vapors, all is vapor" (Ecclesiastes 1:2; see *Tikkuney Zohar*. [The word vapor (*hevel*) is mentioned five times in this verse, alluding to the spiritual vapors or breaths on all five levels of creation] (see *Sefer Yetzirah* 1:5).

Rosh HaShanah is the first of the Ten Days of Repentance. On Rosh HaShanah we sound the shofar indicating that we must cast away all worldliness and live completely for the World to Come (*Likutey Halakhoth, Nedarim* 4:36).

voice. The previous beggar had perfected speech. This one perfected voice, which is more

not involve speech. I have such a wonderful neck and voice that I can mimic any of these sounds.

Regarding this I have the word* of the land [of music]. There is a land where everyone is expert in the science of music. Everyone there studies this discipline, even little children. There is no child there who cannot play some kind of musical instrument. The least person in this land would be the greatest musician any place else. The wise men there, as well as the king and the musicians, are extraordinarily skilled in this art.

Once the leading sages of that land sat down, and each one boasted about his music.* One boasted about his skill on one instrument, while another boasted about his skill on another instrument. One boasted how well he played one instrument, and another boasted that he could play several instruments. Still another one boasted that he was able to play all musical instruments.

Another one then boasted that he could mimic a certain musical instrument with his voice. Still another boasted that he could mimic a different instrument. Yet another boasted that he knew how to mimic many instruments. Another boasted that he could mimic the beating of a drum so well that it sounded exactly like a drum.* Another boasted that with his voice he could mimic the sound of artillery.*

I was also there. I spoke up and said to them, "My voice is better than your voices. This is proof. If you are so skilled in music, let us see if you can help the two lands.

"There are two lands which are a thousand miles apart.* At

---

spiritual than speech. Kabbalistically, speech pertains to Malkhuth, while voice pertains to the six sefiroth of Zer Anpin.

The root of all voice is the seven voices mentioned in Psalm 29 (*Kedushath Shabbath*).

word. *Haskamah,* that is "agreement," as above.

music. *Muzika* in Yiddish. In this story, the third, fourth, and sixth days speak of song (*Likutey Halakhoth, Apitropos* 3:4).

drum. *Poik* in Yiddish.

artillery. *K'neh s'refah* in Hebrew, literally, "burning cane;" *irmatis* in Yiddish.

a thousand miles apart. Some say this is the distance between Uman and Jerusalem.

night, people in these two lands cannot sleep. As soon as night falls, everyone — men, women and children — begins to wail. If a stone were placed there, it would melt [out of pity for this wailing]. They hear a great sound of sobbing, * and because of this, all the men, women and children wail. [This is true in both lands.] The same sound of sobbing is heard in both lands, even though these two lands are a thousand miles apart.

"If you are so skilled in music, I would like to see if you can help these two lands, or if you can mimic their sound. [Let's see if you reproduce the exact sound of the wailing that is heard there.]"

[The wise men] said to me, * "Will you bring us there?"

"Yes, I will," I* replied.

They all set out, and eventually came [to one of the two lands]. At night, when everyone began to wail, the wise men also began to wail. [It was quite obvious that they could do nothing to help these people.]

"In any case," I said [to the wise men], "tell me what is the source of the sobbing that is heard here."

"And you *do* know!" they replied.

"I most certainly do," I said. "There are two birds, * one male

---

sobbing. *Yelalah* in Hebrew. It is noteworthy that the word *yelalah* (יללה) has the same letters as *laylah* (לילה), meaning night. The wailing is hence related to the blemish of the moon (*Chokhmah U'Tevunah* 9:3).

to me. The story uses the third person, "to him." It often switches between the third and first persons.

I. "He" in the text.

two birds. The two birds allude to God (Zer Anpin) and the Shekhinah (Malkhuth). The concept of Rosh HaShanah and Yom Kippur is to bring Malkhuth (the feminine aspect of the Divine) face to face with Zer Anpin (the male aspect of the Divine), so that the unification can be complete. This is the concept of uniting "those who dwell on high and those who dwell below," the "Holy One Blessed be He," and His Shekhinah. The "Holy One" is called "Heaven," while the Shekhinah is called "Earth." It is thus written, "God founded the Earth with wisdom, and established the Heaven with understanding" (Proverbs 3:19). It is our task to reunite Heaven and Earth, the Holy One and His Shekhinah (*Likutey Halakhoth, Nedarim* 4:24).

The fact that the two birds are lost to each other alludes to the exile of the Shekhinah.

The exiled Shekhinah is referred to as "a bird who has wandered from its nest" (Proverbs 27:8). The verse continues, "so is a man who wanders from his place." The "Man" in this verse is the Holy One (*Tikkuney Zohar*).

The two birds also parallel the two cherubs on the ark. When the Temple existed, the cherubs were face to face, but when it was destroyed, they were lost to each other, and were back to back.

The Shekhinah is also referred to as the "Congregation of Israel," since it is the Divine Presence that rests on each and every Israelite. It is our task to bring it back to its root in God. The tzaddik can accomplish this by throwing his voice, as we shall see (*Likutey Halakhoth, Nedarim* 4:25).

The shofar includes the sounds of the two birds, the sound from "on high" and the sound from "down below." It thus serves to reunite God and His Shekhinah (*Ibid.*)

The two cherubs were the source of prophecy, as it is written, "[Moses] heard the Voice from between the two cherubs" (Numbers 7:89). The voice of prophecy is also related to the shofar, as it is written, "Lift up your voice like a shofar" (Isaiah 58:1). It is also written, "Your mouth is like a shofar" (Hosea 8:1).

At the revelation at Sinai, the Torah thus says, "The sound of the shofar became continually stronger, Moses spoke and God answered in a voice" (Exodus 19:19). The sound of the shofar indicated that all the Israelites were reaching a level of prophecy. Rashi also notes that God made Moses' voice stronger. This was done through the sound of the shofar (*Ibid.*).

The two cherubs from which prophecy came denote the Holy One and His Shekhinah. As long as the ark with the cherubs stood in the Temple, the relationship between the Holy One and the Shekhinah was perfect, and prophecy could exist. However, after the Temple was destroyed, and the ark hidden, prophecy ceased to exist (*Likutey Halakhoth, Nedarim* 4:36).

The concept of bringing together the two birds, is thus that of reuniting the Holy One and His Shekhinah, which is the redemption (*Rimzey Maasioth*).

The wailing of these birds is alluded to in the verse, "God cries out from on high. He screams from His Holy Habitation" (Jeremiah 25:30). The Talmud states that He cries out like a dove (*Berakhoth* 3a). The Shekhinah is represented by Rachel, regarding which it is written, "A voice is heard in Ramah, lamentation and weeping, Rachel weeping for her children. She refuses to be comforted for her children, because they are not there" (Jeremiah 31:15) (*Likutey Etzoth* B, *Tzaddik* 93).

The two birds were a perfect pair. This is alluded to where the verse refers to the Shekhinah as "my dove, my twin" (Song of Songs 5:2, 6:9). This indicates that God and Israel are like twin birds. Regarding their mutual loss, it is written, "My beloved passed by... I sought Him, but could not find Him" (Song of Songs 5:6). When the Temple was destroyed, the two birds were lost to each other. When it is rebuilt, they will be reunited (*Chokhmah U'Tevunah* 19:3).

Rabbi Nachman also speaks of the "birds" as being the source of voice, and the rectification of malicious speech (*Likutey Moharan* 3). Malicious speech separated the birds, and therefore their rectification is through voice. David became the "shepherd of Israel" because he was worthy of rectifying the song of holiness by writing the Psalms (*Ibid.*).

and one female. They are the only such pair of birds in the world. The female was lost, and the male went to look for her. He searched for her, and she searched for him. They searched for one another for a very long time, until they got completely lost.

"When they realized that they could not find one another, they decided to remain where they were and build themselves nests. The [male] bird made himself a nest near one of the two lands. He was not right next to the land, but he was close enough that the people of the land could hear his voice from the place where he built his nest.*

"The female bird built her nest near the other land. [She too, was close enough that they could hear her voice.] At night, both of these birds begin to wail in a very loud voice. Each one wails for its mate. It is this sound of wailing that is heard in these two lands. [When the people hear this wailing, they too all begin to wail. Therefore, they cannot sleep.]"

[The wise men] did not want to believe me. "Will you bring us there?" they asked.

"Yes," I replied. "[I can bring you there.] But you will not be able to come there. If you come close, you will not be able to tolerate the sound of the wailing. Even here, you cannot stand it, and you are forced to wail along with the others. If you were there, you would not be able to stand it at all.

"It is [also impossible to come there] by day, since it is impossible to tolerate the joy that is there. By day, birds gather around each one of the pair, and they console each one and make it extremely joyful. [The birds] speak words of consolation, telling the pair that there is still a possibility that they will find one another.

---

nest. This is alluded to in the verse, "My soul yearns and pines for God's courtyards, my heart and flesh sing to the living God. A bird has found a house, and the swallow a nest for herself" (Psalms 85:3,4).

The *Zohar* also relates the Shekhinah to a bird in its nest in the commandment telling that when a bird is found on its nest, the mother must be sent away before the young can be taken (*Likutey Halakhoth, Nedarim* 4:25).

"Therefore, during the day, it is impossible to tolerate the great joy that exists there. The sound of the birds who make them rejoice cannot be heard from a great distance, only when one is actually there. However, the sound of the pair's wailing at night can be heard at a very great distance. Because of all this, it is impossible to approach their place."

"Can you rectify this?" they asked me.

I replied, "I can rectify this, since I can mimic any sound * in the world. [With my voice I can reproduce any sound exactly.] Besides this, I can also throw my voice, * so that no sound is heard

---

mimic any sound. The tzaddik must be able to mimic every sound in the world, thus elevating every sound according to its time and place. This is also related to the concept of sounding the shofar on Rosh HaShanah. The shofar includes every sound in the world, as the *Zohar* teaches, "All sounds on high are included in the shofar" (*Zohar* 2:99b; cf. *Zohar* 3:18b).

The shofar is directed at both birds, alluding to God and Israel. The shofar awakens the Israelites and motivates them to repent, saying to them, "Awake, you who sleep." This is the concept of, "Shall a shofar be sounded and the people not tremble?" (Amos 3:6).

The shofar also serves to remind God to have mercy on us. It recalls the binding of Isaac on the altar, and causes God to remember his merit for us.

Thus, the shofar tends to bring Israel to God, and God to Israel. Symbolically, then, it reunites the two birds (*Likutey Halakhoth, Nedarim* 4:25).

throw my voice. The tzaddik can bring God and the Shekhinah together by throwing his voice. One way of doing this is by clothing his lessons in stories. The message is not heard immediately, but when it reaches the person for whom it is intended, it is heard well. Telling stories is therefore throwing one's voice at the Israelites.

The tzaddik can also clothe his prayers in stories. Because of spiritual barriers, he cannot make such prayers directly, and to all practical purposes they seem like stories. But in the place where they are needed, they are heard. In this respect, he is throwing his voice toward God (cf. *Likutey Moharan* 5).

Sounding the shofar is also throwing a voice toward Israel and toward God (*Likutey Halakhoth, Nedarim* 4:24).

Moses was a tzaddik who could throw his voice so that the Israelites heard it wherever they were. Through the sound of the shofar, God helped make his voice powerful so that even those furthest away could hear him. The Torah describes the sound of the shofar as being "very (*m'od*) strong" (Exodus 19:16). The word "very" (*m'od*) is interpreted in the Midrash as denoting death (*Bereshith Rabbah* 9:10). Therefore, Moses' voice, as enhanced by the shofar, could even arouse those who were so evil that they would be considered dead (*Likutey Halakhoth, Nedarim* 4:25).

The concept of the voice from the cherubs was also that of throwing the voice.

here, but the sound is heard at a distance. I can therefore throw the voiçe of the female bird and make it reach the place of the [male] bird, and also throw the voice of the [male] bird and make it reach the place of the female bird. By doing this, I will be able to bring them together. [Through this,] everything will be rectified."

When he saw* that they did not believe him, he took them into a forest. They heard the sound of a door being opened, and then closed and locked with a bolt. They actually heard the click* of the bolt. Then they heard a gun* being shot, and a dog being sent to [retrieve the quarry]. The dog thrashed* around and dragged himself in the snow.*

The wise men heard all this, but they did not see a thing. They also did not hear any sound whatsoever coming from me. Still, I* was the one who was projecting these sounds, and this is why they heard them. They realized that I could accurately produce any sound and also throw my voice. Therefore, I could rectify everything.*

Therefore, the prophet Samuel could hear the voice, but Eli, who was closer, could not hear it (see 1 Samuel, 3:4, Rashi *ad loc.*) (*Likutey Halakhoth, Nedarim* 4:36).

The concept of throwing the voice is also that of the tzaddik who can tell one person something, and not have it have any effect on him, but it can have an effect on other people. Rabbi Nachman thus said, "I tell you something, and sometimes it will not affect you at all. But the words are passed from person to person, from one friend to another. These words finally reach a particular individual and penetrate deeply into his heart. The words then fulfill their mission and inspire him..." (*Sichoth HaRan* 208).

when he saw... Literally, "But who will believe this?"

click. *Klainka* in Yiddish.

gun. *Biks.*

thrashed. *Mith-chabet* in Hebrew.

dragged himself in the snow. *Gegraznit in shnai* in Yiddish. The dog retrieving his quarry alludes to Esau who brought game back to his father (Genesis 27:30). Esau is likened to a dog (*Zohar* 3:124b; *Likutey Halakhoth, Nedarim* 4:24, end).

This shows that this beggar could even throw his voice with regard to mundane matters. Since he could do this, he obviously could do the same with regard to holy matters, and thus reunite the birds (*Rimzey Maasioth*).

I. Literally "the one with the crooked neck." For consistency, we have changed it to the first person.

rectify everything. Since the tzaddik has the voice of the two birds, he can unite them. The

([Rabbi Nachman] did not tell any more about this, and it is understood that he skipped part of the story* here.)

Therefore, I have the word of that land that I have a wonderful voice, and that I can mimic any sound in the world. Now, as a wedding present, I am giving it to you, so that you will be like me.

[When he completed his story] there was very great joy and rejoicing there.

[The Fifth Day]*

On the fifth day, while they were rejoicing, the couple recalled the hunchback beggar. They yearned for him very much, saying, "How can we bring the hunchback beggar here? If he were here, there would be very great joy."*

Suddenly he appeared and said, "Here I am! I have come to the wedding." With that, he fell on them, hugging and kissing them.

He then said to them: Originally, I blessed you that you should be like I am. Now I am giving you this as a wedding present — that you should be like me.

---

shofar is also the spirit-wind of prophecy that comes from the cherubs (birds). Therefore, the shofar will gather the exile (Isaiah 27:13). The gathering of the exile depends primarily on reuniting the birds (*Likutey Halakhoth, Nedarim* 4:36).

skipped part of the story. Rabbi Nachman did not complete the story, since he would not reveal how the redemption was to take place. The redemption, furthermore, depends on all the world repenting. Thus the redemption can only come in its proper time. But, once the others accepted the fact that he can accomplish it, the redemption will automatically come (*Rimzey Maasioth*).

The Fifth Day. Rabbi Nachman told the story of the fifth day on the next Sunday (April 8) (*Sichoth HaRan* 149). Rabbi Nachman was involved in a discussion of a certain cult (*kat*), and spoke about having "broad shoulders" (*breita pleitzes*) [to be able to assume responsibility]. This led to his telling the story of the fifth day (*Sichoth HaRan* 151; *Chayay Moharan* 16b #5).

very great joy. It is only with respect to this beggar that this expression is used. Rabbi Nachman told this part of the story in great joy (*Chayay Moharan* 16b #5).

I am not a hunchback* at all. Quite the contrary, I have broad shoulders.* My shoulders are a case of "little holding much."* I have an affidavit* regarding this.

Once there was a discussion, where people were boasting about this concept. Each one boasted that he was a case of little holding much. Everyone laughed at one of them and made a joke of him, but the others who boasted about being little holding much were accepted. However, in my case, the concept of little holding much is greater than that of all of them.

One of these people boasted that his brain was an example of little holding much. In his brain, he carried thousands and myriads of people, with all their needs, [all their habits], all their

hunchback. He appeared to be a hunchback because he bent his body to accept the yoke of the Torah. He therefore never straightened out his body, which would involve throwing off this yoke. He was like Issachar, regarding whom it is said, "He bent his shoulder to the burden" (Genesis 49:15). This was also the level of the sons of Kehoth, who carried the ark and tablets on their shoulders. If one carries the Torah, one can carry all things, since the ark supported its carriers. This is because the Torah is related to the level that existed before God created space (*Likutey Halakhoth, Sefer Torah* 3:7).

broad shoulders. *Pleitzes* in Yiddish. The expression *breita pleitzes*, or "broad shoulders," denotes the ability to take on large responsibilities, especially with regard to doctrinal matters. A hunchback, on the other hand, appears to have no shoulders at all. Therefore, this beggar was saying that his "nonexistent" shoulders were really very broad, since they were "little holding much."

little holding much. *Muat machzik eth ha-merubah* (מועט מחזיק את המרובה) in Hebrew. This expression occurs in the Midrash (*Bereshith Rabbah* 95). The concept is found in many other places as well (see *Bereshith Rabbah* 5:6; *Vayikra Rabbah* 10:9; Rashi on Leviticus 8:3). It is taught that such a phenomenon occurred among the Israelites on seven occasions (*Ibid., Maaseh Torah* 118).

In general, the concept of "little holding much" is that of transcending space. There are various levels of this, until one reaches the level where space is transcended completely (*Likutey Halakhoth, Tzitzith* 3:8). Sin brings a person under the realm of space. We thus find that after Cain killed Abel, he was condemned to be a "wanderer and a fugitive" (Genesis 4:12; *Likutey Halakhoth, Tzitzith* 3:14).

The concept of "little holding much" applies to the Land of Israel as a whole. It is called "land of the deer," because like a deerskin it can "stretch" to hold all its inhabitants. The Hebrew language is also "little holding much," since a few words can hold many mysteries (*Zimrath HaAretz*).

affidavit. *Haskamah. See above p. 366.*

discussions,* and all their movements. Since his brain carried so many* people, it was an example of little holding much.

The others laughed at him. They said that the people are nothing, and therefore he is also nothing.*

One spoke up and said, "I saw such a case of little holding much. I once saw a mountain which was covered with excrement and filth. I found it very surprising, and I wondered where all this excrement and filth came from."

"There was a man near the mountain, and he said, 'All this came from me.' That man lived near the mountain, and whenever he ate and drank, he would throw his garbage and excrement there. He therefore made it a filthy place, putting a large amount of garbage and excrement on the mountain. Therefore, this man was an example of little holding much, since he was able to produce so much excrement."

"[This is the same concept* as that of the man who boasted that his brain held many people.]"

One boasted that he was an example of little holding much. [He had] an estate that produced much fruit. When the amount of fruit produced by the land was calculated, it came out that the land did not have enough room to hold all the fruit. There was

---

discussions. *Havayoth,* in both in Hebrew and Yiddish. The word can denote "existences," but it also denotes arguments or discussions (see *Sukkah* 28a; *Bava Bathra* 134a).

brain carried so many. A person might boast that he is a great man because he has responsibilities for his family and household. But we see that even one who has responsibility for thousands is not so great, because it is all for vanity and nothingness (*Rimzey Maasioth*).

There are seven levels of people discussed here. These might parallel the seven cases where "little held much" mentioned in the Midrash (*Bereshith Rabbah* 5:6; see above).

he is also nothing. A person can boast that he sustains thousands of people, but what he gives them is physical, and therefore worthless, so his accomplishment is nothing (*Likutey Etzoth* B, *Tzaddik* 94).

the same concept. Rabbi Nachman is speaking here about an unworthy leader. He may have responsibility for thousands of people, but he ruins the souls of those who follow him (see *Likutey Moharan Tinyana* 8:8). What he gives to his followers is like the excrement that the man here spreads around the mountain, and then boasts that it is all from him (*Rimzey Maasioth*).

not enough space in the land to hold all the fruit that it produced. Therefore, it was an example of little holding much.

His words were well accepted.* This was considered an excellent example of little holding much.

One said that [he had] a very wonderful orchard containing fruit. It was such a beautiful orchard that many people and nobles traveled there. In the summer, many people and nobles would come there to take walks. The orchard, however, did not have room for all the people who came there, so it was an example of little holding much.

His words were also well accepted.

One said that his speech was an example of little holding much. He was the secretary* for a great king, and many people came to him. Some came with praise for the king, while others came with petitions. "It is obviously impossible for the king to hear them all," [he said], "so I take all their messages and condense them into a few words that I tell the king. The few short words of mine contain all their praises and petitions. Therefore my speech is little holding much."

One said that his silence was an example of little holding much. Many people were denouncing him and slandering him very much, but no matter how much they did so, he would answer them all with silence. Throughout it all, he remained completely silent. [His silence was an answer for everything.] Therefore his silence was little holding much.

One said that he was an example of little holding much. [He explained,] "There is a man who is poor and blind, and also very huge. I, on the other hand, am very small. But even though I am very small, I lead the poor blind man, who is very huge. Therefore, I am little holding much. The blind man could trip and fall, but by leading him, I am actually 'holding' him up.*

His words were well accepted. Because he actually produced fruit. Thus, he was a great tzaddik, who had the concept of little holding much (*Likutey Etzoth* B, *Tzaddik* 94).
secretary. *Sekretar* in Yiddish.
'holding' him up. In Hebrew this is also *machzik*. Thus it is "little holding much."

Therefore, I am a little 'holding' much. I am little, but I uphold this huge man."

I was also there, and I said, "Actually, you are all examples of little holding much. I understand the true meaning of everything that you said. I know what you truly mean when you boast of being examples of little holding much. [The last of you, who boasted that he leads a blind man, is the greatest of you all.] But I am much higher than any of you.

"When the [last one] boasted that he led a giant, he meant that he directed the orbit* of the moon. The moon is considered to be a blind man, since it does not have any of its own light, and has nothing of its own.* Although [this boaster] is small, he directs

---

orbit. Literally, "leads the sphere of the moon."

nothing of its own. *Leyth lah le-garmei klum* in Aramaic. The expression is from the *Zohar* (1:238a, 1:249b). The moon is therefore also considered a "poor man." In this respect, the moon is also seen as an aspect of Malkhuth, which "has nothing of its own" (see *Likutey Moharan* 1).

The succession of concepts of "the little that holds much" that are introduced here, alludes to successive levels of *teshuva,* repentance.

Rabbi Nachman explains, that *teshuva* is the path to *Kether*, the crown, the glory of God. To achieve this, a person must set aside his own honor, and the way to do this is through being silent. This means the ability to hear himself abused and still say nothing.

The different aspects of *teshuva* are expressed in the form of the letter *aleph* (א). The letter is made up of an upper point, a lower point and a line, which both connects and divides the two points. The lower point of the *aleph*, the *chirik*, alludes to remaining silent. The upper point refers to *Kether*, the concealed throne of God's glory. The *vav* is the *rakiya*, the firmament of many colors, an allusion to *busha*, shame - the shame of one who comes before his Maker after sinning (for the face of one who is embarrassed changes color [*Bava Metzia* 58b]).

When all these levels are brought together (by a person's attaining them) there is "unity between the sun and the moon": the sun (of divine wisdom) shines to the receiving moon. This idea corresponds to the unity between Moses and his disciple, Joshua. For "the face of Moses is like the face of the sun" (*Baba Bathra* 75a) — and Moses is the upper point of the *aleph*. The face of Joshua is like the face of the moon (for all his knowledge was derived from Moses) — and Joshua is the lower point of the *aleph*. Moses and Joshua are united by means of the tent, the stretched out firmament as it were, for "Joshua the son of Nun did not move from the tent" (Exodus 33:11).

These three levels also correspond to the three mitzvoth which Israel was commanded to fulfill upon entering the Land of Israel. The first was to wipe out Amalek. This mitzvah

the moon, which is very large. Moreover, he sustains the entire world, since the world needs the moon. Therefore, he is actually a true example of little holding much."

Nevertheless, my concept of little holding much is much greater than all, including his. This is the proof:

Once there was a group of people who studied the fact that every animal has a shadow in which it likes to rest. Conversely, there is a shadow for each and every animal. Every animal chooses its particular shadow where it wants to dwell.

Every bird, also, has its own unique branch. It is on this particular branch that it desires to live.

Studying this phenomenon, they sought to find a tree* in

---

was particularly associated with Joshua because he had been instructed by Moses to go out and fight Amalek (Exodus 17:9). The second *mitzvah* was to build the Holy Temple. This is associated with Moses, who built the sanctuary. The third *mitzvah* was to appoint a king. This corresponds to the level of the firmament, as it is written, "A star shall step forth out of Jacob" (Numbers 24:17), referring to the king of Israel (Rashi *ad. loc.*). So too is Jacob, who "dwelled in tents" (Gen. 25:27) (*Likutey Moharan* 6).

In the story we also find these three points. First there is the level of silence, referring to Joshua, and corresponding to the lower point of the *aleph*. Next mentioned is the man leading the blind pauper, that is, he is above the moon and is the one to bring it its needs, corresponding to the *vav*. The third level is the one who is higher than this firmament, the upper point of the *aleph* the hunchback himself. He corresponds to the level of Moses, and he himself has the aspect of "the little that holds much," the Holy Temple. (Rabbi Chaim Kramer).

tree. This tree is alluded to in Daniel's vision: "I saw a tree in the middle of the world, and it was very high. The tree grew and was strong, and it was so high that it reached the heavens. Its view was to the end of the earth. Its leaves were beautiful, and it had much fruit, providing food for all. The beasts of the field had shadow under it, and the birds of heaven lived on its branches; all living things had food from it" (Daniel 4:7-9).

This tree is the Tree of Life, which was in the Garden of Eden (Genesis 2:9). Since all animals can live under this tree, it is an example of "little holding much." This tree is the link between space and the realm that is above space. It is through the Tree of Life that souls can travel from the world, which is the realm of space, to the Throne of Glory, which is above space.

If Adam had not sinned, he would have entered into the realm of "above space" during his lifetime. This is the concept of "knowledge." But, "Adam who is in honor understands it not; he is like the beasts who perish" (Psalms 49:21). By sinning, he lost the concept of "knowledge," and was lowered into the concept of space. The rectification for this is

whose shadow all animals live.* All animals would desire to live in its shadow. Similarly, all birds* would live in its branches.

They probed and discovered that such a tree exists. They wanted to go to the tree, since near it there is wonderful delight* that is beyond all imagination. All birds and animals are there, and none harms the other. They all live in harmony and frolic together, so it must be an extraordinary delight to be near that tree.

They then probed to discover which direction they must travel to reach the tree. A dispute* arose regarding this, and none of

---

through repentance, which "reaches up to the Throne of Glory" (*Yoma* 86b). In the time of the Temple, repentance was often accompanied by a sacrifice. The sacrifice related to the animal's place under the tree, and hence brought a person into contact with the tree. The person would then be raised to the level above space (*Likutey Halakhoth, Tzitzith* 3:13).

The Tree of Life is the joy of the World to Come. It is above the concept of space, since it is where souls go up to delight in God.

The Tree of Life is the root of the Torah, which is called, "The Tree of Life to those who grasp onto it" (Proverbs 3:18). One can only approach this tree through the "path to the Tree of Life" (Genesis 3:24). The path is the commandments of the Torah, which are called a "path" (Deuteronomy 5:30) (*Likutey Halakhoth, Sefer Torah* 3:2).

Since the Torah is related to the tree which is above space, the ark which stood in the Temple and held the original Torah and tablets did not take up any space. If one measured from the walls to the ark, it would come out that the ark did not take up any space at all (*Bava Bathra* 99a; *Yoma* 21a; *Likutey Halakhoth, Sefer Torah* 3:6).

It is taught that "all souls come through the great tree" (*Zohar*). The Tree of Life stands under the Throne of Glory, and all souls go up on it (*Likutey Halakhoth, Choshen Mishpat, Sheluchim* 4:16).

The tree also represents the bush in which the ram substituted for Isaac was captured (Genesis 22:13). From this ram's horn, the shofar was made. The sounds of the shofar allude to the four concepts of the tree, as we shall see (*Ibid.*).

all animals live. Since there is room for all animals and birds on this tree, it is above space (*Chokhmah U'Tevunah* 20:2).

birds. Literally, "birds of heaven." In Hebrew it is *tziparey shmaya* (צפרי שמיא), the term that occurs in Daniel 4:9. (Also see Ezekiel 31:13).

delight. This is because the tree denotes the delight of the World to Come, the interface between the physical world, which is spacial, and the spiritual world, which is non-spacial (*Likutey Halakhoth, Yoreh Deah, Sefer Torah* 3:2; see *Likutey Etzoth* B, *Tzaddik* 99).

dispute. This too is caused by sin. After mankind sinned, the path to the Tree of Life was no longer revealed to all.

The breaking of the tablets also caused forgetting, so that there is no longer any clear path to the tree. This brings about disputes between the sages. Even in the time of the

them could come to a conclusion. Some said that they should head east, while others said that it was to the west. One determined that the tree must be in one place, while another said that it was elsewhere. Thus, they could not decide which way to go to come to the tree.

Then a wise man came and said to them, "Why are you trying to discover in which direction the tree lies? Instead, try to find out who will be able to approach the tree. Not everyone can come near it. In order to do so, one must have all the attributes* of the tree. The tree has three roots. The first root is faith,* the second reverence,* and the third, humility.* The trunk of the tree is

Talmud, such disputes existed. But all disputes come about because people do not have the roots of the tree, which are the roots of Torah, that is, faith, reverence, humility and truth (*Likutey Halakhoth, Sefer Torah* 3:1).

God also planted a burning revolving sword along the way to guard the path to the Tree of Life (Genesis 3:24). Because of this sword we do not know where this tree is. There is therefore a dispute as to which direction to take to the tree, and from this all the disputes in the world originate.

Sometimes the motivation behind a dispute can be holy, such as the disputes between Talmudic sages. But at other times, the motivations can be unworthy, and the disputes can lead to causeless hatred. It was such hatred that caused the Temple to be destroyed (*Yoma* 9b). All this comes from the sword, which is a symbol of strife and war.

The sword is therefore described as *mith-hapekheth* which means turning, revolving, or transforming. It is taught that it is called "transforming," because it transforms one opinion into another, causing dispute (*Zohar* 1:121a). This sword came about as a result of Adam's sin.

In the Future World, "The days of My people will be like the days of a tree" (Isaiah 65:22). Strife will no longer exist, even in the animal kingdom, since "the wolf will lie with the lamb..." (Isaiah 11:6). [The sword will be rectified, since "people will beat their swords into plowshares" (Isaiah 2:4).] This is through the power of the tree, regarding which, it is said, "It is a Tree of Life to those who grasp on to it... and all its paths are peace" (Proverbs 3:18) (*Likutey Halakhoth, Sefer Torah* 3:10).

The main concept of dispute arises because of the concept of space. Dispute arises when one party wishes to enter the space or territory of another. But on the level above space, there is no dispute. It is thus taught, "When our love was strong, we found enough room to sleep together on the side of a sword" (*Sanhedrin* 7a). [This was the rectification of the "revolving sword."] (*Likutey Halakhoth, Sefer Torah* 3:11).

attributes. *Middoth.*

faith. *Emunah.*

reverence. *Yirah.* Also translated as "fear," as in "fear of heaven." It denotes the awe of

truth,* and it is from there that its branches come forth. It is

God, as well as the fear of divine retribution.

humility. *Anivuth.*

truth. The Tree represents the Torah, but the five books of the Torah are paralleled by the five books of the Psalms. The Psalms begin by speaking of the path and the tree.

The Psalms begin, "Happy is the man who does not walk in the counsel of the wicked" (Psalms 1:1). This parallels the attibute of faith, since faith comes from the advice of the tzaddik (*Likutey Moharan* 7; *Likutey Moharan Tinyana* 5). One who does not walk in the ways of the wicked will follow the advice of the tzaddik, and will thus gain faith.

"Who does not stand in the path of sinners" denotes reverence and fear of God. Fear is the antithesis of sin, as it is written, "that His [God's] fear be on your faces that you do not sin" (Exodus 20:20). An important trait is "fear of sin."

"Who does not sit in the place of scorners," denotes humility. It is thus written, "If he goes to scorners, then he will scorn, but to the humble he gives grace" (Proverbs 3:34). We therefore see that humility is the antithesis of scoffing and scorning. Scoffing comes from the sin of pride.

"But who desires God's Torah, and immerses himself in it day and night" (Psalms 1:1) denotes the tree itself, which is truth.

The psalm goes on, "He shall be like a tree planted by the streams of water" (Psalms 1:3). This denotes the tree in the story, planted by the supernal streams, regarding which it is written, "God's streams are filled with water" (Psalms 65:10) (*Likutey Halakhoth, Sefer Torah* 3:3).

The four attributes of the tree also represent Abraham, Isaac, Jacob and Moses.

Abraham represents faith, as it is written, "He had faith in God" (Genesis 15:6).

Isaac represents reverence and fear; hence, God is referred to as "the feared of Isaac" (Genesis 31:53).

Jacob represents truth, which is the trunk of the tree, as it is written, "You will give truth to Jacob" (Micah 7:20). This is the body of the Torah, which is referred to as "the Torah of truth" (Malachi 2:6). It is written, "Moses commanded us the Torah, an inheritance of the congregation of *Jacob*" (Deuteronomy 33:4). The Ari teaches that Jacob represented the Torah, but since the trait of humility was not perfected, it could not be given until Moses arrived on the scene.

Moses represents humility, as it is written, "Moses was humble, more so than any man on the face of the earth" (Numbers 12:3). Therefore, he could be the one to receive the Torah (*Likutey Halakhoth, Sefer Torah* 3:5).

All three of these concepts come into play in writing a Torah scroll. The letters themselves represent faith (see *Likutey Moharan* 18). Furthermore, the letters must be perfect, even to the point of a *yod* (*kotzo shel yod*). The *yod* represents humility, because it is the smallest letter in the Hebrew alphabet. Moreover, it represents the World to Come (see *Menachoth* 29b), and the essence of the World to Come is humility (*Likutey Moharan Tinyana* 72).

Finally, the Torah scroll must be written for the sake of God and for the sanctity of the

impossible to go to the tree* unless one has these attributes."

This group had a great sense of unity, and did not want some to go to the tree and some to remain behind. They realized that not all would be able to go to the tree, since some had the needed attributes, but others did not. Therefore, all of them remained so as to give the rest an opportunity to strive and gain the attributes necessary to allow them to come to the tree.

They followed this plan, and they struggled and worked until all of them had these attributes. When all of them had the necessary attributes, they all had the same idea, and all of them agreed* on one way as being the true path to the tree.

They set out, and after a while, they were able to see the tree [at a distance]. However, when they looked at the tree, it was not standing in space.* The tree did not exist in space, and since it did

---

Torah. This represents fear and reverence, as it is written, "[You must] fear the great and awesome Name" (Deuteronomy 28:58). Thus, by keeping the commandment to write a Torah scroll, one brings the tree to oneself (*Likutey Halakhoth, Sefer Torah* 3:8).

The four concepts of the tree also parallel the four sounds of the shofar: *tekiah* (a long sound), *shevarim* (three short blasts), *teruah* (a stacatto), and the final *tekiah*.

The *tekiah* denotes reverence and fear, as it is written, "Shall the *tekiah* of a shofar be sounded in a city and the people not tremble" (Amos 3:6). *Shevarim* is a "broken sound," and it denotes faith and prayer. *Teruah* denotes humility and prophecy like that of Moses (cf. *Likutey Halakhoth, Choshen Mishpat, Sheluchim* 4:15). The final *tekiah* represents the trunk of the tree, which is truth.

The trunk of the tree includes all the plants in the world. All grow through truth, as it is written, "Truth will grow forth from the earth" (Psalms 85:12; *Likutey Halakhoth, Choshen Mishpat, Sheluchim* 4:16).

go to the tree. Through faith, reverence and humility, one can attain truth, which is the trunk of the tree. But the concept of truth is that of unity, since "truth is one" (*Likutey Moharan* 51). But since space derives from multiplicity, both of positions and dimensions, the concept of unity is above space. Therefore, when one attains the attribute of truth, one can approach the tree which is above space (*Chokhmah U'Tevunah* 20:5).

all of them agreed. As long as the groups were far from the tree's attributes, there was no true peace between them. But when they came close to the concept of the tree, they all agreed (*Likutey Halakhoth, Sefer Torah* 3:11). Furthermore since Torah is one, when they all attained truth, they could all be united.

not standing in space. The tree is above space. This is the ultimate level of "little holding much." Since the Torah pertains to this concept, all Israel was able to stand between the poles of the ark, which contained the Torah (see Rashi on Joshua 3:9). In the Temple, also,

not have a place, it was impossible* to approach it.

I was also with them, and I said, "I can bring you* to the tree. This tree does not have any place at all, since it is above the concept of space.* It is also above the concept of little holding

---

people stood crowded together, but when they bowed, they had sufficient space (*Avoth* 5:5). In Jerusalem, no one ever said "the place is too crowded" (*Ibid.*). The land of Israel is called "land of the deer" (Ezekiel 20:6), because it can stretch to hold its populace (*Gittin* 57a). When the Messiah comes, all the Israelites who have ever lived will fit into the Holy Land.

The higher the level of holiness, the less importance space has. The epitome of this was the ark itself, which did not take up any space at all (*Likutey Halakhoth, Sefer Torah* 3:6).

The Torah itself is a paradigm of little holding much, since each letter in the Torah supports many universes. The letters of the Torah were used to create many universes. Furthermore, each word of the Torah contains many concepts. Thus, for example, the Hebrew word for man, *adam* (אדם), contains the forms and attributes of every human being who would ever exist. (Rabbi Nachman said this explicitly to Rabbi Nathan.)

Thus, when somebody writes a Torah scroll, he is bringing the actual letters, which are above space, into the space of the parchment (*Likutey Halakhoth, Sefer Torah* 3:7; also see *Oneg Shabbath,* p. 80).

The Book of Creation (*Sefer Yetzirah* 1:5) speaks of all reality as consisting of five dimensions, the three dimensions of space, time, and the moral, spiritual dimension. The Torah relates to the moral dimension, and hence, is above the dimensions of space.

it was impossible. Literally, "how was it possible to come to it?"

I can bring you. Only a tzaddik who can transcend space can bring people to the tree (*Likutey Etzoth* B, *Tzaddik* 94).

above the concept of space. This tree elevates a person to the Throne of Glory, on the level where God is referred to as *Makom,* meaning "place." God is called this, as the Midrash says, "because He is the 'place' of the world, and the world is not His place" (*Bereshith Rabbah* 68:10). Before the giving of the Torah, God elevated the Israelites to the level of being above space, as He said, "I lifted you on wings of eagles and brought you to Me" (Exodus 19:4). The "wings of eagles," are the wings of the divine commandments, alluded to in the verse, "As an eagle stirs up its nest, hovering over its young..." (Deuteronomy 32:11).

Our sages teach that when God said that He brought the Israelites "on wings of eagles," He brought them from Rameses to Sukkoth, a distance of 120 miles, in a single day. He did this by allowing the Israelites to transcend space.

The concept of transcending space is realized through the commandment of tzitzith (tassles, as on the tallith). The Talmud states that the meditation involving tzitzith brings a person up to the Throne of Glory, which is above the concept of space (*Likutey Halakhoth, Tzitzith* 3:8).

It is therefore taught that, through tzitzith, the exiles will be gathered. They are now

much, since this concept is also an aspect of space. It is obvious that the concept of little holding much always involves the concept of space, no matter how little space is involved.

"However, the concept of little holding much that I have is at the very end of space,* beyond which there is no space at all. Therefore, I can carry you to the tree, which is totally above space."

separated by space, because they are in different places. But when they transcend space, they will all be together (*Likutey Halakhoth, Tzitzith* 3:9).

This is also related to the concept of sacrifice. An animal does not have "knowledge" (Daath). The concept of "knowledge" is that of joining and unification, as in the verse, "Adam knew Eve his wife" (Genesis 4:1). Therefore, when a person has full knowledge, he is able to transcend space. An animal, however, does not have knowledge, and therefore is bound totally by space.

The Holy Temple, however, was an aspect that transcended space, as discussed earlier. It is thus taught, "Jerusalem is higher that the entire Land of Israel, and the Land of Israel is higher than all other lands" (*Zevachim* 54b). This is derived from the verse, which says of Jerusalem, "You shall go up to the place" (Deuteronomy 17:8). This indicates that Jerusalem is related to God, who is called the Place of the universe. All lands and all places are united in the Temple through the Foundation Stone (*Evven HaShethiyah*).

When animals are sacrificed in the Temple, it is as if the animals are finding their place in the shadow or in the branches of the tree. They are elevated from the arena of space to the arena that is above space. When the person bringing the sacrifice vicariously identifies with the animal, then he, too, transcends space (*Likutey Halakhoth, Tzitzith* 3:13).

On Rosh HaShanah, through the sounding of the shofar, we also ascend on the tree to the Throne of Glory, which is above space. Since sin only exists in the realm of space, when we transcend the arena of space, we also transcend the boundaries of sin, and God can judge us for merit. This is also the concept of *teshuvah*-repentance (*Likutey Halakhoth, Choshen Mishpat, Sheluchim* 4:16).

very end of space. The hunchback therefore existed in space, but just barely. He actually existed on the interface between the realm of space and the realm above space. Thus, he could enter the realm above space, and also transport others there.

This is alluded to when Abraham told the angels to rest "under the tree" (Genesis 18:4), rather than inviting them into his house. He wanted to bring them under the Tree of Life, above the concept of space.

This is alluded to in the expression "under the tree." In the Hebrew "the tree" is *ha-etz* (העץ). Since *vav* follows *heh*, *peh* follows *eyin*, and *kof* follows *tzadi*, the letters "under *ha-etz*" are *vav peh kof*, (ו-פ-ק) which have a numerical value of 186. This is the same numerical value as the word *makom* (מקום), meaning place. This indicates that the tree is "above" the concept of place (*Oneg Shabbath*, p. 80).

(The hunchback was on the level of the intermediate concept between space and that which is above space. He possessed the highest possible concept of little holding much, at the end of space, above which the word "place" does not apply at all. Anything higher than this is totally above the concept of space. Therefore, he could carry them from within space to a concept that is above space. Understand this well.)

I took them and carried them to the tree.* Therefore, I have the word of [these men] that I possess the highest concept of little holding much. (He appeared to be a hunchback because he carried much on his shoulders, being a case of little holding much.)

I am now giving you this as a gift — that you should be like me.

[When he finished] there was great joy and very great rejoicing.

[The Sixth Day]*

On the sixth day they were also rejoicing, and they yearned very much [saying], "How could the one without hands be brought here?" Suddenly, he appeared and said, "Here I am! I have come to your wedding!" He spoke to them in the same manner as the other [beggars], and kissed them.

---

carried them to the tree. The tzaddik who transcends space can overcome the limitations of space, and unite all peoples. He can bring them to the ultimate peace (*Likutey Halakhoth, Sefer Torah* 3:11). This is the concept of the Messiah, who will bring peace to all the world. This is why the couple said that there would be great joy if the hunchback was there. Furthermore, he could bring people to the tree, which was the source of great joy and delight, as we see in the story.

The Sixth Day. Rabbi Nachman completed the story of the sixth day on the next Tuesday (April 10) (*Sichoth HaRan* 149). It was shortly before Passover, and his house was being replastered for the festival. He had gone to Rabbi Aaron, the official rabbi of Breslov, and a group was around him. When they told him an anecdote, he said that it was related to the story of the sixth day, and he immediately told it (*Sichoth HaRan* 151).

Then he said: [You think there is something wrong with my hands.] Actually, there is nothing wrong with my hands. I have great power in my hands.* But I do not use the power in my hands in this physical world, since I need this power for something else entirely. Regarding this, I have the word of the Water Castle.*

Once, a number of men were sitting together and each one boasted about the power in his hands.* One boasted that he had a certain power in his hands, and another boasted that he had a different power.

Finally, one boasted that the power in his hands was such that if an arrow* were shot he could retrieve it.* He had such great

---

hands. Although this beggar appears not to have any hands, he actually has tremendous powers in his hands. It is just that his hands are above the physical plane and therefore cannot be seen (*Likutey Etzoth B, Tzaddik* 96).

Water Castle. *Vassiriken schloss* in Yiddish.

power in his hands. There are four powers discussed here: the power to retrieve an arrow, giving by receiving, conferring wisdom, and holding back the wind. These are discussed individually.

arrow. In one sense, shooting an arrow refers to sexual misdeeds. It is thus taught that the sperm "shoots like an arrow" (*Yebamoth* 65a). A sexual misdeed is like an arrow shot at the Shekhinah, which is the paradigmatic Feminine Principle. A tzaddik can undo the damage done by sexual misdeeds, and hence "retrieve" the arrow (*Likutey Halakhoth, Evven HaEzer, P'ru U'R'vu* 3:10).

retrieve it. This is an attribute of God, as He said, "My hand will grasp judgment... I will make My arrows drunk with blood" (Deuteronomy 32:41,42). "Grasping judgment" denotes grasping the instrument of judgment and retrieving it. Rashi thus says that this means that God can shoot an arrow and then make it come back (end of story). In this context, the arrow denotes divine punishment.

Rabbi Nathan likens God's shooting arrows to giving the Holy Land to the seven Canaanite nations. He then retrieves the arrows by taking the land from these nations and giving it to Israel (*Likutey Halakhoth, Pesach, Roshay Perakim* 9:3).

One may raise a general objection here. Why does the story say that he has the power to *shoot* the arrow and then retrieve it? Why does it mention shooting? Would it not be better not to shoot the arrow in the first place?

But actually, shooting the arrow is in itself part of the healing process. If the tzaddik can shoot the arrow, then he can undo the spiritual damage at its very root. The tzaddik does this by identifying with the evil deed, and thus "shooting the arrow."

A good example of this is bringing a sacrifice, which is meant to rectify the world of Asiyah. The slaughter-knife comes from the same root as the arrows (cf. Proverbs 25:18),

power in his hands that even after an arrow had been shot, he could return it and bring it back to him.

I challenged him, "What kind of arrow can you retrieve? There are ten types of arrows.* This is because there are ten types of poisons.* When a person shoots an arrow, he first coats it with some type of poison. There are ten types of poison. When one coats [the arrow] with the first type of poison, it does a certain degree of harm. If the [arrow] is coated with the second type of poison, it does worse harm. Thus, there are ten types of poison, each one more harmful than the other.

and are the instruments of Esau, as Isaac blessed him, "By your sword you shall live" (Genesis 27:40). The name Esau (עשו) comes from the root *asah* (עשה), which is the same as the root of Asiyah; Esau is the evil aspect of Asiyah. By applying the knife to the animal, however, one rectifies the evil of Esau at its very root. This is also the reason that we recite the sacrificial readings as the first part of the morning service. This portion of the service corresponds to Asiyah (*Likutey Halakhoth, Tolaim* 4:7).

It is taught that a person should draw people close with his right hand, and repulse them with his left (*Sotah* 47a). This is also the concept of shooting an arrow and bringing it back.

ten types of arrows. The ten types of arrows denote ten types of spiritual damage caused by sin. It is thus written, "Your arrows have gone deep into me, and Your hand has come down upon me" (Psalms 38:3). These arrows of sin caused the exile of Israel, as it is written that the Israelites said to God, "You made me a target for the arrow" (Lamentations 3:12) (*Likutey Halakhoth, Rosh HaShanah* 6:12; for other references to arrows, see *Likutey Halakhoth, Pesach, Roshay Perakim* 6:5, 9:4).

As we shall see, water is associated with the power of healing. The arrows, on the other hand, are associated with the element of dust. The closer something is to the earth, the greater the power of evil (*Likutey Halakhoth, Tolaim* 4:6).

The arrows denote the powers of evil, which come from the Breaking of the Vessels. This is associated with the expansion of the Tetragrammaton which adds up to 52, known as *BaN* (בן). As we shall see, this expansion parallels the element of dust (*Likutey Halakhoth, Tolaim* 4:8). The ten arrows then allude to the ten sefiroth of BaN.

The ten arrows can also allude to the ten nations that originally occupied the Holy Land (mentioned in Genesis 15:18-21). The *Targum* thus renders the verse, "he crushed their arrows" (Numbers 24:8), as "he vacated their land" (*Zimrath HaAretz*).

poisons. The *Zohar* speaks of ten unclean Crowns (*Tikkuney Zohar* 69, 108b). "Crown" is the highest of the sefiroth, and the ten unclean Crowns are the root forces of all evil. The ten poisons in the story denote these Crowns (*Likutey Halakhoth, Tolaim* 4:2).

The poisons represent the different ways that a person can defile the covenant of Abraham through sexual misdeeds (*Likutey Halakhoth, P'ru U'R'vu* 3:10).

"That is why there are ten types of arrows. All the arrows are actually the same, but since there are different poisons with which the arrows are rubbed, and there are ten types of poison, it is considered as if there are ten types of arrows."

I therefore asked him, "What kind of arrow* can you bring

What kind of arrow. The remedy for the arrows is through repentance. This parallels the verse, "In the beginning God created the heaven and earth" (Genesis 1:1), which the Talmud speaks of as being the first of the Ten Sayings of Creation (*Rosh HaShanah* 32a). Since the verse does not say that God said anything, this is a "hidden saying." As a hidden saying, it includes all ten (cf. *Likutey Moharan Tinyana* 12). [This parallels the sefirah of Kether, which is the highest sefirah, and includes all ten sefiroth.] (*Likutey Halakhoth, Rosh HaShanah* 6:12).

Since the first verse of the Torah includes all sayings, it also includes evil. The Torah therefore continues "The earth was desolate and void" (Genesis 1:2). But the verse then continues, "The spirit of God hovered over the face of the water." The Midrash states that this is the "spirit of the Messiah" (cf. Isaiah 11:2). The Messiah works with water, which denotes repentance, as it is written, "Pour out your heart like water" (Lamentations 2:19) (*Likutey Halakhoth, Rosh HaShanah* 6:3).

Thus, Kether includes everything, even evil. Since it can include evil, it can also rectify evil, and therefore, it is the root of repentance. This beggar had the powers of Kether, just as the Messiah will, to rectify all ten levels of evil. Since Kether contains all ten levels of holiness, it can rectify all ten levels of evil (*Likutey Halakhoth, Rosh HaShanah* 6:7).

The first saying of creation is hidden; thus, it represents God's hidden power, which also sustains evil. Therefore, this hidden saying is also the source of all ten arrows. These arrows are shot at the Princess, who represents the souls of Israel. The arrows come from the realm of the unclean.

The one who heals the Princess has the power both to shoot the arrows and to retrieve them. This is the power of the hidden saying.

This also answers the question, "If he can remove the arrows, why does he shoot them in the first place? Would it not be better not to shoot them at all?"

But he "shoots the arrows and retrieves them" because he is associated with the hidden saying, which is the source of both evil and its rectification. The arrows are needed so that free will and free choice exist in the world. But once evil exists, and the arrows have been shot, there must also be the means of retrieving and removing them.

This beggar has no hands precisely because he is associated with the hidden saying. Just as God's power is not detectable in this saying, so the beggar's hands are not detectable. Nevertheless, they have the greatest power of them all (*Likutey Halakhoth, Rosh HaShanah* 6:12).

The first word of this hidden saying is *Bereshith* (בראשית). The *Tikkuney Zohar* states that this has the same letters as *yira bosheth* (ירא בשת), which means, "fear, shame." This is the concept of repentance, whose main ingredients are fear of God and shame for one's

back?" I also asked him if he could retrieve the arrow only before it hit its victim, or if he could bring it back even after it hit.

To the second question, he replied, "I can retrieve an arrow even after it hits* its target." However to the first question he said that he could only retrieve one type of arrow.

I said to him, "If this is true, then you cannot heal the Queen's Daughter.* If you can only turn back one type of arrow,* you

---

sins (see *Likutey Moharan Tinyana* 72). Therefore, the first word, *Bereshith*, includes the concept of repentance, which removes the arrows.

God therefore gave us ten days of repentance between Rosh HaShanah and Yom Kippur. The ten days of repentance serve to remove the ten arrows through our repentance. The arrows are the blemish that we make in the Shekhinah through our sins (*Likutey Halakhoth, Rosh HaShanah* 6:13; cf. 6:4; also see *Ibid., Roshay Perakim* 6:7).

On Yom Kippur we recite the confession ten times. This also serves to remove the ten arrows. The arrows have injured the Shekhinah, but with our confessions, we are able to remove them.

While reciting the confession (*viduy*, וידוי), it is a custom to strike the heart with the fist. This alludes to the fact that the arrows are removed through the power of the hands. Closely related to this is the custom of lifting one's hands to God when praying for forgiveness (*Likutey Halakhoth, Rosh HaShanah, Roshay Perakim* 6:9).

Our sages teach that, "It was not necessary to begin the Torah with *Bereshith*" (cf. Rashi on Genesis 1:1). But it was done "to show the strength of His deeds" (Psalms 111:6). This is the strength of God's "hand," which is contained in *Bereshith*, alluded to by the handless beggar. This, as Rashi explained, was to remove the ten nations, who occupied the land previously (see Genesis 15:18-21). These ten nations, as we have seen, parallel the ten arrows (*Likutey Halakhoth, Pesach, Roshay Perakim* 9:3).

As we have seen, the concept of slaughtering a sacrifice rectifies the effects of the ten arrows. The ritual slaughter involves a back and forth movement of the knife. This back and forth movement is also related to the concept of shooting and retrieving.

Rabbi Nachman also speaks of praying with the Attribute of Justice. This takes the arrow, which is the means of punishment, and uses it as a means of healing. Prayer is also called an arrow. Jacob thus said that he captured the land of the Amorites with his "sword and bow," and the "bow" is interpreted to mean prayer (*Likutey Halakhoth, Tolaim* 4:7).

In general, there are four aspects of ten here; ten arrows, ten walls, ten types of pulse, and ten types of song. We shall discuss their relationship shortly (*Likutey Halakhoth, Pesach, Roshay Perakim* (9).

after it hits. It would seem to be a difficult enough task to retrieve an arrow after it was fired. But to retrieve an arrow and undo its effects after it has hit its target is truly remarkable. This is obviously to be interpreted on a spiritual level rather than on a physical plane (*Likutey Halakhoth, Evven HaEzer* 3:10).

Queen's Daughter. The Divine Presence (Shekhinah), which is identified with the souls of Israel. See Story #1.

cannot heal her."

One [of the men present] boasted that he had such power in his hands that whenever he took or received something from another, he was actually giving to him.* [For him the very act of receiving was an act of giving.] Therefore, he was a master of charity.*

I asked him what type of charity he gave, [since there are ten types of charity]. He replied that he gave a tithe.*

I said to him, "If this is so, you cannot heal the Queen's Daughter. You cannot even approach the place where she is; you can only go through one wall* [in the place where she is staying].

---

one type of arrow. We thus see that some tzaddikim can rectify some evil, but it takes an extraordinary tzaddik to be able to rectify all types of evil (*Rimzey Maasioth*). Elsewhere, Rabbi Nachman writes that in order to take a *pidyon* (redemption) a tzaddik must know how to plead before all twenty-four heavenly courts (*Sichoth HaRan* 175; *Likutey Moharan* 215).

actually giving to him. The Talmud thus says that when a person gives a gift to a very important person, the acceptance of the gift is in itself a gift. Thus, when a woman gives an important man a gift, it is counted as if he had given her something of monetary value (*Kiddushin* 7a).

Rabbi Nachman also once said, "When I take money from someone, I am actually giving him something. My taking is actually giving" (*Sichoth HaRan* 150). This is the ultimate level of the tzaddik (*Likutey Etzoth* B, *Tzaddik* 96).

charity. Every time he accepts something, he is actually giving. Since there is no limit to how much he can accept, his "giving" is limitless.

However, this is also the concept of charity. When a person gives charity, the spiritual benefits that he receives are much greater than any amount that he gives.

This concept of charity is most important, since the entire world was created for the sake of charity. Moreover, the very creation of the world was an act of altruism and charity on the part of God It is thus written, "I have said, the world is built on charity" (Psalms 89:3). Furthermore, the paradigm of charity was Abraham, and it is thus taught that the world was created for the sake of Abraham (*Likutey Halakhoth, Pesach, Roshay Perakim* 9:4).

As we see in the story, the walls of water stand through charity. This charity is the logic of the Vacated Space that God will reveal in the Ultimate Future (see *Likutey Moharan* 64; *Likutey Halakhoth, Tolaim* 4:10).

tithe. *Ma'aser.* That is, one tenth of his income. This is the concept of "tithe of money" (*ma'aser kesafim*), which is discussed in Jewish law.

one wall. That is, through one of the ten walls of water surrounding the Water Castle, as we

You cannot get to where she is."

One [of the men present] boasted about the power in his hands, saying that there were officials in the world. [These are highly placed people who are in charge of cities and nations.]* Each one needs wisdom. Through his hands he could give them wisdom.* He did this by laying hands on them.

---

see later in the story. These walls consist of waves in the water, as the story later states explicitly.

Charity is associated with water, as it is written, "Your charity is like the waves of the sea" (Isaiah 48:18) (end of story). Rabbi Nachman also taught explicitly that charity is water (*Likutey Moharan Tinyana* 15; *Likutey Halakhoth, Rosh HaShanah* 6:8). Charity is related to the sefirah of Chesed, which is also associated with water.

Therefore, one can only enter the walls of water through charity. If one can grant all ten types of charity, one can enter through all ten walls leading to the Water Castle (*Likutey Halakhoth, Rosh HaShanah* 6:8).

Both charity and the entire Torah are likened to water. It is for this reason that charity includes all of the Torah. The Torah itself is referred to as charity, as it is written, "It will be charity for us if we keep all this Torah" (Deuteronomy 6:25). Charity, however, is given only through the tzaddik, as it is written, "The tzaddik has mercy and gives" (Psalms 37:21).

Since the environment of the tzaddik is charity (*tzedakah*), which is likened to water, the tzaddik is likened to a fish. It is therefore said of the children of Joseph (the paradigm of the tzaddik and personification of Yesod), "They shall increase like fish..." (Genesis 48:16). When a tzaddik takes charity, he is able to grow spiritually, through his worship and study of the Torah. This is great merit for the one who gives him charity. Thus, whenever the tzaddik takes. he gives, as we saw earlier.

Since fish represent the tzaddik, who is completely holy, everything in a fish is kosher. With mammals and birds, some parts of their bodies are not kosher, such as forbidden fats, the sciatic nerve (*gid ha-nasheh*) and the blood. In the case of a kosher fish, on the other hand, everything is kosher.

This is also the reason that a fish does not require any kind of ritual slaughter. Other animals need this rectification, but fish are inherently holy, just like a tzaddik (*Likutey Halakhoth, Yoreh Deah, Dagim* 4:1).

These are... This appears only in the Yiddish.

give them wisdom. Laying of hands confers wisdom. Thus, Moses laid his hands on Joshua to give him wisdom. The Torah says, "Joshua, son of Nun, was full of the spirit of wisdom, because Moses had laid his hands upon him" (Deuteronomy 34:9). Joshua thus became a man "who has wind-spirit in him" (Numbers 27:18). This meant that he knew how to determine each person's wind-spirit (*ruach*), which is manifested in that person's pulse (*Likutey Halakhoth, Tolaim* 4:2).

I asked him, "What type of wisdom can you confer with your hands? There are ten types of wisdom."

When he replied what kind of wisdom, I said to him, "If this is the case, you cannot heal the Queen's Daughter. You cannot understand her pulse, since there are ten types of pulse.* [You can only confer one type of wisdom, and therefore only understand one type of pulse]."

One [of the men present] boasted that he had such great power in his hands that when there was a storm, he could hold it back* with his hands. Then with his hands he could make the wind blow with the proper force* so that the wind was beneficial.

I asked him, "What kind of wind can you hold with your

---

ten types of pulse. This is discussed at length in the Zoharic literature (*Tikkuney Zohar* 70, p. 108a; see *Shaar Ruach HaKodesh*, p. 14). These ten types of pulse beats correspond to the ten Hebrew vowel points. The pulse beat is related to the shape of the vowel point.

In Hebrew, the word for pulse is *defek* (דפק), from the word *dafak*, meaning to knock (as on a door). This is alluded to in the verse, "The sound of my beloved knocks..." (Song of Songs 5:2) (*Likutey Halakhoth, Rosh HaShanah, Roshay Perakim* 6:2).

The ten types of pulse relate to the vowel points, which are associated with the universe of Beriyah (*Likutey Halakhoth, Pesach, Roshay Perakim* 9:3).

Human life depends on the pulse. The ten pulse types parallel the ten types of song (see *Likutey Moharan Tinyana* 24). Therefore, healing requires knowing the pulses, and then knowing what song to use as a remedy (*Likutey Halakhoth, P'ru U'R'vu* 3:1).

hold it back. This is alluded to in the verse, "Who gathers up the wind in His palm" (Proverbs 30:4). Rabbi Nachman taught that this was related to the concept of melody, as we see in the story (end of story).

The wind relates to air, the highest of the four elements. This relates to the expansion of the Tetragrammaton that adds up to 72, known as *AB*, the highest of the four expansions. It is on the level of Chokhmah and Atziluth. This is also the level of the cantillations, which are an aspect of song. (This is discussed at greater length below.)

The concept of song comes from the wind and breath in the lungs. The Talmud also notes that a north wind blew on David's lyre (Aolean harp), and caused it to play music (*Berakhoth* 3b; *Likutey Halakhoth, Pesach, Roshay Perakim* 9:3).

Holding the wind is an attribute of God, as it is written, "The storm wind does His bidding" (Psalms 148:8) (*Likutey Halakhoth, Pesach, Roshay Perakim* 9:3).

proper force. *Mishkal* in Hebrew, which denotes balance. The Yiddish says, "With the hand, He can make the wind with a measure, so that there should be a wind as we need it, and the [proper] measure."

hands? There are ten kinds of winds." He described the type of wind that he could hold, and I said, "If that is the case, you cannot heal the Queen's Daughter. You can only play one type of melody. She can only be healed through melody,* and there are ten types of melody.* But you can only play one type of melody, out of these ten."

healed through melody. From this we see, in general, the importance of song and melody. The tzaddik must know all ten categories of song, because the Princess can only be healed through song and joy (*Sichoth HaRan* 273).

This healing takes place in the Water Castle. Joy and song, however, are associated with water, as it is written, "You shall draw water with joy from the well of salvation" (Isaiah 12:3). Therefore, when water was drawn for the special Sukkoth libations, it was a special time of rejoicing, known as *Simchath Beth HaSho'evah*. On the seventh day, people would take the willow (*hoshanah*), which also grew by water, since the Torah describes it as "willow of the brook" (Leviticus 23:40) (*Likutey Halakhoth, Rosh HaShanah, Roshay Perakim* 6:2).

This is also the concept of Purim, which is a festival of joy. Passover is the first of the three festivals, but preparations for it are made on Purim, which occurs a month earlier (see *Megillah* 32a; *Orach Chaim* 427). Mordechai is the tzaddik who can heal even those who are very ill spiritually, and he does it through joy and song. He heals the Princess, who denotes the souls of Israel (*Likutey Halakhoth, Basar BeChalav* 5:19).

Both song and the pulse depend on wind and breath. Therefore the energy of song gives strength to the energy of the pulse. The wind associated with music and the pulse also upholds the walls of water. The Princess also escapes the arrows by running into these walls of water. Therefore, all four concepts in this story are interdependent, and hence all four major powers are in the hands. These correspond to the four concepts of written Hebrew: cantillations (*taamim*), vowel points (*nekudoth*), crowns (*tagim*), and letters (*othioth*), referred to collectively as *TaNTA*. All of these are interdependent. Everything, however, ultimately depends on melody, which corresponds to the cantillations, and hence is the highest level of the four (*Likutey Halakhoth, Tolaim* 4:11).

ten types of melody. Rabbi Nachman himself taught that the Ten Psalms were a "general rectification" (*tikkun kellali*) for all sins, particularly sexual sins, and especially those involving emitting semen in vain (*Likutey Moharan* 205; *Likutey Moharan Tinyana* 92; see end of story). These involved the ten types of melody found in the psalms. The Ten Psalms are numbers 16, 32, 41, 42, 59, 77, 90, 105, 137, 150.

It is highly significant that the Ten Psalms were revealed during the week before Rabbi Nachman began to tell the story of the Seven Beggars (*Alim Leterufah*, letter of Tulchin at end of book; cf. *Sichoth HaRan* 141, *Parparoth LeChokhmah* on *Likutey Moharan Tinyana* 75). It is significant that the concept of the Ten Psalms is also related to the power of charity mentioned here in the story, since Rabbi Nachman said, "If someone comes to my grave, gives a penny to charity, and recites these Ten Psalms, I will yank him out of Gehenom by his *peyoth* (earlocks)" (*Chayay Moharan* 45a #41; cf. *Nevey Tzaddikim*, p. 66).

It is also significant to note that this relates to the sixth day. The sixth day parallels the sefirah of Yesod, which pertains to the sexual organ. Hence, the rectification for sexual misdeeds is part of this day's story.

The sixth day was also the day when man committed the first sin. This was the shooting of the ten arrows. The rectification must go to the root of the evil, and therefore takes place also on the sixth day.

The psalms as a whole also contain all ten different types of song (*Tikkuney Zohar* 13; *Likutey Moharan Tinyana* 92). King David ended the book with Psalm 150, which contains the expression " *halelu-hu* ("praise Him") ten times. The last of these is, "Praise Him with cymbals of *teruah*" (Psalms 150:5), because the *teruah* (stacatto) also includes all ten types of song (*Likutey Halakhoth, Evven HaEzer, P'ru U'R'vu* 3:10).

Through the ten types of song, we can balance the ten types of wind. The ten winds, however, form the ten types of waves, which are the ten walls around the Water Castle. Therefore, when one knows the ten songs, one can penetrate the ten walls (*Likutey Halakhoth, Rosh HaShanah, Roshay Perakim* 6:3).

Sin and spiritual damage are associated with sadness and depression. The healing is therefore through song, which brings joy. With his hands this beggar could enter the nine chambers of joy (cf. *Likutey Moharan* 24; *Likutey Halakhoth, Orach Chaim, Hodaah* 6:20; cf. *Likutey Halakhoth, Evven HaEzer, P'ru U'R'vu* 3:1).

The "hidden saying," *Bereshith*, also contains all ten types of songs. It is therefore taught that *Bereshith* (בראשית) has the letters *shir taev* (שיר תאב) (*Tikkuney Zohar* 10; *Likutey Halakhoth, Rosh HaShanah* 6:14).

The sacrifice and libation offerings were meant to refine fallen souls and raise the sparks of the souls that had fallen deep into the realm of evil. While the libation offerings (*nesakhim*) were being poured, the Levites would sing. This was because the healing of the Princess was through song (*Likutey Halakhoth, Rosh HaShanah* 6:14).

The ten songs were also alluded to in the ten sounds of the shofar. On Rosh HaShanah the shofar is sounded in the following manner:

tekiah shevarim teruah tekiah
tekiah shevarim tekiah
tekiah teruah tekiah

Thus, there are a total of ten sounds. These allude to the ten types of song.

Furthermore, on Rosh HaShanah, in the mussaf service, ten verses of *malkhiyoth* (kingship), ten verses of *zikhronoth* (remembrances), and ten verses of *shofroth* (shofar sounds) are said. Each set of ten verses also parallels the ten types of song.

Rosh HaShanah is the beginning of the ten days of repentance; therefore it has these ten types of song. Song is the basis of repentance, since song leads to joy, and joy brings one to the side of merit (*Likutey Moharan* 282). It is only through the ten types of song that those who are far from God can be brought back (*Likutey Halakhoth, P'ru U'R'vu* 3:10).

The ten days of repentance also parallel the ten types of song. We begin these ten days with Rosh HaShanah, where all ten types of song are brought into play through the ten sounds of the shofar. Shofar is the rectification of these ten types of song, as it is written, "Make song good with the *teruah* sound" (Psalms 33:3). The psalm says, "God will rise in

[All the people there] spoke up and asked me, "What is your ability?"

I replied, "I can do what you cannot do. [In each of the cases that you discussed] there are nine portions that you cannot accomplish. I can accomplish them all."*

---

teruah, God in the sound of the shofar. Sing to God sing..." (Psalms 47:6). This indicates that after sounding the shofar, one can sing all types of songs properly (*Likutey Halakhoth, P'ru U'R'vu* 3:10).

The ten days of repentance end with Yom Kippur. This completes the ten types of song (*Likutey Halakhoth, P'ru U'R'vu* 3:11).

I can accomplish them all. The handless beggar thus had four powers: (1) to remove the arrows; (2) the power of charity, to go through the ten walls; (3) the power to confer wisdom and know the pulse; and (4) the power to control the wind and play all types of music.

On Sukkoth, we take the four species in hand to strengthen the hands of this beggar. Then on Simchath Torah we perfect the concept of joy and song when we complete the Torah and begin it once again. We begin the Torah with the word *Bereshith*, which is the hidden saying (*Likutey Halakhoth, Rosh HaShanah, Roshay Perakim* 6:2).

The four species are the palm (*lulav*), willow (*aravah*), myrtle (*hadas*) and citron (*ethrog*) (Leviticus 23:40). The lulav has the form of an arrow, and this strengthens the power to remove the arrows. The "willows of the brook" strengthen the power of the handless beggar to penetrate the walls of water. The myrtle parallels the life of the soul in Chokhmah (Wisdom), and this gives the power to understand the ten pulsebeats. Finally, the ethrog perfects the concept of joy and song.

The Torah is then completed on Simchath Torah, with the verse, "... and all the mighty hand... which Moses wrought in the sight of all Israel" (Deuteronomy 34:12). This strengthens the concept of the hand. We then immediately begin the Torah with *Bereshith*, the "hidden saying" (*Likutey Halakhoth, Rosh HaShanah, Roshay Perakim* 6:5).

There are four groups of ten in this story: ten arrows, ten walls (charity), ten types of pulse (wisdom in hand), and ten songs (power to hold back wind). All are ten.

These four parallel the four supernal universes, Atziluth (Nearness), Beriyah (Creation), Yetzirah (Formation), and Asiyah (Making). These parallel the four letters in the Tetragrammaton (YHVH, יהוה).

They also parallel the four expansions of the Tetragrammaton. They are:

YOD HY VYV HY	(יוד הי ויו הי)	72	AB
YOD HY VAV HY	(יוד הי ואו הי)	63	SaG
YOD HA VAV HA	(יוד הא ואו הא)	45	MaH
YOD HH VV HH	(יוד הה וו הה)	52	BaN

They also parallel the four concepts involved in writing, referred to as *TaNTA*: *taamim* (cantillations), *nekudoth* (vowel points), *tagim* (crowns), and *othioth* (letters).

In addition to this, they parallel the four elements: fire, air, water and dust.

They also parallel the four levels of creation: the inert, plants, animals, and humans (speaking creatures).

The final parallel is the four parts of the daily morning service, the *Korbanoth* (the sacrificial readings), *Pesukey deZimra* (the Introductory Psalms), the Sh'ma and its blessings, and the Amidah.

All these groups contain four elements, and they parallel the four elements in this story.

The four expansions of the Tetragrammaton relate to the highest levels of creation, known as Adam Kadmon. AB is above all comprehension, and nothing can be said about it at all. SaG was the beginning of all revelation, from which the Universe of Nekudim (points) came into existence. These points were the original vessels. BaN represents the breaking of the vessels. Finally, the Broken Vessels were rectified when MaH and BaN were unified. [This parallels the unification in Atziluth, which is lower than Adam Kadmon, of Zer Anpin and Malkhuth.]

The Princess denotes Malkhuth, which is God's kingdom. The main purpose of creation was to reveal Malkhuth. God therefore brought forth the original Vessels, which were known as the Kings (from Genesis 36:31-39). As a result of the imperfections built in creation, these Vessels were broken. This was to bring the concept of evil and free will into the world. The Breaking of the Vessels created the forces of the Other Side, represented in the story by the king who tried to capture the Princess. This king is the counterpart on the Other Side, of Malkhuth, the Kingdom of God. This evil king wants to capture the Princess, denoting the inner holiness of all things, this being the mystery of the verse, "All glorious, is the Princess inside" (Psalms 45:14).

The Princess is thus in each of the seven Kings of Edom (Genesis 36:31-39), who represent the vessels which were shattered. When the vessels were shattered, and the kings died, the Princess was captured by the evil king. The Princess represents the sparks of holiness that fell down into the realm of the evil husks (*klipoth*), from which the Kings of Edom draw their power.

The Princess can only escape when she goes through the walls of water. This is the rectification, involving the light of MaH. Water is the third element, just as MaH is the third expansion of the Tetragrammaton. It is also for this reason that water cleanses all impurities (*Likutey Halakhoth, Pesach, Roshay Perakim* 9:1).

The ten arrows parallel the Universe of Asiyah, the lowest of the four universes. This is the universe where the powers of evil have their strongest hold. It also parallels the element of dust and BaN.

The ten walls of water parallel the Universe of Yetzirah. It also parallels the expansion known as MaH, and the element of water. [Thus, Rabbi Akiba told the four who entered *Pardes* that when they ascend they should not say "water water" (*Chagigah* 14b). Yetzirah is the domain of "water," but it is not physical water.]

The ten pulses parallel the Universe of Beriyah. This relates to the *nekudoth* (vowel points), which are the second highest level. It also parallels the expansion SaG.

Finally, the ten types of song parallel the Universe of Atziluth. This parallels the *taamim* (cantillations) which are the highest level of expression. Cantillation and song involve the same concept. This is related to the expansion AB (*Likutey Halakhoth, Tolaim* 4:5).

This is the story:

Once there was a king* who desired a Queen's Daughter.* He made all kinds of plots to capture her until he was finally successful and took her captive.*

Then the king had a dream. The Queen's Daughter was standing over him, and she killed him.*

The four powers of the hands are alluded to in the four times that hands are mentioned in the poem "A Woman of Valor" (Proverbs 31:19,20) (*Chokhmah U'Tevunah* 21:5).

king. The king is a manifestation of the Evil Urge (*Yetzer Hara*), who is known as an "old and foolish king" (Ecclesiastes 4:13) (*Likutey Moharan* 1; *Likutey Halakhoth, Tolaim* 4:2).

As is known, evil came into existence basically with the Breaking of the Vessels. The Vessels are represented by the "Kings of Edom" (Genesis 36:31-39). Therefore, the power of evil that came into existence when the vessels broke is appropriately represented by a king (*Likutey Halakhoth, Pesach, Roshay Perakim* 9:1; *Tolaim* 4:3).

This evil king was personified by Pharaoh, who tried to keep the Israelites captive (*Likutey Halakhoth, Tolaim* 4:4).

Queen's Daughter. This is the same as the Princess described in Stories #1 and #2. See Introduction.

In general, this Princess represents every Jewish soul, which is attacked by the forces of evil (*Sichoth HaRan* 273; *Likutey Halakhoth, Basar BeChalav* 5:19).

In more general terms, the Queen's Daughter is the Shekhinah, which is referred to as the Congregation of Israel (*Knesseth Yisroel*) (*Likutey Halakhoth, Rosh HaShanah* 6:12; *Ibid. Roshay Perakim* 6:7; *P'ru U'R'vu* 3:10). This is the sefirah of Malkhuth (kingship, royalty), the Kingdom of God (*Likutey Halakhoth, Pesach, Roshay Perakim* 9:1). This is the root of all souls, and the root of all worlds, since all were created to reveal God's Kingdom (*Likutey Halakhoth, Tolaim* 4:3).

This concept of the Princess is personified in many ways. In one sense it is personified by the entire nation of Israel. It was personified by Pharaoh's daughter, a holy person, whose holiness had been captured by an evil king, her father. Just like the Princess in the story, she tried to rid herself of the king's influence, by going to bathe in the water (Exodus 2:5) (*Likutey Halakhoth, Pesach, Roshay Perakim* 9:3).

took her captive. The Evil King represents the broken pieces of the shattered vessels. These are the forces of evil which are nourished by the 288 sparks of holiness, which represent the Princess in their power (see Story #1). This is alluded to in the verse, "The earth was desolate and void, with darkness on the deep" (Genesis 1:2). (*Likutey Halakhoth, Tolaim* 4:3).

The capture of the Princess was re-enacted on a physical plane when Sarah was taken captive in Pharaoh's palace (Genesis 12:15), and later, when she was taken to Abimelekh's house harem (Genesis 20:2). It was manifested when the Israelites were enslaved in Egypt (*Likutey Halakhoth, Tolaim* 4:4).

killed him. The Evil One realizes that in the end, evil will be destroyed by the souls of Israel.

When he woke up, he took this dream to heart. He summoned all the dream interpreters, and they all said that it would come true in its literal meaning, that she would kill him.

The king could not decide what to do with her. If he killed her, it would grieve him. If he sent her away, this would anger him, since another man would then have her. This would frustrate him very much, since he had worked so hard to get her, only to have her belong to another man. Furthermore, if he exiled her and she ended up with another man, there would be all the more chance of the dream coming true. With an ally, it would be even easier for her to kill him.

Still, he was afraid because of the dream, and did not want to keep her near him. Therefore, the king did not know what to do* with her.

As a result of the dream, his love for her gradually began to wane. As time passed, his desire for her grew less and less. The same was true of her. Her love for him declined* more and more until she hated him.* Eventually, she fled.*

God thus said, "I will remove the unclean spirit from the world" (Zechariah 13:2). It is thus taught that in the ultimate future, the Evil Urge will be slaughtered (*Sukkah* 52a). This is also the concept of the thanksgiving offering, which involves destroying the evil within the individual bringing it (*Sanhedrin* 43b; *Likutey Halakhoth, Tolaim* 4:2).

Thus, the Kingdom of Evil sees that it will be cast off and destroyed in the end. This was manifested on the physical plane when "God made great plagues for Pharaoh because of Sarai" (Genesis 12:17). Similarly, God came to Abimelekh in a dream (just as the king saw a dream), and told him, "You will die because of the woman you took" (Genesis 20:7) (*Likutey Halakhoth, Tolaim* 4:4).

did not know what to do. The *Yetzer Hara* (Evil Urge) thinks of ways to destroy the soul, even when the soul is in its power (*Likutey Halakhoth, Tolaim* 4:2).

Her love for him declined. At first there was some love between the soul and the Evil Urge. As a result of her exile, she forgot her lofty status, and felt some love and closeness to the Evil One. But when she began to realize that he no longer loved her, her love for him also grew weaker (*Likutey Halakhoth, Tolaim* 4:2).

she hated him. The soul also begins to realize that the Evil One wants to destroy her. She therefore begins to hate him and plans how to escape (*Likutey Halakhoth, Tolaim* 4:2).

fled. This had its parallel on the physical plane when Jacob fled from Laban (Genesis 31:20-21). Jacob contained all the souls of Israel, and was fleeing from Evil, which was personified by Laban.

The king sent* his men to search for her. When they returned, they reported that she was near* the Water Castle.*

It was repeated when the Israelites fled from Pharaoh. It is thus written, "Pharaoh heard that the people had fled" (Exodus 14:5).

King David, also, said, "If I only had the wings of a dove, I would fly away and be at rest... I would rush myself to a shelter from the stormy wind and tempest" (Psalms 55:7,9) (*Likutey Halakhoth, Tolaim* 4:2).

The king sent. Evil wishes to recapture the internal holiness in all things (*Likutey Halakhoth, Pesach, Roshay Perakim* 9:1). This was expressed on the physical plane when the Egyptians wanted to place the Israelites under their dominion, and said, "Let us deal wisely with them... lest they increase, and when there is a war, fight against us, and go forth from the land" (Exodus 1:10) (*Likutey Halakhoth, Tolaim* 4:4).

she was near... As on the physical plane, it was reported to Pharaoh that the Israelites had fled and were on the shore of the Red Sea (Exodus 14:5) (*Likutey Halakhoth, Tolaim* 4:4).

Water Castle. When the Princess wanted to escape the king, she went to water, since water cleanses all things. This is why an important step toward purification and repentance is immersion in a mikvah.

Rashi notes that water was created before heaven and earth, and for this reason, the creation of water is not mentioned explicitly in the Torah (Rashi on Genesis 1:1). This is because the creation of water is included in the word *Bereshith* ("In the beginning"), which is the "hidden saying." Water is thus the root of all creation, but the creation of water is concealed in the word *Bereshith*.

As we have seen, *Bereshith* includes the creation of all things, even evil. Therefore, since water comes from this saying, water has an affinity for evil and becomes unclean very easily. Thus, even though a "second level defilement" (*sheni le-tumah*) will not render food unclean, it will not only make water (and other designated liquids) unclean, but will make them a "first level defilement" (*rishon le-tumah*), which can defile foods (*Parah* 8:7; *Pesachim* 14b).

Conversely, however, water can cleanse evil at its root. Therefore, in a mikvah, water is needed to cleanse all things.

Water thus involves a joining of good and evil, through which evil can be rectified. Such a joining is referred to as "Knowledge" (Daath), as in the verse, "Adam knew Eve his wife" (Genesis 4:1). The final rectification will take place through the cleansing power of water-knowledge, as it is written, "The world will then be filled with knowledge, as water fills the seas" (Isaiah 11:9).

Since the main rectification of evil is divine reward and punishment, this also comes about through water. It is thus written, "[God] spreads His light on it, and He covers the depths of the seas; since by these He judges peoples..." (Job 36:30,31; cf. Rashi *ad loc.*).

When one immerses in a mikvah, one brings oneself back into the hidden saying. In doing so, one totally annuls oneself for God.

As we have seen, a person goes through the ten walls of water through charity. The

This was a castle made of water.* It had ten walls* one inside

hidden saying, *Bereshith*, is said to refer to various priestly portions, such as *challah*, *bikurim*, and *terumah*, all of which are called *reshith* (beginning). This is the concept of charity, which is the first money a person must spend. Through charity, one can enter the hidden saying, and thus enter the ten walls of water (*Likutey Halakhoth, Rosh HaShanah* 6:14).

Since water represents knowledge, which is the joining of good and evil, it was the root of the Tree of Knowledge. There are four elements, fire, air, water, and dust, and also four levels of life, humans, animals, plants, and inert objects. The third level is water and plants; therefore, the two are parallel. For this reason, Knowledge was embodied in a tree, which is a member of the plant family. This is also associated with the expansion MaH.

Since water is the joining of good and evil, it is the source of free will. It is also the source of all cleansing.

The fourth level is dust, which corresponds to the expansion BaN. Water is MaH. [Indeed, some say that the Hebrew word for water, *mayim* (מים), is the plural of the word *mah* (מה), meaning "what."]

It is taught that, at first, God wanted to create the world with the Attribute of Justice. This was BaN, which corresponds to dust, the source of the King's arrows. But God then added the Attribute of Mercy, which is the expansion MaH, and created the world from both. Therefore, the world is created from MaH and BaN, that is, from dust and water. Man was also created from dust and water, and this is why man has free will.

It is written, "the spirit of God hovered over the face of the water" (Genesis 1:2). The Midrash states that this is the "spirit of the Messiah." The Messiah works through the primeval water that came from the hidden saying, and thus will rectify and cleanse the world. But tzaddikim in all generations also participate in this process.

This is why Pharaoh's daughter, when she wanted to escape from the defilement of the palace, went to wash. She wanted to cleanse herself in the concept of water (*Likutey Halakhoth, Pesach, Roshay Perakim* 9:3).

The Torah itself is also likened to water, since the Torah is also the means through which evil is elevated and transformed. It is therefore said regarding the Torah, "Let all who thirst come to water" (Isaiah 55:1) (*Likutey Halakhoth, Tolaim* 4:2).

made of water. When the Princess fled, she ran to water. This was the world as it was first created, as the Midrash says, "When the world was first created, it was water in water" (*Yerushalmi, Chagigah* 2:1). Water was the first thing created, and the rest of creation was based on it, as it is written, "[God] spread the earth on the water" (Psalms 136:6). This indicates that the earth and everything on it originated in water (*Likutey Halakhoth, Pesach, Roshay Perakim* 9:2).

The Water Castle is alluded to in the verse, "God will open His good treasury to give you rain in due time" (Deuteronomy 28:12). This good treasury is the Water Castle, which is the source of rain and bounty.

This is why Moses rested by a well after fleeing to Midian (Exodus 2:15). The Midrash states that he was emulating Jacob, who found his wife by a well. All wells pertain to the

Water Castle, where the Princess fled. Therefore, Moses and Jacob knew that they would find their aspect of the Princess, that is, a wife, at a well. The Princess includes all virtuous wives.

This is also why Moses was cast into the water as an infant, and then drawn from the water (Exodus 2:3-5). He had to enter through all ten walls of water. This is something that only Moses and the Messiah, the first and last redeemers of Israel, would be able to do. Moses was thus cast into the water to show that he had the ability to pass through the ten walls of water in safety. He could then bring about the redemption, which was the healing of the Princess.

For this reason, the Patriarchs dug wells (Genesis 26:18). Wells are derived from the ten walls of water, where the Malkhuth of holiness is found. This is personified by the Princess, who is faith. Since the Patriarchs saw their task to be revealing faith in God to the world, they dug wells (*Likutey Halakhoth, Rosh HaShanah, Roshay Perakim* 6:3).

As mentioned earlier, the Breaking of the Vessels was through the expansion of BaN, while the rectification is through MaH. Since the four expansions are AB, SaG, MaH and Ban, and the four elements are fire, air, water and dust, MaH parallels water, and BaN parallels dust. Therefore, the Breaking of Vessels is associated with dust, while their rectification is through water.

Dust is therefore the place where all the forces of evil have a grasp. It is thus written, "The serpent's bread is dust" (Isaiah 65:25).

Water, on the other hand, cleanses all impurities. It is for this reason that, before entering the Temple or any other holy place, one must immerse in water. Similarly, before a woman can be with her husband, she must immerse. All Israel, similarly, entered the covenant of the Torah through immersion, and a proselyte relives this by immersing in a mikvah (*Kerithuth* 9a; *Likutey Halakhoth, Tolaim* 4:3).

ten walls. The ten walls of water parallel the ten measures of wisdom given to the world (*Zimrath HaAretz*).

As we have seen, water denotes knowledge and wisdom. Through the ten types of knowledge embodied in the ten walls of water, this beggar could know the ten pulses (*Likutey Halakhoth, Rosh HaShanah. Roshay Perakim* 6:2).

Actually, the ten walls may be alluded to by the fact that the word "water" (*mayim*) occurs eleven times in the account of creation (Genesis 1:2, 1:6 [3], 1:7 [2], 1:9, 1:10, 1:20, 1:21, 1:22). Ten of these parallel the ten sayings with which the world was created, and the eleventh parallels the eleventh saying, "It is not good for man to be alone" (Genesis 2:18), which is the root of evil. These eleven times thus parallel the eleven ingredients in the incense.

Thus, the ten walls parallel the ten sayings of creation (*Avoth* 5:1). The constriction (*tzimtzum*) of God's power that was necessary for creation is represented by the ten walls. The forces of creation involved God's wisdom (Chokhmah), as it is written, "They were all made with wisdom" (Psalms 104:24). Wisdom is represented by water.

Furthermore, the world cannot endure God's wisdom (Chokhmah) unless it is constricted. This constriction is represented by the ten walls of water (*Likutey Halakhoth, Rosh HaShanah, Roshay Perakim* 6:4).

The Ten Walls and Ten Sayings also represent the Ten Sefiroth. These Ten Sefiroth can only be revealed because God constricted His light to the sides, creating a Vacated Space (see *Likutey Moharan* 64). One cannot enter the castle without drowning, since no one can enter the Vacated Space.

All creation was thus constricted from God's wisdom, which is likened to water. Thus, all physical creation also came into being through water. It is thus taught, "at first the universe was water in water" (*Yerushalmi, Chagigah* 2:1). God then created all things from water, as He said, "Let the water be gathered, and let dry land appear" (Genesis 1:9). Therefore, the element of dust also originates from water (see *Sefer Yetzirah*, Long Version 1:12). After that, everything came from dust.

The original light was God's wisdom, which is alluded to by water. The constriction, however, also took place through God's wisdom, and is also water. Therefore, the castle is water, and the walls are also water. This is a paradoxical situation which cannot be understood.

The main creation, however, was the earth, which would be an environment for man. Man was created from "the dust of the earth" (Genesis 2:7). Therefore, the water must be constricted into dust so that we can survive.

We cannot survive on water; similarly, we cannot understand the wisdom (water) and logic of the *tzimtzum* (constriction). But in the Ultimate Future, "The earth will be covered with knowledge of God, just as the water covers the sea" (Isaiah 11:9). We will then understand the wisdom and the logic of the *tzimtzum* (*Likutey Halakhoth, Tolaim* 4:5).

Since the entire *tzimtzum* is alluded to in the word *Bereshith*, this word contains all ten walls of water (*Likutey Halakhoth, Rosh HaShanah* 6:14).

The generation of the flood blemished these ten walls, and, since there was nothing to hold back the water, the flood occurred. Still, the world was not destroyed completely; the walls of the ark remained so that Noah and those with him were able to survive. The Hebrew word for Noah's ark is *teyvah* (תיבה), which also has the connotation of a word. This was like the walls of water, which were the ten words or sayings of creation.

When God then swore that He would not send another flood, He showed the rainbow as the sign of His covenant (Genesis 9:13). This bow pertains to the arrows of holiness, which are the antithesis of the arrows of the Evil King. It was seen in the clouds, which are the source of water and rectification. It was also for this reason that the Torah was given in a cloud.

Therefore, in the beginning of the *zikhronoth* (remembrances) on Rosh HaShanah, we recall Noah's ark (*Likutey Halakhoth, Rosh HaShanah, Roshay Perakim* 6:4).

As we have seen, the ten walls of water represent the Vacated Space. Rabbi Nachman teaches that the only way to enter the Vacated Space is through the power of song (*Likutey Moharan* 64). Therefore, the way to enter through these ten walls of water was through the ten types of song (*Chokhmah U'Tevunah* 21:2).

The Torah is likened to water, and the ten walls of water parallel the Ten Commandments, which include the entire Torah. [The entire Torah contains 613 commandments, but if one adds up the digits of 613, one obtains 10.] This also parallels the ten degrees of prophecy (see *Likutey Moharan Tinyana* 8).

It is impossible to enter the waters of knowledge except through the Torah. The walls are the barriers in the waters of knowledge, which are like the sea; whoever enters them without proper preparation is drowned. This is because there is too much water; there is so much knowledge that one cannot accept it. It is therefore impossible to enter this knowledge to know God. "Too much oil extinguishes the lamp."

The only way one can enter is through faith. This is the power of the Torah, as it is written, "All Your commandments are faith" (Psalms 119:86). Faith is called a wall, as it is written, "I am a wall" (Song of Songs 8:10), and Rashi comments, "My faith is as strong as a wall" (*Likutey Halakhoth, Tolaim* 4:2).

Since the Ten Walls parallel the Ten Sayings of creation, it is fitting that they be mentioned on Rosh HaShanah, which is the time the creation of the world was completed. For this reason, on Rosh HaShanah we recite the psalm, "The earth and everything in it belongs to God, for He founded it on seas..." (Psalms 24:1-2). This alludes to the Ten Walls upon which the world was founded. These Ten Walls are the constriction of wisdom through which God's essence and kingdom could be revealed (*Likutey Halakhoth, Rosh HaShanah, Roshay Perakim* 6:6).

From Rosh HaShanah until Shemini Atzereth we are engaged in rectifying Malkhuth and faith. As mentioned earlier, during the ten days of repentance, we remove the ten arrows from the Princess (Malkhuth).

Then comes Sukkoth, which alludes to the Clouds of Glory that accompanied the Israelites in the desert. The first mention of cloud came when a "mist arose from the earth and watered the garden" (Genesis 2:6). This was the first "awakening from below." This parallels charity, which causes the clouds to produce rain and water from the ten walls.

All revelation is from cloud. When God gave the Torah, "He spoke to them from a pillar of cloud" (Psalms 99:7). These were clouds of water, which denote knowledge (*Likutey Halakhoth, Rosh HaShanah, Roshay Perakim* 6:4).

The rectification of water was also accomplished on Sukkoth through the water libation (*nisukh ha-mayim*) that was done on this festival. The water went down to the depths, through a channel in the altar known as the *shith*. The Talmud states (*Sukkah* 49a) that this *shith* is alluded to in the word *Bereshith*, which can be broken up into *bara shith* (ברא שיח), "He created a *shith*." Thus, the water libations can affect the hidden saying of *Bereshith*. These libations pass through the ten walls of water, to bring up the souls that have fallen through the ten levels of defilement.

While a sacrifice is to refine fallen souls in general, the water libation is meant to raise up the sparks of souls that have fallen into the depths of the realm of evil. They therefore go down to the depths through the *shith*, which is alluded to in the word *Bereshith*, the hidden saying (*Likutey Halakhoth, Rosh HaShanah* 6:14).

The rectification culminates on Shemini Atzereth when we bring the prayers for rain. We want the clouds to bring the right amount of water, and this is regulated by the ten walls. These ten walls stand up through wind, which, as we see, is the song of joy. Since the walls stand up through wind, we first say, "who makes the wind blow," and only then, "who makes the rain fall."

Since the walls are rectified through joy, we pray for rain on Shemini Atzereth, which is a particular time of joy, as it is written, "You shall be only happy" (Deuteronomy 16:15). The second day of Shemini Atzereth is Simchath Torah, when we celebrate the joy of completing the Torah (which is also water on a higher plane), and beginning it again.

the other, all made of water. The floors inside this castle were also made of water. [This castle] also had trees and fruit, all made of water. *

It goes without saying how beautiful this castle was, and how unusual. A castle of water is certainly something wonderful and unusual.

It is impossible for anyone to enter the Water Castle. It is made entirely of water, and anyone entering it would drown. *

Meanwhile, the Queen's Daughter, who had fled to the castle, was going around the Water Castle. The king was informed that she was circling the castle.

The king took his army * and set out to capture her. When the

---

This joy is the ten types of song. Through these songs, one can hold and balance the ten types of wind, and thus support the ten walls of water, which regulate all rain (*Likutey Halakhoth, Rosh HaShanah, Roshay Perakim* 6:3).

The King's Daughter who fled to the sea represents the entire nation of Israel. The walls of water were therefore like the walls that existed at the splitting of the Red Sea, regarding which it is said, "The water was to them as a wall, to their right and their left" (Exodus 14:22) (*Likutey Halakhoth, Tolaim* 4:4; cf. *Sichoth HaRan* 151).

all made of water. The Water Castle alludes to the Vacated Space that God created in the midst of His Light and Wisdom. As Rabbi Nachman points out, we cannot say that God's wisdom exists in this space, since God vacated it of His wisdom. Yet, we must also say that His wisdom does exist in the space, since the Vacated Space only came into being through God's wisdom. This is a paradox that will not be resolved until the Ultimate Future.

This is like the Water Castle, whose ground, trees and fruit were all made of water. We cannot find God's wisdom (water) in the Vacated Space, but the space itself is also an aspect of God's wisdom (*Likutey Halakhoth, Tolaim* 4:8).

would drown. The water alludes to wisdom. If one goes into it and does not know one's way one will drown. This is what happened to many philosophers and scientists, who entered the realm of wisdom, but drowned in atheism. This is especially true because, when one is approaching the Water Castle, one is entering the Vacated Space, which contains wisdom that appears to demonstrate the absence of God. But through the power of Torah, one can enter and not be harmed (*Likutey Halakhoth, Tolaim* 4:2).

took his army. When a person flees from the Evil Urge, the Evil Urge gathers all his host and pursues that person. The more a person flees, the more the Evil Urge pursues. That is why, "Whoever is greater has a greater Evil Urge" (*Sukkah* 52a) (*Likutey Halakhoth, Tolaim* 4:2).

On a physical plane this was re-enacted by Pharaoh, who pursued the Israelites, taking all his armies (Exodus 14:9; *Likutey Halakhoth, Tolaim* 4:4).

Queen's Daughter saw them coming, she decided that she would flee into the castle.* She would rather drown than be captured by the king and have to remain with him. There was also the possibility that she would survive and be able actually to get into the Water Castle.

When the king saw her fleeing into the water, he said, "If this is how it is..." and he gave orders to shoot her, [saying], "If she dies, she dies."

[The soldiers] shot her and hit her with all ten types of arrows,* rubbed with the ten types of poison. She ran into the

---

flee into the castle. She ran into the Torah, which is likened to water. This is the teaching, "If you meet the Evil Urge, drag him to the house of Torah study" (*Sukkah* 52b) (*Likutey Halakhoth, Tolaim* 4:2).

The Torah is life and healing, as it is written, "God's Torah is complete, it restores the soul" (Psalms 19:8). It can bring a person from the ways of death to the ways of life (*Likutey Halakhoth, Tolaim* 4:4).

On the physical level, this was represented by Nachshon ben Aminadav, who jumped into the Red Sea, and led the Israelites into the sea to escape Pharaoh.

ten types of arrows. (See *Sichoth HaRan* 273). These arrows are the Forces of Evil, the Husks (*klipoth*) and dregs of creation (*Likutey Halakhoth, Pesach, Roshay Perakim* 9:2).

These ten arrows come from the Ten Crowns of Defilement (see *Tikkuney Zohar* 69, 108b; *Likutey Halakhoth, Rosh HaShanah* 6:14).

The King was strong enough that, even though the Princess had run into the water, he was able to hit her with his arrows. He was able to do so because the rectification (*tikkun*) is not complete, and there are still 288 sparks of holiness captured among the forces of evil, giving them strength. It is because of these sparks, that evil can have power even over the cleansing power of water and Torah. This is also the reason that water can become defiled very easily, as mentioned earlier. As long as the rectification (*tikkun*) is not complete, evil has power even there (*Likutey Halakhoth, Tolaim* 4:3).

The fact that the King shoots at her after she has fled into the water, indicates that the Evil Urge attacks most strongly when people try to immerse themselves in Torah. [It is thus taught that the Evil Urge strikes out against Torah scholars more than anyone else (*Sukkah* 52a).] Although Torah is a protection against the Evil Urge, as soon as the Torah scholar puts aside his studies, he is particularly vulnerable (*Likutey Halakhoth, Tolaim* 4:2).

These arrows, in particular, represent sexual misdeeds, which are a blemish of the Holy Covenant of Abraham (*pegam ha-b'rith*). This particularly involves emitting semen in vain, which injures the Divine Presence like an arrow (*Likutey Moharan* 29). This is alluded to in the verse "Your arrows have gone deep into me, and Your hand has come down upon me" (Psalms 38:3) (*Likutey Halakhoth, P'ru U'R'vu* 3:10).

The arrows shot into the Princess are reflected in the sadness and depression that affects a person. Rabbi Nachman (*Likutey Moharan Tinyana* 24) taught that the main exile of the Divine Presence comes about primarily through sadness (*Likutey Halakhoth, Rosh HaShanah* 6:8).

This sadness comes from the element of dust (see *Likutey Moharan* 189). This is the advice of the serpent, since "The serpent's bread is dust" (Isaiah 65:25). Moreover, the main power of evil over man is through his illicit sexual urges. The *Zohar* teaches, "The main Evil Urge is illicit sex" (*Zohar* 3:156). This, however, is usually brought about through sadness and depression (*Likutey Halakhoth, Tolaim* 4:2).

As mentioned earlier, the ten arrows come from the Breaking of the Vessels. This comes from the expansion BaN, the lowest of the expansions, paralleling the element of dust. This is also the absence of God from the Vacated Space. But water is the logic of the Vacated Space, which is God's wisdom inside it. This is the beginning of the rectification. The reason the vessels were broken was because the logic and wisdom in the Vacated Space was hidden after the *tzimtzum*. There was some rectification after creation, but it was not complete.

The arrows struck the concept of Malkhuth, which is the Messiah. It is thus written, "He was wounded for our sins" (Isaiah 53:5), which speaks of these arrows. This occurred after the Princess ran into the water, as it is written, "Your breach is like the sea, who will heal you?" (Lamentations 2:13) (*Likutey Halakhoth, Tolaim* 4:8).

These arrows are alluded to at the very beginning of creation, where the Torah says, "The earth was desolate and void, and with darkness on the face of the deep" (Genesis 1:2) (*Likutey Halakhoth, Pesach, Roshay Perakim* 9:2).

These arrows of sin are rectified by the arrows of holiness, which denote proper sexuality in a holy context. Regarding this it is written, "Like arrows in the hand of a mighty man, are the children of one's youth" (Psalms 127:4).

Arrows also denote prayer (*Likutey Moharan Tinyana* 83; see *Tikkuney Zohar* 13, 29b). In order to rectify the ten arrows, prayer must be said with a minyan of ten men (*Likutey Halakhoth, Rosh HaShanah, Roshay Perakim* 6:4).

The Princess absorbing the arrows was also paralleled by the angel absorbing the arrows that the Egyptians shot at the time of the Exodus. Regarding this it is written, "The angel of God which went before the camp of Israel, moved and went behind them, and the pillar of cloud moved from behind them, and stood between them, coming between the camp of Egypt and the camp of Israel, (Exodus 14:19,20). Rashi notes that it came between the two camps to absorb the arrows that the Egyptians were shooting at the Israelites. This "cloud" represented the Shekhinah, which absorbed the ten arrows of the Evil King.

The battle down below was a counterpart of the war on high. Just as the Egyptians were firing arrows down below, the Evil One was firing his arrows on high. These arrows were arrows of doubt and disbelief, causing the Israelites to rebel against God. It is thus written, "They rebelled at the Red Sea, they crossed a sea of woes" (Psalms 106:7; Zechariah 10:11).

As a result of these ten arrows, the Israelites were injured spiritually, so that they rebelled against God ten times in the desert (*Avoth* 5:4). We are still not healed from the effects of these arrows. From them, all heresy and doubt come. It is thus written, "The

castle,* and entered into it. She went through the gates in the
walls of water. The walls of water have such gates. She passed
through all ten walls of the Water Castle, until she came to its
interior. When she got there, she fell unconscious.*

I heal her.* Someone who does not possess* all ten types of

wicked bent the bow, they made their arrow ready on the string, that they may shoot the
upright in the heart with darkness" (Psalms 11:2).

It would have been utterly impossible for the Princess to tolerate the poison arrows so
long if God had not made the remedy before the sickness, helping her to flee into the ten
walls of water. These represent the Torah, which is life and healing (*Likutey Halakhoth,
Tolaim* 4:4).

The arrows are therefore shot only after the Princess runs into the sea. This was alluded
to when, in the first plague, the water turned into blood. God then took the Israelites
through the sea to escape the Egyptians. The King attacked the Israelites in the sea at the
very beginning, too, by having all their sons cast into the Nile. Moses had to be cast into
the Nile as well, since he would have to enter the ten walls of water to heal the Princess
(*Likutey Halakhoth, Pesach, Roshay Perakim* 9:3).

ran into the castle. Her running into the Water Castle represents the Israelites fleeing evil
by immersing themselves in the Torah. Torah is life and healing, as it is written, "God's
Torah is complete, it restores the soul" (Psalms 19:8). When the Israelites run to the
Torah, they have the power to tolerate the exile, which is a result of the ten arrows. It is
thus written, "[The Torah] is your life and the length of your days" (Deuteronomy 30:20)
(*Likutey Halakhoth, Tolaim* 4:4).

However, even though she ran into the water, the arrows hit her. Even though water is
purification, it was not entirely rectified. Therefore, it did not offer complete protection
against the arrows (*Likutey Halakhoth, Tolaim* 4:8).

unconscious. The Israelites are weary and faint because of their sins (*Sichoth HaRan* 273).

The fainting of the Princess is alluded to by "the darkness on the face of the deep"
(Genesis 1:2). She almost died, but was sustained by the spirit of the Messiah. The verse
thus continues, "The spirit of God hovered on the face of the waters" (*Ibid.*) and the
Midrash states that this is the spirit of the Messiah. [Kabbalistically, this also represents
the sparks of holiness that give life force to everything that has fallen into the *klipoth*.] In a
sense, it is the Messianic hope that gives hope even to those who have fallen into the lowest
realms of evil. (*Likutey Halakhoth, Tolaim* 4:3; cf. *Likutey Halakhoth, Pesach, Roshay
Perakim* 9:2).

The Princess would remain unconscious in the Water Castle for hundreds of years
(*Likutey Halakhoth, P'ru U'R'vu* 3:10).

Some say that the reason she fainted was because the walls of water were not
completely rectified; therefore, there was too much light (*Chokhmah U'Tevunah* 21:2).

I heal her. Only a great tzaddik, who has the power to enter every place where the soul has
fallen, and remove all ten arrows, can heal the Princess (*Sichoth HaRan* 273). Of course,
the final healing will be accomplished by the Messiah (*Likutey Halakhoth, Tolaim* 4:4).

charity cannot enter all ten walls; he will drown* in the water there. The king and his army tried to pursue her, but they all drowned* in the water. I, on the other hand, was able* to go through all ten walls of water.

These walls of water are like the waves of the sea which stand like a wall.* The winds support the waves* and lift them up. These waves constitute the ten walls which stand there permanently,* but they are lifted up and supported by the winds. I, however, was able to enter through all ten walls.

I was also able to draw all ten types of arrows* out of the Queen's Daughter. I also knew all ten types of pulses,* and could detect them with my ten fingers. Each one of the ten fingers has the power to detect one of the ten types of pulse. I could then heal her through the ten types of melody.*

---

possess. Literally, "have in his hands," alluding to the power of the hands.

he will drown. If a person has a tradition from his master, he can enter all ten walls without being harmed. But if he does not, he can drown. This refers to the walls of water of wisdom, which can drown a person in atheism and heresy. This is what happened to many philosophers and scientists (*Likutey Halakhoth, Tolaim* 4:2).

they all drowned. Just as Pharaoh and his army drowned when they pursued the Israelites into the Red Sea (Exodus 14:28; *Likutey Halakhoth, Tolaim* 4:4).

was able. This is alluded to in the verse, "The spirit of God hovered on the face of the waters" (Genesis 1:2). This is the spirit of the Messiah, which entered into the water where the Princess had fled (*Likutey Halakhoth, Pesach, Roshay Perakim* 9:2; *Likutey Halakhoth, Tolaim* 4:3).

stand like a wall. They stand up through the wind, which denotes joy (*Likutey Halakhoth, Rosh HaShanah, Roshay Perakim* 6:3).

winds support the waves. Alluded to in the verse, "Your charity is like the waves of the sea" (Isaiah 48:18) (end of story).

stand there permanently. The walls stand up through the same spirit-wind that produces the pulsebeat. The wind of song also gives strength to the wind of the pulse. Hence, everything depends on song. This is the level of cantillations (*taamim*), which is the highest of the four levels (*Likutey Halakhoth, Tolaim* 4:11).

all ten types of arrows. Taking out the arrows is the process of purification, transforming uncleanness into purity. It is the task of all the Israelites, and especially the tzaddikim, to remove these arrows (*Likutey Halakhoth, Pesach, Roshay Perakim* 9:2).

all ten types of pulses. So that he can recognize the spiritual sickness of each and every person (*Likutey Halakhoth, Tolaim* 4:2).

through the ten types of melody. This healing is primarily through joy. It is thus written

I thus heal her.* Therefore, I have this great power in my hands.* I am now giving you this as a gift.

[When he finished his speech,] there was great joy and tremendous rejoicing.

[Rabbi Nachman concluded:]
It is very difficult for me to tell this story. However, since I

regarding the Messianic age, "It is good to give thanks to God... with a ten stringed instrument (denoting the ten songs), with a lute, with meditation on the harp. For You, God, have made me happy through Your works" (Psalms 92:1-5).

The joy of these ten types of songs comes through the Ten Psalms of the *Tikkun HaKelali*. Defilement of Abraham's covenant (sexual misdeeds) comes as a result of sadness. Therefore, when "all flesh had corrupted their way" (Genesis 6:12) through sexual immorality, God "was *saddened* through His heart" (Genesis 6:6). The covenant is therefore rectified through joy (*Likutey Halakhoth, Tolaim* 4:2).

The ten types of songs are included in the Song of the Red Sea, which, according to the Talmud (*Sanhedrin* 91b), Moses will sing in the Messianic age. Therefore, the song literally begins, "Then Moses will sing" (Exodus 15:1). The Messiah is an aspect of Moses, and when he comes, he will sing this song which includes all ten songs, and the Shekhinah will be healed. Regarding this it is written, "Sing to God a new song, for He has done wonders" (Psalms 98:1).

The song of the Red Sea ends, "God will reign forever and ever" (Exodus 15:18). This is speaking of God's kingdom in the Messianic age, when the attribute of Malkhuth (royalty, the Princess) will be rectified. Regarding this it is written, "Let the heavens rejoice and earth be glad, and let nations say, 'God is King' " (Psalms 96:11). Then we will, "Sing to God, sing to our King, for God is King of all the earth" (Psalms 47:7).

The Princess is thus healed primarily through song. It is thus written, "Praise God with the harp, with a lyre of ten (songs); sing to Him, sing to Him a new song" (Psalms 33:2) (*Likutey Halakhoth, Tolaim* 4:4).

I thus heal her. It is thus written, "Is there no balm in Gilead? Is there no physician there? Why then is the daughter of my people not healed?" (Jeremiah 8:22). God likewise says, "I have stricken down and I will heal" (Deuteronomy 32:39) — in the Ultimate Future. The commentaries note that God heals with the same thing with which He strikes, this being the concept of shooting the arrow and then retrieving it. This is the concept of rectifying evil at its very root (*Likutey Halakhoth, Tolaim* 4:8).

The Princess can thus be healed only through a very great tzaddik (*Likutey Etzoth* B, *Tzaddik* 96). However, the final healing of the Princess is the final redemption, regarding which it is said, "On that day, God will heal His people's wound, and heal them of their bruise" (Isaiah 30:26) (*Kedushath Shabbath*).

power in my hands. Like the story of the fourth day, the story of the sixth day is not completed. This is a process that is still ongoing. However, when other people realize how far they are from the handless beggar, the rectification can be complete (*Rimzey Maasioth*).

have begun it, I am forced to end it. There is not a single redundant word in this story. One who is versed in the sacred literature will be able to understand some of the allusions.

The story speaks of arrows, and a certain power in the hands to turn back arrows. This is related to [God's statement], "My hand will grasp judgment" (Deuteronomy 32:41). Rashi explains this verse saying, "When a human being shoots an arrow, he cannot turn it back, but when God shoots an arrow, He can."

The concept of charity is seen as being related to the walls of water, which are the waves of the sea. This is alluded to in the verse, "Your charity is like the waves of the sea" (Isaiah 48:18).

[The story] speaks of the power of grasping the winds in one's hand. This is alluded to in the verse, "Who gathers up the wind in His palm" (Proverbs 30:4). This is related to the concept of melody as mentioned elsewhere *(Likutey Moharan I 54)*.

The ten types of melody and ten types of pulses have been discussed earlier.*

[Rabbi Nathan adds:]

All this I heard explicitly. However, regarding [the meaning of] who, what and when, the story is very deep. This involves the primary concept of the story itself. Who were the [beggars]? What were they? When were they? All this is too deep to be understood.

[Rabbi Nathan continues:]

The end of the story would involve the Seventh Day* and the

---

discussed earlier. The source cites *Likutey Moharan Tinyana* p. 32a. This reference denotes the first edition of the second part of *Likutey Moharan* (Mohalov, 1811). The reference is to *Likutey Moharan Tinyana* 92.

the Seventh Day. A group was standing around Rabbi Nachman after he finished the story of the sixth day, and someone told him an anecdote. He said, "This is the story of the seventh day. It seems that people are already telling my story. I would very much like to finish it." However, the story was never finished (*Sichoth HaRan* 149; cf. *Ibid.* 151; *Yemey Moharnat*, p. 32b).

This story would involve the beggar without feet. From the lessons of Rabbi Nachman, it seems that his power would be through dancing. Rabbi Nachman thus taught that by

beggar without feet.* However, we were not worthy of hearing it. The same is true of the end of the first part of the story, regarding the king [who gave over his kingdom to his son during his lifetime]. [Rabbi Nachman] said that he would not tell any more. This is a great loss. We will not be worthy of hearing it until the Messiah comes.* May this happen quickly in our days, Amen.

Rabbi Nachman also said, "If I knew nothing else other than this story, it would still be very extraordinary."*

dancing with one's feet, one can restore lost faith (*Likutey Moharan Tinyana* 81). However, in the beginning of the story, Rabbi Nachman told how the King's Son had lost his faith. Thus, the story of the seventh day, might involve the restoration of this faith (*Chokhmah U'Tevunah* 15:1).

beggar without feet. The time before the Messiah is known as *Ikvatha deMeshicha*, which literally means "the heels of the Messiah." Therefore, the power of rectification of the Messiah comes from his feet.

This is related to the story of the Prince at the beginning of this story. The king tells him that the main thing is joy, which is expressed by the feet in dancing. In the World to Come, it is taught that God will make a dance for all the righteous. All of them will then point to God, and say, "This is God, I have hoped for Him" (Isaiah 25:9; *Taanith* 31a). This is the concept of the complete restoration of faith (*Chokhmah U'Tevunah*).

The beggar with no feet is the one who will effect the ultimate rectification of the Princess, who is the Shekhinah. Regarding the Shekhinah it is written, "Her feet go down to death" (Proverbs 5:5). This is because the feet of Malkhuth go down to the realm of evil, giving it existence until the Messiah comes and rectifies all things. Thus, the ultimate rectification is through the feet.

until the Messiah comes. When Rabbi Nachman left Breslov for good, and was traveling to Uman, he said that we would not be worthy of hearing the end of the story until the Messiah came (*Yemey Moharnat*, p. 32b).

very extraordinary. Elsewhere, this is presented as, "If I only told the world this one story, I would still be very great" (*Likutey Halakhoth, Tefillin* 5:1). He indicated that this story contains many lessons regarding many ancient tzaddikim (*Likutey Halakhoth, Evven HaEzer, P'ru U'R'vu* 3:10).

The following appears after the story in Hebrew:

The concept of King David and the above mentioned verse "From the ends of the earth" which alludes to the story. This pertains to the third day, for there they spoke about the Heart and the Spring. See there. And you will see wonders, how in each concept wondrous things are alluded to. Of the great awesome things of this story it is impossible to speak at all, for this is above all. Happy, happy is he who is worthy, even in the World to Come, of understanding a little of it. If a person has any brain, his hair will stand on end

He said explicitly that this story is wonderful and unusual. It contains many moral lessons and Torah lessons, and has in it many Torah concepts and many teachings.

It also speaks of many ancient saints. Thus, King David stood at one end of the earth, and screamed out to the spring which issues forth from the stone on the mountain. It is thus written, "From the ends of the earth, I call to You. When my heart is faint, lead me to a rock that is too high for me" (Psalms 61:3).

All this, I heard from [Rabbi Nachman's] own mouth explicitly. From his words, it is obvious that King David is the heart mentioned in the story, where the heart of the world stands at one end of the world facing the spring, and screams out in constant desire... Still the ideas are obscure. Happy is he who is worthy of grasping the mystery of these stories.

when he looks well at this awesome story; and he will understand a little of the greatness of the Creator and the greatness of the true tzaddikim, for nothing like it has ever been heard.

I heard the concept of the verse "From the ends of the earth..." mentioned above, which pertains to the story of the third day, explicitly from [the Rebbe's] holy, awesome lips (may he rest in peace). I also found that most of the words of this Psalm 61 in which this verse is written, allude to lofty mysteries of the story of the third day.

"Days on the days of the king shall be increased..." because he constantly needs that days should be added on his days... as mentioned above.

"Kindness and truth will preserve him" (Psalms 61:8). This is the true man of kindness... *der groiser man der emeser ish chesed.* For all time and days are made through the great man, who is a true man of kindness, as noted in the story. He continues and increases the "days of the king." This is the Heart mentioned above, which is the concept of King David, and this is the meaning of "he will preserve him." He watches and preserves it so that as soon as it comes very close to the end of the day when the Heart of all the world would die, then this true man of kindness protects and watches it, when he comes and gives a day to the Heart...

And this is the meaning of "Thus I will sing to Your name forever to pay my vows of each day" (Psalms 61:9). For every day that he gives comes from the hymns and songs.

"I will take refuge in the cover of Your wings selah" (Psalms 61:5). When the Heart needs to rest, the Great Bird comes and spreads its wings over it... This is "I will take refuge in the cover of Your wings..."

This pertains to the first day, the concept of the old men. Each one boasted about what he remembered. One remembered even when they cut his navel... and he was the least of them...

The Rebbe, of blessed memory, said that in the Talmud there is a similar concept where Shmuel boasted that he remembered the pain of circumcision...(*Yerushalmi Kethuboth* 5).

ADDITIONAL
STORIES

14

THE CHANDELIER*

Once a son left his father, and remained in a distant land for many years. When he returned home, he boasted about how he had learned the art of making chandeliers.* He told [his father] to invite all the [local] masters of this craft, so that he could demonstrate his skill.

His father invited all the masters of the craft to see the skills that his son had learned during the time he was away. However, when the son took out a lamp that he had made, they all realized that it was very ugly. The father later went to them, and asked them to tell him the truth. Since they had no choice but to tell the truth, they told him that [the lamp] was very ugly.

Later the son boasted [to his father], "Didn't you see the wisdom of my craft?"

The father replied that the other craftsmen considered it to be very inferior work.

The son replied, "They have it backwards. Through this lamp, I have demonstrated my skill. I have shown each one of them his shortcomings. In this lamp, I included the shortcomings of all the local masters of this art. You did not realize that one considered one part ugly, but another part very well made. The next one, however, considered the first part beautiful and wonderful, while for him, the second part was poorly made.

"This is true of all of them. What one considers bad, is good to another, and vice versa.

"I made this lamp out of shortcomings and nothing else, to

The Chandelier. This and subsequent stories are only in Hebrew.
chandeliers. *Heng leichter* in Yiddish.

demonstrate to all of them that they do not have perfection. Each one has a shortcoming, since what is beautiful to one is deficient to the next. But if I want to, I can make a perfect [lamp]."*

If people knew all the shortcomings and deficiencies in a thing, they would know the essential nature of that thing, even if they had never seen it before.

"Great are God's deeds" (Psalms 111:2). No man resembles another. Adam had every human form in the world. Moreover, the Hebrew word for man, *adam*, includes all these forms. The same is true of all other things. In the Hebrew word for light, *or*, all lights are included.

The same is true of everything else in creation. Even in a forest, no two leaves are alike.

[Rabbi Nachman] spoke of this at length. He then said, "Types of wisdom exist* that [can sustain a person completely].

I can make a perfect [lamp]. Thus, the Land of Israel is perfect; it lacks nothing. It is thus described as, "A land in which you will lack nothing" (Deuteronomy 8:9). If one sees any shortcomings in the land, it is merely because of one's own deficiencies, which prevent one from recognizing its good. The *Sifri* thus says that everything that the spies (*meraglim*) saw as shortcomings in the land were actually advantages (*Zimrath HaAretz*).

Types of wisdom exist... Another time, Rabbi Nachman said, "I know wisdom that cannot be revealed. If I were to reveal this wisdom, people would be nourished by the delight of comprehending it, and they would no longer eat or drink. Every soul in the world would long to hear this wisdom, and everything in the world would stop. People would seek the sweet beauty of this wisdom, and would leave this mundane life. But I cannot reveal this wisdom to mankind. As soon as I begin to speak of it, I hear lofty things in the words of the listener. I then stop speaking so that I can listen and receive from him" (*Sichoth HaRan* 181).

He also said, "There are categories of wisdom, even in this physical world, which can sustain a person without any other nourishment. Such awesome, wonderful categories of wisdom exist even in the mundane world. With this wisdom alone, a person could live without eating or drinking" (*Sichoth HaRan* 306).

Rabbi Nachman's follower, Rabbi Naftali, told that once the Rebbe's mother asked him, "Why do you push yourself not to eat? With what will you live?"

Rabbi Nachman replied, "I now live with 'wisdom gives life to its owners' " (Ecclesiastes 7:12).

A person could live with such wisdom, without eating or drinking." He then spoke at length of this awesome concept.

[Rabbi Nachman's followers] spoke of a person who was in a large gentile city, and remained there a long time. He was trying to reach a certain goal there, and each time, it appeared as if he would accomplish it. But in the end he remained there a very long time.

[Rabbi Nachman] said that this often happens to people. Each time a person thinks that he will accomplish something. He says, "Now I will accomplish it." Then later, "Now I will finally accomplish it." This goes on and on.

He also said, "I have men with me who know things with which they can live without eating or drinking" (*Shevachey Moharan* 3b #9).

The *Zohar* thus speaks of "being nourished by the radiance of the Divine."

15

THE HORSE AND THE PUMP*

Once there was a man who did not believe in *letzim* (jokers).*
These are demons from the Other Side, who sometimes come and
lead people astray. Although there have been many encounters
with such beings, this man did not believe in them.

One night a *letz* (joker) came to him and called him, asking
him to come outside. When he went outside, the *letz* showed him
a beautiful horse that he had to sell. Examining it, he saw that it
was indeed a very beautiful animal. "How much do you want for
it?" he asked.

"Four rubles,"* replied the *letz*.

The man realized that the horse was worth at least* eight
rubles. It was a prime horse in very good condition. He bought
the horse for four rubles, and felt that he had got an excellent
bargain.

The next day, he took out the horse to sell it. People came, and
immediately wanted to give him the asking price. He said to
himself, "If they want to give me that much, it is obviously worth
twice as much." Therefore, he refused to sell it.

He brought the horse elsewhere, and people were ready to give
him twice his original price. He said to himself, "Most probably,
it is worth more than twice this amount."

The Horse and the Pump. Rabbi Nachman told this story on Shavuoth, 5567 (Friday, June
12, 1807) (*Chayay Moharan* 15d #59). Rabbi Nachman had taken his fateful journey to
Navritch, and his wife had died in Zaslev just before Shavuoth. That Friday night, Rabbi
Nachman put on his shtreimel for the first time that festival. He then sat until morning
with Rabbi Nathan and a few other men. It was then that he told this story (*Yemey
Moharnat* 19b, 20a).

letzim. Jokers. Apparently these are a type of poltergeist (see *Kav HaYashar* 69).

rubles. *Adumim* in Hebrew.

at least. Approximately, *be-shufi* (בשופי) in Hebrew.

He kept on bringing the horse further and further, until its price was in the thousands. He still would not agree to sell it to anyone, no matter how much he was offered. He always said, "Most probably it's worth twice as much." Finally, he could not find anyone who could afford it other than the king.

When he brought the horse to the king, the king offered him a huge sum of money for it. Everyone agreed that it was a very fine horse. However, he could not come to an agreement with the king, since he said, "Most probably it is worth even more." Thus, even the king could not buy the horse from him.

He left the king, and brought the horse to a pump to give it water. The horse immediately jumped into the pump and vanished. [Of course, this was only an illusion made by the *letzim*. The entire horse was such an illusion, and they made the horse appear to jump into the pump.]

The man began to scream because of what had happened, and people heard the screams and gathered around him. "Why are you screaming?" they asked.

He replied that his horse had jumped into the pump.

The people hit him and beat him; they thought he was mad. The pump's opening was very small. How could a horse possibly jump into it?

He realized that they were beating him because he appeared to be a madman, and he wanted to leave. Just as he was preparing to leave, however, the horse stuck its head out of the pump. Thinking that he had his horse, he began to scream again.* Again the townspeople gathered around him and beat him as a madman.

Again he wanted to leave, but as soon as he was preparing to leave, the horse stuck its head out of the pump. He began to scream again, and again the people gathered and beat him.

The Other Side constantly fools a person for no reason, with absolute falsehood that does not have any substance. The person

---

scream again. "Hah! Hah!" in the source.

is tempted, and goes after it. Each time it appears that he will make more profit, and he desires all the more. He pursues it many times, and suddenly it vanishes. As he runs after it, everything he desires is taken away from him.

Sometimes, the desire goes away a little. But when he wants to separate himself from it completely, the desire sticks out its head again, and once again he pursues it. This keeps on happening. Every time it sticks out its head, he runs after it.

[Rabbi Nachman] did not explain this concept further. Understand it well.

There was once a great saint, who had completely overcome his sexual desires. When he had perfected himself sexually, he ascended to the highest worlds. There he saw a pot full of flesh and bones.

"What is this?" he asked.

He was told, "This was once an extremely beautiful woman. But she would warm up her body to sin. Therefore, she is being 'warmed' here in this pot."

He wanted to see what she looked like. He was given Divine Names, so that he was able to reassemble her as she was during life. He saw that she was a very great beauty.

From this, we can see how improper this type of desire is. If a woman were cut into little pieces, how much desire would be left for her? ....

16

THE MELANCHOLY SAINT

Sadness is a very despicable trait. One must keep oneself from it completely. One must encourage and uplift oneself. A person must realize that every time he makes even the slightest motion to serve God, it is very precious in God's eyes. This is true even if that person only moves himself by a single hairsbreadth.

This is because a person exists in a physical body in the lowest of the worlds. Therefore, every movement is extremely difficult for him, and is very precious in God's eyes.

There was once a tzaddik who became very depressed and melancholy.* This depression and melancholy caused the tzaddik great difficulty, and it became worse and worse. He fell into lassitude and heaviness, where it was literally impossible for him to move.

He wanted to make himself happy and uplift himself, but it was impossible for him to do anything. Whenever he found something that would make him happy, the Evil One would find

---

depressed and melancholy. This is the version that Rabbi Nathan heard. Another of Rabbi Nachman's followers heard the following version: There was a tzaddik who felt that he had to serve God perfectly each day. He calculated exactly what he had to do, down to the number of steps he would take each day in his house. When things did not work out as he planned, he became very depressed (*Chayay Moharan*, p. 16b #6).

The main reason a person becomes depressed is because he is proud. He therefore feels that he should be able to accomplish much more than he does. But in the end the tzaddik realizes that the only thing that can make him happy is the fact that God did not create him as a gentile, which was something over which he had no control. He was then humble, and this led to joy, as it is written, "The humble shall have increased joy in God" (Isaiah 29:19). It is also written, "The humble shall listen and rejoice" (Psalms 34:3), and "The humble will see and rejoice" (Psalms 59:33) (*Likutey Halakhoth, Pesach* 9:15).

sadness in it. Therefore, it was impossible for him to do anything to make himself happy, since in everything he found sadness.

Finally the tzaddik began to meditate* on the [fact that God] had not created him* as a heathen. This could certainly be the source of unlimited joy. It is impossible even to imagine the thousands of levels of separation between the lowest possible Israelite and the unclean spiritual level of the idolator.

He pondered God's kindness that "He did not make me a heathen" and realized that this could be a source of great joy, without any sadness.*

When a person tries to find joy in something that he himself did, it is possible to find sadness in every joy. No matter what he does, he can find shortcomings, and he will not be able to uplift himself and be happy. But in the fact that "He did not make me a heathen," there is no sadness. This is from God; God made him the way He did, and had pity on him, not making him a heathen. Since this was God's deed, there are no shortcomings in it, and hence there is no defect in this rejoicing. No matter what, there is an unimaginable difference between him and an idolator.

The tzaddik began to make himself happy with this. He rejoiced and uplifted himself little by little, continuing more and more, until he came to such a level of joy that he was on the same level of joy that Moses experienced when he went on high to receive the Tablets.

---

began to meditate... When a person is on the lowest level, it is easy for him to find something with which to uplift himself (*Likutey Halakhoth, Yoreh Deah, Reshith HaGez* 4:6).

had not created him... *Shelo asani goy* (in the first person). This is the wording of one of the morning blessings.

joy, without any sadness. The main thing, then, is to make a small beginning. God thus said, "Open for Me like the eye of a needle, and I will open for you like the gates of the Temple" (*Shir HaShirim Rabbah* 5:3) (*Oneg Shabbath*, p. 48).

Thus, no matter how low a person is, if he makes even a single motion to serve God, it is something very great on high, and it can bring him back completely (*Likutey Halakhoth, Tefillin* 5:43).

The main thing is to make the first move. If one begins even a little bit, one can go very high (*Parparoth LeChokhmah* 6:8).

Through this uplifting and joy, he was able to fly many miles into the supernal universes. He saw himself, and he was very far from the place where he had been originally. This bothered him very much. He felt that when he descended, he would be very far away from his original place. When it was discovered that he had disappeared, people would consider it a great wonder. The tzaddik [did not want such publicity] since he always wanted to "walk modestly [with God]" (Micah 6:8).

The joy came to an end, since joy has a limit. Therefore, joy begins automatically and ends automatically. When joy begins to end, it ends little by little. [The tzaddik] therefore descended little by little, coming down from the place to which he had flown during his time of joy. He eventually returned to the place from which he had ascended. He was very surprised, since he was in exactly the same place where he had been at first.

He realized that he had returned to the exact same place where he had been at first. Looking at himself, he realized that the had not moved at all, or if he had moved, it had been at most by a hairsbreadth.* He had moved so little, that no one other than God could measure it. The tzaddik was very surprised at this. Here he had flown so far, through so many universes, and at the same time, he had not moved at all.

This showed him how precious in God's eyes is even the slightest motion. When a person moves himself even a hairsbreadth in this world, it can be considered more than thousands of miles, and even thousands of universes.

This can be understood, when we realize that the physical

---

hairsbreadth. The hair on the head is the gate to the intellect. In Hebrew, the word *sa'ar* (שער) meaning hair, and *sha'ar* (שער) meaning gate, are the same. Therefore, if a person improves himself by a hairsbreadth, it can bring him back completely. Similarly, if a person strays from God by a hairsbreadth, it can do much damage (*Likutey Halakhoth, Choshen Mishpat, Nezikin* 4:3).

For this reason, even the smallest amount of leaven (*chametz*) is forbidden on Pesach. *Chametz* represents the side of evil, and even the smallest amount is extremely harmful (*Likutey Halakhoth, Nezikin* 4:4).

world is no more than the central point* in the midst of the spheres.* This is known to masters of astronomy. Compared to the supernal universes, the entire physical universe is no more than a dot.

When lines extend from a central point, the closer they are to the point, the closer they are to one another. The further they extend from the point, the further such lines get from each other. Therefore, when the lines are very far from the point, they are also very far from each other. This is true, even though near the central point, they are extremely close to each other.

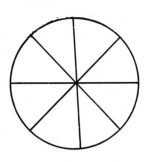

If one imagined lines drawn from the earth to the upper spheres,* one would see that even if one moved a hairsbreadth, the movement would be reflected as a motion of thousands of miles in the upper spheres. It would be in the same ratio as the spheres are higher than the earth. The spheres must be very huge, since there are stars without number, and each star is at least as large as our planet.

This is all the more certainly true when one considers the supernal universe, compared to which, even the highest astronomical spheres are like nothing. Therefore, the distance

---

central point. Therefore, the physical earth upon which we walk is the ultimate constriction (*tzimtzum*). Wherever a person walks, he comes to other points, where there is a different *tzimtzum*. Therefore, traveling and doing good brings Godliness into new areas of *tzimtzum*. For this reason, the Israelites traveled for forty years in the desert. With every step, they created new faith, thus rectifying Adam's sin (*Likutey Halakhoth, Eruv Tavshilin* 5:20).

spheres. The orbits of the planets around the earth. This takes a relativistic geocentric view of the universe.

to the upper spheres. Therefore, even holiness that is like a hairsbreadth down below is more precious than millions of universes on high (*Likutey Halakhoth, Chol HaMoed* 4:13). Since a person lives in a physical body, and has many obstacles in the physical world, moving away from evil by even a hairsbreadth is something very precious to God (*Likutey Halakhoth, Yoreh Deah, Reshith HaGez* 4:1).

between these extending lines in the supernal world is without measure. A movement of less than a hairsbreadth, so small that only God can estimate it, can consist of a passage through thousands of universes and thousands of miles in the supernal worlds.

How much more is this true when one travels a mile or more to serve God. "No eye has seen it..." (Isaiah 64:3).

17

TWO PALACES*

There are two types of palaces, and the two are very much the same. However, in one a king lives, and in the other, a slave lives. Obviously, there is a great difference between the palace of the king and the palace of the slave. Nevertheless, it is possible to confuse the two.

This is because there is a knot that binds many souls together, until a house and palace are made from them. One is bound to another, and one to another, until they make a foundation. Then a tent is made, until finally, out of them are built a house and a dwelling place.

This dwelling place is a habitation for truth. When one needs to seek the truth, it can be found in that dwelling place, made of the knots of souls. They make up the dwelling place of truth.

It is for this reason that the Torah commands, "Incline after the majority" (Exodus 23:2). Since many are bound together, it is a place of truth.

This is also the concept of, "All the souls of the house of Jacob" (Genesis 46:27). This teaches that out of the souls, the house of Jacob was made. This is the house and dwelling place of truth, which is Jacob's quality, as it is written, "You will give truth to Jacob" (Micah 7:20).

Opposing this, however, is the knot of the wicked, where the souls of many wicked are bound together to form a house and dwelling place for falsehood. Regarding this, the prophet warned,

---

Two Palaces. This is related to the story of "The Exchanged Children." The king's son can forget his status to such an extent that even he cannot discern between the two palaces (*Likutey Halakhoth, Birkath HaShachar* 3:11).

"Do not say that everything that people call a knot (conspiracy) is a knot" (Isaiah 8:12).

The knot of the wicked does not count. Regarding it, it is written, "Do not follow the multitude to do evil" (Exodus 23:2).

It is possible, however, to confuse the two houses, confusing truth and falsehood. Falsehood often disguises itself as truth. [In falsehood] there is also a knot of many souls. Therefore, it is possible for a person to be mistaken and confused, and not know where the truth is. He then does not know what [group] to join.

However, through the commandment of redeeming captives* *(pidyon shevuyim)*, one is worthy of discerning between the two houses, between truth and falsehood, and between the king and the slave. Falsehood is the concept of the slave and the concept of the accursed.* This is the concept of "Cursed is Canaan, he shall be a slave of slaves" (Genesis 9:25).

There are two types of intelligence. They are an aspect of "before and after" (Psalms 139:5).

There is a type of intelligence that comes to a person in the course of time. The older he becomes, the more he knows. This is the concept of "days speak" (Job 32:7). This type of intelligence is an aspect of "after," since it comes *after* time has elapsed. For such intelligence, time is needed.

But there is a type of intelligence that comes to a person as a sudden influx *(shefa)* in an instant. This type of intelligence is higher than time, and does not need any time to develop. This intelligence is an aspect of "before." [In Hebrew, this is *panim* (פנים), which also means "face."] This is the concept of Jacob, and the concept of the truth, alluded to in the verse, "They seek your face, Jacob, Selah" (Psalms 24:6).

---

redeeming captives. Captives are like slaves. Therefore, when they are redeemed, they are brought out of the aspect of being slaves (*Chayay Moharan* 16c #7).

accursed. Even if a man serves God, but he is still a slave, he is accursed. However, there is also a concept of a holy slave, such as that of "Moses, God's slave" (Deuteronomy 34:5; see *Likutey Moharan* 5).

After the Sabbath of the portion of *VaYechi*, [Rabbi Nachman] said:

At the third meal (*Shalosh Seudoth*), there was revealed to me a specific remedy (*segulah*) for the pox.* Take some chalk.* Then take an amount of soap weighing three times as much as the chalk. Make a bath from both of them, and bathe the infant. This must be done as soon as the child begins to have a fever. If there is not a powerful decree against the child, [it will be successful]. However, if it is a powerful decree, heaven forbid, then it will not help.

Pox is a result of the sin of the Golden Calf.

It may be difficult to understand this, since gentiles are also affected by this disease. However, the Midrash teaches that the gentiles really should not be affected by any sickness, [since the physical world is their portion]. But so that they would not denigrate the Israelites, God gave them all the sicknesses that the Israelites have.

Rashi expresses a similar thought in his commentary on the verse, "Make me not a reproach for the degraded ones" (Psalms 39:9). The prayer was that the degraded ones should also be stricken with disease and pain, so that they would not be able to say, "You are stricken and we are not stricken." This prayer caused pain and sickness to come to the gentiles.

Another difficulty arises because this sickness must have also existed before the sin of the Golden Calf. However, before that time, it was not a serious illness. Pox results from the food that the infant absorbs in its mother's womb, as physicians say. However, it was originally not a fatal illness as it is now. This was caused by the sin.

This is alluded to in some degree in the verse, "You may wash yourselves with *nether*, and use very much *borith*, but your sin is

---

pox. *Pakin* in Yiddish.
chalk. *Kreid* in Yiddish. The word also denotes lime or whiting.

still written before Me" (Jeremiah 2:22). Rashi explains that the sin in this verse is the sin of the Golden Calf.

Nether is chalk. *Borith* is soap.

(Therefore, this verse alludes to a specific remedy for an illness that comes because of the sin of the Golden Calf. It must be washed away with *nether*, which is chalk or lime, along with a greater portion of *borith*, which is soap.) Understand the wonders here.

From the days of [Rabbi Nachman's] youth:

Once people came to him with a redemption (*pidyon*), [asking that he pray] for a child by the name of Sarah Esther *bat* Yehudith. He said that she would die, and she did.

He said that he knew this from the Torah itself. It is written, "The fish that were in the Nile died and stank (*metah va-yive'ash*, מיתה ויבאש) (Exodus 7:21). The last words, "died and stank" have the initial letters of "*Sarah Esther bat Yehudith, vay metah* - (וי מיתה שרה אסתר בת יהודית) - Sarah Esther bat Yehudit woe has died." May God protect us!

[Rabbi Nachman] told his followers that whenever they experienced a nocturnal emission, they should immediately immerse in a mikvah. As a result of this nocturnal pollution, whatever [damage] was done, was done. However, before a permanent impression is made, one should immerse and purify oneself.

[Rabbi Nachman] warned that one should not be frightened by this at all. Fear, worry, and depression are very harmful as far as this is concerned. This is especially true now that he has revealed the Ten Psalms that have the specific power to rectify this sin.

[The Ten Psalms] are Psalms 16, 32, 41, 42, 59, 77, 90, 105, 137, and 150, as discussed in our printed works.* If a person

---

our printed works. See *Likutey Moharan* B 92; *Sichoth HaRan* 141. The Ten Psalms are published separately as *Tikkun HaKelali* (The General Rectification).

recites these ten psalms on the day that he has had a nocturnal emission, his sin is rectified, and he need not have any further concern.

[Rabbi Nachman] laughed at Chasidim and God-fearing men who were terrified whenever they had an untoward thought, lest they experience a nocturnal pollution. However, the fear itself can often bring that which they wished to avoid. He therefore mocked this.

His main teaching was that a person not be afraid or terrified by this. One should not think about it at all. One should be like a mighty warrior, standing up against one's desires, utterly fearless, and not thinking of them at all. Then, "God will do what is good in His eyes" (I Samuel 3:18), as He desires.

In his discussion, Rabbi Nachman hinted that this was the blemish of King David and Bathsheva... However, he did not explain this very clearly.

However, a man must strengthen himself in joy at all times, and not let anything depress him, no matter what happens. If he is strong in his resolve, he will not be afraid at all, and will not dwell upon such thoughts. He will travel in his simple way with joy, and he will overcome everything in peace.

It is impossible to put such words into writing. However, "a prudent man will follow the right path" (Proverbs 14:15).

On the Sabbath of Chanukah he told a story that was partially forgotten. It involved the son of a king who was far away from his father,... and yearned very much... He received a letter from his father, and was very happy because of it. He yearned very much at least to reach out a hand, and if a hand were extended, he would hug it and kiss it.

[The son] then made up his mind that the letter was the handwriting of the king himself. Therefore, it is the "hand" of the king... (All of this was not written exactly, since it was not recorded at the time it was said.)

תם ונשלם שבח לאל בורא עולם
ברוך הנותן ליעף כח, ולאין אונים עצמה ירבה

Finished and completed, praise to God Creator of the Universe. Blessed is "He who gives power to the faint, and who increases the strength of one who has no energy" (Isaiah 40:29).

RABBI
NACHMAN'S
PARABLES

18

THE THIEF*

Once there was a poor man who sat in the synagogue and studied Torah. An astrologer* came to the city, and the entire populace ran to him. The poor man, however, did not go. When his wife came to the synagogue, she did not find anyone there other than her husband, since everyone else had gone to the astrologer. She began screaming at him, "You are a lazy, hapless beggar! Why don't you go to the astrologer?"

He did not want to go, but his wife kept pressing him until he had no choice. When he finally got to the astrologer, the astrologer told him that it was his destiny to be a thief.

The man returned to the synagogue, to his Torah study. His wife came to him and asked, "What did he tell you?"

"He told me that I am a poor man and I will remain a poor man," replied her husband.

That night, he came home and ate a piece of bread as his main meal. During the meal, he began to laugh. His wife asked him, "Why are you laughing? You must know something that you're not telling me."

"No," he replied. "He did not tell me anything. I'm just laughing for the fun of it."

He continued eating, and suddenly, he laughed again. When his wife asked him why, he replied to her as before. Then, all of a sudden, he began to roar with laughter. She said to him, "Now

---

The Thief. This collection of stories is not in *Sippurey Maasioth*, but in *Maasioth U'Meshalim*, in *Kokhavay Or*, beginning on page 14. They were originally found in a notebook of Rabbi Naftali, one of Rabbi Nachman's close disciples (see *Ibid.*, p. 13). These stories are only in Hebrew, with some Yiddish phrases thrown in.
astrologer. *Rosh bit* in Yiddish.

I'm sure that you know something." He replied, "Yes, it's true. The astrologer told me that it is my destiny to be a thief."

His wife replied, "I do not want you to be a thief. It is better that we remain poor. Let us accept what God gives us. Don't become a thief."

When the Sabbath came, they had everything that they needed. They had bread, and everything else. When they sat down to eat, they had four or five girls, and the girls grabbed the bread, since there was not enough for all of them. The wife said, "Lord of the Universe. It is so disgusting to me to be so poor!" Addressing her husband, she said, "I would rather have you be a thief, so that we should not be so poor." The poor man did not have any choice but to obey her.* [He wanted to, he did not want to, but he went all the same. The Rebbe used this expression several times when he told this story.]

The husband went out to steal. His first victim was the wealthiest man in town. When he got there, he found the watchmen sleeping, and no one asked him a thing. He went to the store, and found the lock open, since this was his destiny. When he went to the strongbox, it was also unlocked. He took four or five rubles, just enough to support himself, and brought them to his wife.

"I did as you asked," he said. "This should be enough to support us. But I don't want to have to steal again!"

"I agree with you completely," she replied. "I also don't want you ever to steal again. We only had to do it this time, since things were so tight."

But then, once again, an occasion arose when she screamed at him, "Beggar! Hapless fool! You were in the store already? Why didn't you take enough to buy me a coat."*

The man had to go steal again. When he got there, he found another thief.

"Who are you?" he asked.

---

to obey her. In parentheses in Yiddish, "Whether he wanted to go or not, he went anyway."
coat. *Yupa.* See the story of "The Sophisticate and the Simpleton."

"A thief," replied the other. "Who are you?"

"Also a thief," replied the poor man. "Let's be partners in crime. This is my destiny, and I know that I will be successful."

They agreed. However, the poor man began to think, "If we steal here, we will impoverish our victim. When I was alone, I would only steal enough for a coat for my wife. But now we will steal very much, and the victim will remain without anything."

"Why should we make a fellow Jew suffer a loss?" he said to the other. "Better let us steal from a gentile."

They agreed to this, and decided to steal from the king (who lived in that city). [The poor man] was sure that he would be successful, since that was his destiny.

The thief said, "The best thing to steal would be the outfit the king wore at his coronation. This is so valuable that it would suffice us for many generations. I know where these clothes are kept."

The poor man agreed. He was sure that he would be able to steal them, since this was his destiny.

They went to the palace, and went from one room to another and finally came to the garments. The garments were very precious, and this is what they took.

They then began to argue. There was one large garment and one small garment. The thief said that since he was the one who knew about them, he should get the larger one. The poor man, on the other hand, said that he deserved it, since he was the man of destiny, and it was because of destiny that the theft was successful.

"Let us take our dispute to the king," declared the poor man.

"How could you possibly do that?" asked the thief.

"It does not matter," said the poor man. "I will go and ask him."

"If you do that," said the thief, "and actually ask the king, then I will give you the large garment of my own accord."

The thief went with him to the king. Reclining next to the king was a man who told the king stories to put him to sleep. The two of them took the bed with the king sleeping on it, and carried it to another room. When the king woke up, he thought that he was in his usual place.

The poor man began to tell the king the story of the two thieves. When he ended, he asked the king, "Who deserves the larger garment?"

The king became very angry. "Why are you asking me such a simple question?" he said. "It obviously should go to the poor man, since it is because of his destiny that the theft was successful. Now, you'd better tell me a story!"

[The poor man] told him a story, and the king fell asleep. They then carried the bed back to its original room.

In the morning, it was discovered that the king's royal garments had been stolen. The king remembered that the one reclining near him had asked who should get the larger garment. [The regular story teller] was therefore beaten, but he said that he knew nothing about it. They beat and tortured him very much, but he kept on insisting that he did not know anything about the theft.

The king sent for the archbishop* to ask him about these strange happenings, and if it was possible that the storyteller really was not the thief. The archbishop said that it was possible that he was ignorant of the crime. He also said that the king was foolish to say that the larger garment belonged to the poor man. The king became very angry with the archbishop, and wanted to punish him, but he could do nothing.

Meanwhile, the thieves were being sought, but they could not be found. Finally, the king ordered that an announcement be made that whoever had perpetrated the theft should come out, and he would not be harmed. The king felt that he had to satisfy his curiosity as to how the garments were stolen. There were many people around him talking about the case.

Finally the poor man came, and asked the people what they were speaking about. When they told him, he said, "What's the fuss? The one who stole will return."

---

archbishop. Leader of priests, called *archriga*.

The people rebuked him. When he asked a second time, they rebuked him again. "Beggar! You deserve to be killed. It is being said that you know something about the theft."

"Yes," replied the poor man, "I know who the thief is."

"If you know, then you must tell," they said.

"I will tell," he replied.

The poor man came to the king, and said, "I know who the thief is."

"I would very much like to see the thief," replied the king.

"I am he!" said the poor man.

The king kissed him and asked, "How did you do it?"

The [poor man] told him the entire story. They caught the other thief, and he had to return the second garment which he had.

The king then said to the poor man, "I would like you to play a similar trick on the archbishop, since I am very angry with him."

The poor man said, "Give me a set of vestments like the archbishop wears during his service. I will also need a large number of turtles* captured for me. Besides that, I will need many candles."

The poor man put on the vestments, and attached a candle to each turtle. He then stood at the altar, and began to scream. Everyone gathered, and the archbishop came with them. The archbishop was very frightened, since he saw fires and heard a voice crying out, but did not know what it was.

[The poor man] said to the archbishop, "I have come for you. I want to bring you into paradise immediately."

The archbishop fell on his face.

"Before I take you to paradise," said the poor man, "I must first bring you through purgatory for a short time. Then I will bring you to paradise. First you must get into my sack."

When the archbishop was in the sack, [the poor man] carried

---

turtles. *Rakis.*

him to the king. The sack was hung up in the palace courtyard, and the king was informed. People came and saw the sack hanging with someone obviously inside it, and they began to throw stones at it. The archbishop was severely wounded and all his teeth were broken. The archbishop did not know what was happening; was this purgatory as he had been told, or was it all a trick?

After he had been well beaten, the king gave orders to cut him down. The sack was cut down and opened, and [the archbishop] left in humiliation.*

---

humiliation. In another version, "In the end, he was hung, since 'the end of a thief is hanging.' While he was being brought, the Evil One walked alongside with a sack of shoes, and he said, 'I wore out all these shoes until I finally brought you to this.' "

19

FAITH

There was once a poor man who earned a living by digging clay and selling it. Once, while digging clay, he discovered a precious stone which was obviously worth a great deal. Since he had no idea of its worth, he took it to an expert to tell him its value.

The expert answered, "No one here will be able to afford such a stone. Go to London, the capital, and there you will be able to sell it."

The man was so poor that he could not afford to make the journey. He sold everything he had, and went from house to house, collecting funds for the trip. Finally he had enough to take him as far as the sea.

He then wanted to board a ship, but he did not have any money. He went to a ship's captain and showed him the jewel. The captain immediately welcomed him aboard the ship with great honor, assuming that he was a very trustworthy person. He gave [the poor man] a special first class cabin, and treated him like a wealthy personage.

[The poor man's] cabin had a view of the sea, and he sat there, constantly looking at the diamond and rejoicing. He was especially particular to do this during his meals, since eating in such good spirits is highly beneficial for the digestion.

Then one day, he sat down to eat, with the diamond lying in front of him on the table where he could enjoy it. Sitting there, he dozed off. Meanwhile, the mess boy came and cleared the table, shaking the tablecloth with its crumbs and the diamond into the sea. When he woke up and realized what had happened, he almost went mad with grief. Besides, the captain was a ruthless man who would not hesitate to kill him for his fare.

Having no other choice, he continued to act happy, as if nothing had happened. The captain would usually speak to him a few hours every day, and on this day, he put himself in good spirits, so that the captain was not aware that anything was wrong.

The captain said to him, "I want to buy a large quantity of wheat and I will be able to sell it in London for a huge profit. But I am afraid that I will be accused of stealing from the king's treasury. Therefore, I will arrange for the wheat to be bought in your name. I will pay you well for your trouble."

The poor man agreed. But as soon as they arrived in London, the captain died. [The entire shipload of] wheat was in the poor man's name, and it was worth many times as much as the diamond.

[Rabbi Nachman] concluded, "The diamond did not belong to the poor man, and the proof is that he did not keep it. The wheat, however, did belong to him, and the proof is that he kept it. But he got what he deserved only because he *remained* happy."

20

KAPTZIN PASHA

Once there was a court Jew who was very much favored by the Turkish Sultan, more than any of the other ministers of state. The Sultan was very fond of him, more than anyone else in his government. Every day, the Sultan would invite him to his palace to spend time with him.

The other royal ministers grew jealous of him, and devised plots to denounce him to the Sultan and destroy him.

Among the ministers, there was a pasha named Kaptzin Pasha, who hated this Jew more than anyone else in the government. When he was with the court Jew, he behaved like a close friend. But every day he would devise plots to denounce the Jew before the Sultan.

Once the Pasha came to the Jew and began to speak to him. He maliciously told him, "I was with the Sultan, and I heard him say that he is very fond of you. There is, however, one thing that bothers him. Whenever you come to him and speak with him, he can't stand your bad breath. Since he does not want to avoid you, this troubles him very much. My advice is that when you come to the Sultan you should place a perfumed handkerchief over your mouth. This will cover up your bad breath, so that it will not disturb the Sultan."

In his innocence, the Jew believed him, and agreed to follow his advice.

The Pasha then went to the Sultan and told him that he had heard the Jew say that he suffers very much since whenever he speaks to the Sultan, he has to smell the Sultan's bad breath. "Therefore," [said the Pasha], "Whenever the Jew comes to you, he will place a perfumed handkerchief over his mouth, so that he will not smell your breath. And if you don't believe me, this is proof. Tomorrow when the Jew comes, he will have a handkerchief over his mouth."

When the Sultan heard this, he became very angry. He said, "I will see if you are telling the truth! If it is true, I will destroy that Jew!"

The next day, when the Jew came to the Sultan, he placed the handkerchief over his mouth, just as the Pasha had advised him, since he had believed him. When the Sultan saw that, he understood that the Pasha had been telling the truth. He immediately wrote a note saying, "When the bearer of this note arrives, immediately throw him into the furnace where all those who are sentenced to death are cast." The Sultan then sealed the letter with his signet, and said to the Jew, "Do me a favor and personally deliver this note to the man whose address is written on the envelope."

The Jew took the letter and promised the Sultan that he would do as he requested, not knowing what was written in the letter.

The [court Jew] was very diligent to keep the commandment to circumcise Jewish children. Whenever he was honored to perform a circumcision,* he would not pay attention to any obstacle, since this commandment was very precious to him.

On that very day, when he was supposed to deliver the Sultan's letter to the place it was sent, God arranged to save His good friend. He made it happen that a man came from a village, and honored [the court Jew] to travel with him to the village to circumcise his son. The custom of [the court Jew] was not to avoid performing this precept, no matter what the circumstances. He began to think, "What will I do to fulfill the Sultan's request that I deliver the letter?"

God then arranged that he should meet [Kaptzin] Pasha. [The court Jew] told the Pasha that he had been with the Sultan, and

---

to perform a circumcision. *Chitukh* in Hebrew. This is the cutting off of the foreskin. Often, another person would be honored to pull it back (*periyah*). In those times, it was a custom to give honor to people by having them perform these ceremonies.

that the Sultan had given him a letter to deliver. But now God had arranged that he could perform a circumcision, and his custom was not to set aside this commandment for any reason whatever. "Therefore," he said, "I am asking you to do me a favor. Please, if you would, take the letter, and deliver it there."

The Pasha was very happy at the turn of events, since now he would also be able to denounce the Jew for not delivering the letter as the Sultan had ordered. He immediately took the letter and delivered it to the one to whom it was addressed. The recipient was the executioner in charge of burning those who had been sentenced to death by the Sultan. He immediately grabbed the Pasha and threw him into the furnace. He was burned as he had been judged by God, and was thus punished "measure for measure." *

The Jew, meanwhile, did not know anything about this, and the next day he appeared before the Sultan as if nothing had happened. When the Sultan saw him, he was very surprised. "Didn't you deliver the letter that I gave you?" he asked.

The Jew replied, "Your Majesty, I gave the letter to Kaptzin Pasha to deliver. God gave me the opportunity to perform a circumcision, and my custom is not to pass over this opportunity whenever it presents itself."

The Sultan then understood that there was a reason that the Pasha had been burned, and that it was because he had slandered the Jew. The Sultan asked him, "How come you hold a perfumed handkerchief over your mouth when you speak to me?"

"The Pasha advised me to," replied the Jew. "He told me that he heard you saying that you couldn't stand my bad breath."

The Sultan then told him how the Pasha had slandered the Jew. He said, "The Pasha said that you couldn't stand my bad breath, and that you were putting the perfumed handkerchief over your mouth to avoid smelling it."

The Sultan then revealed to the Jew the contents of the letter.

---

measure for measure. *Middah ke-neged middah.* The concept that God always makes the punishment fit the crime; it is found in many places in the Talmud (see *Sotah* 9b).

He said, "Now I know that God has power over the world, and He saved His friend from all evil. What the Pasha wanted to do to you was done to him. He was paid back as he deserved."

The Jew was now all the more esteemed by the Sultan, more so than any of his ministers of state. He was very highly esteemed and dear to him.

21

SIMPLICITY

God wins battles merely because of the simple folk who recite psalms with simplicity, and not through those who use sophisticated means.

A king once went hunting,* and he traveled like a simple man, so that he would have freedom of movement. Suddenly a heavy rain fell, literally like a flood. The ministers scattered in all directions, and the king was in great danger. He searched until he found the house of a villager. The villager invited the king in and offered him some groats.* He lit the stove, and let the king sleep on the pallet.*

This was very sweet and pleasant for the king. He was so tired and exhausted that it seemed as if he had never had such a pleasurable experience.

Meanwhile, the royal ministers sought the king, until they found him in this house, where they saw the king sleeping. They wanted him to return to the palace with them.

"You did not even attempt to rescue me," said the king. "Each one of you ran to save himself. But this man rescued me. Here I had the sweetest experience. Therefore, he will bring me back in his wagon, in these clothes, and he will sit with me on my throne."

Rabbi Nachman concluded by saying that it is said that before

hunting. *Navlavi.*
groats. *Graetz.*
pallet. *Pieklik.*

the Messiah comes, there will be flood. (People will be flooded with atheism.) It will not be a flood of water, but of immorality. * It will cover all the high mountains, * even in the Holy Land, where the original flood did not reach. * But this time, it will come with such strength that the water will splash over the land. This means that it will have an effect even in virtuous hearts.

There will be no way to combat this with sophistication. All the royal ministers will be scattered, and the entire kingdom will not be firm on its foundation. The only ones who will uphold it will be the simple Jews who recite Psalms in simplicity. Therefore, when the Messiah comes, they will be the ones to place the crown on his head.

---

immorality. The abbrevation here is *Mem Zayin* (מ"ז), which can denote *mayim zedim, makhshavoth zaroth.*
cover all the high mountains. Genesis 7:21.
Holy Land... There is an opinion in the Talmud that the flood did not cover the Land of Israel (*Zevachim* 113b).

22

VERDA

Once a man was traveling with his teamster (to Berlin and other large cities). The man went aside to attend his needs, and the driver, whose name was Ivan, remained with the coach in the middle of the street. A soldier came along and asked, "Why is it standing there? Who is it?" [In German, "who is it" is *wer da*, or as pronounced in Yiddish, Verda.]

The driver thought that the soldier was asking his name, so he replied, "Ivan."

The soldier gave him a blow to the head. "Verda!" he demanded.

"Ivan!" screamed the driver.

The soldier hit him again, and shouted "Verda!"

Finally, the soldier took him and the wagon to a side street. When the man came back, he looked around until he found his coach. He said to the driver, "Ivan..."

The driver was terrified. "Don't call me Ivan!" he said. "Call me Verda."

When they finally left the city, he said, "Now you can call me Ivan. There my name was Verda, but here my name is Ivan."

Rabbi Nachman concluded by saying, "By me it is Verda." (That is, "who is it.") One knows his lowly status. Also when the body (Ivan) is purified, it is called, "who" and "what." But when people leave me, then they become Ivan again, since the physical remains physical.

23

THE BITTER HERB

Once a Jew and a German gentile were traveling as hoboes together. The Jew told the German to make believe that he was a Jew (since their language was similar), and the Jews would have pity on him. Since Passover was approaching, he taught him how to act (when he is invited to a Seder). He told him that at every Seder,* Kiddush* is made, and the hands are washed. However, he forgot to tell him about the bitter herb.

He was invited to a house, and being very hungry from all day, looked forward to the fine foods that had been described by the Jew. However, first they gave him a piece of celery* dipped in salt water, and other things served at the Seder. They then began to recite the Haggadah* and he sat there longing for the meal. When the matzah was served, he was very happy.

Then they gave him a piece of horseradish for the bitter herb.* It was bitter to taste, and he thought that this was the entire meal. He ran from the house, bitter and hungry, saying to himself, "Cursed Jews! After all that ceremony, that's all they serve to eat!" He went to the synagogue and fell asleep.

After a while, the Jew arrived, happy and full from a good meal. "How was your Seder?" he asked.

The other told him what had happened.

"Stupid German!" replied the Jew. "If you had waited just a little longer, you would have had a fine meal, as I had."

Seder. The traditional Passover night feast.
Kiddush. The prayer over wine that begins the Seder.
celery. *Karpas.* Celery is dipped in salt water and eaten at the very beginning of the Seder, before the Haggadah (story of the Exodus) is recited.
Haggadah. The story of the exodus from Egypt.
bitter herb. It is eaten just before the meal.

The same is true when one wants to come close to God. After all the effort to begin, one is given a little bitterness. This bitterness is needed to purify the body. But the person might think that this bitterness is all there is to serving God, so he runs away from it. But if he waited a short while, and allowed his body to be purified, then he would feel every joy and delight in the world in his closeness to God.

24

THE TREASURE

A man once dreamed that there was a great treasure under a bridge in Vienna. He traveled to Vienna and stood near the bridge, trying to figure out what to do. He did not dare search for the treasure by day, because of the many people who were there.

An officer passed by and asked, "What are you doing, standing here and contemplating?" The man decided that it would be best to tell the whole story and ask for help, hoping that [the officer] would share the treasure with him. He told the officer the entire story.

The officer replied, "A Jew is concerned only with dreams! I also had a dream, and I also saw a treasure. It was in a small house, under the cellar."

In relating his dream, the officer accurately described the man's city and house. He rushed home, dug under his cellar, and found the treasure. He said, "Now I know that I had the treasure all along. But in order to find it, I had to travel to Vienna."

The same is true in serving God. Each person has the treasure, but in order to find it, he must travel to the tzaddik.

25

THE TURKEY PRINCE

A royal prince once became mad and thought that he was a turkey. He felt compelled to sit naked under the table, pecking at bones and pieces of bread like a turkey. The royal physicians all gave up hope of ever curing him of this madness, and the king suffered tremendous grief.

A sage then came and said, "I will undertake to cure him."

The sage undressed and sat naked under the table next to the prince, picking crumbs and bones. "Who are you?" asked the prince. "What are you doing here?"

"And you?" replied the sage. "What are you doing here?"

"I am a turkey," said the prince.

"I am also a turkey," answered the sage.

They sat together like this for some time, until they became good friends. One day, the sage signalled the king's servants to throw him shirts. He said to the prince, "What makes you think that a turkey can't wear a shirt? You can wear a shirt and still be a turkey." With that, the two of them put on shirts.

After a while, he signalled them again, and they threw him a pair of pants. Just as before, he said, "What makes you think that you can't be a turkey if you wear pants?"

The sage continued in this manner until they were both completely dressed. Then he signalled again, and they were given regular food from the table. Again the sage said, "What makes you think that you will stop being a turkey if you eat good food? You can eat whatever you want and still be a turkey!" They both ate the food.

Finally, the sage said, "What makes you think a turkey must

sit under the table? Even a turkey can sit at the table."

The sage continued in this manner until the prince was completely cured.

26

THE TAINTED GRAIN

A king once told his prime minister, who was also his good friend, "I see in the stars that whoever eats any grain that grows this year will go mad.* What is your advice?"

The prime minister replied, "We must put aside enough grain so that we will not have to eat from this year's harvest."

The king objected, "But then we will be the only ones who will be sane. Everyone else will be mad. Therefore, they will think that we are the mad ones. It is impossible for us to put aside enough grain for everyone. Therefore, we too must eat this year's grain. But we will make a mark on our foreheads, so that at least we will know that we are mad. I will look at your forehead, and you will look at mine, and when we see this sign, we will know that we are both mad."

---

mad. There are fungi of the ergot family that attack grain, and can cause hallucinations and other bizarre experiences when ingested. These fungi contain substances very similar to LSD.

27

THE DEER

Once a king was pursuing a deer, but he could not catch it. The royal ministers caught up with him and said, "Your Majesty, let's go back."

"I must capture the deer," replied the king. "But whoever wishes to go back can go back."

28

THE BIRD

There was once a king who was a great astrologer. One year he saw in the stars that if the wheat was not harvested before a certain time, all the wheat would be ruined. He saw that there was not much time.

He came up with the idea that he would give the harvesters every possible pleasure and all their needs, so that they would have a clear mind to work day and night. Then they would finish the harvest before the deadline.

However, the workers took what the king sent them, and they enjoyed themselves so much that they forgot to work on the harvest. The time came, and the wheat was not harvested, so that it became completely ruined.

The people did not know what to do. They realized that the king would be terribly angry with them.

A sage gave them an idea. The king was very fond of a certain type of bird. If they could bring him such a bird, he would have so much pleasure from it, he would forgive everything. However, it was very difficult to capture this bird, since it lived very high up. They did not have a ladder, and there was no time to get one.

The sage once again gave them an idea. Since they were many men, one would be able to stand on the shoulders of the other, making a human ladder to reach the bird.

They liked the idea, but began to argue, since each one wanted to be on top. They wasted time arguing, until the bird flew away. The king then remained angry at them for neglecting to harvest the wheat on time.

The idea is that God created man, and gave him every

pleasure, all so that he should "cut the grain" before he is harmed through blemishing the covenant of Abraham (*pegam ha-b'rith*). People would then be able to serve God with a clear mind. But they neglected it through their enjoyment, until they forgot the grain, and let their minds be ruined. Nevertheless, there was still hope through the bird, who is the tzaddik, since through him everything could be forgiven. But then there was arguing and strife, since each one wanted to be on top. They were thus kept from binding themselves to the tzaddik.

29

TRUST IN GOD*

There was once a king who said to himself, "Who can have fewer worries than I have? I have everything good and I am a king and a ruler."

He went to investigate this. He walked around at night, standing behind the houses, to listen and determine what people were saying. He heard each one's worries, and how things were not going well in their business. At one person's house, he heard that the person had troubles, and had to obtain an audience with the king. In this way, he heard each one's complaints.

Then he saw a very low house, that was sunken in the ground, so that its windows were literally at ground level. Its roof was fallen and broken. Inside he saw a man sitting and playing his fiddle, but he had to listen very well to hear the sound. The man was very happy. He had a plate and drink in front of him. The drink was wine, and he had other food before him. The man appeared very happy, full of joy, without any worries.

The king went into the house, and asked how the man was getting along. The man replied. The king saw the pot, the wine and the food in front of the man, and saw the joy on the man's

---

Trust in God. This story was first printed in Jerusalem around 1905 by Rabbi Tzvi Dov ben Avraham of Berdichev. It was printed in both Hebrew and Yiddish. It seems that it was either preserved in manuscript or told orally in Uman.

At the beginning of the story, it states that Rabbi Nachman told this story on 4 Elul, 5566 (August 18, 1806). Shortly before this (July 27), Rabbi Nachman had spoken of how one can accept all suffering with love and faith (*Likutey Moharan, New Sayings,* at end of volume, p. 4; *Shevachay Moharan* 35a #124; *Likutey Halakhoth, Geviyath Chov* 4:10).

This story was also told just about a month after the story of "The Lost Princess," which was told on July 25, 1806.

face. The man gave the king some wine, and drank to the king. Out of love, the king also drank.

The king then lay down to sleep. The king saw that he was totally happy, without any worries whatever.

In the morning the king got up, and the man also got up and accompanied the king.

"Where do you get all this?" asked the king.

"I am a repairman," replied the man. "I can fix anything that is broken. I can't make anything, but I can fix things. I go out in the morning, and I fix things. When I have five or six gulden, I buy myself food and drink."

When the king heard this, he said to himself, "I will ruin him."

The king returned home, and issued a decree that if anyone has anything broken, he should not give it to anyone to fix. He must either fix it himself, or buy something new.

The next morning, the fixer went out, and looked for things to repair. He was told that the king had issued a decree that nothing be given to others to fix. This was bad for him, but he had trust in God.

He walked a while, and saw a wealthy man cutting wood. "Why are you cutting the wood yourself?" asked the fixer. "Isn't it beneath your dignity?"

"I tried to find someone to cut the wood for me," replied the rich man, "but I couldn't find anyone. I had no choice but to cut it myself."

"Let me," replied the fixer. "I will cut the wood for you."

He cut the wood, and the rich man gave him a gulden. He saw that this was a good way to earn money, so he went to cut more wood, until he had earned six gulden. He took the money and bought himself his meal. The meal was a feast and he was very happy.

The king went out again that night, and stood outside the fixer's window to see what had happened. He saw the fixer sitting with food and drink in front of him, very happy. The king came in, and saw the same as the previous time. They then went to sleep as they had done previously, and in the morning the man got up and accompanied the king.

"Where did you get your food?" asked the king. "How did you earn money for it?"

"My usual work is to repair things," replied the fixer. "But the king made a law that nothing can be given to another to be fixed. So I went and chopped wood until I got enough money for what I needed."

After leaving the fixer, the king issued a decree that no one should hire anyone to cut wood.

When the man heard this, he was upset, since he had no money. But still, he trusted in God. He walked a while, and saw a man cleaning out his stable. "Who are you to be cleaning out a stable?" he asked.

"I looked all over, " replied the other, "and I couldn't find anyone to do it for me. Therefore, I had to do it myself."

"Let me," replied the fixer. "I will clean it out for you."

When he was finished the man gave him two gulden. He cleaned out a few more stables, and earned himself the six gulden that he needed. He bought his entire meal, and returned home. The meal was for him a feast, and he was very happy.

The king went out again to see what had happened, and again saw him happy. The king came in, spent the night, and in the morning, the fixer accompanied the king. The king asked him how he got the money, and he explained what he had done. The king then issued a decree that no one may be hired to clean out barns or stables.

That morning, the fixer went out to clean stables, but he was told that the king had made a law that no one be hired to do such work. Not having any choice, the fixer went to the recruiting officer and joined the national guard. Some soldiers are drafted, but others volunteer for pay.

The fixer hired himself out as a soldier, and made a condition with the recruiting officer that he would only join temporarily, and that he would be paid every morning. He immediately put on his uniform, and put his sword at his side. At night, he took off his uniform, and with his pay, he bought himself his meal and went home. The meal was a feast for him, and he was very happy.

The king went out to see what had happened. He saw that everything was set before the fixer, and that he was very happy. He entered the house, and spent the night with him as before. The king then asked him how he was getting along, and the fixer told him the whole story. The king called the officer and told him that he should not lift a finger to pay any of the men from the treasury that morning.

When the fixer reported for duty, he asked the officer for his pay for the day. When the officer would not pay him, he said, "But we made an agreement that you would pay me every day."

"True," replied the officer, "but the king decreed that no one get paid today."

The fixer pleaded and argued, but to no avail. "I'll pay you tomorrow for two days," said the officer. "But today it is impossible to pay you."

The fixer devised a plan. He removed the blade from his sword, and replaced it with a wooden blade, so that no one could tell the difference. He then pawned the sword blade and bought his meal as usual. The meal was a feast.

The king came back again, and saw the fixer completely happy. He came to visit and spent the night, and asked him how things were doing. The fixer told him the whole story, how he had removed the sword blade from the handle, and had pawned it to buy his meal. "When I get paid today," he finished, "I will redeem the blade and fix it. No one will know the difference. I can fix anything! The king will have lost nothing."

When the king returned to his palace, he summoned the officer in charge. He said, "I have a criminal who was sentenced to death. Call this fixer whom you recruited as a mercenary, and give him orders to cut off this criminal's head."

The officer went and summoned the fixer. The king gave orders that all the officers should see this joke. He told them that one of his soldiers had replaced the blade of his sword with a wooden substitute.

When the fixer came before the king, he fell on the ground

before the king, and pleaded, "Your Majesty. Why did you summon me?"

"To decapitate a criminal," replied the king.

The fixer begged and pleaded. "But I have never killed a man," he said. "Please! Get someone else to do it."

"That's just why I'm ordering you to do it," replied the king.

"Is the case really that clear?" asked the fixer. "Maybe the case is not clear. Maybe he doesn't deserve to die. I never killed a man in my life. How can I now kill someone who might not even deserve to die?"

"There is no question whatsoever that he deserves to die," replied the king. "The verdict is unanimous. And you must be the one to carry out the sentence and execute him."

The fixer saw that he would not be able to dissuade the king. He looked up toward heaven and said, "God Almighty. I never killed a person in my life. If this man does not deserve to die, let the blade of my sword turn to wood."

With that, he drew his sword, and everyone saw that the blade was a piece of wood. All those present had a good laugh. The king saw what a fine man the fixer was, and he let him go home in peace.

BIBLIOGRAPHY

❧ ❧ ❧

INDEX

BIBLIOGRAPHY

Adir BaMarom. Important work on Kabbalistic thought by Rabbi Moshe Chaim Luzzatto (1707 — 1746), first published in Warsaw, 1882. The author was considered one of the most important of all Kabbalistic thinkers, and is best known for his *Mesillath Yesharim* (*Path of the Upright*).

Adney Kesef. Biblical commentary by Rabbi Yosef (ben Abba Mari) ibn Caspi (1279 — 1340), first published from manuscript by Yitchak Last, London, 1911. The author was a leading Jewish thinker in Spain.

Alim LeTerufah. Collection of letters by Rabbi Nathan (ben Naftali Hertz) Sternhartz of Nemirov (1780 — 1845), first published in Berdichev, 1896, and with editions in Jerusalem, 1911. A more complete edition was published by Rabbi Aaron Leib Tziegelman in Jerusalem, 1930. [We have used the Jerusalem, 1968 edition.] Rabbi Nathan was the foremost disciple of Rabbi Nachman, and publisher of many of his works, including the Stories.

Anaf Yosef. Commentary on *Eyn Yaakov* (q.v.), by Rabbi Chanokh Zundel ben Yosef (died 1867), first published together with his other commentary, *Etz Yosef*, in the Vilna, 1883, edition of *Eyn Yaakov*. The author, who lived in Bialystok, Poland, wrote commentries on numerous Midrashim.

Arba Meyoth Shekel Kesef. Important work on the Kabbalah of the Ari (Rabbi Yitzchak Luria, 1534 — 1572), by Rabbi Chaim Vital (1542 — 1620), first published in Koretz, 1804. [We have used the Cracow, 1886, edition.] See *Etz Chaim*.

Arukh. One of the earliest and most popular dictionaries of the Talmud (q.v.) by Rabbi Nathan (ben Yechiel) of Rome (1035—1106), first printed in Rome, 1472. The author was a colleague of Rabbenu Gershom, leader of Ashkenazic Jewry, and corresponded with Rashi (q.v.).

Avanehah Barzel. Stories and teachings of Rabbi Nachman and his disciples, collected by Rabbi Shmuel Horowitz (1903—1973), first printed in Jerusalem, 1935. [We have used the Jerusalem, 1972, edition, printed together with *Kokhavey Or* (q.v.).] The author was an important Breslover leader in Jerusalem.

Avkath Rokhel. Ethical and escatological work by Rabbi Makhir, first printed in Constantinople, 1516.

Avodath HaKodesh. Important Kabbalistic work by Rabbi Meir ibn Gabbai (born 1480), first published in Venice, 1567. Born in Spain, the author lived in Egypt and Safed after the expulsion.

Avoth deRabbi Nathan. A running commentary on *Avoth*, by the Babylonian sage, Rabbi Nathan (circa. 210 c.e.). It is printed in all editions of the Talmud. We follow the paragraphing of the Vilna, 1883, Romm edition of the Talmud.

Bahir. An important ancient Kabbalistic work, attributed to the school of Rabbi Nechunia ben Hakana (circa. 80 c.e.), first printed in Amsterdam, 1651. An English translation by Rabbi Aryeh Kaplan was published by Weiser (York, Maine, 1979).

Batey Midrashoth. A collection of ancient Midrashim and similar material from manuscript by Rabbi Shlomo Aaron Wertheimer (1866—1935), first published in Jerusalem, 1893-97, and with additions, Jerusalem, 1950.

BaMidbar Rabbah. Part of the *Midrash Rabbah* (q.v.) dealing with the Book of Numbers.

Bereshith Rabbah. The section of the *Midrash Rabbah* (q.v.) dealing with the Book of Genesis. It is a commentary on the Scripture, based on Talmudic material.

Belbey HaNachal. Commentary on *Likutey Moharan* (q.v.), by Rabbi Barukh Ephraim (ben Yitzchak), first printed together with *Parparoth LeChokhman* (q.v.) in Lvov (Lemberg), 1876. It was later printed with *Likutey Moharan*, New York, 1966.

Beth Halevi. Commentary on the Torah (two volumes) by Rabbi Yoseph Dov (ben Rabbi Yitzchak Zev) Halevi Soloveitchik. Rabbi Yoseph Dov was a descendant of Rabbi Chaim of Volozshin, and a leading rabbinical authority in Lithuania. The first edition was printed in Vilna.

Biur HaLikutim. Commentary on *Likutey Moharan* (q.v.) by Rabbi Avraham (Chazan HaLevi) ben Reb Nachman of Tulchin, (1849—1917) printed in part in Jerusalem, 1908, and in greater part, B'nei B'rak, 1967.

Burstyn, Rabbi Nachman. Oral teachings, by a leading figure in Breslov in Jerusalem.

Butril, Rabbi Moshe. Commentary on *Sefer Yetzirah* (q.v.) written in 1409, and first printed in the Mantua, 1562, edition of *Sefer Yetzirah*. The author was an important Kabbalist, and quotes a number of sources no longer in existence.

Chayay Moharan. Important biographical work on Rabbi Nachman, by his chief disciple, Rabbi Nathan of Nemerov (see *Alim LeTerufah*), printed with notes by Rabbi Nachman of Tcherin, Lemberg, 1874. [We have used the Jerusalem, 1962, edition.]

Chayay Nefesh. Kabbalistic discussion of Breslover principles, by Rabbi Gedalia Aaron (ben Eleazar Mordechai) Koenig (1921—1980), published in Tel Aviv, 1968.

Chokhmah U'Tevunah. Kabbalistic commentary on the Stories by

Rabbi Avraham ben Nachman of Tulchin, first published in B'nei B'rak, 1962.

Choshen Mishpat. Fourth section of the *Shulchan Arukh* (q.v.) dealing with judicial law.

Daath Chokhmah. Penetrating Kabbalistic work by Rabbi Moshe Chaim Luzzatto (see *Adir BaMarom*), first printed as part of *Pith'chey Chokhmah VeDaath,* Warsaw, 1884. [Reprinted with *Klach Pith'chey Chokhmah*, Jerusalem, 1961.]

Dan Yadin. Commentary on *Karnayim* (q.v.) by Rabbi Shimshon (ben Pesach) Ostropoli (died 1648), first published in Zolkiev, 1709. [We have used the Amsterdam, 1765 edition, reprinted in B'nei B'rak, 1971.] The author was the leading Kabbalist in Poland in his time.

Derekh HaShem. Key work on Jewish thought by Rabbi Moshe Chaim Luzzatto (see *Adir BaMarom*), first printed in Amsterdam, 1896. Translated into English by Rabbi Aryeh Kaplan as *The Way of God* (Feldheim, New York, 1977).

Emunath Uman. Letters by Rabbi Nathan ben Reb Yehuda Reuven of Nemerov, (a leading disciple of Rabbi Nathan of Nemerov), and other Breslover leaders, edited by Rabbi Nathan Tzvi Koenig, and published in B'nei B'rak, 1966.

Etz Chaim. The major classic of Kabbalah, based on the teachings of the Ari (Rabbi Yitzchak Luria, 1534—1572), and written by Rabbi Chaim Vital (1542—1620), and first published in Koretz, 1782. Both the Ari, and his disciple Rabbi Chaim Vital, were the leaders of the Safed school of Kabbalah. Many consider the Ari to be the greatest of all Kabbalists.

Evven HaEzer. Third section of the *Shulchan Arukh* (q.v.) dealing with marriage and divorce.

Evven Shethiyah. Biographies of the Chasidic leaders of Kosov and Viznitz, by Rabbis Chaim Kahana and Chaim Yessachar Gross, published in Minkatch, 1930.

Eyn Yaakov. Collection of aggadoth (non-legal portions) of the Talmud, by Rabbi Yaakov (ben Shlomo) ibn Chabib (1433—1516), first published in Salonika, 1515-22. [We have used the Vilna, 1883, Romm edition, reprinted in New York, 1955.]

Hagah. Gloss on the *Shulchan Arukh* (q.v.), presenting the Ashkenazic customs, by Rabbi Moshe (ben Yisrael) Isserles (1525—1572). Originally known as *HaMappah,* it was first published together with the *Shulchan Arukh* in Cracow, 1578, and in virtually every subsequent edition. The author was a leading rabbinical figure in Cracow, and one of the greatest halakhic authorities of all time.

HaGra. Commentary on *Shulchan Arukh* (q.v.) by Rabbi Eliahu (ben Shlomo, known as the Vilna Gaon (1720—1797), first printed with the *Shulchan Arukh* in Gorodna, 1806. The author was the greatest genius of his time, and the acknowledged leader of all non-Chassidic Jewry in Eastern Europe.

Handbook of Jewish Thought. Concise, encyclopedic work on basic Jewish theology, by Rabbi Aryeh Kaplan (Maznaim, Brooklyn, 1979).

Hekhaloth Rabathai. Important meditative work from the Merkava school of Kabbalah, attributed to Rabbi Yishmael (First Century), and also known as Pirkey Hekheloth. First printed as part of *Arzey Levanon*, Venice, 1601. We have used the edition published as part of *Batey Midrashoth* (q.v.), Volume 1, p. 67 ff.

Idra Rabbah. Portion of the *Zohar* (q.v.) dealing with the dynamics of the supernal universes, presented as a lecture by Rabbi Shimon bar Yochai to his ten disciples. Found in the *Zohar* 3:127b ff.

Idra Zutra. "The Lesser Gathering," so called because three of Rabbi Shimon's disciples had passed away. In the *Zohar* 3:287b ff.

Karnayim. Kabbalistic work by Rabbi Aaron ben Avraham of Cordein, first published with commentary *Dan Yadin* (q.v.).

Kav HaYashar. Ethical classic by Rabbi Tzvi Hirsch (ben Aaron

Sh'muel) Kaidanover (1648—1712), first published in Frankfurt am Main, 1705. The author lived in Frankfurt.

Kedushath Shabbath. Breslover teachings regarding the Sabbath, by Rabbi Nachman (Goldstein) of Tcherin 1823—1898, published with *Yekara DeShabbatta,* Lemberg, 1876. The author was a student of Rabbi Nathan and a grandson of Rabbi Aharon, the Rabbi in Breslov during Rabbi Nachman's life.

Kehillath Yaakov. Dictionary of Kabbalistic terms, by Rabbi Yaakov Tzvi Yolles (died 1825), published in Lemberg, 1870. The author, who is best known for his *Maley Ro'im* on Talmudical concepts, was rabbi in Dinov.

Kohelleth Rabbah. Section of the *Midrash Rabbah* (q.v.) dealing with the book of Ecclesiastes.

Kokhavay Or. Stories and teachings of Rabbi Nachman and his disciples, by Rabbi Avraham ben Nachman of Tulchin, (see Biur HaLikutim) first printed in Jerusalem, 1896.[We have used the Jerusalem, 1972, edition.]

Kramer, Rabbi Chaim. Oral teachings. Rabbi Kramer is the director of Yeshivath Chasidei Breslov and its affiliated *ba'alei teshuvah* and research institutes in Jerusalem.

Kramer, Rabbi Shmuel Moshe. Oral teachings, by a leading figure in Breslov in Jerusalem.

Likutey Etzoth B. See *Likutey Etzoth, Mahadura Bathra.*

Likutey Etzoth, Mahadura Bathra. Concise teachings and advice based on the works of Rabbi Nachman, by Rabbi Nachman of Tcherin, first pubished in Lemberg, 1874.

Likutey Halakhoth. Monumental work on Breslover thought and Kabbalah, following the order of the *Shulchan Arukh* (q.v.) by Rabbi Nathan of Nemerov. Rabbi Nachman's foremost disciple. First part printed in Jasse, 1843, with subsequent sections published through 1861. [We have used the eight volume, Jerusalem, 1970, edition.]

Maaver Yaavak. Laws and customs involving visiting the sick and funeral preparations, by Rabbi Aaron Berakhiah (ben Moshe) of Modina (died 1639), first printed in Venice, 1626. [We have used the Zhitamar, 1852, edition, reprinted in B'nei B'rak, 1967.] An important Kabbalist, the author lived in Italy.

Maggid Mesharim. Kabbalistic teachings given over by an angelic instructor (*maggid*) to Rabbi Yosef Caro (see *Shulchan Arukh*), first printed in Lublin, 1646, and completed in Venice, 1654. [We have used the Jerusalem, 1960, edition.]

MeAm Lo'ez. Monumental running commentary on the Torah, written in Ladino (Judeo-Spanish) by Rabbi Yaakov (ben Makhir) Culi (1689—1732), first published in Constantinople, 1730—33. Upon the author's death, the set was completed by Rabbi Yitzchak (ben Moshe) Magriso and Rabbi Yitzchak Agruiti, as far as the portion of Ekev in Deuteronomy. A Hebrew translation, *Yalkut MeAm Lo'ez* was completed by Rabbi Sh'muel Kreuser (Yerushalmi), Jerusalem, 1967—71, and an English translation is being completed by Rabbi Aryeh Kaplan under the name of *The Torah Anthology* (q.v.). Rabbi Yaakov Culi was born in Jerusalem, and later moved to Constantinople, where he was a leading figure in the Sephardic community.

Megaleh Amukoth. Kabbalistic interpretation of Moses' prayers by Rabbi Nathan Nateh (ben Shlomo) Spira (1585—1633), first published in Cracow, 1637. [We have used the Furth, 1691, edition, reprinted in Brooklyn, 1975.] The author was one of the foremost Kabbalists in Poland.

Mekhilta. The earliest commentary on the Book of Exodus, by the school of Rabbi Yishmael (circa. 120 c.e.), often quoted in the Talmud. First printed in Constantinople, 1515.

Midbar Kedemoth. Alphabetical listing of important concepts, by Rabbi Chaim Yosef David Azzulai, known as the Chida (1724—1806), first printed in Lemberg, 1870. The author was one of the leading scholars and most prolific writers of his time.

Midrash Lekach Tov. Also known as *Pesikta Zutratha*. A

Midrashic work by Rabbi Tovia (ben Eliezer) HaGadol (1036—1108), first printed in Venice, 1546. This work incorporates many earlier Midrashim which were circulating in fragmentary manuscripts. The author lived in Bulgaria and Serbia.

Midrash Rabbah. The most important collection of Midrashim, assembled during the early Gaonic period. The component Midrashim vary from almost pure commentary to pure homelies. All, however, are based on the teachings of the sages of the Talmud. The *Midrash Rabbah* on the Torah was first printed in Constantinople, 1512, while that on the five *megilloth* was printed in Pesaro, 1519.

Midrash Sh'muel. Commentary on *Avoth*, by Rabbi Shmuel (ben Yitzchak) Uceda (1538—1602), first printed in Venice, 1579. Often quoted by the *Tosefoth Yom Tov* (q.v.). The author studied Kabbalah under the Ari and Rabbi Chaim Vital (see *Etz Chaim*). He established a major yeshiva in Safed where both Talmud and Kabbalah were taught.

Midrash Shochar Tov. See *Midrash Tehillim.*

Midrash Tehillim. Also known as *Midrash Shochar Tov.* An ancient Midrash on the Psalms, first printed in Constantinople, 1515. A critical edition, based on manuscript was published by Shlomo Buber, Vilna, 1891.

Nachath HaShulchan. Work on the *Shulchan Arukh* (q.v.) based on the first lesson of *Likutey Moharan* (q.v.), by Rabbi Nachman of Tcherin, first published in Jerusalem, 1910. [We have used the Jerusalem, 1968, edition.]

Nachaley Emunah. Letters of Rabbi Nachman of Tulchin (the foremost student of Rabbi Nathan of Nemerov) and other Breslover leaders, edited by Rabbi Nathan Tzvi Koenig, first printed in B'nei B'rak, 1967.

Nevey Tzaddikim. Historical bibliography of all Breslover works, by Rabbi Nathan Tzvi Koenig, published in B'nei B'rak, 1969.

Oneg Shabbath. Collections of letters and lessons explaining Breslover teachings, by Rabbi Ephraim Tzvi (ben Alter Ben-Tzion) Krakavski of Pshedbarz (1880—1946), published in New York, 1966.

Or HaGanuz. Commentary on the *Bahir* (q.v.) by Rabbi Meir ben Shalom Abi-Sahula, written in 1331, and published anonymously in Vilna, 1883, together with the Bahir. The author was a student of the Rashba (q.v.).

Orach Chaim. First section of the *Shulchan Arukh* (q.v.) dealing with prayers and holy days.

Othioth deRabbi Akiva. Commentary on the letters of the Hebrew alphabet, attributed to Rabbi Akiva (circa 100 c.e.), first published in Constantinople, 1516. We have used the version in *Batey Midrashoth* (q.v.).

Pardes Rimonim. Major kabbalistic work by Rabbi Moshe Cordovero (1522—1570), first published in Salonica, 1583. The author was the head of the Safed school of Kabbalah before the Ari (see *Etz Chaim*).

Parparoth LeChokhmah. Major commentary on *Likutey Moharan* (q.v.) by Rabbi Nachman of Tcherin, first published in Lemberg, 1876.

Peney Moshe. Standard commentary on the *Yerushalmi* (q.v.) by Rabbi Meir (ben Shimon) Margolioth (died 1781), first published in Amsterdam, 1754. Printed together with most editions of the *Yerushalmi*.

Pirkey deRabbi Eliezer. Important Midrashic work by the school of Rabbi Eliezer (ben Hyrcanos) HaGadol (circa 100 c.e.), first published in Constantinople, 1514). [We have used the Warsaw, 1852 edition, which includes a commentary by Rabbi David Luria, the Radal.]

Pri Etz Chaim. Important Kabbalistic work on meditations for various prayers and rituals, based on the teachings of the Ari (see

Etz Chaim), by Rabbi Chaim Vital, first published in Koretz, 1782.

Rabbi Nachman's Wisdom. Translation of *Shevachey HaRan* and *Sichoth HaRan* (q.v.) by Rabbi Aryeh Kaplan, published in New York, 1973.

Ramban. Acronym of Rabbi Moshe ben Nachman (1194—1270), denoting his commentary on the Torah, first printed in Rome, 1472. The author was a leading spiritual leader of his time, writing over fifty major works. He maintained a yeshiva in Gerona, Spain.

Rashba. Acronym of Rabbi Shimon ben Avraham Adret (1235—1310). His commentaries on the aggadoth of the Talmud were published together with *Eyn Yaakov* (q.v.) in Salonika, 1515. A student of the Ramban (q.v.), the author was rabbi of Barcelona, and one of the major Jewish leaders of his time.

Rashi. Acronym of Rabbi Shlomo (ben Yitzchak) Yarchi (see Shem HaGedolim) or Yitzchaki (1040—1105), author of the most important commentaries on the Bible and Talmud, printed in almost all major editions. His commentary on the Torah was the first known Hebrew book to be published (Rome, cira 1470). He headed yeshivoth in Troyes and Worms, France. His commentaries are renowned for being extremely terse, immediately bringing forth the main idea of the text.

Recanti. Torah commentary of Rabbi Menachem (ben Binyamin) Recanti (1210—1305), first published in Venice, 1523. [We have used the edition with the commentary of Rabbi Mordechai Yaffe, Lemberg, 1880.] The author was one of the leading Kabbalists of his time, and the first to quote the *Zohar* (q.v.).

Reshith Chokhmah. An encyclopedic work on morality (mussar), drawing heavily on the *Zohar* (q.v.), by Rabbi Eliahu (ben Moshe) de Vidas (1518—1592), first published in Venice, 1579. A student of Rabbi Moshe Cordovero (see *Pardes Rimonim*), the author had a reputation as a sage and saint.

Rimzey Maasioth. Commentaries on the Stories, by Rabbi Nachman of Tcherin. First printed in Lemberg, 1902, and with all subsequent editions of the Stories.

Rimzey Maasioth, Hashmatoth. Additional commentaries on the Stories by Rabbi Abraham ben Nachman of Tulchin, printed in the Lemberg, 1902, edition of *Sippurey Maasioth*.

Rokeach. An important code of Jewish law and pietistic practice by Rabbi Eleazar (ben Yehudah) Rokeach of Worms (1164—1232), first printed in Fano, 1505. Besides being a leading authority in Jewish law, the author was one of the foremost masters of Kabbalah in his time.

Rosenfeld, Rabbi Tzvi Aryeh Benzion (ben Yisrael Abba) (1922—1978). A descendent of Rabbi Aaron, rabbi in Breslov in the time of Rabbi Nachman, and of Rabbi Shmuel Yitzchok of Tcherin, one of Rabbi Nachman's leading disciples, Rabbi Rosenfeld was one of the leaders of Breslover Chasidim in America. He left numerous tapes of lectures and lessons on the Stories, as well as handwritten marginal notes on his private copy of *Sippurey Maasioth*, now in the hands of his son-in-law, Rabbi Noson Maimon.

Sefer Baal Shem Tov. Anthology of writings of the Baal Shem Tov (1698—1760), founder of the Chasidic movement, by Rabbi Shimon Mendel Vidnik of Givarchav, first published in Lodz, 1938.

Sefer Chasidim. Laws and customs of the Chasidey Ashkenaz (German Pietists) by Rabbi Yehudah (ben Shmuel) HaChasid (1148—1217), first printed in Bologna, 1538. The author, who lived in Speyer and Regensberg, was a master Kabbalist, and a leading rabbinical authority.

Sefer HaMiddoth. Alphabetical listing of concise practical lessons, by Rabbi Nachman of Breslov, first published in Mogolov, 1811.

Sefer HaPeliah. Kabbalistic classic, also known as *Sefer*

HaKanah, attributed to the school of Rabbi Nechunia ben Hakana (see *Bahir*). Thought to have been written by Rabbi Elkana ben Yerocham, first published in Koretz, 1784.

Sefer Tekhunah. Astronomical work by Rabbi Chaim Vital (see *Etz Chaim*), first published in Jerusalem, 1866. [We have used the Jerusalem, 1967, edition.]

Sefer Yetzirah. One of the earliest and most important mystical works, thought to have been written in Talmudic times or earlier. [There are some who attribute the authorship to Abraham.] First printed in Mantua, 1562, it has been the subject of over a hundred commentaries.

Sefer Zerubavel. Ancient eschatological work, first printed in Constantinople, 1524, and in *Batey Midrashoth* (q.v.), Volume 2, p. 495 ff. Probably written in late Talmudic times, it was used by Saadia Gaon (882—942 c.e.).

Shaar HaGilgulim. A detailed work on reincarnation, the last of the "Eight Gates" (*Shemonah Shaarim*) based on the Kabbalah of the Ari, by Rabbi Chaim Vital, first published in Jerusalem, 1863. [We have used the Ashlag edition, Tel Aviv, 1963.]

Shaar HaKavanoth. Kabbalistic meditations on the worship service and rituals, the sixth of the "Eight Gates," by Rabbi Chaim Vital, first published in Salonika, 1852. [We have used the Ashlag edition, Tel Aviv, 1962.]

Shaar HaMitzvoth. Kabbalistic interpretations of the commandments, the fifth of the "Eight Gates," by Rabbi Chaim Vital, first published in Salonika, 1852. [We have used the Ashlag edition, Tel Aviv, 1962.]

Shaar Ruach HaKodesh. Meditative methods, the seventh of the "Eight Gates," by Rabbi Chaim Vital, first published in Jerusalem, 1863. [We have used the Ashlag edition, Tel Aviv, 1963.]

Shaarey Orah. Major Kabbalah classic, by Rabbi Yosef (ben

Avraham) Gikatilla (1248—1345), first printed in Riva de Trento, 1561. The author, who lived in Italy, was a student of Rabbi Avraham Abulafia.

Shaarey Tzion. Important collection of Kabbalistic prayers, by Rabbi Nathan Nata (ben Moshe) Hanover (died 1683), first published in Prague, 1662. The author was a leading Kabbalist.

Shaarey Zohar. Index and commentary of the Talmud, cross-referenced to the *Zohar*, by Rabbi Reuven Margoliot (1889—1971), published in Jerusalem, 1956.

She'erith Yisrael. Collection of letters by the elders of Breslov, edited by Rabbi Nathan Tzvi Koenig, published in B'nei B'rak, 1963.

Shefa Tal. Important Kabbalistic work by Rabbi Shabathai Sheftel (ben Akiva HaLevi) Horowitz (1561—1619), first published in Hanau, 1612.

Shemoth Rabbah. Section of the *Midrash Rabbah* (q.v.) dealing with the Book of Exodus.

Shir HaShirim Rabbah. Section of the *Midrash Rabbah (q.v.) dealing with th Song of Songs.*

Shivechey HaRan. Highlights of Rabbi Nachman's life, including his pilgrimage to the Holy Land, by Rabbi Nathan of Nemerov, first published in Ostrog, 1816. Translated into English as part of *Rabbi Nachman's Wisdom* (q.v.). Parts are included in the *Gems of Rabbi Nachman*, by Rabbi Aryeh Kaplan, New York, 1980.

Shiur Komah. Book of Kabbalistic concepts by Rabbi Moshe Cordovero (see *Pardes Rimonim*), published in Warsaw, 1883.

Shivechey Moharan. Anecdotes and teachings of Rabbi Nachman, compiled by Rabbi Nathan of Nemerov, printed together with *Chayay Moharan* (q.v.).

Shulchan Arukh. The standard code of Jewish Law, by Rabbi Yosef (ben Ephraim) Caro (1488—1575), first published in Venice, 1564. Divided into four parts, *Orach Chaim, Yoreh Deah,*

Evven HaEzer, and *Choshen Mishpat.* Born in Spain, the author migrated to Turkey after the expulsion in 1492, and then to Safed, where he served as chief rabbi. With the addition of the *Hagah* (q.v.), the *Shulchan Arukh* became the standard work on Jewish Law for all Jewry.

Sichoth HaRan. Short teachings and sayings of Rabbi Nachman of Breslov, collected by Rabbi Nathan of Nemerov, first published together with *Sippurey Maasioth,* Ostrog, 1816. An expanded edition, including much new material, was published in Zolkiev, 1850. Translated into English as part of *Rabbi Nachman's Wisdom* (q.v.). Selections are included in *Gems of Rabbi Nachman* by Rabbi Aryeh Kaplan, New York, 1980.

Sichoth VeSippurim. Exposition of Rabbi Nachman's teachings, including commentary on the Stories, by Rabbi Avraham ben Nachman of Tulchin, published in Jerusalem, 1913. Reprinted as part of *Kokhavey Or* (q.v.).

Sifethey Cohen. Commentary on *Yoreh Deah* and *Choshen Mishpat* (q.v.) by Rabbi Shabethai (ben Meir) HaCohen (1621—1662), usually refered to as the Shakh. First published alone in Cracow, 1646, and later with most standard editions of the *Shulchan Arukh* (q.v.).

Sippurey Maasioth. The Stories of Rabbi Nachman, translated here in this volume. First published in Ostrog, 1816, and with a new introduction, in Lemberg, 1850.

Sippurim Niflaim. Anecdotes and teachings involving Rabbi Nachman of Breslov, as well as previously unpublished stories, collected by Rabbi Shmuel Horowitz (1903-1973). First published in Jerusalem in 1935.

Sternhartz, Rabbi Avraham (ben Reb Naftali Hertz) (1862-1955). A great-grandson of Rabbi Nathan, and grandson of Rabbi Nachman of Tcherin, he was one of the most important elders of Breslov in Uman, USSR, and Jerusalem. Among his many students were Rabbi Tzvi Aryeh Rosenfeld (q.v.), Rabbi Gedaliah

Koenig and Rabbi Nachman Burstyn who included many of his teachings in his lectures (see *Tovoth Zikhronoth*).

Talmud. The embodiment of the Oral Torah, as taught by the great masters from approximately 50 b.c.e. until around 500 c.e. The first part to be codified was the Mishnah, set in its present form by Rabbi Yehudah the Prince, around 188 c.e. Subsequent discussions were redacted as the Gemara by Rav Ashi and Ravina in Babylonia around 505 c.e., and it is therefore often refered to as the *Babylonian* Talmud. Next to the Bible itself, it is the most important work on Jewish law and theology. Individual volumes of the Talmud were printed in Soncino, Italy, as early as 1482, but the entire Talmud was first printed by David Bomberg in Venice, 1523, along with the commentaries of Rashi and Tosafoth (q.v.). (Also see *Yerushalmi.*)

Tana deBei Eliahu Rabba and **Zuta.** An early Midrash attributed to the teachings of the prophet Elijah, first printed in Venice, 1598.

Tanchuma. An early homiletic Midrash on the Torah, attributed to Rabbi Tanchuma bar Abba (circa 370 c.e.), but added to until around 850. First printed in Constantinople, 1522.

Targum. Authorized Aramaic translation of the Torah, by the proselyte Onkelos (around 90 c.e.). In Talmudic times, it was read along with the Torah, so that the congregation could understand the reading.

Targum Yonathan. Aramaic translation of the Torah, attributed to Yonathan ben Uzziel (circa 50 c.e.). Portions appear to have been amended in Gaonic times.

Tifereth Yisrael. Theological work, discussing the significance of Israel and the Torah, by Rabbi Yehudah (ben Betzalel) Loew (1424—1609), first published in Venice, 1599. The author, known as the Maharal of Prague, was one of the most respected rabbis of his time, and is credited with having made the Golem.

Tikkun HaKelali. The Ten Psalms prescribed by Rabbi Nachman as a "General Rectification" for sexual and other sins, first published by Rabbi Nathan of Nemerov, Breslov, 1821. Available in English as "Rabbi Nachman's Tikun" published by Yeshivat Chasidei Breslov, 1982.

Tikkuney Zohar. Part of the Zoharic literature, consisting of seventy chapters on the first word of the Torah, by the school of Rabbi Shimon bar Yochai (circa 120 c.e.), first printed in Mantua, 1558. However, a second edition, Orto Koy, 1719, provided the basis for all subsequent editions. The work contains some of the most important discussions in Kabbalah, and is essential for understanding the system of the *Zohar* (q.v.).

Tikkuney Zohar Chadash. Additions to the *Zohar Chadash* (q.v.) in the manner of *Tikkuney Zohar.*

Toledoth Yaakov Yosef. The first Chassidic work, by Rabbi Yaakov Yosef of Polonoye (died 1782), first published in Koretz, 1780. The author was the senior disciple of the Baal Shem Tov, founder of Chasidism.

Torah Anthology, The. Translation of *MeAm Lo'ez* (q.v.) by Rabbi Aryeh Kaplan.

Tosafoth. Collection of commentaries, using Talmudic methodology on the Talmud itself. The work was a product of the yeshiva academies of France and Germany between around 1100 and 1300, begun by the students of Rashi (q.v.) and his grandsons, most notably, Rabbi Yaakov Tam (circa 1100—1171). It is printed in virtually all editions of the Talmud.

Tosefoth Yom Tov. Important commentary on the Mishnah (see Talmud) by Rabbi Yom Tov Lipman (ben Nathan HaLevi) Heller (1579—1654), first published in Prague, 1614—17). The author, who served as rabbi in Prague and Poland was a student of the Maharal (see *Tifereth Yisrael*).

Tosefta. Additions to the Mishnah (see Talmud) by Rabbis Chiya and Oshia (circa 230 c.e., published together with most editions of the Talmud. The *Tosefta* is often quoted in the Talmud itself. [We have used the paragraphing found in the Romm edition of the Talmud, Vilna, 1880-86.]

Tovoth Żikhronoth. Breslover traditions, by Rabbi Avraham (ben Naftali Hertz) Sternhartz (Kokhav Lev) (1862—1955), published in Jerusalem, 1951. The author was one of the Breslover elders in Jerusalem.

VaYakhel Moshe. Important Kabbalistic work by Rabbi Moshe (ben Menachem) Graff of Prague (1650-1707), first printed in Dessau, 1699.

VaYikra.Rabbah. Section of the *Midrash Rabbah* (q.v.) on the Book of Leviticus.

Yad. Short for *Yad Chazakah,* otherwise known as *Mishneh Torah,* the monumental Code of Jewish Law by Rabbi Moshe ben Maimonides (1135-1204), better known as the Rambam. The work was so named because of its fourteen divisions, the numerical value of *Yad.* It was the first systematic codification of Jewish law, and the only one that encompasses every aspect of the Torah. Considered one of the great classics of Torah literature, it was first printed in Rome, 1475. It has been printed in many editions, and is the subject of dozens of commentaries.

Yagel Yaakov. Collection of letters and lessons on Breslov teachings, by Rabbi Yaakov Gedaliah (ben Nethanel) Tefilinsky (1941—1971), published by Rabbi Nathan Tzvi Koenig, B'nei B'rak, 1972.

Yalkut Shimoni. Also known as the Yalkut, one of the most popular early Midrashic collections on the Bible, compiled by Rabbi Shimon Ashkenazi HaDarshan of Frankfort (circa 1260), first printed in Salonika, 1521—27. Many Midrashim are known only because they are cited in this work. The author was a preacher in Frankfort.

Yemey Moharnat. Biography of Rabbi Nathan of Nemerov. The first section was printed in Lemberg, 1876, and the second part, dealing with Rabbi Nathan's pilgrimage to the Land of Israel, was printed in Jerusalem, 1904.

Yerach HaEthanim. Breslover teachings about the power of a Tzaddik, Rosh Hashana, Yom Kippur and Succoth based on*Likutey Moharan*, by Rabbi Nachman of Tcherin, published in Jerusalem, 1951.

Yerioth Sh'lomo. Monumental work on Hebrew synonyms and language, by Rabbi Shlomo (ben Zelligman) Pappenhiem (1760—1840), in three parts, published in Dyherenfurth, 1784, 1811, Roedelheim, 1831. The work is often quoted (as the Rashap) in *HaKethav VeHaKabbalah*, and is said to have influenced Rabbi Shimshon Raphael Hirsch. The author served as a *dayyan* (rabbinical judge) in Breslau.

Yerushalmi. Or *Talmud Yerushalmi.* An earlier version of the Talmud, thought to have been redacted around 240 c.e. by Rabbi Yochanan (182-279 c.e.) and his disciples in Tiberias with the concurance of the sages of Jerusalem. A work of major importance, although considered secondary to the Babylonian Talmud. It was first published in Venice, 1523. [We have used the Romm, Vilna, 1922-28, edition.]

Yoreh Deah. Second section of the *Shulchan Arukh* (q.v.), dealing with dietary laws and other areas requiring rabbinical decision.

Zera Berakh. Torah commentary by Rabbi Berakhia Berakh (ben Yitzchak) Spira (1598—1666), published in Cracow, 1646, with additions in Amsterdam, 1662. The author was a son-in-law of Rabbi Yom Tov Lipman Heller (see *Tosefoth Yom Tov*), and served as preacher and *dayyan* (rabbinical judge) in Cracow.

Zimrath HaAretz. Breslover teachings regarding the importance of the Land of Israel, by Rabbi Nachman of Tcherin, published in Lemberg, 1876. [We have used the Jerusalem, 1968, edition.]

Zohar. The primary classic of Kabbalah, from the school of Rabbi Shimon bar Yochai (circa 120 c.e.), compiled by his disciple, Rabbi Abba. After being restricted to a small, closed circle of

Kabbalists and hidden for centuries, it was finally published around 1290 by Rabbi Moshe (ben Shem Tov) de Leon (1239—1305). After considerable controversy, Rabbi Yitzchak Yehoshua (ben Yaakov Bonet) de Lattes (1498—1571) issued an opinion that it was permitted to print the *Zohar,* and it was published in Mantua, 1558—1560. It has been reprinted in over sixty subsequent editions, and is the subject of dozens of commentaries.

Zohar Chadash. The "New *Zohar*," by the school of Rabbi Shimon bar Yochai, consisting of manuscripts found in the possession of the Safed Kabbalists, assembled by Rabbi Avraham (ben Eliezer HaLevi) Barukhim (1516—1593), and printed in Salonika, 1597. It was called the "New *Zohar*" because it was printed after the original Zohar.

Zohar HaRakia. Commentary on the *Zohar* by the Ari (see *Etz Chaim*), and edited by Rabbi Yaakov Tzemach, first published in Koretz,ʼ 1785.

INDEX

A

B

C

D

E

F

G

H

I

J

K

L

N

O

P

Q

R

S

T

U

V

W

Y

Z

BIBLICAL QUOTATIONS

Genesis

1:1	413, 414, 424	2:19,20	40
1:2	34, 63, 309, 413, 422, 425, 426, 431 432, 433	3:1	20, 161
1:3	279	3:3	317
1:4	371	3:5	161
1:5	34	3:6	19, 20, 41
1:6	426	3:11	162
1:7	426	3:15	236
1:9	426, 427	3:16	242
1:10	426	3:17	279, 284
1:16	119, 154, 158	3:18	86, 347
1:20	426	3:19	317, 345
1:21	426	3:24	232, 307, 344, 404, 405
1:22	426	4:1	56, 409, 424
1:26	150	4:2	279
1:26,27	1	4:5	19
1:27	13	4:6	19
1:28	317	4:12	67, 399
1:30	86	5:24	302
1:31	171	6:6	35, 434
2:6	428	6:9	162
2:7	427	6:12	434
2:9	403	7:21	474
2:18	35, 69, 426	9:2	249
		9:6	13